Illustrated history of New Zealand

SELECTED BOOKS BY MATTHEW WRIGHT

Hawke's Bay: Lifestyle Country (Cosmos, June 1991)
Wonderful Wairarapa (Cosmos, October 1991)
Wellington/Kapiti Coast (Cosmos, December 1992)
Hawke's Bay — The History of a Province (Dunmore Press, Palmerston North, 1994; reprinted 1995)
Havelock North — The History of a Village (Hastings District Council, Hastings, 1996)
Napier — City of Style (Random House, Auckland, 1997)
Kiwi Air Power — The History of the RNZAF (Reed, Auckland, 1998)
Working Together — The History of Carter Oji Kokusaku Pan Pacific Ltd 1971–1993 (Pan Pac, Napier, 1999)
New Zealand's Engineering Heritage (Reed, Auckland, 1999)
A Near-Run Affair — New Zealanders in the Battle for Crete, 1941 (Reed, Auckland, 2000; reprinted with new title 2003)
Quake — Hawke's Bay 1931 (Reed, Auckland, 2001; reprinted with revised photographs 2006)
Town and Country — The History of Hastings and District 1860–2001 (Hastings District Council, Hastings 2001)
Blue Water Kiwis — New Zealand's Naval Story (Reed, Auckland, 2001)
Desert Duel — New Zealand's North African War (Reed, Auckland, 2002)
Wings Over New Zealand — A Social History of New Zealand Aviation (Whitcoulls, Auckland, 2002)
Italian Odyssey — New Zealanders in the Battle for Italy 1943–45 (Reed, Auckland, 2003)
Rails Across New Zealand – A Social History of Rail Travel (Whitcoulls, Auckland 2003)
Pacific War — New Zealand and Japan 1941–1945 (Reed, Auckland, 2003)
The Reed Illustrated History of New Zealand (Reed, Auckland, 2004)
Western Front: The New Zealand Division in the First World War (Reed, Auckland, 2005)
Freyberg's War: The Man, the Legend, and Reality (Penguin, Auckland, 2005)
Cars Around New Zealand — A History of Kiwi cars (Whitcoulls, Auckland, 2005)
Escape! Kiwi POW's on the Run in World War II (Random House, Auckland, 2006) (Editor)
Fighting Past Each Other — The New Zealand Wars 1845–1872 (Reed Childrens Books, Auckland, 2006)
Two Peoples, One Land — The New Zealand Wars (Reed, Auckland, 2006)
Trucks Around New Zealand (Whitcoulls, Auckland, 2006)
Fantastic Pasts: Imaginary Adventures in New Zealand History (Penguin, Auckland, 2007)
Torpedo! Kiwis at Sea in World War II (Random House, Auckland, 2007) (Editor)
New Zealand's Military Heroism (Reed, Auckland, 2007)
Motorbikes Around New Zealand (Whitcoulls, Auckland, 2008)
Big Ideas: 100 Wonders of New Zealand Engineering (Random House, Auckland, 2009)
Old South: Life and Times in the Nineteenth Century Mainland (Penguin, Auckland, 2009)
Behind Enemy Lines: Kiwi Freedom Fighters in WWII (Random House, Auckland, 2010) (Editor)
Shattered Glory: The New Zealand Experience at Gallipoli and the Western Front (Penguin, Auckland, 2010)
Historic Hawke's Bay and East Coast (Bateman, Auckland, 2010)
Guns and Utu: A Short History of the Musket Wars (Penguin, Auckland, 2011)
New Zealand on the Move: 100 Kiwi Road, Rail and Transport Icons (Random House, Auckland, 2011)
Convicts: New Zealand's Hidden Criminal Past (Penguin, Auckland, 2012)

Illustrated history of New Zealand

MATTHEW WRIGHT

Historical illustrations from the
Alexander Turnbull Library

David Bateman

Text copyright © Matthew Wright 2013
Matthew Wright photographs copyright © Matthew Wright 2013
Typographical design copyright © David Bateman 2013

The moral rights of the author have been asserted.
Alexander Turnbull Library picture copyrights as credited.

Published in 2013 by David Bateman Ltd
30 Tarndale Grove, Albany, Auckland, New Zealand
www.batemanpublishing.co.nz

ISBN 978-1-86953-841-5

An earlier edition of this book was published as *The Reed Illustrated History of New Zealand*, Reed NZ Ltd, Auckland 2004.
This fully re-written and re-originated second edition with revised photographic selection published by David Bateman Ltd, 2013.

This book is copyright. Except for the purpose of fair review, no part may be stored or transmitted in any form or by any means, electronic or mechanical, including recording or storage in any information retrieval systems, without permission in writing from the publisher. No reproduction may be made, whether by photocopying or by any other means, unless a licence has been obtained from the publisher or its agent.

Cover design: Shelley Watson/Sublime Design
Printed in China through Colorcraft Ltd, Hong Kong

Contents

Introduction		7
1	Deep time	11
2	Agents of change	31
3	Shadows of empire	61
4	The road to Erewhon	97
5	Desperate times	147
6	Prelude to a century	185
7	God's own country	251
8	The quest for security	317
9	Slices of heaven	363
10	Extreme decades	421
Notes		451
Glossary		471
Bibliography		472
Index		483

Introduction

New Zealand has a short history by world standards. Archaeological discoveries show that it is less than 800 years since our lands were first settled by humanity. The first settlers, Polynesians, probably arrived around 1280 AD.[1] Elsewhere in the thirteenth-century world, cathedrals were being raised, the Italians were inventing the watermark and new colleges were being established at the University of Oxford. Arab astronomers were mapping the skies, and the Chinese had known gunpowder for perhaps three centuries.[2]

New Zealand's human history, then, is but an eyeblink by world standards. Yet although brief, it is dense with meaning, event and colour. The advent of the British colony in 1840, particularly, kicked the pace into high gear; and the decades that followed were filled with fast-moving trends, from colonial ambition to a renewed love affair with Britain, to the first hesitant steps as an independent nation on the world stage, all overlaid with a race-relations story that had a unique basis in world history. The wider experience encapsulated the essence of the human condition; a rich tapestry woven of hope, ambition, wars, utopian dreamers, rogues and occasional heroes. Few countries offer such combinations of immediacy, accessibility and depth in their histories.

No one book can pursue all the lines of enquiry offered by this remarkable and concentrated past—a point highlighted by the very different offerings of Keith Sinclair and W. H. Oliver, published at the end of the 1950s.[3] Since then historians have pivoted general accounts of New Zealand around race relations,[4] politics and nationalism,[5] or the human narrative.[6] All are complementary; history is an additive field, and where they overlap is also of value. Deeper truths can often be teased out of co-operative discussion.

History also demands an effort to abstract. Despite the conceit that each new generation of historians has 'corrected' the old, our understanding of New Zealand's past has usually been framed by contemporary priority, a reflection

ABOVE

Romanticised imagery from another century: George Baxter's take on missionary Reverend J. Waterhouse's landing on the Taranaki coast in 1844.

George Baxter, coloured print, Alexander Turnbull Library, B-088-004

ABOVE

Map by John Ryland (1753–1825) from Cook's original.

John Ryland, Alexander Turnbull Library MapColl833aj/1773/Acc.422

of changing views of ourselves. In most cases it has been a process not of de-mythologising, but of re-mythologising. That is not particularly useful if we are to understand what events meant to the people who lived through them. We share language, heritage and relations with the past, but to assume we share meanings is misleading. The challenge is to understand that past in its own terms—showing how it stands relative to other times, including our own. By nature, this challenge can never be completely met; history is always a prisoner of the time when it was written. But we can, at least, be aware of the issue.

A few words are needed to explain the thrust of this book. It is a book of theme and explanation, looking at some of the trends that made New Zealand what it was in the past, and what it is today. One focus is to show and understand the way that our past has been mythologised and re-mythologised by the mind-set of successive generations, including the revisionist or 'post-colonial' history of late twentieth century academia. Historical newspapers, archival documents, reports and other material can be found with a few mouse-clicks. The question is not what this material is—but what it means for us. What does it tell us about the human realities of its day? What are some of the social truths of New Zealand's history as a whole?

The answers follow no single region, and I have not attempted to produce a narrative that deals homogenously with every moment and every geographic area. That is not the aim or intent, and the text should not be mistaken for an attempt to do so, or judged against such criteria. This is a book about the shapes and patterns of our history at the broadest level. I have covered much of New Zealand's detailed story, regionally and thematically, elsewhere—including books I have written focussing on South Island settler idealism, on pastoral life in Hawke's Bay, the New Zealand Wars, the musket wars, and on New Zealand's experience of both World Wars. I have covered transport and engineering stories elsewhere. I have written technical papers on economic history, covered the social experience of the Hawke's Bay earthquake in significant detail, and delved into a range of other aspects of the past. There is no need to repeat every detail of that work here; this book has a different purpose. Indeed, in many respects, all this material—including this book—forms part of one over-arching work which can be read together.

This is also an illustrated history. Pictures offer a perspective that words seldom convey. The subjects selected by artists and photographers, and the way they represented them, add meaning. From these we can learn much about the way people of historical times saw themselves—literally how they framed their world. The pictures chosen for this volume are not always the best known or iconic images; but they have been selected for a reason. There are pictures of families standing before their houses in their Sunday best, prize possessions spread out before them, their prosperity frozen in time by the photographer. There are pictures of triumphal railway construction, of celebrating crowds; of depression-era hardships. From the photographs themselves, from the nature of the subjects, and from the way they were framed and presented, we can learn how the photographers—and hence, indirectly, the people of their age—viewed their world. All of these speak to us in more ways than we perhaps imagine at a casual glance, and in more ways than can be conveyed in text alone.

Elements of this book were originally written in 2003 and published the following year as the *Reed Illustrated History of New Zealand*. This second edition offers a thoroughly revised text throughout, fully re-styled and completely re-written and re-cast in many key places. I have also revised some of the picture selections, including the last chapter, which has been fully re-illustrated with twenty-first-century imagery. Although technically a second edition, the level of change renders this, in many ways, a new book.

There are reasons why this labour has been so important. Although some kinds of histories can be happily reprinted without amendment, this book is one of broad pattern interpretation; and our understanding of history never stands still. It is not a matter of simply adding a few pages to 'update' a chronology. New data sometimes emerges to challenge deeper ideas, or to add depth to what we know. Even where the data is well known and established, the kinds of questions we ask and the answers we look for are constantly reframed, as our ideas and perspectives change with time. This does not mean earlier work by an author is 'wrong', for it is not. It is right in terms of the questions. perceptions, ideas and knowledge of that time. But the quest for understanding never stops. The chance to revise, to re-think, to re-examine and to explore new 'truths', must be seized with both hands. In the case of this book, new research on New Zealand's pre-history, particularly, had to be taken into account. Elsewhere there were places where further understanding could be teased out of events, or where the passage of time had given a better perspective; or even where nuances needed, on reflection, to be better expressed.

New Zealand's general history is a broad topic, and while researching and writing this book I consulted a wide range of books, academic papers, theses, primary documents, diaries, manuscripts, private papers, official reports and statistical records from diverse sources including the Alexander Turnbull Library, the Auckland War Memorial Museum, the Christchurch Public Library, the Hawke's Bay Museum, the Hastings District Council, the National Library and Archives New Zealand among others. Quoted material per the first edition is used according to permissions given then; and quoted material added for the second edition is believed on the basis of copyright duration, authorship and age to be in the public domain. Photographs have been captioned according to information supplied by the Alexander Turnbull Library, as required when publishing from their collection, and I ask that any readers who have documentation that may query that detail, or which might add further information, directly contact that library with their material.

I again extend my thanks to those who generously gave their time in 2003 to comment on aspects of the original text, who gave me permission to quote from their work, and to use images supplied, including Barry Gustafson, Richard Jackson, Nigel Prickett, and the late Sir John White.

I am grateful to Tracey Borgfeldt of David Bateman Ltd for her support of this revised edition. The historical pictures, paintings, sketches and ephemera in this book are from the collection of the Alexander Turnbull Library, part of New Zealand's Natonal Library, and I am grateful to National Library staff for their unstinting support, particularly Heather Mathie who took on the challenge of processing my orders for 600-odd images in both the first and second editions. All reasonable efforts have been made to locate copyright holders, if applicable. Most of the photographs in Chapter 10 are my personal work.

Matthew Wright
December 2012

CHAPTER ONE
Deep time

Our journey through New Zealand's history begins with the journey of New Zealand itself, a voyage through deep time in which the very fabric of the land was remoulded and recast. The largest 'New Zealand', Rangitata, eroded almost to nothing as it carried its cargo of birds, plants and insects away from a fracturing Gondwanaland around 85 million years before the present. New lands rose. Five million years ago, 'Cook Strait' was in the Manawatu. Natural climate change intruded. Around a million years before the present, the world entered an era of intermittent ice ages. Great glaciers rumbled down from the Southern Alps into Otago and Canterbury. It was an age of fire. The North Island was dominated by the Oruanui volcanic field near Lake Taupo, where an immense eruption 30,000 years ago obliterated much life in the central plateau.

So much of the world's water was locked up in ice during these years that the seas dropped. At the most recent glacial maximum some 20,000 years ago, it was possible to walk overland from Taranaki to Golden Bay. Cook Strait was a deep bay battered by ferocious winds. Much of the country around was scrubby, though forests grew on sheltered slopes and in Northland.[1] The world entered a further inter-glacial period fourteen millennia ago, bringing a sea level rise that separated North and South Islands and inundated coastal plains. At one stage the seas were higher than in the early twenty-first century. Forests came and went, but by around 2000 years before the present—as Julius Caesar conquered ancient Gaul—both North and South Islands were heavily forested, mainly podocarp in the north and beech in the south.[2] Another Taupo eruption in the second century AD changed the pattern again, covering 20,000 square kilometres of the North Island in ignimbrite and a further 30,000 with tephra. It had a global impact; and for a while the Romans and Chinese were able to admire spectacular sunsets.[3]

No human eyes directly saw this disaster. As late as 1960 historians could argue that readers had the 'luxury of choice' when deciding precisely how and when

ABOVE

James Cook's artist Sydney Parkinson drew this 'Representation of a war canoe of New Zealand, with a view of Gable End Foreland'.

Sydney Parkinson, Alexander Turnbull Library, B-085-013

ABOVE

Moa captured the imagination of Victorian-age settlers. Reconstructions such as this *Illustrated Sydney News* effort of 1865 owe more to fantasy than any scientific reality, even as known then; but they are still valid history, for they tell us a good deal about the mind-set of the mid-nineteenth century.

Artist unknown, Alexander Turnbull Library, B-158-026

New Zealand was first settled.[4] Stories of pakepakeha (fairy folk), moa hunters and pre-Maori 'Moriori' added myth to popular understanding, but perhaps the biggest problem was the persistence of settler-era beliefs, some of which were still being promoted in fringe literature of the early twenty-first century.[5]

Just when Maori arrived puzzled the European mind from the first. The notion that Maori might have arisen locally was swiftly dismissed, and early settler thinkers pored over genealogies, finally pinning the arrival to around 300 years before Tasman on the basis of descent.[6] Linguistic comparison and a broad commonality of looks and culture suggested that they had come from east Polynesia; and in that, these earliest settler-thinkers such as William Colenso and others got it basically right. Specifically where, when and how was another matter, but for a while the question was academic, for this early analysis was overtaken towards the end of the nineteenth century by one of the greatest myths of New Zealand's history; the idea that Maori had arrived in a huge, heroic canoe migration from an undefined 'Hawaiki', around 1350. Like the contemporary myth of two-race settlement and the late twentieth-century myth that Maori invented trench warfare,[7] the great canoe migration was a fantasy born of the collision between Pakeha scholarship and period idealism. It was largely devised by late nineteenth-century ethnographer S. Percy Smith,[8] and had less to do with reality than with Smith's rationalisation of Maori tales, framed by the demands of late settler age thinking—the evolution of societies by displacement, the ranking of peoples from lowest savages to highest Tory-voting English gentlemen.

Michael King has suggested that what followed also keyed into late nineteenth century settler ideas of nation-founding. Smith's thinking was framed by the priorities of a time when Pakeha were styling themselves as the greatest of Britain's children, 'chief junior' in the wider empire, with origins—vicariously provided by Maori—that were at least as heroic as those of the mother country. Maori bought into it too; Te Rangi Hiroa (Sir Peter Buck) was certainly a leading advocate.[9] So the canoe migration myth became a new historical truth, popularised in the *School Journal*,[10] and still taught in primary schools into the 1960s.

The heroic migration theory joined the other Pakeha misapprehension of the age—that New Zealand had been colonised twice before Europe arrived. Maori had, apparently, displaced an earlier people—Moriori. It was untrue. Earlier thinkers—notably Colenso—recognised that Maori stories of pakepakeha were mythic. The settlers also knew that Moriori were not pre-Maori New Zealand settlers; they were a people who lived in the Chathams.[11] So where did the two-race theory come from? Part of it was bedded in the period notion of 'diffusion'—the idea that only Europeans could innovate, that indigenous cultures changed only through invasion. Another part of the myth came from the fact that moa had obviously been eaten to extinction, but nobody was prepared to believe Maori had done it. Julius Haast attributed the midden heaps he found at Glenmark to earlier 'moa hunters'.[12] All this gained power on the back of Smith's general re-framing of Maori mythology to suit late nineteenth-century Pakeha needs. As Kerry Howe observes, it was a way of legitimising the Pakeha settlement; Maori had displaced Moriori. Now the British were displacing Maori.[13]

It was not the first time views of New Zealand's past had been re-framed around contemporary ideology, nor the last; and the close fit to the ideals of

LEFT

Late nineteenth-century myth-making: Otago university registrar Augustus Hamilton reconstructed this moa around 1899, put it into the Dunedin Botanical Gardens, and persuaded Te Rangi Hiroa (left), medical student Tutere Wi Repa and missionary Koroneho Hemi Papakakura to attack it. The 'Ostrich' posture is noteworthy, since discredited.

Photographer unidentified, Alexander Turnbull Library, PAColl-1308, F-2887-1/2

the period lent credibility that these notions did not really deserve. The actual evidence for both a canoe migration and for settlers other than those who gave rise to Maori was flimsy. Only Ngati Kahungunu spoke of a 'fleet',[14] and this may have referred to coastal voyages.[15] Earlier settler-era thinkers had heard the same tales and given little credence to them—Colenso dismissed the whole concept of canoe migration as a myth, a product of the 'inventive mind of man ever seeking to understand the why and wherefore of things around him'.[16] However, thanks to Smith, this mythology was heavily entrenched in the Pakeha mind by the early twentieth century. It was not seriously questioned until the 1970s, when David Simmons demonstrated that Smith had reorganised Maori tradition to create a coherent but misleading tale.[17]

One of the outcomes of these gyrations, including the gaps in Smith's story, was a widespread popular notion that Maori origins could never be known. This gave undue credence to a wild array of fantasies by autodidacts and fringe thinkers about 'pre-Maori' arrival by everybody from the Chinese to the Celts.[18] Much of this was based on uncritical and out-of-context acceptance of old writings and ideas, sometimes filtered through 'new age' theology.[19] Some of it, unpalatably, appeared to be driven not by abstract enquiry but by a backlash to the Maori renaissance of the late twentieth century.

In fact there were explanations for Maori origin, and they were much more exciting, filled with all the dimensionality of human drama, than any enthusiast dreams. But the hard evidence took a while to find. The detail eventually began emerging as systematic archaeology got under way in the wake of the Second World War, bolstered by technical developments that transformed the ability of archaeologists to reconstruct timelines, further helped by the discovery of the facts underpinning Pacific island settlement. The Maori story was integral with the wider spread of humanity across the Pacific; and by the twenty-first century only the smaller and more academic details were in contention.

New Zealand was the last large land mass in the world settled by humanity. Just as Colenso and other pre-Smith observers had suspected, the first settlers were from East Polynesia,[20] specifically the Society, Cook and Austral Islands.[21] Just when they arrived took a while to pin down, helped by archaeological work in the Pacific islands which revealed that the places Maori came from in East Polynesia were settled between 800 and 1000 AD.[22] New Zealand clearly had to be settled after that. But the picture was still muddied by false alarms, such as the claim that rat bones found in New Zealand dated to the first century AD. That stood out from the bulk of the evidence, but was later re-visited and shown to be incorrect.

New Zealand's Polynesian settlers arrived not as a great migration, but sporadically over some years, near the end of the great voyaging epoch that had taken Polynesians as far as South America and back. The timing was largely driven by the fact that New Zealand lay behind contrary winds unsuited to Polynesian navigational techniques—it was easier to reach South America.[23] The earliest significant arrivals were late in the thirteenth century, around 1280, probably bringing Polynesian settlers to the Wairau bar. There is no evidence of human occupation in northern New Zealand below an ash layer deposited by an eruption of Tarawera, initially dated to 1260,[24] later pinned to 1314.[25]

Curiously, what this meant was that the 'about 300 years before Tasman' identified by pre-Smith studies of the genealogical record in the 1860s—around 1340–1350—was generally right. So was Smith's date of 1350, roughly, which he had worked out on the same basis. This was indeed the period when Polynesians were arriving. Late twentieth-century scientific methods, including pollen analysis, revealed a national picture consistent with a late thirteenth-century arrival and expansion through the country.[26] There was sustained forest loss in the Bay of Plenty around 1350–1400; Taranaki around 1550; and Northland by 1450–1500. North Canterbury was denuded from around 1400; and Otago around 1300–1550.[27] There were some dates outside these ranges, and natural

ABOVE

Maori fishing on the Whanganui River around 1844, a scene little changed from pre-settler days.

John Alexander Gilfillian, Alexander Turnbull Library, E-273-q-018 fires complicate the picture; pollen analysis draws no distinction between deliberate and accidental burning. However, the broad picture was clear.

Settlement may have sprung from an initial exploratory voyage, followed by multiple arrivals from several East Polynesian islands.[28] The 'starting population' could have been as high as 500, though genetic analysis suggests Maori could also be descended from a smaller group.[29] The fact that Polynesian pigs and chicken are absent from the archaeological record suggests that settlers arrived in a few small groups over a short period and that return or repeat voyaging was minimal;[30] though some have argued that tropical pigs and chickens did not survive the voyage, or perished in the New Zealand environment.[31]

For a while there seems to have been some interchange with Polynesia. The Kermadecs provided a way-point for the return journey.[32] But that ended, for all practical purposes, around the fifteenth century.[33] While there may have been occasional later interchanges, New Zealand's Polynesian settlers were isolated in any practical sense. This may have been due to natural climate change. New Zealand's first settlers arrived towards the end of a climatic optimum, locally known as the Waiherere warm period.[34] The world changed. An era of troubled weather—often cooler, especially in Europe—began around 1300 and did not end until the mid-nineteenth century.[35] Other events, including volcanic activity, added to the environmental pressures of this 'little ice age'. And it had its downstream effects, especially on societies that relied on subsistence agriculture or marginal food sources. While climate change could not solely determine human fortunes, it certainly added layers of complexity to the calculation.

ABOVE

Maori fascinated the British public after Cook's first voyage in 1769.

Sydney Parkinson/R.B.Godfrey, Alexander Turnbull Library, A-111-105.

Maori, moa and fire

New Zealand's Polynesian settlers found a temperate world very different from the tropical one they had left. The early era is sometimes named after Tamatea, the legendary figure associated with exploration, extensive fires[36] and the longest place name in New Zealand.[37] There was little disease, apparently because the early population was too low to support viruses.[38] A rich diet of birds, seals and other wildlife fuelled a rate of population growth estimated by some analysts at up to 3.7 percent.[39]

The settlers made new homes for themselves, semi-permanent settlements that included gardens, where the Polynesian crops could grow.[40] Plants such as kumara and yam were not well suited to New Zealand's cooler climate. That threw the focus on to New Zealand's bird and animal life—but it was, in any case, there for the plucking. The birds had no fear of humans, including the largest of all, the moa. Some estimates suggest that up to half the total food supply at this time was provided by moa.[41] And in this last great collision between humanity and Pleistocene fauna, some species were quickly hunted to extinction.[42] There was a good deal of collateral impact in the process. Up to half New Zealand's forest cover was apparently burned off in the process, partly as a means of flushing game, partly by accident when cooking fires or blazes set to clear land got away. The Polynesian settlers arrived at the end of the Waiherere warm period,[43] an 80-year climatic optimum shared by the rest of the world. While the cool

ABOVE

'The inside of a Hippah, in New Zealand'. Artist John Webber (1851–1793) depicts part of Queen Charlotte Sound, near Motuara Island.

John Webber, hand-coloured engraving, Alexander Turnbull Library, B-098-023

Spörer Minimum that followed from about 1350 had only minimal effect on air temperature, the shorter growing season and drier weather made gardens that much harder to keep. The South Island, where much of the moa hunting took place, was particularly ill-suited to tropical plants by this time.

Moa remain one of the best-known extinct birds in the world. Species ranged from the 250-kg *Dinornis giganteus* to the 20-kg *Euryapteryx curtus*,[44] but it took years to sort out how they disappeared. Walter Mantell found evidence of fires, human habitation and moa bones in Taranaki during a 'dig' in 1847, but did not think moa were on the menu, and it was the early 1850s before he found enough remains to demonstrate the point.[45] Julius Haast 'put the pot on' [?] in 1869 when he announced, on the basis of his excavations around the Rakaia River mouth, that ancient inhabitants had eaten moa in vast numbers, taking just the choice cuts and leaving the rest to rot.[46] This caused a sensation. But Haast did not think Maori had done it, hypothesising a 'moa-hunting' people who he believed preceded them.

Work during the twentieth century left no doubt as to what had gone on. Remains such as 'industrial' cooking and processing complexes painted a picture of a bird with a low reproductive rate falling prey to a burgeoning Polynesian population.[47] There was nothing surprising about this. Neolithic humans had reduced many species through over-hunting, and the idea that it might have happened in New Zealand was suggested by Roger Duff in the 1950s, who divided Maori pre-history into 'moa-hunting' and 'classical' eras. However, that was controversial at the time and it was the 1960s before Polynesian migrants were widely accepted as the main cause in the disappearance of moa.[48] The problem was the way the argument was framed; either Polynesians had eaten moa to extinction, or it was due to natural causes. Reality, inevitably, defied reduction to simple causes; multiple effects were at play, including natural ones. But the fact remained, nonetheless, that a New Zealand biota which had been stable for hundreds of thousands of years suddenly bent and finally collapsed when humans arrived. Extreme estimates have suggested that moa vanished within a generation of settlement. Other studies propose up to 200 years.[49]

The main problem was sparse evidence. Carbon dating was only a partial help because of wide uncertainties associated with the system, particularly at first.[50] But the broad picture was clear; hunters would venture into the high country during incubation season, snacking on moa eggs while capturing prey with snares and dogs. Some moa were butchered on the spot and the joints carried to great oven complexes, where the meat was cooked in its own fat.[51] Other birds were portaged mostly intact for dressing at the cook-site, leaving a few wasted parts—particularly heads and necks—to rot. This diet was leavened in some areas with Polynesian plants, notably taro, yams and kumara.[52]

For all that, the demise of moa was not simply dine-to-destruction. The human impact on the environment was surprisingly complex. Moa populations were depleted not just through consumption but also by over-hunting, waste and the simultaneous destruction of eggs during the hunt. At the same time, the forests in which moa lived were also dwindling in the face of human impact.[53] And there were losses of eggs to the dogs and rats brought in by the Polynesian settlers. All this compounded to devastating effect, and it was not even necessary to eat the last moa; reducing them below a viable breeding population sufficed. They died out region by region, and moa hunting appears to have been virtually at an end by the beginning of the seventeenth century.[54] Early European settlers were excited by suggestions that they still lived,[55] but these claims were soon dispelled and alleged sightings since are not credible.[56] The key issue, again, has been that moa could not survive singly; there had to be a reasonable breeding population.

Debate over moa diverted popular attention from the fact that they were but one symptom of a much wider human impact on the environment. Other birds on the menu included shag, kaka, penguin, weka, pukeko, shearwaters, tui, kiwi, wattle-birds, parakeets, albatross, hawk, falcon, quail, owls, geese, swans and oystercatchers among others, all of which have been found in midden heaps.[57] Around 35 species became extinct during the period; by comparison, 11 species are known to have become extinct since 1840. The Polynesian-era number included Finsch's duck, already in decline for natural reasons—but whose residual population 'succumbed very quickly to human hunting'.[58] The discovery underscored the fact that, irrespective of the vagaries of natural change, humanity had a dramatic effect.

ABOVE

'A New Zealand Warrior in his Proper Dress a[nd] Compleatly Armed, According To Their Manner'.

Sydney Parkinson, Alexander Turnbull Library, PUBL-0037-15

Similar arguments flowed around loss of New Zealand's natural forest cover in the same period.[59] Studies confirmed that it had been destroyed fairly quickly over significant areas,[60] and debate was always polarised between natural causes[61] and human intervention.[62] In fact both were true. Volcanic activity, climatic variations, storms and droughts had devastating effect.[63] But these were compounded and overlaid by fire-lighting, evidenced by the increase in forest destruction which became apparent around 600 years before the present.[64] This was a new factor, and estimates indicate that up to half the total forest cover in New Zealand was burned off after the Polynesians arrived.[65] Destruction varied from rapid and widespread annihilation to a more piecemeal approach, as in Palliser Bay where bush was nibbled back as the new settlers made room for gardens.[66]

What it boiled down to was that New Zealand was the venue for the world's last collision between humanity and the Pleistocene. A biota of plants, birds, insects and animals that had been relatively stable for millennia—subject only to the pressures of natural climate change and occasional natural disasters—suffered a devastating and rapid decline within a few decades of human arrival. It does not take rocket science to work out what happened.

Tangata whenua

Maori culture emerged indigenously in New Zealand out of Polynesian settler society. The evolution came piecemeal during the fifteenth century, a shift identified by archaeologists through new styles of artwork and gardening patterns.[67] It did not happen overnight; there has been debate over whether there was a multi-stage shift. But change did happen, and for many reasons, not least the fact that by the late 1400s New Zealand's natural bounty had been cropped. The fifteenth century was also a chilly and tumultuous one for New Zealand, with volcanic activity, earthquakes and even tsunamis around the coasts. Wave height at Kapiti Island was estimated at 11–15 metres,[68] which could have dislocated local coastal settlements.[69] As in Europe, climate was not a determining arbiter of human change, but it was one of the factors contributing to the historical pattern,[70] and cannot be ignored.

The evolution of distinctly 'Maori' culture in New Zealand meant they became indigenous. They occupied and drew identity from the whole country, but there was no 'Maori nation'—Maori had no formal name for either themselves or the land. The North Island was sometimes called Te Ika a Maui. Some hapu referred to it as Aotea or Aotearoa—though the name was also applied to Great Barrier Island. Sometimes the South Island was Te Waka a Aoraki or Te Wai Pounamu.[71] These were functions of isolation; there were no peoples or places to distinguish. For Maori, the distinctions lay within their own society, and they took great care in defining those structures. These were derived both from location and ancestry, itself sometimes traced back to a founding canoe or event.[72]

Maori life was based around semi-permanent settlements usually associated with resource sites,[73] people often migrating with the seasons as food supplies shifted.[74] Maori made tools and utensils from available resources, including

'Native bridge with swing and pa in the distnce', an engraving by J. W. Wood from an original artwork by Cyprian Bridge

Cyprian Bridge, Alexander Turnbull Library, PUBL-0144-1-209

stone, wood, flax, bone, shell and vegetable fibres.[75] Clay was available, but the art of pottery had been lost during the earlier migration to East Polynesia and was not rediscovered in New Zealand. One key difference between the new world of Maori and the older world of Polynesian settlers were pa—wood and earth defences which emerged largely after 1500, probably a response to a more settled and resource-limited lifestyle with the need to protect particular areas and resources.[76] Many different types emerged, most of them in the North Island.[77]

This society was divided—like Polynesian and, for that matter, European— into elite and commoners. Upper strata included ariki and rangatira, both standing above tutua. Experts—tohunga—had status of their own, as did elders or kaumatua. Status was intimately related to mana, a personal attribute that could be won or lost through behaviour, achievements, defeat, victory or even turns of fortune, and which was generally more important to ariki and rangatira than to tutua. Mana helped define rights to resources, and in this way the resource dynamic continued to intensify, underpin, create and refine custom.

Food was always the main priority, as it was, indeed, for all societies around the world in this pre-industrial time, Britain's included. And it was sometimes a struggle, particularly as the 'little ice age' began to bite, cutting down the range of places where the Polynesian crops could grow. Once the original biota had been exploited, New Zealand's remaining 'package' of plants and animals was not well suited to supporting people. It could be done; but as William Colenso observed even in the 1860s, the task demanded 'a large amount of daily labour'.[78]

In fact, food production soaked up most of the available labour for extended periods, and archaeological investigation of middens has revealed that the range and quantity Maori had for most of the pre-European period was far less than during the bounteous archaic era.[79] Polynesian vegetables—taro, yam, kumara— were grown where possible in carefully tilled gardens, their size sometimes maximised by excavation.[80] Archaeological work has revealed an 'experimental' period, varying from region to region, before all the horticultural methods and systems were fully developed. Fern root was eaten but not cultivated, though there is evidence that natural bracken regrowth occurred in older gardens, forcing Maori to find new horticultural land but providing a good resource for the root.[81]

Hunting was important. Birds sought out included shag, kaka, penguin, weka, pukeko, shearwater, tui, kiwi, wattle-birds, parakeets, albatross, hawk, falcon, quail, owls, geese, swans and oystercatchers.[82] Most were snared, some caught with slings.[83] Waterways and swamps were key resource areas because of their fat eels—tuna—and lampreys. Shellfish were collected from beds. Ocean fishing was important; there was mackerel, mullet, cod and snapper to be had for venturesome waka.[84] All this was particularly important in the south, where Polynesian plants did not grow; this remained a hunter-gatherer world. The distinction emerged in subtle differences in social structure, language and custom—and in numbers. Population estimates suggest there were fewer than 3000 Maori in the South Island even by the late eighteenth century, most of them in the northern reaches, although the total Maori population was perhaps 100,000.[85]

By contrast with people in Europe, Asia, Africa and the Americas, Maori had no domestic animals that could become beasts of burden. All the work had to be done with human muscle power alone; a point played out in the archaeological record which reveals that Maori were strong, robust, relatively tall and highly active, but short-lived because their lifestyle took its toll on their bodies. Some skeletons reveal damage to the spine and collarbone caused by carrying heavy loads.[86] Others show signs of neck arthritis, suggesting extended arm use, as from paddling.[87] Average life expectancy at birth was about 24, though someone who survived to their teens might live into their early thirties. This was not radically different from contemporary Europe. Sites excavated on the Wairau bar reveal that many women there died aged around 23–25,[88] suggesting that, as elsewhere, childbirth was a killer.

ABOVE

Woman and child during the 1840s.

Joseph Jenner Merrett, Alexander Turnbull Library, A-275-002

BELOW

A 'cabin' in Torrent Bay on the northwest coast of the South Island.

Louis Auguste de Sainson, hand-coloured engraving, Alexander Turnbull Library, PUBL-0038-1-18r

Hard living helped shape the nature of Maori society as it evolved, combining with other human and cultural values, structures and customs inherited from Polynesia. As always, the environment did not determine Maori culture; but the challenges Maori had to meet and conquer did provide a context within which society evolved. This was evident to the first Pakeha: Maori were, early nineteenth-century 'pakeha Maori' Frederick Maning decided,

> …pretty much like what almost any other people would have become if subjected for ages to the same external circumstances. For ages they have struggled against necessity in all its shapes. … It has even left its mark on their language… The necessity of labour, the necessity of warfare, and a temperate climate, gave them strength of body, accompanied by a perseverance and energy of mind perfectly astonishing…[89]

There was a particular emphasis on balance, on managing resources—and on reciprocity between kin groups and individuals. The cultural importance of this for Maori is underscored by the number of words that emerged to specify different flavours of reciprocal transactions, utu and muru among them. It ran through most social interactions, starting with exchanges of food and gifts, to specific responses in warfare. Reciprocity was also abstracted, emerging when customary expectations were broken, including breaches of tapu, insults or slights.

Warfare was integral to society, though it is wrong to suggest that Maori were innately savage. Early Pakeha settlers thought they were; but it is more accurate to say that the relationship between society and war differed from that of eighteenth and nineteenth-century Europe, where warfare was glorified but where combatants were also specialists. Maori did not have professional full-time soldiers. Toa (warriors) were also farmers, fishermen, hunters, builders and labourers. They were trained in fighting arts as one of the tasks they were expected to do; and the warrior tradition formed part of the social order.[90]

TOP LEFT

Although Joseph Banks found a carved meeting house at Tolaga Bay, large and elaborate permanent buildings were more widely a nineteenth-century development for Maori. In pre-contact times decoration was more restrained, and some houses were temporary, designed to provide shelter for short periods while people gathered food. These buildings, and the 'cabin' opposite, were sketched by Dumont D'Urville's artist Louis Auguste Sainson in 1827.

Louis Auguste Sainson, Alexander Turnbull Library, C-010-024

ABOVE

Waimate pa, Taranaki, during 1839.

Charles Heaphy, Alexander Turnbull Library, A-164-008

ABOVE

'The head of a chief of New Zealand, the face curiously tatow'd, or marked according to their manner'. Sydney Parkinson was tasked with accurately recording what he saw. Moko patterns differ from those observed by later explorers, underscoring the fact that Maori styles did change over time, a point often lost after patterns were snap-frozen by the advent of the Pakeha colony in the nineteenth century.

Sydney Parkinson/T. Chambers, Alexander Turnbull Library, PUBL-0037-16

To that extent Colenso was right in looking on war as a core focus of society; fighting was important at a social and political level, as were individual fortunes in battle. Mana could be won or lost depending on the outcome. But fighting was also subject to a range of controls generally derived from the fact that conflict was an expensive luxury.[91] Although settler-era British observers often judged Maori warfare by British values, it had its own range of social controls. Most were geared towards limiting the economic cost, which was that of labour lost from food production. While it is an overstatement to suggest that classic-era battles were 'trials of strength' akin to football matches,[92] there were many mechanisms to reduce the cost of warfare to resource-limited Maori. They included proxying through death of slaves, single combat, or negotiation—all valid ways of dispute settlement instead of fighting. Negotiation and the customs of utu and muru—formalised systems of exchange—were integral to the mix.

Maori society also carried what, to British observers, was a dark side. Maori ate each other. Cannibalism—kai tangata—was discovered by James Cook and his crew as early as 1769–70, and repeatedly observed by Pakeha during the next 80-odd years, although Maori quickly realised it stood against British values and became rather coy about it. Te Pahi told New South Wales Governor Philip King, in 1805, that his own hapu did not indulge in it, but others did. King was sceptical, reporting that 'everything I have heard and observed' told him 'that this practice most certainly prevails in New Zealand.'[93] Cannibalism died out in the 1840s, apart from a brief revival for terror purposes during the late 1860s. However, its pre-European reality stood against the post-colonial idealisation of indigenous behaviour to the point where some scholars of the late twentieth century tried denying that cannibalism had ever been a traditional practice,[94] typically by casting intellectualised but ultimately specious methodological doubt on the source material.[95] A thoughtful 2008 analysis of the topic even provoked an anonymous complaint to the Race Relations Conciliator.[96]

All this revealed a good deal about the mind-set of late twentieth century scholars, but very little about Maori. The reality was that Maori did practise cannibalism in pre-European times—the practice was inherited from Polynesia. It was, however, not the uncontrollable frenzy imagined by European observers. The whole was thoroughly hedged and framed with cultural rules, principally tied up with spiritual and moral reciprocity—a form of ultimate utu. Relatives were never eaten. Nor were the early Europeans liable to be devoured, unless they transgressed. But it took a little while for the British to realise that Maori had cultural rules. Cannibalism was well outside normal British rules and

ABOVE

Canoes on the Whanganui River.

Thomas William Downes, Alexander Turnbull Library, A-036-001

social conventions; British observers looking in regarded those who practised it as worse than savages, uncontrollably lusting after human flesh. Maori lining beaches to welcome arriving Pakeha were thought more likely to be sizing the visitors up as a British gentleman might assess a prime steer. Reality was far less lurid, and it did not take long to discover. John Savage insisted as early as 1807 that Maori were 'not so horrible as represented'. The cultural frameworks of kai tangata were obvious even then; it was integral with utu, part of the wider system of reciprocity. 'Thus, after a conquest, the victors do not devour the whole of their prisoners, but are content with shewing [sic] their power to do so…It is probable that an [sic?] European, who should act with hostility towards them, would be treated in the same way, but if cast defenceless upon their shores… would meet with far different treatment.'[97] That was a fair assessment.

Maori society itself was structured around dynamic relationships that flowed from kin groups. The basic building block was whanau, an extended family; numbers of whanau formed a hapu, which became the key structure through the period.[98] Sometimes groupings of hapu refocussed as a wider organisation usually known as iwi. They occupied rohe (territories), but there was significant flexibility between all these groups. Hapu and iwi formed and broke up over time. This was partly a function of the way customary values played out, partly a function of resource limitation. As some have argued, the main social group— the hapu—had to be large enough to collect the food and raw materials it needed, without overstraining what was available. Seasonal resources such as shellfish or

ABOVE

William Ellis' picture of a 'New Zealand warrior' from 1778.

William Webb Ellis, pencil and ink, Alexander Turnbull Library, A-264-002

rookeries also implied mobility, which was not conducive to large-scale political structures.[99]

These structures were in constant flux through the period, and a lot of the oral record picked up by late nineteenth-century 'recovery ethnographers' and through the land court evidence effectively described these changes in operation. Kin groupings would come together, co-exist, then perhaps split a generation or two later. The best example is Ngai Tahu. This iwi began as what Harry Evison has called a 'loose association' of hapu in the southern North Island.[100] They began moving south during the early eighteenth century and by around 1730 were at Horomaka (Banks Peninsula).[101] Other groups, such as Ngati Irakehu of the Wairarapa, joined them; and new kin groupings emerged including Ngati Kuri of Kaikoura, Ngati Tuahuriri of Kaiapoi and the West Coast, Ngati Irakehu of Horomaka, and—further south—Ngāi Te Ruahikihiki.[102] This was playing out as Europe arrived.

The great southern land

Towards noon we saw a large high-lying land, bearing south-east of us at about 15 miles distance; we turned our course to the south-east, making straight for this land… We resolved to touch at the said land as quickly as at all possible…
– *Abel Tasman's Journal*, 13 December 1642.[103]

The early seventeenth century was an age of upheaval in Europe.[104] New religious beliefs, patterns of thought and fresh political ideals were given force by a subsistence crisis brought on in part by the onset of the little ice age.[105] Long-standing political, economic, social and religious structures bent or broke, and as T. K. Rabb tells us, war compounded the drama.[106] Politics, philosophy and religious thought were reshaped, setting the scene for the 'age of reason' and, with it, the philosophies that Europe's first explorers and settlers brought to New Zealand.

Much of this crisis bypassed the Netherlands, seven provinces which drew strength from their 1588 unification and a sustained effort to make Amsterdam the financial heart of Europe. The Vereenigde Oostinsche Compagnie (VOC)—the Dutch East India Company—was established to work the East Indies spice trade in 1602. Based at Batavia, it fought its own wars and made its own treaties to secure Dutch trade against British and Portuguese interests. The world beckoned.

By the fourth decade of the seventeenth century much of Asia was known, Japan was contacted, and the VOC began looking further afield into areas that mapmakers had yet to chart. Legend hinted at lucrative trade with the wealthy inhabitants of a huge continent thought to exist as a counterweight to Europe, a land of wonder filled with everything from men with faces in their stomachs to people who walked on their heads. Other heads prevailed in the VOC, where Jan Carstenz charted part of west Australia in 1623, and Francoijs Thyssen mapped a portion of the south coast four years later.[107] Spanish and Portuguese explorers had crossed the Pacific on five occasions, and Ferdinand de Quiros penetrated to 26° south, finding Espiritu Santo but no continent.[108] In 1615, Willem Schouten and

Jacob le Maire rounded New Guinea and cast across the Pacific at a latitude of 30° south—again without finding the fabled continent.[109] Around 1641, Abel Tasman (1603–1659) and fellow officers Isaac Gilsemans (c1606–c1647) and Francoijs Visscher (c1600–1645) decided to explore the waters south and east of Australia, and in January 1642 Visscher prepared a 'Memoir Concerning the Discovery of the Southland'.[110]

The Batavia Council authorised the voyage in August. Tasman was given the fluyt *Zeehaen* (Seacock) and larger *Heemskerck*, 'victualled at all points' for a year, with 'a quantity of precious and other metals for bartering purposes'. The plan called for a journey to the VOC base at Mauritius, then south to 52°, 'or at most 54°', before sailing east to the longitude of the Solomons 'or somewhat farther east'.[111] Trade was uppermost in the minds of Governor-General Antony van Diemen and his council. Separate instructions urged Tasman not to tip off locals to the value Europeans placed on gold, and to 'prudently prevent all manner of insolence' from the sailors.[112]

Tasman set out from Batavia in mid-August 1642 and reached Mauritius in late September.[113] Bad weather forced them to abort the run south at 49°, and they sailed east, sighting the south coast of Tasmania on 24 November. They struck east again on 5 December and eight days later the lookouts sighted Punakaiki. Needing to replenish water, firewood and fresh food, Tasman closed with Cape Foulwind but kept clear of the rugged shoreline. By 16 December they were off Farewell Spit, spending the next day running 'along a low-lying shore with dunes'.[114] Late on 18 December the fleet dropped anchor in Taitapu (Golden Bay), east of the Takaka river mouth. Soon after dark, two waka—'prows', to Tasman—approached the Dutch vessels, and the occupants 'began to call out to us in a rough, hollow voice.' Although equipped with a 'vocabulary' that VOC administrators thought might be useful, Tasman's men 'could not understand a word'.[115]

These people were Ngati Tumatakokiri, whose seventeenth-century population has been estimated at between 400 and 500. Although one historian has suggested the blasts they blew on pukaea may have been intended to frighten away ghosts,[116] they were actually challenging the unknown strangers.[117] Tasman's innocent order to 'one of our sailors (who had some knowledge of trumpet-blowing) to play them some tunes', was taken by Ngati Tumatakokiri as accepting the challenge.[118] They repeated their calls, answered from the *Zeehaen* as well. Tasman had no idea about the import of all this, but ordered 'double watches... and to keep in readiness all necessaries of war.'[119] His priority was fresh water, and he ordered a meeting on board the *Heemskerck* next morning to discuss ways of getting it. The *Zeehaen*'s senior officers crossed in a cock-boat, and were still on board the flagship when Ngati Tumatakokiri approached, ready for the fight. Tasman's journal recorded people of 'ordinary height' with 'rough

ABOVE

An eighteenth-century rendition of Abel Tasman's ships *Zeehaen* (left) and *Heemskerck*.

John Watt Beattie, Kinnear Collection, Alexander Turnbull Library F-14565-1/2

Bay'. It was New Zealand's first example of cultural miscommunication, and it was not the last.

Tasman still needed water, but they were beset by a five-day storm in the Taranaki bight. This probably prevented them finding Cook Strait,[125] though Tasman suspected there was 'a passage through' on the basis of tide.[126] Christmas was marked with fresh pork and wine, and as the weather settled the Dutch sailed north. They anchored off the Three Kings on 5 January and found a bay with a freshwater stream, but surf and 'men of tall stature' on the hills above deterred a landing.[127] An attempt next day to get water also failed, and Tasman decided to quit 'Staaten Land' altogether, shaping course for Tonga.

A British endeavour

Tasman's reception at Golden Bay quashed further Dutch effort to explore the southern continent. The partial coast of 'Nieu Zeeland', possibly coined by map-maker Johan Blaeu—hung like a question mark on European charts.[128] It took Europe more than 130 years to find the answers. By the eighteenth century the British and French were at odds with each other in Europe, India and around the world; rivalry translated after the Seven Years War into a fresh effort to explore the globe. However, competing expeditions to the Pacific in the 1760s invariably took advantage of equatorial winds to sail from the Horn through Polynesia—missing the South Pacific.[129]

A journey into those southern waters was not long in coming. Philosophy, arts and the sciences flourished under the power of reason. Geographers wanted maps of the world, botanists and biologists hoped to find and classify new species, and the Royal Society wanted to measure the distance between Earth and the sun by observing a transit of Venus. An effort to take advantage of a 1761 transit failed, and calculations revealed that another would be visible in 1769.

ABOVE

Yorkshire-born James Cook (1728–1779) joined the Royal Navy in 1755. Discharged when peace came in 1762, he married Elizabeth Batts and began a career as a maritime surveyor. He was made captain of the *Endeavour* for his first voyage to the South Pacific. He made a second world-spanning journey in 1773, commanding HMS *Resolution*, which he also took to the Pacific for his third voyage in 1776. A tall man, 'above six feet high', he had a face 'full of expression' and heavy eyebrows which apparently 'gave his countenance altogether an air of austerity.' This portrait is from a painting by John Webber, at the Cape of Good Hope, though few images apparently bear close resemblance.

John Webber, Alexander Turnbull Library, A-218-009

LEFT

HMS *Endeavour* leaving Whitby for the Thames, where she was fitted out for the long voyage to the South Pacific.

Lionel T. Crawshaw, Alexander Turnbull Library, A-110-019

NEW ZEALAND
AN ILLUSTRATED HISTORY

View of the North Side of the Entrance into Poverty Bay, & Morai Island, in New-Zealand.
1. Young Nick's Head
2. Morai Island

View of another Side of the Entrance into the said Bay.

ABOVE

Two views of the entrance to Poverty Bay as seen by Cook's artist Sydney Parkinson (1745–1771).

Sydney Parkinson/R.B.Godfrey, Alexander Turnbull Library, PUBL-0037-14

In late 1767, Society officials—wanting widely spaced observations—proposed that hydrographer Alexander Dalrymple should lead an expedition to observe it from the Pacific. The Admiralty concurred, but proposed Lieutenant James Cook instead. The scientific contingent was led by Joseph Banks, a wealthy Fellow of the Royal Society,[130] who assembled a group that included astronomer Charles Green, artists Sydney Parkinson and John Buchan, and naturalists Dr Solander and Herman Spöring.

Cook raised his pendant on the *Endeavour*, ex-*Earl of Pembroke*, at the end of May 1768 and began preparing for sea.[131] Anti-scorbutics were in vogue, and in addition to the usual salted meats, flour, pulses, biscuits and livestock, Cook was ordered to take pickled cabbage, thinned orange juice, carrot marmalade and malt, and to report the effects back to the Admiralty.[132] These joined the private stores, scientific equipment, water and other gear needed for a long ocean voyage, all shoe-horned with 94 men—including the scientists and a dozen marines—into a vessel just 106 feet (32 metres) long.

'Secret' instructions—published shortly after he left Britain in July 1768—required Cook to look for the missing continent by running south to 35°, then west 'until you discover it, or fall in with the Eastern side of the Land discover'd by Tasman...'[133] *Endeavour* reached Tahiti in April 1769, where Cook observed the transit. They sailed south with Tahitian chief Tupaia on board, found nothing at the specified latitude, and turned east. Early in October the *Endeavour* reached Turanga-nui—Poverty Bay. Here, by a riverbank, Cook had his first meeting with

ABOVE

'View of the Moordenaer's Bay, as you [are] at anchor there in 15 fathoms,' the artist wrote on this well-known drawing from Tasman's voyage. Text translates: 'A. Our ships; B. The prows which came alongside of us; C. The cock-boat of the *Zeehaen*, which came paddling towards our ship, and was overpowered by the natives, who afterwards left it again owing to our firing; when we saw that they had left the cock-boat, our skipper fetched it back; D. A view of the native prow with the appearance of the people; E. Our ships pulling off to sea; F. Our pinnace bringing back the cock-boat.'

Isaac Gilesmans, Alexander Turnbull Library, PUBL-0086-021

voices and strong bones', whose hair was tufted and 'tied fast in the manner of the Japanese... surmounted by a large thick white feather...'[120]

Nine waka were soon paddling around, carrying more than 100 toa. Tasman's men 'held up and showed to them, as before, white linens', but Gerrit Janszoon, skipper of the *Zeehaen*, was becoming uneasy. Maori outnumbered the soldiers on the vessels, and he decided to send the cock-boat back to the *Zeehaen* with a warning not to let 'too many of them on board'. The cock-boat crossed safely, but as its crew began the return journey to the *Heemskerck*:

> ...those in the prow [waka] before us, between the two ships, began to paddle furiously towards us...struck the *Zeehaen*'s cock-boat so violently... with the stem of their prow that it got a violent lurch, upon which the foremost man in the prow of villains, with a long blunt pike, thrust the quartermaster Cornelis Joppen, in the neck several times with so much force that the poor man fell overboard...[121]

The toa 'fell upon' the crew of the boat and 'overcame them by main force', killing three and fatally wounding a fourth. Three survivors, including Joppen, swam to the *Heemskerck*, where they were picked up by the pinnace. The Dutch 'diligently fired our muskets and guns' as the Maori paddled away, while the pinnace 'well-manned and armed', collected the cock-boat.[122] Tasman ordered his small fleet to sea, and as they hoisted their sails, counted 22 waka, half of which, 'swarming with people, were making for our ships.'[123] More shots were fired. Tasman, angered by the 'outrageous and detestable crime',[124] dubbed the area 'Murderers'

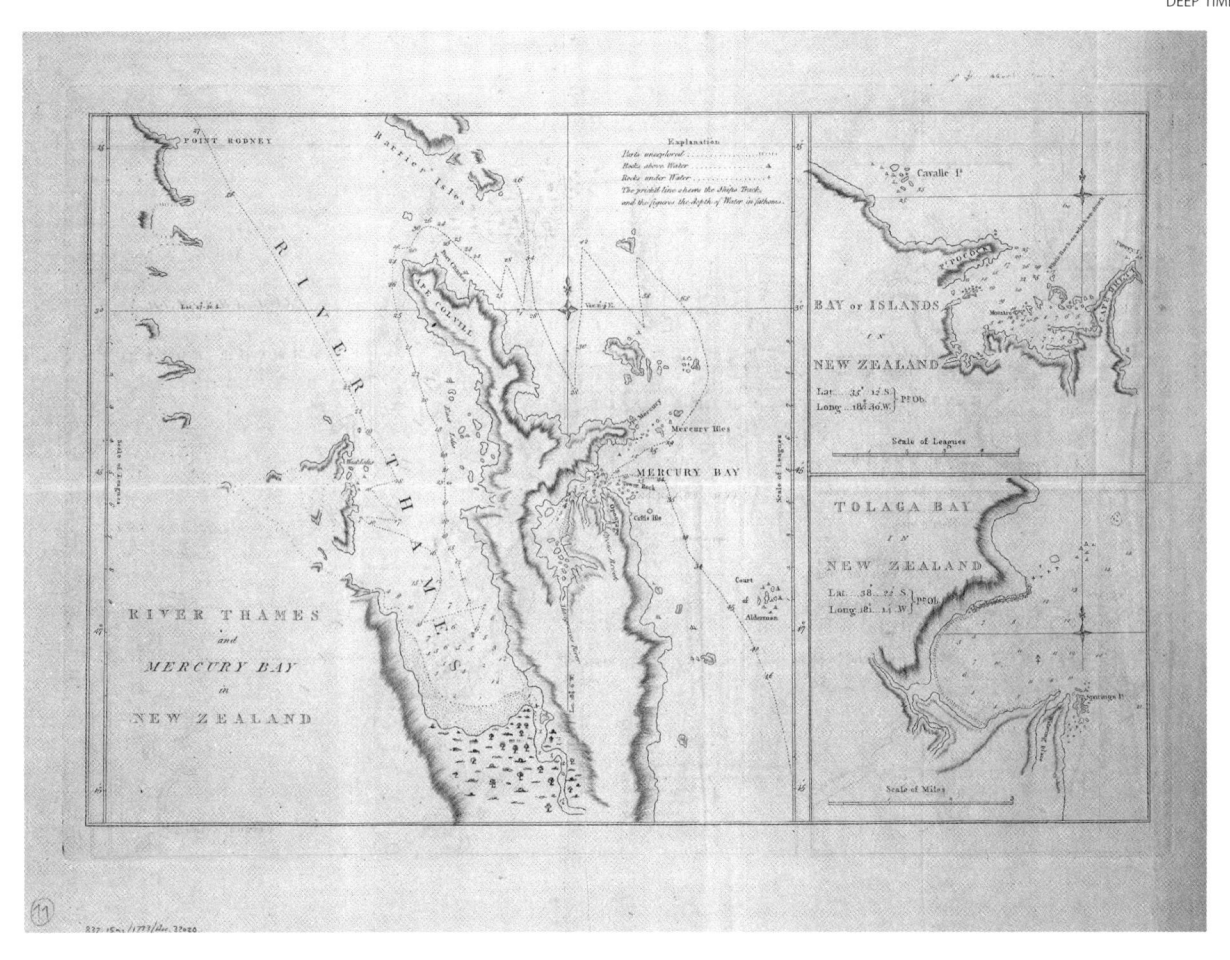

Maori, the Rongowhakata. As at Golden Bay, the *Endeavour* was outside Maori experience; they first thought it was a floating island or bird, the Englishmen initially regarded as gods.[134]

Cook had no reciprocal illusions. He had been given 'hints' which were no more useful than Tasman's 'vocabulary', but had the advantage of three months in Tahiti. Tupaia was also to hand, and it was 'an agreeable surprise' to find that Maori 'perfectly understood him.'[135] In fact both Maori and Tahitian were derived from the same language, proto-Tahitic.[136] Maori responded to initial calls in Tahitian by 'florishing [sic] their weapons over their heads and danceing [sic]... upon this we retired until the marines had landed.'[137] One of the Englishmen recognised the challenge as a 'Dancing War Song' which was 'Calculated in my opinion to Chear [sic] Each Other and Intimidate their Enemies...'[138] Unfortunately, such early rapport did not prevent bloodshed. By the end of the day two Maori—Te Maro and Te Rakau—were dead at the hands of the British and their firearms.[139] Next day there was more shooting. So began six months in New Zealand, during which the industrious British obtained a unique 'snapshot' of classic pre-contact Maori society.

Cook arrived just one step ahead of the French; Jean de Surville reached the South Island three weeks after Cook touched Poverty Bay. Cook had already claimed New Zealand in toto for Britain—a paper claim, but even had the French pushed, the spectre of 'southern men' sipping wine and devouring canapés in France's southernmost department was less likely than an eighteenth-century

ABOVE

James Cook's voyage attracted huge interest back in Britain and a significant number of books were published about the adventure. These charts of the 'River Thames and Mercury Bay, Bay of Islands, Tolaga Bay in New Zealand' appeared in John Hawkesworth's 'An account of the voyages undertaken by the order of his present Majesty, for making discoveries in the southern hemisphere, and successively performed by ... Captain Cook....'

Alexander Turnbull Library, MapColl 832.15aj/1773/Acc.32020

political accommodation with Britain. Cook himself reached the South Island in January 1770, discovering a refuge in Queen Charlotte Sound which he used as a base during his two later voyages into the Pacific.

Cook has usually received the proverbial good deal from New Zealand historians, in part because of the exaltation of all things British during the mid-twentieth century. In a wider context this is less justified. Cook was an innovative and skilled commander, yet arguably many of his brother officers had similar traits—skills deriving from the need for any naval captain to act independently, responsibly and successfully during long months out of contact with the Admiralty. Although more sensitive than many of his peers towards indigenous people, Cook mishandled some contacts, with fatal consequences. His greatest strength was as a navigator—he was in the same league as his near-contemporary William Bligh, competent and sure-footed. His first voyage was achieved without the aid of the Harrison chronometers, a device too experimental for Cook to take in 1768, though he had one for his second and third voyages. He mapped most of the New Zealand coastline and a significant proportion of the Australian, and some of his charts were still in use more than a century later. The errors over Stewart Island and Banks Peninsula were minor given that he did not have an opportunity to examine these areas in detail.

ABOVE

Sir Joseph Banks (1743–1820), seen here in later life, was a botanist who inherited a fortune when his father died in 1764 – always a good start in eighteenth-century Britain. When he joined James Cook's ship to lead its scientific contingent he was just 26. After Cook's first voyage he was elected President of the Royal Society, a post he held until his death.

Thomas Phillips, Alexander Turnbull Library, A-038-017

CHAPTER TWO
Agents of change

European explorers nosed into New Zealand's coasts and inlets towards the end of the eighteenth century. Marion du Fresne, George Vancouver, Alejandro Malaspina and Antoine-Raymond-Joseph de Bruni d'Entrecasteaux led expeditions to New Zealand in the last two decades of the century. Settlement was another matter. John Thomson tried to interest Secretary of State Henry Dundas in a New Zealand colony in 1792. He thought 'fifty sober men', a hundred sepoys, and the same number of convicts could get in by setting 'one tribe against another' and allowing the British to force the loser to terms. Maori would be forced to cooperate via hostages, who 'by being taught and well treated' would 'introduce civilisation and render the country… an asylum for distressed mariners.'[1]

This idea was ridiculous even by period standards. The British Empire of the eighteenth century was a trading entity. New Zealand was a remote archipelago; and Britain had other priorities as the American Revolution, French Revolution and the rise of Napoleon threw their world into chaos. The push into the South Pacific came, eventually, on the back of the American Revolution, which cost Britain its dumping ground for convicts. Australia beckoned as a possible alternative—and not merely for its remoteness. Plans floated in the mid-1780s envisaged the penal colony also becoming a focus for developing trade into the South Pacific.

New Zealand had its place in these schemes as a potential resource centre. Britain's huge merchant marine and navy devoured masts, sails and rigging, and proposals to obtain flax rope from Norfolk Island for Indian merchant shipping were floated in 1785 by Sir George Young and Sir John Call.[2] Young waxed lyrical about the qualities of New Zealand flax, which 'may be obtained at a much cheaper rate' than Russian cordage.[3] Thomas Townshend, Lord Sydney,

TOP

French explorer Jules Sebastien Cesar Dumont D'Urville made several voyages to the South Pacific in the late 1820s. Here, D'Urville's artist Louis Auguste de Sainson depicts Tolaga Bay Maori 'dancing' aboard D'Urville's ship *Astrolabe*.
Louis Auguste de Sainson, Alexander Turnbull Library, B-052-021-1/2

ABOVE

D'Urville discovered French Pass the hard way in 1827, nearly losing his ship *Astrolabe* to a combination of tidal rip and shallow water.

Louis Auguste de Sainson, Alexander Turnbull Library, B-052-004

BELOW

D'Urville's 'schooner', as the original caption put it, surrounded by 'New Zealand canoes'.

Louis Auguste de Sainson, Alexander Turnbull Library, PUBL-0034-2-350

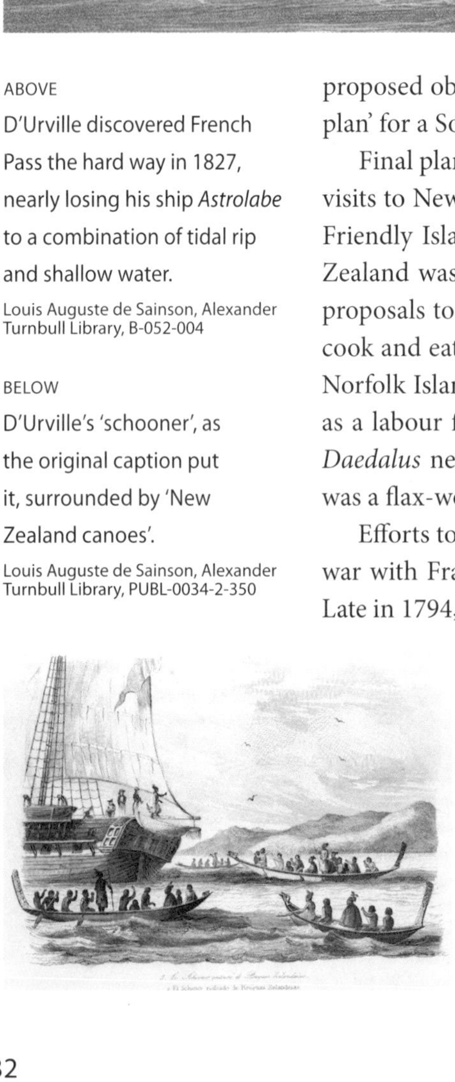

proposed obtaining flax and masting timber from New Zealand in his 'heads of plan' for a South Pacific penal colony.[4]

Final plans for a penal colony at Botany Bay, floated in March 1787, called for visits to New Zealand 'for the flax-plant'—though Maori escaped the fate of the Friendly Islanders, where colonial authorities hoped to procure women.[5] New Zealand was never a serious contender as a prison venue, and Arthur Phillip's proposals to exile sodomites to New Zealand, where Maori would be invited to cook and eat them, were absurd. A satellite prison was, however, established on Norfolk Island where Lieutenant-Governor Philip King planned to use convicts as a labour force to process local flax. Two Maori captured by the crew of the *Daedalus* near the Cavalli Islands in 1793 were brought there to help. Neither was a flax-worker.[6]

Efforts to exploit New Zealand's resources gained momentum when renewed war with France interrupted supplies of mast and spar timber from the Baltic. Late in 1794, William Bampton sent the *Fancy*, under Edgar Dell, into Doubtless Bay to get timber for refitting a ship in India. Dell sailed on to the Hauraki Gulf and the Thames (Waihou) River mouth, where Cook had reported stands of trees. In three months, his men felled 213 of them, mostly kahikatea.[7] Other ships followed, the *Hunter*, *El Plumier* and *Betsey* among them. Ultimately, however, New Zealand timber did not prove durable and the trade was virtually at an end by the early 1800s. Flax was also less a benefit than initially thought; tests at the Chatham Rope Yard in 1818 revealed that 'New Zealand hemp bore little more than two thirds the weight' of equivalent rope from Riga and Chile.[8]

CHAPTER TWO
AGENTS OF CHANGE

Hunters had better luck. Seals were to be had for the taking – the animals had no knowledge or fear of men, who had merely to walk up to these animals and club them. Captain William Raven took the *Britannia* into Dusky Sound late in 1792 to begin the slaughter. The seal skins he brought back to Australia opened the flood gates. The following year Bampton took his *Endeavour* across the Tasman—not Cook's ship, but a creaky old East Indiaman, that basically collapsed and is often considered New Zealand's first shipwreck. Bampton, his crew and a handful of convicts who had stowed away made it back to Norfolk Island on their consort, *Fancy*.[9]

Many more sealers arrived after the Australian rookeries were hunted out, a rough bunch who generally worked away from the main centres of Maori population. They were later joined by whalers, a polyglot band of Americans, British, Spanish and Russian ne'er-do-wells, some of them ex-convicts with their Certificates of Freedom, looking to make a life for themselves. And so the Australian colony, effectively, arrived in New Zealand. For all their distance and a subculture that included its own argot, these whaling ventures were extensions, in effect, of colonies in New South Wales and Tasmania. They were

ABOVE

Interior of a pa. A lithograph from artwork by Louis Auguste de Sainson.

Louis Auguste de Sainson, Alexander Turnbull Library, B-052-008

LEFT

Joseph Toms, Thom or Thoms, also known as Geordie Bolts (1798–1852), established a whaling station next to Ngati Te Ra pa at Paremata, early in the nineteenth century. By the time artist Samuel Charles Brees (1810–1865) sketched these pictures in the early 1840s, Toms was also running an inn and cross-harbour ferry.

Samuel Charles Brees, Alexander Turnbull Library, A-343-005

33

RIGHT

This painting of Te Kopi whaling station in Palliser Bay probably dates to 1844.

Samuel Charles Brees, watercolour and gum arabic, Alexander Turnbull Library, B-031-025

closely integrated; ships plied the Tasman with cargoes of whale oil and bones. For all their rough edges, the whaling stations were subject to British law, and major transgressors were packed off back to Sydney or Hobart Town for justice to be done. It was not cheap to set up a whaling venture, but it was a lucrative trade, immensely profitable on relatively modest capital if all went well. Where it did not, there was a risk of sudden-death loss, and some investors crashed and burned. Many did not. There were whaling stations in Dusky Sound by the 1790s, but their heyday came in the 1830s when many stations opened around the southern South Island and eastern North Island.

Trade and prejudice

Contact during the early nineteenth century came mainly in the far north and deep south. And it brought a new age of unprecedented change and novelty for both peoples. While southern exposure was principally through whalers and sealers, the northern revolved more around trade. Merchants gravitated to the Bay of Islands and Ngapuhi particularly. It was not by chance. Sydney authorities introduced the potato there in 1794, hoping to develop the place—with Maori help—as a trading and supply centre for Sydney and for ships embarking on cross-Pacific journeys. The strategy worked; by 1805 Governor Philip King was able to trumpet that the 'frequent intercourse' had been 'very advantageous', and that Maori were using it 'not only for their own advantage' but also to supply the whaling ships 'very liberally'.[10]

Such sentiments understated a complex and steadily unfolding relationship. British traders, whalers, drifters and convicts arrived in New Zealand filled with the ideas and prejudices of their age. Maori welcomed them, swiftly seeing every advantage for their own lives in the tools, blankets, goods and products of industrialising Britain. The fact that Maori were active agents was not always obvious to British thinking channelled by 'fatal impact' notions and other period ideas about race and intellect.[11] In fact Maori went out of their way to learn all they could about British technologies and culture. Some sought passage to Australia.

Others went to Paris and London. Most did so with the help of patrons, such as Thomas Kendall, but the real question was who was patronising who. Eager trade deals, which King took to mean that Maori were 'very tractable',[12] were actually Maori proactivity.

Te Pahi—'Tippahee' to contemporary Europeans—a rangatira of Hikutu, took an early lead in the contact race. So did Ruatara—'Duaterra' or 'Dewaterra' in contemporary British spelling—who sailed to Port Jackson on board the *Ferret* in 1805. He returned with a variety of animals and European products.

None of this was done for British purposes or because Maori particularly admired British culture. It was to meet Maori needs. British industrial goods— hoes, rakes, shovels, hammers, nails, saws, blankets, cloth, needles, thread, tobacco, rum, guns, munitions, buckets and all the panoply of things nineteenth-century technology had at its disposal—were drawn into the Maori world, reframed by Maori within their own systems and values, and used to improve the Maori lot. And so Maori came into collision with the industrial age and all the forces that brought with it. These were turning British society upside down, even as the British came into contact with Maori; the effect on Maori life was as profound, though not quite the destructive culture-annihilation that it has sometimes been portrayed to be.

These early years—what we might call the 'contact era'—brought a sharp learning curve for both peoples. Each culture found the other strange, and early Pakeha who tried to live in New Zealand often trampled on key Maori values without even realising it. Frederick Maning discovered that all he had to do was pick up a skull he had found. Linguistic gaffes were rife; neither people spoke the other's language particularly well in the early nineteenth century—indeed, Colenso reported as late as 1868, three generations later, that few Pakeha even then spoke Maori 'correctly; still fewer idiomatically'.[13] R. G. Jamieson reported that even frowning at a Maori was insulting, and 'to swear and rail at him is an offence for which he will demand immediate payment'.[14]

Maori also posed a paradox for the British. At a time when indigenous

LEFT

Maori bartering pigs and potatoes with a merchant, thought to be Joel Polack, probably at Kororareka.

John Williams, Alexander Turnbull Library, A-079-017

ABOVE

It did not take long for Europe's industrial-age goods to spread through New Zealand from the contact points. Edward Ashworth (1814–1896) made this pen-and-ink sketch of Waingaroa Maori in the early 1840s, by which time blankets, tools, seeds, plants, ironware, tobacco and rum were well entrenched in Maori life. European observers, however, often misinterpreted the way this adoption worked; Europe's goods were acculturated, drawn into Maori life and given a Maori context. In the process they changed aspects of Maori life, but they did not destroy old values, despite European notions of the day that this was what was happening.

Edward Ashworth, Alexander Turnbull Library, A-208-022).

peoples were regarded as ignorant, childlike savages, Maori had many of the characteristics that the British admired. William Yate thought them 'uncivilised' but 'industrious…a hard working race.'[15] Augustus Earle thought Maori were 'cast in beauty's perfect mould…the intellects of both sexes…of a superior order … eager for improvement, full of energy, and indefatigably industrious…'[16] William Marshall admired what he saw as restraint, contrasting with the 'gluttony and drunkenness' of British civilisation, lures with which to 'deprave the habit of body of those who indulge therein'.[17] All these, and more, were characteristics which the British reserved to define their own superiority. The paradox was resolved via the curious notion of the 'noble savage', people who defied prevailing ideas about racial ranking and jumped the queue to be almost—but, naturally, not quite—as good as the British.

But Maori were still savage, to the British mind. They were not Christian—they lived, as one missionary put it, in the 'dark night of heathenism'.[18] Customs such as utu and muru were often interpreted by the British as theft. Maori were also swift to anger, hot on revenge, and the clincher was their reputation for dining on human flesh. Cannibalism. That one side of Maori life, at a stroke, wiped out any notion that Maori might be in the British league.

For their part, Maori found British culture equally odd by their own standards. British customs crossed every cultural boundary. And Maori were not slow to condemn it. When Te Pahi visited Sydney in 1805, he 'spared no pains to convince us that the customs of his country were in several instances better than ours, many of which he looked on with the greatest contempt, and some with the most violent and abusive disapprobation.'[19] 'Cannibal' Jack Marmon discovered that Maori were curious about his own values, but only as a 'foil to the superior Maori'.[20]

Maori capability did not stop the British slotting them into period theories, particularly 'fatal impact'. This widely held notion was linked into concepts of market competition, suggesting that Maori would become helpless victims of a 'superior' culture, with lethal results—a fear expressed by the Church Missionary Society (CMS) in particular.

To some extent Maori were victims of Europe. Disease was an indiscriminate and uncontrollable killer. Epidemics in the late 1790s had devastating effect, and early missionaries recorded waves of whooping cough, influenza, tuberculosis, measles, the common cold and venereal disease.[21] Maori helplessness in the face of ills that even European science did not fully understand, coupled with exaggerated accounts of depopulation, helped fuel 'fatal impact' thinking, though disease was not thought decisive. 'Many other causes combined at the same time to work the destruction of the natives,' self-confessed 'Pakeha Maori' Frederick Maning wrote:

> ...continual excitement, over-work, and insufficient food, exposure and unhealthy places of residence, together with a general breaking up of old habits of life, thinned their numbers. European diseases also assisted, but not to any very serious degree...[22]

The period notion that contact destroyed indigenous peoples was enduring. Even when time and experience gave the lie to the conceit, the supposition still fed into ideas that pre-contact Maori society, at least, had been somehow broken by the impact. This remains one of New Zealand's more intense historical debates, polarised between camps; either Maori society was bent and broken as they dropped old values, or tikanga sailed through untouched. The reality, inevitably, was somewhere between. Change occurred within existing frameworks—the rules were bent, twisted, driven to supercharged levels, but tikanga was resilient enough to survive. The point is made clear by the way religion was received. The Church Missionary Society and other evangelists were quick to introduce the gospel to Maori, swiftly followed by claims of 'conversion'. Reality was different. Not all chiefs picked Christianity up. As William Yate noted at the time, Hongi Hika rejected Christianity as fit only for slaves.[23] Conversion was only nominal well into the nineteenth century. Even in the late 1830s, a generation after the CMS arrived, A. N. Brown was told by Maori that the Bible did not 'come down from Heaven', it was written by missionaries and 'sent to Paihia to be printed.'[24] 'What was all that nonsense about?' a dying Te Rauparaha told a minister who had just given him the last rites. 'It won't make any difference to my health.'[25] Christianity took its place alongside other European customs, selectively adopted by Maori to overlay—but not supplant—traditional beliefs. The identification of sectarian difference with inter-hapu rivalry underlines the point.

ABOVE

The 'flogging Parson', Samuel Marsden (1765–1838), in 1833.

Richard Read, pencil and wash, Alexander Turnbull Library, A-039-038

LEFT

Samuel Marsden's vicarage at Parramatta, west of Sydney, around 1810. By May 1818 a dozen Maori were at the associated school, 'occupied in the acquisition of useful arts', including 'rope-making and twine-spinning'.

Edmund Thomas, Alexander Turnbull Library, G-19192-1/2

ABOVE
Mission station at Kerikeri, established in 1819, and seen here around 1830.

Artist unknown, Alexander Turnbull Library, PUBL-0031-30

ABOVE RIGHT
Waimate North mission station, near the Bay of Islands, based on a drawing by Cyprian Bridge around 1845.

Cyprian Bridge/J. Whymper, Alexander Turnbull Library, PUBL-0144-1-330

Partly for these reasons, Maori response to Christian teachings did not develop as the missionaries expected, but this was not through lack of trying. The Church Missionary Society—Anglican, evangelistic, devoted to saving indigenous peoples from the evils of British settlement—led the charge. And in the process they dominated the early Pakeha settlement in the northern point of contact around the Bay of Islands.

The push was led during the second decade of the nineteenth century by Samuel Marsden, CMS head in New South Wales—a complex character who reputedly got his jollies from watching men being flogged until their bones showed, and who classified all Australian women as either whores or wives. To him, New Zealand was a land ripe for the gospel; but the Governor, Philip King, refused to entertain such notions. New Zealand seemed too dangerous in the wake of the *Boyd* massacre of 1809. Marsden pushed, inspired by a visit from Bay of Islands chief Ruatara, who studied at the missionary school at Parramatta in 1809–10. King finally lost his power of veto in 1814 when Marsden bought a ship.

Carpenter William Hall, rope-maker John King and schoolteacher Thomas Kendall pioneered the way, setting up a station at Rangihoua under Ruatara's protection, and the missionaries followed soon afterwards. Marsden and his ministers, meanwhile, pressured the New South Wales administration of Lachlan Macquarie to bring wayward Bay of Islands visitors into line. Macquarie

RIGHT
William Bambridge (1819–1879) sketched the mission house and church at Waimate North, near the Bay of Islands. Haymaking goes on in the adjacent field.

William Bambridge, William Bambridge Diary, 1843–1845, Alexander Turnbull Library MS-0130-203

concurred and, although New Zealand was outside British authority, made Kendall a Justice of the Peace, while Ruatara ('Dewaterra'), Hongi ('Shungee') and Kawakawa ('Korra Korra') were given 'power and authority' to carry out Macquarie's orders.[26]

Kendall's school opened in 1816 with 33 pupils, rising to 50 before the children were diverted to food-gathering. More than 60 attended during 1817,[27] and Maori also attended Marsden's school across the Tasman at Parramatta. He thought exposure to 'civilized life' [sic] in Australia would be useful, apart from any skills they might pick up at the school.[28] How successful the 'conversions' were is debatable; to some extent Maori converted the missionaries sent to New Zealand, rather than the other way around. Both Kendall and William Yate found sexual partners among Maori, and Kendall was tempted by Maori beliefs almost to the point of abandoning Christianity.[29]

The missions entered a world of often divisive politics. Contact had become a mark of status for Maori, a door to prosperity, new ideas and new goods. Chiefs vied to have a mission under their own jurisdiction, and when Hongi took control of the second station at Kerikeri in 1819, war almost followed. Other missions were slower to arrive, in part because of fractious inter-hapu politics; one opened at Te Puna in 1822 and another at Paihia the following year. The Methodist Missionary Society set up a Wesleyan station at Kaeo in 1823; but it was sacked in 1827 and shifted to Mangunu on the Hokianga, under the patronage of Tamati Waka Nene. Catholicism arrived later in the 1830s.

ABOVE

New Testaments donated by the British and Foreign Bible Society are distributed to Taranaki Maori, 1842. Translating the Bible and distributing it was a priority for CMS missionaries. However, it was the early 1840s before even the New Testament was widely available in quantity.

Working Men's Educational Union, Alexander Turnbull Library, F-029.

ABOVE RIGHT

European industrial-age goods transformed Maori economics, switching the focus to producing potatoes and flax for trade.

Louis Auguste de Sainson, Alexander Turnbull Library, PUBL-0034-2-387

ABOVE

Cyprian Bridge sketched this 'ordinary New Zealand pah with potato plantations around it' in 1845.

Cyprian Bridge, Alexander Turnbull Library, A-079-031

However, the fact that Maori were active agents in the contact process did not mean they could always control the outcome. European trade goods did not, as some observers assumed at the time, cause Maori to drop their old ideas like hot potatoes. Instead, the new products were acculturated, drawn into Maori culture and used for Maori purposes. But they were nonetheless a change from what had gone before, a novelty, influencing Maori in many ways. The biggest impact was economic; Europe's plants and tools transformed the basis of Maori subsistence economics, and many hapu swung their productivity into producing flax and potatoes for trade.[30]

This rising demand for consumables, including tobacco, clothing, liquor, seeds and munitions, locked Maori into an economic relationship with industrial-age Britain. European goods—blankets, mirrors, needles, pipes, pots and clothing—also became part of a new 'currency of mana', a way in which status could be asserted. Europeans often missed the point. 'The great madness,' Maning wrote in 1863, 'was for muskets and gunpowder. A furious competition was kept up… After the demand for arms was supplied, came a perfect furore for iron tools, instruments for husbandry, and all kinds of Pakeha manufactures…A few years ago the madness ran upon horses and cattle; and now young New Zealand believes in nothing but money…'[31] Such thinking missed the cultural context in which European products were placed by Maori.

In this barter economy, goods were usually paid for with potatoes, pigs, flax and access to women, often via temporary marriages—though this was probably not what Governor Phillip King had in mind in 1805 when he referred to 'frequent intercourse' in the Bay of Islands.[32] Whether the women were willing is another matter. There were reports of ships' crews 'forcing the women to prostitute themselves',[33] and there is some evidence that Maori men required some women to do so for trade purposes. Progeny seldom survived; women were reported to 'generally procure abortion', though a few children were 'preserved'—apparently on the promise that the father would return.[34]

Maori initially held the whip hand in this trade—as Kendall protested, 'They dictate to us!'[35] But that changed as supply routes grew and Maori began placing increasing reliance and value on British goods—notably guns and munitions. Prices fell with growing volumes of trade. 'It used to be 25 hogs for a single musket', Ensign McCrae of the 84th Regiment reported in 1821, but it was 'now generally 15, or 200 baskets of potatoes.'[36] This was still steep. Much depended on negotiating skill; another trader at the same time exchanged a musket and 'some powder' for 18 pigs.[37]

Contact wars

War swept New Zealand for a generation from the 1810s, provoking a significant dislocation. Popularly these tumultuous events were always known as 'musket wars', because that was the main weapon Maori used; but the musket was neither cause nor driver of the fighting. Despite impressions, the wars were not initially fought with muskets. Most taua in the northern wars of 1817–21 had two or three—numbers with propaganda value only. Nor were the weapons forced on Maori. Muskets were a currency of rivalry well before they were available in tactically useful numbers, and Maori sought to procure the weapons from the British—in the face of missionary protests—and American sailors, who were 'free from restraint'.[38] The quality of these weapons was questionable, but this was less crucial to Maori than possession.

Some historians have tried to dub them 'potato wars', though they were much more than that. Certainly the potato did not fuel the long-range fighting parties that featured in the earlier part of the era—when one Ngapuhi taua ran out of food at Pipitea, for instance, they began killing slaves ' … we had made an agreement that each chief should kill some of his slaves for all our party to eat in his turn, we stayed in this place for some time till most of our slaves had been eaten …'.[39]

BELOW
William Strutt (1825–1915) made this pencil-and-wash drawing of 'the Maori war dance', probably in the late 1850s. The imagery was similar to that of the 'musket wars', two generations earlier.

William Strutt, pencil and wash, Alexander Turnbull Library E-453-f-001

ABOVE

A 'war speech, previous to a naval expedition'. Te Rauparaha, in particular, launched campaigns over water during the musket-war era.

Augustus Earle, Alexander Turnbull Library, PUBL-0015-09

BELOW

A 'New Zealand war speech', originally engraved in sepia by J. Stewart after another Earle original.

Augustus Earle, Alexander Turnbull Library, PUBL-0022-160

One post-colonial historian has suggested that the wars never really happened at all—proposing that they were an exaggeration, an illusion of colonial-age perception applied over tikanga that sailed on immutably. In fact the wars did occur, and were a significant shift of pace and scale from what had gone before. Their expression was entwined with the impact and reception of Britain's industrial-age technology and to this extent they were a symptom of what was going on, rather than the only expression. However, there was no denying them under any circumstance. There were over 500 battles, some so lethal that, a generation later, settlers carried bones away by the cartload. Muskets did not feature much in the earlier part of the wars, but did later; and war parties, many eventually armed with muskets, roamed massive distances.

In the face of them entire peoples undertook heke (migrations) on a scale that had not been seen in 200 years or more. Some areas, such as those around the Manukau and in Hawke's Bay, were virtually deserted by their traditional occupants, some of whom did not return until well into the settler period.[40] The numbers involved have never been precisely determined, but some estimates suggest that up to 40,000 Maori were dislocated, either through enslavement or migration.[41] To this can be added casualties of perhaps 20,000 spread over the period—about 19 or 20 percent of the estimated late eighteenth-century population.

The meaning of these events has been tied with changing views of history. For British observers of the day—and later into the nineteenth century—the only question was whether Europe should take some of the blame. The instrument of destruction was always held to be the musket, and Franciscan monk Domenico Vaggioli summed it up by condemning what he called the 'thoughtless, nay stupid introduction of arms and ammunition into New Zealand by Europeans' which 'caused incredible harm and bloodshed'.[42] Fighting, he insisted, had been further fuelled by what he called the 'erroneous view Maori had of natural justice'; muskets made the wars lethal, and the driving forces of utu intensified the struggle. Giving Maori muskets, he declared, had been 'like putting razors into babies' hands.'[43]

That thinking was a fair summation of the settler-age attitude, further filtered in Vaggioli's case by his sectarian opposition to the CMS. However, this wider mind-set was reversed in the late twentieth century by the 'revisionist' effort to re-shape our past around prevailing post-colonial ideology. By this argument, tikanga drove ahead through all the storm forces of the contact age, controlling every aspect of Maori life.[44]

Neither approach, of course, was entirely satisfactory. The reality was that the musket wars were a reaction to contact—but not in the patronising way imagined by settler-age observers and duly denied by post-colonial revisionists. A complex interplay was at work. Contact brought the shock of the new to Maori, who had never been exposed to outside culture in quantity before. Maori society adapted to the impact of Britain's industrial goods, technologies, ideas and thinking. Much of it was acculturated; but the practical reality was that British tools and vegetables changed the Maori labour and economic calculation. There was also a social impact; as with any society facing the new, the novelty became idealised, elevated—turned into a race for status. Guns were drawn in as status objects, underscored by the fact that many early weapons were given names. The double-barrelled fowling piece given by George IV to Hongi Hika, for instance, was 'Patu Iwi', the 'killer of tribes' or 'peoples'.[45]

In the end, though, guns—and the fighting that followed—were merely symptomatic of the wider process of contact. Europe's goods and products were swiftly drawn by Maori into their own society and world, but that process also provoked changes of behaviour. Europe's goods, ideas and technologies—including guns—altered the economic calculation and introduced forces to Maori that did not dislodge or destroy tikanga, but did change the way that it operated. The economic calculation, in particular, was materially shifted. More food could be produced for less labour, freeing toa up for fighting; but at the same time, the onus was on hapu to produce yet more in order to buy the consumables. One source of labour was slaves. Many intertwined forces combined to create

ABOVE

'Meeting of the artist and Hongi at the Bay of Islands, November 1827', one of the most famous images of the musket-war era.

Augustus Earle, Alexander Turnbull Library, G-707

ABOVE

Te Rauparaha (c1760s–1849), the Ngati Toa chief who dominated much of central New Zealand for a few years from the late 1820s. He was also responsible for introducing British-style trench warfare to New Zealand, during the siege of Kaiapoi in 1830.

Charles Heaphy, Alexander Turnbull Library, A-146-006

RIGHT

An idealised image of Te Rauparaha's forces at sea. From his base on Kapiti Island, the Ngati Toa chief was able to dominate much of the southern North Island, Cook Strait and significant parts of the northern South Island, from the late 1820s.

William Menzies Gibb, Making New Zealand Collection, Alexander Turnbull Library, F-652-1/4-MNZ

BELOW LEFT

Henry Williams trying to reach Matamata in 1836. The original caption identifies the Europeans, left to right, as Henry Williams, Alfred Nesbit Brown, Dr Fairburn and Mr Morgan.

Henry Williams, Alexander Turnbull Library, PUBL-0031-1836-1

BELOW RIGHT

This 'night scene in New Zealand' was published in 1837, capturing the imagery of missionary work as the missionaries liked to see it.

William Wade, Alexander Turnbull Library, PUBL-0031-37

the change. The result was that while Maori continued to frame their lives within tikanga, including many of the rationales for the wars—in some cases reflecting utu demands going back years or decades—Britain's goods allowed traditional systems of reciprocity to run at supercharged speed, feeding wars of unprecedented scale that rolled out from the main contact point in the north.

Once the momentum had begun to develop, it was difficult to stop.[46] Muskets increased the lethality of battles, particularly during the 1830s when the new weapons became widespread. Although death rates during this period were not as high as has sometimes been claimed, wounds often proved fatal, sometimes months afterwards as Hongi Hika discovered the hard way in 1828. In a society where relationships were based on reciprocity, the higher death-rate perpetuated grievances, and under these circumstances the question is not why did the wars occur, but how did they end? Fighting intensified during the late 1830s, growing in lethality as taua gained muskets, and even the 1839 battle of Te Kuitianga on the Kapiti Coast can be considered part of the cycle.[47] However, although there were tussles over the next few years, as in 1842 when Ngati Tamatera and Te Arawa attacked Ngaiterangi,[48] fighting was over for practical purposes by the early 1840s.

Missionaries, rather grandly, credited themselves. The CMS spread to Kawhia during the period—plus two isolated missions on the Kapiti Coast[49]— and ministers were invariably regarded as peacemakers. They also brought opportunities for trade, though the flow was not a significant factor behind

Maori queue to receive the Word in this idealised image of missionary work. There was a significant gulf between missionary claims of 'conversion' and the reality of the way that Maori adopted Christianity during the early nineteenth century.

Artist unknown, Alexander Turnbull Library, PUBL-0151-2-014

war's end because the primary dynamic was not access to European products. One historian has suggested that land sales helped defuse tensions by removing disputed territories,[50] but this is less convincing. Although these factors affected Wellington and the Bay of Islands as early as 1840, it was the 1850s—well after the wars ended—before European land purchases became widespread enough to be decisive across wide swathes of New Zealand. Furthermore, the act of defining boundaries in order to transact them was itself sometimes a trigger for conflict. The more crucial settler influence, in this regard, was the fact that the British actively intervened to prevent or end fighting, as at Pakiaka during 1857.[51]

We have to seek other reasons for the conflict petering out, and the main factors seem to have been exhaustion and the rising tide of European settlement. Huge casualties, coupled with migration and the drain warfare placed on resources meant Maori had fought themselves to a standstill by the late 1830s, just as the British began appearing in numbers. Maori did it themselves; more often than not, wars and some struggles were ended by the intervention of lay preachers. It was from this that the missionaries believed conversion responsible for ending the war, though what counted was the institutional mechanisms— the structures—that the church offered, which stood outside Maori tikanga and could be adapted to frame peace-making without further inflaming the fighting.[52]

By the early 1840s Maori were swinging to the relationship with British government and settlers, a relationship which was affected at many levels by the legacy of the wars, not least the way in which the dislocations of the wars were preserved by the advent of land sales. Migrations turned traditional occupation on its head, and occasionally—as Richard Barrett and William Wakefield discovered in Wellington—the occupier was not the only claimant.[53] Traditional loss of rights associated with defeat in battle produced a skein of precedents which complicated government land purchases. War-weariness also affected attitudes to colonisation. Ngati Whatua unease at possible attack from the north prompted them to invite William Hobson to establish his capital on the Waitemata shores in 1840. In some places, settlers were seen as a new tangata whenua, as in Hawke's Bay, where Ngati Whatuiapiti chief Te Hapuku asked 'to have Europeans to replace my tribes now nearly extinct.'[54]

The wars gave Maori relatively up-to-date weapons and not only introduced them to European-style field tactics, which they modified to suit local conditions, but also British-style trench warfare. Musket pa emerged, geared against muskets and often actively defended with cannon, which made an appearance during the 1830s. The step from these to the pa Maori built during the war against the British of the mid-1840s was minimal. One historian has also proposed that the musket wars were unifying, prompting new iwi identities which were then 'frozen' as a result of the colony arriving.[55] However, while pre-contact changes in socio-political structures were to some extent brought to a halt by the arrival of the settlers, the dynamic of socio-political change emerged later in different forms, such as kingitanga, syncretic religions such as Pai Marire, and other responses to the arrival of Europe.

A reputation for lawlessness

Europe settled in New Zealand while the 'musket wars' flared. Around 60 Pakeha were living in the CMS stations at Rangihoua, Kerikeri and Paihia by 1827. The number jumped when the Waimate station opened four years later. Others

BELOW

Dumont D'Urville's expedition artist Louis Auguste de Sainson made this picture of Kororareka beach in 1827, when the town was already well established as a trading post and a reputed centre of riotous lawlessness.

Louis Auguste de Sainson, Alexander Turnbull Library, B-052-006

CHAPTER TWO
AGENTS OF CHANGE

ABOVE

S. C. Brees' painting of the 'town of Kororareka', 1840s.

Samuel Charles Brees, Alexander Turnbull Library, B-031-017.

LEFT

An engraving based on Joel Polack's 1838 picture of Kororareka township. According to Polack it was the best anchorage in the Bay of Islands, 'possessing the best holding ground', and 'sea room for beating in and out of the bay and out of a strong tideway' lay opposite the town.

Joel Samuel Polack, Alexander Turnbull Library, PUBL-0115-1-front

settled at Kororareka (Russell), a trading community on the east side of the bay. The Hansen family tried to make a living there from 1819, joined in the mid-1820s by a motley crew of traders, beachcombers, deserters and convicts.

Some were there because the Empire always leaked; there was trouble the world around with the lawless moving beyond the fringes of British authority. But some of the more enterprising were hoping to turn a profit from trade. During the 14 months from January 1830, 60 vessels carried exports worth £37,980 and imported goods valued at £23,350.[56] These figures translate to early twenty-first century values of around $7.5 million and $4.6 million respectively, and most of the profit ended up in the pockets of Australian merchants. Figures for January to September 1830, for instance, reveal that £18,426 worth of New Zealand goods were imported into Sydney, including just over 500 tons of flax, 35,200 linear feet (10,700 metres) of timber, 36 tons of maize and 500 gallons of whale oil.[57]

Kororareka became New Zealand's first town, with a population of around 100 by 1830. Its floating population was higher. As many as 30 ships could bring

PARRAMATTA, KORORARIKA BAY, THE RESIDENCE AND PROPERTY OF MR. POLACK, BAY OF ISLANDS.

ABOVE

Shipping in Kororareka bay, 1840.

Artist unknown, Alexander Turnbull Library, PUBL-0064-2-TP

two or three hundred sailors ashore at once. Most wanted grog, food and women, usually in that order; and lack of these—or an excess of drink—led to trouble. The problem was that Kororareka was outside the jurisdiction of New South Wales, and settlers thumbed their noses at precedent which suggested that the law applied to them outside Australia. A lock-up in the form of a well-ventilated sea chest was little deterrent.

When trading opportunities were saturated, a few merchants tried to gain a competitive edge by theft, sabotage and assault. Debts were often uncollectable—on one occasion a Sydney-based debt-collector was set upon, tarred and raupo-feathered. Another loser was Jewish merchant Joel Polack, run out of town after losing a gunfight on the beach. This went on against a riotous background of drunken high-jinks, street brawls, prostitution, gambling, occasional theft, and corruption on the part of visiting transients. By 1838 the town had a church, but perhaps more important were the 'five hotels, innumerable grog-shops, a theatre, gambling-saloons, and skittle alleys'.[58] Justice was erratically enforced by what one observer later called an arbitrary 'club-law system.'[59] Kororareka gained the epithet 'hell-hole of the Pacific', and the real question is how functioned so well under the circumstances. Part of the answer is that it was never quite as bad as made out. Even the earliest historians of the place drew distinctions between 'the lawless band of Europeans congregated at Kororareka' and honest traders.[60] Others put all the trouble down to visiting sailors.[61] Certainly a lot of the worst trouble was imported—as in January 1827, when a ship captured by convicts arrived and was tackled by two visiting whalers in New Zealand's only 'fighting sail' style naval battle. Respectable citizens did what they could to curb excesses.

The real problem was that lack of legal government allowed the more boisterous to thumb their noses at authority. As early as 1819, John Bigge, leading an enquiry into the Australian colony, queried the allegation that sailors were mistreating Maori in the Bay of Islands.[62] Statutes were passed in 1817, 1823 and 1828 with the intent of improving behaviour in New Zealand, but none had any effect. The final straw was the *Elizabeth* affair of 1830, when Te Rauparaha paid John Stewart a small fortune in processed flax to take a taua, secretly, to Banks Peninsula where they revenged themselves against Ngai Tahu. Stewart was considered an accomplice in the kidnapping and murder that followed, and while these were in line with Maori values, they were 'atrocious crimes' by British standards. Efforts to prosecute Stewart, however, were unsuccessful, and he drowned at sea before a final legal effort against him could be mounted.

On the back of the scandal, New South Wales Governor Ralph Darling suggested appointing a Resident. However, New Zealand was not legally British territory, nor was the Colonial Office enthusiastic. James Busby finally reached the Bay of Islands in May 1833 with a letter of authority from King William, but had no legislative power and no practical means of asserting British law or protecting Maori. A Colonial Office bill intended to give him legal standing failed to pass the New South Wales legislature, and Darling's successor Richard Bourke refused to provide either troops or special constables.[63]

Busby's lack of teeth soon prompted a crisis. The *Harriet* was wrecked on the Taranaki coast in mid-1834, local Maori held several survivors hostage, and Bourke responded by despatching HMS *Alligator* to rescue them. The fracas that followed underscored the darker side of Empire; trusts offered by Maori were betrayed, a chief was almost murdered after arriving to parley, and Arthur Thomson later thought the British conduct 'resembled the operations of insulted buccaneers more than an expedition of his Majesty's forces'.[64] Busby bore the brunt of local fallout for not reacting first—though he had not been told of the *Harriet's* misfortune and had nothing to respond with in any case. This did not prevent talk of his ineffectual character and possible sacking. Bourke finally decided not to replace him, but Busby continued to suffer from lack of real power. He could have been made a magistrate, as Allan Gardiner was in Natal during the same period, but nothing was done.[65]

Europe came to the rest of New Zealand while Busby sat at Waitangi. Whaling spread dramatically during the mid to late 1830s. Traders—including the itinerant Polack—sought opportunities inland. A few Europeans settled with Maori, among them Barnet Burns, who was left standing nervously on Mahia Peninsula with his trade goods.[66] He allowed himself to be tattooed. Burns was not the only European to do this, but tales of Europeans becoming 'chief' of various tribes reflected European thinking rather than actuality. The process was assisted by missionary evangelism, a shift from the commercial ideals of the 1810s largely driven by the arrival of Henry Williams as head of the CMS in New Zealand. He initiated, among other things, an effort to translate the Bible. Fragments of the Old Testament were prepared in the late 1820s, but the focus switched to the New Testament in the early 1830s. Henry's brother William Williams took on the task of translation, and 23-year-old William Colenso arrived at Paihia in late 1834 to print the texts. Some 5000 copies of the New Testament were handed out after Williams finished the job in late 1837.[67] Colenso translated elements of the

TOP

HMS *Alligator*'s boats off the Taranaki coast, late September 1834, allegedly trying to 'get Mrs Guard and her children from the New Zealand savages'. In fact the British were the ones who behaved savagely.

Thomas Woore, Alexander Turnbull Library, A-048-008

ABOVE

Early European traders settled with Maori, among them Barnet Burns, who landed on the Mahia coast in the 1820s and gained a moko.

Artist unknown, wood engraving, Alexander Turnbull Library, PUBL-0074-front

ABOVE

Page from the journal of Edward Markham (1801–1856), showing the flag Busby organised for Ngapuhi in 1835.

Edward Markham, Alexander Turnbull Library, MS-1550-120

Old Testament, but Robert Maunsell's full translation was not available until 1858.[68]

Improvising a treaty

The Treaty of Waitangi is always seen as pivotal in New Zealand's history—a national founding document that remains the pivotal divider between past and present, helping define the nature of race relations in New Zealand. And in a historical sense it has evolved to become that. However, while at the time it was certainly seen as a founding document of the colony, the way that this colony might pan out was never anticipated; the Treaty itself was a largely arbitrary and certainly hasty measure taken to meet an immediate need, framed by an uneasy fusion of British pragmatism, administrative weakness, penury and humanitarianism. The problem was balancing the hands-off approach espoused by the CMS with pressure to formally control the growing European settlement. This seemed at first to be in the 'too hard' basket; Britain had many world priorities in the 1830s, and New Zealand initially seemed more liability than asset. Money was unavailable to underwrite a colony,[69] and Busby was left to handle European rampancy alone.

He turned to Maori for support, trying to draw them in via the issue of New Zealand-built ships lacking registration papers and flags. Flagged vessels, registered via Busby's office, were less likely to be impounded when they got to Sydney, and in March 1834, just over two dozen local chiefs assembled on the lawn outside Busby's Residency at Waitangi to select the flag.[70] Busby hoped this would lay the groundwork for unity, but although Maori were finally prodded into picking an emblem, most did not subscribe to the British view of flags.[71] Busby persisted, envisaging a 'tribunal' of chiefs, which would allow New Zealand to evolve into a British protectorate.[72] This did not go down well in the Colonial Office, where Lord Glenelg—former CMS vice-president—felt Europe had a responsibility to 'civilise' non-Europeans for their own protection. An 'Aborigine Protection Society' had already been formed in response to reports of Maori mistreatment, and in this environment Glenelg could not endorse settlement.

Chance provided Busby with his next opportunity. New Zealand was part of the British sphere, but without a formal declaration of British government the country was legally open to claim, and there was a scare in 1831 when the French warship *La Favourite* was reported to be on her way to annex New Zealand for France.[73] That crisis passed, but then in 1835 the self-styled Baron Charles Phillipe Hippolyte de Thierry loomed into view. He had purchased land near the Hokianga, apparently intending to establish an independent French enclave, perhaps with help from Tahiti. Busby responded with a 'Declaration of Independence', signed by thirty-odd chiefs in October, and which he continued to peddle until the late 1830s. The declaration was accepted by the Colonial Office to the extent that its signatories were sought for the Treaty of Waitangi, which superseded it.[74]

The severity of the French threat was always unclear. De Thierry reached New Zealand in late 1837, with colonists he had picked up in Sydney, to find his land had been sold. This prompted a bizarre tirade in the *Sydney Gazette*. 'I am an Englishman at heart,' he wrote, 'but the study of my life will be to support the independence of New Zealand under some civilised ruler ... and to save this fine people from the degradation and destruction which would inevitably follow its subjection to the British crown.'[75] There was talk of him being appointed French Consul in 1838, prompting a brief effort in London to remind the French that New Zealand was a British sphere.[76] Parisian officials concurred. In the end, de Thierry proved a chimera; Busby suspected he was mad.

Reconciling the humanitarian concerns of the CMS and Colonial Office with the need to establish colonial government in New Zealand remained a problem, intensified by Busby's weakness. 'He has no power, no authority,' the Aborigines Committee of 1836 concluded.[77] Colonial Office officials thought Busby was incompetent, and although the Secretary, James Stephen, ruled out action as late as November 1837,[78] renewed inter-hapu warfare in the Bay of Islands prompted Busby to request a warship. Bourke despatched HMS *Rattlesnake* from Sydney with Lieutenant William Hobson on board. The crisis had blown over by the time Hobson arrived, but European numbers in New Zealand were approaching 2000 and Hobson suggested a 'trading factory' system similar to the one used earlier in India, though he knew the idea was probably unworkable.[79]

But the pressure was on to do something. Long drought and regulations

BELOW

Rawiri, a 'fully tattooed chief' of Taranaki, drawn here in 1856 by William Strutt (1825–1915).

William Strutt, Alexander Turnbull Library E-452-f-006-3

fixing Australian land at 12 shillings an acre—roughly around $100 in early twenty-first century money—prompted many would-be pastoralists to seek new opportunities in New Zealand's wide grasslands. Some deals were made remotely in Sydney, as when W. C. Wentworth and his partners purchased 20 million acres from visiting South Island chiefs.[80] However, the prospect of cowboy land sales and an independent, private government was unacceptable—for slightly different reasons—to the CMS, Busby and the Colonial Office. Hobson's 'factory' proposal joined a missionary petition and a report from Busby on Glenelg's desk,[81] and in late 1838, Glenelg proposed a consul who would report directly to the Colonial Office.[82] But nothing had been done by the following February, when Glenelg relinquished office to the Marquis of Normanby. The leisurely pace was partly a consequence of three-month communications between New Zealand and London, partly due to staff shortages—the office had only 25-odd clerks to deal with 50 colonies.[83]

In light of hints that Normanby intended to act, the New Zealand Company sent the *Tory* scurrying around the world—though her hasty departure was not, as legend has it, to forestall a Colonial Office effort to stop them. The Colonial Office found out in advance, but the only response was a fresh flurry of bureaucracy.[84] Stephen thought colonisation 'inevitable'.[85] Events took a new pace in May when Stephen canvassed legal opinion, telling the Attorney-General that the Colonial Office intended to get a 'cession of sovereignty' from 'the chiefs of New Zealand' and wondering whether the colony could be temporarily attached to New South Wales.[86]

In mid-June Stephen went to the Treasury for authority to fund the cession, specifically budgeted at £4,005—around $800,000 in early twenty-first century New Zealand dollars—of which a quarter was for 'presents for [the] natives.'[87] He got the cash—with one rider. Nothing could be done without the 'indispensable preliminary' of the 'amicable negotiation with and free concurrence of the native chiefs.'[88] Treasury Pro-Secretary G. J. Pennington was less concerned with humanitarianism than finances. Forced annexation had led to war before, and wars were expensive.[89]

This laid the groundwork for instructions to Hobson, drafted by Stephen and signed by Normanby. Hobson would get the 'free and intelligent consent' of Maori to accept British sovereignty, negotiating with 'principles of justice, sincerity and good faith'.[90] Unruly Europeans would be rescued from 'the evils of a lawless state of society'.[91] Stephen also intended to halt the 'dangers' posed by 'mere land jobbers'.[92] This drove the policy of pre-emption, copied from earlier precedent on the American frontier where the Crown had acquired sole right to buy land. It had a double benefit. By giving the colonial administration a land monopoly and an injunction to buy cheap and sell high, Normanby also hoped to make land acquisitions self-funding from a relatively small investment, and the Colonial Office justified this with the argument that most of the land was 'of

ABOVE

A Maori woman from Taranaki, mid-1850s.

William Strutt, Alexander Turnbull Library, E-452-f-009-2

no actual use' and 'possesses scarcely any exchangeable value'.[93]

Much of the approach was underpinned by humanitarian concerns, evidenced in Colonial Office insistence that Hobson organise schools and crush the 'savage practices of human sacrifice and cannibalism.'[94] Hobson was in London and quick to query the instructions. Did the orders apply to both North and South Islands? If he could not persuade Maori to stop cannibalism, was he authorised to 'repress these diabolical acts by force'?[95] Normanby admitted that too little was known about the South Island to make a decision, but if it was 'uninhabited except by a very small number of persons' who were of 'savage state, incapable from their ignorance of entering intelligently into any treaties', then British occupation might become a 'matter of ... duty to the natives.'[96]

Hobson left London in late August 1839 intending to secure sovereignty over New Zealand by treaty. He reached Sydney four months later to discover an awkward situation. Rumour that the Colonial Office was intending to pre-empt land purchase in New Zealand had been circulating for months, spurring local merchants to rush across the Tasman and secure land themselves. One of the most prolific was William Barnard ('Barney') Rhodes, who sailed from Sydney on his barque *Eleanor* in October 1839 and toured New Zealand, making extensive purchases in both the North and South Islands. The deals were hasty, shoddy and vague—typified by Rhodes' Hawke's Bay experience. He 'bought' territory from the Mahia Peninsula to Cape Turnagain, but failed to negotiate with the appropriate people, and the exact details of what changed hands seemed unclear even to Rhodes himself. To some extent boundaries had to be unclear; as Edward Jerningham Wakefield found out, Maori were 'unused to dealing in land according to our notions.'[97]

However, the variations in Rhodes' claims also suggest sloppiness and certainly haste on his part. He told his partners he had bought 1,401,600 acres in a thirty-mile deep block between Cape Turnagain and Mahia. When he registered his purchase with the government of New South Wales, however, the deeds specified 1,228,000 acres and a depth of 20-odd miles (32 km). Nor was he clear about the price. He told his partners that he had spent 'about £150', but revealed to the

ABOVE

William Hobson (1792–1842), joined the Royal Navy in 1803 and rose to the rank of Commander by 1824. He was appointed to command HMS *Rattlesnake* in 1834. He was dogged by ill-health, in part a legacy of yellow fever. This, with the strains of governing a penurious colony, may have contributed to a stroke he suffered in 1840. He succumbed to another stroke in September 1842.

James Ingram McDonald, Alexander Turnbull Library, G-826-1

ABOVE

Tamati Waka Nene.

Joseph Merritt, Alexander Turnbull Library, A-255-019

BELOW

Henry Williams, translator of the Treaty of Waitangi.

Charles Baugniet, Alexander Turnbull Library, C-020-005

Land Claims Court that he had handed over £50 in cash and goods to the value of £323—translating to roughly $73,000 in early twenty-first century money. It was paltry even by nineteenth-century standards.[98]

The New Zealand Company also 'purchased' central New Zealand during late 1839. From the British perspective this was likely to undermine the effort to gain sovereignty by agreement. The merchants viewed Colonial Office policy as interference, protesting to Hobson in early January.[99] Governor George Gipps responded by proclaiming jurisdiction over New Zealand and reserving all land purchases to the Crown, a declaration that reached New Zealand with Hobson late that month. The pressure was on to get the treaty organised. Hobson and his secretary J. S. Freeman had prepared notes, broadly echoing Normanby's instructions, which Busby reworked into something slightly different. He submitted the first draft to Hobson on 3 February,[100] transforming Hobson's notion of having New Zealand ceded in stages into a plan by which Maori would accept British sovereignty from North Cape to the Manukau estuary and the Thames. In exchange they would be treated as British and guaranteed possession of their 'forests, fisheries and other properties', until they wanted to sell them to the Crown. Those were explicitly only the areas on which Maori actually lived or which they used; other lands were defined as 'waste' and, as far as the British were concerned, were up for grabs.[101]

Busby and others on the ground in New Zealand were under no illusion that Maori identified with all of the land. In the final version of 4 February, restricted sovereignty disappeared, as did the explicit claim on 'waste lands' and with it the implicit restriction on what was—and was not—Maori property. Conceptually, this was less a problem than the distinction between sovereignty and land ownership, the more crucial intellectual issue in the British mind. None of the drafters were sure that Maori understood the difference, and efforts to come up with wording to clarify it were flawed by haste and the lens of nineteenth-century rationalism.

The three clauses of the final treaty were further muddied by translation. Late on 4 February Hobson asked Henry Williams to translate the treaty ready for a meeting with Maori next morning. Williams did the job with the help of his son Edward, apparently fluent in everyday Maori but not a trained translator, and they sat down to preserve the 'spirit and tenor' of Busby's wording in just a few hours. Inexperience was not the only pitfall; there is some evidence that the draft Williams had been given did not include the words 'forests and fisheries'.[102]

Irrespective of this blunder, the final result was coloured by Williams' motives and inexperience. He used 'ratou taonga katoa' to refer to property—a term which meant a good deal more to Maori than Williams apparently thought it did. The result, as one historian has pointed out, was that Maori later argued for rights to resources that the British drafters did not intend, and which were not in the English version.[103] The main problem was Williams' use of 'kawanatanga'—'governorship'—to mean sovereignty. In the Declaration of Independence, the translation had been 'mana', a word with obvious implications for Maori. The mistranslation was compounded when Williams came to the clause guaranteeing Maori possession of their lands until they sold them. For 'possession', he selected 'rangatiratanga', which was actually a better match for 'sovereignty'.[104] Hobson used it in that sense two months later,[105] and it was also translated that way by missionaries in other Maori documents, such as a letter by Tamati Waka Nene that has survived in Colenso's papers.[106]

In short, Williams' translation was problematic even by the standards of his day, a point so well recognised that there were accusations of deceit. In the 1890s, Catholic monk Domenico Vaggioli even classified Williams as the 'treaty's arch-manipulator'. Sectarian difference played a part in Vaggioli's thinking.[107] Williams' motives were extensively debated during the late twentieth century re-analysis of the treaty,[108] and there has been suggestion that he may have felt the treaty would not be accepted if chiefs thought they were going to lose their authority.[109] There seems some truth in this, but it is also clear that the situation was further complicated by the cultural gulf. John Flatt, for instance, told a Lords Committee in 1838 that Maori: '…do not think anything of sovereignty… Their simple view is, that their land may be cultivated, and that they may be benefitted by that.'[110]

Charitably, Williams—a former naval officer—was doing his best to resolve these issues in wording that Maori would be likely to accept; but irrespective of any intent to dissemble, it seems clear from his choice of vocabulary that he did not have the wit to truly translate the treaty even if it had been the right version. His apparent effort to 'spin' the whole in order to sell it to Maori simply compounded the problem. Colenso—the more capable intellectual—might have done better. But he also suffered from cultural centrism and was never asked.

Williams' translation did not survive unadulterated. On the morning of the 5th, Busby wanted amendments. By this stage Maori were assembling on the Residency lawn, and Busby ended up in the house with Hobson and Williams making changes. They finally emerged on to the 'delightfully situated lawn' in front of the house, where a 'spacious tent … tastefully adorned with flags' had been set up.[111] Even the weather cooperated. 'Nature', Colenso wrote, '[had] consented to doff her mantle of New Zealand grey.' Colourful policemen, sailors and officials wandered about on the emerald lawn, contrasting with Maori who turned out in the more muted tones of their own formal dress, leavened with 'woollen cloaks of foreign manufacture.'[112] Inside the tent, Hobson and his officers arranged everything to impress:

ABOVE

William Colenso (1813–1899, missionary, printer, botanist, linguist and pugillist. A settler-era 'renaissance man', temperamental, opinionated, and one of New Zealand's most capable intellectuals of the day, Colenso was also one of the few to write down what he saw at Waitangi in February 1840. This picture was taken in 1868, some time after his career with the Anglican church came to its tumultuous end.

Photographer unidentified, Alexander Turnbull Library, F- 5028-1/4

In the centre of the narrow raised platform were the Governor and captain of the man o' war in full uniform, on the Governor's left were Mr Busby, and the Roman Catholic bishop in canonicals, his massy gold chain and crucifix glistening on his dark-purple-coloured habit, on the right of his Excellency were the members of the Church of England Mission, in plain black dresses…[113]

Williams read the treaty aloud, and the rangatira spent the day considering the proposals, with supplementary explanations by Hobson. All did not go as smoothly as it could have. At least one European fluent in Maori complained to Hobson that the 'native speeches were not half interpreted by Mr. Williams, neither were His Excellency's remarks fully interpreted to the natives.'[114] He apparently portrayed the treaty as an 'act of love' by Queen Victoria towards Maori.[115] That did not wash well with Maori, who initially disliked the arrangement, though to some extent this was also a function of hui, where all points of view were expressed before being considered. During the morning Te Kemara pointed out 'in his energetic, peculiar manner' that Busby and the missionaries had already bought land[116]—an embarrassing point. Other points of view followed, including those of Tamati Waka Nene of Ngati Hao, who believed there would be commercial opportunities. His arguments ended the meeting that evening, and Hobson announced that they would reconvene on the 7th.

Next morning, however, 'not less than 300' Maori were back at the Residency, 'talking about the treaty, but evidently not clearly understanding it.' There had been confusion over times. Hobson arrived from the ship 'in plain clothes', and decided to 'take the signatures' of those who wanted to sign. However, as it was not a 'regular public meeting' he refused to accept further debate.[117] Pompallier then 'pushed forward' and asked: 'That the natives might be informed that all who should join the Catholic religion should have the protection of the British government.' Hobson agreed, 'with much blandness', adding that he was sorry Pompallier had not asked earlier, as 'your desire should have been embodied in the Treaty'.[118]

Williams objected; this protection applied to all denominations by default, but Hobson insisted and Williams 'accordingly commenced' to write a 'grave announcement … for the benefit of all', declaring that Maori who joined the Anglican, Wesleyan or Catholic churches—or who retained what Williams called their 'heathen beliefs' ('ritenga Maori'), would all receive the same protections under the treaty. He read it out in silence, 'the Maories [sic] being at a perfect loss, [as to] what it could all mean.'[119] As one historian has noted, some early twenty-first century commentators suggested this was a 'fourth' clause of the treaty.[120] In fact the clarification was for Pompallier's benefit and he left as soon as it was read out.[121] Williams' objections were also correct. Although Anglicanism played an important role in the life of the day, Britain was a secular state in 1840. In any case, the remarks were neither on the treaty that was signed that morning, nor had been raised when the treaty was considered by Maori.

Once Pompallier's objection was out of the way, Hobson had Williams re-read the treaty. At first no one wanted to sign, so Hobson decided to call out names, starting with Hone Heke Pokai—'known to be most favourable' towards the treaty.[122] As Heke was about to place his mark, Colenso interrupted and

OPPOSITE

A 1949 reconstruction of the signing of the Treaty of Waitangi. Although idealised in many respects, and inaccurate in specific details such as Hobson's clothing, Leonard Mitchell's artwork captures the essential theme of a British ceremony conducted with all due pomp and circumstance.

Leonard Mitchell, Alexander Turnbull Library, A-242-002

Journal of Agriculture

JANUARY · 1949

ABOVE

An 1880s reconstruction of the signing of the Treaty of Waitangi—but probably not intended to represent the main ceremony. The Treaty was signed in many places around the North Island under circumstances like this.

Artist unknown, Alexander Turnbull Library, A-114-038

asked whether Maori actually understood it. 'I have spoken to some Chiefs,' he continued, 'who had no idea what ever as to the purport of the Treaty.' Hobson remarked that he had done all he could to make sure they did, 'and I really don't know how I shall be enabled to get them to do so. They've heard the Treaty read by Mr W.'[123] After some discussion with the others he threw the onus for explaining it back on the CMS.

Heke then signed, the first of more than forty Maori who placed their marks that day, while two others made 'long speeches against the signing' in the background.[124] Twenty-six had signed the 1835 Declaration of Independence—which the new Treaty was explicitly designed to supersede, and accepting the new treaty was a significant legal step. Hobson waited out the 7th, and the following day proclaimed the new colony with a 21-gun salute and flourish of flags from the *Herald*.

Hobson then circulated the treaty around New Zealand, with results reflecting the way European authority had penetrated the hinterland. Northland, the Waitemata and the Waikato were well covered by government officials, but other regions relied on ad hoc measures. William Williams, now at Turanga (Gisborne), was told to get signatures from the East Coast and collected about 40 in Poverty Bay during April, but abandoned plans to visit Ahuriri for the rest.[125] Coverage elsewhere was thin. Hobson was laid low with a stroke, and Willoughby Shortland sent Bunbury off around the country in the *Herald* to get more signatures. He annexed the South Island by cession on 17 June, but otherwise the main targets were the remaining signatories of the 1835 declaration. This brought Bunbury to Hawke's Bay in June, looking for Te Hapuku, who had signed the Declaration of

Independence as late as 1839. The chiefs Waikato and Mahokai happened to be visiting and also signed,[126] but Bunbury did not seek out others in the area and most Ngati Kahungunu did not sign.[127] National patchiness was compounded by the fact that not every chief was prepared to sign, but over 500 signatures were nonetheless collected on multiple sheets, including several to an English-language version.

Maori had various reasons for signing. Tamati Waka Nene saw the treaty as a means of extending the trading relationship with Britain.[128] For Hone Heke, signing was apparently an assertion of mana.[129] Others saw it as a means of getting the blankets and tobacco offered during the ceremonies, though this sometimes prompted dispute. 'Next morning,' one signatory recalled, 'the things came with which the Governor intended to pay us for writing our names'—a disappointment, because 'there was not much tobacco, and only a few blankets.'[130] This prompted a 'fierce squabble',[131] an argument repeated around the country, causing some nineteenth-century critics to classify it as a 'blankets treaty.'[132] A few changed their minds, motivated in one case by the paucity of blankets,[133] returning the gifts in an effort to nullify their decision.[134] In the Waitemata, British military protection was arguably a motive—a legacy of the musket wars.[135] Hobson's point that the treaty guaranteed land ownership left some 'very much alarmed...for they thought that perhaps a great war expedition was coming...'[136]

As at Waitangi, the problem was cross-cultural misunderstanding. The frames of reference rendered a lot of what the British were saying either meaningless or irrelevant to Maori. Waitemata Maori, listening to the explanation of the treaty, felt the 'meaning ...was so closely concealed we never have found it out'. As Frederick Maning noted, this was a 'polite Maori way of saying that ... [the speaker] was talking nonsense'. One message was 'understood well', however:

ABOVE

William Williams, East Coast missionary and brother of Henry Williams.

Charles Bauginet, Alexander Turnbull Library, PUBL-0031-37

BELOW

HMS *Herald*—literally the herald of the Treaty of Waitangi for many Maori around New Zealand—in Sylvan Cove, Stewart Island.

Edward Marsh Williams, Alexander Turnbull Library, A-083-005

...he told us plainly that if we wrote on the Governor's paper, one of the consequences would be that great numbers of Pakeha would come to this country to trade with us, that we should have an abundance of valuable goods, and that before long there would be great towns, as large as Kororareka, in every harbour in this whole island. We were very glad to hear this, for we never could ... get half muskets or gunpowder enough, or blankets...[137]

Some did perceive what the British had in mind, though within the framework of Maori understanding. When Bunbury explained the treaty to Te Hapuku, the chief suggested that Maori would be made slaves, and demonstrated what he meant by drawing a 'sort of diagram' on a board, 'placing the Queen by herself over the chiefs as these were over the tribes.' Bunbury assured him 'it was literally as he described it, but not for an evil purpose ...but to enable her to enforce her execution of justice and good government equally amongst her subjects.'[138]

CHAPTER THREE
Shadows of empire

If anyone could be called New Zealand's founding father, it would probably be amateur hypnotist, convicted kidnapper and would-be social climber Edward Gibbon Wakefield. Half a dozen towns from New Plymouth to Christchurch were directly or indirectly established as a result of his efforts, and he brought nearly 9000 settlers to New Zealand in the process. Propaganda issued by his New Zealand Company guided the public perception of Wakefield well into the twentieth century, building the myth of a glorious nation-founder. In truth he was not. Stripped of myth, the facts about both Wakefield and his enterprises have a tawdry banality well removed from the image of pioneering settlement. The company was a hollow edifice, jacked up on minimal capital and maximum talk by idealists who used a sense of entitlement as a lever to convince others of their right to power and success. It did not last. Greed, incompetence and wild misconception about the realities of the human condition created a witches' brew of deed and misdeed that brought the company to its knees in around a decade. It was New Zealand's first experience of socio-economic engineering, and it was not the last.

It is easy to demonise Wakefield on the back of this explosive collision between ideology, personal conviction and the greed of those he found to back his social crusade. But we must not do the man an injustice; as his biographer Philip Temple has argued, the truths of Wakefield's life were both better and worse than we imagine.[1] He was a complex character. His lack of scruples, perhaps, were an outcome of a dysfunctional family upbringing. An early belief in a basic immorality of humanity was probably heightened by his exposure to post-Napoleonic politics from 1815. Ill-health crippled him after 1840 and, on the basis of volatile behaviour and wild mood swings, he may have suffered from bipolar disorder. Certainly he was complex, defying efforts by biographers to reduce his character to a few clear traits.[2] And for all his faults, for all the appearance of

ABOVE

The New Zealand Company survey ship *Cuba* at anchor in a north-westerly breeze off Port Nicholson heads, 1840. Barrett's reef is visible to the right in this watercolour by New Zealand Company draughtsman Charles Heaphy (1820–1881).

Charles Heaphy, Alexander Turnbull Library, A-144-003

ABOVE

Edward Gibbon Wakefield (1796–1862) around 1823. London-born Wakefield abducted a wealthy Cheshire industrialist's daughter in 1826, married her, and fled to France. It was apparently part of a plan to let him enter Parliament, but the ploy backfired. Sentenced instead to three years' jail, he turned to social theory, writing *A Letter From Sydney* which was both serialised and published as a book. The settlement in New Zealand followed from it. Wakefield left England for his colony in 1852 and was elected to the Wellington Provincial Council, but contracted rheumatic fever in 1855 and never recovered. He withdrew from public life and died at his Wellington home a few years later.

Abraham Wivell/B. Holl, engraving, Alexander Turnbull Library, A-042-023

fraud with which his under-capitalised, over-ambitious company launched its business, one point remains crystal clear: Wakefield genuinely believed in his social theories, and very genuinely intended to build colonies around them. He never stopped trying, even as his company collapsed around him.[3]

Wakefield developed his colonial ideas during the late 1820s while in Newgate prison. He produced 'Sketch of a proposal for colonising Australasia'[4] in which he presented a bold vision of a neo-feudal colonial arcadia in which what he called the 'better attributes'[5] of old England—meaning the edifices of rising middle-class society such as clubs and athenaeums—would be transplanted into the new world. Land, he envisaged, would be sold by the company to settlers at a 'uniform price per acre … without exception'.[6] This central control over the wholesale supply would give the founding company a lever with which to keep prices at the point where the labouring poor could not afford to buy. As the New Zealand Company eventually put it, the 'great object of the price is to secure the most desirable proportions between people and land'.[7] Even if he had to bring Maori into the scheme to placate CMS and Colonial Office demands, he imagined he could use the same levers to create a Maori nobility within his new society.[8]

To keep a pool of cheap labour available, Wakefield envisaged profits would be ploughed back into the enterprise, paying to bring out migrant labourers from the 'thousands and tens of thousands of half-starved semi-maritime' people in the 'north and west of Scotland.'[9] But they would not be prisoners of their class; he imagined that those who were suitably 'industrious and thrifty' could eventually own land and even become 'an employer of hired labourers, a master of servants,'[10] replaced by other workers brought in by the company.[11]

It was a quintessential effort to use untrammelled free-market forces to engineer a society suffused in the thinking of the day—portraying labourers as shiftless and lazy, authors of their own misfortune. Privately, he remained scathing about these 'ignorant and imprudent wastrels'.[12] His ideas were radical, but the idea of building a new society around the new principles of pure capitalism, free of the troubles of the old world, struck chords. He was wooed by the National Colonisation Society when released from prison in 1830, launching into his new occupation with a good deal of enthusiasm. However, an effort to establish an Australian colony foundered in 1835 after a dispute over land prices, and in the face of opposition from James Stephen.[13]

New Zealand seemed a good alternative. A 'New Zealand Company' had been established as early as 1825, sending two ships under James Herd to the South Pacific. But the government refused to issue a charter and the proprietors gave up with a dead loss of £20,000.[14] Wakefield decided to try himself, and formed the New Zealand Association, but the jump from that to colonising company required parliamentary approval, and was opposed by the Colonial Office, where Stephen thought the colony would 'infallibly' exterminate Maori, and in any case considered Wakefield's idea too vague.[15] Wakefield then published specific plans, alarming both Colonial Office and the CMS with his fantasies of Maori desperate to be colonised and a conveniently hospitable New Zealand aching to be purchased.[16]

The idea remained in abeyance until early 1839, when news came of the Colonial Office proposal to obtain pre-emptive purchase rights.[17] Wakefield

LEFT

Joseph Somes, New Zealand Company Secretary.

John Wood, Alexander Turnbull Library, C-043-007

ABOVE

Edward Jerningham Wakefield (1820–1879) was the only son of Edward Gibbon Wakefield. Although described by his father as a 'faithful lieutenant', his appetites militated against success. He visited New Zealand with the Tory in 1840 and was appointed resident magistrate, but his behaviour prompted Robert FitzRoy to dub him the 'devil's missionary' and withdraw the commission. He returned to England, but then emigrated to New Zealand in the early 1850s, entered politics, and after a brief term spent the next quarter-century intermittently trying to be re-elected. He married in 1863 and died in Ashburton in 1879.

Artist unknown, engraving, Alexander Turnbull Library, PUBL-0128-001

hastily formed the New Zealand Land Company on a capital of £100,000,[18] attracting some of London's leading bankers and capitalists—Joseph Somes, Francis Baring, Viscount Ingestre, Lord Petrie, Henry Allenby, John Boulcott, John Buckle and others[19]—whose motives, arguably, were less idealistic than greedy. They hired most of Wakefield's extended family for senior positions, and got to work. It was a classic exercise in leveraging and talking up—the company was grossly undercapitalised for its intended scale of operations. Early proclaimed profits of £99,000 on expenses of just over £20,200[20]—an absurd return—revealed the hollow nature of the whole edifice. That was further underscored when they advertised the first properties on the London market, 1100 sections in the first town at £1 per acre, promising that 'extensive tracts' of the 'most fertile' land had been 'already purchased and secured.'[21] Investors swallowed Wakefield's promise of a profitable Arcadia, and a thousand sections were bought by people who had no intention of moving.

There was only one small problem. It was a lie. And the deceit was well known. There was an investigation, and *The Times* condemned the 'system of monstrous plunder' created by men whose 'passion for money' had 'unhappily superseded their love of honest fame'.[22] Wakefield actually had rights to virtually nothing in New Zealand—merely a few scraps left over from the original New Zealand Company of the 1820s. All rested on the company ship *Tory*, which he sent with his younger brother William Wakefield on board to secure more territory. The mission had to succeed or the whole company venture was going to be revealed for the hollow shell it was. It was an indictment of the company mind-set that—despite lack of news—they offered more land on the London market in August, this time in the 'Hokianga, Kaipara, Manukau' and 'the islands of Waiheke and Paroa' among other places.[23] Meanwhile, the company sent the *Cuba* racing to New Zealand with a surveying team. The colony ships *Oriental*, *Aurora* and *Adelaide* followed in mid-September filled with 'labourers especially of the agricultural class.'[24] The *Glenbervie* left in October, loaded with 'Machinery, mills, steam-engines, agricultural implements ... and goods of various other descriptions'.[25]

The whole edifice rested on the younger Wakefield managing to obtain land. There was no backup plan.[26] As it happened, the *Tory* reached New Zealand on 16 August after a 96-day passage. They watered at Ship's Cove, then sailed for Port Nicholson.[27] This area was occupied by hapu of Te Ati Awa, who had migrated from Taranaki during wars a few years earlier and felt far from secure. Te Rauparaha's loose Ngati Toa empire stood to the west. He was not a safe ally, and two hapu, Ngati Mutunga and Ngati Tama, had already left for the Chathams in 1835.[28] Wakefield offered another form of escape and was delighted with their 'lively satisfaction' when he offered to buy land in the area.[29] His instructions, penned by Gibbon Wakefield, exhorted him to:

... constantly bear in mind that the profits of the Company must, in a great measure, depend on the judgement which you may exercise in selecting places of future location ... it should be your especial business to acquire spots which enjoy some peculiar natural advantage... Wilderness land ... is worth nothing to its native owners... We are not, therefore, to make much account of the utter inadequacy of the purchase money according to English notions of the value of land...[30]

Maori were nevertheless needed onside, and to sweeten the deal, the company intended to hold back a tenth of any purchase 'in trust ... for the future benefit of the chief families of the tribe.' The idea that this was actually to 'benefit' Maori was yet more company elasticity with the truth; it was effectively an additional cost to the company which they introduced explicitly to placate Colonial Office concerns about the impact their settlement would have. Wakefield intended to use it as a cynical means of drawing chiefs into his iron-clad market society. That meant they had to be divided, and he told his brother not to 'make reserves ... in large blocks' as this would cause Maori to 'continue savage.'[31]

The waters were thoroughly muddied by translation. George Clarke later dismissed interpreter Richard Barrett's 'whaler Maori' as pidgin, and doubted that the ex-whaler even understood the English version of the deeds he was presenting.[32] Certainly the real reasons for sale by vendors Te Wharepouri and Te Puni Kokopu did not surface.. But by late September they had settled on a price of about £400 worth of goods for the district.[33] Te Wharepouri divided them into six, though there were seven hapu in the area,[34] and this was not the only problem. Wakefield had been exhorted to 'most clearly set forth' the boundaries, 'not merely in words, but in a plan attached to the written contract.'[35] However, when it came to the crunch, they discovered it was 'almost impossible ... to buy a large and distinct tract of land, with fixed boundaries.'[36] Maori did not define land in such terms. The combination of uncertain borders, uncertain tenure and inequitable division of the goods was a time-bomb for which the fuse was lit even as the first settler ships left Britain.

Wakefield moved on in October, arriving off Kapiti just after a battle between Ngati Toa on one side and Te Ati Awa and Ngati Raukawa on the other, spurred

ABOVE

Te Wharepouri, also known to New Zealand Company agents as 'dark horse'.

Charles Heaphy, Alexander Turnbull Library, PUBL-0011-02-1

by the sale of land in Port Nicholson. The ship's doctor, Ernest Dieffenbach, tended the wounded. Wakefield had heard of Te Rauparaha in England and, as Temple argues, probably left the old chief until last so as to be preceded by rumour of the *Tory*'s power.[37]

What Wakefield did not anticipate was the political complexity of the world he was crashing. Te Rauparaha had lost much of his grip on his loose empire after the 1834 battle of Haowhenua, a little way up the coast,[38] but he still had a good deal of mana and dominated a large slab of the trans-Tasman trade from his Kapiti base. A good deal of his remaining power came from a near-monopoly over weapons supply, and his problem was how to stop the new arrivals distributing muskets to anyone but himself.[39] What followed was bizarre. By Wakefield's account, he secured much of the Ngati Toa empire, over 20,000,000 acres (8,094,000 hectares).[40] Te Rauparaha thought he had 'sold' only a few pieces. It was sloppy—the deed defined some borders as merely being 'about' certain latitudes, and place names included 'Ngatiruanui'— which was actually a South Taranaki hapu.[41] Clarke later dismissed the whole thing as being of 'very hasty and hugger mugger character'.[42]

Wakefield sailed on, and by November was in the South Island, where he 'purchased' more land. A few days later he took three Wanganui chiefs on board the *Tory* and 'purchased' land from them. The deal was completed later by Arthur Wakefield, who thought he had secured 40,000 acres for £700. Other deals in Taranaki were left for Barrett to conclude in his iconoclastic 'Maori'. Before year's end the company had laid claim to virtually the whole of central New Zealand, twenty million acres from the north of Taranaki to Pito-one (Petone) and into the northern South Island.

The company ship *Cuba* arrived off Petone in early January 1840, bringing surveyor William Mein Smith; but the settler ships were just days behind and Smith had no time to complete his work. Hopeful migrants poured on to Pito-one beach with their cases, trunks, goods and furniture—including 25,000 bricks and at least one piano—to discover they would have to camp. The cargo was dumped below high-tide mark and ended up 'washing about in the sand'.[43] There

ABOVE

Te Ati Awa leader Honiana Te Puni Kokopu was born in Taranaki in the late eighteenth century and, with other Te Ati Awa chiefs, led his people to the Wellington region in 1832 as a result of the musket wars. Their tenure was not secure, which is why Te Puni and Te Wharepouri welcomed the Wakefield settlement. Pallbearers at his funeral in 1870 included Native Minister Donald McLean.

Charles Heaphy, Alexander Turnbull Library, PUBL-0011-02-2

ABOVE

Henry Petre's residence at Petone.

Samuel Charles Brees, Alexander Turnbull Library, PUBL-0020-14-1

were surprises all round. Te Wharepouri had been promised settlers as part of the deal,[44] but assumed this meant 'nine or ten' Europeans—one in each pa, who could 'barter with the people'. When he saw 200 or more pouring from every ship he almost decamped.[45] The farrago was emblematic of the enterprise, and to cap it off the settlers discovered the hard way that the valley was a flood-plain.[46]

Smith had been instructed to 'adhere to the conditions on which the land orders have been sold', though the form of the town was 'left to your own judgement and taste.'[47] Faced with swamp in the Hutt Valley, William Wakefield thought the colony might fare better on the south side of the harbour near Pipitea pa, which he called Thorndon. Precious little land was to be had there either, but there was no going back, and more than 1300 settlers were deposited in the Hutt Valley and Wellington that year alone, complete with their furniture, ploughs,

RIGHT

Company propaganda displayed the Hutt Valley as flat, open and fertile with a navigable super-Thames running through it. In fact the region was a swampy alluvial valley dominated by a shallow and wandering river.

Samuel Charles Brees, Alexander Turnbull Library, PUBL-0033-1847-168

CHAPTER THREE
SHADOWS OF EMPIRE

LEFT

When Petone and the Hutt Valley proved unsuited to the large-scale settlement to which the New Zealand Company had committed itself, company officials turned to flat land in the south of the harbour. Wiremu Tako Ngatata had led his people to the Thorndon flat after Ngati Mutunga departed a few years earlier and by 1840 about 80 Maori lived in the Piptea Pa, seen here; and there were other settlements in the vicinity, some of the residents of which had not agreed to the 'sales' made by Te Puni and Te Wharepouri.

William Mein Smith, Alexander Turnbull Library, C-011-005

ironmongery by Cottam and Hallen, and an array of 'Manning's Portable Cottages'—prefabricated homes that came complete with 'joists, floors, doors and glazed windows'.[48]

This land shortage knocked Company plans over almost at once. Wellington had little land for the 'country sections' Wakefield had promised—in effect, 'lifestyle blocks'. A lucky 30 settlers got what was available, by lottery; and in late 1840 William Wakefield had to offer the rest land in Whanganui. Dubious title there laid the foundation for a long dispute.

Capital remained short. The Britannia Hotel and Store opened in mid-1840, and owner J. Pierce deigned to list prices, declaring that the 'competitive system of puffing, much practised in the old world' had no place in New Zealand, and he therefore refrained 'from introducing prices', instead inviting 'a trial'.[49] He was joined by others; T. Roskell's store 'at the west end of the beach' offered 'spirits

LEFT

Much of the Wellington area was clad in forest. The land was sold as farm sections and the trees cut down. Some of the timber disappeared into the maws of sawmills such as this one at Kaiwharawhara.

Samuel Charles Brees, Alexander Turnbull Library, A-109-033

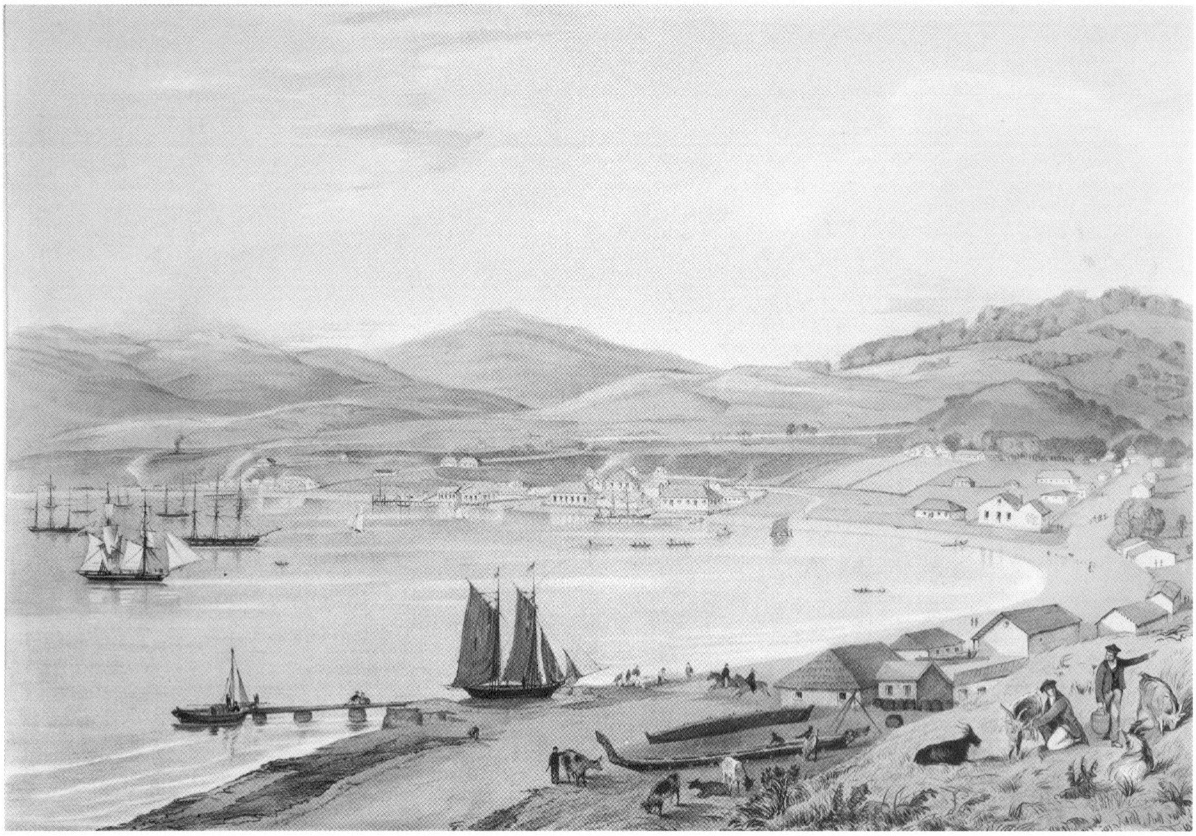

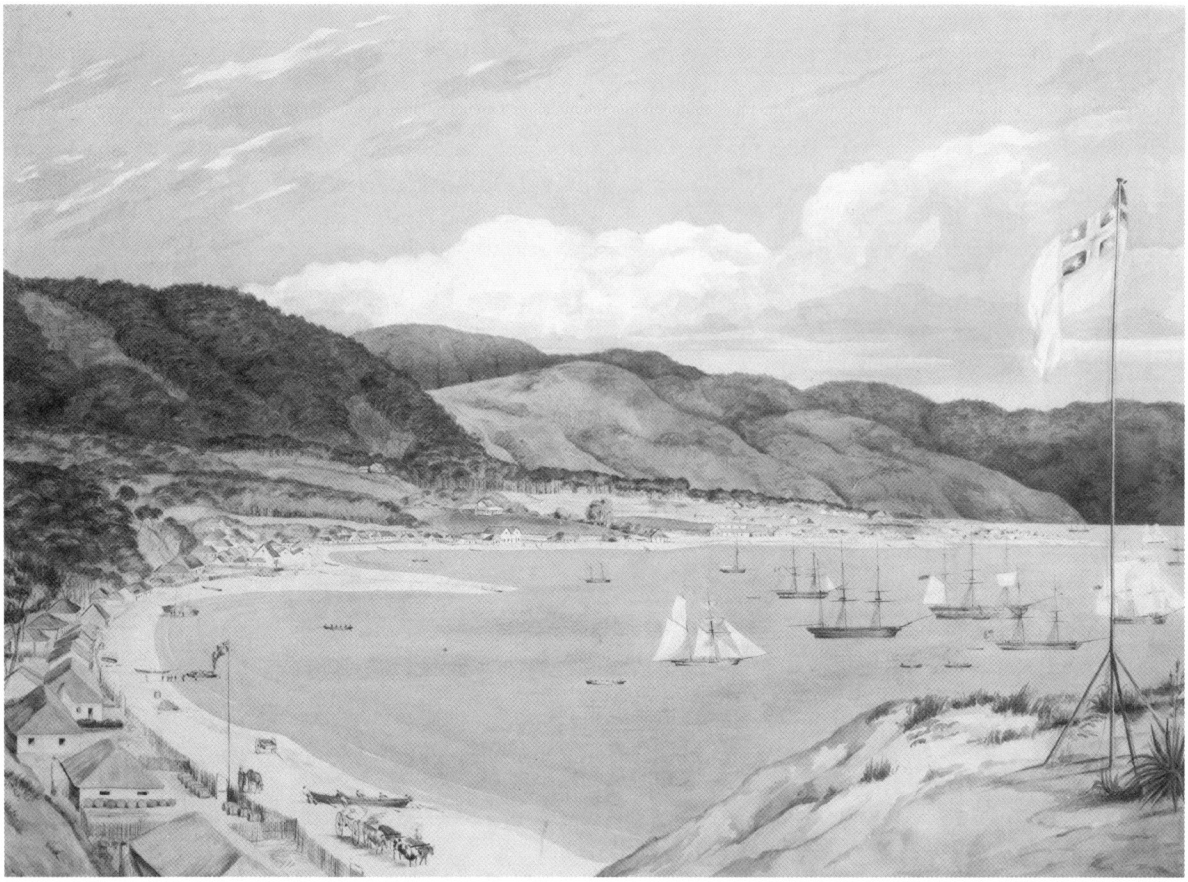

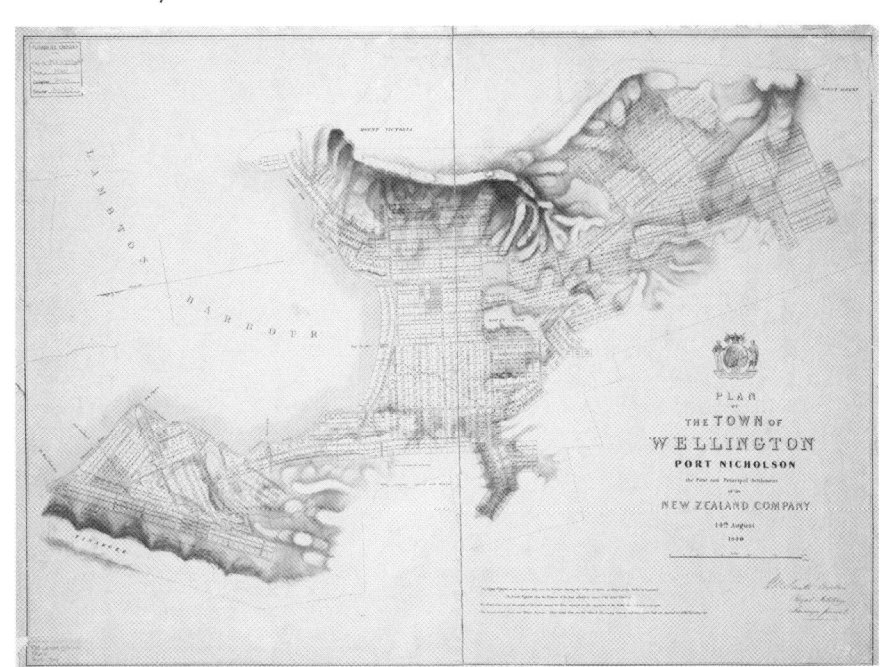

OPPOSITE ABOVE

Te Aro flats provided early Wellington with most of its flat land, seen to advantage in this 1841 Heaphy watercolour. Mount Victoria rises to the left of the frame, with the Aro Valley to the right.

Charles Heaphy, Alexander Turnbull Library C-026-002

OPPOSITE BELOW

Charles Heaphy titled this watercolour 'Thorndon flat and part of the city of Wellington' when he painted it in 1841—an overstatement, but the town nonetheless had an air of establishment barely a year after it was founded, helped along by the prefabricated buildings.

Charles Heaphy, Alexander Turnbull Library C-025-010

(wholesale and retail), tea, coffee, sugar, tobacco and cigars… butter, cheese, hams and pork' among other stores.[50] J. Telford's shop, at the other end of the beach, offered a similar range. R. W. Elsdon opened a 'commercial inn and tavern' offering 'wines, spirits, ale and porter' along with 'cold joints'.[51] But until the hinterland was settled there were few customers.

Wellington stuttered, but to Company officials back in London the problem was not that their purist socio-economic ideas were flawed. They had simply not been pushed hard or fast enough. And the lure of fast and vast profit from borrowed capital was tempting. The result was a second Wakefield colony, this time on an even larger scale. It was the brain-child of Bryan Duppa, fraught with politics and hoisted on another edifice of grand promise and self-entitled conviction.[52] The new colony was eventually dubbed 'Nelson' in a further effort to lend the repute of Napoleonic war heroes to the scheme, but dogged with trouble the whole way—even down to location, which ran afoul of Hobson's undeclared

ABOVE LEFT

William Wakefield's house, on the hill behind Barrett's Hotel, Wellington.

Samuel Charles Brees, hand coloured engraving, Alexander Turnbull Library, A-109-032

LEFT

Company officials came to Wellington armed with an ideal urban grid-plan, though this seems to have been more inspiration than serious proposal. Practical reality tempered social perfection, though the actual plan still draped straight roads and oblong sections over rugged terrain and Maori settlements alike.

Alexander Turnbull Library MapColl832.4799gbbd/1840/Acc.316

BELOW

Artist unknown, Making New Zealand Collection, Alexander Turnbull Library, 119NMZ-1/4)

war with the company. Company authority on the ground, Arthur Wakefield, had to accept a location in Blind Bay. It lacked a proper harbour; one of the early ships to arrive—the *Fifeshire*—piled up on rocks and sank, and Arthur Wakefield's hopeful letters to his brother William—running Wellington—were filled with post-fact efforts to paint Nelson Haven as something other than a disaster. The harbour, he insisted, could be made safe at 'a trifling expense' and was capable of 'considerable improvement whenever the place shall have commerce and population which would require it.'[53] In fact, within a few months, he had to accept an offshore anchorage along the coast, which he dubbed 'Bolton roads'.[54]

The bigger problem was London speculators, who forced up prices on local land and derailed opportunities for the settlers who did arrive. By mid-1842 there were 2000-odd settlers on site, but only 526 of the 1000 allotments had been sold, and 364 of these belonged to absentee landlords. The result was inevitable; the colony lacked capital, the poor squatted and Wakefield struggled. His situation was not helped by the fact that the company, back in London, was staggering. Money ran out. Wakefield needed cash to pay workers who had taken up promise of company employment if there was no other available. It was not good. A petition launched against the company by disaffected settlers summed it up; by mid-1843, even 'pretended capitalists' had been 'reduced already to all but starving point'.[55] Arthur Wakefield was killed in the 'Wairau Affray' of mid-1843—an own goal of catastrophic proportion. Sir Everard Home, commanding HMS *North Star*, spoke with local Maori a few weeks later and concluded that Nelson was in greater danger from its disaffected workers.[56]

The town survived, but not because it had followed the dictates of company theory. That was true of all the Wakefield settlements—Hutt Valley, Thorndon, Nelson and later New Plymouth and Whanganui. Prefabricated buildings created a swift air of permanence, the building boom provided initial employment, and early trade with Maori was lucrative. Settlers arrived at regular intervals, some drawn by the propaganda of company secretary John Ward, whose portrayal of a flourishing Eden might be considered New Zealand's first work of fiction:

> The extensive forests offer an inexhaustible supply for the wants of many generations... Flax ... appears to be indigenous and inexhaustible ... an almost incalculable source of riches... Peaches are plentiful in the season at Hokianga; figs, grapes, oranges, melons and the Cape gooseberry, thrive uncommonly well... Strawberries and raspberries grow in abundance... the latitude and climate are suitable to the olive...[57]

Nearly 9000 would-be migrants swallowed these words and were disappointed.[58] Nor did early successes resolve deeper problems ranging from the failure of Wakefield's social dream to the incompetence of company officials. There was a divergence between a simplistic theoretical construct, and the fuzzy truths of a complex real society. The emigrants were more capable than Wakefield imagined, and came to better themselves, not re-enter a world of semi-slavery at the hands of industrialists and landowners. Some left as they could afford to do so. Within a few years many were looking beyond company lands, derailing the control of land, and hence its prices, with which Wakefield had hoped to lock his society into place.

ABOVE AND OPPOSITE TOP
An 1842 panorama of Nelson harbour and town. One of the features of Wakefield's colonisation scheme was his plan for 'instant towns', rising up almost overnight with the help of prefabricated buildings carried out from England. Others were quickly built by settlers eager to move out of tents and temporary accommodation.

John Waring Saxton, Alexander Turnbull Library PUBL-0011-06-2

TOP

New Plymouth in 1843.

Emma Ancilla Wicksteed, Alexander Turnbull Library, PUBL-0011-09-1

ABOVE

Settlers arriving at New Plymouth were initially housed in these barracks, built with Maori labour.

Charles Heaphy, Alexander Turnbull Library, PUBL-0048-01

RIGHT

Samuel Charles Brees (1810–1865) produced many paintings and drawings illustrating the life and landscapes of the Wakefield colonies for an 1847 book, including this 'Town of Petre, Wauganui' [sic].

William Mein Smith, Alexander Turnbull Library PUBL-0020-06-5

Hobson's choices

William Hobson faced a multitude of problems as he recovered from a stroke during early 1840. His infant administration was penniless, commanded 90 soldiers and had yet to peddle the Treaty of Waitangi around the country. Pre-Treaty land claims had yet to be tackled, and New Zealand Company officials were uneasy about the potential loss of their 1839 'purchases'.[59] There was talk of a private French colony at Akaroa, under the aegis of the Nanto-Bordelaise Company. Captain Langlois of the whaler *Cachalot* had 'purchased' 30,000 acres on Banks Peninsula in 1838, and eventually persuaded the French government to support a private venture to exploit fishing opportunities. The colonists were on their way by early 1840. To cap it off, the New Zealand Company declared self-government in May.

Hobson dealt with it systematically. He sent two magistrates and several constables to welcome the French and remind them that New Zealand was British. The New Zealand Company prompted more decisive steps. Hobson was informed of their declaration of self-government late on 21 May, considered it treason,[60] and before the day was out issued a proclamation seizing the North Island by cession. Shortland was despatched on the *Integrity* to raise the Union Jack over Wellington. Thomas Bunbury formally annexed the South Island three weeks later off Cloudy Bay. The immediate driver was Hobson's political problems, but sovereignty was also explicit in the British understanding of the Treaty of Waitangi—this had been its key intent from their perspective. The Colonial Office began promoting the Treaty around Europe to forestall other efforts to steal the march on Britain's newest colony. Meanwhile the British government issued a post-fact charter for the New Zealand Company, legitimising the operation within the gamut of colonial sovereignty.

These difficult beginnings set the theme for successive colonial governments in the early 1840s. The bold assertion that British power had been declared over New Zealand—and the assumption by the Colonial Office that this was true—was at odds with local reality. Actually, Hobson and his successors William Shortland and Robert FitzRoy had to balance Colonial Office requests, the increasingly strident demands of the New Zealand Company, and difficult race-relations matters against a penurious reality. Lack of funds, military weakness and lack of settler numbers highlighted the fact that Crown control was only nominal in the face of superior Maori numbers and power.

One of the bigger issues of the day was the 'waste land' argument. It stemmed in part from a Colonial Office interpretation of the Treaty of Waitangi. To the new Secretary of State, Lord John Russell, indigenous property rights extended only to the lands which Maori actually occupied and cultivated, and he asked Hobson to 'define on the maps of the colony the lands of the aborigines.'[61] This was not

ABOVE

Auckland was founded as colonial capital more by chance than design. William Hobson intended to site the capital at Okiato, near Russell, but it was tied up with land purchases made illegal by the Treaty of Waitangi. A power vacuum in the Waitemata, legacy of the musket wars, made settlement easier there. Felton Mathew surveyed a site in late 1840 and the new capital was set up early the following year. New Zealand Company officials in Wellington were bitterly disappointed. The fact that the colonial administration could be housed in this modest structure is indicative of the nature of government at that time. The building was destroyed by fire in 1842.

Edward Ashworth, Alexander Turnbull Library, E-216-f-005

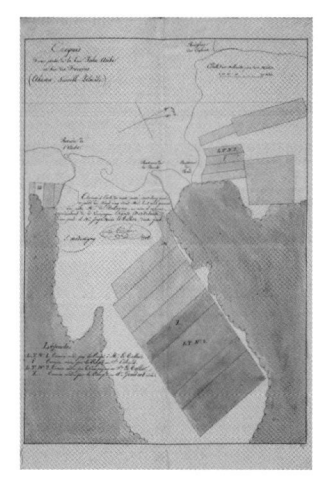

ABOVE

Akaroa was tipped as the site of a Nanto-Bordelaise Company colony. Hobson sent magistrates to remind the French that New Zealand was British.

Artist unknown, Nanto-Bordelaise Collection, Alexander Turnbull Library, qMS-1407-080

Hobson's understanding of what Maori had agreed to, but the Colonial Office played into New Zealand Company hands. Agitated by the potential loss of their purchases, company officials claimed that the law did not recognise anything other than ownership by occupation, and the Treaty was nothing more than 'a praiseworthy device for amusing and pacifying savages for the moment.'[62] Quite.

Hobson's lack of effective clout goes far towards explaining his apparent spinelessness, his premature death in 1842, and the bad press delivered by historians both to his regime and those of his successors Shortland and FitzRoy. All three have been portrayed as preludes to a heroic George Grey (1812–98), a crusading, eccentric idealist whose controversial administration shaped the country from the late 1840s.

There were substantial contrasts between these figures, but one of the more pragmatic reasons for the difference in style between Hobson and Grey was the ongoing administrative development of New Zealand's government structures at the hands of the Colonial Office, back in London. By the early 1840s it was clear that Auckland-based Crown government could not keep close tabs on Wellington, still less anywhere further south. The Wairau incident, when Nelson settlers illegally tried to assert ownership of the Wairau plains by force and provoked a battle with Ngati Toa, prompted calls in Wellington for local government. FitzRoy—by contrast with Hobson or Shortland—viewed the idea favourably. But his concept of municipal powers fell short of what the company had in mind, and they were further alienated in 1844 when he abandoned the pre-emption provisions of the Treaty of Waitangi, playing into the hands of Auckland landowners.[63]

Grey's New Zealand Government Act of 1846, following Colonial Office instruction, split New Zealand into two provinces. The southern, New Munster, was based on Wellington, and came under a Lieutenant Governor—explorer and adventurer Edward Eyre. Both provinces had their own two-house legislative assembly that reported to a General Assembly in Auckland; and most of the

RIGHT

Life at home in the new colony: Sonia Bambridge and son William (1842–?), at Purewa in the mid-1840s.

William Bambridge, sepia ink, Alexander Turnbull Library, qMS-0122-074.

LEFT

Nelson, 1845: an air of prosperity belies the faltering Wakefield scheme.

Francis Dillon Bell, Alexander Turnbull Library, A-252-019

Wellington administrators—with the exception of Colonial Secretary Alfred Domett, a career civil servant, were company men. This compromise provided an on-the-spot administration, reinforcing the authority of the Crown and providing better control of the European settlers. It all came together as the race-relations ground shifted—a consequence of the war that broke out with Ngapuhi in 1844.

Flagstaffs and regiments

Although invariably lumped with the conflicts of the 1860s and 1870s, the war that flared in Northland during 1844–46 was very different from its successors. The struggle set Hone Heke Pokai and Te Ruki Kawiti against Tamati Waka Nene and the British. In some respects it reflected traditional Ngapuhi relationships, in which the British played a third party. However, historians have struggled to explain why fighting erupted, or what it meant. To T. L. Buck, writing in the 1920s, it was a 'rebellion',[64] though this is not how Heke saw it. Causes transcended personalities; had Heke not sparked the war, trouble would probably have brewed one way or another.

The main issue was the conceptual gulf between notions of sovereignty and chieftainship. As far as the British were concerned, Maori had signed over sovereignty, though they were still free to run their people within the framework of British laws. Maori, however, interpreted British duties and ordinances as interference with their own power. In the Bay of Islands the issue was compounded by the fact that Ngapuhi felt abandoned after Hobson moved the capital to the Waitemata. Many had signed the treaty expecting to receive settlers and trade. However, 'in our part of the country ... the Pakeha did not increase in numbers, but on the contrary, began to go away to the town at Waitemata... Tobacco began

ABOVE

'Potie' of 'Port Nicholson' was apparently the mistress of Nelson hotelier William Wright. Maori-settler liaisons of this kind were not uncommon.

Isaac Coates, Alexander Turnbull Library, A-286-017

ABOVE

Robert FitzRoy (1805–1865) visited New Zealand in 1835 as captain of HMS *Beagle*, the scientific research ship. In 1843 he was appointed Governor of New Zealand, but the dire financial situation of the colony put him in an impossible position.

Artist unknown, H. J. Schmidt Collection, Alexander Turnbull Library, PAColl-3059, G-1318-1/1

BELOW

Kororareka 'on the morning before the assault', 10 March 1845.

G. T. Clayton, Alexander Turnbull Library C-010-022

to be scarce and dear; the ships began to leave off coming to Tokerau, Hokianga and Mangonui.'[65] When they discovered that the cause of the price-rises were customs and harbour duties, Maori 'at first did not believe' because 'you all said you were not slaves ... but all free men.'[66]

By 1844 Heke was determined to do something about it, though he did not want to destroy his economic relationship with the British.[67] Quite the reverse; in fact his gripe was with the way colonial duties had interfered with what he regarded as Maori authority, to their financial detriment, and then with the way that the trade had been taken away to Auckland. The point was underlined by his target—the symbol of British sovereignty, fluttering from the flagstaff above Kororareka, which Heke himself had given to the British. On the night of 8 July, he sent his men to fell it. It was provocative, and Maori certainly 'expected there would be fighting'.[68] However, FitzRoy had no force to hand, and in any event preferred diplomacy. He sent Archbishop Selwyn to meet Maori, then came to the Bay of Islands himself, removing customs duties in September.

At first all seemed well, but FitzRoy's concession did not relieve the underlying tensions, and Heke knocked the flagstaff down a second time in early January 1845. FitzRoy responded by putting a price on Heke's head and asking Nene to guard the pole. The latter agreed, but although Nene's men boasted of capturing Heke and 'smoking him'—spending the reward on tobacco—they made no effort to stop Heke when he brushed past them on the night of 19 January. He hacked the staff down a third time and sauntered back to his canoe with the words 'Heoi ano.' ('That's enough.')[69] The British did not agree—to them it was a 'brazen declaration of war'.[70] FitzRoy called for more troops and sent 30 men of the 96th Regiment to guard the flagstaff—now re-erected with reinforcing. Meanwhile Williams circulated 300 copies of the Treaty of Waitangi around the Bay of Islands. The arrival of the regulars also had an effect. Maori in this district had not seen British troops in number, and the demeanour required of line soldiers in this age of regimented battle stood in sharp contrast to the norms of a toa, even in the musket wars era:

> Now, these soldiers had red garments; they did not work, or buy and sell, like other Pakeha people; they practised every day with their weapons, and some of them were constantly watching as if they expected to be attacked every moment. They were a very suspicious people, and they had stiff, hard things round their necks to keep their heads up, lest they should forget, and look too much downwards, and not keep their eyes continually rolling about in search of an enemy.[71]

The soldiers were joined by around 250 marines and 'special constables', but Heke was undeterred. 'I will cut down the flagstaff... The soldiers are not gods; lead will kill them.'[72] Kawiti joined him, and they launched a joint attack on the night of 9 March. British forces included 45 sailors from HMS *Hazard*, anchored offshore. Heke's men took the blockhouse and felled the flagstaff, but the battle devolved to a pot-shot struggle in the town and Maori did not advance even after Joel Polack's powder store was accidentally blown up.[73] This gave the British time to evacuate to ships anchored in the bay, and the *Hazard* opened fire as Maori and settlers alike surged forward to pillage the wrecked town.[74]

Heke had not intended things to go so far—this was wrecking the trading relationship he had been trying to recapture—and he insisted that the looters were neither his nor Kawiti's.[75] FitzRoy waited for elements of the 58th Regiment to reach Auckland from Sydney and in late April launched an expedition under Lieutenant-Colonel William Hulme. The British landed in the Bay of Islands in early May, attacked Pomare's pa, then marched inland through rain to Lake Omapere, where they were joined by Nene's men outside Heke's incomplete Puketutu pa. Heke had 200-odd men to hand, and Kawiti provided a force variously cited as 140 or 300,[76] which camped outside the pa. Hulme opened fire with rockets, then sent the bulk of his men to

ABOVE

Heke Pokai (c1807–1850), adopted the first names Hone Wiremu (John William) when he and his wife were baptised in 1835. Here he stands with his second wife Hariata, daughter of Hongi Hika, and Te Ruki Kawiti.

Joseph Jenner Merrett, Alexander Turnbull Library, C-012-019

LEFT

Major Cyprian Bridge (1808–1883) led this attack on a pa on the Waikare River on 16 May, which was believed to hold some of the plunder from Kororareka.

Cyprian Bridge, Alexander Turnbull Library, A-079-004

NEW ZEALAND
AN ILLUSTRATED HISTORY

78

LEFT

Battle for Ohaeawai, July 1845, ink and wash sketch by Sergeant John Williams of the 58th Regiment. The battle was a defeat for the British, but late twentieth-century efforts to portray the pa defences as a pioneering invention by Maori were overstated.

John Williams, Alexander Turnbull Library, E-320-f-002

take the incomplete rear, where they were engaged by Kawiti's force. The British got the better of it, but by arrangement Heke sortied into British forces in front of the pa. The storming party rushed to help, Kawiti attacked them in the rear and Hulme decided to withdraw. It was a tactical Maori victory, but at the same time it was clear that Maori ran second to the regiments in open battle. Neither Heke nor Kawiti missed the lesson.

A tussle between Heke and Nene's forces followed at Te Ahuahu while the British regrouped, now under Colonel Henry Despard. By June they were ready to attack Kawiti's new pa at Ohaeawai, south of Waimate, and some 600-odd soldiers and 250 of Nene's men set out from Kerikeri. Just getting there was a struggle; Despard remarked that 'Scarcely a rivulet was passed that some of the guns did not upset...'[77] They battled their way to Ohaeawai, but a five-day siege did not crack the defences, and Despard's decision to storm the pa produced only disaster. With 70 wounded and ammunition running short, the beleaguered Colonel had to abandon the attempt. Kawiti's forces slipped away, and Despard got the blame.

FitzRoy decided to negotiate, but his failures were the final straw for the Colonial Office, and he was sacked in September. His replacement was Captain George Grey, the ruthless, autocratic and idealistic administrator of South Australia, who reached Auckland in November 1845. Negotiations had reached a point where FitzRoy believed peace could be organised, but Grey thought the chiefs' letters were merely a device to gain time, demanding a fresh expedition to attack Kawiti's new pa. The force that left Auckland on 7 December included 800 regulars and a naval brigade, backed by three 32-pounders, an 18-pounder, two 12-pounders and other artillery. This arsenal was pitted against Kawiti's new fortress of Ruapekapeka—'The Bat's Lair'—another modified musket pa built on a hillside south of Kororareka. Grey asked Nene's ally Makoare Te Taonui to detain Heke at Hikurangi, while Despard advanced across 18 miles (30 km) of rugged terrain. It took days, in part because Despard insisted on building staging

OPPOSITE ABOVE

96th and 58th Regiments in action at Puketutu, 8 May 1845. Lieutenant Egerton's rocket battery is visible to the right in this painting by Major Cyprian Bridge of the 58th Regiment.

Cyprian Bridge, Alexander Turnbull Library, A-079-008

OPPOSITE BELOW

Colonel Henry Despard (c1784–1859) led British forces and kupapa against Ohaeawai in mid-July 1845. Cyprian Bridge drew this 'view of the left angle' from 'breastwork adjoining our main battery.' Flax masking the pekerangi (outer fence) is noteworthy.

Cyprian Bridge, Alexander Turnbull Library, A-079-005

RIGHT

John Williams drew this picture of Ruapekapeka after the British had taken it on 11 January 1846, after a sketch by Colonel Wynyard.

John Williams, Alexander Turnbull Library, E-320-f-010

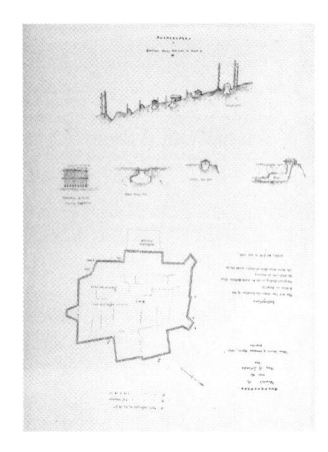

ABOVE

Charles Heaphy's diagram of the Ruapekapeka defences, noting the flagpole knocked over by a lucky shot early in the siege. What this does not show is the slope that gave the defenders a significant advantage.

Charles Heaphy, Alexander Turnbull Library, B-043-015-3

posts, but they were in position by Christmas and began a massive bombardment. Maori were 'almost deaf with the noise ... the air was full of cannon-balls', and the palisades 'began to disappear like a bank of fog before the morning breeze.'[78]

Heke arrived with 60-odd men on 10 January, but Despard did not move until the next day, when he discovered that the defenders had withdrawn—only Kawiti and a dozen men remained behind, exchanged brief shots with the British, then withdrew. Stories circulated that the Maori had left the pa because it was Sunday and they intended to pray.[79] There were also suggestions that Kawiti and Heke planned to draw the British into the bush behind the pa, then ambush them 'as if they were wood-pigeons.'[80] There was a skirmish in the bush, but the loss of 12 dead and 30 wounded did not dent British strength and this 'ambush' theory has been dismissed by some historians.[81]

Actually the battle ended the war—neither Heke nor Kawiti felt able to continue. The two chiefs arrived at Pomare's pa a week after the battle and agreed to cease hostilities. Their people 'could not live on fern-root and fight the soldiers at the same time.' Nor was dispersing among Ngapuhi an option. 'After talking over this plan for some time,' an observer recalled, 'it was found it would not do, for already some chiefs ... had said they would give up anyone who came to them ... rather than bring war against themselves.'[82] The only other option was peace. It was a clear concession; Britain had won. In this respect the war was closer to the old inter-tribal conflicts; a limited struggle where lack of resources forced a negotiated end. Grey offered a pardon,[83] Heke and Kawiti kept their looted property, and the flagstaff remained down.

The meaning of this outcome has been debated; in the late twentieth century and early twenty-first, some historians took Grey's magnanimity as a sign that this war was a Maori victory.[84] Actually that was not so. The British were in a military position to continue the war in 1845, whereas Heke and Kawiti were forced to a halt. Grey's subsequent actions have to be seen in context of the British approach of the day—to seek negotiation before warfare, and to settle with what FitzRoy called 'justice and clemency'.[85] It was practical as much as ideological. War was

LEFT'

'View of Pomare's new pah at the Karetu off the Kawa Kawa River, New Zealand, June 1846'.

Cyprian Bridge, Alexander Turnbull Library, A-079-002

costly for the indebted colony, and other flashpoints demanded attention. When the opportunity came to make an expedient peace, Grey did so. The fact that he continued to investigate ways of keeping Heke and Kawiti under control through 1846 is an indication that he recognised the threat they still posed, not sudden military impotence.

This war—and particularly the siege of Ohaeawai—gained new meaning in the twentieth century because it was used to make the claim that firearms-age trench defences, as a world phenomenon, were largely invented by Maori of the 1845–1869 era. The idea became pervasive in New Zealand's non-military academic circles during the late twentieth century,[86] upheld as a 'truth' just as the great canoe migration and two-race notions had been upheld a century earlier. It was eventually simplified into the nonsense assertion that Maori had invented trench warfare and the British stole it for the First World War. The origins of western positional warfare and field defences are very well documented. The world pioneers were fourteenth and fifteenth-century Europeans such as Leonardo da Vinci, who developed most of these techniques during the Renaissance.[87] Artillery-proof structures intended to shield the garrison were integral to Europe's fortresses from the early sixteenth century, further developed by Sébastien le Prestre, Marquis of Vauban.[88] By the late eighteenth century, 80 years before the siege of Ohaeawai, the British had calculated the depths of earth needed for fieldworks to deflect specific weights of artillery.[89] The techniques of firearms defences, both permanent and field, and firearms-age siege warfare in general were being taught in places such as the Woolwich Royal Military Academy and the Royal Military College at Sandhurst.[90] All this is well documented in basic texts, and the real question is how the 'Maori invention' fantasy gained traction amongst the late twentieth-century New Zealand historical community.

The idea actually originated with two historians of the 1920s. T. Lindsay Buick directly compared Maori defences of the 1840s to some First World War dugouts.[91] James Cowan similarly compared Ngati Raukawa communications trenches of the 1860s with purpose-dug structures on the Western Front of 1916–18,[92] and

ABOVE

Te Ruki Kawiti (c1770s–1854) of Ngati Hine was known to the settlers as 'The Duke', and had a formidable reputation as both fighting chief and peacemaker. He was heavily involved in the musket wars and refused at first to sign the Treaty of Waitangi. He changed his mind, but then sided with Heke in 1845.

Artist unknown, Alexander Turnbull Library, F-37353-1/2

took that further with his description of Ohaeawai which, he argued, reflected a parallel invention by Maori of artillery bunkers.[93] This idea was also discussed by James Belich in 1986[94] and at a time when historians were questioning old shibboleths, the notion struck chords with late twentieth-century non-military academics, gaining surprising currency despite flying in the face of documented military history.[95]

It was an excellent demonstration of the way history is mythologised—where meanings are forced through contemporary intellectual lenses and given apparent credence in the process because the resulting pattern so closely fits contemporary ideas. In fact there was a much more complex process going on in early nineteenth-century New Zealand, and one that generally highlighted the relationship Maori had with the whole raft of introduced British technologies and ideas. Despite British conceits of the day, this process was not one of automatic adoption of their 'superior' ideas. Maori were very selective, and there was a good deal about British society that they did not like. Governor Phillip Gidley King discovered that first-hand when Te Pahi visited Sydney in 1805. The chief 'spared no pains to convince us that the customs of his country were in several instances better than ours, many of which he looked on with the greatest contempt, and some with the most violent and abusive disapprobation.'[96]

However, industrial goods and the ideas that went with them had obvious uses for Maori. So did matters military. But it was not a process of simple copying, as colonial-age observers assumed and as post-colonial historians were as eager to deny. Maori merely needed to understand the principles; they could run with those to create systems inspired by British methods, but adapted to New Zealand's conditions and local tactical demands, often with specific Maori innovations

BELOW

Some 400 men of the 58th, 96th and 99th Regiments arrived in the Hutt Valley during March 1846 to enforce martial law after raids by Ngati Toa.

Samuel Charles Brees/Henry Melville, hand coloured engraving, Alexander Turnbull Library, E-070-007

Fort Richmond in the central Hutt Valley was designed by Captain Compton on US blockhouse practice and first occupied in April 1846 by part of the 58th Regiment. The bridge is an 1844 structure built for the New Zealand Company.
S. C. Brees/Henry Melville, Alexander Turnbull Library, A-109-030

built into the mix. This was recognised at the time; as Auguste Berard declared in 1846, Maori had 'shown great military talent', drawing 'the highest praise' from British observers.[97]

Key players in the military acculturation process included Hongi Hika, who visited the military college at Woolwich in 1820 and pumped them for details, then adopted British firearms techniques—modified to New Zealand needs—when he got back.[98] Te Rauparaha learned about assault saps and then applied the system to his own siege techniques, acculturated to fit his political needs. At Kaiapoi in 1832, for instance, he had three saps dug and assigned one to each of his allied iwi.[99] Other information flowed steadily as Maori pestered Europeans for all they knew of military matters. Jack Marmon found Maori were eager to 'have a resident Pakeha amongst them' largely so he could be pushed to reveal 'all the methods of warfare and offence known to him'.[100] Pa took on many of the defensive features the British had developed in consequence of firearms experience, built in earth rather than European-style masonry, but conceptually designed for the same purpose. The process was clear at Ohaeawai, which was a modified musket pa that had a good deal in common with British field forts of the seventeenth century, using many of the same tactical features.[101]

In a military sense the failure of Heke's war to spread among Ngapuhi makes clear that the British had checked northern Maori. In open combat fought on their own terms, the professional soldiers were extremely capable, and British artillery counted for much even in battles fought on Maori terms. Non-combatant Maori had been eager to see the 'full strength of the soldiers put forth, that we might see what the utmost of their power was,'[102] and they got it at Ruapekapeka in a storm of noise and fire. Restraint also carried a practical benefit; war damaged the

ABOVE

Boulcott stockade after the Battle of Boulcott's Farm, graves of the regimental soldiers in the foreground.

George Hyde Page, Alexander Turnbull Library, B-081-002

economic relationship with the settlers, and few chiefs were prepared to sacrifice what they had gained.

Grey withdrew half the force to Auckland, but they had not been there long before they were sent to a new war in Wellington. This southern tussle broke out largely as a result of the shoddy land purchases of the late 1830s, which trampled over Maori rights already in flux on the back of the musket wars. Formal investigation under William Spain dragged on, the settlers collided with Maori. There were newspaper calls for Te Rauparaha's death.[103] The northern war raised tensions still further. FitzRoy decided to prioritise that struggle, but by early 1846 Ngati Toa were directly threatening settlers in the Hutt Valley and there was unease across the colony as administrators from Nelson to New Plymouth began looking sideways at their own local iwi. By this time Grey was in charge. A brief skirmish in the Hutt Valley in March 1846 prompted him to declare martial law across the Wellington region, which he enforced with the help of 400 men of the 58th, 96th and 99th Regiments under Hulme.

That did not prevent the Battle of Boulcott Farm in May, when Upper Whanganui chief Te Mamaku led around 200 toa against 45 regulars of the 58th under Lieutenant G. H. Page, pinning the British in a stockaded barn. After about an hour Page led his men to engage the foe directly and, with the help of a small party of militia that happened to arrive soon afterwards, drove Te Mamaku's much larger force back over the Hutt River.[104]

Tensions remained high. Te Rangihaeata built a pa at the head of the Pauatahanui Inlet. What followed demonstrated Grey's ability to find lateral answers. Amidst talk of Maori reinforcements arriving from Whanganui, Grey had Te Rauparaha seized on pretext of treason. This coup de main effectively decapitated the Ngati Toa empire. He then sent forces against Te Rangihaeta's pa, but abandoned that on news that the chief had withdrawn from it and gone inland. A British force that included some 250 regulars from the 58th, 65th and 99th Regiments, backed by local militia, constables and around 150 Te Atiawa, pursued Te Rangihaeata's group inland to a ridge, where the chief had a small field fortification built. The British could only tackle him by a long uphill climb into heavy fire—but they had the advantage of a mortar, which was brought up from Porirua; and after about 80 rounds had been lobbed into the Maori position, Te Rangihaeata took advantage of darkness to escape.

He was pursued by Te Atiawa and took refuge in the Horowhenua. However, Grey—as in the north—did not prosecute the fight. He portrayed himself as magnanimous, even humanitarian: 'I do not make war against women and children'.[105] Reality was different. Cost played a part. But the more crucial issue was that he had pushed the boundaries of British power; it had been a war, in effect, of cheek, and in the process Grey had effectively replaced Te Rauparaha's loose empire with one of his own. But the military aspects were only a part of the wider assertion of power, a point underscored by the rather disgraceful sequel to the fighting. Eight Ngati Hau under Hohepa Te Umuroa were captured by Te Atiawa during the war.[106] Grey had them charged with rebellion and convicted in a show trial, conducted in English, and all but two were packed off to the convict settlements in Tasmania. The inequity was manifest even by period standards; there was an outcry on both sides of the Tasman. The issue reached the Colonial Office. Grey's behaviour had been well out of line and the convictions were quashed; but justice came too late for Te Umuroa, who died of tuberculosis at the Darlington Probation Station.[107]

This appalling episode highlighted the changing nature of the power balance in New Zealand. Grey's strategies were coloured in detail by his personality but broadly reflected wider British thinking of the day—and the demands of the Colonial Office. Wars were expensive. Effective power was not wrested from indigenous peoples by the sword, but by a broader range of strategies. It was a question of speaking softly and carrying a stick. Demonstrations, followed by negotiation and conciliation on British terms, were the order of the day. And in this sense both the northern and southern wars were significant for New Zealand. They underscored—and to some extent pushed—a change in the balance of power. The Pakeha population was growing, the colony gaining dimension as the

ABOVE
The fight on what was later named Battle Hill, inland from Paremata. This impression by George Page (1823–1908) underestimates the extreme slopes up which the British attacked.
George Hyde Page, Alexander Turnbull Library, G-525

towns expanded and became better established, as the local economy emerged, as pastoralists began expanding outwards into the grasslands. British presence was still a shadow of empire; but the balance was shifting. By the end of the 1840s, Maori still held the balance of power in a practical sense, but the settler state was in a position to assert itself with caution.

Shades of Grey

Mr Colenso told me they [Ngati Kahungunu] seemed doubtful about selling the whole of Moturuahou [sic] Island that they wanted several reserves on the island, and Mr Colenso advised them to have a clause inserted in the deed giving them free rights to their vessels entering and leaving the harbour besides such other rights as would no doubt be to their advantage, although it does not appear to me essential that the natives require such advice when they are in treaty with the British Govt.
–Donald McLean, 11 November 1851[108]

Government attitudes to Maori and the Treaty of Waitangi steadily hardened during the 1850s. This reflected a general Empire-wide transition from more humanitarian ideals that followed the end of the Napoleonic wars, towards the tougher imperialist sentiment of the later nineteenth century, itself a function of changing British thought. In New Zealand, the shift was made possible by Grey's policies and the ongoing influx of settlers, which tipped the balance just enough to give Grey leverage that Hobson had not enjoyed. What followed was a combined outcome of misfired plans, misunderstandings and the workings of fate, along with cynical efforts to drive land purchase deals.

Grey had his own ideas about how to handle the land purchase process, but he inherited problems that required drastic action, not least of which was the mess left by William Wakefield. An added complication was the Colonial Office interpretation of the Treaty of Waitangi, reflecting the 1844 opinion of a House of Commons Committee. Under pressure from the New Zealand Company, this committee concluded that the Treaty of Waitangi represented 'injudicious proceedings'. The problem was 'waste lands'—territory not physically occupied by Maori. As Colonial Secretary Lord Stanley told Grey, 'all lands not actually occupied in the sense in which alone occupation can give a right of possession, ought to have been considered as the property of the Crown.'[109] These attitudes drew protest in New Zealand from Sir William Martin, who argued that 'the whole surface of these islands ... has been appropriated by the Natives... Nowhere was any piece of land discovered or heard of which was not owned by some person or set of persons.'[110]

Grey did not dissent; as he remarked to Colonial Secretary Earl Grey, 'even in the most densely inhabited portions ... are very large tracts of land claimed by contending tribes to which neither of them have a strictly valid right.'[111] In practice, however, he could not seize the 'waste' lands, and instead set up mechanisms for Crown purchase, abolishing the Protectorate Department and putting the protection of Maori rights into the hands of officials such as Donald McLean. He intended to maximise returns to government, pushing land sales 'so

ABOVE

A 'terrible and fatal man', George Grey (1812–1898) was just 28 when he was appointed Governor of South Australia. He became Governor of New Zealand in 1845, after FitzRoy's dismissal, and made an early splash with his handling of the wars. He followed this with controversial 'flour and sugar' policies and introduced representative government to New Zealand. He was appointed Governor of South Africa in 1854, a post he held until 1861 when he returned to New Zealand,. By this time he was offside with the Colonial Office, and was dismissed in 1868 amid remarks that he was unlikely to be re-employed. He entered New Zealand politics in 1874 and became Premier in 1877.

Photographer unidentified, Alexander Turnbull Library, PA2-2509, F-92895-1/2

far in advance of the wants of the European settlers as to be able to purchase the lands required by the Government for a trifling consideration...'[112] Agents such as McLean, Henry Kemp and Walter Mantell came under pressure to drive sales at the lowest price. Grey envisaged the main payment would be through ongoing trade and his 'flour and sugar' policies—a deliberate effort to educate Maori and provide them industry; in short, to 'assimilate' them into the British economy.

From a twenty-first-century perspective it was flat-out colonialism, but to Grey the plan was also a way of helping Maori help themselves. As early as April 1851, Donald McLean noted in his diary that 'it would be an excellent thing if the natives would join with the Europeans in purchasing sheep, or shares. It would be a yearly revenue to them, which would always be increasing, and ... lead to their eventual wealth and improvement.'[113] Such sentiments defined the way the British saw Maori; official reports for decades afterwards invariably began with descriptions of 'industrial pursuits'.[114] What Grey, McLean and their successors variously missed or hoped to change was the point that Maori economics were geared around traditional social structures. This society had clearly not collapsed—though it had to adapt to the new environment—and Maori certainly had no intention of taking up British systems which, from a Maori perspective, were not better than their own.

Grey facilitated flour mills and other factories, and set up 'industrial schools' to teach Maori how to use them. Costs were significant; the 'Wanganui Industrial School'[sic] of 1853 absorbed more than £1,500 in government money and a further £200 from the CMS for the land. Most were effectively small farms. By 1856, Te Aute had more than six acres in wheat, four in potatoes and 13 in grass. Principal Samuel Williams believed he could 'confer a benefit' on Maori by 'teaching them to cultivate their land in a proper manner, also to look after their

BELOW
Wellington waterfront mid-1840s, about the time the town became politically prominent as capital of New Munster, Grey's southern province. The hotel in centre-frame was owned by Richard Barrett and was one of the prefabricated buildings brought from England, originally intended as a schoolhouse.
Samuel Charles Brees/Henry Melville, Alexander Turnbull Library, A-109-027

ABOVE

Yorkshire-born Edward John Eyre (1815–1901) reached Sydney in 1833 with £400 and settled on the Hunter River. His restless spirit drove him to explore the interior, including a pioneering 13-month continental crossing from Adelaide to Albany in 1840–41. He returned briefly to England before being appointed Lieutenant-Governor of New Zealand under George Grey. The two fought a near-continuous turf war until 1853, when Grey displaced Eyre. The latter left for England, where he embarked on a controversial career as colonial administrator in the West Indies.

Artist unknown, Alexander Turnbull Library, F-11991-1/2

RIGHT

Pastoralism exploded into the Wairarapa during the late 1840s, derailing New Zealand Company monopolies on land and creating fortunes for those who got in on the ground floor of this new money-spinner.

S. C. Brees/Henry Melville, hand coloured engraving, Alexander Turnbull Library, E-070-009

stock, milking &c.'[115] But Te Aute staggered and folded—15 pupils in 1856 had fallen to just four by 1859, when Williams closed it. He put the failure down to poor accommodation, hard work demanded of the pupils, temptations of high wages in adjacent stations—and the 'excited state of the native mind on the Land question.'[116]

Actually it reflected deeper issues. Grey's policies broadly reflected the general British belief of the day that their own society was, by nature, not only superior, but a desirable end point in a linear chain of social development that began with the stone age and ended with gentlemen's clubs. Indigenous peoples would, the belief went, automatically want to adopt these 'higher' values and customs; and the best thing the British could do was to help them along the way by educating them in it. However, that stood well apart from what was actually going on in New Zealand, and the reality of the 1850s was that Maori were very much their own people; tikanga and ritenga had been bent but not broken by the impact of British industrial goods, systems and ideas; and old values still held strong. Maori certainly could not be 'assimilated' by having British values rammed down their throats.

This did not prevent the British trying long after the assimilation horse had bolted. As late as 1862, William Baker decried the indiscipline he saw at the Turanga church school as symptomatic of Maori social systems, condemning the lack of 'prompt and cheerful obedience' as 'one of the greatest evils', making it 'more imperative that it should be strictly enforced at their public schools.'[117]

The irrelevance of British culture to Maori hampered Grey's efforts to kick-start Maori industry on the British model, but the real problem was that by the mid-nineteenth century Maori were reliant on income to buy the British goods and consumables that had been adopted and acculturated over the previous couple of generations. In earlier times this had been possible through trade; but the unfolding local Pakeha economy changed the calculation. By the early 1850s many hapu and iwi were hobbled by debts and the fact that the majority of their income went on consumables—some of which were purchased because European goods had become part of a currency of rivalry, which the British misinterpreted as 'frivolous' spending, but which reflected the way colonial pressures were being received amidst traditional systems. Industry, in any case,

Big sky, big country. The 'great Wairarapa district' contrasted sharply with the narrow valleys of Wellington. Hunters soon gave way to pastoralists eager to strike leasing deals with Maori—thumbing their noses at government in the process.
S. C. Brees/Henry Melville, hand coloured engraving, Alexander Turnbull Library, E-070-008

was not cheap. A mill set up at Warea in 1846–47 cost £150, paid in pigs to the builder, William Henwood. He was also the operator, and Maori found that the cost of construction and operation outstripped returns; the mill was abandoned in the early 1850s. Nor were mills always set up for economic reasons; in the late 1840s mills became a brief focus of rivalry, as a result of which uneconomic numbers were set up in some areas, none in others. Hapu in Taranaki even came to blows over siting one.[118] Government assistance helped improve returns, but the wheat market crashed in 1856. Prices fell from 12 to 3 shillings per bushel and Maori agriculture effectively collapsed.[119]

Some British were puzzled by the failure of Grey's system, but the only explanation officials could come up with was that Maori had 'got into dissipated habits and squandered the money in debauchery at Auckland and Wellington, and in the purchase of useless, and extravagant articles.'[120] Efforts to rectify the problem reflected this attitude, as at the Kohimarama conference of 1860 where chief government land buyer Donald McLean told chiefs that:

> The education of your children, greater attention to the cultivation of the soil, the erection of better houses to live in, and the acquisition of European property will, I sincerely trust, claim your chief attention, when you return to your people.[121]

One of the problems was that the playing field was not quite as level as Grey and his government imagined. It was difficult for Maori to get credit; nor could their goods command the prices fetched by the same products grown by settlers. Another issue was Grey's personal influence; he insisted on distributing the funds. More crucially, however, was the fact that Maori received and interpreted these initiatives within their own values and systems. The initiative ultimately foundered on the dissonance between Maori cultural priorities, Grey's British culture-centric expectations of what Maori should do, and the difficult realities of the emerging colonial economy with which Maori were trying to engage.

Partly for these reasons, the bulk of Maori income during the 1850s derived from land sales, and these arrangements had a built-in end point, quite apart

ABOVE

A party explores the shores of Lake Wairarapa in the early 1840s.

William Mein Smith, watercolour, Alexander Turnbull Library, B-062-021

OPPOSITE BELOW

Sheep grazing on a Wairarapa run, late 1840s. Former New Zealand Company Surveyor General William Mein Smith (1799–1869) painted this watercolour in the late 1840s. He was one of the first pastoralists in the Wairarapa, setting up a run at Huangarua in 1845, in partnership with Samuel Revans.

William Mein Smith, watercolour, Alexander Turnbull Library, B-062-022

from the other issues that flowed from the jagged edge of cultural dissonance. Government land-buyers envisaged sale in the British sense, but Maori did not share that vision. Maori had several means of transferring rights; take tupuna—ancestral rights; take raupatu—by conquest; and tuku whenua—by gift.[122] British requests to buy territory did not fit this framework, and many Maori concluded that the British only wanted the 'shadow of the land.'[123] Some government land buyers understood the issue, particularly Donald McLean, who began couching deeds of sale in the language of a tangi, to indicate a complete separation. However, the distinction was not obvious to all Maori and after a sale, some used the land as they always had, which caused ructions. When Ngati Kahungunu hunted on government land in Hawke's Bay during 1855, Resident Magistrate Alfred Domett admonished them:

> It is not your land. The white people do not go upon your land without your leave. In like manner, you would not go on the Queen's land ... without leave of the white men who are living upon it & paying for it to government. ... This conduct of yours is very bad.... If you had no land of your own there might perhaps be some excuse for you. But you have plenty of land at Te Apiti, Kairakau, Waimarama and elsewhere you can hunt.[124]

The process was further complicated by the tangled skein of confused land rights that emerged across much of the North Island and northern South Island, particularly, on the back of the musket wars, coupled with the fact that rights over land were inevitably complex in any event, because they reflected the way they had evolved over deeper time. Disentangling this complex network of kin-related issues was time-consuming, and land buyers such as McLean frequently tried to shortcut the process. That provoked criticism from CMS officials who, in any event, viewed the land sale process as one likely to destroy Maori. In 1851, for instance, Ahuriri missionary Colenso told McLean that 'land originally given as a gift from one chief to another does not empower the recipient to sell but to hold for himself and successors.'[125] The Scot almost certainly knew this already; he was intimately familiar with Maori life and the more compelling idea is that he was choosing to ignore it.

All of this was a recipe for trouble, but the colonial hardening of attitudes to land purchase from the late 1840s was partly driven by necessity.[126] Colonists were flooding in. Land had to be found for them. Land was also a source of income; government derived a good deal of its funding during this period by buying land cheaply from Maori, in effect at wholesale rates, and then on-selling or leasing to settlers.

By the early 1850s the Crown focus was fixed on the Wairarapa, a direct consequence of unauthorised pastoral expansion out of the Wellington region, combined with New Zealand Company ambitions in the same area. These purchases into populated Maori areas allowed government officials to develop and refine policies later applied at national level, and the initiative came from the New Zealand Company. By the mid-1840s it was clear to Edward Gibbon Wakefield that his dream had misfired; but he was far from defeated and concocted the idea of a Church of England colony. This was brought to fruition by John Robert Godley, whose Canterbury Association was formed in 1847 on promise of land in New Zealand. Wakefield imagined they could settle in the Wairarapa, open grassland that Robert Stokes had reached as early as 1841.[127] But although Shortland's suspension of pre-emption—the exclusive Crown right to purchase land wholesale from Maori—gave the company a free hand, William Wakefield would not commit to purchase.[128]

ABOVE

The 'brown-eyed, lion-faced' poet, Alfred Domett (1811–1887) struck comment from those he met. Charlotte Godley thought him 'quite a gentleman, and clever'; but others felt he had a 'slight ruggedness of character'. He was a student at St John's College, Cambridge 1829 to 1833—though he did not complete his degree. He published his first book of poems in 1833 and befriended Robert Browning, then moved to New Zealand in 1842. George Grey persuaded him to join the Legislative Council in 1846, and in 1848 he became Colonial Secretary for New Munster. He was elected MP for Nelson in 1855, married Mary George in 1856, and became Premier in 1862–63. Domett held various other offices until 1871, when he retired and returned to England.

Herman John Schmidt, Schmidt Collection, Alexander Turnbull Library, PAColl-3059, F-1298-1/1

ABOVE

Donald McLean (1820–1877), the archetypal 'canny Scot' and chief land buyer in Hawke's Bay and the Wairarapa. Controversial even at the time, he became known to Maori as the 'great Taniwha', and his activities eventually produced grievances from Wanganui to Napier. Yet he exhibited sensitivity towards Maori in other respects and gained a reputation as a race-relations fire-fighter, the national 'Maori doctor'.

Photographer unidentified, Alexander Turnbull Library, PA2-2603

Some settlers, led by C. R. Bidwill, Frederick Weld and his business partner C. Clifford, decided to make their own deals with Ngati Kahungunu. Few of them knew anything much about sheep, but Weld leased an area for £12 per annum and put merinos on it in May 1844. By 1846 there were nearly 20 privately leased pastoral stations in the Wairarapa. Early difficulties managing the flocks were resolved by hiring shepherds, and within two years Weld made a personal profit of around £4,000,[129] around $800,000 in early twenty-first century money. This was a simply stunning return at a time when many Wakefield settlers were struggling to make ends meet. Grey's reimposition of pre-emption rendered these leases illegal, but the pastoralists metaphorically thumbed their noses at him—they knew, as well as Grey did, that the government had to tread a fine line between enforcing the law and stifling settlement.

Wakefield asked Grey to grant the New Zealand Company land in the Wairarapa that year, an area that briefly became the new focus of settler expansion at national level. Francis Dillon Bell and interpreter George Clarke approached Ngati Kahungunu in February 1847 and discovered no one was prepared to sell while they could get a return by leasing. All Grey could do was issue a circular letter threatening to force the Europeans off if Maori did not sell. This stalled at the first recipient,[130] and in October government warned settlers that further leasing could result in prosecutions.[131] However, Grey did not push the effort and instead turned to the South Island, where the Wairau was purchased during 1847 and slabs of land in Canterbury and Otago a year later.[132] The Company was still eager to secure land in the Wairarapa, and a second government effort got under way in mid-1848,[133] despite staunch opposition from Colenso, who was running the Ahuriri mission. Domett thought the minister might 'feel a peculiar interest in the formation of this [Church] settlement,'[134] but Colenso turned down a request to butter up chiefs, penned a dire warning to the CMS, then wrote to Eyre and Domett that he:

> ... cannot conscientiously aid or assist or ... use any influence which I may possess over the native chiefs to prevail upon them to alienate the whole of their Lands to the Crown, or to accept ... scattered or detached parcels or blocks among the whites.[135]

Eyre—diplomatically—put this down to a misunderstanding,[136] but in the end it was academic. Ngati Kahungunu wanted £16,000, four times Kemp's budget. Grey turned his attention to the more sparsely populated Akaroa and Canterbury, a decision that simply spurred the pastoralists of the Wairarapa in their drive to lease illegally from Maori. What was more, some had already

CHAPTER THREE
SHADOWS OF EMPIRE

spilled north into Hawke's Bay and it looked like more would follow.[137] Ngati Kahungunu wondered about sales to the Crown as well, and in mid-1849 Eyre received several letters offering land.[138] Armed with this proposal, the Lieutenant-Governor hit on the idea of surrounding the Wairarapa with lands that could be leased to settlers at lower prices than Wairarapa chiefs were prepared to accept, and nominated the gadabout, moa enthusiast and sometime government land official Walter Mantell to make the deal. However, Grey viewed Hawke's Bay as a sideline, preferring more direct ways of undercutting leasing in the Wairarapa. The job went to Donald McLean, the rising star of the land purchase system.

McLean went on to dominate the style of land purchase arrangements in New Zealand—particularly the North Island. The Scot had arrived as the Treaty was being signed, spent some years in the Coromandel and Bay of Plenty in various business ventures, then moved to Taranaki where he began a meteoric ascent of the land purchase department ladder. A remarkable fluency in te reo ('the language') and a surprising identification with Maori as a colonised people—perhaps driven by his own experiences as a Scot—gave McLean an edge. But he never lost sight of his goals for the colony; he dispossessed Maori even as he was making friends with them, and by late 1849 he was halfway through negotiating with Ngati Te Upokoiri for part of the Manawatu.[139]

ABOVE

Ahuriri lagoon, watercolour by Clive settler Joseph Rhodes. Settlement had spread this far north from the Wairarapa by 1850, well in advance of effective government control. The pa is noteworthy; this was the site of a massacre and cannibal feast in 1824.

Joseph Rhodes, watercolour, Alexander Turnbull Library, A-159-033

93

RIGHT

An 1858 view of Waipukurau Pa, central Hawke's Bay, site of the 1850 meeting that led to the sale of three significant blocks of land in Hawke's Bay.

Joseph Rhodes, Alexander Turnbull Library, A-159-027

If Grey had thought that McLean would turn attention to the Wairarapa, however, he was mistaken. McLean's success as land buyer drew in part on his ability to discover, follow and exploit kin ties. He was embroiled in negotiations with Ngati Te Upokoiri in the Manawatu, who he believed gave him an opening into Hawke's Bay through their relatives there, in turn opening up links to the Wairarapa via Ngati Kahungunu and associated iwi. This was out of line with Grey's idea of buying the Wairarapa directly at all cost; but McLean was determined—possibly for personal reasons to do with securing his career and with it an income[140]—and so when Eyre told him to investigate purchases in the Manawatu and Wairarapa, McLean replied that he would go to Ahuriri 'where some of the Principal Chiefs concerned in the sale of the Districts ... are residing.'[141] Grey rejected it.[142] However, Eyre passed the message to McLean with an out-clause; he was to 'report what steps you consider it desirable to take' to buy land in the Manawatu and Wairarapa.[143] As far as McLean was concerned, this meant pushing Ahuriri, and it appears McLean finally sold the strategy to the Governor.[144] What was more, when he reached Waipukurau pa in December 1850 to talk turkey, opening offers included 'Haretaonga [sic] and Ahuriri from end to end'.[145]

In a practical sense that translated into three blocks across Hawke's Bay – still an unprecedented succession of sales. However, when serious bargaining began in earnest for the Waipukurau block in April 1851, McLean discovered that Ngati Kahungunu knew all about Grey's intentions, and paramount Ngati Whatuiapiti chief Te Hapuku talked McLean up to £4,800 for the Waipukurau block,[146] around $980,000 in early twenty-first century terms and significantly more than McLean wanted to spend. The result was that he had to push both the subsequent Ahuriri and Mohaka deals to the edge of failure.[147] Grey's 'flour and sugar' assistance and an economic relationship with settlers were considered part of the payment.[148]

This did not prevent significant grievances flowing from the arrangements, although one study pointed out that McLean offered concessions to keep the door open for future sales.[149] The point has also been made that some of the problems that followed can be attributed to mismatch of culture rather than an intentional attempt to defraud.[150] Certainly the major issue—the belief by McLean that he had purchased the Ahuriri lagoon, and the belief by Maori that they had not sold it—has been shown, from the perspective of investigative general history, to be due to unintended miscommunication and unspoken assumption, not deliberate intent.[151]

McLean turned his attention to the Wairarapa in 1852, using his connections with Te Hapuku as a lever. Although other land was sold around New Zealand, notably in Canterbury and Otago, Wairarapa and Hawke's Bay remained the main focus of the government purchase strategy in the North Island for years, partly because the politics of buying it were so much more complex than in the sparsely populated South Island.

Grey made a lightning trip through the Wairarapa and Hawke's Bay in early 1853, and the result was a general arrangement to sell further blocks. Negotiations were apparently complete by the end of 1853, when Ngati Hawea chief Kurupo Te Moananui wrote to McLean to explain that he was organising the lands for sale and intended to come to Wellington for payment. Four sales followed while Te Moananui and Te Hapuku were in Wellington over Christmas 1853, without consultation with their people.

This presaged a national policy of pressure on chiefs to sell directly. Speed was of the essence as settlers poured in. In this, McLean stood apart from some of the ideals of his day—but in others, he did not. This was period of hardening attitudes by the British, a generational shift which was eventually reflected across the Empire. McLean was promoted to head the Land Purchase Department, and he shortly gained the ear of the new Governor, Thomas Gore-Browne, who decided that Maori relations were an Imperial matter, putting them under his own authority. In a practical sense, that left McLean alone to proceed.[152] The sales that followed were unprecedented; in the 21 months from mid-1856 to March 1858, some 771,673 acres in the Bay of Islands, Whangarei, Auckland, Thames, Kaipara and Wellington districts changed hands for a grand total of £24,870.[153]

There were two interrelated outcomes for Maori. Land sales became part of a currency of rivalry, but McLean's system led to the promotion of one chief over

ABOVE

Te Hapuku (c1797–1878), Ngati Whatuiapiti rangitira, cultivated by McLean as a prominent land-seller in Hawke's Bay, a move that led ultimately to war in the district.

Samuel Carnell, S. Carnell Collection, wet collodion glass negative, Alexander Turnbull Library, PAColl-3979, G-22221-1/4

another as agent, causing old oppositions to flare. The process damaged chiefly authority, because many parted with land without properly discussing it with their people. This was evident early on when various Waikato hapu protested the activity of Te Wherowhero, among other chiefs, who had sold the Waitemata and Manukau blocks without adequate consultation.[154] Trouble flared in Hawke's Bay, which provided four-sevenths of the total sold by Maori in the 1855–56 period. Selling land had evidently become part of a 'race for mana' between Ngati Kahungunu, led by Kurupo Te Moananui; and Ngati Whatu-i-apiti led by Te Hapuku.[155] War broke out between them in late 1857. McLean hastened to distance himself, but it was a direct outcome of his purchase system, and Samuel Williams rammed the point home at the time. McLean, who was by this time also dogged by conflict-of-interest problems associated with his personal land purchases in the area, brokered a settlement in March 1858.[156]

That war came at a moment when Pakeha, for the first time, outnumbered Maori in New Zealand. The pivot came some time in the late 1850s; in 1851, there were 26,707 Pakeha, but by 1859—the first census to also include Maori—there were 59,413. The Maori population had dropped to just 56,049,[157] though distribution was not even and areas such as the Waikato and the East Cape of the North Island were almost wholly populated by Maori. Still, it was a significant shift in practical demographics and, with it, effective power. This relatively sudden imposition of Britain across New Zealand was made possible, in part, through the land obtained by McLean's Land Purchase Department.

The settlers brought with them a society that was very different from that of Maori—but also very different, at least in aspiration, from the one they had left behind in Britain. It also contrasted with the purist market-controlled society envisaged by Wakefield, and this new world—a world that drew from its British roots but which also shared a good deal with other emerging colonial societies around the Pacific Rim—did not take long to unfold.

ABOVE

Grasmere Station, probably during the 1860s.

Daniel Louis Mundy, Alexander Turnbull Library, F-50828-1/2.

CHAPTER FOUR
The road to Erewhon

Settlers poured into New Zealand during the mid-nineteenth century in a relentless movement of people from halfway around the world, punctuated by two great booms in the early 1860s and 1870s, and by dips during the depths of depression in the late 1860s and 1890s. The rate was explosive, boosted by all the power of an industrialising world and the capacity of nineteenth-century British sea power—a scale of shipping that underscored the depth of their worldwide commercial empire. By the late 1850s the population balance had shifted in favour of Pakeha—relentlessly and in ways that Maori never anticipated.

Settler society was shaped by a potent mix of industrial ideology, new philosophies of reason, new evangelism and new economic theory.[1] This combination goes a long way towards explaining both why settlers came to New Zealand and the society they built—with its nod to egalitarianism, the do-it-yourself ethos, dreams of private home ownership, the 'quarter-acre paradise', gridwork street patterns, and emphasis on job security.

New worlds

The forces that shaped New Zealand's mid-nineteenth-century settler world can be traced to industrial-age Britain. The industrial revolution was one of the major discontinuities of Western history. In just two or three generations from the 1750s, British society—and then, that of Europe—was turned upside down by a heady brew of technical, economic and political change, all underpinned with new philosophies and the rationalism that emerged from the unfolding 'age

ABOVE

Oakes colliery explodes.

Artist unknown, author collection

of reason'. For those at the forefront of the wave it was an exciting time to be alive. But it was also a very uneasy age as people spun out of the turmoil, victims of change they could not control, treated as authors of their own misfortune and criminalised by a frightened government.

Nothing like it had been seen before in the history of the world, a collision of forces, circumstances and ideas where new thinking and technology helped drive a revolution of economy and social structure. The 'early modern' world of tenant farmers, semi-sufficient rural communities and self-employed town artisans was swept away in favour of an economy in which the majority had to find paid work in order to survive. It was an age of urbanisation, which meant more than just fast-expanding towns and cities, but a mind-set and subculture that was soon shared by those living in country areas.

The cycle was pushed from the country, where landowners began obtaining land for 'rational' farming by turfing off tenants and 'enclosing' common fields. Change was also pulled from the cities, where a combination of new engineering techniques and labour shortages prompted inventors to devise machines intended to meet demand for cloth, machines that required a retinue of unskilled supplicants to tend them.[2] The dispossessed rural poor drifted into

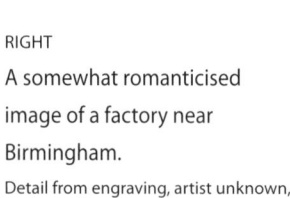

RIGHT

A somewhat romanticised image of a factory near Birmingham.

Detail from engraving, artist unknown, author collection.

smoky industrial towns, such as Manchester or Sheffield. The mews and narrow streets of these places—the only open areas amid a 'forest of chimneys'[3]—filled a dual role as community gathering places and sewers.[4] Some town workers' homes did not even have kitchens; meals were pies and hot potatoes purchased from street vendors.[5]

The new economy was as iniquitous as it was vicious for those who did not have money. Factory owners made vast profits by paying 'Johnnie' but a 'penny a day', masking the fact that the British economy expanded little between 1760 and 1820,[6] a reality which meant that the new wealth came not from increased productivity, but from the poor. Food shortages triggered by inclement weather systems compounded the problem. Poaching and theft became the only way some country folk could keep their families fed; but government response addressed only the symptom.[7] Songs, nursery rhymes and stories mourned a lost rural idyll, and excoriated captains of industry and sponsors of the 'Inclosure' Laws who had profited from the dislocation on such a huge scale that it was viewed not as theft, but enterprise. 'The law locks up the man or woman,' a rhyme of the day insisted, 'Who steals the goose from off the common/But leaves the greater villain loose/who steals the common from off the goose'.[8]

Many people found succour in religion. John Wesley evangelised the Word to northern, Midlands and South Wales working classes. When the Anglicans rejected 'Wesleyanism', he founded the Methodist church. The Evangelicals infused new life into Anglicanism. The upheavals of industrialism, the ethos that went with it, and food shortages caused by oscillating weather patterns[9] helped prompt new emphasis on the more abstemious teachings of Protestantism. The link was explicit. As R. Vaughan declared in 1843; the 'strength of Protestantism' was a 'strength on the side of industry, of human improvement....'[10]

One of the first to rationalise these upheavals was Adam Smith (1723–1790), who is credited with inventing the 'invisible hand' of 'the market'—though he only mentioned the concept once, in the context of foreign trade.[11] His ideas were further developed by David Hume (1711–1776), who drew on the economic doctrine of Jean Bodin—a sixteenth-century advocate of burning witches—to lay the groundwork for a philosophy based on the assumption that human interactions were based on self-interest and open competition.[12] During the early nineteenth century these ideas were extended by clergyman Thomas Malthus (1766–1834) and financier David Ricardo (1772–1823) into dogma, and as Eric Hobsbawm has pointed out, it is impossible to argue that their motives were anything but partisan.[13] At the time, William Cobbett decried Malthus as a 'monster' whose theories 'furnished unfeeling oligarchs' with ammunition.[14] This was also true of Ricardo's 'iron law of wages', which suggested that employer benevolence would distort the labour market—a point seized upon by industrialists seeking to maximise profits.

Such theories derived from and fitted the puritanical mood of the day, and did not take long to implement. In 1820 the London Merchants offered a petition to Parliament urging 'freedom from restraint'.[15] They found an ally in the people, who funded taxes on corn through higher bread prices. Successive bad seasons following on from the calamitous 'year without a summer' in 1816 had helped put food at a premium,[16] and by linking abolition of the 'Corn Laws' to the free market, Britain's industrial elites were able to push their philosophy to society.[17] The edifice was given validity in the 1850s when Charles Darwin—inspired by Malthus—built market competition into his theory of natural selection. Herbert Spencer then championed the notion as proof that pure competition was a natural state.[18] Such circularities helped entrench dogma that blamed the misfortunes of the poor on their own failings. The notion that they should be punished for it followed. 'The workhouse,' Reverend H. H. Milman declared in 1832 to Edwin Chadwick, 'should be a place of hardship, coarse fare, of degradation and humility; it should be…as repulsive as consistent with humanity.'[19]

The problem was that these theorists were observing a world in disarray—and based their thinking on simplistic assumptions. It was naive to expect that simple market exchange and contract could wholly explain or supplant complex social interactions.[20] The German philosopher Karl Marx—whose theories were founded in the same chaos—produced explanations that were just as impractical.

There was fallout as disaffected, disempowered and hungry people protested their lot. The British government almost collapsed in the face of social change in 1816 and again in 1830. Popular opposition by the 1830s was oriented around the Chartists, a cause that emerged from Robert Owen's failed union movement and as a reaction to the moderate Parliamentary Reform Bill of 1832.

Crop failures between 1838 and 1843 prompted the epithet 'hungry forties', a situation not helped by the fact that purist liberal capitalism was profoundly anarchic. The industrial economies of the period swung wildly between violent booms and catastrophic busts. The 'railway mania' of the 1840s gave Britain multiple competing railways between a few centres, but failed to provide a national transport network, and then the railway stock bubble burst. This contributed to the general economic crisis of 1847, which fed into political crisis in 1848.[21] Britain avoided calamity by a whisker in the face of Chartist agitation. European governments fell over, helping prompt some thinkers to temper early

RIGHT

'Here and there; or, emigration a remedy'. This Punch parody of July 1848—one of Britain's crisis years—contained a fair dollop of truth about the realities of nineteenth-century Britain and the colonies.

Artist unknown, wood engraving, Alexander Turnbull Library, PUBL-0043-1850-01

The Needlewoman at Home and Abroad.

AT HOME. ABROAD.

LEFT

More emigration parody with its biting criticism of the fate of the poor in Britain.

Alexander Turnbull Library
F-148MNZ-1/4

theories. John Stuart Mill suggested that minimal education, state protection of start-up industry, and regulated working hours would be needed to make the economy operate properly.[22]

Britain's poor faced an insecure future and the wealthy feared revolution. Many saw migration as the answer,[23] and Robert Horton organised systems to export paupers as early as the 1820s. The poor pushed, flocking to the migrant ships in the hope of finding a better future for themselves elsewhere. Some of the wealthy also felt impelled to seek better fields; those with a little capital felt they could make better use of it in virgin territory.

Whether all settlers were trying to build a perfect world in New Zealand is debatable. Some were. Jerusalem may not have appeared among England's dark satanic mills, but optimists hoped it might be built in the green and pleasant lands of the colonies. Dilettante theorists such as Wakefield held high hopes for building idyllic societies around pure market forces. But he had trouble getting colonists, and although one historian has argued that New Zealand's settlers were Arcadian,[24] the reality for most migrants was that they simply hoped to better themselves. The point is made clear by the fact that Chartists and radicals were among those who went—including to New Zealand—and there is evidence that the radical agenda was dropped as soon as they emigrated.[25]

The voyage to New Zealand

The rate at which New Zealand was settled during the mid-nineteenth century was simply extraordinary. The first government census in 1851 revealed a European population of 26,707. Most had arrived in the previous 15 years, many by subsidised passage with the New Zealand Company. By the next head-count in 1858 their numbers had doubled, and by 1864 there were just over 171,000.[26]

ABOVE

'The emigrant's daughter': although families usually emigrated together, this 1861 sketch captures the pain of parting forever from friends, family and home. Only the wealthy could afford a return journey from halfway round the world.

Thomas Graham, Making New Zealand Collection, Alexander Turnbull Library, F-84-1/4-MNZ

Only a small proportion was natural growth; in 1861—65, for instance, about 15,000 settlers were born in New Zealand but another 90,000-odd arrived by sea.[27]

Not all stayed. Tens of thousands of people poured into New Zealand during the gold rush days—and tens of thousands poured out, part of a gigantic floating population that surged around the Pacific in pursuit of the precious metal. It was a demonstration of the raw scale of Britain's merchant marine by the mid-nineteenth century. In the year to 31 March 1862, some 29,454 men arrived in New Zealand, of whom 24,243 came from Australia. Only 794 were from Britain,[28] though these were more likely to be permanent; the tyranny of distance translated into a return cost that few could meet. In other respects, New Zealand—however bad—was an improvement on 'home'. This was particularly so in the 1870s, when many migrants were labourers.[29]

The reasons why people were leaving Britain are clear; but why they chose New Zealand are not. The 90-day journey under sail compared unfavourably with the ten it took to cross the Atlantic by steamer.[30] Land was more expensive in the antipodes, and even with assisted passage, New Zealand offered fewer prospects than Canada, the United States or Australia. New Zealand intercepted less than one percent of the total emigrating from Britain during the period.[31] Still, the fraction who made the journey had reason for it. Proselytising by officials and colonial boosters such as Charles Hursthouse, Richard Taylor and Thomas Cholmondeley played a part in the decision. Frederick Campbell, working for a company that acted as broker for the New Zealand Company and the Canterbury Association, recalled years later that:

> ...it was necessary to know as much as possible about the colony, from books, from the tales by people who had been there, and from 'other sources'. These other sources, I found to be from the fertility of their own imagination, and I am afraid I soon became an apt scholar....I knew more about New Zealand in those days, than I do now after 44 years residency here. Yarns like how easy it was to: 'Go into the bush, catch a pig, and kill it for dinner.' 'Throw a line with a hook into the river and pull out a fish for breakfast.' 'Make a few holes in the ground, cut up a bucketful of potatoes, plant them, then dig up enough to last you for a year.' 'Live outdoors, as houses were superfluous,

ABOVE

John Robert Godley (1814–1861), instrumental mover-and-shaker behind the Canterbury Association, was inspired by Ireland's plight during the potato famine. Plans to settle a million Irish in Canada were dropped, but a meeting with Wakefield triggered a new plan for an Anglican church settlement in New Zealand.

Photographer unidentified, Alexander Turnbull Library, F-1079-1/2

RIGHT

Farewelling the Canterbury Association colonists, Gravesend, September 1850. Although often considered the real pioneers of Christchurch, when the first four settler ships reached Lyttelton they were met by customs officials—a sign that New Zealand's Pakeha colony was not the blank canvas they imagined.

Alexander Turnbull Library PUBL-0033-1850-199

and all you needed was a blanket to lie down and sleep out anywhere—all year round.' 'Grow roses which were always in bloom'....We used to say what jolly fellows the natives were, so the Wairau Massacre came as quite a shock, but we did make light of it to clients...[32]

The extent to which settlers were deceived by the hype is unclear. Raw percentages suggest not many were. Fantasy New Zealand did not compare with the well-reported realities of New York, Sydney or Cape Town as a place of opportunity—or as a road to the frontier for die-hards who wanted to hack a living from virgin soil. Those who found New Zealand appealing may have had a healthy cynicism. Propaganda raised expectations but did not convert. 'I left England because I was sick of it,' William Hay wrote in 1865, 'and believing that I should better my condition by so doing...'[33] The fact that dips in migration to New Zealand correlate with depression and war in the colony suggests a pragmatic reality behind the decision. At individual level there were many reasons for making the journey, including 'betterment'. Campbell himself took the decision 'at some evil hour in November 1850', making the voyage on the *Bronte*.[34]

Alternately portrayed as an ocean rest-cure or a duel with hunger and disease, the three months from Gravesend or Plymouth to Auckland, Wellington, Lyttelton or Port Chalmers was a remarkably constant experience—the difference between the cabin passages of the 1840s and 1850s and those of the 1870s and 1880s was not great. Steam sped the Atlantic crossing, but sail remained the prime mover for the journey to New Zealand until the end of the settler period in the late 1880s; the usual route took them to the Cape of Good Hope and east through the Roaring Forties.

A few came out in style. Thomas Tanner chartered a ship to carry his servants, gold plate, pedigree animals, furniture, books and family.[35]

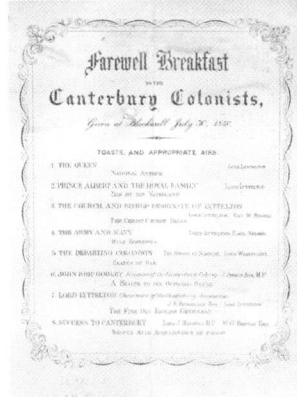

CHAPTER FOUR
THE ROAD TO EREWHON

ABOVE

Guest list for breakfast farewelling the 'Canterbury Colonists' in 1850.

Creator unknown, Alexander Turnbull Library, F-1213-1/2-MNZ

ABOVE LEFT

'The emigrant's farewell', a scene repeated time and again as settlers departed for destinations afar.

James Fagan, Alexander Turnbull Library, C-015-001

BELOW

The *Lady Nugent*, by G. R. Hilliard, en route to New Zealand. 'Our ship at times appearing to fly up into the clouds and again as if to descend from a watery Mountain into the very bottom of the sea,' he scribbled in his journal. 'Felt very qualmish.'

George Richard Hilliard, Alexander Turnbull Library, A-113-016

RIGHT

A romanticised and likely over-scaled view of life on board the *Randolph*, a Canterbury settler ship en route to New Zealand in late 1850.

Artist unknown, Alexander Turnbull Library, F94-1/4-MNZ

He was a rare breed, but for those with enough cash, cabin passage offered a comfortable, entertaining, genteel and relaxing journey of gastronomic excess.[36] During one voyage at the end of 1861, F. W. Hamilton reported living 'in the very best style having fresh meat of all kinds every day, fresh fish, sweet cream, and all kinds of fruit preserved in bottles.'[37] A succession of feasts was part of the sales-pitch, and actually appears to have materialised for the wealthier passengers. Breakfast, lunch, dinner and supper were seldom less than banquets. Various hot boiled or roast meats—joints and choice cuts from onboard livestock—were invariably accompanied with cold or jellied meats, roast fowl, hams, cheeses, boiled vegetables, pies, broths, bread, biscuits, jams, conserves, puddings and nuts, all laid on the groaning board for cabin passengers whose appetites had been whetted by deck games and sea air.

Some of this gluttonous cornucopia came from private supplies, renewed where opportunity permitted. Occasionally cabin supplies ran out, forcing passengers to subsist on steerage rations; but while some captains preferred non-stop passage, others were prepared to stop for food along the way if fortune permitted, including the English Channel. Deal boatmen 'bought oranges off from shore' at '20 a shilling' when the *Palala* anchored offshore in early 1880, bound for New Zealand. Later, as migrant schoolmaster William Rainbow

RIGHT

Dinner time 'on board the first emigrant ship for New Zealand'. Real ships, even in 'cuddy' class, were considerably more cramped.

Artist unknown, Alexander Turnbull Library, A-109-054

LEFT

Although steamships regularly crossed the Atlantic by the mid-nineteenth century, the journey to New Zealand was by sail for decades.

Artist unknown, Alexander Turnbull Library, G-17245-1/2

recorded, boatmen delivered 'macaroni, haricot beans, lentils, & a suit of oilskins and boots for me.'[38] There were certainly opportunities to stop further along the way. 'The captain had promised to heave to off Tristan d'Acunha [sic]', Charlotte Godley wrote from the South Atlantic in March 1850, 'and send off a boat for potatoes and pigs...unluckily...the wind changed when we came pretty near it...'[39]

Cabin passage still had its hazards. 'Woke in the night and found rat sitting on my face,' Rainbow wrote a few days out from Deal in early 1880.[40] Seasickness was another problem. Most thought the storms 'wretched',[41] though the results could not be confided in genteel society; as Godley wrote to her mother, the 'wretchedness' of the first days at sea were 'not a thing to be spoken of'.[42] Things improved further south. 'Everything soft & mild & ship heeling over like a rocking chair,' Rainbow penned a week or two out of Deal.[43] Quoits, reading, chatting and lessons helped fill the hours, but 'ship life became monotonous after a time.'[44] Night offered entertainment. 'Tonight I have been sitting on the poop for a time watching the phosphorescence of the sea,' Rainbow wrote in February, 'I have seen the Southern Cross... not so striking as it is reputed. Orion is glorious...and the Milky Way & Magellan Cloud [sic]—a cluster of stars dim thro' great distance. There are others—glorious, but I don't know them.'[45]

At times the ships sailed in company. 'Twenty-six ships all in sight together from the mast,' Charlotte Godley wrote early in 1850 after being becalmed on board the *Lady Nugent*.[46] Cyrus Davie took the opportunity to swap ships, jumping from the *Sir George Seymour* to the *Randolph*.[47] Off the Cape of Good Hope it was a different story. They had been

BELOW

Settler ship at sea. 'Frigate' construction was in vogue by the mid-nineteenth century, complete with fake gunports.

Artist unknown, Alexander Turnbull Library, G-2543-1/1

ABOVE

Settlers bound for New Zealand celebrate New Year's Eve 1864.

Artist unknown, Alexander Turnbull Library, B-064-022

promised 'dusty weather' and got it, 'tremendous waves, as they seemed to me, and we sprang our fore-top mast and lost some ropes, and a sail or two much torn.'[48]

For those without the means, the voyage was another matter. A steerage passage was an ordeal amid cramped, damp and airless spaces below decks, relieved by time on deck. Food was supplied as part of the ticket, but some captains failed to stock promised supplies, either through incompetence, or deliberately to reduce costs. A steerage diet was usually boiled salt beef or pork, potatoes or rice and sometimes peas or lentils, prepared in giant cauldrons and doled out. On some ships hours might pass before everybody was fed, and if the food ran out steerage went hungry. Nutrition was marginal at the best of times, and there was at least one reported death by starvation.[49] Dysentery was common. Scarlet fever, mumps, measles and chickenpox were sometimes rife. Pneumonia sometimes followed otherwise minor colds. Close-packed conditions and the fact that many of the poor were not in good physical order to begin with compounded the dangers. Children were particularly vulnerable, and for many families the voyage was one of unrelieved tragedy as their offspring died, one after another.

The voyage often threw together folk from disparate walks of life. William Rainbow's fellows in 1880 included a 'German couple' and three children; a 'tall slip of a Scotch boy' on his way to visit his uncle; and a doctor. The cabin next door was 'highly mixed' and included a 'gas engineer...with a crank about him that we are the lost tribes of Israel.'[50] Charlotte Godley's fellow passengers on the *Lady Nugent* of 1850 included wealthy aristocratic scion Algernon Tollemache, on his way to see £15,000 worth of land he had bought in New Zealand. He brought with him his dog, 'three maids', and a 'family whom he is helping to emigrate…with five very naughty, dirty children.'[51] Others included:

> …one lady, Miss Borton, quite young and rather pretty, though neither aristocratic nor very bright…Mr. Bulkeley, cousin to Sir Richard, going out to New Zealand to join his regiment, the 65th; Mr. Nicholson, who has just left Oxford—his father is some rich man near Leeds…Mr. Robinson…has been a merchant at Calcutta…and a smart young Mr. Lee, one of many brothers, going out as a settler, Mr. Wakefield…and a Mr. Elliott, who knows all about everything but is careless about his h's and is taking out a steam engine.[52]

Aristocrat, merchant, engineer, officer and one of the prestigious Wakefields seemingly had little in common, but even Elliott's Cockney origins and his interest in engineering did not prevent him joining other 'cuddy' passengers at dinner, or in the six a.m. wash on deck. Wealth—not breeding—defined status, and folk of very different lives mixed and mingled. Despite efforts by cabin passengers to keep the poop deck to themselves, steerage inevitably met cabin settlers. Some of the latter deliberately sought the company of 'emigrants'.[53]

In some respects this reflected British society of the day, which was redefining itself around middle-class values, wealth and behaviour. On-board life refined and focussed the phenomenon, putting disparate people into contact in a way that could not have happened in London, Leeds or Liverpool. For this reason, although fleeting, the voyage to New Zealand cannot be discounted as one of several factors behind new social structures in the antipodes. Certainly

Cabin plan of the *John MacVicar*.
Artist unknown, Alexander Turnbull Library, F-48401-1/2

BELOW
Divine service on board the *Pegasus*, New Zealand-bound in 1865.
Artist unknown, Alexander Turnbull Library A-277-020

ABOVE

Jane Maria Atkinson, nee Richmond (1824–1914).

Photographer unidentified, Alexander Turnbull Library, F-79203-1/2

BELOW

'Miss Absolon', a sketch usually attributed to Charles Heaphy.

Charles Heaphy, pencil and watercolour, Alexander Turnbull Library, qMS-0613-096

the voyage was a symbolic rite of passage, literally highlighting the shift from a comfortable society to the new world of the colonies. In short, the settler ships were more than a means of transport; they were devices for making a social transformation—and at this level, the journey was a voyage of permission.

An egalitarian society?

The colonial world into which Britain's migrants poured was very different from the one they had left. It took pride in its sense of egalitarianism. And to the extent that settlers lived on a cheerful first-name basis irrespective of standing, and that British-style notions of birth and 'station' did not prevent people getting ahead, it was. Charlotte Godley's discovery that New Zealand's aspirant genteel folk included wealthy butchers[54] highlighted social prospects that New Zealand shared with the unfolding United States frontier of the day, and Australia, but not mother Britain.

To this extent, New Zealand enjoyed a flatter society than nineteenth-century Britain—despite Britain's own widening of class in the same period. In part it was integral to being a colony, the sense of leaving the old world behind and making a new one. The arbiter of status in colonial New Zealand and other Pacific Rim colonies was not birth but self-made wealth. It was an insidious measure; the easy familiarity between people in most walks of life and the fact that there were no obvious barriers to getting ahead—other than self-motivation—lent power to the growing mythology.

The hardships of the first settlements acted as a further leveller of behaviour, as did early back-country work when would-be wealthy and poor worked shoulder-to-shoulder. To be on first-name terms became a mark of respect, and anything that smacked of the old ways was protested. When Napier shopkeepers and mechanics were barred from a ball run by Donald McLean in March 1868, 'A Napier Tradesman', writing to the *Hawke's Bay Herald*, complained that 'snobbishness' was 'now rampant'. Shop owners and tradesmen were being sneered at by 'sheepocrats' and 'devotees' of the Hawke's Bay Club.[55] Vertical familiarity of the emerging New Zealand kind was familiar enough elsewhere. From the historical perspective it underlined the general point that New Zealand settler social structures were not the tight horizontal European 'brotherhood' imagined by Karl Marx, but a more nebulous and flexible arrangement defined by behaviour and economic standing.

The ambition of those who emigrated to better themselves, and the fact that there were no overt barriers to progress, also led to the other great social feature of the emerging colony—and the other great contribution to the myth of equality: there were very few servants.

This was not due to any shortage coming in. Nearly 70 percent of a sample of 4028 single women who emigrated during the 1857–71 period had been employed in some form of domestic service in Britain.[56] But they had not come half way around the world to carry on with that career. It showed. Figures from 1851 indicate that domestics made up just 2.85 percent of the workforce in Auckland and a miserable 2.02 percent in Nelson.[57] Typical servants' wages hovered around £25 per annum in Wellington in 1847–48, rose to a maximum of £40 in 1850, and by 1852 some domestics were earning £50. In Nelson, the rate doubled between 1847 and 1852.[58]

This suggests both a sellers' market and a sustained effort to attract and retain staff. Actual servant numbers have not been well captured in the statistics. Although 1858 figures reveal 1927 'domestics', out of a European population of 59,238, this included those working in lodging-houses. For the 17 years after 1874, the 'domestic' classification included wives, widows, sons and daughters at home, and the 8795 women and 3582 men who listed themselves as 'domestics' out of a total population of 299,514 in 1874 were not all servants.[59]

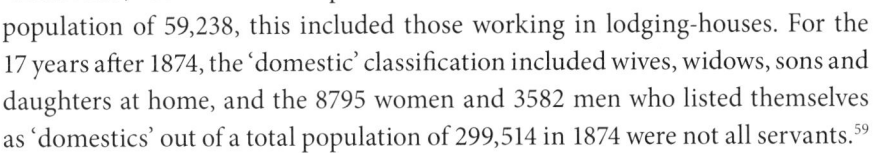

A more useful picture emerges from the chorus of complaints by the would-be elite, for whom domestic staff were not only a sign of status but also essential help in the early days when trying to set up. 'The first thing necessary was to procure a servant,' early Canterbury settler Sarah Courage declared in her memoir.[60] That was the hard part. Taranaki settler Jane Atkinson thought she could handle being servantless 'provided I have not more than three people besides myself to do for.'[61] She eventually hired Ann Foreman—an efficient, capable woman who became pregnant and left.[62] 'Things have come to a pretty pass here,' Conway Rose declared to his sister in 1853, 'quantities of people are obliged to do without a servant & farming operations are limited for want of labour'.[63]

Agencies sprang up to find home help, but the other problem was that servants never stayed long anyway. Jane Moorhouse hired nine different servants over a three-year period between 1867 and 1870.[64] Mary Hobhouse, wife of the Bishop of Nelson, first hired a 'very nice creature of 14', then a 'young lady as housemaid'—but the latter 'soon captivated the soft-hearted Mr Philpotts' and Hobhouse had to replace her with 'a little girl of 15'.[65]

The picture seems clear. Poorer migrants found work as domestics, but they had come to the colony to improve their lot and stayed only until they could 'get on', often by marriage. And this was not unusual on the Pacific Rim or, indeed, across the Empire. New Zealand's domestic percentages were down by comparison with those at 'home' or in other colonies, but servant numbers had been dropping around the British Empire since the eighteenth century. Ultimately, self-appointed local elites had to grin and do their own laundry. Many did so without complaint. After all, hard work was also a mark of Calvinist-inspired colonial gentility.

Did broad origin in the rising middle classes and the fact that old arbiters of status no longer applied mean that New Zealand lacked class structure? Settler society has been sliced and diced many times by historians. One argued that the 'undiluted' application of Marx is fraught with difficulty because his theories

ABOVE

The 'great plain' of Canterbury in 1851, as seen by William Fox. The 'Canterbury Papers' described the scene as a 'complete wilderness, with the exception of the farm of Messrs Deans...' adding that wide grasslands would require 'no labour' to maintain livestock.

William Fox, Alexander Turnbull Library A-195-014

ABOVE

Short on stature, big on status: Dr Isaac Earl Featherston (1813–1876) emigrated to New Zealand in 1840 as surgeon-superintendent on the *Olympus*, settling in Wellington where he ran a medical practice alongside his political interests. He returned to Britain in 1871 as Agent-General for New Zealand.

Photographer unidentified, Alexander Turnbull Library, F-5051-1/2

RIGHT

Isaac Featherston lays the foundation stone of the Houses of Assembly, Wellington, 1857. The former Wakefield colony won the hard-fought battle to become national capital in the mid-1850s, a decision pushed in part by the difficulty of governing New Zealand from its northern end at a time when communications were poor.

(William Fox, Alexander Turnbull Library, A-018-021)

emerged from old industrial society, not colonial.[66] Certainly it seems clear that New Zealand did not have a class society in the popular Marxist sense, though perhaps the Weberian cultural-economic definition might be made to apply.[67] Much of the debate depends on what is defined as 'class'. Deference, impassable social barriers and birth had been traditional definitions in Britain, and their apparent lack in New Zealand—combined with powerful evidence of social mobility, lack of inherited barriers, and the way settlers were on familiar terms with each other—has often been seen as betraying a lack of real class structures.

In fact we have to be cautious about trying to apply European class ideas to New Zealand—or trying to interpret New Zealand's history in Marxist 'class struggle' terms. Marx, Feuerbach and their colleagues founded their theories on what they saw in Europe's turbulent industrial societies and the collapse of France's *ancien régime*—not the colonial world of the nineteenth-century Pacific.[68] New Zealand society ultimately defined much of its own reality

The fact was that New Zealand's frontier world shared a good deal with the rest of the Pacific Rim colonial society of the day, also unfolding in Australia and across the US frontier at the same time. And a class structure did emerge— one unique to the colonies, mediated not by birth but by wealth. The sense of familiarity across income levels and the idea of open opportunity masked very real inequalities within New Zealand's frontier world. The arbiter was money— and the layers emerged rapidly as the earliest aspirants rose, often via their own boot-straps, to fill the very highest ranks of society. Once there, they were hard to dislodge; and they did what all middle-class British folk were aiming for— they actively aped the British nobility, just as the rising captains of industry and other wealthy middle-class folk did in Britain.

The gates to the very top opened with the explosion of pastoralism at the end of the 1840s; and they closed as sharply within about ten years. Late-comers found that out the hard way. David Balfour fell from gold-prospecting to swagging in the 1860s, worked his way back to become a respectable and respected station manager and family man by the mid-1870s—but could advance no further.[69] Others had the same experience. There was only so much room at the top, and once the middle-class gentry and elite oligarchs had established themselves, poorer settlers had little real opportunity beyond a certain point.

In settler-era New Zealand, then, a sense of creating opportunities and of shedding the past removed the hard barriers of class-stratified British society, as well as weakening the 'horizontal' links that people of the same 'class' had felt. A good deal of apparent success at 'getting on' instead reinforced the 'vertical' element, but this did not mean that a genuine society of equals emerged. Jocularities and first-name familiarities hid the point that New Zealand settler society was stratified.

Life at the top

New Zealand's main currency of social rivalry during the settler period was wealth, self-made, often expressed as land.[70] The earliest pastoralists quickly accumulated most of it to themselves, exploiting early growth to entrench themselves at the top of the heap. This uppermost rank was virtually a closed shop, an oligarchy that was financially and politically so far ahead of the pack as to beggar comparison even with their nominal peers. They dominated provincial and national life for decades. One historian has even gone so far as to suggest they were stunned by their own success,[71] and while others suggest that the power of these groups should not be overestimated,[72] the oligarchs held sway where it counted. It was not without reason that William Rolleston asked whether Minister of Defence and Auckland businessman Thomas Russell represented the government—or whether the government was there to represent Russell.[73]

This group gained power early. Wakefield's effort to control property access

BELOW

Pastoral wealth was built on the sheep's back. This is shearing, 1864 style, complete with manually-pressed wool. The station owner looks on.

Ilustrated Sydney News, Alexander Turnbull Library, PUBL-0169-1864-001

ABOVE

Mary Elizabeth Hobhouse, nee Brodrick (1819–1864)

Photographer unidentified, Alexander Turnbull Library, F-46810-1/2

came to nothing when there was territory to lease beyond company lands. The first snake in his ideological Eden was the Wairarapa, where Ngati Kahungunu concluded deals with would-be pastoralists spreading north from Wellington during the mid-1840s. This group was a mixed bunch, initially ignorant of their trade, but all with ambition. Nearly half were from Scotland, and there were three doctors, a lawyer, six surveyors and two self-proclaimed gentlemen among them.[74] The fleece soon turned to gold; wool reached 11¾d per pound in Wellington auctions during 1845, and by 1850 typical prices had topped a shilling.[75] Estimates suggested that £540 starting capital— around $110,000 in early twenty-first century money—could return net profits of £1,200 after five years. Some did better. Early Wairarapa settler Frederick Weld made £4,000 profit from a turnover of £6,000 in 1850.[76] This was a simply mindblowing level of return.

Pastoralists surged into Hawke's Bay, Otago, Canterbury and Marlborough from the early 1850s, sometimes squatting, later with regular leasehold on the back of new land regulations. Much of the initial impetus came from established Wairarapa pastoralists—notably Henry Tiffen, who pushed north to Hawke's Bay; and Weld, who expanded south to Marlborough. As time went on and these pastoral provinces became better established they attracted interest from British investors, all hoping to multiply their cash faster in the colony than they could at home. Hector Smith reached Hawke's Bay in 1858 with £8,000, which he spent on 12,000 acres near the Ruahine Ranges. Just four years later Algernon Tollemache offered to acquire the property on a lease-to-buy arrangement of £1400 per annum for 11 years, followed by a cash settlement of £14,000. Smith 'very nearly took' the 'good offer'. Instead he 'did a wise thing' and bought an adjoining run for £12,000.[77] It was all part of an exciting and unfolding game—one that had every potential to create gigantic rewards for the bold and the savvy.

Others boot-strapped themselves from nothing, including Hebridean shepherds Allan and John McLean, who held half a million acres of Canterbury by 1858.[78] William Rolleston (1831–1903) reached Lyttelton in 1858, decided to 'turn shepherd at once,'[79] and within three years had his own run, Mount Algidus. Once Laurence Kennaway (1834–1904) had got his coastal land into 'comparatively habitable order' he hastened inland in search of 'available sheep-country', finding 40,000 acres near the Rakaia.[80] It was a case of the quick or the dead; as Kennaway wrote, late-comers lost out or ended up in 'furious dispute' with neighbours over the boundaries.[81] Often the effort to leverage a fortune out of nothing demanded cheek and guts in the face of uncertain leaseholds, often

ABOVE

William Bishop's home, Matai valley, around 1844.

Charles Heaphy, Alexander Turnbull Library A-144-011.

hostile climate, and all the troubles and tribulations of the infant colony.

By 1861 national wool exports were valued at £524,000, second only to gold and streets ahead of the next highest, timber, which stood at a miserable £19,000.[82] This bounty was produced and handled by a tiny minority. Less than a fifth of all settlers worked in the agricultural and pastoral sector, and numbers on the stations were smaller still.[83] Differential fortunes highlighted the relationship between oligarch runholder and lesser gentry. In 1878 there were 215 flocks of more than 10,000 sheep in Canterbury and Otago; but only 11 were of 50,000 or more. One, Morven Hills, ran up to 130,000 sheep and had one of the largest woolsheds in the world.[84] Holdings were not always private—New Zealand's largest landowner of the day was the New Zealand and Australian Land Company, which had stations totalling nearly 600,000 acres by the 1870s.[85] Australians also bought land privately, as in March 1876 when the Joshua brothers of Melbourne bought part of the Kereru and Otamauri estates, some 33,000 acres and 26,000 sheep, for £35,000.[86] At least part of the success of these enterprising boot-strappers came from a dynamic adaptation of diverse cultures; as one historian has noted, farm management and pastoral business practices were American.[87]

Pastoralism was not the only road to riches. There was nearly as much to be made from supplying the stations, trading their wool, and acting as agent for the shipping companies. Again, the window did not stay open for long. By the late 1850s the oligarchs—among them several McLeans, Ormond, Molesworth,

ABOVE

The essence of settler New Zealand pastoral life—a 'good house amidst well-planted grounds, surrounded by its square miles of sheep-run'.

Artist unknown, wood engraving, Alexander Turnbull Library, PUBL-0199-01

Riddiford, multiple Williamses, various Campbells, miscellaneous Rhodes and several unrelated Russells—had gained an unshakeable position from which they also derived political status. They were characterised by their wealth and also, initially, by their youth. Many were no more than 30 when they accumulated their fortunes, and few bettered John Ormond. This 'resolute' man of 'great mental power' was just 17 when Eyre appointed him Clerk of the New Munster Executive Council. He had his first pastoral run by age 20; and by 27 was on the Hawke's Bay Provincial Council, a body he had been instrumental in creating.[88]

The oligarchs were joined by other pastoralists, agents, industrialists and merchants. They were a wide group, occasionally divided by historians into multiple sub-classes and strata,[89] but it is misleading to over-classify and intellectualise. In reality all were part of wider 'middle-class-derived' settler society, wealthy gentry of often widely varying fortunes who included back-country pastoralists, others who operated lowland mixed farms, and businessmen, agents or merchants in the towns. Most regarded themselves socially—though not financially—in the league of the oligarchs. They frequented the same clubs, aspired to the same ideals, and hobnobbed whenever possible.

At first the self-appointed status of the elite had more to do with aspiration than reality. Mary Hobhouse remarked that there were 'some rich sheep owners' around in 1860, but 'most of the gentry here' lived in conditions no better than that of 'a comfortable farmer or tradesman at home...'[90] Elitism implied behaviour as much as money, and as always was framed in terms that—to outsiders—seemed paradoxical. Gentility stood against the puritanical middle-class exaltation of self-denial and a hard day's work. The New Zealand answer was to reconcile the difference with symbols and rituals such as a change of clothes after work, itself practical yet symbolically underlining the shift of role. A settler housewife could remove her house-soiled apron and replace it with a decorative example at the end of a day.[91]

Timing also played a part. Hands-on activity in working hours was replaced

ABOVE

Samuel Butler (1835–1902) sold 'Mesopotamia' to William Parkerson in 1864, who on-sold to the Campbell family. Each new owner built a new home; in this 1871 picture, Butler's original cottage is just visible behind the house on the right. Family pose for the photographer on the lawn.

Photographer unidentified, Making New Zealand Collection, Alexander Turnbull Library, F-386-1/4-MNZ

by genteel behaviour in the evenings or on Sundays. That survived settler times and emerged during the twentieth century in, for instance, the ability of a Prime Minister to hands-on renovate his own bach, clear the section or indulge in a spot of weekend house-painting without being frowned upon.[92] These rituals were also one way that the self-made elite identified and reinforced their difference from the poor.

Aspirations were dictated by the layer above, a point summed up by the Otago Witness in 1874. 'There is … no impassable barrier separating these gradations of gentility. There is a gate from the one to the other, and the open sesame is money …'[93] This was probably not something the elite of the day wanted to hear. George Bell of Wantwood held himself aloof, as did G. H. Moore of Glenmark, who typically received his estate manager in the library and, if he had to get into his 77,000-acre run, took his carriage.[94] Waipukurau pastoralist Henry Russell was so imperious he gained the nickname 'Lord H'. Others adopted trappings of patronage, as in 1892 when staff and residents of John Harding's station 'assembled in full force' at his house on Boxing Day to 'partake of that gentleman's hospitality and receive the Christmas gifts he so liberally provides for them...'[95] A cut-off point of around ten staff has been suggested for this sort of behaviour,[96] but we must not over-analyse; styles were also personal, sometimes reflecting the aspirant 'would-be' rather than the more confident 'have'. The majority of New Zealand's self-styled elite derived no shame from soiling their hands or consorting with workers. George Carlyon—a veteran of Crimea and the archetypal officer and gentleman—insisted on directing his staff on his sprawling

ABOVE

An 1860s addition has been tacked on to the original structure on this Taranaki property.

Photographer unidentified, Alexander Turnbull Library, F-61457-1/2

RIGHT

William Hort Levin (1845–1893), right, championed Wellington—including the Te Aro reclamation, for which he is being pilloried here—and was one of the principal shareholders in the Wellington and Manawatu Railway Company.

William Hutchison, Alexander Turnbull Library, A-095-022

Gwavas property despite knowing nothing about sheep.[97]

Inevitably this society was riddled with what—from other times and perspectives—seem to be contradictions. The middle-class ethos of Presbyterian-infused personal restraint sat awkwardly with the opulent displays of wealth that helped assert status on the frontier. Individuals found their own answers; while some gentry displayed the fruits of fortune in houses, buggies, clothing and a lavish lifestyle, others drew pride and a sense of personal satisfaction from being seen to be frugal—though this did not mean doing without. Ultimately the decision was personal, and there were wide variations, most obvious in the homes many built for themselves.

Low, sprawling, single-storey dwellings sprang up across Hawke's Bay, Otago, Marlborough and Canterbury, in particular, during the 1850s and 1860s. With verandahs and floor-to-ceiling French windows opening into rooms of opulent luxury, these 'colonial mission' homes were a perfect match for the social demands of the time. Drawing rooms, servants' quarters—even ballrooms in some of the later incarnations—along with wide grounds, occasionally a tennis court, croquet ground or other sports facility, helped set station homes apart from the dwellings of the staff. Early homesteads were often supplanted by

'The Grange' on Napier's hill, Mataruahau, mid-1870s.

Photographer unidentified, Alexander Turnbull Library, F-110489-1/2

mansions imitating the country homes of England. Most were fashionably in wood, but a few were cob, concrete or—as in the case of John McLean's huge North Otago home—brick. Most were architect-designed, many in Queen Anne style, others neo-Gothic, still others classical. Almost all the elite had one, the difference between 'frugal' and 'extravagant' often emerging as a predilection to extend an existing home instead of building a new one.

Many were surrounded with pleasant gardens and English-style woodlands. Canterbury's Telford family preferred an 89-acre block of native bush, but they were in the minority. Most who could afford it planted English trees, and the Rhodes family imported English birds to sing in theirs.[98] Sports facilities were de rigeur; William Pember Reeves had lawn tennis courts installed at Risingholme, his mansion near Christchurch. In Hawke's Bay, R. P. Williams had a 'very elegant and chaste' house at Mangateretere, surrounded by ornamental gardens and a croquet lawn.[99] John Ormond owned two pastoral mansions—one on his Porangahau property and another near Hastings—as well as a Napier town house. Thomas Tanner spent tens of thousands on a mansion on his Riverslea property. When Sir William Jervois came to stay in 1883, Tanner spent a fortune redecorating.[100] Canterbury sprouted other grand homes, many with English names, grounds and gardens. All were outstripped by Dunedin-based W. J. Larnach, who poured perhaps £125,000 into a Gothic mansion on the outskirts of town—a home that, in name at least, became his castle.[101]

Much of the inspiration for a pastoral lifestyle—with its middle-class aping of British nobility—came from British cities, themselves creations of Britain's urbanising middle class of the day.[102] Town houses were a focus for urban social life and rivalry. Dunedin's genteel homes congregated on Maori Hill;

ABOVE

Wealthy Hawke's Bay pastoralists, including Donald McLean and John Ormond, sought places on Napier's hill for their town houses, but they had to compete with the jail—lower left—and Hukarere, centre. This picture was taken in the late nineteenth century.

Photographer unidentified, Alexander Turnbull Library, F-29565-1/2

RIGHT

Many urban elite made fortunes on the backs of import businesses and industries. This is a group of Dunedin businesses in the 1870s. Details such as the locomotives are fanciful, but the image underlines the more crucial point that rail was important to the economy at the time.

Working Men's Educational Union, Alexander Turnbull Library, D-010-012

OPPOSITE BELOW

Coaches crossing the Maungatoetoe stream, between Waiouru and Tokaanu, central plateau.

Photographer unidentified, Alexander Turnbull Library, PAColl-5155, F-19571-1/4

in Christchurch they clustered around Fendalton.[103] Some houses were rented for a few hundred pounds per annum, or built for under a thousand, but some people went further. Former Dundee businessman James Watt had a £7,000 mansion built on Napier Hill during the 1870s.[104] Watson Shennan's Threave soared to three storeys above Dunedin's High Street in 1904. Not all the 'town' houses were necessarily in the towns. John Bathgate's was 10 miles (16 km) from Dunedin and set in 240 acres of park-like gardens; while Thomas Tancred grew wheat in the rural grounds of his 'town home' near Christchurch.[105] Elsewhere, town houses were built amid wide grounds between urban streets, sprinkled with fountains and ornamental shrubs, and sometimes the town house became the main family dwelling.

The pastoralists were joined in the towns by an urban gentry of bankers, brokers, speculators, moneylenders, agents and small-scale industrialists. Many had boot-strapped their wealth on the back of pastoral fortune; Thomas

Cawthron made an estimated £240,000 from his 30-year stranglehold on Nelson's shipping agencies.[106] The urban elite often gained government offices ranging from Provincial Superintendent—in the case of Wellington's Dr Isaac Featherston—to Agent General. James Fitzgerald was immigration agent, police sub-inspector and then editor of the *Lyttelton Times* before becoming Christchurch Provincial Superintendent in 1853.[107]

One of the pivots on which all genteel life turned was 'the club', another institution inherited from middle-class urban Britain. Gentlemen's clubs were one-stop social institutions with dining rooms, private bars, ballrooms, libraries, reading rooms, office facilities, billiards rooms and places for large-scale social functions. Socially they reinforced the gap between the haves and the have nots, providing a framework within which rivalry for status could be played out. Pastoralists often spent the bulk of their time there when in town. Important deals were hammered out in clubs, and disgrace there was tantamount to social suicide. Stiff entrance fees and subscriptions denominated in guineas, the currency of the elite, were powerful gatekeepers. But this was not something military men had to worry about; membership was usually free to officers.

Clubs were not the only way the colonial elite made their aspirations felt. Another was marriage—an essential ticket to higher social circles. Many self-styled elite were married when they emigrated. Others married in New Zealand, and self-made New Zealand settlers could also go 'home' to find a spouse. Colonial pastoralists were accorded immense status in England, where there was a surplus of women. Colonel George Whitmore, a widower, went to England to meet and marry his second wife in 1865. Wakarara pastoralist Hector Smith married while on a visit to Scotland the following year.

Status intruded into elite lifestyles, often rudely. Visitations were usually announced with a calling card, received by a servant who could tell the would-be visitor that the owner was 'not at home', even if everyone knew that they were. Elegant parties were another means of showing status and spending spare cash. Adela Stewart recorded one soirée for 60 at her Katikati home that began with two hours of dancing. Dinner was served at 10.00 p.m., followed by dances—28 in all—before soup was offered at 2.00 a.m. There was more dancing before tired partygoers dispersed into the dawn, except for the ones found 'coiled up in floor corners all over the rooms' late next morning.[108] Such overnight roistering was

ABOVE

Algernon Gray Tollemache (1805–1892), brother of the First Earl of Dysart, was one of the few English nobles among New Zealand's self-made elite and became one of New Zealand's wealthiest men during the settler period. He was one of the early investors in the New Zealand Company, buying land for speculation as early as 1839, and finally made the journey around the world in 1850, sailing from Gravesend on the *Lady Nugent* with the Godleys.

Photographer unidentified, Alexander Turnbull Library, F-5090-1/2

common enough in an age of difficult transport. In 1892 the McHardy family, living at remote Blackhead station, brought a 100 guests by coach from Waipawa to a woolshed ball that lasted until the following morning.[109]

Exotic destinations beckoned for those with enough cash. Hawke's Bay pastoralist Henry Tiffen went to Japan during the 1870s, just a few years after it was opened up to the west. Other wealthy settlers toured the United States, Africa or Europe. Often these were interim stops on a journey 'home', where the New Zealand elite slotted into the top of middle-class British society. Sometimes they stayed for years in the Imperial capital, coalescing in a New Zealand enclave in Kensington. Others drifted back 'home' to retire. There has been the suggestion that a triumphal return to Britain was often the rationale of the drive to make a colonial fortune, and the exodus of aged and wealthy boot-strappers from New Zealand certainly suggests so.[110]

Among the oligarchs who made the return journey was a fabulously wealthy Algernon Tollemache, whose assets were estimated at more than £1,267,000 when he died in 1892—a figure that translates to approximately $250 million in early twenty-first century money, but in terms of buying power was far higher by period standards.[111] Less well-heeled gentry who retired to the 'old country' included Herbert Meyer, worth £41,000 by 1869, and Christchurch's J. C. Aitken. A few, such as Henry Russell, were less well-heeled; he spent a fortune in the vain hope of demolishing his political enemies, was hammered by the downturn of the 1880s, and returned to Scotland poorer though perhaps wiser.[112] Elite settlers who stayed in New Zealand were often as wealthy. Sir David Monro (1813–1877) was worth more than £50,000 when he died,[113] a typical fortune of the self-made and easily enough to keep them in comfort. Their numbers were leavened by the handful of oligarchs who took wealth to a higher plane. John Ormond was estimated to be worth £400,000 when he died, and G. H. Moore's Glenmark estate was valued at £350,000 in 1882.[114]

Roads to the top: pastoralism

Many of New Zealand's early elite made their fortunes from the first big growth industry of the colony: pastoralism. It was predictable. For those in on the ground floor in the mid-1840s, pastoralism was a road to instant fortune. That remained true into the early 1850s, on the back of government land lease regulations. There was a further boost in 1860s New Zealand when the United States Civil War cut cotton supplies to British manufacturers. Some turned to wool. Most pastoralists also dabbled in meat, but early experiments with salt, oats and other preservatives were dismal. Carcases were often boiled down for fat; Hawke's Bay pastoralist R. P. Williams, for instance, processed around 30,000 in the 1875 season. His 300 tons of tallow was exported the following year at £48 per ton.[115]

Pastoralism was the 'scientific' farming of the age, often inspired by American practice as much as British, and demanding huge areas of back-country. The main cost and labour was in the pasture, though even that was relatively low intensity. Pastoralists would set light to huge areas of scrub, letting roving flocks trample the remains into the soil and follow them with hand-strewn grass seed—typically

Moving sheep in the late 1880s.
Edward Roper Stapleton Sandys,
Alexander Turnbull Library, C-075-008

Yorkshire fog, cocksfoot, couch or danthonia. This was cheap, but had a built-in end-point because burning and grazing exhausted poor back-country topsoil. D. P. Balfour wrote that the sheep were 'in the last stages of starvation' when he arrived at Gwavas in 1873. The difficulty was that as 'crushing' was a spring activity, farmers kept every animal they could through the winter. This was a sin, according to Herbert Guthrie-Smith, transgressing 'the first and greatest of pastoral commandments.'[116] Yet most had no choice.

There was a cost. Within a few decades some back-country areas were suffering shingle slides. By 1910 large parts of Guthrie-Smith's Tutira, crushed and burned for 30 years or more, were inundated with manuka. Hector Smith had a problem with thistles on his Wakarara property and set his staff to work pulling them while he concentrated on fern crushing. He recorded how on one day in January 1864 he, James Smith and Alick Duff burned 5000 acres of fern—'as good a job as destroying thistles.' But John Chambers told C. W. Richmond that thistles had been worth £10,000 to him in improvements, because they prevented fern regrowth.[117]

One of the biggest problems was roaming stock. Tutira station owners C. H. Stuart and T. C. Kiernan suffered 30 percent losses in 1877,[118] but at up to £50 a mile, fencing often lagged. Shepherds were employed at station borders, doubling as hunters. Once or twice a year musters were taken to get the wool. David Balfour's musters at Mangawhare typically took a fortnight. Stragglers missed in earlier years could often add to a flock—in February 1874, Balfour found he had

RIGHT

Bullock teams in the Stratford district. These beasts were the heavy haulers of the nineteenth century.

James McAllister, James McAllister Collection, Alexander Turnbull Library, PAColl-3054, F-12361-1/1

OPPOSITE TOP

A classic settler-era shearing shed, Rangitikei district.

William James Harding, W. J. Harding Collection, Alexander Turnbull Library, PAColl-3042, G-313-1/1

OPPOSITE BOTTOM

Dipping at Clayton Station, Canterbury, January 1892. Few nineteenth-century treatments were effective. Arsenic worked against fly-strike but damaged the wool and was dangerous to sheep and farmers. Other chemicals were no better; C. J. Nairn once treated rams with a concoction so toxic he had to lie down afterwards to recover from the fumes. The main enemy was scab, a burrowing parasite not conquered nationwide until the 1890s.

Photographer unidentified, Alexander Turnbull Library, PAColl-4624, F-2358-1/2

100. Another year there were more than 1000.

One of the key advantages of pastoralism was that it did not take too much labour to get results, a huge advantage at a time when would-be pastoralists needed to keep costs down. That was particularly true for starting pastoralists; some began their ventures with only their own labour and perhaps one or two shepherds or farmhands to assist. But even well-established runs were usually under-manned and, in some places, either under-stocked or set out on land that could only carry one or two sheep to the acre. Te Haroto, mid-way between Napier and Taupo, reached 160,000 acres by 1890—yet ran only 24,000 sheep with four permanent staff to manage them. Gallomy Station, in Otago, ran 75,000 sheep on its 129,000 acres in the 1870s, but after rabbits tore through the area stock levels dropped to less than 30,000.[119]

Under-manning compounded the problems most pastoralists had controlling the threats to their grassy empires. Anything that competed with the sheep—or which damaged the wool—threatened profits. Rabbits were a particular problem, largely because they bred like, well, rabbits; and they took to the New Zealand back country rather better than ducks took to water. Phosphor-radium poison evidently had an impact in Otago,[120] but general efforts to control the problem with rabbit-proof fences, hunting and poisoning were not very effective.

Scab—a burrowing parasite—appeared in Nelson in 1845. By 1846 it was in the Wairarapa, and cases were recorded in Riccarton in 1848.[121] Imported sheep also had it; F. W. Hamilton discovered an outbreak in a flock he was bringing out from Britain in late 1861.[122] Government introduced legislation to limit stock movement around New Zealand in an effort to control the problem, but what was really needed was better medication. Footrot, a fungal infection, was attacked by running sheep through blue-stone or lime-filled yards—though to little effect. Guthrie-Smith was one of many who endured 'endless labour in paring the hoofs of the limping brutes.'[123] Up to a quarter of his ewes were

CHAPTER FOUR
THE ROAD TO EREWHON

ABOVE

This mail coach negotiates the Waimakariri river bed.

Photographer unidentified, Alexander Turnbull Library, PAColl-5155, F-19613-1/4

BELOW

Sarah Ann Cameron, daughter of Riverton founder and utopian social dreamer Captain John Howell.

Photographer unidentified, Wallace Museum Collection, Alexander Turnbull Library F-44078-1/2

lame during the early 1880s. Lungworm was another problem. Guthrie-Smith lost three-quarters of his weaners to the parasite when the problem was at its height. 'Everywhere sheep-farmers were dosing their young sheep with turpentine and oil, or attempting the smoke cure with sulphur.'[124]

Even getting the sheep into New Zealand was fraught with problems, as Hamilton found. The flock he brought in from Britain survived scab during the journey only to be poisoned on landing:

Last Saturday we landed the sheep...all over the Country here is an onerous shrub called Tute which affects all sheep newly landed. Sunday nearly all of ours were tuted, they were taken with spasms and lockjaw and seem to be in awful pain. We bled nearly all of them and gave them ammonia, but in spite of all we could do we lost thirty of them which amounts to something at £65 a head.[125]

The quest for a breed that could cope with New Zealand conditions ran through most of the available types. Romneys were introduced to Wellington in 1852. Gilbert merinos were described as 'one of the finest results of rational breeding of the present time' in a November 1861 advertisement, while Henry Tiffen, G. G. Carlyon, G. Hunter and W. Lyon bought Negretti merinos in Wellington a month later at an average price of £43.10.00 per head—about $8,700 in today's money. Merinos fell out of favour during the following decade, replaced in the North Island largely by Lincolns; and in 1877 one newspaper reported that there had been a 'complete usurpation' of long-wool breeds in Hawke's Bay.[126] The same was not true in Canterbury, where merinos reigned supreme into the late nineteenth century.

The prices commanded by breed-stock underscored one of the key realities of the business. Pastoralism offered huge returns, but it also carried huge costs, particularly once everybody was trying to jump on the pastoral bandwagon. In the settler era, that reduced it to something of a closed shop.

Middling along

The middle ranks of New Zealand's society were filled with folk who shared origins, aspirations and familiarity with the upper strata, but not the income. That happened for a number of reasons, mostly to do with opportunity. In an academic sense they could be dubbed 'respectables', though it is misleading to impose an intellectualised social structure across settler society. There were divisions, some of them quite sharp; but like all the unfolding frontiers of the Pacific Rim, New Zealand's settler society was a good deal flatter, and a good deal more amorphous, than the British world the settlers had left behind. Those of modest income in mid-nineteenth-century New Zealand were not a socioeconomic 'class' to themselves in the strict European sense. Social ties and socioeconomic ambitions were not horizontal but vertical; and the key value of the frontier was one of opportunity and ascent.

That ideal, of course, did not entirely translate into reality. As we shall see, there was a clear status ladder inherited from the middle-class values of urbanising Britain; and there was also a distinction between hopes and the practical experience of frontier life. In the realistic sense there were indeed barriers to 'getting on', and sharp ones to boot. Some of them were attitudinal, flowing from efforts by wealthier settlers to ape British elite society with its distinct 'places' for rich and poor; but for the most part, colonial barriers to advancement were created by the frontier world itself, usually because the local economic pie was of limited scale. Once a handful of elite had their hands on the larger pieces it was difficult for others to break in.

But this did not reduce the fact that settlers had an expectation and belief that they had cast off the old world, and that there were opportunities on the frontier for anybody, whatever their origin, to rise by their own effort to any level.

The other reason why we cannot over-divide New Zealand's middle-income settler world into close-structured classes is that for all the pretensions to nobility expressed by some of the self-made elite, very few settlers actually were of noble origins and most were simply ordinary British folk who shared much the same socio-cultural background, broadly the rising 'middle class' ethos of the day. The ambitions, aspired lifestyles, attitudes and general expectations of

BELOW

This family pose outside their cob house, Canterbury, in the 1860s.

Photographer unidentified, Making New Zealand Collection, Alexander Turnbull Library, F-172-1/4-MNZ

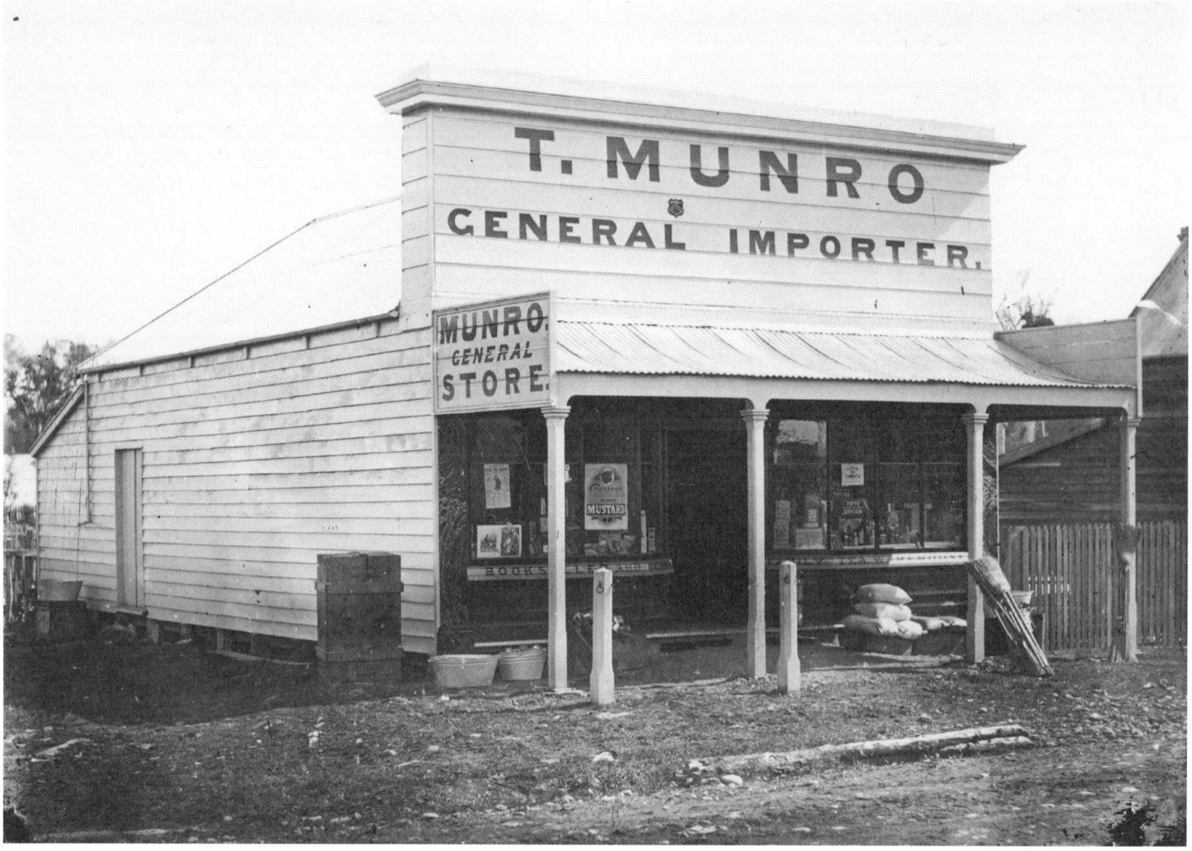

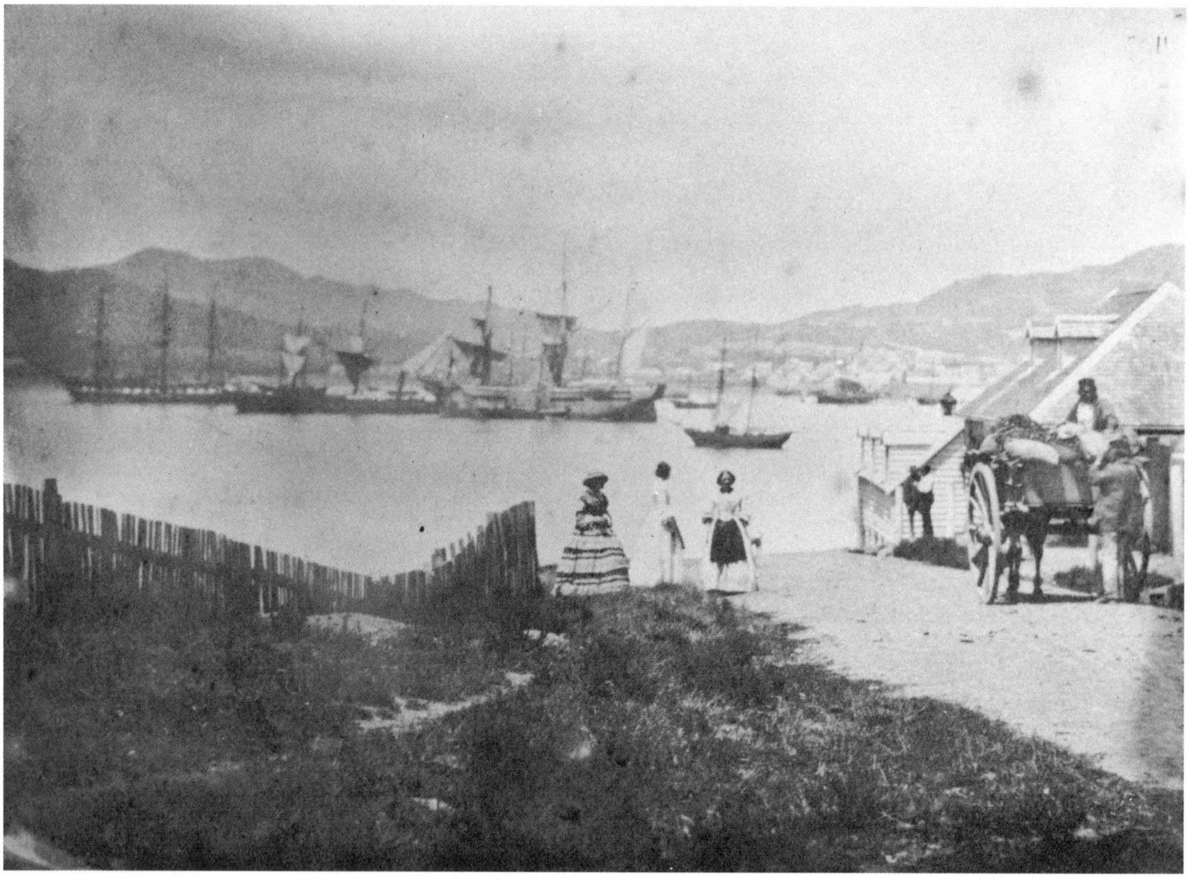

Huts on Mesopotamia during the late 1860s.

William Packe, Alexander Turnbull Library, A-196-015

settlers from doctors to bankers to storekeepers to businessmen were all much the same at the broadest level.

For these reasons, we are probably better to look on New Zealand's 'middling' settlers as a single broad group, rather than trying to over-classify them into sub-classes. From this perspective, the lifestyles of New Zealand's middle-income settlers fanned across a wide spectrum, shading at the top into the world of the self-made pastoral elite, and at the bottom into skilled tradesmen. The distinctions were blurred by social mobility and the ethos of familiarity.

Like all societies it had its dissonances. The notion that anybody could 'get on' stood against a clear social ladder that put academics, teachers, doctors, lawyers and bank managers somewhere near the top of the middling continuum—along with small businessmen and small-to-medium landholders, agriculturalists and mixed-farmers. Publicans, farm managers, store-owners, and self-employed

OPPOSITE TOP

T. Munro's Whanganui store during the 1870s. Hitching posts outside are noteworthy; there was a good deal of the 'wild west' about New Zealand's colonial world.

William James Harding, W. J. Harding Collection, Alexander Turnbull Library, PAColl-3042, G-1595-10x8

OPPOSITE BOTTOM

Respectable women pose with labourers in this late-1850s photograph of Wellington, possibly by Richard Taylor. Scale of shipping in the harbour is noteworthy; a vigorous coastal trade to other centres such as Christchurch, Nelson, Auckland and Napier was joined by an equally brisk trans-Tasman flow. Other ships came and went direct from Britain and the United States. All this kept the significant deep-water harbours such as Port Nicholson turning over briskly. The papers were filled with daily news of arrivals and departures.

Photographer unidentified, Alexander Turnbull Library, E-296-q-170

LEFT

Mr and Mrs W. Bell, Mrs Porter and family pose for the camera in Auckland's St Martin's Lane.

Photographer unidentified, Mrs Banks Collection, Alexander Turnbull Library, F-36960-1/

tradesmen or artisans, such as tailors, carpenters, farriers and saddlers, were usually assigned to the middle or lower end. In practice, income and behaviour counted as much as occupation. Ambition fuelled movement: in the case of Robert Cole, the Ross publican who saved enough to buy pastoral property in Timaru, or Meeanee publican R. D. Maney, whose rags-to-riches-to-rags career on the back of Maori debt spurred national controversy.[127] Savvy tradesmen, such as Henry Shacklock or Josiah Firth, could become big businessmen without being thought 'above' their station. Others were not able to move so far. John Hislop, educationalist extraordinaire, took an active role in Dunedin's civic affairs after retiring—but public office in the town was a lateral shift from his former career as first Secretary of Education.[128]

Middling settlers also lived in the country, often as agriculturalists or in small mixed-pastoral lowland areas. Most were helped by policy as government sold small blocks of land in the hope of creating an agricultural economy to rectify the lack of such basics as vegetable supply. During the 1870s, Canterbury's lowland mixed farms multiplied from 300 to around 1000 holdings.[129] This does not mean that smallholders were a kind of 'sturdy yeomanry' predestined to become the farmers of the twentieth century. In fact, close settlement was patchy for decades. However, like the urban respectables, most smallholders were ambitious, and the more successful were able to elevate themselves. Some did so by founding towns, a vehicle for social advance even for the elite.[130]

Others worked for pastoralists. Managers were at the top of the scale, often considered halfway elite themselves. Reputation was everything at this level; a skilled station manager such as Balfour could demand £200 per annum or more. Managers and senior staff were often 'poached' by other station owners, and Balfour turned down offers while he was at Gwavas. Although £100 was an adequate annual wage for much of the latter nineteenth century, only overseers and head shepherds approached this figure. Ordinary shepherds, bullock drivers, ploughmen and other skilled hands could receive anything between £40 and £80, though some were paid less.

TOP
Edward Dobson (1816–1908) became Canterbury Provincial Engineer at a time when such professions were becoming respectable occupations.
Photographer unidentified, Alexander Turnbull Library, PA2-2445, F-32835-1/2

ABOVE
Arthur Dobson (1841–1934), one of Edward's sons, discovered Arthur's Pass while exploring west of Otira in 1864, though he did not name it himself. Later he was involved in a project to build an east-west rail link through the pass.
Photographer unidentified, Alexander Turnbull Library, F-5041-1/2

ABOVE

Business and politics often went together in the middling settler world.

Lyon and Blair Ltd, Alexander Turnbull Library, B-034-024

TOP LEFT

Ohiwi Brown's house at Muritai, near Gisborne, encapsulated the essence of settler aspiration to respectability: the insular house, fenced garden and air of financial success suggested by the horse and buggy on prominent display for the camera.

Photographer unidentified, Feickert Collection, Alexander Turnbull Library, PAColl-4198, F-36310-1/2

OPPOSITE BOTTOM

Houses and gardens on Napier's hill, probably 1870s. Picket fences, limed streets and organised gardens give an air of establishment, barely 20 years after the town was founded.

Photographer unidentified, Williams Family Collection, Alexander Turnbull Library, F-29576-1/2

It was a male-dominated society, but some women did join the ranks, among them Mary Taylor (1817–93) who had an 'objection to sedentary employment'. She and a friend were helped by 'gifts and loans' to buy land in Wellington, where she set up a shop in 1850. 'How we work!' she wrote.[131] Other women had to enter the world of the wealthier by marriage though, at first, married women had no rights and were effectively property-less. Some got around this by signing contracts with their husbands. The New Zealand Married Women's Property Protection Act of 1860 gave limited rights. These were broadened by a further act in 1870, though New Zealand still lagged behind Britain.

Bottoming out

The lower-income echelons of New Zealand's settler-age society encompassed a range of people, occupations and skills, ranging from semi-skilled or unskilled labourers who eked out a living from piecework or temporary jobs, to bottom-of-the-range farmers, and servants.[132] Many worked at anything they could find from hay-carting to general labouring, tree-felling, road-making, rail-laying and tunnel-digging. Some were able to set up households and even own homes if they did well enough. Some were given a mild hand-up along the way, notably the assisted settlers of the 1870s, who hacked a living out of virgin bush in central Hawke's Bay and the Manawatu.

Unlike the middling groups and elite, many of New Zealand's labouring poor had not come from Britain's rising middle classes; they had come from nothing in Britain and were hoping to better themselves. However, although the colony had no declared barriers, reality imposed practical limits as we have seen, and both origins and education also helped define behaviour and opportunities. The working classes and labourers of the colony were often less well educated than the middling classes, and their behaviours and aspirations alike were shaped by

ABOVE

Living in a raupo whare did not reduce the need for a washing line. This soldier's family were photographed around 1863, probably in the Waikato.

Lieutenant-Colonel William Temple, Alexander Turnbull Library, F-4135-1/2

RIGHT

Charles and Elizabeth Kerr pose outside their cob cottage with Elizabeth Ritchie and a Mr Hill, around 1870.

Photographer unidentified, Murray Collection, Alexander Turnbull Library, F-55441-1/2

their working-class origins back in Britain. Language was coarser—respectables preferred not to say words that the working classes used with abandon. These were not quite the offensive terms of the twentieth and twenty-first centuries. One of the worst expletives in the evangelical settler age was 'damn', politely censored to a dash—itself becoming a mild obscenity, 'dash it'.

Part of what shaped this life came from the limits of income. Typical workers' wages in Auckland, for instance, hovered around seven shillings a day in the late

Government landing terrace at Timaru during the 1860s.

Photographer unidentified, Alexander Turnbull Library PAColl-7489, F-5329-1/2

1840s—this when a pound of tea was two shillings and sixpence, and bread two shillings a loaf.[133] Making do was often the name of the game; stews and scrag-ends took the place of joints, dripping substituted for roast beef as a sandwich filling. Household furniture and equipment was repaired rather than replaced. All this was essential to survival at the bottom.

Working-class women had a particularly hard life. Many had to keep house at a time when every task was done by hand, then put in a day's work on their farm, family store, or on the piecework that gave them 'pin money'. A few found other paid work. Sarah Self, who emigrated to Auckland with her husband in the early 1860s, got a job as a seamstress in an Onehunga dress shop at six shillings a week with promise of more once she had learned the trade.[134] Self used the cash to make her own life more comfortable. 'I do not earn much at present as I do not know much about the trade,' she wrote, 'but I earn more than my washing comes to.'[135] Sometimes women were the only breadwinners. Like men, women in every walk of life had to adapt to the new environment, and in so doing found new strengths.

For all that, being working class was not quite the trap it had been in Britain. Some, such as Balfour, rose into the ranks of the respectables. Most were eager to at least be seen to have ambition—and not to be classified at the bottom. In 1851 Auckland, some 491 men put themselves down as labourers out of a workforce of 8840. In Russell there were six out of a workforce of 402.[136] Pride, self-promotion, misclassification and falling through the statistical net undoubtedly contributed to an understatement. But these figures are indicative. It was a consequence, in part, of early ambition to 'get on' and the fact that Britain's working poor could not afford to migrate. The shortages were keenly felt—not least in the Wakefield

RIGHT

A settler puts out a chimney fire, mid-1850s.

William Strutt, Alexander Turnbull Library, E-453-f-003

colonies. A sustained effort to import labour during the 1870s bore fruit, and one historian has suggested that the rural labour pool stood at around 60,000 by the early 1890s. This included labourers who worked elsewhere in the off-season, railway- and road-builders, coal miners and fowlers.[137]

Country poor included the smallest landholders, settlers brought in often by assisted passage and set up, by policy during the 1870s, in North Island bushland. Some worked for the government on railway construction and were paid in part by land grants, which they then had to clear with backbreaking effort. Many set up dairy farms, though it was the 1880s before this became truly viable. Many rural families made ends meet collectively. Rural and small-town schools were often short of pupils as a result. In 1886, the Havelock (North) school even had to delay opening because most of the pupils were working on the Riverslea hop garden.[138]

Unskilled workers often found employment on the stations. It was an arduous life. Wages were low, the hours long, accommodation frequently dubious.[139] Without much time off or the means to go anywhere, station hands frequently spent their evenings drinking. Some stations had permanent staff of up to 50, but others were itinerant, moving from station to station in gangs as the work came and went. Ploughmen, shearers and wool classers booked themselves ahead with station owners and worked at a variety of locations Many developed a regular clientele, and the better known had good connections across wide areas of New Zealand. Seasonal or short-term threshers, harvesters and shearers could earn around 30 shillings a week.[140]

The bottom end of the working scale included swaggers and ne'er-do-wells who sought work wherever they could find it. They were a minority, but could be found in many parts of the back-country, sometimes alone, often in pairs or groups. Numbers swelled in the early 1860s as miners fell out of the gold rush; shrank in the 1870s; and grew again in the mid-1880s as the economy bent.

Urban boosters

All the threads of settler society came together in the towns. Here the settlers could find the markets, banks, industries, shops and hotels essential to the colonial world. Towns offered opportunities for skilled workers: plumbers, farriers, smiths, carpenters. Early Wellington traders included three cabinetmakers, one turner, two fishmongers, three coffee-house keepers, one lithographic printer, four bakers, four butchers—and nine publicans.[141] Centres such as Christchurch, Auckland or Dunedin with their bustling shopping streets, theatres, hotels, parks, gardens, museums, libraries and up-to-date newspapers, contrasted sharply with

ABOVE
Settler towns were bustling venues for colonists from all walks of life. This is 1860s Dunedin, a dense-packed and vigorous provincial capital in the midst of a gold boom, much to the horror of local authorities who saw the influx of miners as liable to derail ambitions to build an abstemious and God-fearing Scottish society in Otago. The number of vessels in the harbour is noteworthy.
Alexander Turnbull Library F117581-1/2

ABOVE

Insular middle-class Christchurch around 1860. These views from the Provincial buildings highlight gridwork streets with fenced, insular residential sections—still rough-hewn at this stage, but harbingers of a quarter-acre future.

Photographer unidentified, Alexander Turnbull Library, F-346367-1/2

the imagined rural idyll. Dunedin's Vauxhall Gardens offered diversions ranging from a 'pavilion of pleasure' to ballrooms and flower gardens.[142]

Towns were the pivot, focus and rationale of settler life, and the urban ideals they represented were shared by all settlers, irrespective of where they made their homes. New Zealand's rural dwellers of the nineteenth century were not the 'country folk' of eighteenth-century Britain. They came from an urbanising society, and the middle-class ideals they shared or aspired to were irredeemably 'urban' at every level. This did not mean location so much as aspired lifestyle. Yet although this ideal was shared by virtually every settler who reached the country—regardless of where they ended up living—New Zealand was surprisingly urbanised from the outset. More than 40 percent of all settlers lived in towns as early as 1881, nearly a fifth in towns of 25,000 or more.[143] By 1911 half the population lived in towns,[144] but these statistics understate the importance of the urban centres. Towns were the pivot-point and life of New Zealand, including the rural districts, which relied on them as social hubs, as supply centres, and as venues for business, employment and politics. Country gentry, itinerants, labourers and seasonal workers swarmed into town for social contact, to buy clothes, food, tobacco, alcohol and the necessities of life, to get entertained, pleasured, and drunk. Labourers often oscillated between town and country, following work as the seasons changed.[145]

Left
A heavily retouched view of Christchurch from around 1854. The town had been in existence less than five years, yet already called itself a 'city', and in aspiration embodied much of the social idealism that characterised the provincial frontier. The grid street pattern is noteworthy. When surveyor Edward Jollie drew the original sketch plans of the town he tried something a little different. 'Gingerbread!' cried his boss, Thomas, and scrapped them. Jollie was, however, able to retain two long avenues along the Avon, which he called the 'lungs' of the city.
Photographer unidentified, Alexander Turnbull Library 75389-1/2

Wealthy settlers with political ambition looked to provincial capitals, such as Christchurch, Dunedin, Napier, Auckland, New Plymouth and Wellington as places to vie with one another for power and status. Even after the provincial system was abolished in 1876, towns reflected the entrenched political, economic and social interests of the gentry. A few even saw their own priorities as synonymous with those of their town—business rivalry was sometimes commuted into town rivalry, which found expression in competition for major town monuments and buildings. For any aspirant landowner, founding towns was a ticket to social status as well as profit, creating opportunities to become the prominent town patron. These places littered the New Zealand colonial landscape. Not all worked. Some did, even immortalising the name of their founders. Wellington businessman William Levin drew status from the Manawatu town named after him. Once a town had been established the chance of a newcomer successfully setting up another nearby was slim, though many tried—evidenced by adjacent centres such as Levin and Shannon.

This combination of ambition, personal identification with place, and the pivotal nature of urban life to New Zealand had a sharp effect. Towns, like the colony as a whole, were promoted by residents as desirable, go-ahead places even when they were not. Boosters typically included the local newspaper editor, whose motives inevitably included circulation. Similar commercial motives drew storekeepers into the town promotional mix. Politicians, too, were often town boosters, at least up to the turn of the twentieth century when the rise of a new farming class pushed rural interests ahead of urban.[146]

There was much of the wild west in New Zealand's settler-age towns, again underscoring the Pacific Rim culture that was shared, with variations, by unfolding Australia, New Zealand and the United States in the mid-nineteenth century. It was overt; the minor visual differences between Hastings, Minnesota and Hastings, Hawke's Bay—or for that matter Palmerston North, Christchurch, Invercargill or Hamilton—were academic. Most shared a gridwork street pattern or some near adaptation, their town centres bristling with grand-fronted shops, clapboard hotels with wide verandahs, sash windows and hitching posts. Moleskin or canvas trousers were in vogue on both sides of the Pacific, including the 'jean' cut developed by Levi Strauss. Even spelling reflected a common cross-Pacific theme. Honor was preferred to honour in settler New Zealand, clamor instead of clamour, druggist instead of chemist shop.[147]

RIGHT

Quarter-acre paradise, 1850s style: another rather crudely retouched—but historically important—view of Christchurch. Enclosed sections were an early feature of the New Zealand townscape

Photographer unidentified, Alexander Turnbull Library F-75383-1/2.

CHAPTER FOUR
THE ROAD TO EREWHON

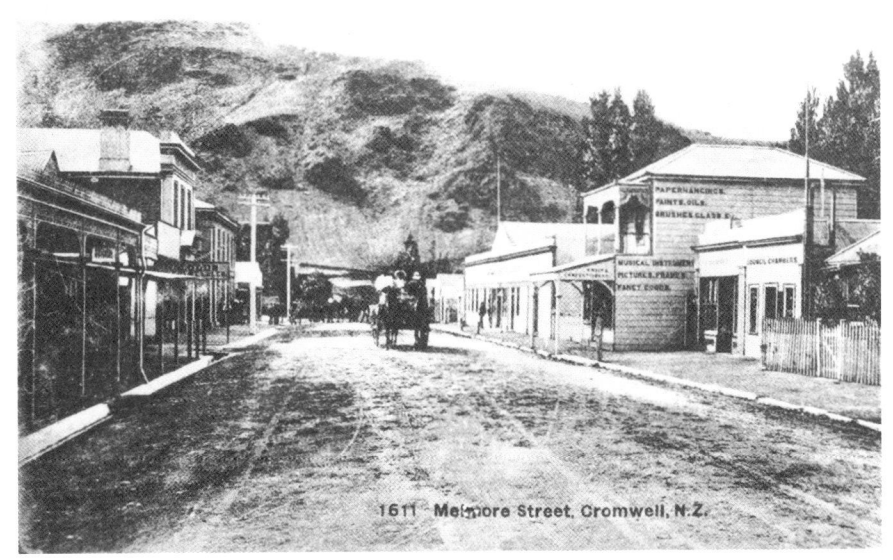

ABOVE

Tiromoana, seen here around 1870, could have been transplanted from the US frontier of the same period. Here were the same limed streets, the same clapboard buildings with their grand frontages, hitching posts and general air of immediacy that marked the US frontier. The similarities underscored the fact that New Zealand, for all its British origins, was also part of a wider Pacific Rim culture during the mid-nineteenth century.

Photographer unidentified, Alexander Turnbull Library, F-17145-1/4

ABOVE LEFT

Another townscape during New Zealand's 'wild west' era, this time Cromwell.

Photographer unidentified, Alexander Turnbull Library, F-122529-1/2

LEFT

More limed streets and clapboard hotels; this is Princes Street, Dunedin, 1864.

William Meluish, Alexander Turnbull Library, F-4373-1/2

RIGHT

Social dreaming: Robert Pemberton's 'Ground Plan of a model town for the happy colony to be established in New Zealand by the workmen of Great Britain'. This 1854 design, intended to map spheres of existence—terrestrial and celestial—reveals that idealism had not died. The centre was designed to hold a miniature farm. Beyond lay the first circle with four colleges, conservatories, workshops, swimming baths and riding schools. Outer circles held factories and workshops, with orchards separating housing areas. The fourth carried an arboretum and horticultural gardens, while the whole was surrounded by a three-mile circumference park.

Robert Pemberton, Alexander Turnbull Library, Plans-80-077

New Zealand's urban landscape embodied a good deal of settler hope—hope that they might build a better and more prosperous future for themselves and their families. It was physically expressed in urban sections, which became the essence of New Zealand's urban landscape. The classic quarter acre emerged immediately, embodying the middle-class notion of insular privacy, concepts of 'progress', a desire to reject the congested mews of Britain's industrial cities, and theories about street layout and social structure. While town planners, such as Auckland designer Felton Mathew, drew on British cities for inspiration—in his case, Bath[148]—the majority applied grids. These were the vogue pattern for cities, an expression of the utopian dreams of the day, a conscious effort to eliminate the perceived causes of England's urban problems and physically provide what James Buckingham called 'social balance'.[149] Frontier paradise was defined by neat gridwork town plans with wide symmetrical streets, encompassing clearly delineated and separate spaces for the rich, for the poor, for public buildings, for parks, for schools, for prisons, and for rubbish. The concept explicitly rejected the conditions found in London, Manchester, Leeds, Sheffield and other long-

CHAPTER FOUR
THE ROAD TO EREWHON

ABOVE

Frederick Carrington's design for early New Plymouth slammed the grid across the available landscape, making concessions only for waterways.

Frederick Alonzo Carrington, Alexander Turnbull Library, MapColl-832.295a/1842/Acc.1928

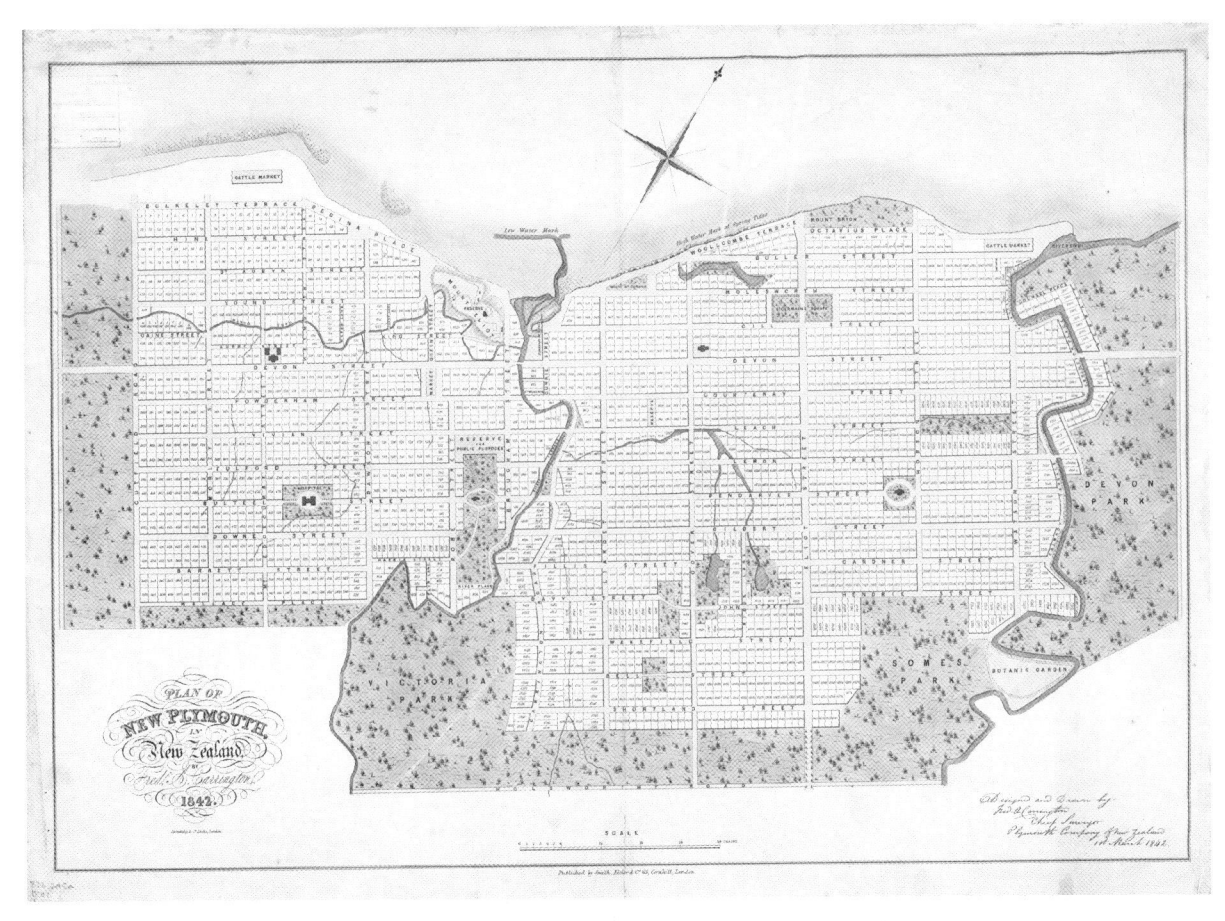

established English cities, where urban expansion had often been little-planned, and where the poor congregated in filthy cul-de-sacs.

Grids offered more than just a physical imposition of ideal social order. Hopeful nineteenth-century town planners, suffused with the notion that physical dirt was associated with moral corruption, also argued that wide streets offered social, moral and physical advantages. In the conceptual sense they were buoyed on the notion that the 'bad' air that engendered moral turpitude could be literally blown away. Cities, it seems, literally had to breathe; Edward Jollie even referred to the avenues he plotted down the banks of the Avon as 'lungs'. On a more pragmatic note, however, the grid also made it impossible for poor communities to use the streets as living spaces, as they did in London's narrow cul-de-sacs. They also did not act as dirt traps, and at a time when cholera dogged many ill-sanitised cities, but when nobody quite knew what caused it, that had practical benefit.[150]

In New Zealand the wide streets that went with the idea were embodied in law—the Municipal Corporations Act 1876 required roads to be 66 feet wide.[151] Although this included footpath and berm, it was far in excess of the needs of foot and horse traffic. Wider streets were occasionally reserved to separate industrial zones from residential, rich from poor. F. W. Engels referred to such districts as 'separate territories, assigned to poverty.'[152] It was an apt observation; Frederick Utting's 1866 plan for Tauranga, or Jollie's plan for Christchurch, included manicured green belts and parks as a way of splitting zones.[153] The key to ideal living, it seemed, was functional separation.

139

RIGHT

This 'Plan of the City of Wellington' was drawn for the New Zealand Company in 1839 to the latest concepts: gridwork street layout with functionally separate regions and an overall physical order that contrasted with the chaotic mews of London. It was likely more talking point than serious scheme; New Zealand Company surveyor William Mein Smith was instructed to use his own judgement on-site, making 'ample reserves for all public purposes; such as a cemetery, a market place, wharfage and probable public buildings...' in such a way that the 'beautiful appearance of the future city' would be 'secured'—even at the expense of profit to the company. Idealism nonetheless featured, including an instruction to create a broad town belt— which became a well-known feature of Wellington.

Samuel Cobham, Alexander Turnbull Library, MapColl 832.4796a/(1839)/Acc.1269, F-51659-1/2

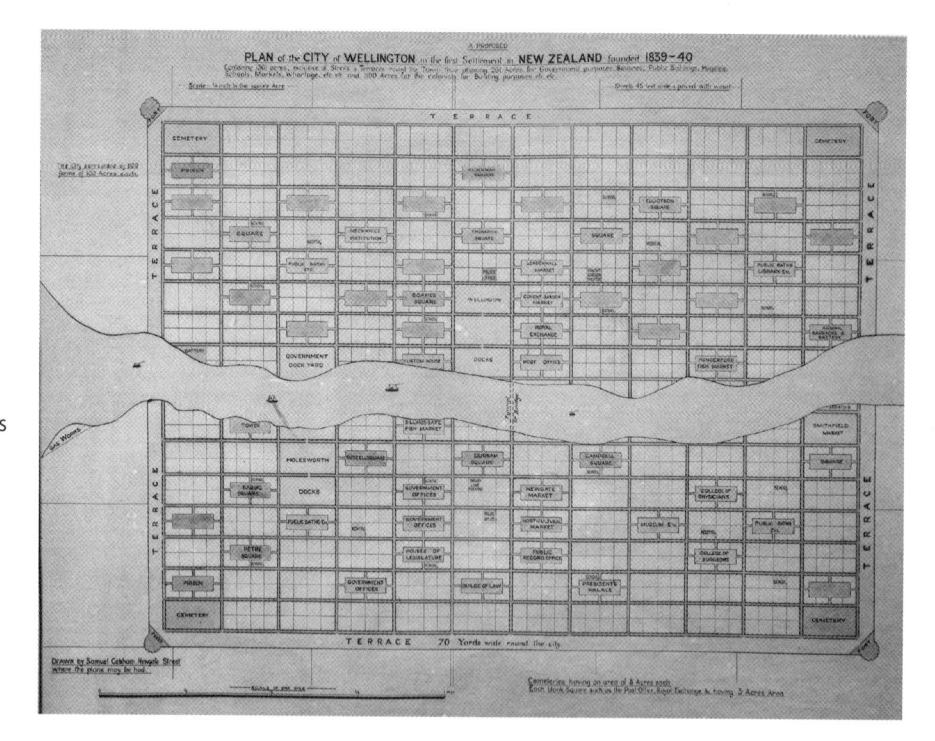

The grid did not always work. The New Zealand Company crossed the world with plans for Wellington which, naturally, did not fit the terrain,[154] though there is good evidence that this was an ideal, an expression of hope rather than a serious town layout. The actual plans, drawn up locally, embodied much the same style of thinking with its grids and its separated functional areas, but the whole was built around the nature of the local geography, compromising to conform to its patterns. Indeed, landscape often forced designers to compromise. Some towns, such as Invercargill, were built with a little leeway as to location; and when J. T. Thomson cast about for a place to site Invercargill, his first priority was terrain well suited for 'sanitary operations'. The grid, with its streets a full two chains wide as a way of keeping 'good' air flowing through the town, duly followed.

However, some planners had to work with what they were given. Wellington was one example, gridded around the curving shoreline of Thorndon Bay and the expected boat harbour in Basin Reserve. In Nelson, Frederick Tuckett created colliding grids as the only way he could get the new town to work. Alfred Domett put another grid into his 1853 plan for Napier, but only insofar as he could get it to fit. Two of the main streets of the original plan curved to fit the Tutaekuri river. Others bent with the hill and dale of Mataruahou, Napier's 'hill'. Not all planners succumbed to geography; in 1842, Frederick Carringtom rammed the New Plymouth grid heedlessly across hill, dale and stream.[155]

At other times the grid was compromised for patriotic reasons; both Havelock North, designed by Henry Tiffen, and Martinborough featured grids tempered with a Union Jack.[156] Plains offered better opportunity for gridwork perfection. Other examples included Hastings, Christchurch, Hamilton, Gore, Hokitika, Invercargill and Palmerston North.

Although towns by any reasonable measure of scale, these colonial urban centres inevitably gained the epithet 'city', a title that embodied more than just pretensions to grandeur; it was also a word that implied ideal living, a word that captured all the hopes and dreams of the nineteenth-century frontier.

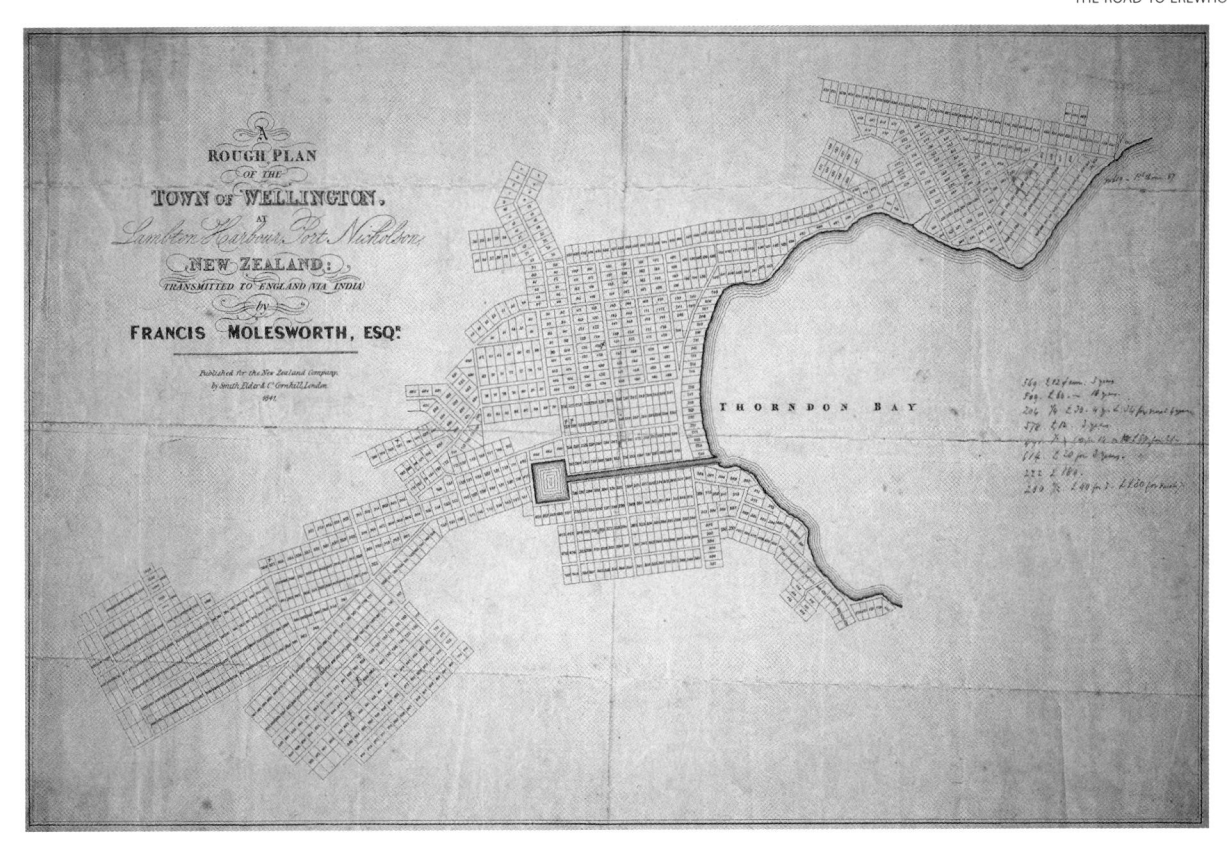

In New Zealand, these nascent cities encapsulated the property thought ideal for middle-class urban life, where settlers could bring their families up in the privacy demanded by the middle-class ethos. The suburban section was also a device by which working classes could elevate themselves. If they could afford one, they could adopt some of the lifestyles of the genteel. Another driving force behind the urban section, as one historian has argued, may have been survival. The quarter-acre provided enough land for a subsistence garden, hens and perhaps a goat or a sheep; working-class families who relied on piecework or seasonal employment were less likely to starve.[157] Indeed, domestic poultry and the vegetable patch remained a feature of suburban gardens into the 1970s. It was an old pre-industrial tradition transplanted to the Antipodes, given particular impetus by the fact that industrial working-class Britishers suffered for lack of it. This argument must be tempered with the fact that many urban sections were an eighth of an acre, and some workers could not afford to buy or rent even this much land. But that is not to diminish the importance of the ideal in the settler mind.

This was the origin of New Zealand's 'quarter-acre' ideal—driven from below, pushed from above—a utopian dream for middle-class and workers alike. The fact that many settlers had emigrated in search of security also provides insight into the other New Zealand phenomenon—owning the house and quarter acre. Suburban house ownership in New Zealand was traditionally higher than elsewhere in the world, remaining so to the end of the twentieth century. So important was getting property in one's own name that generations of New Zealanders were prepared to get heavily into debt for it. This phenomenon was

ABOVE

The real plan of Wellington laid gridwork streets over swamp and hill. Some aspects never materialised, including canal access to Basin Reserve, then projected as a harbour. The 1855 earthquake put paid to this scheme.

Francis Molesworth, Alexander Turnbull Library, MapColl-832.4799gbbd/1841/Acc.16266, F-124686-1/2

ABOVE

Wellington's Thorndon waterfront around 1860. Shops from left to right are: unknown, W. James furniture, Johnsons, Prossors, the Crown and Anchor Hotel, Ashton's, E. W. Mills, unknown, Lewis Moss, unknown. The prominent house on the hill is Hoggard's. Tinakori hill behind is part of the town belt.

Photographer unidentified, Alexander Turnbull Library, F-31733-1/2

unprecedented, its origins unprosaic. The poor of industrial Britain had been reliant on indifferent employers and landlords for livelihood and housing, never knowing when they might not end up on the street. Settlers came to New Zealand to escape this fate.

Settler society and its anomalies

Various theories about how settler society fitted together have been offered by New Zealand historians over the years. One has been that, in an absence of easy transport, settler New Zealand consisted of clusters of local communities. The evidence certainly seems to point that way, particularly as some areas developed special community spirit—notably Havelock North, 'our village' to its people for decades.[158] And that did not, also, preclude wider connections between families or friends who, at times, ended up at widely separated ends of the colony. Coastal traders carried mail and passengers; and by the 1860s many inland routes were being served, for those who could afford it, by stage coach.

An attempt was made in the 1980s to 'harden' the way settler society was understood—to bring it into the ambit of the sciences by analysing from the numbers.[159] British efforts to study their own history that way in the 1960s had met mixed results. The New Zealand effort explicitly rejected traditional evidence, such as newspapers, letters, diaries and memoirs, which showed that colonial New Zealand had a boisterous and vigorous social life. Instead, the historian presented mobility, crime and litigation statistics and argued that many settlers spent their time moving about the country hitting, drinking and suing each other.[160] He interpreted this as symptomatic of a society that lacked society—a lonely world in which settlers were socially isolated 'atoms', psychologically damaged examples of humanity who took out their frustrations on others accordingly.[161]

This idea caused a minor sensation across the academic historical community when published in the early 1980s, although there were obvious problems with a philosophy that denied such a large part of the evidence. Indeed, even taken in its own terms, 'atomisation' did not explain why colonial-age 'atoms' went to the time, expense and effort of suing each other if they had only passing social contact. Why did they care enough about their victims? This was not the only built-in paradox: court action, by definition, demanded ongoing contact with a well-organised society—certainly with a solicitor and witnesses.

The other point raised against the theory was that, if settlers were eager to take out their frustrations on each other, the obvious option was not proxying their differences in expensive and abstract intellectual-academic fashion through the courts. All they had to do was open fire. This was New Zealand's wild-west era, after all. Back-country folk of the day toted an extraordinary arsenal of revolvers, shotguns and rifles. But settlers seldom used their firearms on each other. Furthermore, one of the well-known psychological responses to real loneliness—suicide—was at its historic low during the period.[162]

Surprisingly, it took time for the academic historical community to debate the point. One study suggested that the data reflected only one aspect of New

ABOVE

New Zealand's settler society enjoyed a dynamic life. Country areas were linked in part by stagecoach services, many of them using United States-style 'thoroughbrace' technology. This is S. J. Harding's coach outside the Club Hotel, Masterton. This scene, like so many from settler-age New Zealand, could have taken place anywhere on the Pacific Rim frontier.

Photographer unidentified, Alexander Turnbull Library, PA1-q-269-06-1, F-110626-1/2

ABOVE

New Plymouth, probably during the late 1850s. Limed streets and footpaths give an air of settlement.

Photographer unidentified, Making New Zealand Collection, Alexander Turnbull Library, F-1098-1/4-MNZ

Zealand's settler world—specifically, the behaviour of the lumberjacks, road-builders, navvies, shearers and milling gangs who migrated together around New Zealand in search of employment. Academic studies of women's culture later revealed a society that was the very antithesis of atomisation.[163]

In the end it is difficult to see why the 'atomisation' theory gained ground or provoked any debate at all; the kinds of statistics collected by period bureaucrats were never going to be a complete explanation for the human condition even if the data was complete, which it was not. Statistics were always going to be fragmentary at best, always framed by the intent of those collecting them. Any credible interpretation of the settler period was going to have to incorporate the equally hard facts about human emotion, feeling and expression available from letters, newspaper reports, diaries, memoirs and photographs from the period.

This material reveals that New Zealand enjoyed a dynamic, vibrant and well-connected settler society during the nineteenth century—and even the statistics showed it. The socially desirable building block was the nuclear family—and in spite of a huge demographic imbalance, marriage rates were at an all-time high during the 1855–1874 period, some 8.97 percent per thousand, peaking in 1864–1866 at over 10 percent three years running. This contrasted with the average 6.78 percent of the 1875–1894 period when New Zealand was in depression.[164] By comparison, apart from a brief peak during the Second World War, twentieth-century rates were typically around 7–8 percent. In 1858, more than 49 percent of European males over 15 were either married or widowed, though the figure varied regionally. In underpopulated and pastoral Hawke's Bay, the figure was 27 percent.[165] Around 30 percent of the population in the 1871–1891 period were married,[166] which was a reflection of the high percentage below marriageable age. In 1881, of 185,941 unmarried males, some 104,876 were under 15.[167] This suggests a social pattern in which those who could get married usually did, although the figure remained skewed because there were more men than women.

The importance of family and marriage to the settlers is underlined by the fact that the very moment when women were at their rarest was also the period when the highest percentage of men and women met and married each other. Given the ratio of men to women, that demands some explanation. Part of the reason was that the demographic imbalance was not as severe as raw numbers suggest. In the 1840s and 1850s the ratio of men to women was around three to one, not helped when thousands of gold-hungry men poured into the country during the 1860s.[168] Unfortunately, knowing that 29,884 women joined 63,285 men during the 1861–65 period is not very useful, because a good number of the miners moved back to Australia.[169] A better indication is in the ratio of the 9369 women and 11,167 men who arrived during the 1867–70 period.[170] The imbalance was not even, either across age-brackets or from region to region. Pastoral provinces generally had a lower than average percentage of women.[171]

But there was still a major imbalance at national level; some back-country areas were almost wholly male, and settler authorities did something about it, importing single women in their thousands. They were viewed as potential wives and domestic servants. One study has shown that nearly 70 percent of a sample of 3737 single women who arrived between 1858 and 1871, were aged between 15 and 24, and 95 percent were under 30.[172] Many sought marriage to better themselves, and were often very young; Ellen Hewitt, for instance, married 'only three weeks' after her fifteenth birthday and was a mother at 16.[173] Men actively looked for wives, evidenced by such pleas as that of 'A Bachelor', who wrote to the *Otago Witness* in 1870 with a call to 'inaugurate a marriage office in connection with the Labour Exchange' as a way of getting 'respectable single men' to meet potential wives.[174]

Unmarried men had a society of their own. When not looking for wives, they actively sought the company of their peers, evidenced by the proliferation of boarding houses, which were decried by the *New Zealand Times* as 'crowded dwellings' whose denizens were 'glad to escape to the public house'[175]—where drinking with good mates and punching well-known rivals were popular social activities. One historian, taking kauri bushmen of the Auckland province as a case study, demonstrated that this culture of up to 1000 men was family-oriented to a point, hard-drinking, and looked after each other in the towns—particularly when fights broke out.[176] This suggested a single men's society of close-knit groups. Much of New Zealand's tradition of 'blokes together' originated in this period.

LEFT

Suburban Auckland, 1858; this is Grafton road.

Photographer unidentified, Mrs Lyon Collection, Alexander Turnbull Library, PAColl-5079, F-36268-1/2

Being an itinerant certainly did not mean being isolated. Ernest Weston (1866–1926) and his brother Harold (1865–1958) took to the road as swaggers, but stayed in close contact with each other and their families.[177] Settlers such as David Balfour—who ended up alone out of circumstance—built social ties with their neighbours. Distance was no barrier to comradeship. Indeed, these far-flung back-country communities were in many ways more closely knit than those of the urban centres. Balfour's memoirs and diary reveal much about this kind of community.[178] Occasional loneliness on his back-country leasehold did not drive him to drink—if anything, his experience hardened his thinking the other way. 'Beware drink, it is a treacherous thing,' he later intoned to his children, adding: 'To avoid running into debt you must be sober.'[179]

This was the very antithesis of 'atomisation', and the conclusion is clear. Settler society was built around and relied on a broad range of social connections, particularly marriage and family ties, those of 'work gangs', friendship, club, sports and business associations. This was as true in the back country as it was in the urban areas, if not more so. People moved about in this volatile world of linked communities, but they also kept in touch even when apart from those they knew. The result was a complex, socially active, closely interconnected and vibrant settler world.

CHAPTER FIVE
Desperate times

The intrusion of Britain into New Zealand during the mid nineteenth century can only be described as explosive. Colonies that numbered just a few thousand souls in the mid 1840s grew with impetuous haste. But it was a curiously unbalanced settlement. Physically, Pakeha New Zealand of the 1860s consisted of isolated clusters of Britain scattered across North and South Islands. That was particularly so in the north, and the growing settlements butted against a hinterland which in places was little known to Europe. In the North Island particularly, these settlers came into direct collision with Maori who felt increasingly threatened by developments that they had not anticipated and which they were not able to halt or control. These were curiously unbalanced settlements in other ways, too, particularly given New Zealand Company plans to create instant civilisation with all its accoutrements. Private enterprise had not built an effective infrastructure; communication was poor and funding to build roads and rail unavailable.

Successive governors wrestled with the realities of a colony that consisted of disparate and isolated parts, all struggling to build that essential infrastructure, all desperately short of capital. That highlighted another challenge—administration. The capital, Auckland, was several days by steamer from the southernmost major district of the day, Otago. The practical answer to the problem was devolution. Grey had already divided New Zealand into two provinces, on Colonial Office urging. In 1852 he took that further. The Constitution Act of that year created a system of semi-autonomous districts. The two provinces of his earliest years were replaced by several, including Auckland, Wellington, Marlborough, Nelson, Canterbury and Otago, each under an elected Superintendent—an all-powerful administrator answerable to the local Provincial Council and inevitably elected from the ranks of the gentry or oligarchs. Provincial Councils controlled their own immigration, education and public works policies, along with their debts. They were not fixed; Hawke's Bay split from Wellington in late 1858 after an

ABOVE

British artillery at Gate Pa just after sunrise, 29 April 1864. General Sir Duncan Alexander Cameron, bearded and holding a shooting-stick, leans on the gun carriage wheel. The soldier to his right straddles a Cohorn ('Coehorn') mortar.

Photographer unidentified, Alexander Turnbull Library, F-29252-1/2

ABOVE

Government House, Auckland, soon after opening in 1856. The transfer of central government to Wellington less than ten years later was a coup for the former Wakefield colonists, who had been agitating since 1840 to have government moved there.

Photographer unidentified, Alexander Turnbull Library, F-2657-1/1

argument over the Wellington provincial debt—none of which had been spent in Hawke's Bay. Southland split for similar reason from Otago—but soon re-amalgamated as a way of restoring a tremulous fiscal position.

This was a pragmatic effort to resolve practical problems, but it carried its own issues. The provinces established territories for the rising elites—small territories for small and insular groups of newly wealthy, but the social and financial rewards for those who dominated were high, and they vied for power and status, colliding ambitions that frequently exploded into showers of vituperation. The top office was usually the most hotly contested—exemplified in Hawke's Bay where Alexander Alexander—a man whose parents, it seemed, singularly lacked imagination—told Donald McLean that while Alfred Domett had 'no wish to become superintendent of Hawke's Bay', he would 'act if called'. Domett was opposed by a significant faction, but Alexander's opinion of them was not high. Henry Tiffen had 'considerable official influence', Henry Russell was 'disliked by everybody', Joseph Rhodes was a 'donkey', and T. H. Fitzgerald a 'scheming Jesuit'.[1] A few years earlier Fitzgerald had also been dismissed by Domett as a 'desperate sneak',[2] but he got the job despite such sentiments. There was no love lost between them—Fitzgerald soon decried Domett as 'indolent'.[3]

In theory the provinces were subsidiary to central government, elected on a property-based franchise that included about 20 percent of all settler males. In practice the General Assembly—based in Wellington after 1865—was less effective, particularly as parliamentarians were drawn from the same elites who ran the provinces. Central government, all too often, became a vehicle for the elite to push their parochial interests. These battles for power were not helped by the chaotic nature of early colonial politics. There were no parties as such, and the response to the first elections for central government in 1853 was apathetic to the point where there were problems even finding candidates in Otago. Politics were splintered, and even efforts to reinforce central government, championed by E. W. Stafford and C. W. Richmond among others, were arguably de facto methods of improving the lot of particular provinces.[4]

This was not the only weakness of the provincial system. Public works were poorly coordinated, erratic, and often geared to support the interests of the elite. Many were pursued less for practical value than for their use as sources of provincial pride and status, particularly rail—the symbol of nineteenth century progress. This became an election-winning issue in Christchurch. William Moorehouse was made Superintendent in 1857 on the back of grand promises to build a railway across Canterbury, starting with a link to Lyttleton—by tunnel through the old volcano. Fearless Victorian-age railway engineers were up to the task; the greater challenge was paying for it. Christchurch was less than a decade old and its founding Association still wallowing in the detritus of its debts. Moorehouse's political career did not survive the battles that went with it. But the so-called 'Moorehouse tunnel' was finished—an impressive display of engineering chutzpah by world standards.[5] At a time when status was measured by such feats, other provinces scrabbled to find ways of developing their own rail systems in the wake of it. But less glorious public works languished despite soaring provincial debts—sewage systems, water supplies and hospitals among them. Canterbury was not alone. In Hawke's Bay, the Provincial Council elected in 1859 voted money for roading and £125 for the prison, but £250 voted towards a hospital was barely sufficient. Patients were charged for their stay, and it took an outbreak of typhoid in 1876 to provoke agitation for a bigger institution.[6]

New Zealand Wars: Waitara to Waikato

Race relations reached crisis in the 1860s on the back of ongoing land sales and long-standing disputes. Some stemmed from the volatile combination of circumstances swirling around the hectic 1839–1840 efforts to buy land ahead of the Treaty. Those stomped across the legacies of musket wars upheavals; and officials as William Spain, tasked with settling the issues, often failed to take into account all possible claimants. During the early 1850s a new raft of similar grievances erupted on the back of a pernicious land purchasing system developed by Donald McLean, in which the onus was largely thrown on to the chiefs to settle matters with their people. This system effectively dispossessed many Maori without their consent and drove a wedge between the rangatira and the people. In Hawke's Bay, it triggered a turf war.

All these issues were compounded for Maori by their poor economic position. By the early 1850s most hapu were reliant on British industrial goods and consumables, but lacked the income to buy them. Land sales were the only way to make good the difference; the pressure to sell stood uneasily against growing determination to put a halt to those same sales. One outcome was a level of

ABOVE

Thomas Gore-Browne (1807–1887) and family around 1859. Left to right: Mabyl, Thomas, private secretary Captain F. G. Steward, Harriet, Harold.

Photographer unidentified, Urquhart Album, Alexander Turnbull Library F-2658-1/1)

unified purpose, as iwi facing common pressures drew together to find common answers.[7] Te Heuheu called meetings near Taupo in 1856 to discuss what British agents described as a 'Maori Parliament', principally as a device to halt land sales. Te Heuheu also hoped to implement changes to British law, by treaty, putting them 'on a footing more satisfactory to the Native race.'[8]

The gathering attracted rangatira from much of the North Island, laying the groundwork for what became known as the King movement. In early 1858, at the urging of Wiremu Tamihana, Te Wherowhero was elected as Potatau I. Adherents were required to place their territory under protection of Te Wherowhero's mana. It was considered co-rule with the settlers.[9] However, at least one historian has noted that although the symbols of power were easy to set up, maintaining an institution new to Maori was more difficult.[10] Perhaps the more crucial issue was that, once again, the legacies of musket-war events intruded and shaped the way that the movement emerged. Not all Maori responded—the enemies of Waikato were notably absent—and some hapu joined or left as expedient.[11]

One of the key priorities was halting land sales, which Kingitanga recognised as a mechanism of disempowerment. The difficulty was that Maori relied on sales to fund consumables, and efforts to restrict expenditure included bans on drinking. Some settlers thought Maori were 'ingenuous' for thinking that 'simply making a King would be enough to heal their wounds.'[12] Yet Te Wherowhero provided a focus, and was succeeded in 1860 by his son Tawhiao, underlining the persistence of the movement. A land buyer's report of early 1860 offered one reaction; while the movement 'effectually put a stop to sales of land to the Government...', it would also stop 'further bloodshed, by preventing lands from being sold by claimants with doubtful titles; or...by rightful and acknowledged claimants, against the wishes of the majority of those interested.'[13] These sentiments were lost amid the government notion that Kingitanga was separate sovereignty—illegal under the Treaty of Waitangi.

All this might have led to fighting, but the war that actually broke out in Taranaki reflected local disputes that had been going on since the New Zealand Company 'purchase' of 1839–1840, facilitated by Barrett. It was distinctly dodgy, as we have seen. However, Land Commissioner William Spain reached a 'verdict in favour of the Company's having effected a valid purchase' in 1844.[14] The issue was further complicated by a difficult rights situation that followed the musket wars; territory was sold that was claimed by Te Atiawa, who had been driven out of the area by Waikato. The settlers also wanted more land and in particular a proper harbour, which New Plymouth lacked. The prospect of sale or otherwise, coupled with the rights situation, provoked tensions between local iwi. A dispute between Maori over selling in the Bell Block area led to a 'fatal affray' in August 1854,[15] followed by a larger-scale battle in December. Native Secretary C. L. Nugent thought there was no danger to the settlers, and that government interference might be 'fatal to the prosperity' of the district.[16] Browne issued a

BELOW

Map showing major engagements.

Artist unknown, Alexander Turnbull Library, MapColl-832.16hkm/1868-1869/Acc.5862

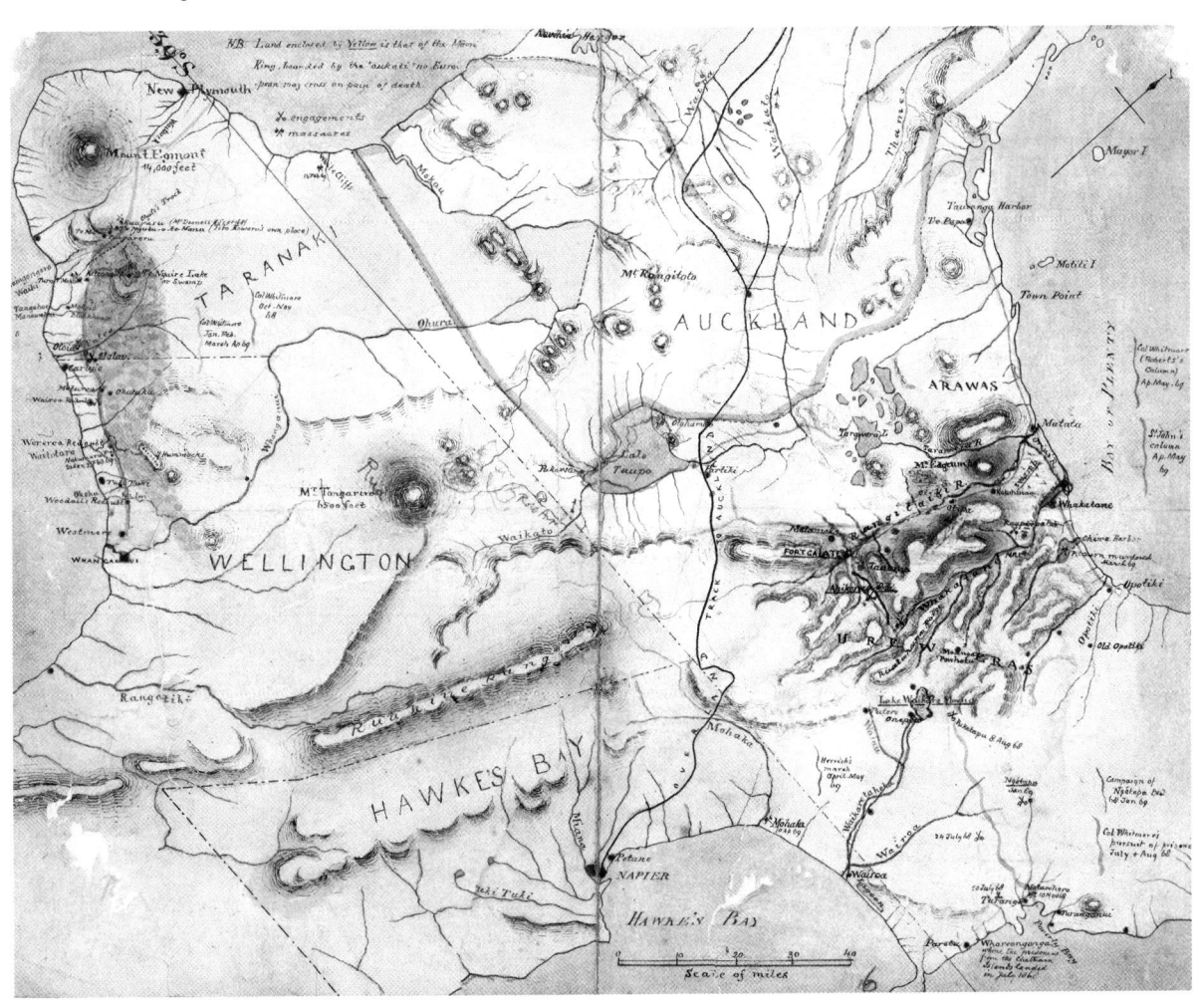

NEW ZEALAND WARFARE.—ASSAULTING A PAH.

ABOVE

A rather fanciful image of Taranaki militia and the Royal Marines, supported by sailors from HMS *Niger* during the first Taranaki War, attacking Waireka pa on 28 March 1860.

Artist unknown, Alexander Turnbull Library, PUBL-0098-02-24-06-lower

proclamation declaring that any Maori fighting in the district would be 'treated as persons in arms against the Queen's authority.'[17] Meanwhile there were calls to confiscate the land of Kingite supporter and Te Atiawa chief Te Rangitake, also known as Wiremu Kingi.[18]

The eventual casus belli was the 600-acre Waitara block, which contained the harbour New Plymouth lacked. Te Teira was prepared to sell; Te Rangitake was determined not to. In early 1859 Browne went to New Plymouth to see if he could settle their differences. There is some evidence that both McLean and local land buyer Robert Parris failed to brief Browne adequately. After addressing Te Teira, Browne received an offer of sale, which he accepted—out of ignorance, according to one historian. McLean did not correct him.[19] Te Rangitake was still staunchly opposed to sale, and when surveyors arrived in February 1860 to start marking out the block, his people intervened. Browne responded vigorously, sending HMS *Niger* to stand offshore while part of the 65th Regiment under Colonel C. E. Gold took punitive action. Tensions spiralled. Settlers began pouring into New Plymouth, and the town was soon bursting with refugees, including Te Teira's people.

The war that followed was the first of a series that engulfed the central North

Island over the next 12 years. They can be divided, for general historical purposes, into two broad phases: the early 1860s, when the economy was booming and Imperial regiments bore the weight of the fighting; and the late 1860s, when New Zealand was in depression and local militia took up the sword, with the help of allied Maori.

Interpretations of what this meant have ranged from heroic nineteenth-century views founded in fatal impact and fantasies of glorious British victories, to the post-colonial reversal of that idea and, with it, the assertion that the settlers only just won in the face of Maori resistance.[20] The problem was that while 'revisionist' thinking provided a compelling rebuttal of the old view of the wars and keyed into prevailing late twentieth-century intellectual priorities, it did not replace it with an informed military evaluation.[21]

The first Taranaki War surged through 1860. Most of the fighting took place in and around the Waitara block, some of it pivoting around various field fortifications thrown up by the engineers of both sides. The war ended with a long assault against a chain fortress built by Hapurona, Te Rangitake's gifted strategist, which stretched back into the hills upland from the Waitara block. Major-General Thomas Pratt declined to expend his men in fruitless frontal attacks and instead threw an assault trench forwards, taking the Maori forts one by one. By mid-March the siege was over,[22] and so was the war; Te Atiawa had been driven from the disputed territory, and Te Rangitake sought peace.

It was a decisive British victory. Maori had shown themselves masters of the firearms-age field techniques they had originally picked up from the British during the musket wars and then adapted to Maori purposes. But the British

BELOW

Maori fire into British positions at Pukerangiora in this drawing by Lieutenant H. S. Bates of the 65th Regiment.

Henry Stratton Bates, Alexander Turnbull Library, NON-ATL-0121

ABOVE

Rewi Manga Maniapoto (1815–1894).

Photographer unidentified, Alexander Turnbull Library, F-52801-1/2

knew very well how to counter these—and in the battle of attrition that followed had every advantage of supply.

The disputed ground shortly switched to the King Country. Settlers were putting pressure on available land. Grey was reappointed Governor in 1861 and tried to negotiate with Tawhiao in January 1863. Further fighting in Taranaki mid-year, in which Waikato were implicated, gave Grey a pretext to act. Maori north of the Waikato refused an ultimatum and, on 12 July, part of the 14th Regiment crossed the Mangatawhiri River. So began the Waikato War, which ultimately drew in a significant proportion of British regimental forces outside India, mostly at British cost.[23] Maori initially held the Hunua Ranges, flanking British positions and bringing pressure to bear on Manukau settlers, and the first thrust in September brought 200 Ngati Maniapoto and Ngati Pou to Pukekohe. British forces were supported by irregulars, including a force under mercenary commander Gustavus Ferdinand von Tempsky. Skirmishing continued while Cameron waited for the 12th Regiment to arrive from Australia and for new shallow-draught gunboats to be completed.

In late October the British advanced up the Waikato. The gunboats helped Cameron reduce the defences at Meremere, and the decisive battle took place in late November at Rangiriri, a bottleneck between the Waikato and Lake Waikare. Around 500 Maori held the fortifications, against which Cameron could bring 1500 soldiers. However, he made the mistake of launching a frontal assault and took heavy losses. What followed was surprising; Cameron belatedly ordered a sap, but next day a white flag rose over the defences. Cameron took it as a sign of surrender and sent the troops in. Maori, however, simply wanted to negotiate—they had run short of ammunition. Cameron insisted on surrender, and over 180 Maori were taken prisoner.[24]

This opened the way into the Waikato, and by mid-December the regiments were in Ngaruawahia. Tawhiao withdrew to the Waipa Valley, unwilling to accept the British demand for total surrender of his land. However, the British did not immediately follow. Cameron had 7000 men, but many were occupied keeping his logistics line open, and he could not advance far or fast until the supply situation improved. This gave Tawhiao time to prepare defences in the crucial Rangaiowhia agricultural district. Cameron declined to engage and sent just over 1200 men on a flank attack into Te Awamutu, which they reached on 21 February. This forced Tawhiao to pull out of Paterangi; but he declined to engage in open battle and threw up fresh defences at Rangaiowhia, just east of Te Awamutu. They did not hold when the British approached, and the vital agricultural area fell to Cameron.[25]

CHAPTER FIVE
DESPERATE TIMES

LEFT
HMS *Pioneer* shells Maori positions at Meremere. The paddle steamer drew around 3 feet (1 metre) and was designed for river service.
Illustrated London News, Alexander Turnbull Library, PUBL-0033-1864-093

The British now controlled the economic heart of the Waikato, and the war ended at Orakau, which Rewi Maniapoto reluctantly fortified under pressure from Ngati Raukawa and Tuhoe. At the end of March, von Tempsky's Forest Rangers and part of the 18th Regiment, the Royal Irish, launched an assault on the pa, which had about 300 defenders. It was a bitter struggle tinged with moments of chivalry, its end driven by lack of water in the pa. Although Maori declined a call to surrender on 2 April, the only other option by this stage was a break-out. In one of the salutary moments of the war—underscoring just how good Maori

BELOW
Attack on Rangiriri, 20 November 1863. This 1890 engraving appears to show the second assault by Captain Henry Mercer and men of the Royal Artillery. Mercer was killed during the attack.
Thomas Redmayne, Alexander Turnbull Library, PUBL-0046-4-39

155

ABOVE

British forces in Ngaruawahia, early 1864.

George Pulman, Alexander Turnbull Library, A-044-017

RIGHT

King Matutaera's whare, Ngaruawahia, 1864.

Daniel Manders Beere, D. M. Beere Collection, wet plate glass negative, Alexander Turnbull Library, G-96092-1/2

were in the field—they successfully punched through the British lines, but were pursued by cavalry, suffering heavy casualties.[26] As always, fighting on British terms was risky; but on this occasion, Maori had little choice.

Tawhiao threw up more fortifications in the southern King Country and there was talk of further military action, but Grey sought a settlement. This was standard British practice at the time. The fact was that by April 1864 the regiments had staged a successful invasion of the Waikato and achieved all the tactical and strategic aims, but achieving this absorbed many of the regiments outside India; in 1863–1865 the British were also fighting in Umbeyla, the Peshawar valley, Bhutan, Jamaica and Arabia.[27] Trouble was brewing in Abyssinia.[28] To have a portion of the British field force tied up in a corner soaking up Imperial funds was impractical, and the main factor behind their withdrawal.

The military reality was that Cameron had met Grey's declared objectives of July 1863 by the time he attacked Orakau. Maori put peace feelers out after Ngaruawahia was occupied. 'I don't say that peace is made', Tamihana explained to Cameron—but he would not continue the fight unless Grey brought it to him by attacking Waipa.[29] Grey was in a position to enforce terms, confiscating land north of the Puniu River. In a wider sense this was consistent with Imperial strategy, which often resolved the problem of the 'thin red line' by switching to diplomacy.[30] Maori wanted peace for their own reasons; Tamihana wrote to Pompallier in August to say that the war was over—adding that it 'would have ceased had it ended at Rangiriri.'[31]

Attention turned to Tauranga, where the harbour had been occupied by the British in January to cut off supply to Waikato. Some tribes in the district, notably Te Arawa, were supporters of the Crown, but Ngaiterangi were not, and there was talk of illegal munitions sale. British forces at the Monmouth Redoubt were told not to provoke Maori; but there was skirmishing in early April.[32] Local chief Rawiri Puhitake decided to build a pa and invited the British to attack it—even offering to construct a road. Colonel H. H. Greer did not rise to the bait, so Puhitake built a new fieldwork just outside Tauranga, Pukehinahina—Gate Pa. By late April Cameron had assembled 1700-odd men at Tauranga, backed by the Royal Navy and with artillery that included howitzers,

ABOVE

A fanciful reconstruction of Maori answering William Mair's offer to let the women and children go free from Orakau. The act was usually, but wrongly, attributed to Maniapoto.

Wilson and Horton, Alexander Turnbull Library, C-033-004

LEFT

Cavalry of the Defence Force charges at Orakau, after a painting by Frank Malone. Out of food and water, Maori had no choice but to break out in a bold move that aroused admiration among the British and went down in legend.

Frank P. Malone, Alexander Turnbull Library, PUBL-0197-3-569

ABOVE

H. G. Robley (1840–1930) sketched Gate Pa early on 30 April 1864, revealing the tactical features of the defences. Palisades were intended as delaying obstacles, while the defenders remained safe behind earthworks and in trenches, some linked by tunnels.

Horatio Gordon Robley, pen and wash, Alexander Turnbull Library, A-033-007

8-inch mortars and a monster Armstrong gun hurling 110-pound shot.[33] Only the mortars were effective against earthworks, which demanded plunging shot; but the sheer size of the Armstrong cannon impressed those ignorant of the way weapons work, including the *New Zealand Herald* correspondent.[34] The reality was that cannon fire, with its flat trajectory, had no chance of doing damage to the earthworks—and in the event, most of the shells simply skittered beyond, at times even into British forces lining up behind the pa.[35]

In the mid-1980s, James Belich argued that Gate Pa was built as a trap to lure the British to their slaughter,[36] and that it was a defence capable of standing in the Ypres salient of the First World War.[37] This was nonsense. British defences half a century later in Ypres were very different in form, intent and technology, pivoting on above-ground pill boxes to meet a different and later tactical need, notably including later technology such as widespread machine guns.[38] Nor could the Ypres defences be flanked. Whereas in Tauranga, Gate Pa was not only flanked—it was surrounded.

More crucially, Gate Pa was not built as a trap. The place to kill the enemy was not inside the last ditch of the defence, but in the clear ground ahead. Maori understood this and set up their fortification accordingly, even creating hindrances with palings stolen from town fences to keep the advancing enemy at bay in the killing ground. It did not work—the British assault on the pa pushed the Maori out of it and the regiments burst clean through the defence. But the defenders were then driven back into the earthworks by members of the 68th Regiment, stationed behind the pa and surrounding the defences. It is hard to see being pushed out of the defence by a British assault, into encircling British forces, as a 'trap' being sprung by Maori. Only after Maori had been driven back into the defences by the British did the melee break out inside, and it was desperate; Hori

Ngaitai's account makes clear that Maori stood firm only at one end.[39] The fact that they prevailed amid the confusion is an endorsement of the sheer capability of the toa involved, helped by the fact that some of the British soldiers had never been in battle before. The result was a confused melee, and the British force inside the entrenchment was repulsed.

Ngaiterangi knew they had met near-defeat. They slipped away during the night, leaving the British in possession of the field. Cameron went back to Auckland, leaving Greer with orders to attack at once if Ngaiterangi started to build a new fort. This led to a battle at Te Ranga in June, where Maori tried to defend a half-completed structure and lost nearly 120 toa, including Puhitake. British casualties were nine dead and 39 wounded. It was decisive; a settlement was reached in July.

Booster engines

The wars of the early 1860s were fought against a background of vigorous economic expansion. This was a paradox in many ways; the settler economy had minimal infrastructure, widely separated main centres, virtually no national communication other than coastal shipping, and relied heavily on non-renewable resources such as gold. Yet the economy expanded with near-explosive haste. To some extent this growth was an illusion born of arithmetic; the settlers had started from nothing and a shift from one timber mill to two represented 100 percent growth in that sector. After the economy was established, a shift from 99 to 100 mills represented only a 1 percent increase. However, New Zealand's initial colonial growth was spectacular even when stripped of its statistical illusions. The main reason was that the population was expanding, and new arrivals wanted land, housing, shops, business opportunities, farms, entertainment, clothing and goods. These demands created lucrative opportunities, and as long as dynamic expansion continued, massive returns became possible from very little capital. Investors who were in at the right time surfed the wave as the economy unfolded.

It was a fairly standard frontier pattern—and like all bubbles it disguised the fact that the underlying economy was not in good shape. The balance of payments was appalling. Annual deficits soared during the early 1860s from £1,123,000 in 1861 to £3,599,000 in 1864, and there was a deficit most years from 1861 to 1876.[40] The distortions created by debt, bad balance of payments and no sustained income were compounded by the fact that the mechanisms that allowed a handful of ambitious middle-class settlers to super-boost their fortunes also affected the way everything else developed.

In theory, the provinces were part-funded by profit from state land purchase, but this was never enough, and the difference had to be borrowed via legislation such as the Loan Act 1856, which obtained £500,000 from debentures offered at 4 percent on the London market.[41] In 1863 the New Zealand government tried to borrow £3 million at 5 percent, but when the British government refused to underwrite the loan, the only way of getting the money was to issue £1 million worth of short-term debentures at 8 percent as bridging finance. Provincial governments also created debts, as in 1860 when Canterbury borrowed £300,000

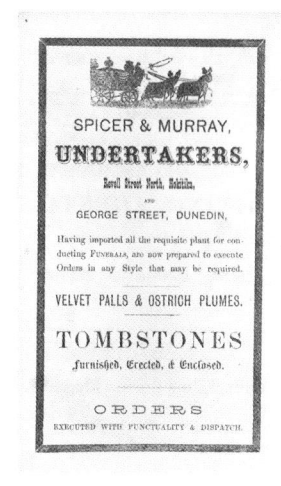

ABOVE

For all its imbalances, New Zealand's settler society still had what it needed to function — including newspapers and, of course, undertakers.

Artist unknown, Alexander Turnbull Library, F-31932-1/2

RIGHT

Frederick Aloysius Weld (far left) and his wife Filumena Mary Anne Lisle Phillipps Weld (second from left) with Sir Charles Clifford (right, back), Jessie Cruickshank Crawford and Francis Louise Tollemache. As Premier briefly between 1864 and 1865, Weld inherited the politics of the New Zealand wars.

Photographer unidentified, Alexander Turnbull Library, F-34967-1/2

to pay for its spectacular tunnel and railway system. Auckland borrowed £500,000 three years later. Political tensions rose with the debts; Hawke's Bay separated from Wellington and Southland from Otago in response to the fiscal position of the parent province. Independent borrowing spurred wider worries about New Zealand's credit rating, and in 1867 central government moved to consolidate the debt—borrowing another £7 million for the purpose.[42]

Private capital flowed in through trading banks, family connections, or companies established for the purpose. These included the New Zealand Loan and Mercantile Agency and the Northern Investment Company, formed by leading pastoralists with the aim of borrowing money from Scottish investors.[43] Other money came from former Australian pastoralists, among them William 'Ready Money' Robinson of Cheviot, whose 93,000 New Zealand acres were worth a quarter of a million pounds in 1882.[44] Several Australian-backed companies operated runs, including Robert Campbell & Co. of Otago.[45]

The provincial system, which split New Zealand into competing and semi-

ABOVE

A slightly romanticised and mildly piratical image of early gold mining. The sidearm is noteworthy.

Working Men's Educational Union, Alexander Turnbull Library, D-010-010

autonomous regions, added further strain. Provincial development was lumpy. Auckland became the prime industrial-agricultural region, with 60,201 acres under cultivation in 1858.[46] This was about half the national total and produced, among other things, 28 percent of the national potato crop in 1869.[47] Auckland also housed 102 of the 406 factories in national operation by 1867, including 30 sawmills—a third of the national total—11 grain mills, seven breweries, seven brickworks, four fellmongeries and ten flaxworks among others.[48] The value of this plant was double that of the next highest province, Otago.[49] Pastoral and agrarian products, such as wool, oats, hay and wheat, were focussed in Canterbury, Otago, Marlborough and to some extent Hawke's Bay. In 1869, nearly half the national oat crop—the 'fuel' for New Zealand's horses and beasts of burden—came from Otago and most of the rest from Canterbury. Almost two-thirds of the wheat was grown in Canterbury, and more than half the barley.[50] Getting this from place to place depended on coastal traders. Efforts by provincial governments to rectify these issues were limited, in part because governments were dominated by oligarchs whose focus was on their own interests.

The economy was initially trans-Tasman. In 1861 some 61 percent of all exports by value went to Australia and 37 percent to Britain. However, the British share rose at the end of the decade and on into the 1870s, hitting 80 percent by 1876.[51] This emphasis pre-dated the frozen meat boom, which has been erroneously given as the driver of new attention to Britain,[52] by nearly a decade. The reality—which was that the growth of that industry did not drive

RIGHT

Gabriel's Gully, mid-1860s. It did not take long for Gabriel Read's discovery to become the hot news of the South Pacific. This 'tent city' was one result.

Photographer unidentified, Alexander Turnbull Library, F-31007-1/2

BELOW

Gabriel's Gully transformed into a bleak landscape of pit and heap.

Photographer unidentified, Alexander Turnbull Library, F-2662-1/4

ABOVE

A glimpse of New Zealand's 'wildest west': Ahaura goldmining settlement at Napoleon Hill, Grey County, looking down Prince's Street East. Shanty towns, complete with casinos, burst into life near the diggings.

Photographer unidentified, Alexander Turnbull Library, PA-0-530-25

New Zealand's late nineteenth-century love affair with the motherland—is given greater weight by the fact that much of the exported material by value in the 1860s was gold, initially sold to Britain via the Melbourne market and thus appearing as an Australian export.[53] Eliminating gold from the equation shows an even earlier New Zealand bias in favour of the mother country.

Imports painted a different picture; just over half came from Australia during 1861, and trade was still significant in 1876.[54] In 1870, imports to New Zealand from all sources included £114,188 worth of apparel; £215,164 worth of boots and shoes; £636,936 worth of drapery and £61,789 worth of hats. This compared with £175,210 worth of ironmongery, £9,125 worth of gin, £25,114 of whisky, and rum to the value of £16,104.[55]

The other problem was that New Zealand's settler economy was extractive. Pastoralism exploited the dwindling fertility of the soil. Timber, kauri gum and gold could only be harvested once. Yet gold, in particular, was the foundation of New Zealand's fortunes in the early 1860s. Most of the precious metal came from Otago. Dunedin was established by the Lay Association of the Free Church of Scotland in 1848, on a modified Wakefield system where lack of capital and minimal farming activity restricted settlement to the town and environs. The pastoralists who spread into the hinterland during the 1850s were migrants from Australia and Canterbury, let in particularly by new grazing regulations in 1856. Infrastructure was minimal—roads were 'canals of liquid mud'—and European exploration of the interior was patchy.[56]

Maori knew of gold in Otago, but the metal had little value in pre-European times. Settlers were tantalised by stories of nuggets the size of 'a small potato' being tossed back into the Molyneux River. There was one effort to discover the 'El

RIGHT

Chinese miners came to New Zealand, following the gold, and did so despite a level of prejudice by Pakeha of the day against Asians that plumbed the worst depths of bigotry. Some settled, frequently becoming market gardeners. Here, Ah Sam and Joe Quin prepare goods for market.

Photographer unidentified, Alexander Turnbull Library C6165

RIGHT

Banks quickly followed the gold miners. This is a BNZ branch on the diggings in 1864.

Photographer unidentified, Alexander Turnbull Library, F-594-1/1

Dorado' in 1852.[57] Another, led by Thomas Archibald, spent three weeks scouring Otago rivers in the hope of finding the precious metal. Other parties, including one led by Alexander Garvie, were more successful; but their small finds were apparently 'suppressed, as likely to cause mischievous results' or 'neglected, as of trivial import.'[58] Otago authorities faced an uphill battle to preserve the ideals of their neo-Scottish settlement.

By the end of the decade, however, the idea that gold might rescue a flagging economy was gaining ground. In early 1861 roadmen found gold in the upper Lindis Gorge. There was a 'small rush', but the 'general yield was not encouraging'.[59] Then in late May the prospector Gabriel Read, armed with a butcher's knife, tin dish, spade, and 'about a week's supply of provisions', checked a 'large area of country' in the Tuapeka district, discovering 'prospects which would hold out a certainty that men with the proper tools would be munificently remunerated.'[60] There was a rush with 'highly satisfactory' results; and when the first shipment

Gold mining at Addison's Flat, Buller.

Photographer unidentified, Alexander Turnbull Library, F-14986-1/4

of 5056 ounces came down to Dunedin the floodgates opened. As an official report remarked, 'thousands were bitten by the gold fever, and abandoned their ordinary pursuits to "try their luck" at the diggings.'[61]

By Christmas there were 14,000 gold-seekers in the district, though numbers fluctuated radically. Discoveries near Cromwell prompted a surge there; and other prospectors moved up the Mataura Valley. More checked the Clutha headwaters, and William Fox found gold in the Arrow. Over the next few years, tens of thousands of men arrived, prospectors whose working lives spanned the Pacific from California to Victoria and Otago. By far the majority came from Australia—24,243 in the year to July 1862.[62] Almost as many hurried back the other way; 16,386 to Australian destinations in the year to 31 July 1862. Some re-crossed the Tasman when more gold was found soon afterwards in Otago, a movement decried officially as 'senseless panic'.[63] But the two-way trade continued; 7303 moved back to Australia in the following twelve months, crossing paths with 31,762 coming in, followed by 31,762 in and 7477 out respectively in the year to December 1863. By then the boom was largely over, and miners poured back across the Tasman in 1864, while incoming hopefuls dropped to fewer than 2000.[64] The population of Otago oscillated violently on the back of these wild surges. However, some estimates suggest the population on the fields peaked at around 24,000.[65]

The statistics make several things clear. Although some fortune-hunters came from America, Britain and from within New Zealand, around 80 percent came from Australia; many went back there when the New Zealand lodes were worked out. A few stayed, moving on to prospects in Nelson, the West Coast and Thames. Still others—like David Balfour, or Australian businessman Alexander

ABOVE

Industrial-scale mining with floating dredges dominated the long-term gold industry, notably on the West Coast and near Alexandra. This example—known as the Manuherika Dredge—operates on the Manuherika river just outside Alexandra.

Photographer unidentified, Alexander Turnbull Library, F-62537-1/2

Burt, entered the New Zealand workforce. How much the miners made is debatable. There is an oft-quoted shibboleth that only shopkeepers and publicans made money on the gold frontier; but the 500,000-odd ounces extracted in 1862–63 implied an average annual yield of around 21 ounces per miner. Most seem to have been able to make ends meet.

The discoveries revolutionised New Zealand. One historian has argued that anti-Chinese prejudice was introduced with the gold-miners; that the influx of labour accentuated egalitarianism—and that it introduced new 'fondness for gambling.'[66] Gold became a significant export; the £753,000 worth exported in 1861 was New Zealand's single biggest income-earner that year, outstripping wool at £524,000 and timber at £19,000.[67] A report at the time claimed that Dunedin 'assumed the dimensions of a city', 'agricultural villages' became 'important inland towns', and the 'large and important town of Queenstown' was established. Much of this was puff; Dunedin still lacked a proper sewer system and was prone to epidemics.[68]

Provincial revenue soared on the back of export duty and miners' licences, reaching some £78,587 in 1862. Against this had to be netted the costs of running the fields, £35,270 in 1862 for Gold Field Department staff salaries, escort services, buildings, hospitals—and the £1,000 reward to Gabriel Read 'for discovery of Tuapeka'.[69] Most of the gold went to Melbourne; in 1863 the amount shipped to Australia amounted to four-fifths of the total. This was credited with obscuring the importance of the Otago field in Britain, an 'error…not confined to the illiterate.'[70]

The Otago rush marked the beginning of New Zealand's golden years. Other gold was found elsewhere in the South Island and in Thames, and for a few years the metal was New Zealand's most valuable export. Some 674,499 ounces went overseas in the year to 31 March 1866.[71] But the auriferous nirvana did not last long. By 1867 the Otago 'rush' was over. Gold still came from the west coast, around Havelock, and the Thames fields, but further practical extraction demanded large-scale industrial processes. This did not stop an ongoing national search for easier lodes. In 1867 the Hawke's Bay Provincial Government offered £1000 to whoever discovered gold there, and George Whitmore secretly sent parties to look. Gold eventually was found in the province, but in no great quantity.

The end of the Otago gold boom coincided with a crunch in the wool market, as prices were forced down by a glut of cheap products from the expanding American frontier, which was shaking down after the end of the Civil War.[72] Some historians have suggested that the downturn was the start of 30 years of economic stagnation alleviated only by an artificial upturn in the 1870s. It has sometimes even been given a proper name—'The Long Depression', though some economic historians dispute that it existed at all in that form. But by any measure, the late 1860s brought a downturn. An editorial in the *Hawke's Bay Herald* in early 1868 attributed the depression to over-government, bankruptcy of provincial governments, and a falling market for surplus sheep. The solution proposed by the paper was fresh industries and direct taxation of absentee landowners.[73] George Maunder, who emigrated to New Zealand in the late 1860s, lost his job as a wool presser at Ahuriri in 1870. 'I do not know what I shall do next,' he wrote to his sister. He had already decided not to go to Auckland 'as things are very dull there'. Optimistically, he thought flax, sheep and cattle offered hope.[74]

Pai Marire and Te Kooti

New Zealand's first major economic crisis came just as the New Zealand wars entered a new phase. Fighting flared in north Taranaki during late 1863. However, the military details of the 1864–66 period—notably war in South Taranaki and the 'Lame Seagull' march by Cameron—are less crucial than a context that included the withdrawal of the regiments after a spat over cost, and arguments over local militia driven by personal rifts within the governing oligarchy.

Maori feeling was refocussed by a new movement that emerged in Taranaki during 1862, called Pai Marire by founder Te Ua Haumene. He portrayed Maori as a lost tribe of Israel and spoke of revelations from the angel Gabriel. This emergent intersection of Old Testament teachings and culture contact was not unusual; similar phenomena occurred many times around the world, and more than once in New Zealand. One study has identified coincidental similarities between traditional Maori and Hebrew cultures, providing a likely mechanism by which the connection was made in Taranaki.[75] However, while Te Ua saw the movement as peaceful, militarist adherents gained power after the battle of Te Ahuahu in April 1864, and began seeking wider support. Their strategies included taking the dried head of Captain Thomas Lloyd around local tribes.

OPPOSITE BELOW

Gold rush days in Thames. The North Island attracted its share of hopeful prospectors, and when the yellow metal was found at the south end of the Coromandel there was a rush there. These structures stand at Moanataiari Creek around 1868, with the chimney of the Moanataiari Battery just visible up the valley in the centre frame. The Prince Alfred Hotel stands to the right, on the corner of Coromandel Street.

Photographer unidentified, Alexander Turnbull Library, F-65407-1/2

ABOVE

Hori Kingi te Anaua, John White and Te Ua Haumene, around 1860. As founder of Pai Marire, Te Ua was demonised by the settlers; but his original aims were peaceful. Born around 1825, he became a lay reader in the Wesleyan mission, where he discovered the Old Testament. He was inspired to found the Pai Marire after a vision in September 1862. John White (1821–1891) was Resident Magistrate in the Wanganui district, former interpreter and a key figure in the government effort to resolve Maori issues peacefully. He wrote extensively on Maori life and times, and edited the repudiation newspaper *Te Wananga*.

Photographer unidentified, Alexander Turnbull Library, PA2-2856, F-103545-1/2

Practices such as speaking in tongues and dancing around a mast-like Niu pole confirmed the image of Pai Marire as savage killers in the settler mind, a concept not challenged until the twentieth century.[76] All this struck horror into local settlers. Lloyd's head was eventually retrieved by regimental interpreter Charles Broughton, who—with what can only be called a sense of the disingenuous—rode into Waitotara and asked for it.[77]

In battle, Pai Marire used the cry 'Hau Hau', which the settlers used as a name for the movement. Like adherents of other syncretic movements around the world—including the Yihequan of late 1890s China—Pai Marire believed that faith, symbolised by a physical movement, could protect them from Europe's weapons. However, the teaching that an upraised hand deflected bullets did little good at Sentry Hill in April 1864. Nearly 300 Pai Marire attacked the British redoubt, over 30 were killed and as many wounded.

The movement assumed a new dimension in early 1865 when Kereopa Te Rau arrived in the Bay of Plenty, intending to win over Hirini Te Kani, principal Heretaunga chief. They still had a British head, which one witness saw 'with a cap of the 70th on. They pretend to make it speak.'[78] While in the district Kereopa's people killed the Reverend Carl S. Volkner in his Opotiki church. Kereopa drank his blood from a chalice and ate Volkner's eyes—an act that inevitably sent shock waves through the Pakeha colony on many levels. Much of the often hysterical settler response to Pai Marire can be traced to these events. Kereopa was later tried for murder in Napier, and hanged.

Pai Marire spread down the East Coast of the North Island during the next few months, but violence did not reach Hawke's Bay until mid-1866.[79] The movement was adopted by Ngati Hineuru of Te Haroto, part way between Napier and Taupo. By mid-1866 they were effectively at war with Ngati Kahungunu, a conflict driven by longstanding disputes over distribution of the original Ahuriri purchase money.[80] Tough talk seemed likely to give way to violence several times during the year, but Donald McLean sought to negotiate. He had significant mana in the district with Maori, and his efforts prevented any fighting until October, when two battles were fought on the same day at Omarunui and Petane between settlers and Ngati Kahungunu kupapa on one side, and Ngati Hineuru and Pai Marire on the other.

The settler victory at both locations was so decisive that there was talk of a massacre. Post-colonial analysis has portrayed Pai Marire at Omarunui, particularly, as innocent victims.[81] However, events have to be seen in the context of the politics of the land issue, of the settler image of Pai Marire, and of the fact that the Pai Marire force openly rejected multiple offers of surrender.[82] As far as settler authorities were concerned, the group at Omarunui meant mischief. This was confirmed, to their minds, when McLean was tipped off about '...a plan... under which a general movement of the disaffected Natives was to take place... and that this place [Napier], if feasible, was to be the point of attack, but if not, then an attempt was to be made to attack Wairoa and Poverty Bay.'[83] Napier

LEFT

'Savage dance', a lurid reconstruction of Carl Sylvius Volkner's death at Opotiki.

Illustrated London News, Alexander Turnbull Library, PUBL-0033-1865-47-080-2

was the largest town along the east coast of the North Island at the time, and a significant colonial centre of the day. Given the reputation of Pai Marire, McLean took such reports in deadly earnest. As he told Stafford, he intended to collect a force:

> ...to be able to deal conclusively with the intruding Hau Haus, which I trust may be done without bloodshed, for able as I shall then be to surround them with an infinitely superior force, I trust to obtain their submission, and by that means to absolutely crush out the danger which at present menaces the district.[84]

The desire to avoid battle was genuine; and a show of force, with or without a fight, also served McLean's need for a moral victory over hapu wavering towards Pai Marire.

The next crisis on the East Coast did not come for several years—ironically, triggered by McLean's follow-up to the Omarunui incident. Meantime, fighting

LEFT

Battlefield at Omarunui, October 1866: colonial forces and kupapa crossed the Tutaekuri river, foreground, to attack the village.

Photographer unidentified, Alexander Turnbull Library, F-111457-1/2

ABOVE

Major-General Sir George Stoddart Whitmore (1830–1903) came to New Zealand as military secretary to General Sir Duncan Cameron, sold his commission and bought property in Hawke's Bay, then became prominent as colonial militia commander, leading campaigns against Te Kooti and Titokowaru in the late 1860s.

William Henry Whitmore Davis, E. Ellis Collection, Alexander Turnbull Library, PA2-0604, F-5306-1/2

BELOW

Wiremu Tamehana te Waharoa and Josiah Clifton Firth, seated centre top row, in mid-1865, just after Firth had purchased land near Matamata.

Photographer unidentified, Firth Family Papers, Alexander Turnbull Library, MS-Papers-1491-09/1-3-04, F-93195-1/2

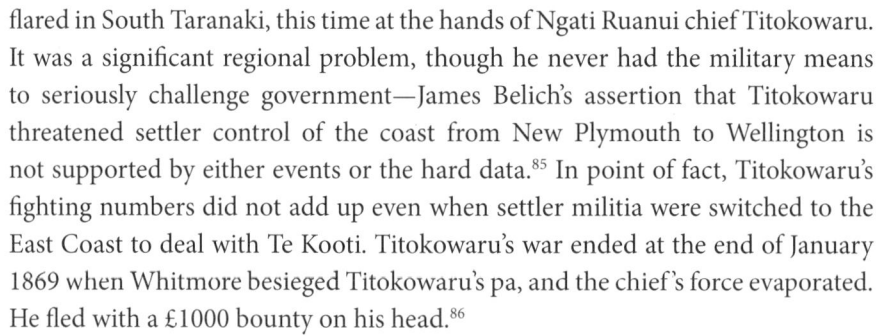

flared in South Taranaki, this time at the hands of Ngati Ruanui chief Titokowaru. It was a significant regional problem, though he never had the military means to seriously challenge government—James Belich's assertion that Titokowaru threatened settler control of the coast from New Plymouth to Wellington is not supported by either events or the hard data.[85] In point of fact, Titokowaru's fighting numbers did not add up even when settler militia were switched to the East Coast to deal with Te Kooti. Titokowaru's war ended at the end of January 1869 when Whitmore besieged Titokowaru's pa, and the chief's force evaporated. He fled with a £1000 bounty on his head.[86]

The last phase of the New Zealand wars revolved around Te Kooti Arikirangi Te Turuki (c1830–1893), who founded another syncretic religion, Ringatu, and was one of the most complex and multi-dimensional characters of settler-era New Zealand. He was a charismatic leader, intellectual, loyal to his friends, and—despite efforts of post-colonial historians to downplay the point—a master of terror, who was directly or indirectly responsible for a good deal of death and suffering.[87] He had worked for the settler authorities, fallen out with his employers in 1866, and McLean exiled him to the Chathams. Te Kooti believed he had been wrongly imprisoned, but his calls for a trial fell on deaf ears. In mid-1868 he and his followers seized the schooner *Rifleman* and landed near Gisborne. He was pursued as an escaped prisoner, attracting support from disaffected Maori.[88]

Te Kooti was more guerilla leader and terrorist than military commander, and his two largest engagements—Ngatapa and Te Porere—were poorly handled. However, he ran an effective terror campaign, discomfiting settlers on back-country stations with the power of rumour alone. David Balfour, on his leasehold property midway between Napier and Wairoa, recalled that 'for about four years I very rarely lay down at night without a loaded rifle for my bedmate…my pen entirely fails me now to paint the fears, troubles and anxieties that I (and all others in the district) had during these next four years, principally through undefined dangers…in my case, as I was often alone, imagination would often conjure up something to be afraid of and render me truly miserable.'[89] Government response was torpedoed by a feud between Stafford and McLean, and further undermined by arguments between McLean and Whitmore. This led to both McLean and Ormond joining the opposition party of William Fox in late 1868, action decried by the *Advertiser* as the 'most unconscionable instance of ratting ever known in the Colony.'[90]

When Te Kooti struck Poverty Bay at the end of the year, McLean tried to get a relief expedition sent from Wairoa, but argued with the local commander, and meanwhile Te Kooti established a stronghold at Ngatapa. Whitmore was authorised to lead a force against it, although the *Hawke's Bay Herald*—the mouthpiece of the Ormond-McLean faction—suggested that he possessed 'neither the confidence nor the goodwill of either Maori or European.'[91] McLean feared the Colonel might alienate the kupapa and asked government to rescind their decision, but Native Minister J. C.

CHAPTER FIVE
DESPERATE TIMES

Richmond told him it was too late. In response McLean withdrew his support from the Poverty Bay campaign, and with it the Hawke's Bay militia and around 700 Ngati Kahungunu. He also organised a separate campaign into the Urewera, defying a government ban on independent provincial action.

Whitmore 'had relied on the Napier natives to complete the investing force' at Ngatapa,[92] complicating a difficult siege which ended with Te Kooti's escape. Some of the defenders were summarily executed by kupapa, to the horror of the militia. As one recalled: '...8 had that morning been shot in camp...we saw the bodies...lying out in a row, amongst whom I recognised Renata Tupara, Wi Kipa etc; altogether some 150 are supposed to be killed.'[93] This 'Ngatapa massacre' was prosecuted by Maori against Maori, and it is arguable whether Whitmore could have stopped them—but in any case, he did not try. This was revenge by proxy for the Marawhero massacre of a few weeks earlier. Te Kooti escaped, and the Wairoa

ABOVE
This picture has been variously identified but appears most likely to be a group of Maori prisoners on board a hulk in Wellington harbour.

Photographer unidentified, Alexander Turnbull Library, F-4134-1/2

LEFT
Ngatapa, where Te Kooti was besieged by colonial militia and kupapa at the end of 1868.

James Crowe Richmond, Alexander Turnbull Library, A-048-011

ABOVE

Officers and men of the Colonial Defence Force at Waikaremoana, 1868.

George Henry Swan, Alexander Turnbull Library, F-106151-1/2

campaign did not achieve anything either, because Te Kooti did not retreat from his stronghold when Whitmore approached, and the Wairoa group could not intercept him inland as intended.[94]

As a result Te Kooti was able to raid Rauporoa, near Whakatane, in March 1869. Immediately afterwards he led about 100 followers to Mohaka in northern Hawke's Bay, massacring 57 Maori and seven settlers, including John Lavin and his family. Balfour and several others reached Mohaka with a relief column and joined a group looking for Lavin. They found the family dead, and Balfour reconstructed what happened from the positions of the bodies. The three children, aged about four, six and eight, had been playing by the river when Te Kooti's men appeared. The children fled, but had not gone far before they were tomahawked from behind. Lavin apparently realised something was wrong and hid with his wife in manuka scrub on a flat behind the house, but they were quickly located. Lavin returned fire with a revolver, but a

> ...half-caste Hauhau [sic], who knew Lavin well...called out 'Lavin, come and take your children with you.' They (the Lavins) thinking it was some friend...showed themselves and were instantly shot dead and died in each other's arms.[95]

Post-colonial analysis has tried to paint the attack as utu against Lavin,[96] but the argument is not compelling. The children had been murdered in cold blood by any standards. Government response to the raid was decisive. Whitmore and 600 armed constabulary were transferred to the East Coast and, against McLean's objections, launched a systematic scorched-earth invasion of the Urewera with the support of kupapa. This response, as brutal in its own way as the murder by Te Kooti's men of fleeing children, ended Te Kooti's threat to the East Coast. However, a change of government later in the year introduced more political complications. McLean became defence minister under Fox. Whitmore was sacked, and responsibility for a campaign to crush Te Kooti fell on Ormond, who organised it from Napier in his capacity as Hawke's Bay Provincial Superintendent. The embittered Whitmore later claimed that Ormond was so obsessed with cost-cutting that the appointed commander, Thomas McDonnell, 'rarely had a complete day's ration at all, never knew when to expect a convoy, and was always absolutely without reserve.'[97] Ormond, for his part, told McLean that he was 'positively getting ill with work and worry.'[98]

McDonnell met the Hawke's Bay kupapa at Moawhango and advanced across the Rangipo desert in heavy rain while Ngauruhoe belched ash and smoke. It was an apocalyptic start, but Te Kooti was no battlefield strategist, and the settler forces had little real difficulty taking his iconoclastic field defence at Te Porere. Te Kooti fled to the King Country. Never missing a beat, the *Hawke's Bay Herald* took the opportunity to blame his being 'let loose in our midst' on the 'criminal neglect of the late Ministry'[99]—an attack on Stafford. McLean tried to negotiate with Tawhiao, but thanks to what Whitmore called 'our imbecile management of affairs'[100] was unable to persuade him to hand Te Kooti over. McDonnell became the scapegoat because, according to the bitter Whitmore, 'Mr Ormond was too influential a member of the party, and Mr McLean too necessary to it, to be called to account.'[101]

Te Kooti left the King Country and was pursued by Ngati Kahungunu, Te Arawa and Ngati Porou. After a final engagement in mid-February 1872 the religious leader fled again into the King Country, where he remained until his pardon in 1883.

ABOVE

Horonuku Te Heu Heu Tukino IV (1821–1888), paramount chief of Ngatu Tuwharetoa, joined Waikato against the British invasion in 1864 and subsequently supported Te Kooti. Aftter the settler victory at Te Porere he was persuaded to surrender to the British and taken to Napier, where Donald McLean placed him under house-arrest, in the care of Ngati Kahungunu.

Samuel Carnell, S. Carnell Collection, Alexander Turnbull Library, G-22227-1/4

Priming the fires

New Zealand was in dire straits by the late 1860s. The economy was faltering and the combination of King Country, Te Kooti and Titokowaru showed that the state had yet to penetrate the North Island. It was a complex plight which Julius Vogel—Colonial Treasurer from 1868—hoped to resolve with a grand strategy to build an infrastructure, bring in settlers, and reduce the North Island hinterland. Keith Sinclair has argued that his policy was a precursor to twentieth-century state intervention.[102] That is debatable. Vogel occasionally espoused his own brand of social idealism, but he was a man of his time, and his main motives were a response to the 1860s.

The more compelling argument is that he was trying to rekindle the boom years of the goldrush days in the belief it would set the fires of economy burning,[103] a point evidenced by the fact that he saw state spending on rail purely as a trigger for private enterprise to pick up the momentum. Nor were his proposals far

ABOVE

Early train on the Auckland-Onehunga line, December 1873. The locomotive is an F-class 0-6-0 tank, workhorse of Vogel rail and a common sight from Auckland to Bluff during the last decades of the nineteenth century.

Albert Percy Godber, A. P. Godber Collection, Alexander Turnbull Library, PAColl-3039, F-1523-1/2-APG

out of line with prevailing thought. In New Zealand's expanding frontier world, private enterprise could only succeed when working co-operatively with the state; the debate was over the balance point. Vogel was shifting the fulcrum, but not the fundamental structure.

Vogel envisaged a general drive to open up the North Island and develop it, bringing in settlers for the purpose, and building road, rail and telegraph links to draw it all together. In many respects it was a practical move, reflecting the growing power of centralism. The lynch pin was rail. The iron horse had been a particular theme of public debate for years, as much tied to prestige as practical economics. Lines were started by Auckland, Otago and Canterbury, and there were calls for others in Taranaki and Hawke's Bay. The Wellington Provincial Council even surveyed an inland link from Foxton. Everybody wanted rail, in part because of the status, but mainly for its well-established economic benefits. The problem was paying for it. From Vogel's perspective there was also the fact that none of these schemes were particularly co-ordinated. Central government had already convened a Select Committee in 1867 to avert a 'war of the gauges'. However, although underscoring the need for a unified gauge, the Committee nonetheless recommended continuing the fragmented provincial rail system.[104]

Vogel swung to a more centralised approach, though he did not envisage a state rail monolith, wanting some lines run as 'revenue rail' on the American model and anticipating that private lines could spring from the state initiative. There was also a political motive. Vogel had more than just colonial development in mind. Peace had not yet been negotiated with Waikato and the King Country, and a large part of his schemes flowed from a practical drive to push the colony into Maori spheres, whether they wanted it or not. Building rail into the hinterland was one of the key devices for doing this, a motive that stood quite apart from the economic benefits officials presumed it would bring for Maori, and Vogel knew it. Indeed, this was one of the main reasons why the main trunk line was driven through the King Country from the 1880s, and the Prime Minister of the day, Robert Stout, effectively admitted as much during the ceremonies to turn the first sod.[105]

The problem in 1870 was paying for even the branch lines that Vogel envisaged might kick-start the scheme and provide a nucleus for a national network, quite apart from all the other aspects of his general development scheme such as telegraph and the large-scale immigration he needed to bring it all to fruition.

He found some money on the London market, and public works expenditure rose from £284,000 in 1871 to £725,000 in 1872, peaking at £2,332,000 in 1874—around $466 million in today's money. The railways absorbed a large chunk of this cash.[106] Costs were projected to be £7.5 million over ten years, around $1.5 billion in early 21st century money. Vogel hoped to offset expenditure by offering Crown land in part-payment to the builders, John Brogden and Sons. His plans were also penurious; the Railways Act of 1870 authorised lines to the 3 feet 6 inch gauge that the Committee had come down against, largely for cost reasons. Those constraints also meant early Vogel lines were limited to light rail, narrow tunnels and tight curves—all of which made borrowed money go further, but the physical limits restricted speed and rolling stock for decades afterwards.

Along the way Vogel levelled part of the costs directly on the provinces and secured the loans he needed on the security of six million acres of provincial land. That set him against the provincial oligarchs, and George Grey emerged from an eccentric retirement on Kawau Island to lead the attack. Tempers ran high and there was even talk—led from Otago—of separating the South Island from the North. Grey's oligarchs managed to stop part of Vogel's legislation, notably a Forest Conservation Bill. The only way Vogel could undermine them was by making the state bigger than the provinces. The focus of power had already been shifting to central government for some time, and by 1876, using precedent from the 1858 New Provinces Act, Vogel had abolished the provinces, replacing them with a system of smaller counties, boards and local authorities with far less local power. There was more than just a local rationale for Vogel's

ABOVE

Enigmatic social thinker, Colonial Treasurer and sometime Premier Julius Vogel (1835–1899) was prime mover behind the state policies of the 1870s.

Photographer unidentified, Alexander Turnbull Library, PA2-2831, F-92898-1/2

RIGHT

New Zealand's narrow and sinuous track restricted locomotives to small tanks such as the F-class—until the Fairlie Patent arrived. This is one of the engines being reassembled near Wellington's Thorndon station, probably during the early 1880s.

Photographer unidentified, Alexander Turnbull Library, PAColl-7477, F-4671-1/2

BELOW

Mount Victoria, Wellington, in the early 1870s. Fenced sections typified urban life from the earliest settler days.

Photographer unidentified, M. J. Stace Collection, Alexander Turnbull Library, PAColl-5907, F-125984-1/2

focus; the fact was that eight or nine tiny New Zealands could not foot it with six Australias across the Tasman, but one integrated New Zealand was on a par with any one of the Australian colonies.

Rail spread across New Zealand, and by 1874 some £5,575,400 had been allocated for just over 1000 miles (1609.34 km) of line.[107] A little over 808 miles (1300.35 km) had been completed in the South Island alone by 1879. Gross receipts that year topped £601,000.[108] The North Island was less developed, with some 336 miles (540.74 km) of rail—including just over two miles of special three-

Armstrong and Son's Whanganui smithy, early 1870s.
William James Harding, W. J. Harding Collection, Alexander Turnbull Library, PAColl-3042, G-146-1/1

rail incline—pulling in just over £156,000.[109] The North Island's 58 locomotives ran more than 712,000 miles (1.14 million km) and carried 700,000 passengers—many of these repeat journeys, but indicative of the value people placed on rail. Perhaps more critical was the bulk cargo. North Island lines carried just over 176,000 tons of freight that year, including wool, timber, minerals, firewood and merchandise. Livestock—tallied separately—included 65,600 sheep and nearly 11,000 horses and other animals.[110] These figures are made all the more spectacular by the fact that the lines were fragmentary.

Settlers from the Wychwood

The second main lynch pin of Julius Vogel's scheme to develop New Zealand in the wake of the wars was a subsidised emigration scheme. This was broadly intended to open up and populate the 'dark triangle' of the North Island, and to a large extent it did. The influx transformed the demographic landscape and pushed the settler population from just over 297,654 in 1874 to 412,465 four years later.[111] Natural growth did not exceed imported growth until the last four years of the 1870s, and it was not until the depression of the 1880s that the flood of settlers finally fell away.[112]

These new settlers differed from those of earlier decades. The New Zealand government had long coveted labourers, but they were hard to attract until the early 1870s, when they came in droves. Part of the reason was the reduction of rural conditions in Britain, culminating in the 1872 'Revolt of the Fields'.[113] Tenure

ABOVE

A picnic on Craigmore station in 1871.

Photographer unidentified, Alexander Turnbull Library, G-38440-1/2

BELOW

One of the worst disasters of New Zealand's settler era befell the *Cospatrick* off the Cape of Good Hope, when she burned and sank with heavy loss of life.

Samuel Calvert, wood engraving, Alexander Turnbull Library, PUBL-0047-1875-09

in the rural rick was unsteady at best, and the poor did not have the right to enough property to feed themselves. Nor was employment secure, and trouble flared across whole districts. Emigration was often a community phenomenon. Two-thirds of all Oxfordshire migrants of the period, for instance, emigrated to New Zealand in 1874—a statistical glitch among migrants who came disproportionately from south-west England.[114]

The experience of Ascott-under-Wychwood resident Philip Pratley was typical. Pratley worked for tenant-farmer Robert Hambidge, and when they struck for more wages in April 1873, Hambidge tried to bring in outside labour. Local women picketed the farm and 16 were arrested, including Pratley's wife Elizabeth. These 'Ascott Martyrs' were sentenced to short prison sentences with hard labour, souring feeling towards government and employers alike. When New Zealand agent Charles Carter touted the benefits of emigration at nearby Milton-under-Wychwood in mid-November, Pratley listened. Within a few weeks he and his wife had left for Ahuriri on board the *Mongol*. Their move paved the way for others in the extended family, and by the end of the decade Pratley's brothers and several other relations had emigrated, some to Timaru, the rest to Hawke's Bay.[115] Chain migration of this kind was common, and often continued for some time—in the case of the Pratleys, one relation reached New Zealand with his family as late as 1888.[116]

There was a similar pattern in Lincolnshire, where agent William Burton exploited the popular sense of injustice, promising greater rights of free speech and public assembly in New Zealand. Two thousand left, despite efforts by local authorities to dissuade them.[117] One paradox remains: Cornwall, largely unaffected by the revolt of the fields, with Oxfordshire, provided by far the highest proportion of migrants in the early 1870s. The key factors were probably the tin and copper industries; the highest migration correlates with their lowest fortunes.[118]

The journey to New Zealand was different from that of even ten years earlier. Cabin passage was much the same, but Vogel was determined to fix the problems faced in steerage—this was a

ABOVE

Many of the Scandinavian settlers arriving in Hawke's Bay disembarked in Napier, then hemmed in by swamp. This is a view from Hastings Street looking north to Carlyle Street. The river in the foreground was a flood menace.

William Williams, E. R. Williams Collection, Alexander Turnbull Library, PAColl-0975, G-25613-1/2

government effort and the emigrants 'should be made in every way as comfortable as the circumstances of a long sea-voyage will permit…the consideration of expense is in no way to interfere with arrangements for the security of their health.'[119] Ship's surgeons were asked to haul captains into line and the ships— invariably private charters—were inspected on arrival.

This produced some spectacular results, among them the *Salisbury*, which arrived in New Zealand with all on board who had departed Plymouth.[120] 'Everything that was possible seems to have been done for their comfort on board,' Edward Green reported of the *St. Leonards* in September 1873.[121] 'Extreme cleanliness was noticeable in every part of the ship,' another inspector remarked about the *Brerar*.[122] The *Helen Denny* left short on flour, but the captain 'endeavoured, by issuing his cabin stores, to make up the deficiency.'[123]

Other ships did not meet the standard, and at such times even three months in a leaky boat was intolerable. 'In consequence of the ship *Wild Duck* leaking so much,' ship's surgeon H. L. Diver reported, 'many of the immigrants had to crowd into other berths than their own…medical comforts were very short of the quantities ordered…no quicklime…soup very short,…soap ditto, very little charcoal…I consider it a miracle that half my people did not die…'[124] The *Columbus* got a pasting for failing to provide the 'dietary [requirements] of young children' and having a broken water condenser.[125] The *Hovding* ran short of supplies altogether, 11 children died, and the Danes on board made a formal complaint when they reached Napier. The commissioners found no particular

NEW ZEALAND
AN ILLUSTRATED HISTORY

180

evidence of problems, decided to have local immigration officials charge the captain anyway—then had to drop it when they discovered that captains could not be charged under the law. Ormond, as Provincial Superintendent, could not 'enter further into the case' once the commissioners had decided not to pursue it—though he worried about the number of unmarried mothers who had inveigled themselves on board and could not support themselves in New Zealand.[126]

The *Star of India* embarked without the 'cheese, carrots and onions' promised in the dietary scale on the migrants' tickets,[127] and Vogel personally castigated the 'gross carelessness' with which the 'despatching and inspecting officers' had handled this ship.[128] The *Woodlark* reached Port Nicholson in March 1874 with scarlet fever on board. The disease killed 18 children during the voyage, and two more died while the ship was in quarantine.[129] The *Surat* wrecked on arrival at Port Chalmers and the settlers lost all their 'clothing, bedding and effects' because the hulk and all its contents were salvaged and 'sold at public auction' despite protests by the survivors. Vogel rectified the problem after the survivors protested to the Governor.[130] A worse fate befell the *Cospatrick*, which caught fire and sank in the South Atlantic.

Many of the settlers were women, deliberately sought to rectify the demographic imbalance. Scandinavians were considered particularly desirable, and when about 550 Danes were due to arrive in Napier on board the *Hovding* and *Ballarat* in September 1873, one newspaper lasciviously welcomed the 57 single women known to be on board, who with their 'blue eyes and flaxen hair' would 'prove a welcome addition' to the province.[131] How willing these and other

ABOVE

J. G. Wilson drives the region's first buggy in this southern Hawke's Bay scene of the late 1880s.

Photographer unidentified, Alexander Turnbull Library, F-106864-1/2

OPPOSITE TOP

Foxton during the 1870s: a typical settler town in the Vogel era.

William James Harding, W. J. Harding Collection, Alexander Turnbull Library, PAColl-3042, G-333-1/1

OPPOSITE BOTTOM

The Maharahara dairy factory in southern Hawke's Bay.

James McAllister, James McAllister Collection, Alexander Turnbull Library, PAColl-3054, F-3560-1/2)

RIGHT

This 1904 picture of the Gate family reveals the conditions many faced even 30 years after settlement. Left to right: unknown; Alan or Ernest Gate; Anne Gate (nee Mather) holding Hope; Ernest or Alan Gate; Harriett Gate, unknown on horse; Aaron Gate.

James McAllister, James McAllister Collection, Alexander Turnbull Library, PAColl-0975, G-10246-1/1s

Scandinavian women were to emigrate is unclear. Anecdotal evidence suggests some were enticed by subterfuge.

Few found fortune in the new land. Vogel picked Scandinavians to pioneer the dense bush of the Manawatu, northern Wairarapa and southern Hawke's Bay after discovering that a small group did well in Palmerston North in the late 1860s.[132] The popular image of poor settlers hacking lives out of the bush largely emerged from this period, though it was limited both geographically and in time. There were two motives for this invasion of the hinterland. As G. H. Scholefield remarked in 1904, the 'doctrine of progress declared that the bush must be destroyed under the guise of improvements.'[133] However, the more compelling reason was political. In 1870 much of the central North Island remained dark to the colony. Bush had been a friend to Maori during the guerilla phase of the wars. Settling these lands and eliminating the Maori ability to shelter themselves was another step towards enforcing settler power.

The first Vogel migrants were settled on 40-acre lots in the Manawatu during 1871 and given the task of building a road and tramway to Foxton. Others went into the shadow of the Ruahines, where they helped hack a road through the Manawatu Gorge into southern Hawke's Bay. By the early 1880s enough bush had been cleared to begin dairying. Other settlers were sent to the northern Wairarapa, nibbling into the bush from the south.[134]

Not all were Scandinavians; in a demonstration of the power of historical

Dairying spread across Taranaki and southern Hawke's Bay during the Vogel period. This is the Rukuhia factory around 1907.

Photographer unidentified, Alexander Turnbull Library, G-89356-1/2

myth-making, Danes and Norwegians made an impact in southern Hawke's Bay—but were outnumbered by Scottish settlers brought in by similar schemes. Most were dismayed to find their promised farmland clad in thick bush. Access to southern Hawke's Bay was along a bridle track cleared to serve Oringi and Tahoraiti stations, both of which had been operating in the Oringi clearing since the early 1860s. The settlers were expected not only to fell bush to clear their own properties, but also to pay off their passages and land by clearing bush for the railway. Settlement spread from Norsewood and Dannevirke, and more settlers were brought in during 1874, colonising Makaretu. Altogether only around 4000 Scandinavians arrived in the decade after 1872, but they worked diligently with their Scots neighbours and in just 15 years most of the vast tract of bush between Takapau and Eketahuna was reduced to burnt stumps and scrubby pasture, an orgy of government-inspired arson. The scale of it shocked sensibilities even in an age when the ability of humanity to alter the environment was upheld as a barometer of human 'progress'. James Inglis, visiting Hawke's Bay in 1885, condemned the 'wholesale denudation' which, he claimed, would 'exact its retribution in widespread ruin and desolation.' Others had commercial concerns. J. G. Wilson insisted, later, that the destruction of bush in his home district of Umutaoroa 'was premature' and 'would have seen a keen market' ten years later.[135]

For the settlers trying to make a living from the land they had been promised the greater problem was penury. They had emigrated to better themselves, but there seemed very little betterment in their new lot. State wages of around six shillings a day—less land and passage costs—did not go far, and many small migrant farms were just staggering to their feet when depression bit. Nor was dairying a panacea. Butter was initially almost worthless and the newcomers had to find other products. Manawatu settlers found milling lucrative. In Taranaki and Hawke's Bay, edible fungus—*Auricularia auricula-judae*—proved a winner. It had a keen market overseas, and some £375,000 worth was collected and sold nationally between 1872 and 1904, typically at 3 pence a pound.[136]

The wider experience of many of the Vogel-era settlers, and particularly those who found themselves clearing bush in Hawke's Bay, the Manawatu and northern Wairarapa, underscored one of the truths of New Zealand's settler reality. Money had become an arbiter of social division. When sections in Woodville were advertised in November 1874, small settlers were swamped by speculators such as H. B. Sealy, who bought 800 acres at 50 shillings an acre and sold them in December 1876 for £800 profit. This was out of the reach of many smallholders. However, the provincial government set aside 20,000 acres which was taken up by the Woodville Small Farms Association, a Methodist group largely formed from work gangs who had built part of the railway line. This typified nationwide initiatives to make land available for smallholders and underlined a shift in policy. Complaints that too many 'foreigners' were coming in eventually carried enough weight to deter government from seeking settlers outside Britain—in 1883–84, for instance, there were just 55 Scandinavians among 6267 migrants.[137] The hardships faced by all these people reinforced the imagery of a rugged colonial origin, an ethos that became part of New Zealand's founding Pakeha mythology and helped lay the foundations for the twentieth-century ideal of capable, do-anything individualists.

CHAPTER SIX
Prelude to a century

New Zealand changed dramatically between the mid-1880s and the outbreak of the First World War. In some ways the country was moving ahead; the first generation of Pakeha born in New Zealand were growing to adulthood and into positions of office, influence and authority. New social trends rose with them. The rising left, effectively emerging as a prototypical class for the first time, began flexing its muscles in the coal mines of the West Coast and around the railway work gangs. Churchmen urged temperance. Women, too, pushed for national sobriety, national restraint—and the vote for themselves. They got it too, and in this respect New Zealand led the world.

In other ways, though, the country floundered. The economy bumped along from indifferent moment to indifferent moment, a period of either depression or rebalancing, depending on viewpoint. In some respects the progressive social movements of the day were as much response to this as they were to shared ideas brought in from overseas. Economic gloom also put paid to colonial-age notions of building a bigger, better neo-Britain in the South Pacific; and the dashing of that ambition prompted responses ranging from re-assertion of the settler quarter acre and ideal of job security, to an evangelisation of Britain. This rush back to the bosom of the mother country became a defining pillar of New Zealand's early twentieth century.

Maori continued to decline through the latter years of the nineteenth century as settlers penetrated to virtually all useful parts of New Zealand. The turbulent race relations problems of the 1860s were resolved by brute force as the North Island main trunk line slammed through the King Country. Maori did not idly sit back and accept their fate, but for decades lived effectively separate lives. Settler society dominated, certainly in the urban areas, certainly economically. The main problems for New Zealand's settlers by the 1890s were not how two peoples might relate, or how utopian dreams might be brought to fruition; but

ABOVE
Women arriving to vote at Dabinet and Young's store, the polling station at Tahakopa, Clutha, in 1893. New Zealand was the first country in the world to introduce universal franchise.

Photographer unidentified, Alexander Turnbull Library, McWhannell Collection, C-15837-1/2

ABOVE

Light industry played an increasingly important part in the New Zealand economy from the 1880s, particularly in Otago. This is a balling machine in Cruikshank's Mill, Invercargill.

Ross, Alexander Turnbull Library, F-66218-1/2

the difficulties facing a monocultural, male-dominated colony where ambitions to make a bigger and better Britain had come crashing down with economic depression.

What followed was unprecedented. New Zealand went into the 1880s without defined political parties. By the next decade there was a party in power. The same downturn pushed the deprived together—a movement that soon became militant. These shifts swirled with the other changes of the period, many stemming from the switch to an established society, demanding such institutions as a civil service, which had been ad hoc and often personal for much of the settler period. To this was added a change in the position of women and efforts to stop New Zealand becoming, as popular fears supposed, a nation of drunkards.

These changes broadly matched developments around the world, but New Zealand's particular innovations—ranging from the policy of 'estate bursting' to new industrial-relations legislation, the introduction of universal suffrage, and the creation of one of the world's first organised government bureaucracies—led the pack, a point not lost on contemporaries. H. H. Asquith thought the colony was a social laboratory for the world,[1] while Philadelphia academic Frank Parsons went further, declaring in 1904 that New Zealand was the 'birth-place of the twentieth century'.[2]

Swaggers and soup kitchens

New Zealand's twentieth century was very much shaped by the tumult of the 1880s, which has often been referred to as the 'Long Depression'. That has since been debated in the face of strong evidence that there was a vigorous small industrial economy, certainly in places like Dunedin. Elsewhere things were not so black as sometimes painted. But whether a 'depression' or simply 're-balancing' as the distortions of the settler period worked out made little difference for many who lived through it. They still had to do without. And there was certainly a financial crisis in the late 1870s which made things difficult.

The crisis was predictable in hindsight. Vogel borrowed heavily, and New Zealand's six banks and 16-odd private loan companies followed his lead,[3] offering high rates to attract overseas funds, then lending to local borrowers at even higher rates. Bank advances soared from £3.53 million in 1872 to just over £12.8 million in 1878, mostly obtained from Britain.[4] Some of the Scottish loans were secured merely on the good name of the borrower—and with most of it going on speculative land ventures, lenders were becoming edgy. The edifice came crashing down in 1878 when the City of Glasgow Bank collapsed, in part a result of its over-exposure in New Zealand.

New Zealand suddenly became a financial hot potato, credit dried up, and New Zealand banks had to restrict local lending. Merchants, traders and landowners who had relied on the cash suddenly found themselves short. Bankruptcies doubled that year,[5] and there was deflation of 16 percent—a historic record—as the land-price bubble burst.[6] Government revenue dropped from a high of £4,167,000 in 1878 to £3,134,000 the following year, and did not rise much afterwards.

BELOW
Flax mill at Whakaki, near Wairoa, 1889.
William Williams, Alexander Turnbull Library, E. R. Williams Collection, C-9482-1/2, G-25559-1/1

ABOVE

When the government effort to build rail from Wellington to Manawatu stalled, local businessman John Plimmer rallied support and, with William Hort Levin and George Shannon as prominent shareholders, floated the Wellington and Manawatu Railway Company. The line to Longburn opened in 1886, and the company continued operating until 1908, when it was taken over by government. This is a W&MR train on the Thorndon gradient in 1892.

Photographer unidentified, Alexander Turnbull Library, F-18847-1/2

George Grey's government responded with cutbacks. Funds for charitable institutions and hospitals—lumped together in the government books—slumped from 2.5 to 1.4 percent of government spending between 1878 and 1879.[7] The administration of John Hall went further in 1880. In the face of annual deficits that ran over £700,000, Colonial Treasurer Harry Atkinson slashed public works expenditure from 37.5 to 28.7 percent of government spending.[8] This killed the Wellington-Manawatu railway and plans to create a North Island main trunk. Government ran a small surplus during 1881 and 1882, but retractions took money out of the economy. Labourers found themselves destitute. Shopkeepers and businesses who had relied on their custom found their livelihood threatened, and so it went on. In wake of bank credit restrictions, estate agents began advertising themselves as financial dealers. 'Terms very easy,' one agent advised buyers of a Waikato cheese factory. Charles Osmond, an Auckland 'Land and Monetary Agent', offered mortgages and loans, investment services, and estate management alongside his real estate business. So did Edward Wayte, whose 'House, Land and Financial Agency' had both farms and residential properties on sale in early 1884.[9] New Zealand was not alone; there was a downturn across the Empire at the time. But thanks to debt and retraction, coupled with re-balancing as New Zealand's colonial world matured, the colony certainly felt it.

Politics became chaotic. Government of the day consisted of shifting alliances as the fortunes of one would-be leader or another rose and fell. This kaleidoscope changed with ever-increasing speed in the early 1880s; there were as many administrations between 1880 and 1884 as there had been between 1873 and 1880. Neither the Hall nor short-lived Whitaker governments offered much in the way of alternatives, and franchised voters expressed their frustrations at the ballot box. Atkinson's administration lost the next election. However, the bizarre Stout-Vogel alliance that came to power twice in 1884—interspersed with another brief burst of Atkinson's government—inherited the same economic problems, and was kicked out in 1887 in favour of a further Atkinson-led administration, the so-called 'Scarecrow' ministry which renewed its retractive policies.

Unemployment soared, and even the ranks of the land-owning elite and the urban entrepreneur were winnowed. Few fell as hard as Thomas Tanner, bankrupted in 1885 by the Northern Investment Company after he defaulted on an £80,000 debt—around $14 million in early twenty-first century money.[10] Soup kitchens opened in Christchurch during 1880–81 as a stop gap, and there were strident calls for work. This eruption of poor highlighted a weakness of colonial society. Grey's Destitute Persons Ordinance of 1846 had thrown responsibility for supporting the destitute on their 'near relatives',[11] and the state had no role other than to force relatives to pay. Charitable aid was thrown to provincial authorities in New Zealand with erratic results, and support ultimately relied on philanthropy, itself far less well set up in New Zealand than in Britain.[12]

To some extent this was inevitable. One historian has argued that the settler desire to shed British systems such as the poor-house also prompted a decision

ABOVE

Southern Hawke's Bay remained a dismal mass of stumps and ruin during the 1880s, while the Scots and Scandinavians who had arrived there tried to eke a living. The longer term answer was dairying. This Matamau family pose for photographer William Williams in the 1880s, possibly on their way to milking.

William Williams, E. R. Williams Collection, Alexander Turnbull Library, G- 25773-1/1

ABOVE

This family stand in their best for the photographer outside a sawmill house near Invercargill.

Photographer unidentified, Wallace Early Settlers Association Collection, Alexander Turnbull Library, F-66205-1/2

BELOW

The plight of the infirm, old and destitute was often desperate during the 1880s, and welfare was patchy. This is the Newtown Home for the Aged Needy.

Photographer unidentified, Alexander Turnbull Library, C. M. Heine Collection, PAColl-4401-01, G-32552-1/2

to eschew welfare;[13] but in any event the colony had developed in such a distorted way as to make a sustained welfare system unaffordable. There were also philosophic issues. Total annual spending by the Nelson provincial government on hospitals, aid and a lunatic asylum was around £2,700 in the 1860s, but the per capita rate fell.[14] In Otago, the destitute were helped by the local hospital and erratic grants from government—some £200 had been voted in 1860 for the purpose. Julius Vogel helped establish the Otago Benevolent Society to put this on a firmer footing, but this arrangement was rare, and destitution—including old-age— usually meant living in cheaply run and often unpleasant quarters, although these were not numerous. Auckland's total facility amounted to 49 beds in 1880, Nelson's just a dozen. Napier's original building was dismissed in 1875 by the *Daily Telegraph* as 'a miserable refuge in which only the miserable would take refuge'.[15] Women were better catered for in Christchurch, where there was a 25-bed house.[16]

Efforts to implement a formal system began in 1877—well before the crisis erupted—when the first short-lived Atkinson administration toyed with regularising charitable relief. However, fears of creating welfare dependency deterred progress,[17] and the result was that the crisis of the 1880s created social problems which erratic personal generosity could not rectify, even when fuelled by guilt. Some observers of the day even cast these dramatic and chaotic years as a kind of social Darwinism; the downturn, apparently, had purified the ranks of the employed, allowing the fittest to survive while the undeserving and weak were cast out.[18]

For men like Bill Blackie, a station hand suddenly thrown on the scrap-heap, the future seemed bleak. After a stint at pig-shooting he set off from Onga Onga for Wellington, finding 'numerous men' in similar condition, all 'sober, decent workers' who found work 'almost unprocurable'.[19] Blackie eventually reached the South Island and found a few months' work, then returned to the North Island where he oscillated between Hawke's Bay, the Manawatu and Wellington. William Cox spent five years on the road; and even after things began to pick up was unable to find permanent work.

These itinerant men met and mingled, went about in groups or work gangs, and often found lodgings together. Ernest and Harold Weston were among them. The two brothers arrived in New Zealand in 1886, could not find work, and took to the road in 1888. Their trek took them from Auckland to Taranaki, Wellington and Hawke's Bay. There were signs of recession everywhere. A 'troll down the main street of Waipawa' revealed that it had been a 'go-ahead town at one time', but things were 'very quiet now.' They went on to Hampden (Tikokino) where they got permission to sleep in a whare with an old Irishman and somebody else from Shropshire. The former was lifting potatoes at 2 shillings a bag. They felt the towns 'on this side of the Gorge' were 'doing more than the other side. Not so many empty houses, wages higher, general hand on a farm gets 25/- a week, ploughman 30/- and so on.'[20]

As able-bodied men, the Westons were among the lucky ones. The disabled and destitute, the elderly, widows and the infirm had little option but to fall on

ABOVE

An indifferent economy did not prevent the rise of the new tourist industry, born on the back of easier travel worldwide, and the attractions of New Zealand's often remarkable scenery. The delicate Pink and White Terraces on Lake Rotomahana, southeast of Rotorua, were an early draw. They were obliterated in the 1886 eruption of Mount Tarawera, but fragments were found on the bottom of the lake in 2011. This is the Pink Terrace, Otukapuarangi, 'fountain of the clouded sky'.

Photographer unidentified, Alexander Turnbull Library, F-77660-1/2

TOP

Long thought extinct, Mount Tarawera erupted one night in June 1886, a six-hour paroxysm that sent lava, boulders and ash showering into the area, killing 147 Maori and six Europeans. The sound was audible across much of the central North Island; some thought it was the guns of a visiting Russian frigate. Three villages were destroyed. Moura slid into Lake Rotomahana. Te Ariki was crushed beneath 30 feet (10 metres) of ash, while even Te Wairoa—nine miles (16 km) from the mountain—was swamped with ash and mud. Here are the remains of Te Wairoa. McRae's Hotel stands half-crushed amid the bleak landscape of ash and mud.

Burton Brothers, Alexander Turnbull Library, F-20459-1/2

CENTRE

Two survivors beside the 'fowl house in which we spent the night'.

Photographer unidentified, Alexander Turnbull Library, G-23412-1/2

BOTTOM

The Surveyor-General and party on the ashfield at the foot of Tarawera, July 1886.

Photographer unidentified, Alexander Turnbull Library F-80868-1/2

ABOVE

Depression-era capital: Wellington's Te Aro flat in 1884, from Mount Victoria.

Burton Brothers, Alexander Turnbull Library G-2236-1/2-BB

what there was of organised welfare, a system reliant on private gifts to leaven the trickle of cash doled out by impoverished and miserly provincial authorities. Many who could afford it got out altogether; around 125,000 New Zealanders voted with their feet between 1885 and 1892, crossing the Tasman in search of greener fields in Australia.

Rail and race

> We stand here, almost in view of what I might call the classic ground of the Maori war…I think we should remember, in doing work of this class, to contrast it with the old days, the days of the past…it is by works of this character—works which are not to set race against race nor people against people, but to unite them together as one people…
> – Sir Robert Stout at the sod-turning ceremony of the main trunk line, April 1884[21]

The fact that the 1880s were as much a period of social and economic re-balancing as they were of hardship and decline was underscored by the way that many small industries emerged, particularly in southern regions where the prosperity of the gold boom was but memory. Part of the motive was need; enterprising men were looking for new ways to make ends meet, and had to do so within the limits of what they could achieve with often restricted funding. The outcome was an explosion of relatively small but vigorous businesses and industries which gave some areas, notably Dunedin, a quite go-ahead feel. Other areas, notably in the North Island, were given impetus by a new drive to finish long-standing public works. The stalled Wellington-Manawatu railway was picked up by private enterprise; and there was new attention to the North Island main trunk line. This had been long projected as an extension of existing government rail through the Wairarapa and Hawke's Bay, and debate focussed on ways of getting across the rugged Napier-Taupo stretch—an issue that became heavily politicised as local business lobbies played their battles out in newspaper columns.[22] Hawke's Bay agitators were joined by voices from Taranaki, but their clamour fell on stony ground. In the end, while the Commission looking into national railway expenditure in 1880 viewed a Wairarapa-Hawke's Bay rail connection as part of a trunk line, cost considerations killed an immediate link.

The process was kicked into particular action by the demands of race relations. By the early 1880s Maori had neither died off nor been swamped. Efforts to contest disempowerment swung to Parliamentary representation and legal action in the 1870s, and the Parihaka occupation of 1881. What was more, the King Country was still intact, and although Tawhiao made formal peace that year with the government, the region remained nominally independent. Many local Pakeha felt that renewed war could not be completely ruled out—a point recognised by Matamata's Josiah Firth, who built a strong-point next to his house.

Government was eager to eliminate the King Country as a stronghold— and rail offered a way of doing so. They had surprising allies from within the

BELOW

Main trunk line sod-turning ceremony at Puniu, near Te Awamutu. Rewi Maniapoto and Wahanui stand centre-frame in top hats; Robert Stout is to one side in a bowler.

Daniel Manders Beere, D. M. Beere Collection, Alexander Turnbull Library, PAColl-3081, G-96175-1/2

movement, though for different reasons. Both Rewi Maniapoto and Huatara Wahanui recognised the economic benefits of rail for Maori, if it could be brought to them, and agreed to allow government surveyors in, against Tawhiao's wishes. John Carruthers identified routes to Te Awamutu through the King Country— either from the railhead at Waitara, or directly north from Marton. However, Maori were not the only issue. Provincialists in both Hawke's Bay and Taranaki were calling, often loudly, for the line to be routed through their own districts, although the countryside inland from both places posed challenges and potential expense for railway engineers. However, the local voices could not be ignored, and when efforts to locate a route began in February 1883, survey parties were sent to investigate lines from both coasts.

Maniapoto's initiatives were not welcomed by all King Country chiefs, as C. W. Hursthouse's survey party discovered. They left Pirongia (Alexandra) on 12 March to identify a route from Te Awamutu to New Plymouth and headed down the Waipa Valley, but were ordered back by local Maori. A second attempt next day met the same result. On the 20th the surveyors made a third attempt, this time with the consent of Maniapoto and Wahanui. They were escorted by Wetere Te Rerenga, but when they reached Te Uira were:

> stopped by a party of Maoris under the leadership of one Te Mahuki, and violently dragged from their horses...everything was taken from them except the clothes they stood in; they were forcibly led about half a mile, and then thrust into a Maori cook house; their feet were chained, and their hands tied with rope behind their backs; they were then left for forty-one hours, during which time they were kept without food. They were finally rescued by the Natives who had been with them when they were captured, assisted by others and by Te Kooti.[23]

Hursthouse's work and that of his counterparts in Hawke's Bay revealed the impracticability of either coastal route, effectively silencing the provincial lobby. That left only the plateau west of Taupo as a potential way ahead. The North Island Main Trunk Railway Act of 1884 rubber-stamped the plan, and work began that year with the co-operation and blessing of Wahanui. There was a small ceremony

ABOVE

When this J-class locomotive reached Te Aute, central Hawke's Bay, during a trial run of the type on this line in 1887, William Williams was there to capture the moment. This is a detail from one of a series of photographs he took of this moment, including stereograms. Passengers have turned out in their best for the ride and, it seems, for the camera. The well-dressed man and woman in the cab of the locomotive are noteworthy, displacing the driver who stands before the footplate. Motley carriages ranging from Vogel-era six-wheelers to 'clerestory' coaches in American style were typical. Tender locomotives such as this J-class were introduced in the South Island during the 1880s to handle the longer routes being completed by this time. This example was brought north to try out the Hawke's Bay line.
William Williams, Alexander Turnbull Library, PAColl-0975, G-25481-1/1

near Te Awamutu in April, though Hote Tamehana wanted it deferred on the basis that Tawhiao had not given his consent.[24] Stout told a crowd of 1500 that he need not 'point out the good that railways do.' That was not the function of this line; in truth it was a means of linking the diverse halves of the colony:

> He wished the natives to know that the ceremony had nothing to do with the title to the land, nor did it affect their chieftainship...He wished to impress upon them the importance of attending to their health. If they wished to preserve their race they must preserve their health...It was important that they should pay attention to their food, and stop taking alcohol.[25]

The line was a clear challenge to Tawhiao's independence, and he embarked on various strategies to assert himself, including founding a bank and issuing his own banknotes. It did not stop the impact of the line on his people. The Main Trunk Line inched south from Te Awamutu and north from Marton, hampered more by state penury than politics, bringing the trappings of Europe into the immediate hinterland. Labourers built villages along the way, installed their families, and traded with Maori. The permanent way reached Te Kuiti in 1887, and work began on the Waiteti viaduct south of the town the same year. Progress north from Marton was also good; by the same year, track had been laid 18.5 miles (30 km) north of Hunterville.

In many respects this line was emblematic of the way the colony was pushing into New Zealand; it happened whether Maori wanted it or not. Maori continued to decline numerically, settler society continued to expand and consolidate; and government officials continued to exhort Maori to 'better' themselves. Yet in many respects the two worlds were separate and, tacitly, settler government preferred it that way. Expensive works such as the main trunk line hemmed in the remaining centres of Maori life, breaking up territories that might otherwise have become strongholds. However, this did not itself bring Maori into the settler fold. Maori lived mostly in rural settings, and even the ribbons of road and railway did not link all Maori communities with the wider world. When Maori turned up in town, it was often simply to trade.

Maori were by no means quiescent, but responses were hampered partly by the dislocations of the settler period, including the emotional distress of repeated epidemics, and partly by a diffusion of effort. Maori framed responses to settler impact through traditional systems, often re-emphasising existing processes. One of the first was the runanga, known as the komiti to the missionaries, which established what one land purchase officer called 'petty courts' partly in an effort to limit the direct impact of settler goods and social systems on Maori. The system emerged in Waikato but became pan-tribal, evangelised around the North Island during the late 1850s. It was cautiously welcomed by settler authorities:

> As Petty Courts they are really useful; for although the fines and punishments they inflict are generally excessive and, according to our ideas, quite disproportioned to the offences committed, they are always rigidly enforced; and the result has been that drunkenness, which had lately been increasing to a fearful extent among the Natives, has now almost disappeared...[26]

Gore-Browne toyed at one stage with promoting runanga as an opposition to the kingitanga, but settler governments were generally ambivalent. While legislation such as Fox's Native Lands Bill of 1862 contained provisions authorising runanga to sort out land disputes, the legislation passed by the administration of Alfred Domett actually diminished the power of the runanga as arbiter.

Maori were divided as to response and tensions grew between tribalism and movements such as Kingitanga, the drive to promote Maori through Parliamentary representation, or such strategies as the Repudiation Movement of the early 1870s. Other divisions had effect, as around Whanganui where tribes were split between kupapa and kingitanga. Some strategies ended up associated with particular iwi. The Parliamentary drive was largely Ngati Kahungunu, diffused by the competing Repudiation Movement; while Kingitanga became largely Tainui. Syncretic religions such as Pai Marire and Ringatu diffused the response yet further.

Other Maori social systems were eventually transformed by these pressures. As one historian notes, hui gained dimension as forums for discussion—notably to develop strategies for survival and reassertion. Although settler presence prohibited war, Maori began using land courts as a venue to air and resolve grievances.[27] However, this had a downside. Long stays in towns were expensive and, as Parliamentarian Robert Bruce declared in 1885, Maori were exposed there to disease. Discovering that an epidemic had swept through a group of Whanganui Maori after they had been in town for a land court hearing, he added

BELOW
The Maori economic position during the 1880s was often dire. Many formed work gangs and hired themselves to local pastoralists; William Williams took this picture of labourers digging a drainage canal at Whakaki during the late 1880s. The overseer may be John Hunter Brown.

William Williams, Alexander Turnbull Library, E. R. Williams Collection, G-25563-1/2

to the mix what he called the 'demoralizing influences' of the 'lowest class of society'. Government could not, he declared, have devised a 'more ingenious method of destroying the whole of the Maori race'.[28]

Legislation associated with the land courts accelerated Maori dispossession. The system was established by act of parliament in 1865, ostensibly—as Sir William Martin remarked in 1871—to give Maori 'safe and quiet possession of their lands, free to sell them or deal with them as they might think best, without disturbance or interference from their neighbours.'[29] But the act tried to translate communal holding into individual title by arbitrarily dividing the title between up to ten grantees. In theory they held it in trust for the rest of the tribe. In practice—as Justice C. W. Richmond put it in 1873—the certificates provided 'each of the grantees with full property in one undivided tenth part of the block—his share becoming liable at once to be taken in execution for his private debts.'[30]

It was a national issue, but the hot-bed of such sales during the late 1860s was Hawke's Bay, where Napier merchant Frederick Sutton was publicly credited with inventing the 'system of grog accounts and mortgages by which the hapless and improvident natives are gradually but surely being divested of their estates.'[31] He was joined by Meeanee settler Richard Maney, among others,[32] and official concern followed. In 1867, one official warned J. C. Richmond that Maori had begun to sell land 'in every direction' in the face of unlimited credit with local merchants.[33] T. H. Haultain was more explicit, telling the House that 'unscrupulous and dishonest persons' had 'encouraged [Maori] extravagance... to get them into debt, have charged exorbitant prices for the goods they have supplied, and have taken advantage of their ignorance or intemperance to receive mortgage over the lands...a sure preliminary to transfer on their own terms.'[34]

Period sentiment blamed Maori for being at least part-authors of their own misfortune, but the notion that Pakeha had helped push Maori into it—possibly illegally—also stood against period standards. The Heretaunga sale became a national scandal and a general focus for Maori feeling across the country. The crisis broke when Thomas Tanner used the system to purchase the Heretaunga Plains, grant by grant, in 1868–69. The move was entwined in the often vicious faction-fighting of settler politics, and wild claims flew thick and fast as the scandal erupted. The Reverend Samuel Williams was said to have 'prostituted spiritual influence' to help Thomas Tanner make the deal.[35] John Ormond had supposedly used political office as Provincial Superintendent and General Government Agent for Hawke's Bay to gain unfair advantage. When the whole affair was investigated by Commission in 1873, Justice C. W. Richmond judged that this latter allegation had 'no foundation whatever.'[36] But claims that Tanner had illegally dealt with individual grantees were proven.[37]

The Commission did not, however, give Maori what they wanted; and from this came a dual effort by elements of Ngati Kahungunu to improve representation in Parliament, and to 'repudiate' land deals. The Repudiation Movement spread from Hawke's Bay to Whanganui,[38] and became entwined in settler politics at national level. It was bankrolled in Hawke's Bay by Waipukurau landowner Henry Russell, who used it to attack the Ormond-McLean faction. The battle cost him his fortune, and when his funds dried up in the late 1870s the Repudiationists also dwindled.[39] Elsewhere, Maori tried other strategies to retain their property.

Maori Hack Race in full Costume

During the late 1870s Land Court litigants in Wanganui tried—as resident magistrate Richard Woon put it—to '"tapu" several large tracts of country, and to forbid their being surveyed for lease or sale.'[40]

Official opinion that the Maori plight was due to their own 'improvidence'[41] masked the fact that Maori were in an indifferent economic position. To some extent Maori were insulated from the vagaries of colonial economics and the sharp re-balancing of the 1880s, in that individuals in traditional society did not rely on paid employment to survive. Yet in other respects hapu and iwi were doubly hit. The steady whittling away of tribal holdings reduced access to traditional food sources. Meanwhile, three generations of European contact had created an economic reliance on European goods—blankets particularly, and by the 1880s also European clothes, tools and industrial products. Rum, cognac and brandy also featured on some shopping lists. Although liquor was not consumed to anything like the extent imagined by temperance-obsessed settlers,[42] it was certainly used at times as a palliative for the pain felt across whole communities as their way of life crumbled.

Some found seasonal work; Maori could be found around the country hiring themselves out as work gangs for the pastoralists, digging ditches or shearing. By 1891, Maori comprised just 10 percent of the population and held around 17 percent of the land—and that continued to fall.

ABOVE

Maori took a keen interest in horse racing from the earliest settler period. This 'Maori hack race in full costume' is by well-known settler artist C. D. Barraud.

Charles Decimus Barraud, Alexander Turnbull Library, B-080-031-2-2

The road to God's Own

New Zealand's first organised political party came to power in the last decade of the nineteenth century. The Liberals and their policies were a reaction to depression need, and an overdue response to the growing complexity and urbanisation of the period. A new generation was in power, and colonial issues were supplanted

RIGHT

John Ballance, self-confessed 'Fabian Socialist' and New Zealand's first Liberal Prime Minister, with his cabinet, 1891. Back row: Richard Seddon (Public Works), Alfred J. Cadman (Mines), John MacKenzie (lands), Joseph Ward (Postmaster-General), William Pember Reeves. Front row: Sir Patrick Buckley (Attorney-General), John Ballance (Premier).

Photographer unidentified, Alexander Turnbull Library, F-52824-1/2

by such matters as an ageing populace, urban growth, more developed economy and balanced demography—and with this the need to build roading networks and all the other appurtenances of Western society, including a bureaucracy. Any government would have had to tackle these issues by the 1890s, but the Liberals framed their responses around their own thinking. They were helped in part by an economy that prospered on the back of new commodities markets. Annual compound growth in potential GDP during the 1895–1912 period stood at 4.2 percent, up from the 2.6 percent of the depression years.[43]

Local Liberalism had a distinct New Zealand stamp. In Britain, the creed emerged as a political philosophy designed to leaven capitalism with socially responsible government. However, the New Zealand environment with its colonial legacy—including its ideals of security of income and property—was a different beast, and New Zealand Liberals had to manoeuvre between free-market capitalism on one hand and socialism on the other. They neither totally rejected nor accepted either position, though they were criticised both by conservative pastoralists and the radical left. Much was done with the support of the rising Labour Party, which formed in 1910 from the Independent Political Labour League, a left-leaning workers' party. The 'Lib-Lab' alliance crumbled just before the First World War. In some ways it was a difficult match; the Liberal land reform programme and cautious attitudes to social welfare were combined with new militarism and a resurgence of Victorian pro-Imperial sentiment. This contrasted with the same movement in Britain, where peace-hungry Liberals fought guns-versus-butter battles with Conservatives.

Liberalism took time to reach New Zealand; George Grey set up a Liberal Party in the 1870s, but it was the late 1880s before it gained the dimensions needed for government, fronted by such figures as burly West Coast publican Richard Seddon, left-leaning intellectual William Pember Reeves, and self-professed 'Fabian Socialist' John Ballance. They were not a party in the twentieth-century sense—there was initially no apparatus, no organisation, and little to unify members beyond the platform of reform.[44] Party feeling, it has been argued, did not emerge until after the Liberals were in power.⁴⁵ Nor were the Liberals initially very different from the oligarch-based opposition—then called the 'Opposition'—whose own views towards capitalism broadly matched those of the British Liberals. The point was not lost on voters. 'At the ensuing elections,' one *New Zealand Herald* editorial proclaimed in early October 1890, 'the vote will be taken between two sets of politicians, who can hardly be said to have separate political creeds.'⁴⁶ Ballance was identified with the Stout-Vogel camp, and Stout was expected to lead the government if the grouping won.⁴⁷

In the event, New Zealand went into the 1890s with a government under Ballance. Popular support came in part from disillusion; the old system had failed, and governments during the 1880s had made the problems worse. To this extent, the swing was a protest vote. However, a rising tide of radicalism also played a part. New lobby groups emerged in the 1880s with their own methods for solving the crisis. The State Bank League blamed the imprudent lending of banks, calling for government loans at low rates to put the country back on its feet. Radical groups with impressive names such as Knights of Labour or the Trades and Labour Councils blamed labour laws. Others, such as the Anti-Poverty League, thought the oligarch stranglehold on land was the cause of New Zealand's problems. Although no single organisation was particularly large—the Knights apparently peaked at around 5000 members in the early 1890s—they were indicative of a diffuse groundswell of opinion. It was not hard for the Liberals to find support, a point underlined by the collapse of these groups in the 1890s after the Liberals began implementing policies proposed by the Knights in particular. Another factor, at a time when other Liberal policies seemed little different from those of the Atkinson and Stout-Vogel alliances, was the rise of class feeling among the labourers, largely an outcome of the downturn, but in part imported from overseas.

Industrial unrest helped lever the Liberals into power. Strikes rippled through the country in 1890, starting in the Whitcombe & Tombs printing office and spreading to the railways, then the docks—this an import from Australia where there was similar action under way. Stout and Reeves championed the cause, but at a time of high unemployment the labour movement had little clout with employers or government, and the result was a swing to politics by radicalised workers, who threw their support behind the Liberals. This contrasted with the Australian experience where a Labor Party emerged, and to this extent New Zealand reflected expediency rather than ideology. Ballance capitalised on strident calls for labour reform from the industrial sector during his election campaign. Still, the Liberals came to power with what by period standards were radical ideas. Reeves for one had a Fabian agenda, but this was tempered by practicality, and the more dramatic notions could not be achieved overnight or even to their fullest extent—particularly as Atkinson was able to pack the upper house against the Liberals before he left office, frustrating early bills. The Colonial Office had to intervene to resolve the deadlock and, even then, it was 1892 before

ABOVE
'Undesirable Bill'—William Pember Reeves (1857–1932), politician, historian and sometime poet. He introduced compulsory arbitration as part of a raft of industrial reforms in the 1890s. He left politics in 1896 to become High Commissioner in London. His historical works included *The Long White Cloud* (1898) and *State Experiments in Australia and New Zealand* (1912).
A. Vyvian Hunt, Alexander Turnbull Library, A-122-001

RIGHT

A bullock team in Wellington's Cuba Street during the 1890s.

Photographer unidentified, James Smith Ltd Collection, Alexander Turnbull Library F-29256-1/2

RIGHT BELOW

Steam meets the Rimutakas. The best route from the Hutt valley to the Wairarapa left a 1-in-15 gradient on the Wairarapa side, which was tackled with the three-rail system invented by John Fell. The line closed in 1955.

Burton Brothers, Alexander Turnbull Library, C-6614-1/2

OPPOSITE BELOW

Cycling clubs were one key mechanism by which women socialised in the 1880s and 1890s, and the suffrage movement also flowed around these activities.

James McAllister, James McAllister Collection, Alexander Turnbull Library, PAColl-3054, G-12665-1/1

Reeves was made Minister of Labour, and 1894 before he could start some of his significant reforms.

The legacy of turmoil and debt produced other problems. There was a run on the Auckland Savings Bank in September 1893, prompting Seddon to issue a public statement designed to restore confidence.[48] It worked, but the government did not get away so cheaply the following year. The Bank of New Zealand had deposits double those of rival banks in 1878, issuing shares at a premium during the 1880s—adding £200,000 to its profits in the process. This gave the bank confidence to make more advances, but their Australian operation suffered heavy losses in 1887 and the BNZ had to transfer £125,000 to cover it. By 1890, when the decision was made to move the bank to England, total losses included

£349,000 on the sale of its international subsidiary Globo Assets, £54,000 on current business, and a further £28,000 on deals in Sydney. Law changes made redemption of notes and coin a first charge on assets, by which time the bank was in a critical situation. The Liberal administration reluctantly stepped in, backing the bank by £2 million—around $400 million in early twenty-first century money—on a ten-year guarantee.[49]

The most significant development of the first Liberal term was unplanned—indeed, not even on the agenda of the key Liberal leaders. Universal suffrage was introduced in 1893. It was a significant step. Individual colonies and local governments had been giving women the vote for some years, but New Zealand was the first country in the world to do so. Reeves put it down to an expedient alliance with temperance, and it has been argued that the movers-and-shakers thought women might help tip the vote towards prohibition.[50] However, other historians have identified the suffrage movement itself as being the more decisive step behind women getting the vote.[51]

In some senses the push by women for franchise reflected a trend towards greater democracy, itself controversial at the time. All men were given the vote in 1887, which the *New Zealand Herald* condemned on the basis that it put 'power to pledge or to waste the property of the industrious portion of the community' into the hands of 'the idle and worthless.'[52] One of the main forces at work was a broad change in the role of women, buoyed in part by the general radicalisation of the era. By the 1880s women in the Western world were moving away from the

ABOVE

Kate Wilson Sheppard (1848–1934), first President of the National Council of Women.

Photographer unidentified, Alexander Turnbull Library, C-9028-1/2

RIGHT

Agitation to extend franchise to women was grist to the mill for cartoonists. This was published in the *New Zealand Mail* of September 1893.

Artist unknown, Alexander Turnbull Library, F-31495-1/2

stereotype of the submissive and ennui-prone housewife, instead finding work in a variety of roles outside the home, getting involved in organised sport and physical activities—notably cycling—and becoming active as artists, poets and writers. In New Zealand, women found work as teachers, secretaries and clerks; and rate-paying women could vote for local authorities and boards.

To this was added moral evangelism. This emerged in the 1880s and became a driving force behind a cycle of social change that went on into the 20th century. Where Victorian-era middle classes paid lip-service to puritanical self-denial in matters of vice, the moral evangelists—tiring of the double standard—demanded conformity. Restraint was the order of the day; public displays of affection were policed, farmers even forbidden to allow stock to breed within sight of public roadways. Plunket was founded within this moral framework, as was the Scout movement, imported to New Zealand near-complete from Britain.

Temperance had always been a theme in settler society, reflecting in part the ethos of self-denial. George Maunder, though unemployed, resisted the temptation to join his uncle's business in 1867. 'Of course I could not go into the liquor trade,' he wrote later to his sister.[53] However, the gold miners, back-country shepherds, work gangs and a wide slab of others across society had other ideas. It was the age of the hip-flask, when middle-class men routinely carried brandy as a 'restorative'. Sometimes the bottles became marketing gimmicks; at one stage Greymouth's Hibernian Hotel was promoting 'pocket pistols…loaded to the muzzle with the "very finest old SCOTCH MALT WHISKY".'[54] Hotels promoted themselves generally on their range of drinks—closely followed by the quality of their billiards tables and their food.

There was a backlash in the 1880s, buoyed on the wider changes flooding society at the time. Hotels began promoting non-alcoholic wares—even naming themselves to suit, as in 'Jack's Pass Temperance Hotel' near Hanmer.[55] Presbyterian ministers in Riverton urged their congregations to oppose 'intemperate habits' by force.[56] It was a national trend, and the ageing and cantankerous former Premier William Fox even called for outright prohibition.[57]

Women led the calls for restraint, and the Women's Christian Temperance Union also provided an organisational framework for the suffrage movement. The campaign was managed by Katherine Wilson Sheppard, who provided much of the national drive, delegating local affairs to other prominent women such as Helen Nichol, Lily Kirk and Amy Daldy.[58]

The idea found fertile ground on both sides of Parliament, in part as an extension of general support for electoral reform, but also because of genuine support for the cause. Vogel sympathised with women, comparing their treatment with that of the Jews, and introduced a Women's Suffrage Bill in 1887. However, voices against were led by the bullish Seddon, and the bill came crashing to a halt amid his condemnation of 'petticoat government.'[59] Atkinson won the election that year and proposed a new Electoral Bill for 1888, which did not include women's franchise, and the issue was not raised again until the supply debate of 1890, where the majority of the House came down in favour—against Seddon's objections. Again there was no legislative follow-up.[60] By this time there was a groundswell of popular opinion; as Reeves' wife wrote, women were 'intensely anxious'[61] for the vote.

The problem was getting the shift past Seddon and his supporters. An Electoral Bill of 1891 made no provision for women, but Sir John Hall put up a Female Suffrage Bill, and the whole issue was debated again, still without result. Meanwhile Sheppard organised a petition of more than 30,000 signatures as part

Artist unknown, Alexander Turnbull Library, PUBL-0126-1894-01

BELOW

Onehunga women voting in the 1893 general election. Leading campaigner Elizabeth Yates was elected Mayor of Onehunga two months later.

Artist unknown, Making New Zealand Collection, Alexander Turnbull Library, F-2834-1/4

ABOVE

Greymouth cyclists around 1899.

Photographer unidentified, West Coast Historical Society Collection, Alexander Turnbull Library, PAColl-5376, F-96569-1/2

of a skilful campaign by the WCTU and Franchise Leagues to raise the stakes. The effort included personal visits, lobbying, public statements and attempts to woo the media. Women's suffrage was included in the Electoral Bill of 1892 but foundered on the machinations of party politics.

Ballance came down against universal suffrage in early 1893; it was election year and he feared that newly enfranchised women would vote against the Liberals. Seddon became Premier that April when Ballance died; although personally opposed, the portly West Coaster faced a majority opinion in favour. That year's Electoral Bill again included provision for women, which passed the lower house, but the upper was stacked with Seddonites, and this was where the real battle was fought. It was a clever tactic. As one newspaper put it, Seddon's group hoped to 'avoid the appearance of direct treachery...while at the same time...insuring that women shall not vote at the next election.'[62] Seddon argued that the 'political and social revolution' had not gone to referendum,[63] and some observers feared a 'great danger of the measure being wounded to death' as a result of his politicking.[64] However, Seddon's attempt to influence three wavering members backfired, and after coming to a knife-edge the bill was passed. It was 'hardly too much to say,' one newspaper reported 'that the enfranchisement of the women has been accomplished by her enemies.'[65] Six weeks remained before the election, bare time to organise registration. 'Female suffrage must be a reality and not a sham,' the *New Zealand Herald* declared, hoping that the vote might introduce a 'higher and better tone' in colonial government.⁶⁶

Women were wooed by both parties, but it is unclear whether the narrow Liberal victory of 1893 can be attributed to their vote. The other main issue of the day was land reform, and there were swings in some areas for other reasons, as in Hastings where the safe seat of Opposition leader Sir William Russell was almost upset by Thomas Tanner, who put himself forward after being bankrupted by the Northern Investment Company, which Russell part-owned.⁶⁷

Liberal policies gained momentum during their second term, including a sustained effort to build a new public service. Government offices had existed since 1840, but only the Railways Department grew to any scale, and a more extensive general administration was becoming essential by the 1890s as New Zealand society shifted from a relatively small-scale frontier society to an established and urbanised world. The Liberals put their own stamp on the change; their reforms were also part of a general effort to dislodge the personality politics and patronage of the gentry. This had enabled officials such as Donald McLean to impose their stamp on policy—and, in other cases, to feather their own nests. As late as 1885, Thomas Kirk had been made Conservator of Forests by Stout because they knew each other—Kirk was Stout's neighbour in Tinakori Road and drew his water from Stout's well.

Edward Tregear led the Liberal drive to build the public service. Policy was based on Royal Commission findings from 1866 and 1880—with a Liberal spin. To keep the senior public servants in line, Seddon insisted that any salaries of more than £200, around $35,000 in early twenty-first-century money, should come under parliamentary control. Twelve departments were eventually formed, though the old school did not go down without a fight. Nor was the new bureaucracy widely welcomed. 'Our first duty is to ourselves,' one cartoonist captioned a picture of new civil servants.⁶⁸ Another portrayed the new approach as a spider's web of 'red tape' in which the vulnerable 'Zealandia' had been entwined. Old prejudices died hard. Seddon himself was accused of 'jobbery'. There was an attempt to introduce a Public Service Bill in 1904, and many of Seddon's personal appointments had to be regularised post-fact in 1907.

There were, however, bigger issues than the public service on the table. The old settler system of private enterprise and oligarch-dominated local bodies had left many urban centres without sewage systems and, in some cases, lacking proper water supplies. Even when local authorities agreed to build waste disposal systems, the cost was often prohibitive. There was no organised hospital system. It was a national problem, and as towns grew during the late nineteenth century

ABOVE
Independent transport was one way in which the gentry could assert status and show wealth. This gig was probably photographed in the late 1890s.

Photographer unidentified, Alexander Turnbull Library, C-27173-1/2

ABOVE

Lawn croquet, probably in the Wanganui region.

Frank J. Denton, Tesla Collection, Alexander Turnbull Library, PAColl-3046, G-17384-1/1

the risk of disease grew with them. The situation came to a head in 1900 when bubonic plague appeared in Auckland. Although New Zealand only suffered one case, government responded first with a Bubonic Plague Prevention Act, then a general Health Act that created a new government department and gave officials authority to deal with sanitary problems and disease, including tuberculosis. Later, in 1909, the department took over the hospitals, a move that paid off four years later when smallpox broke out—and paid dividends again during the influenza outbreak of 1918.

Other reforms reflected a new relationship between labour force and employers. This was Reeves' initiative, though he had difficulty getting his ideas across. Much of his legislation in 1891 and even 1892 fell victim to the Atkinson-stacked Upper House. It was not until Seddon was in the Premier's chair in 1894 that Reeves made headway; that year, six of his bills were passed through the House, including his key industrial reforms. This Conciliation and Arbitration Act was designed to prod unions into existence, and to cut back strikes by forcing compulsory arbitration. No other country had introduced such legislation, and although there was major industrial unrest in 1912–13, this essentially established a half-century compact between union and employer.

The following year, fearing that Asian migrants might create a pool of cheap labour and undercut his industrial policies, Reeves tried to have an Undesirable Immigrants Bill passed. The effort failed, and Reeves ended up with the nickname 'Undesirable Bill'. Worse, the initiative put him off-side with Seddon, who now considered Reeves too radical—and intellectual—to be of use. In early 1896, the thuggish Premier packed his Fabian-influenced minister off to become Agent-General in London.

The other Liberal innovation was a rudimentary welfare state, beginning with the old-age pension, which Seddon introduced from 1898. This met the legacies both of the depression and of ageing settler society. Many early settlers were approaching retirement age by the 1890s, and while some were able to support themselves, others were not. Reeves was determined to prevent the 'social evils' of the workhouse. In this he was less left-leaning than pro-colonial; it was to escape precisely this fate that many settlers had arrived in the first place. However, there was heavy opposition. Government took four years to implement the pension scheme, and it was finally offered under socially driven criteria designed to restrict it to the so-called 'deserving poor'. Other moves were equally cautious. In 1905 the government initiated the first state housing scheme, limited to Petone. A widow's pension followed in 1908; but here the Liberals, as Michael Joseph Savage later put it, 'left off'.[69]

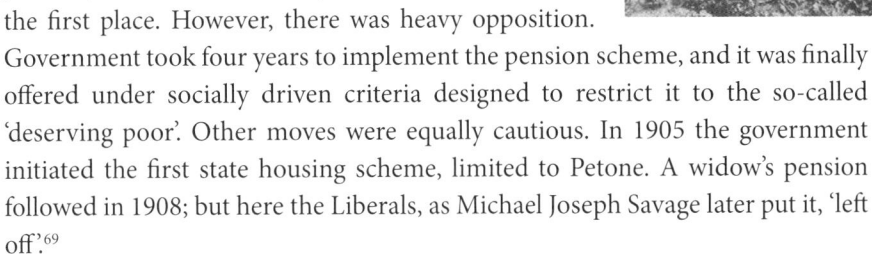

ABOVE

H. A. T. Jackson, J. Alexander and A. S. Jackson with their penny farthings around 1889.

Photographer unidentified, Alexander Turnbull Library, F-25544-1/2

Bursting the estates?

Perhaps the greatest shift of the Liberal period was their drive to 'burst' the estates. Their crusade against the gentry, which was also waged at government level in the effort to regularise the state services, has usually been seen as the cause of profound social and economic change, a final shift from the old world of colonial life. The idea came from Ballance, was put into action by John 'Honest Jock' McKenzie, Minister of Lands from 1891, and was one of the few Liberal policy planks to make much progress during their first term. The conclusion has inevitably followed that the Liberals brought down the oligarchs—indeed, one historian even suggested that gentry political rule was 'done' after the Liberal victory in 1890.[70]

This is one of the great shibboleths of New Zealand history. Estate-bursting was promoted as a radical effort to cut the elite monopoly on pastoral land and open up possibilities for smallholders. But the figures tell a different story. It is untrue to say that the elite were broken—either financially or in terms of their holdings—during the Liberal period. Politically they were far from a spent force in the 1890s. We also have to separate declared aims from the actual policies as implemented. Ballance—a self-professed 'Fabian socialist' inspired by J. S. Mill—envisioned a nation of small landowners. In this he was perhaps the most radical of his peers, but his ideas caught on. Seddon, visiting Walter Shrimpton at Matipiro Station during the 1890s, warned that if Shrimpton did not reduce his holdings, Seddon would do it for him. Aspects of the policy that followed were guided, to some extent, by Reeves' plan to provide perpetual leasehold, allowing smallholders to put all their capital into improvements. These plans were met with horror by the oligarchs; the *Hawke's Bay Herald*—one of several ultra-conservative organs of the gentry—condemned plans for closer settlement and argued that there was no justification for considering landowners 'social pests'.[71]

ABOVE

Grand homes flourished during the 1880s and 1890s. This is Mount Vernon, home of the Harding family in central Hawke's Bay, built in 1882.

Photographer unidentified, Alexander Turnbull Library, F-55213-1/2

In practice, however, the Ballance-Reeves-McKenzie triumvirate had to back off from their more radical ideas.[72] Liberal reforms, as implemented, actually extended many of the policies that governments had been trying to apply since the 1840s, this time adding a financial incentive. All land with unimproved value of more than £500 was taxed at 1 penny in the pound. On top of this Ballance imposed a graduated tax of 1/8 penny in the pound, rising to twopence in the pound for land valued at more than £5000. A few estates were actually burst. Cheviot, with 84,000 acres and 110,000 livestock, was exploded into 150 small farms in 1893.[73] Fourteen South Island estates followed by compulsion. In Hawke's Bay—still a pastoral stronghold—28 were broken by 1912. The main targets were absentee landowners, who were hammered with a further flat 20 percent tax,[74] and those who refused to pay were subject to forced purchase.[75] The national test case came in the mid-1890s. Purvis Russell, a central Hawke's Bay landowner, had moved to Scotland in 1873, and in 1896 the government informed him that his station would be purchased at 'land tax' value. Russell objected, and through prolonged legal battle, postponed the sale until 1900, when he received £21,000 over the tax valuation. Even then he offered £60,000 to retain the land—a tenth of his assets.[76] The station was divided into 57 farms in 1901.

All this created a good deal of high-profile ill-feeling, but appearances were deceptive. In 1891 there were 43,777 landholders with more than an acre, of whom a quarter had holdings of between one and ten acres, 584 had more than 5000 acres, and of these, 24 had more than 50,000 acres. Just seven had more than

100,000 acres.[77] This upper end did not fall significantly—there were 112 holdings of more than 50,000 acres in 1896, and in 1911, after 20-odd years of Liberal 'bursting', there were still 90. The average run size at this level dropped by less than a tenth of 1 percent and still stood at 90,319 acres.[78] The number of holdings of between 5000 and 50,000 acres actually rose from 732 to 926 over the same period.[79]

These figures can be boiled down to a single statistic: in 1896, 2 percent of landholders held slightly over 20.7 million of New Zealand's 33.3 million acres of available pastoral land. By 1911—the last year these statistics were collected—the same 2 percent held just over 19.5 million acres, out of a total national land-holding that had risen to just over 40.2 million acres.[80] Gentry land had dropped from around 61 to 48 percent of the total, absolute holdings had dropped by only 5 percent, and this was hardly sufficient to crumble the land monopolists. Land freed up by 'bursting' amounted to 1.3 million acres.[81] The point is made explicit from the viewpoint of land tax revenue. In a regime that penalised big landholders, the tax take stood at £272,000 in 1896. It rose to £295,000 in 1901, and by 1913 was up to £728,000.[82]

In practice, gentry land was reshuffled rather than diminished, typified by the adventures of Herbert Guthrie-Smith, owner of Tutira Station in northern Hawke's Bay. Alarmed that a Royal Commission had been appointed to investigate tenure of Hawke's Bay properties, he placed his affairs 'unreservedly' in the hands of the Commissioners and resigned the lease on the western half of his station. He was allowed to keep 18,000 acres at quadrupled rent, and the visit ended when the 'Royal Commission, not snatched up to heaven in a chariot of fire as the assembled natives almost seemed to anticipate, proceeded in a cloud of dust on its way to Wairoa.'[83] But in 1905 he was able to lease part of a block north of Te Pohue.[84]

This process of reshuffling also explains how the number of small-holders effectively doubled. The people who gained were principally small farmers and herd-owners; Liberal policies had less effect on agriculturalists—land under close cultivation went up from 8,893,225 acres in 1891 to 10,698,809 just four years later.[85] The leasehold quick-shuffle was aided by the fact that total settler land-holding expanded, particularly in the North Island. A few runs were broken up amid much publicity and high-profile complaint—but, in general, this new land

ABOVE

Oneida homestead hallway: opulence in the latest styles of the 1890s.

Photographer unidentified, Alexander Turnbull Library, F-65812-1/2

BELOW

Town houses reached new levels of luxury as the nineteenth century ended. This is the billiard room of the Coverdale household around 1907.

Steffano Francis Webb, Steffano Webb Collection, Alexander Turnbull Library, PAColl-3061, G-5498-1/1

RIGHT

New Zealand lacked foxes, but hunting was soon modified to match the colonial environment.

James McAllister, James McAllister Collection, Alexander Turnbull Library, PAColl-3054, G-9933-1/1

ABOVE

Gramophones were swiftly acquired by the gentry and picked up as prices fell by white- and then blue-collar workers. Record shops did not take long to emerge; this picture was apparently taken around 1910.

Photographer unidentified, *Evening Post Collection*, Alexander Turnbull Library, F43062-1/2

made it possible both for pastoralists to hold their own, and for small-holders to expand. The new territories came mainly from a Liberal effort to reduce Maori holdings. Between 1891 and 1911, government purchased 3.1 million acres of Maori land in the North Island, on average at just over six shillings an acre.[86] Small-holding in Taranaki, particularly, was markedly accelerated.[87] Maori tried to resist; James Carroll as Native Minister implemented policies designed to at least slow the sales. However, Maori efforts to maintain their position through these years were disorganised.[88]

Pastoral lifestyle during the Liberal years makes clear they were far from a failing breed financially. Rising wool prices after 1895 were coupled with rising yields—more than double per fleece than that of 30 years earlier.[89] Personal profit rather than inability to pay the land taxes seems to have been the key motive to sell. In Hawke's Bay, for instance, J. R. B. A'Deane sold portions of Ashcott, which was valued at £2.16s per acre in 1902, for £5 to £15 per acre in 1906. Other pastoralists who leaped on the profit-wagon included E. J. Watt, who sold Tukituki and Longlands Stations, and Douglas MacLean, who cut up 38,000 acres of Maraekakaho for closer settlement.[90]

Lucrative returns helped restore gentry fortunes after a decade of indifference, and most of the elite had cash to burn even at the outset of the Liberal period. C. G. Tripp of Orari Gorge Station spent some £4700 on luxuries in 1892 alone.[91] Almost without exception, the

LEFT

Family outing in Hawke's Bay, possibly during the late 1880s.

Photographer unidentified, Alexander Turnbull Library, F-137222-1/2

pastoral elite took swift advantage of their good fortune. New houses were the order of the day; great mansions rose, some adjacent to the older houses, others in new and wide grounds, such as the 'large and handsome villa residence' built by Blackhead settler Alexander McHardy in 1894.[92] Many spent vast sums on architect-designed structures, including the 35-room mansion Heaton Rhodes gave his wife in 1895.[93] Allan McLean outdid most with a 54-room town-house in Christchurch.[94]

New inventions offered another way to spend the lucre in which the rich pastoralists were rolling by the 1890s. They vied to buy gramophones, telephones—initially by private line—and anything else that could be run by

LEFT

Lowry Bay Yacht Club picnic, 25 January 1891.

Frederick Halse, Alexander Turnbull Library, PAColl-3041, G-10361-1/2

TOP RIGHT

Early cars were expensive, demanding specialist equipment and either a do-it-yourself mechanical streak or a friendly local engineer.

Frederick Nelson Jones, F. N. Jones Collection, Alexander Turnbull Library, PAColl-3051, G-28502-1/2

ABOVE

Dirt roads did few favours to early cars.

Isaac Jeffares, Jeffares Collection, Alexander Turnbull Library, PAColl-4870, F-80884-1/2

electricity. The younger John Chambers led the way, installing a private hydro-station in 1892.[95] By the turn of the century the 'wonder-fluid' of the age had been widely adopted by those who could afford it, and pastoralists competed to install electric lights, ranges, toasters and refrigerators. Even electric vacuum-cleaners were on the shopping list. As the first years of the twentieth century rolled on the gentry replaced their landaus and broughams with motor cars. No expense was spared; Mason Chambers' Meisse steam car, for instance, topped £450—around $72,000 in today's money.[96] Running costs on these high-maintenance devices were stupendous until garages became widespread. Cars became a focus for new rivalry, and the most powerful in the country for some time was a 24-horsepower Wolseley imported by G. P. Donnelly. New technology did not change the behaviour of coaching days:

> Bill Robin was the chauffeur bedecked in uniform and engineer's cap. You can imagine the scene with all aboard. G. P. in the front seat giving Bill Robin instructions (horn! horn!), Princess Irene in one bucket seat at the back and Maud Perry (her daughter) in the other both wrapped in fur coats, the dicky seats seating Iraia Karauria and others.[97]

This British behemoth was apparently capable of 60 mph (almost 100 km/h)—a frightening velocity in an era of rutted shingle roads and pencil-thin tyres. Other pastoralists bought Continental; Edward Mallaby-Goodwin wowed Ashburton residents with a Benz, while Walter MacFarlane of Amuri preferred a De Dion.[98]

When not belting around in fast cars, the gentry partied—often in public. There was fresh media attention to the new social whirl, as in December 1892 when the *Hawke's Bay Herald* covered a bash held by the McHardys of Blackhead, whose hundred guests were trucked in by the carriage-load to their remote East Coast property.[99] In March 1897, Donnelly hired Napier's Gaiety Theatre and invited 250 guests to a ball marking his daughter's birthday. The 'many tasteful dresses flashing their varied tints' was 'brilliant in the extreme' according to a local paper.[100] There were also 'at homes', as in 1910 when the Theomins of Dunedin gave a soirée at their town house.[101] Even then, public attention was never far away, and the prospect of gentlemen embarking on a 'series of romps' was frowned upon in some media circles.[102]

However, holding their financial position was a different matter from

ABOVE

Early motorists frequently joined clubs, partly because they could get together to procure parts, discuss problems and share interests.

Sydney Charles Smith, S. C. Smith Collection, Alexander Turnbull Library, PAColl-3082, G-20159-1/2

surviving wider social change. By the turn of the twentieth century, the settler political world was giving way to one of boards, government bureaucracy and local bodies. This was partly a function of the government reforms of the day, partly the influx of more smallholders with different social ideas, but also an outcome of the increasing scale, maturity and complexity of society. Settler society had been complex in its own way, but the one that emerged in the 1890s took different directions. Directions that ran against the elite. It was this diminution of social power, and not the land tax, that reduced the elite's influence over society; and beneath the surface arguments, it was this social change, not the reshuffle in landholding, to which the wealthy pastoralists actually objected.

That shift explains why the best organised responses to the change did not coalesce until nearly two decades after the land taxes had been imposed. The loudest protest emerged in 1910, when the younger John Chambers declared that he and fellow pastoralists had 'special duties' that 'included the guiding of public opinions'.[103] That summed up the real issue—the world was changing around them. Not one to pontificate, the Hawke's Bay landowner floated a company and got to work. His ideas were based around Herbert Spencer's principles of human competition and freedom from government interference with private property rights. His initial platform was based around the land reforms. Early settlers, Chambers argued, had taken up land 'in the hope and belief that they would be able to hand on the fruits of their labour to their children.' The number who had survived to 1911 'can probably be counted on one's fingers.'[104] He continued:

ABOVE

Christ's College, 1895. Secondary schools gained importance as the twentieth century dawned; until then, few New Zealanders had gone beyond 'Standard Six'.

Photographer unidentified, Alexander Turnbull Library, Webster Collection, PAColl-0713, F-100476-1/2

The compulsory taking of land from one owner, and handing it over to several others cannot be excused on the plea of public requirements…and what security has a landowner, or for that matter any property-owner?…Non land-owners…appear to have no conception of the sentimental value attached to land long occupied, and on which much labour has been expended…and are all too ready to value everything in terms of gold, or market value…[105]

But land was only the beginning; Chambers attacked socialism and free education, recommending private enterprise in local body affairs and concluding that 'wise laws must be consistent with natural law, and with each other…'[106] These were all symptoms of wider social change, and he put his money where his mouth was. The group bought and shut down the loudest Liberal voice in the district, the *Hastings Standard*, amalgamating it with a new conservative newspaper, the *Herald Tribune*. It was a gallant, determined effort by men who had the wealth and political motive to see their case through. But it was to no avail. They could not fight society. New Zealand's settler world with its great men and its elites, and all its imbalances, was changing in the face of new generations, of a deepening society, of better demographic balance, and of new ideas. The Liberals took the flak; but in a more general sense what was happening was far more profound.

The oligarchs did not disappear. Some, such as John Ormond, shifted gears and continued a prominent career with local bodies.[107] He did not even contest the Liberals, pulling out of the parliamentary race in 1890, to the dismay of many observers. 'Mr Ormond belongs to the class of men who are most needed in

RIGHT

Steamers and pleasure boats on Lake Wakitipu, April 1910.

Photographer unidentified, Alexander Turnbull Library, C-2408-1/2

ABOVE

A travelling party at Te Whati in November 1907. This picture speaks volumes about the contrasts of income in turn-of-the-century New Zealand; Maori had been very much sidelined from a redeveloping economy, even while the elites and rising new-rich of the urban areas partied. Nineteen-year old Kathleen Beauchamp stands second from left at the back.

Photographer unidentified, Alexander Turnbull Library, F-2584-1/2

Parliament,' one newspaper opined. 'If men of his social position…informed by personal experience of the political history of the colony, will abandon public life at the moment when a state of transition is becoming apparent, it is not difficult to understand the process by which Parliament has deteriorated.'[108] Others, such as William Rolleston and William Pember Reeves, remained important figures in national politics. While, as one historian put it, the gentry and their lifestyle had become 'but one form of rural society' by 1914,[109] the fact remains that they retained an enduring core of 'old money' and of prestige that sat uneasily with the myth of a New Zealand society of financial equals.

Frozen economics

> The London market rules the world, and the great distance of New Zealand from this vast city renders it difficult…to compete with other countries lying closer to the British Isles…
> – Editorial, *New Zealand Herald*, 4 November 1890.[110]

The economic problems of the 1880s were in part an outcome of the booster period, which provided mechanisms for a few to make a fortune, but had not given the country a sound basis on which to grow. Once gold, gum, fungus and timber had been exploited there was nothing much to sell beyond wool, and wool markets were depressed by the 1880s. In practice, Vogel's infrastructure was only

ABOVE

Bluff freezing works.

Photographer unidentified, Alexander Turnbull Library, PAColl-0095, F-91861-1/2

OPPOSITE TOP

Inside the Waitara freezing works around 1910.

Photographer unidentified, Alexander Turnbull Library, F-137280-1/2

OPPOSITE BOTTOM

Sheep fair at Ohaupo, 1896.

Reginald Buckingham, Alexander Turnbull Library, J. Atkinson Collection, F-57217-1/2

half the calculation. The country also needed export products beyond wool.

The obvious additions were meat and butter, both under active investigation by the 1870s. Enthusiastic pastoralists from Napier to Invercargill spent years looking into ways of getting mutton to the lucrative London markets without salting. Pioneer settler and engineer John Chambers (1819–1893) was one of the most active in the field.[111] His early experiments with 'warm' preservation—packing the meat with oats and straw—were unsuccessful. In 1879 Chambers and other Hawke's Bay pastoralists set up a large-scale boiling-down works. But he really wanted to export the meat itself, and perhaps inspired by news that frozen meat had been shipped from Buenos Ares to France that year, developed a blast-freezing technique which he attempted to patent.[112] The cost of freezing by the Chambers method was thought to be about a quarter that of rival systems, but the patent office turned him down because he neglected to submit a specification.[113]

In the end Chambers was beaten to the punch by his South Island rivals. The first cargo of frozen mutton left Otago on board the sailing ship *Dunedin* in 1882, fitted with Bell and Coleman refrigerators. Nobody knew whether the cargo would get through the tropics without thawing, but it reached England in good order after a 98-day voyage.[114] Chambers founded the Hawke's Bay Freezing Company in October that year. The company had a paid-up capital of £30,000 and construction began on Napier's Western Spit, but the buildings took some years to complete, and the company ran second to the massive enterprise of William Nelson.[115]

Nelson dominated the early industry. He was already active in the field in the early 1880s, and the advent of refrigeration gave an opportunity to establish a London-based company on 'a large capital', funding a factory outside Hastings to process and freeze 400, later 800, carcases a day. This was unprecedented, and Nelson 'was subjected to a good deal of quiet chaff' for assuming he could get

CHAPTER SIX
PRELUDE TO A CENTURY

ABOVE

Managers and staff of the Wellington-based Union Steamship Company, founded in 1875 as an amalgamation of several earlier organisations. It was bought by the Peninsula and Oriental Steam Ship Company in 1917, but retained its original name.

Photographer unidentified, Alexander Turnbull Library F-60016-1/2

a regular supply of sheep.[116] The first carcases were frozen in February 1884, and at the end of March around 9000 were loaded on to the *Turakina* in Napier Harbour. The refrigerator ship was a novelty—visitors played snowballs on the deck. During the 1884 season Nelson's works shifted 41,000 sheep and ten bullocks. In 1891 the capacity was increased sixfold. For Nelson this was a licence to print money, but he lost no opportunity to reduce costs—one coup was wooing the Tyser Line to carry his produce, cutting freight rates from 11/4 pence per pound to 5/8 pence.[117]

Those with less means pursued dairy products, which the advent of large-scale freezing technology also turned into a potential export. Industrial scale butter production followed the introduction of mechanical separators during the 1880s. The push to improve this machinery continued for decades,[118] and the rise of Taranaki's prosperity can be traced to these developments. Production revolved initially around small co-operative factories, relatively numerous and small-scale because the raw material could not be transported far in carts. Amalgamations followed as transport improved.[119] The thick bush covering much of southern Taranaki was burnt off in a brief orgy of settler arson, opening it up for conversion to dairy farms. Settlements pushed west of Egmont, driving north from Hawera to New Plymouth, often at the expense of Maori reserves.[120]

The key point about all these new industries is not that New Zealand was exporting protein in its various forms, but that—like wool—meat and dairy were agrarian, and they were also being sold largely into a single market. All these products underpinned New Zealand's twentieth-century prosperity, but by contrast with other nineteenth-century frontier economies, such as those of Australia and the United States, New Zealand did not particularly develop anything else to go with farming, such as heavy industry and mining. That contributed to New Zealand's slightly misleading twentieth-century self-image as a land of farmers; but it also carried risks if anything came adrift either with the agrarian world, such as extended droughts or bad seasons, or with the market into which all this produce was being sold.

Meat and dairy were also not an instant panacea to New Zealand's economic problems of the late nineteenth century. Nor did meat and dairy increase the importance of Britain as an export destination. That transition had already taken place in the 1870s, earlier if gold is excluded. Around four-fifths of New Zealand's exports were directly sold on British markets as early as 1876.[121] Part of the reason why New Zealand mutton, lamb, beef, cheese and butter could enter the market there in the 1880s and beyond was because of the business contacts created by wool, gum, flax and gold sales.

Even so, the new products were not an overnight sensation, as an editorial in the *New Zealand Herald* lamented as late as 1890. Distance, competition from other suppliers, and the 'uncertainty of its distribution' in England, discouraged New Zealand farmers from freezing all their eggs into one basket.[122] As late as 1896, meat, butter and cheese exports together still provided only 17 percent of New Zealand's total. Wool still held the lion's share at 47 percent.[123] Percentages of total exports sold to Britain also declined during the 1890s and did not trend back to the 80 percent figure until 1913.[124] This appears—at last—to have reflected the rise of the frozen produce on the London markets. Meat and dairy products combined provided 34 percent of New Zealand's exports and wool alone was down to 35 percent.[125] The key shift for those products did not come until the First World War. Britain commandeered New Zealand produce from 1915, and by 1919 more than 91 percent of New Zealand's exports were going to Britain, of which more than 90 percent were wool, meat and dairy products. Afterwards, the percentage of New Zealand pastoral products sold on British markets continued to climb, trending to nearly 95 percent of New Zealand's total exports during the mid-1920s. Wool and butter dominated sales,[126] and absolute volumes matched the trend, albeit shaped by the downturn of the 1920s.[127]

The picture is clear. Britons who were not eager for New Zealand meat and

ABOVE
New Plymouth breakwater in 1895. Track on the wharf underscores the role of railway in New Zealand's export trade.
William Collis, Alexander Turnbull Library, PAColl-3032, G-6531-1/1

OPPOSITE
The rise of Britain as a key export market from the mid-1870s pre-dated the main rise of the meat and dairy industry. It also gave power to the workforce that handled cargoes, both in and out of New Zealand. Here, watersiders offload coal on the Wellington wharves around 1908.
S. C. Smith, Alexander Turnbull Library, PAColl-3082, G-20028-1/1

ABOVE

This is the Stratford tennis club, probably during the 1890s.

James McAllister, James McAllister Collection, Alexander Turnbull Library, PAColl-3054, G-12490-1/1

dairy during the 1890s began cautiously adopting them during the first years of the twentieth century—and then, when war came, got them by direction. This happened when British society was suffering the trauma of the most lethal war in history. Tastes were moulded by the New Zealand food that arrived every day on British tables, coupled with a moral impact. New Zealand food, however odd it was to pre-war tastes, appeared reliably and consistently, replaced similar products from Europe and the Americas, and did so at a time when the world appeared to have gone mad. New Zealand, whose pre-war contributions to Britain had included the outright gift of one of the world's larger warships, could be relied upon in these uncertain times.[128] In effect the First World War became the mechanism by which New Zealand's agrarian products, particularly butter, were fully accepted by Britain—a point that highlights the role that conflict played in shaping New Zealand's twentieth century.

OPPOSITE

The Reynolds family playing doubles, Christmas 1900.

Frank May Reynolds, Reynolds Album, Alexander Turnbull Library PA-Coll-2772, F-55994-1/2

The dark side of unease

Life in late nineteenth-century New Zealand was very different in many ways from what it had been even 20 years earlier. The population was more balanced demographically, larger, infrastructure was growing, and this developing society leaned towards more organised institutional structures. It was characteristic of the way that the mid-nineteenth-century colonies around the Pacific were developing by this time; an outcome of ongoing efforts to build the road, rail, schools, sewerage, hospitals, clubs, government and all the other things that Britain had and which colonial society lacked. It was symptomatic, too, of the fact that a new generation were coming to adulthood, people born in New Zealand who felt much better grounded in the place, even if Britain was still colloquially called 'home'. And by the 1890s there was also more time and leeway for leisure pursuits by a much wider slice of New Zealand society. There were new community leisure activities, including cycling—translated, for some, into motorcycling by the early twentieth century—picnics, swimming and literary pursuits. Migrant groups, such as the Scandinavians, found unity in organised activities.

A good deal of leisure time, even among blue-collar workers, was put into organised sports, a move buoyed by the rise of sports clubs during the 1880s. Sports had always been part of settler life. New Zealand's classic 'rugby, racing and beer' culture was founded in the settler period, much of the ethos and image of it flowing from the blokeish world of the frontier. But like everything else, sports arrangements matured in the 1880s, further driven by rising prosperity the following decade, a change symptomatic of a maturing society and a growth away from rugged colonial-age structures with their elites.

That shift was particularly clear when it came to racing. Races had always been part of New Zealand's settler life; Samuel Marsden reputedly brought the

ABOVE

Kathleen M. Nunnely, New Zealand Ladies Tennis Champion, serves in 1889.

Photographer unidentified, Alexander Turnbull Library, C-8867-1/2

ABOVE

The All Blacks in a line-out against Midland Counties, October 1905, part-way through a gruelling tour of the British Isles, France and the United States.

Photographer unidentified, Alexander Turnbull Library, 1012-1/4-MNZ

OPPOSITE BOTTOM

Swimming was a popular summer activity in New Zealand, often organised on a club basis. The women in this 1899 picture are members of the Richmond Amateur Swimming Club.

W. E. Sorrell, Alexander Turnbull Library, F-29673-1/2

first horse into New Zealand as early as 1814, and organised races followed hard on the heels of the Pakeha settlements. As in Britain they were socially divided; those with money—the would-be elites—got involved with the bloodstock industry. Races themselves became a venue to display status. But they were also enjoyed by settlers from all walks of life who came for the excitement, both of the race itself and of the chance to enjoy a quick 'flutter'. Then in the 1880s the whole system gained new life and structure on the back of the New Zealand Racing Conference, which emerged largely at the initiative of the Hawke's Bay Jockey Club.

The other hot sport of the day was rugby. Again, this had captured interest and imagination in colonial times, but it gained further momentum on the back of rising institutional structures. The Nelson Football Club reputedly played New Zealand's first organised football game to rugby rules in 1870, at the behest of Charles John Monro. An inter-town match with Wellington followed. Other clubs began organising matches to the same rules during the next few years, and by the end of the 1880s rugby was a national sport with some 700 clubs and 16 unions. The first international game appears to have been played in 1884, when a New Zealand team crossed the Tasman. This began a tradition which, in the early period, culminated in a 1905 tour of Britain by a team eventually known as the 'All Blacks', a moniker, popular mythology insisted, that they gained after a British journalist referred to them as 'all backs'—and the newspaper made a typo.

The rise of organised club sports, particularly rugby, were among the trends of the day that gave New Zealand's twentieth century life its classic shape. But this

CHAPTER SIX
PRELUDE TO A CENTURY

emerging society also carried a dark side. Pakeha New Zealand's character in the two decades leading up to the First World War can best be described as troubled. The new generation of settlers, whose hopes had been cast adrift by the failure of their parents' dreams, struggled with their national image. One outcome was a social inferiority complex, the 'cultural cringe' with its unspoken assumption that anything done locally was, by definition, inferior to the overseas equivalent. This was matched with a 'try-hard' ethos, in which New Zealand policy-makers and people alike compensated by taking up overseas ideals with often painfully over-expressed enthusiasm. The same national mind-set was reflected at personal level with the ethos of personal over-achievement and its flip-side, the 'tall poppy' syndrome in which local achievers were denigrated. All these stood in some tension with each other, and all were underpinned by a transfer of patriotic affection to Britain—itself symptomatic of the 'cringe', though also founded

ABOVE

Racing at Riccarton around 1900.

Photographer unidentified, *The Press* (Christchurch) Collection, Alexander Turnbull Library, PAColl-3031, G-8259-1/1

225

NEW ZEALAND
AN ILLUSTRATED HISTORY

in wider colonial factors. Although not the sole characteristics of New Zealand society, this complex array of behaviours and the factors that drove them answer many questions about the general character of twentieth-century New Zealand.

There were benefits. An ethos that demanded compensation for perceived national inferiority helped create an environment in which some people felt impelled to make genuinely world-beating contributions in their fields. There was genuine personal talent, and an explanation for its apparent concentration in New Zealand can also be found in the frontier ethos, the mind-set that demanded capability simply in order to survive. However, while the cringe helped promote an environment in which people were encouraged and expected to achieve, it also led to the assumption that anything done locally was inferior by definition. The only way to circumvent the problem for much of the twentieth century was to achieve overseas—a rite of passage that purchased validation back home for talented New Zealand scientists, literati, musicians, military leaders and doctors.

The cringe and its flip-side rendered New Zealand very much the over-enthusiastic boy scout of Empire, openly admired as a try-hard but privately ridiculed for a laughable naivety. In the 1890s this was particularly evident in attitudes to Empire itself, which fed the notion that New Zealand was somehow the best of Britain's children, 'chief junior' in the wider Empire. The ethos survived, in part, at least until the Second World War. Its first practical expression came with the Seddon government's efforts to obtain a Pacific empire on behalf of Britain, irrespective of Imperial politics.[129] If we accept the arguments of some historians, this mind-set even helped fuel the late twentieth-century notion that New Zealand was a backward ex-colony which demanded radical reform in order to catch up with the real world.[130]

While the cringe, the transfer of nationalist affection to Britain, and associated phenomena were not the only arbiters of New Zealand society, they deserve explanation. There has been suggestion that one engine driving New Zealand to Britain was the 'protein industry' that emerged in the late nineteenth century, in which New Zealand domestic industries were effectively run as an extension of metropolitan Britain.[131] However, as we have seen, this was not a significant economic factor until the First World War and, to this extent, the meat and dairy connections were the sustainer motors, not the starter or booster. In any event, emotions towards Britain were entwined with the wider issues of cringe, tall poppy and national try-hard, all of which flourished for nigh on a century from the 1890s.

The mind-set that generated them had roots in settler ambition and the way in which ideology, greed and event conspired to collapse the ideal of a better Britain. The dream finally staggered to a halt amid the downturn of the 1880s,

ABOVE

George Mannering (left) and Marmaduke John Nixon tackle Tasman Glacier around 1895.

Photographer unidentified, Alexander Turnbull Library, F-47541-1/2

BELOW

Opoho Cricket Club, 1895.

Photographer unidentified, J. Old Collection, Alexander Turnbull Library, F-56621-1/2

OPPOSITE TOP

Scandinavian community party at the Lowry Bay home of honorary Danish consul Sir Francis Bell, 25 April 1897.

Photographer unidentified, Alexander Turnbull Library, PAColl-4957, F-76847-1/2

OPPOSITE BOTTOM

Camel at Newtown Park zoo, Wellington, around 1908.

Sydney Charles Smith, S. C. Smith Collection, Alexander Turnbull Library, PAColl-3082, G-19622-1/1

ABOVE

'For God's Own Country.' Richard John Seddon (1845–1906), former gold miner, West Coast publican and, by the time this picture was taken, Liberal Premier of New Zealand, wheels away the first sods of the Lawrence-Roxburgh railway. Much of New Zealand's 'jingo' character emerged during the 13-year reign of 'King Dick' as Premier.

Photographer unidentified, Alexander Turnbull Library, F-58363-1/2

TOP RIGHT

Garden pond, 1908, with large double-bay villa behind. This style of housing was in vogue by the turn of the century, a cut-down grand home which itself sometimes reached impressive proportions.

Adam MacLay, Adam MacLay Collection, Alexander Turnbull Library, PAColl-5333, G23924-1/1

RIGHT

End of an era. The last central Otago gold escort changes horses at Roxburgh, 1901.

J. H. Ingley, Making New Zealand Collection, Alexander Turnbull Library, F-1736-1/2-MNZ

giving a rising generation of settlers a shock. New Zealand was emerging by this time as an entity; but in the minds of its inhabitants, it was not a very good entity, and the rectitude with which successive administrations of the 1880s tried to restore prosperity was perceived by some as punishment for that failure. This also came just as a new generation grew to adulthood. They brought new ideas and a new focus of identity, but amid the sense of failure they looked beyond New Zealand for inspiration. They did not have to look far. Most of the movers-and-shakers of the 1890s had been born in New Zealand—or Australia—and knew Britain only as an ideal, a romanticised home spoken of with the rosy tones of distance by their parents. In the face of the failure of New Zealand to surpass Britain, many turned to that idealised Britain for inspiration. To this was added new defence thinking, driven by the growing sense of a national New Zealand which emerged as a general outcome of the end of the New Zealand Wars, Vogel's deliberate efforts to unify, and the overall growth and ageing of society.

All these issues were closely inter-related, but the practical catalyst that turned a cluster of concepts into a headlong rush to the bosom of mother England was defence. Academic work has shown how fears of foreign invasion from the 1870s onwards crystallised both popular and government thinking towards the notion that New Zealand was a small, vulnerable and lone outpost of Empire. At a time of economic stringency, when New Zealand had a clear place within the Empire, policy-makers and public alike inevitably looked 'home' to Britain for assistance.[132] This came just when military force was supplanting economic power as a populist measure of national strength, drawing defence issues into a complex emotional pattern founded in pre-existing ties to Britain.[133] The results reinforced both the sense of inferiority that followed the failure to become a 'better Britain', and the general mind-set that looked to England for inspiration and leadership. All this was further accelerated by the rise of jingoism, an Empire-wide style of thinking that emerged during the latter decades of the nineteenth century, taking its name from a nonsense term used by G. W. Hunt in a popular music hall song.

Jingoism glorified war, refocussed nationalist sentiment at an Imperial level, and popularly redefined Imperial strength around the size and quantity of British military hardware. In many ways it was the antithesis of the 'politically correct' ideals of a century later, but functionally similar in that it prescribed a narrow range of acceptable thoughts and behaviour. Jingoism also provided an underlying framework for many of New Zealand's twentieth-century

ABOVE

A group at Haumurana Springs on Boxing Day, 1912.

R. G. Marsh, Alexander Turnbull Library, PAColl-3405, F-77256-1/2

BELOW

West coasters on an outing near Greymouth around the turn of the twentieth century.

Photographer unidentified, Alexander Turnbull Library, F-96571-1/2

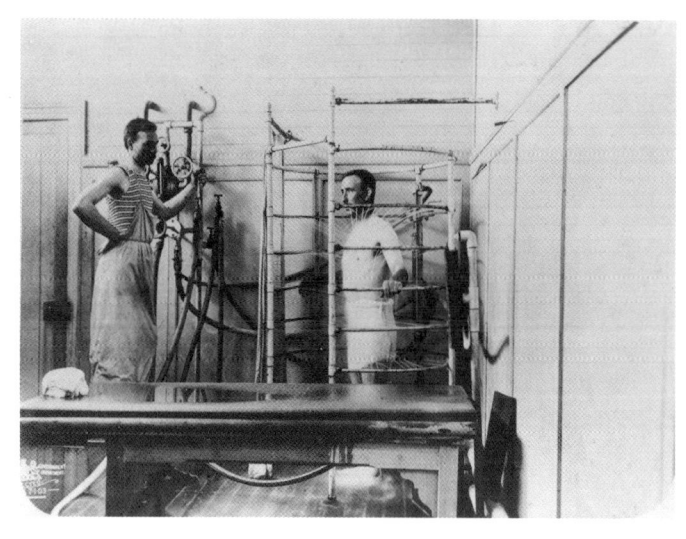

ABOVE

This gentleman 'takes the waters' in Rotorua's Aix Spa around 1903.

Photographer unidentified, Alexander Turnbull Library, Tourist Department Album 11, PA1-o-503-7

OPPOSITE ABOVE

Auckland's Hobson street around 1900, from the spire of St. Matthew's, looking towards the Cook street intersection.

Photographer unidentified, Alexander Turnbull Library G-2807-1/2

OPPOSITE BELOW

Broadway, Stratford, probably during the first decade of the twentieth century. Keeping left seems yet to be a priority in this age of walking-pace transport.

James McAllister, Alexander Turnbull Library, PAColl-3054, G-12236-1/1

RIGHT

Opening day for Christchurch's new electric tramway, 1905.

Photographer unidentified, Alexander Turnbull Library, PAColl-3031, G-8404-1/1

ideals, and its militarist aspects reflected the fact that Britain had last been at war with a European power in 1856. Society at large had forgotten the realities of the battlefield; the confusion and the terror, the desperation, the tragedy. All this was swept away in popular vision, replaced by a curious concoction of ideas drawn in part from public school traditions of sports-field glory—themselves a metaphor—which emphasised heroic deeds in battle as a device for social elevation, possibly posthumously. 'Who would not die for England!' poet Alfred Austin wrote, '...Stern to every voice but Hers...'[134]

Social militarism was all the rage across the Empire by this time. The British organised their boys into Brigades, while the Reverend William Booth's Salvationists called themselves an Army.[135] Soon there were Boys' Brigades in New Zealand, and Booth established an 'outpost' of his army in New Zealand during the early 1880s at the behest of Arabella Valpy, drawing wide support and publishing their newsletter, *War Cry*, from their Dunedin base. There were popular songs and musicals about soldiers, one of the best-known lampooning Garnet Wolseley, the 'very model of a modern Major-General'. Naval officers were lauded like twentieth-century pop stars; and when former Australasian Station commander Rear-Admiral Sir George Tryon went down with the *Victoria* off Tripoli in 1893, New Zealand's Parliament paused in respect. Children were often dressed as soldiers or sailors. Composers devised martial tunes, epitomised by the trumpet marches of John Philip Sousa—whose 1911 tour of New Zealand attracted huge attention—or the military-orchestral tone poems of Edward Elgar.

CHAPTER SIX
PRELUDE TO A CENTURY

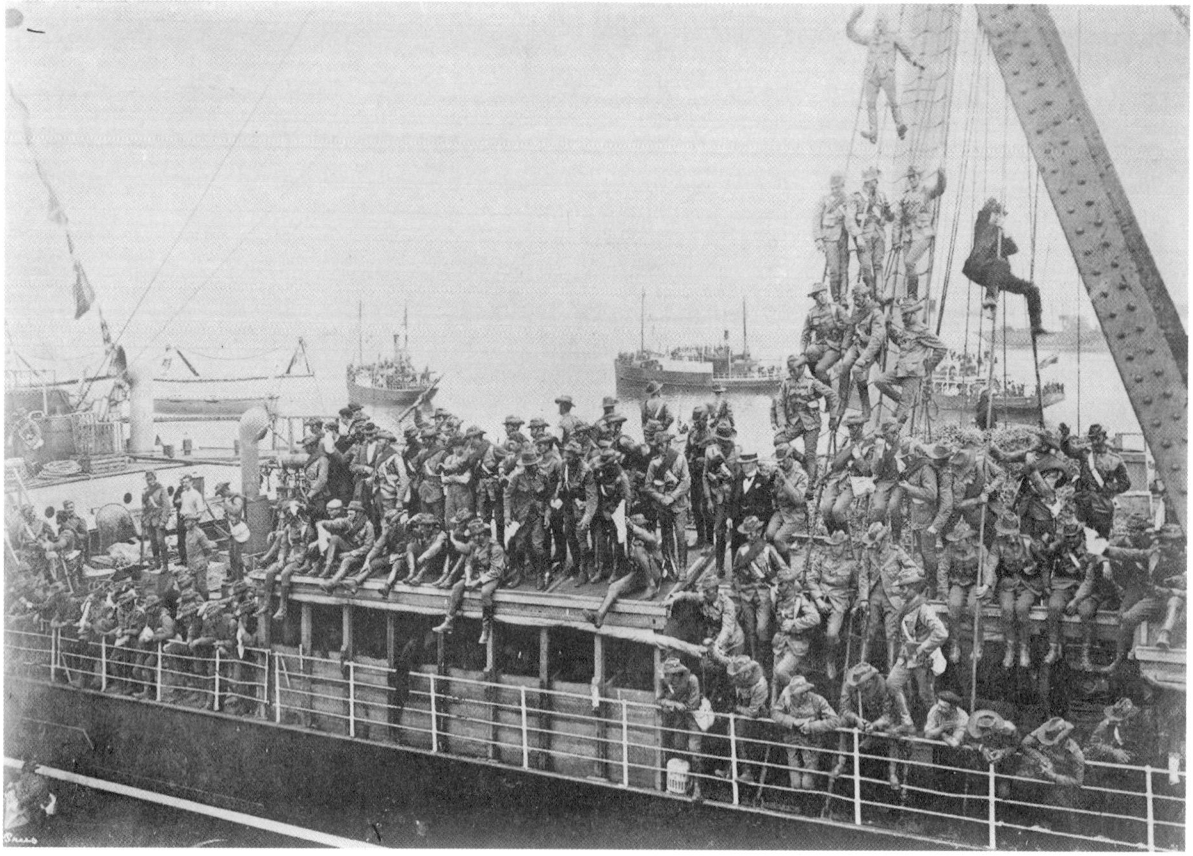

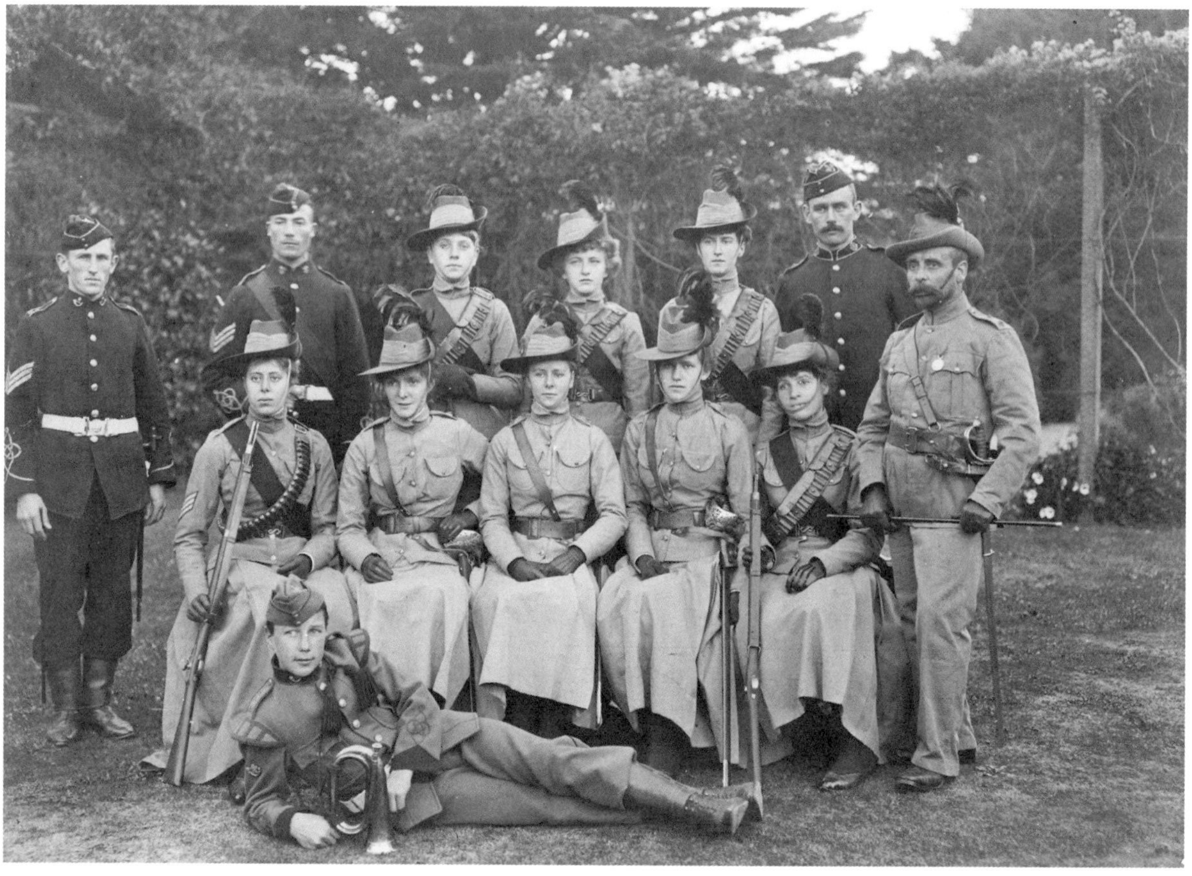

All of this stood rather apart from the hard realities of warfare, and New Zealand's version of jingoism was particularly over the top—evidenced by the eagerness with which government and people welcomed an opportunity to contribute to Queen Victoria's last 'little war', the struggle that broke out between Britain and Transvaal, along with its ally the Orange Free State, in 1899.[136] When news came of it, MPs stood in the House and sang the national anthem—*God Save The Queen*. New Zealand's first contingent of 204 men and 11 officers under Major Alfred Robin was rushed into service as the crisis between Britain and the Transvaal blew up. They hastened to South Africa in time for what was later called the first Boer War. Part of the motive, arguably, was Seddon's intent to play the patriotic card as a device for winning the 1899 election; but the sentiment was genuine, and young Kiwi men flocked to join up in the hope of adventure.

Many did; the three-phase conflict known as the Boer War ran for just over two and a half years, far longer than expected, and the first contingent was joined by a second, third, then a fourth. There was no shortage of volunteers and Maori, too, were eager to go. A total of 6507 New Zealanders eventually served. Public subscriptions to support the war raised over £110,000—nearly $2 million in early twenty-first century money.[137] When Parliamentarian T. E. Taylor tried to question the war, he and his associates were pelted with rotten fruit.[138]

It was New Zealand's first overseas military adventure, the first assertion of self by the colony within the framework of Empire, and it appears that many of the young men went into the conflict with some curious fantasies not only about what warfare was like—but also about what they wanted to get out of it. For George Leece it was glory. which he hoped to obtain through a wound. He

ABOVE

Imperial forces parade along Aucklands' Symonds Street, 1901. A thousand were sent to Australia to help celebrate the Australian Federation, and went on to tour New Zealand.

Photographer unidentified, Alexander Turnbull Library,

PAColl-0614, G-89028-1/2

OPPOSITE TOP

Sailing for South Africa, January 1900.

Photographer unidentified, Alexander Turnbull Library, G-10541-1/1

OPPOSITE BOTTOM

The 'Ladies Rifle Corps' with Wellington militia around 1900. They were recruited by Lady Douglas to raise money for the South African War Patriotic Fund.

Photographer unidentified, Alexander Turnbull Library F-20186-1/2

ABOVE

In the field, South Africa, during the Boer War.

Photographer unidentified, Alexander Turnbull Library, qMS-1676, F-81925-1/2

admitted as much in a letter to his mother, and he got his wish too. What he had not counted on was the likelyhood of such a wound also being fatal. He met his end in August 1901. Yet Leece's death, a tragedy given all the more poignance for his suffering mother, was actually a rare moment for New Zealanders in the Boer war. The infantry weapons were of similar range and lethality to those of the First World War, half a generation later; but the fighting was different, characterised by open and fast-moving battles between forces that, by continental European standards, were small. Of the 6507 New Zealanders who went, just 71 died in battle or from wounds sustained in battle. Another 16 were killed in a railway accident in South Africa, and 133 succumbed to disease.

The contingents came back to dinners, cheers, and gongs; one soldier, Kaiapoi-born Henry Coutts, was even awarded a scarf, one of four knitted by Queen Victoria herself and awarded to the most deserving soldiers from the far-flung colonies for deeds of heroism. Popular sentiment gave this rather iconoclastic award the status of the Victoria Cross; but British officials frowned on the idea and Coutts never did get to add 'QS' after his name. Memorials bore the names of all who went, not just the dead. And amidst the apparent proof that war was

RIGHT

Programme for a Boer War fundraising matinee, Wellington Opera House.

Artist unidentified, Alexander Turnbull Library, Eph-A-WAR-SA-1900-01-cover

ABOVE

The 1st New Zealand Rifles are welcomed home in Dunedin, 23 January 1901.

Photographer unidentified, Alexander Turnbull Library, PAColl-6075-02, F-18796-1/2

merely a ripping adventure, a heady mix of tourism, blokeish excitement and glory, New Zealand's sense of jingoism sailed on unabated.

Like most ideologies, this mind-set also carried a flip-side of unease. The origins could be traced back a generation or more, both in New Zealand and across the British Empire. Victory over Napoleon in 1815 had cemented Britain's place as a pre-eminent world power, but by the late nineteenth century the laurels were a little wilted, and the apparent ease with which the regiments quashed trouble did not compensate. By the 1870s the naval scales had been re-set by the development of steam-driven ironclads. The advantage now went to the nation with the highest industrial capacity, and Britain was not holding ground in the face of German, French and Russian industrialisation. Tension with Russia over the border between Afghanistan and Russia helped prompt fears of a sudden crisis that might plunge the Empire into war. At popular level the British welcomed the idea. 'We don't want to fight,' G. W. Hunt penned in his popular music-hall song, 'but by Jingo, if we do, we've got the ships, we've got the men, we've got the money too.'[139]

Braggadocio of this kind put a brave face to the wider public sense of vulnerability. It also gave the world a word that broadly summed up the whole complex mind-set of the day—jingoism. It was a populist concept. British officials and military strategists took a more sober view; knowing the realities of warfare, about the expected realities of new hardware, and knowing that popular fears of nemesis following hard on the heels of Imperial hubris were more imagined than real. But this did not deflect explosive public 'panics' in Britain, based on imagined lack of naval hardware—still less efforts by politicians to capitalise on the populist sentiment. New Zealand's protector, in short, was suffering an inferiority complex of its own, and this fed into New Zealand's own sense of inferiority, helping shape the emerging 'cultural cringe'.

This heady mix was given spice by the geographical realities of being an island nation half a world away from the motherland. New Zealand was 1200 miles from Australia and more than 10,000 from Britain, seeing itself as a lonely outpost of Empire in the South Pacific. Successive New Zealand governments feared that war might leave Britain's South Pacific colonies vulnerable, a feeling that intensified as the New Zealand wars ended and the colonial focus swung from internal to wider issues. The Admiralty disagreed; a Russian fleet coming south would be cut off by British naval forces in Hong Kong. But isolated raids or attacks on shipping were another matter, and the British set up the Australian Station in March 1859 partly for this reason. The Admiralty thought this was an efficient answer; however, these views were not shared in New Zealand where there was wide feeling that only ships on the spot could protect the country against a bolt from the blue.

Efforts to deal with the problem were hampered by penury. Coastal defences were mooted as early as 1869, but the cost was prohibitive, and hints that Britain should donate old weapons fell on deaf ears. The irascible but capable George Whitmore—by this time in charge of colonial defence—demanded coastal defence guns again in 1870.[140] Options discussed along the way included 'Whitehead automobile torpedoes' to protect the harbours. Spar torpedo boats were eventually procured—truly heroic vessels designed to ram an explosive charge, conveniently kept at the end of a pole, into the side of an enemy vessel. They were kept in pairs in some of New Zealand's main harbours, but mercifully never tested in war. Nor could they be anything other than a last-ditch defence, and ultimately New Zealand had to rely on Britain—a point rammed home in February 1873 by the *Kaskowiski* adventure.

This, briefly, was the sensation of the colony. Aucklanders opening the *Daily Southern Cross* were amazed to read that their city had been held to ransom by a captured British warship. Helped by 'mephitic water-gas' and a 'submarine pinnace', the Russian cruiser *Kaskowiski* had slunk into Waitemata Harbour, taken control of the British ship, and demanded £250,000 from authorities. They apparently got away with £131,096 17s 6d, leaving a prize crew on the British ship to extort further cash from helpless Aucklanders as the day wore on. 'WHERE IS THE BRITISH NAVY?' thundered the editorial.

It was all a fabrication by editor D. M. Luckie, and anybody who actually read the name of the alleged Russian ship aloud probably got the joke at once. But for a day or two the *Kaskowiski* and its apparent crew of ravening pirates caused a sensation.[141] The reaction highlighted

BELOW

Some pillars of colonial-age life changed little even as New Zealand society evolved around it, particularly the the quarter-acre with garden. Even country home owners subscribed to the urban-style fenced section with vegetable patch; this impressive example dates to 1905.

James McAllister, James McAllister Collection, Alexander Turnbull Library, PAColl-3054, G-9841-1/1

'When the last guest says goodbye', cartoonist E. F. Hiscocks' 1902 swipe at Seddon's overblown, boy-scout brand of imperialism.

E. F. Hiscocks, Alexander Turnbull Library, PUBL-0201-050

the mood of New Zealanders, and Luckie pushed his more serious message over the next few weeks. New Zealand lacked any seaborne defence, and the parent Empire was apparently not providing it.

The British lurched on, seeing crisis around every corner despite the practical reality of commanding a global Empire that was approaching its high-water mark of prestige and wealth. There was a fright in 1878 that prompted panic buying of warships, and Britain seemed on the brink of war with the great bear again in 1884. New Zealand's reaction was sharp; a Russian squadron that appeared off China was thought to pose a direct threat,[142] requests for volunteers prompted huge response, and an alarmed colonial government placed panic orders for arms.[143] This backgrounded discussions at the 1887 Colonial Conference, where the Admiralty agreed that Australia and New Zealand could pay for five fast cruisers and two torpedo boats to supplement the Australasian Squadron.[144] New Zealand's actual contribution—starting in the 1891–92 financial year—varied between £20,304 and £21,534.[145]

The problem was that torpedo boats were no substitute for a battle fleet. New Zealand's defence needs were 'blue water'—yet, having failed to become a 'bigger Britain', the colony could not pay for the 'blue water' forces needed to protect vital trade lines. This added to the social and economic issues that were pushing New Zealand back to Britain during the last decades of the nineteenth century.

New Zealand's rush into the arms of the mother country was not a simple admission of lesser status. The idea of a 'bigger' Britain might have failed, but New Zealand still entertained dreams of being a great child—though the first strategy for achieving this did not go down well. Liberal thinking revolved around notions of a federated Empire, with the result that Seddon and Joseph Ward found themselves at successive Colonial and Imperial conferences arguing for such things as a reduction of Dominion trade tariffs and increase in federal defence, in what one historian called a 'minority of one.'[146] Another consequence was a vigorous effort by New Zealand to gain Pacific island territories, for Britain, in the face of German, French and American expansion. Even Hawai'i was coveted. Fiji turned Seddon down in 1900–01, though the Cook Islands and Niue

BELOW

Joseph George Ward (1856–1930) in topee hat outside the Christchurch Club, probably around 1912. Seddon's former Finance Minister became Premier on Seddon's death in 1906. Although a career politician he became a wealthy man in his own right, son of a Melbourne merchant and owner of J. G. Ward & Co., which eventually reaped a fortune from rising meat prices.

Photographer unidentified, Alexander Turnbull Library, G-3775-1/1

were annexed.[147] This did not go down so well in London. Britain was using the islands as a diplomatic bargaining tool back in Europe, and Seddon's pugnacious efforts to take Samoa in particular were not welcomed by the Foreign Office, whose officials had to juggle the delicate balance of European politics.[148]

The decision not to amalgamate with the six Australian states when they federated at the end of the decade was another result of this thinking. In some ways it should have been an obvious step—Pakeha New Zealand had been administratively, socially and economically integral with New South Wales up to 1840, and afterwards was reliant on Australian resources and trade. Wellington was closer to Sydney than Perth. Britain treated Australia and New Zealand as a single strategic entity. And yet when the moment came—as F. L. W. Wood has observed, all seven Australasian colonies tottered towards union; but in the end, New Zealand tottered away from the other six.[149] Even in 1900, Parliamentary opinion was balanced, and abstentions outnumbered individual pro or con voices. Australian-born politicians such as Ward favoured it, and late arguments to join were considered by Royal Commission in 1901.

To some extent the decision was pragmatic; New Zealand's economic star was rising in the late 1890s, whereas Australia was hammered by drought. And jingoistic voices were loud. Seddon prevaricated, arguably to avoid upsetting anti-federation elements in the electorate. Eventually he began arguing that a federated New Zealand would be run from across the Tasman—striking a chord.[150] However, the real issue in 1900 was that federation stood at odds with New Zealand's new view of itself. Ties with Britain were more significant;

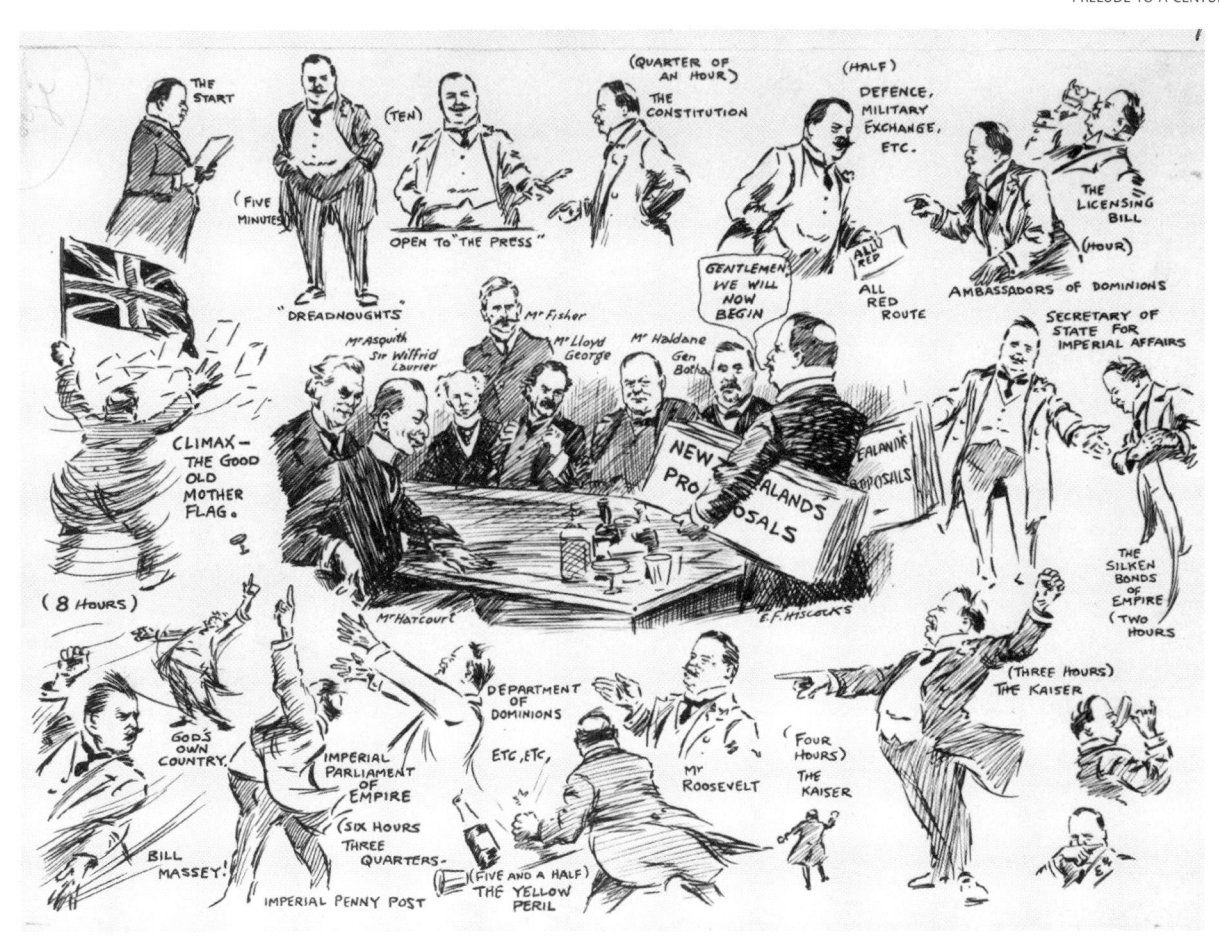

the Australian colonies had far less value by this time as import or export destinations. The decision meant that New Zealand had become the smaller of two Australasian colonies. That had disadvantages within the Imperial structure, particularly as Britain treated Australasia—including New Zealand—as a strategic entity.

The Prussia of the Pacific

New Zealand's self-image as chief of Britain's children emerged just as the Empire was evolving into a looser structure, decisively away from the very ideas that New Zealand had suddenly latched on to. Under British Liberal guidance the colonies became self-governing Dominions. The ultimate goal was a permanent alliance between independent nations tied by common ancestry, and it was not exactly a request. New Zealand had little option but to go along with the administrative side of it, and the rejection of the opportunity to federate with Australia on the back of pro-Imperial thinking did not mean rejection of Dominion status when it was offered in 1907.[151]

It was no paradox; societies can seldom be reduced to a single voice. Yet even the ardent pro-Imperialists of the day saw themselves as asserting New Zealand's identity within the framework of Empire, and being a Dominion was not entirely out of line with that idea. Still, New Zealand's view of Empire was unique, and

ABOVE

Like Seddon, Ward was ruthlessly lampooned for his wordy pro-Imperial braggadocio. This is E. F. Hiscocks' take on Ward's performance at the 1911 Imperial Conference.

E.F. Hiscocks, Alexander Turnbull Library, PUBL-0200-25

NEW ZEALAND
AN ILLUSTRATED HISTORY

240

the architect of its official expression in the years before the First World War was largely guided by Joseph Ward, who became Premier on Seddon's death in 1906.

Described by his contemporary A. R. Barclay as running an 'India rubber' government, Ward—Premier and Minister of Defence from 1906 to 1912—has generally been dismissed as an impulsive character with a liking for abrupt policy turns,[152] a view echoed by historians who have seen Ward's activities as little more than a series of headlong rushes to help his beloved Empire.[153] In fact, while Ward stood in the vast shadow of his predecessor, his ideas were framed by the same federal concepts that Seddon had peddled from the 1890s. As Wood has argued, these notions probably originated as a means of keeping out of federation with Australia, and were unpopular in an Empire moving towards permanent alliance between independent nations.[154]

Seddon's failure to find support at the Colonial Conferences of 1897 and 1902 did not stop Ward calling for an 'imperial council' and closer naval links at the 1907 conference. 'There is but one sea around our shores,' he argued 'and...with one sea and one Empire, there should in reality be but one Navy.'[155] His proposals were turned down,[156] perhaps predictably in an environment where Britain saw Australia and New Zealand as a single strategic entity, and where Australia—by virtue of a larger economy—held the whip hand. First Lord of the Admiralty, Lord Tweedmouth, grudgingly agreed that Australia might build a small fleet to supplement British forces.[157]

ABOVE

Crowds waiting to board the gift ship HMS *New Zealand* at Lyttleton, 1913.

Photographer unidentified, *The Press* (Christchurch) Collection, Alexander Turnbull Library, G-2276-1/1

OPPOSITE TOP

Sailors and crowds mingle in Queen Street during the week-long celebration marking the visit of a US Navy battle fleet.

William Archer Price, W. A. Price Collection, Alexander Turnbull Library, PAColl-3057, G-1234-1/2

OPPOSITE BOTTOM

Cadets from the Wellesley Street Normal school.

Photographer unidentified, Alexander Turnbull Library, *Auckland Star Collection*, PAColl-2752, G-2929-1/1

ABOVE

Joseph Ward at Westshore, Napier, turning the first sod on the East Coast Railway Line in 1912. War, depression and earthquake dashed hopes of an early link to Gisborne. and the line did not open until 1942.

Photographer unidentified, Alexander Turnbull Library, PAColl-6075-57, F-51050-1/2

OPPOSITE TOP

Military camp at Oringi, near Woodville. Bell tents had been characteristic of army camps since the mid-Victorian period, remaining so well into the twentieth century.

S. C. Smith, Alexander Turnbull Library, PAColl-3082, G-20108-1/1

OPPOSITE BOTTOM

Another side of jingo-era life: picnic at Nelson racecourse.

Frederick Nelson Jones, Jones Collection, Alexander Turnbull Library, G- 26680-1/2

Ward was aware of Admiralty opinion that Australian proposals might be more acceptable if New Zealand co-operated,[158] and his response was a sudden announcement that the New Zealand naval subsidy to Britain would be increased from £40,000 to £100,000 a year.[159] It looked like more impulsiveness. He justified it as an effort to improve general naval defence,[160] but the timing makes obvious it was a ploy to torpedo Australian fleet proposals and curry British favour. New Zealand's later treatment by the Board of Admiralty certainly stood out in contrast to the way Australia was handled.[161]

This colliding mix of policy, politics, hopes and strategic perceptions was further complicated by fears in both Australia and New Zealand of Asian ambition. Nineteenth-century notions about China translated, virtually overnight, into a more direct fear of Japanese ambitions in the South Pacific, after the Japanese victory over Russia in 1905. The problem was that Japan was also Britain's sole ally, and attitudes in Australasia embarrassed policy makers in Whitehall. That did not stop the Ward administration welcoming the 'Great White Fleet' in 1908, a very significant United States naval force based around 16 battleships. The name explicitly referred to the paint scheme; the warships all had white hulls and tan upperworks. But it also had obvious racial overtones given the fact that Washington officials had authorised the cruise in part to assert American interests over Japan's in the Phillipines.

That role made the visit by this force to Auckland, Sydney and Melbourne particularly pointed in political terms, underscored by the effusive welcome New Zealand gave to the ships. Massive public celebrations, dubbed 'Fleet Week', marked the moment. Government officials even pressured railway engineers to complete the main trunk line ahead of schedule so that a train could bring parliamentarians north to Auckland in a single day from Wellington, symbolising New Zealand's own capability and visions of status.

CHAPTER SIX
PRELUDE TO A CENTURY

243

Fear of Imperial nemesis continued to suffuse public minds from London to Wellington, and fresh public panic brewed during early 1909 amid fears that Germany was about to overtake Britain in a new naval race, which at popular level was based around a numbers game associated with dreadnoughts, the new super-battleships of the day. These vessels had not merely re-set the naval start-line between rival European powers, but had also become synonymous with naval strength and, apparently, the sole arbiter of national power. They were also the most expensive pieces of military hardware yet concocted, and when it looked like the ruling British Liberal Party would not authorise six dreadnoughts for the 1909–10 financial year, the Conservative opposition led a counterattack with the catch-cry 'we want eight and we won't wait.'[162]

This was the apparent background against which Ward abruptly offered Britain a dreadnought, by telegram from Woodville, one Sunday in March 1909, without calling either Cabinet or Parliament. It was an astonishing gesture, committing New Zealand—a tiny colony of less than a million souls—to a new debt of disproportionate scale. The move has been regarded by contemporaries and historians as Ward once again rushing to the aid of his beloved Empire. He told the House that 'prompt action was absolutely desirable—was, indeed, essential—if the moral effect which we had in view was to be secured.' But he was hammered for not following proper procedure afterwards and tried to get himself off the hook with hints that he had 'confidential information relating to the pressing danger of the situation'. That too was revealed as bluff when the correspondence was published in Australia and cabled to New Zealand.

All of this erupted amidst the naval scare in Britain, which essentially ended on 29 March with an attempt to censure the British government for failing to properly defend the Empire. But Ward had clearly not been in that loop. Reform party leader William Massey capitalised on Ward's embarrassment, and even the Governor-General, Lord Plunkett, thought Ward had made an 'error in tactics'.[163] Neither Ward's contemporaries, nor historians since, have questioned the assumption that Ward acted on personal motives.

RIGHT
William Massey's defence policies set him apart from Australia and Britain, a point on which he had to compromise, foreshadowed in this Trevor Lloyd cartoon.

Trevor Lloyd, Making New Zealand Collection, Alexander Turnbull Library PUBL-0166-1914-100

In fact it was another attempt to undermine Australia and push the consistent federal Imperial view forward. His subsidy increase had not had the effect he wanted, so he played his ace. As he told Plunkett, New Zealanders 'would take much greater pride and interest in knowing that HMS "So-and-so" and HMS "Something Else" were their ships and a visible tangible object lesson of their Dominion's part in the Empire's defence than in merely paying £100,000 a year in ignorance as to how the money was spent.'[164] Ward had, he insisted, been thinking of making an offer for some time for these reasons.

What he did not say was that his hand had been forced by the annual meeting of Australian Commonwealth leaders in mid-March 1909. On the 18th, just two days after the British First Lord of the Admiralty triggered the crisis by indicating the Estimates that year would contain just four dreadnoughts, Australian Prime Minister Andrew Fisher remarked that Australia and Canada could best help British defence by offering to pay for a dreadnought each, as an indication that the 'relatively rich young Dominions' would be prepared to help the mother country. It was only a talking point, but the remark drew attention.[165] Knowing that an Australian offer would trump his own, Ward made the offer as soon as he heard the news. He could not afford to wait even a day to call Cabinet, in case the Australian government decided to make an announcement before the conference ended.[166]

The gamble paid off politically. The Australian stock exchange called on the Commonwealth to make a similar offer, sentiments echoed by the Premiers of New South Wales and Victoria who announced that if the Commonwealth government did not make a dreadnought offer, they would.[167] Ward had touched a deep-held sentiment across the Tasman, and had good reason to feel pleased with himself as he left for the Imperial Conference in July 1909. But his strategy quickly unravelled. Although the new Australian government of Alfred Deakin fulfilled its election promises and gave Britain a dreadnought, Australian thinking remained focussed on a local fleet and Colonel J. F. G. Foxton was sent along to argue the toss.[168] The Admiralty were keen to settle, but the compromise— degrading the gift ships to battlecruisers and integrating them into Pacific-based 'fleet units'—was geared towards Australia.[169]

It was a slap in the face for the Empire's self-appointed chief junior. Ward was 'rather sorry that the Admiralty has recommended that a [naval] unit be formed for Australia', and realised New Zealand would be denuded of the second-line protection he had expected in exchange for his gift. This forced him to compromise his 'federal' principles and, purely for pragmatic reasons, follow the Australian lead by having ships stationed in New Zealand waters.[170]

Although New Zealand's local forces were subsequently administered under legislation passed in 1913, this 1909 arrangement defined the basic shape of the naval force until 1941.[171] What Ward also seems to have missed was that this settlement inflicted a double blow to his intent. He had offered a first-class battleship; but what New Zealand bought was a battlecruiser. Although touted as the wonder-vessels of the age, battlecruisers were not in the league of dreadnoughts, and opinion within the Admiralty was growing against them by 1909 because of their lack of armour. And it was worse than that; the gift ship, inevitably dubbed HMS *New Zealand*, was not even of the latest design.

ABOVE

Drama in the streets. Black Tuesday—the morning of 12 November 1912. Strike-breakers attacked striking miners at Miners Hall, Seddon Street, Waihi. A good number were injured in the scuffle that followed, and Frederick George Evans was fatally wounded.

Photographer unidentified, H. E. Holland Collection, Alexander Turnbull Library F-44240-1/2

None of this was so obvious in the moment; but even so, there was no question that New Zealand had come off second-best in the Fleet Unit arrangement. And that underscored the real problem. Ward's defence policies foundered, in the end, on the dissonance between New Zealand hopes and British realities, and the pragmatic nature of the power balance meant that New Zealand had little choice but to toe the Imperial line. The outcome, a million-plus pound debt for an obsolescent warship, coupled with the eventual arrival of second-class cruisers in local waters, underlined the fact that Ward's concepts were out of line. At a time when Britain was beginning to shed its Empire, New Zealand was clinging ever-tighter to the motherland. The dissonance characterised the relationship for the first two thirds of the twentieth century.

Red Feds and Massey's Cossacks

Jingoism stayed strong as the twentieth century entered its second decade. Thousands flocked to see Ward's gift ship, HMS *New Zealand*, when she came to New Zealand shores in 1913, amid a new outburst of patriotic fervour for the motherland.[172] But the tides of change were already adding a dimension to this world of glorious Empire. The late nineteenth century was the age of the radical left, a generational reaction to the inequities of power, money and

Socialist party demonstration at Waihi, in support of striking miners.

Photographer unidentified, Nash Collection, Alexander Turnbull Library, PAColl-5792, F-70458-1/2

opportunity that had flowed from the industrial revolution. The Communards of Paris dramatically politicised the image of the left in 1870, and by the end of the century there was widespread agitation across Europe and Britain, demanding change on the basis of class unity. British Liberal policies were at least partly geared to meeting these demands. Radicals, reactionaries and anarchists were all feared to lurk in coffee shops and bars, planning assassinations or bombings, while others held public meetings to discuss revolution. As always, popular fears overstated the threat—bearded radicals with Homburg hats and smoking cherry bombs did not actually hide around every corner. But there was genuine trouble in Russia, where industrialisation lagged; and massive strikes led to an attempted revolt in 1905.[173] The fact was that, popular fears or not, working-class society had swung to the left.

In New Zealand, however, local radicalism was tempered by the structure of colonial society, which differed from that of Europe. Social mobility and lip-service egalitarianism diffused the feeling, and class unity in the Marxist sense, insofar as it emerged at all, took its lead from colonial structures and values—not European patterns. Despite occasional efforts by historians to make the New Zealand experience fit the radical European mould, there was little to closely compare the 'Red Feds' with the contemporary Mensheviks led by Leon Trotsky, and New Zealand's labour left was framed within the values of its own society. It was based on small-scale organisations, including early trade unions. Their influence in the labour force was restricted by Reeves' labour legislation, which forced compulsory arbitration, although that was changing by the first decade of the twentieth century under such radicals as Robert Semple—'Battling Bob', as he was called at the time—Michael Savage, Bill Parry and Paddy Webb. They were

ABOVE

Maritime strikers and sympathisers marching along Mansfield Street to Newtown Park, Wellington, 1913.

S. C. Smith, Alexander Turnbull Library, G-48931-1/2

not as radical as some of their European counterparts and it has been argued that they were less inspired by the teachings of Marx than by moderate labour leaders such as Edward Bellamy.[174]

They were broadly opposed by a new union of farmers, the small-holders created by the Liberals, who defected from the Liberal cause in droves during the first decade of the twentieth century. This group coalesced initially around the New Zealand Farmers Union, formed in 1902 at Kaitaia, which evolved into a new political grouping, the Reform Political League. That filled the vacuum left by the demolition of Russell's oligarch-based Opposition in 1900. They were led after 1903 by former Tamaki dairy farmer William Ferguson Massey, a bluff figure not unkindly dubbed 'Farmer Bill'. Disillusioned with Ballance's policies, he became involved in politics as farmers' advocate for the National Association in the early 1890s, and stood for the Waitemata seat in 1894.

This new grouping made little headway against Seddon in the 1905 elections. They did better against Ward, though the Liberals won in 1908 despite a swing to the right. Massey renamed the group the Reform Party, garnering support from a centre-right base. The main gripe was with McKenzie's 999-year leasehold system. The lessee could not use land as security on loans, and that was crippling. Nor could the lessees take advantage of rising land prices, although goodwill on the lease was transactable. Ward's curative offers did not slow erosion of his support from the right, and his policies also alienated him from the left. The elections of 1911 left Ward without a working majority, and he resigned the following year.[175]

The results of this election broadly set the pattern for New Zealand politics until the mid-1980s; it was fought out between a centre-right that drew support from the conservative rural farming vote, matched against a largely urbanised centre-left that drew its vote from the workers. Both tended towards the centre, and neither were strictly comparable with overseas equivalents. This did not prevent the usual efforts to classify for political purposes and, in the 1900s, New Zealand's left were regarded as dangerously radical by the conservatives. The losers during the same period were the Liberals, who by this time represented a more centrist party that did not really address the demands of an increasingly diversified electorate.

Labour militants emerged as a significant force during the later 1900s, particularly on the West Coast where they dominated the Blackball mines and later disrupted work on the Otira rail tunnel. The New Zealand Federation of Miners was formed in 1908, the Federation of Labour (FOL) in 1909. They were dubbed 'Red Feds' by their opponents and regarded as communist, but their demands were modest enough—mostly reflecting a living wage and a reasonable old-age pension. Seddon's Old Age Pensions Act of 1898, though later lauded as founding the welfare state, actually provided token payments under such exclusive terms that many could not take advantage of them.[176]

Tensions rose when the FOL rejected the arbitration system, becoming effective war in early 1912, when the 1200-member Waihi Miners Union aligned itself with the FOL, but the engine drivers and winders withdrew from the Waihi Miners Union to form their own group. The miners went on strike in protest

BELOW

Maritime strikers' protest, 1913. Confrontations followed, which were broken by force.

William Archer Price, William A. Price Collection, Alexander Turnbull Library, PAColl-3057, G-186-1/2

amid calls to disband the new Engine Drivers Union. At first the dispute merely simmered against the background of a failing Liberal administration under caretaker Prime Minister Thomas McKenzie, but Massey became Prime Minister in July and was able to manoeuvre the Waihi situation into a 'law and order' issue. Police were deployed to the town in September and arrested some striking miners for 'obstruction'. The strike dragged on. In November, police raided the miners' union hall in Waihi, an armed struggle followed and two men died—Constable Gerald Wade and miner Frederick Evans. The strike was forcibly ended and the miners and their families were ordered to leave town. New workers were brought in, employed only if they agreed to abide by the old arbitration system.

It had been a decisive victory for Massey, but as far as the labour movement was concerned this was only the first round. The Waihi clash helped spur the United Federation and the Social Democrat Party into existence. Trouble erupted on the Wellington waterfront, where there was a lock-out in late 1913 after a dispute over travel expenses. Sympathetic strikes followed in the Huntly coal mines and in other docks. The FOL tried to extend it into a general strike, to which Massey responded by appointing special mounted constables—'Massey's Cossacks'—to help keep law and order. The strikers did not have the sympathy of the farmers, and the crisis came to a head on 8 November with what has been called the 'battle of the wharves'. In simultaneous operations, the 'Cossacks' took the Auckland wharves, backed by a contingent of farmers and with the cruisers *Psyche* and *Pyramus* providing visible backing. Skirmishing spilled into surrounding streets. Another force of 'Cossacks' tackled the Wellington strikers with a flurry of batons. They were met by revolver fire, but the results were perhaps inevitable. The strike was broken after 58 days, and the labour movement cracked. Two-thirds of the FOL resigned.

A general election loomed in 1914. Massey had a bare majority, and the Liberal–Labour wing offered a credible threat. It would have been an interesting contest; but fate intervened. A new international crisis erupted in July. At first it did not seem too serious. But a volatile mix of alliance ties, bloody-mindedness and the mechanisms of war planning and railway timetables swiftly stepped Europe, and with it the Briish Empire, into the conflict that had always been feared, which had always been perversely encouraged by the jingoes, and during which—as Tutira station owner Herbert Guthrie-Smith put it—the 'old world crashed and passed away.'[177]

ABOVE
Ilex at sea, 1913.

James Hutchings Kinnear, Kinnear Collection, Alexander Turnbull Library, G-17015-1/2

CHAPTER SEVEN
God's own country

New Zealand's twentieth century was a roller coaster of depression, booms, disease, and unimaginably lethal wars, through which evangelised settler ideals of security, equality and the quarter-acre dream rode like a ship on a turbulent sea. It was also a short century. Trend and theme seldom match convenient dates, and British historian Eric Hobsbawm has argued that the twentieth century as a socioeconomic and political cycle actually began in 1914 and ended with the fall of the Eastern Bloc around 75 years later.[1] His arguments are compelling; and although he wrote from a world perspective, New Zealand shared the broad experience through its imperial and international ties—with indigenous twists, including local start- and end-points, generated by domestic causes.

The First World War—which opened this great century-spanning social and political cycle for Europe and then the world—has been classified as the first act in a 31-year conflict, fought out in two steps with a 20-year interval between them.[2] It is a compelling view, and not just because of the direct causality between the two. These were the first industrial-scale wars in the history of the world, drawing in not merely combatants but whole populations, and they had a profound effect. The old European order fell, and from the chaos emerged the patterns that dominated the twentieth century—including the great oppositions between democracy, totalitarianism and communism that did not finally resolve until the Cold War effectively ended in 1990–92.[3]

These developments also framed New Zealand's twentieth century—but local pressures added their own twists. The First World War, here as elsewhere, drove social change. Shifts that had been implicit suddenly swept into being, along with a sense of social and national unity that overlaid feelings towards Britain and stood in uneasy tension with them; a plural loyalty sometimes called 'double patriotism'. Arguably, the popular cycle began with the Gallipoli experience, but it was also profoundly shaped by the campaign on the Western Front; between

ABOVE

Bridge building and heliograph instruction at the Canterbury Engineers annual camp before the First World War.

Photographer unidentified, Alexander Turnbull Library G-8484-1/1

them they drew in half of all young New Zealand men and exerted a huge shaping force on the generation that followed.

During the inter-war decades New Zealand matched worldwide swings between 'big' and 'bigger' government, adding twists of its own, underpinned and moulded by the legacy of settler society. It was a heady mix into which idealism, the 'cultural cringe', jingoism and the concept of being 'chief junior' to Imperial Britain fed in complex ways, and were themselves changed by it. It was also a blokeish world in which women and Maori were sidelined—but from which both re-emerged, buoyed by a sea-change in attitude as the cycle ended in the 1960s and 1970s. New Zealand responded to the uncertainties of the early century, and Britain's steady disengagement from Empire, with a swing to security, to protectionism. In the 1930s it was called 'applied Christianity' by the Prime Minister of the day, Michael Joseph Savage. Government was not hostile to the ordinary people; it was there to help them.

It worked. Helped by a direct effort to exploit the economic potential of the Second World War, New Zealand's mid-twentieth century was the most prosperous age the country had known—bringing to reality the quarter-acre paradise that the settlers had sought so many decades earlier. But there were costs, and the policy was inevitably pushed to extremes and well past its use-by date, contributing to an equally extreme swing in the opposite direction from the mid-1980s which brought dramatic—and traumatic—change of its own. Aspects of that were more reaction to and reversal of what had gone before than anything new, and in 1999 a newly elected Labour administration declared the 15-year crusade in purist socio-economic theory over. With that the great cringe-driven cycle of tension over dual nationalism, the argument between big and small government—the difficult disengagement from a colonial past—that had broadly defined so much about New Zealand's twentieth century, approached one possible end point. From the historical perspective it was only coincidental that these trends came precisely in late 1999, at the popular end of the millennium. But it was also, somehow, apt.

Poppies and mud

The First World War stands as a tragic monument to the end of one era and the start of another, soaked in the blood of a generation who never wanted to die, but who were slaughtered in their thousands across the fields of Flanders, at Gallipoli, in Russia, the Alps, and in Palestine among other places. New Zealanders were among them, young men whose lives stretched into an unknown future in 1913, but who—as Lawrence Binyon's words remind us, never lived to grow wearied by age.

None of this was anticipated during the glorious northern summer of 1914. Long-standing tensions between Europe's powers seemed quiescent, and even the assassination of Archduke Franz Ferdinand of Austria at the end of June was at first a local affair. But that changed in the face of Europe's volatile combination of alliances, economic rivalries, national competition, personality politics and

BELOW

Crowds outside *The Press* office, Cathedral Square, Christchurch, 1914.

Photographer unidentified, Alexander Turnbull Library, F-103409-1/2

the legacy of the 1871 Franco-Prussian war.[4] Britain wavered, reluctant to see a German-dominated continent, equally reluctant to get involved in war. But when German forces crashed through Belgium, Britain honoured an 1839 neutrality guarantee and declared war. So did the Empire.[5]

Nobody expected the fighting to last beyond Christmas; but the 'miracle of the Marne' stopped a lightning German push to Paris in October 1914, and the Franco-British and German armies outflanked each other to the Channel. As winter began they dug in. So began three years of soul-destroying trench warfare that remains the enduring image of the First World War. This theatre—and not Gallipoli—was also the reality of it for most of the New Zealanders. The problem was that the methods of defence—trench, wire and machine gun, which drew both from technical developments since the 1860s and the half-millennium long European tradition of military fieldwork—could not be overcome by infantry alone. It took the British three years to develop the new technologies and tactics needed to break the deadlock.[6]

Until then the war in Europe, which was the decisive front on which the whole conflict could be won or lost, descended to a battle of attrition. And in one of the more tragic expressions of the way that human endeavour so often collides the good with the bad, the armies needed to feed this industrial-age killing machine were available as another consequence of the same general developments that had led to the scale of war and its subsequent technical deadlock in the first place. It was a lethal mix into which New Zealand was inexorably drawn. Rising populations and technical capacity had been matched during the late nineteenth century by a rise in state organisational power, a combined outcome of communications technology, new social structures, and the cult of patriotic nationalism. Seddon's

BELOW

Crowds farwell the 2nd (South Canterbury) Regiment from Timaru, 21 August 1914.

Photographer unidentified, Alexander Turnbull Library, F- 49274-1/2

CHAPTER SEVEN
GOD'S OWN COUNTRY

DEPARTURE OF 6TH REINFORCEMENTS

reformed public service led the world, but it was not the only bureaucracy by the first decade of the twentieth century—and wartime governments, in any case, were adept at creating authority. The result was a state ability to direct populations in ways that had been only hinted at during Europe's last big war a century earlier. War became more than just a fight between professional combatants. It drew in total populations, affecting every walk of life—one way or another.

New Zealand contributed principally on land, a consequence of pre-war policies that handed naval defence to Britain and focussed local attention on the army. However, to this were added air and sea contributions via the Royal Flying Corps, the Royal Navy and Royal Naval Air Service, New Zealand's own tiny naval forces, and in local forces and training establishments. The human aspect has been accounted for in various ways, but one analysis based on the official tally put the national effort at some 91,941 volunteers and 32,270 conscripts.[7] Total losses in all theatres—heavily skewed towards the army division deployed to Flanders—amounted to just over 41,000 wounded and more than 16,500 dead.[8] Of these, 10,245 were killed outright and 3958 died of wounds, while 2351 were listed as dying of 'other causes', including disease. Some 227 others died in New Zealand 'before discharge', some of them casualties of the influenza epidemic of 1918.[9] Hundreds of others died in the 1920s from the after-effects of gas or the lingering results of their injuries, a number not captured by official records—though around 3000 servicemen were still being treated in New Zealand hospitals as late as 1920.[10]

ABOVE

Effusive farewells for soldiers departing for the great adventure overseas became bittersweet as the realities of the First World War hammered home. Here, crowds farewell the Sixth reinforcements.

Photographer unidentified, Alexander Turnbull Library G17071-1/2

None of this was anticipated in 1914, when New Zealanders saw war as an opportunity for adventure and to show that the loyal Dominion would do its part for the Imperial cause. The Boer War had shown the way, and once again New Zealanders brought up on a diet of jingoism and glory flocked to war, among them Aubrey Tronson who joined 'principally through a pure love of adventure and travel.' He had always harboured an ambition to see London and attributed his enthusiasm for war to his father, and a military descent. Tronson's interest in the military was aroused during boyhood by the Boer War; strengthened by the Russo-Japanese war of 1904–05; and when the First World War broke out he was so eager to volunteer that he badgered the recruiting office twice a day for a week.[11]

Haste was demanded for a conflict expected to last only a few months. The British asked the government to send a force to Samoa within a fortnight of war breaking out. The convoy with its light cruiser escort took the German colony in late August, fortunately without running into the powerful East Asiastic Squadron of Vice-Admiral Graf von Spee, which was at sea—whereabouts unknown.[12]

Plans went ahead for a significant contribution in the European theatre. The framework had been laid by the Defence Act 1909 and Defence Amendment Act 1910, which established territorial forces whose training began at school with a new Cadet system. Registration was compulsory, and by mid-1911, three months after the legislation came into force, 21,838 Territorials and 29,991 Cadets had been registered.[13] The army—with a theoretical establishment of 30,000—was organised under Major-General Sir Alexander Godley, British-sourced commander and nephew of John Godley. They were short on experienced officers, but some 8700 men and 3800 horses left New Zealand late in 1914. One of the convoys taking them to Egypt ran foul of SMS *Emden*, a cruiser from the East Asiastic Squadron; the German vessel was defeated in classic ship-to-ship combat by HMAS *Sydney*, one of the escorts.[14]

The men went to war with the cheers of a nation bored with the dreary round of peace and ignorant of the awful realities of fighting, but their enthusiasm was not mirrored in London. Louisa Higginson, a nurse at Napier Hospital, sailed to England with her friend Mary Collins on board the *Corinthic* in early 1915 in the hope of volunteering for war work. They were surprised by what they saw in the Imperial capital, confiding to the diary then being kept by Mary that they could not understand the apparent lack of English patriotism.[15] By this time Turkey had entered the war against Britain, and as far as Churchill and the British War Cabinet was concerned, this opened up an opportunity to bypass the stalled Western Front, relieving the pressure on the Russians at the same time.[16] Plans to send the New Zealanders on to France were shelved; they got as far as Cairo, and a Turkish thrust into the Syrian desert resulted in New Zealand's first combat death of the war as early as February 1915, when Private William Ham succumbed to wounds after a tussle at Ismailia.

Many of the Kiwis saw themselves as tourists. George Bollinger eagerly anticipated the teeming streets of Cairo,[17] though the realities were often disappointing and Tronson found the city interesting but grubby.[18] Cairo also brought the men into direct contact with Egyptians. It is, however, over-simplistic to condemn their reactions as racism—a mistake made by at least one historian.[19]

At the time their behaviour was thought normal, and the New Zealanders were ridiculed for being at the softer end of the spectrum. It was also a two-way street; Louisa Higginson thought the Egyptians were rude and rather irritating.[20] Tensions escalated, and all came to a head during Easter 1915 in a major riot.

The Kiwis were shortly drawn into Britain's plan to strike Turkey out of the war by taking the Dardanelles and surging into Istanbul. The attack was launched in early 1915, initially as a purely naval effort—this last against the advice of First Sea Lord Admiral Sir John Fisher, who felt the assault had to be combined with a land attack on the peninsula to succeed.[21] When the attempt to force the Dardanelles with old battleships failed, that land assault had to be launched against alerted Turkish defenders. It was meant to be over in a day or two—all the army had to do was take the peninsula and neutralise the forts protecting the Dardanelles, letting minesweepers clear the waters to let the battleships through. Available forces included the Australasian contingents in Cairo, which assembled as the Australia and New Zealand Corps. They landed on 25 April 1915, following the Australians.

The plan failed; the attack bogged down like the Western Front. The Kiwis sat in their little lodgement beside the Australians, hanging on for months amidst flies and death. They took a prominent role during a final effort to take the peninsula in early August, when the 760-strong Wellington Battalion under Colonel William Malone reached their objective atop Chunuk Bair. But they could get no further; and Malone—killed by 'friendly' fire during the battle—was posthumously blamed.[22] Historically it was a decisive moment for New Zealand—the first real assault while fighting for Empire—and the foundation of the long-standing myth of Kiwi soldiers who punched above their weight and fought against terrible odds, but who could never achieve more than near-run

BELOW

Landing at Anzac Cove, 1915. Mythology later had the New Zealanders arriving at dawn; in fact, they did not land until mid-afternoon and some not until the next day. By then the Turks had already hemmed the Anzac forces into a narrow coastal strip, which became the key battlefield for the next eight months.

Photographer unidentified, R. W. Crofter Collection, Alexander Turnbull Library PAColl-4318

RIGHT

Outpost No.1 on the Gallipoli front.

James Cornelius Read, J. C. Read Collection, Alexander Turnbull Library, PAColl-1655, F-58066-1/4

defeat. It was a further expression of the cultural cringe, but it shaped the way New Zealand's military results were seen through both acts of the great twentieth-century world war.

The Kiwis were finally pulled out of Gallipoli in December, after eight miserable months. The withdrawal, at least, was triumphal; nobody died getting away. But Gallipoli itself had been a charnel house for New Zealand with a final official total of some 7453 casualties—of whom 2721 were killed outright. Louisa Higginson saw some of the despondent survivors back in Egypt, mourning the lives that had been sacrificed for nothing.[23]

The defeat on Gallipoli brought the true cost of modern warfare home to New Zealanders—shattering pre-war expectations of battlefield glory for Britain. That same mind-set also turned the tragedy into triumph, a sleight-of-hand transformation that emerged in 1916 during events to mark the first anniversary of the landing. In Auckland, Archbishop A. W. Averill insisted that 'our boys' had not 'died in vain' on Gallipoli. 'They represented New Zealand's sense of honour and gratitude…the worthiness of the nation to take its place in the great family of free nations in the Empire'.[24]

That was the first meaning of Gallipoli for New Zealand, and it was not the last. Later the battle became a moment for nationalism, the birthplace of New Zealand as an identity of its own. This was true only in hindsight. Sentiment at the time was more focussed on asserting a place within the framework of Empire. Ideas of nationalism certainly emerged from the First World War experience, but they took time and a wider campaign than Gallipoli to take popular root.

The real shaping force behind the First World War was the Western Front. This was where the whole conflict pivoted; defeat here for either side meant defeat in the war. This was where the New Zealand Expeditionary Force had been heading in 1914 when it was delayed in Egypt; the journey resumed in early 1916 with a full division, assembled from the forces in Egypt. Command went

By the time the New Zealanders reached Ypres – 'Wipers' – it had been on or near the front line for two years.

Henry Armitage Sanders, gelatin dry plate negative, RSA Collection, Alexander Turnbull Library, PAColl-5311, G-12950-1/2

to Major-General Andrew Russell, Napier-born scion of a military family who had given up a promising career in the British army to run the family station near Hastings. He had distinguished himself in command of the Mounted Rifle brigade at Gallipoli and, in March 1916, was given the ultimate honour—command of New Zealand's primary overseas field force. The New Zealand Division was one of the largest fielded during the war, in part a result of careful government management of 'manpower' issues back in New Zealand. Conscription—although not greatly popular—eventually evened up the flow of men into the forces. It was so well managed that even in late 1918 New Zealand was in a position to 'go on till the end of 1920 supplying reinforcements to our army at the front.'[25] Maori contributed a Pioneer Battalion, on a voluntary basis but pushed by Maori members of Parliament—notably Maui Pomare of Te Ati Awa—who hoped to elevate the status of Maori in the process.[26] Around 2200 eventually served.

The net result was that socially significant numbers of New Zealanders—up to half the cohort of young men of the day—were thrown together under adverse conditions for a far longer period than Gallipoli, and their experiences defined the reality of the war for New Zealand. It was a shattering time. Young New Zealanders, some fresh out of school, fought, bled and died in places that most had not even known as names on a map: Flers, Messines and Passchendaele among them. These tiny villages and the fields between them became irrevocably associated with an endless, inhuman and de-humanising world of mud, filth, bullets, shells, bombs, mines and the corrupting remains of earlier casualties.

ABOVE

'Hellfire corner', on the road out of Ypres towards the front. Hessian sacking was intended to mask passers-by from being targeted by German snipers. It was down this road that many New Zealand soldiers marched when the New Zealand Division was stationed in this part of the Western Front.

Photographer unidentified, Alexander Turnbull Library, F-51945-1/2

The spectre of it haunted the generation who fought through it—and defined all that was wrong with war for half a century afterwards or more.

Although this apparently mindless deadlock has puzzled non-military historians, it was an inevitable outcome of technology. In 1914–17, new systems for battlefield defence—machine gun, minefield, pill-box, trench and barbed wire—had not yet been countered by systems of offence. Part of the reason was that the scale of the battlefield expanded dramatically with the increasing range of small arms. The net result was that men could not advance across the field to their objectives without being slaughtered. Until the necessary assault techniques were developed it was unlikely that one side or the other could prevail. Early efforts using gas were unsuccessful,[27] and it was not until the British developed systems for combined warfare involving artillery, infantry, aircraft and tanks, all connected by a detailed command-and-control system, that the deadlock was broken.[28] It was also an asymmetric struggle, because the Germans had taken the policy decision in 1915 to run a mostly defensive war in the west until they had defeated Russia in the east. The onus was thus on the British and French to crack defences that had been particularly well set up, often, quite literally, in concrete. And the pressure to keep on trying came at political level.

New Zealand's black month came in 1917. Between 4 and 30 October, the division suffered 952 killed, 3052 wounded and 1300 missing.[29] 'Life is not worth a minute's purchase here,' Kiwi soldier Jesse Stayte later wrote, 'and some of our men are being killed and blown to pieces every few minutes.'[30] By far the majority

LEFT

Staged scene at 'Clapham Junction', Ypres salient, November 1917. New Zealanders cheer a wounded comrade with jokes from *New Zealand at the Front*. The reality of the front, particularly in this dismal region, was very different. Wounded men were sometimes not picked up; stretcher parties waded through knee-deep mud, risking their own lives, to get them.

Henry Armitage Sanders, RSA Collection, Alexander Turnbull Library, PAColl-5311, G-12979-1/2

LEFT

The funeral of Sapper J. F. Haynes, New Zealand Engineers, early May 1917.

Henry Armitage Sanders, RSA Collection, Alexander Turnbull Library, PAColl-5311, G-12761-1/2

of these losses, some 3200 killed, wounded or missing, came on 12 October when the division took part in the abortive attack on Passchendaele. Although it is wrong to single the battle out as a massacre—for it was no different in essence to any other of the abortive infantry-artillery efforts, including New Zealand's other main thrust at Flers in 1916 —it was the most lethal for New Zealand. The blow was so heavy that, even a quarter-century later and in another war, New Zealand commanders had merely to mention 'Passchendaele' to prompt a rethink of any apparently failing strategy.[31]

Germany returned to the offensive in spring 1918 after the collapse of Russia and armistice in the east. It was a moment of crisis; Erich Ludendorff hurled 43

ABOVE

Meal time in a front-line New Zealand trench, April 1918.

Henry Armitage Sanders, Alexander Turnbull Library, PAColl-5311, G-13087-1/2

divisions against 12 British in the Somme, more against the Armentieres sector.[32] New Zealanders were swept up in the whirlwind, but Ludendorff's offensive staggered to a halt in July. Later in the year, it was the Allies' turn to attack, with their new tactics,[33] and for a few weeks the war became a fast-moving struggle. Revolution erupted in Germany, spreading from a mutinous High Seas Fleet; and although their army had not quite been defeated in the field—something historians argued about afterwards—Germany agreed to an armistice on 11 November 1918. For the numbed soldiers at the front it was an emotionless moment. Nobody knew what to do, and N. E. Hassall wrote that he and the other New Zealanders 'just wandered aimlessly about doing nothing'.[34] Others, elsewhere, were more joyous. 'Peace, blessed peace,' Kiwi nurse Fanny Speedy told her diary, as the bells of London rang out around her. But even then she had to admit that the moment was 'too big to realise and too sad to understand'.[35]

Temperance, pacifists and influenza

War came home to New Zealanders in letters and casualty lists, in the return of mutilated soldiers from hospitals, in shortages of imported goods, in the suspicion of Germanic migrants, and in patriotic quests for funds, gifts and 'comforts'. It struck the hearts of every family with sons or brothers at the front, and that was most of them. Conscription—when it came in 1916—was promoted

ABOVE

Farewell luncheon for New Zealand soldiers at Trentham Camp, 1916.

Photographer unidentified, Kenneally Collection, Alexander Turnbull Library, F-106752-1/2

as a way of equalising the sacrifice. Certainly it minimised disruption, producing around 32,000 for the army, about a third of the total who served, selected by random marble-draw in Wellington. Some, like Bourke, were happy enough to go. Others slipped the net by omitting to register. Others did register, but then refused to go—among them a good number of Labour supporters, including Peter Fraser. Jingo-era New Zealand treated such dissenters harshly. Many were imprisoned under poor conditions, even stripped of voting rights for a decade. Opposition in the King Country—the only area where Maori conscription was enforced—was organised by Tawhiao's grand-daughter Te Puea Herangi, who urged passive resistance.[36]

The struggle affected everyday life in many ways. New Zealand imported virtually all its clothing, textiles, metal, machinery, sugar, tea, liquor, tobacco, paper and books, among other things. Forty percent by value came directly from Britain, and availability varied dramatically during the war years. It reached its lowest ebb in 1917 when the Germans launched their second round of unrestricted U-boat warfare in the Atlantic. Prices skyrocketed.[37] Car imports from Britain were restricted, prompting some firms to look to the United States. New Zealand also imported £8,000 worth of German goods in 1915, and even in 1917 some £700 worth came into the country, probably through third-party neutrals.

Patriotism was nonetheless the order of the day. Shopkeepers advertised that their products were not German. An Empire Defence Fund was organised to supply New Zealand soldiers with 'comforts', Patriotic Committees raised funds, there were concerts to support the wounded, and drives to raise money for those in Belgium. Overseas charities and aid organisations also sought support from New Zealand. The Over-Seas Club, a London-based organisation backed by *The*

Times, sought donations to its Tobacco Fund. 'The brave soldiers in the fighting line are asking for something to smoke,' the advertisement advised. 'Will you help us to supply it?' A typical parcel included fifty cigarettes, a quarter-pound of 'smoking mixture', and matches.[38]

Sectarianism gained surprising ground during the war. New Zealand had never been a particularly religious society; certainly the ill-feeling between Protestant and Catholic in Britain was little in evidence here. But that changed during the war. The trauma of the struggle had some effect; so too did external forces such as the Irish Easter Rebellion of 1916. Former Baptist minister Howard Elliott formed the Protestant Political Association in 1917, backed by the Grand Orange Lodge. They were closely tied to the Reform Party and membership flourished, growing by some accounts to 200,000 by 1919; but that dwindled rapidly after 1921, a move one historian has put down to a combination of British settlement in Ireland and the fact that post-war, Massey's party gained the upper hand.[39]

Temperance gained new momentum, in part reflecting overseas trends, in part stemming from a feeling that stay-at-homes had no right to live in luxury when New Zealand's young men were suffering and dying overseas. Prohibition seemed a very real prospect, and by way of compromise 'six o'clock closing' was introduced in 1917. It did not seem to curb drinking; that year some 3116 New Zealanders were arrested for offences under the liquor acts, including

BELOW

Sheep farming flourished during the First World War, largely on the back of a wartime 'commandeer' of New Zealand's production by the British. This is a yard in Northland.

Northwood Brothers, Alexander Turnbull Library, G- 10744-1/1 drunkenness.[40] Nor did the practice of 'dry' areas make much difference; some 276,510 gallons (1.257 million litres) of alcohol were sent into no-licence districts, most of it beer and stout.[41] This was a rising trend—more than 381,000 gallons of liquor (1.732 million litres), again mostly beer and stout, was taken into no-licence districts in 1919.[42]

Six o'clock closing was intended to help curb drinking habits in general, and stop family men spending evenings getting drunk at the pub. In reality it simply added speed to a growing cult of drinking in quantity, reinforcing beer as a currency of New Zealand manhood. The new rule did not particularly reduce alcohol consumption at all, but what it did do was fill New Zealand streets at five minutes past six with half-intoxicated men looking for a punch-up. With typically only half an hour between 'knock off' time and 'closing time', haste was of the essence and many public bars became male-only swilling venues with concrete floors, geared to dispense the maximum quantity of beer in the shortest possible time to as many patrons as possible. The ability to 'hold' liquor, to be able to drink without apparently suffering the effects, became a mark of personal status which, in due course, translated to the notion that it was all right to drive drunk.

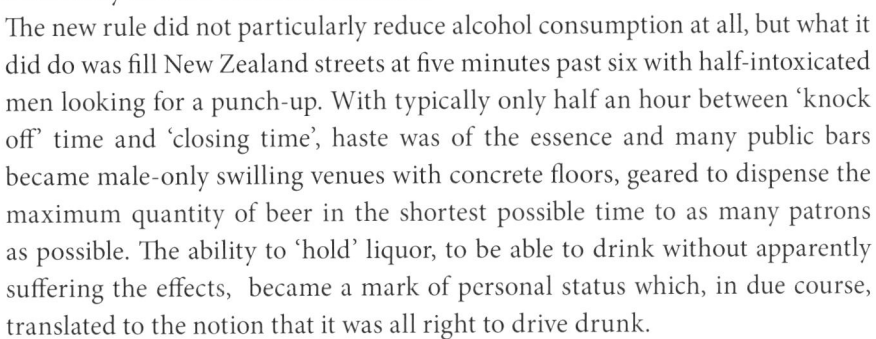

However, early closing was only a halfway measure as far as many campaigners were concerned. War also brought rules against 'shouting'—the practice of bars buying occasional drinks for their patrons—and against barmaids. Women, it seemed, became vile strumpets once armed with a till and bottles of liquor, temptresses who induced men to drink. The prohibition on women serving in bars was indicative of the way the temperance movement had been given emotional depth by the rising voices of the 'socially pure', increasingly removed from any real threat to their ideals posed by New Zealand drinking, and highlighting the way that such social causes, once intellectualised, emotionalised and radicalised, could grow out of all proportion to practical reality.

War exigencies gave power to these ideas, however, and in 1919—faced with such intonements as 'alcohol is…one of the chief causes of cruelty, crime and vice',[43] New Zealanders voted in favour of outright prohibition by a majority of 3263. It seemed decisive. But then soldiers overseas tipped the balance. They were not going to forego their drink, and New Zealand remained a nation of drinkers. The army was regarded as 'debauched' in some circles,[44] but it was difficult for the socially pure to threaten Western Front veterans with hell. The soldiers' vote probably saved New Zealand from the violence and black marketeering of the United States; but as late as 1925, 47 percent of New Zealand voters remained in favour of prohibition. This view was not shared across the Tasman. In 1928, for instance, New South Wales residents voted 5:2 in favour of staying 'wet'.[45]

A new killer emerged in 1918; an invisible death transmitted in part by the

ABOVE

Although posed, this scene of people 'drinking' at Macetown in 1902 highlighted popular fears about the demon drink.

Photographer unidentified, Lambie Collection, Alexander Turnbull Library, F-38592-1/2

ABOVE

District nurses outside their South Durham Street headquarters, Christchurch. Left to right: C. Browne, Sister Constance, M. Palmer, M. Rogers, S. Maude, C. Savory, L. Laing and Tolerton.

Steffano Francis Webb, Steffano Webb Collection, Alexander Turnbull Library G-5293-1/1

mass travel associated with the war. 'Spanish' flu, a mutation of bird flu, erupted in a worldwide pandemic with a toll estimated at between 25 and 40 million. It reached New Zealand in two waves, the first in July 1918. That produced no more deaths than the usual winter ills, and authorities only realised it had happened in hindsight. The second was far more virulent. It struck Auckland during late October and was carried south 'by rail and shipping'. Within a fortnight there were cases in Bluff, though the 'wave seems to have lessened in virulence as it advanced.'[46] Perhaps a third of all New Zealanders caught it, with fatalities variously quoted at between 6500 and 8600. The precise number remains unknown, partly because health authorities could not differentiate between pandemic deaths and those caused by usual strains of influenza. Many deaths came about from secondary infections, which some doctors listed as the primary cause of death. An official report noted that several hundred deaths officially put down to pneumonia, bronchitis and pulmonitis 'should have been' attributed to the pandemic.[47]

Excluding these, but including deaths attributed to influenza and 'cerebro-spinal fever', suggests that 5471 non-Maori and 1130 Maori died from the pandemic between October and December 1918.[48] This was a severe blow; war casualties of over 16,500 had been significantly higher, but they had also been spread across the years of conflict. The flu, by contrast, swept the country in months and hit families hard. What was more, at 226 per 10,000 of population the official Maori death rate was more than four times the European, a point that health authorities could not explain beyond the remark that Maori were 'exceptionally liable to attack'.[49] The young also fell in disproportionate numbers; almost half those who died were between 25 and 40, 'although only 24 percent of the population are between those ages.'[50]

Popular opinion put the late-1918 outbreak down to cases that reached Auckland on board the SS *Niagara* in October. This ship—with '100 crew down'—had Prime Minister William Massey and Sir Joseph Ward on board as passengers, and the popular story went that their pressure to get off prompted the authorities to let the ship dock.[51] However, Auckland health authorities had already noted cases before this ship arrived,[52] and an investigating Commission could not prove that the *Niagara* had been the trigger. A more crucial issue for the country had been a 'general disregard of precautionary measures in the initial stages, due to want of knowledge regarding the nature of the disease.'[53] The mechanisms of disease transmission were known, as was the fact that most people died from secondary infections such as pneumonia.[54] All this was made clear in Public Health Department guidelines:

> …no form of inoculation can be guaranteed to protect against the disease itself. But the chief dangers of influenza lie in its complications, and…much can be done to mitigate the severity of the infection and to diminish its mortality by raising the resistance of the body against the chief secondary infecting agents. …The liability of the immediate attendants to infection may be materially diminished by avoiding inhalation of the patient's breath, and particularly when he is coughing. …The risk of conveyance of infection by the fingers must be constantly remembered.[55]

ABOVE

'Nurse Maude's relief depot and emergency motorcars', during the influenza epidemic of late 1918.

Photographer unidentified, *The Press* (Christchurch) Collection, Alexander Turnbull Library, PAColl-3031, G-8546-1/1

OPPOSITE BOTTOM

Christchurch medicine depot during the influenza epidemic, December 1918. 'Stimulants' on sale at the Central Medicine Depot included small bottles of brandy, whisky and stout, this at a time when temperance was on the rise and New Zealand teetered on the verge of prohibition.

Photographer unidentified, *The Press* (Christchurch) Collection, Alexander Turnbull Library, G-8542-1/1

ABOVE

A 'medicine department' in the Wellington Town Hall, where tonics were prepared for influenza victims.

Photographer unidentified, New Zealand Free Lance Collection, Alexander Turnbull Library C-16207-1/2

Masks were considered, following overseas example, and the department recommended keeping away from public areas, adding that 'the virus of influenza is very easily destroyed.' If everybody had followed this advice, the spread of the disease might have been reduced. Unfortunately there was little popular distinction between viral and bacterial infection, all of which were usually categorised as 'germs', and mechanisms for transmission were misunderstood.

Popular thinking was not helped by the profusion of remedies—which were on the market irrespective of epidemics and designed to lift cash from the fearful. These included 'Zam-Buk' ointment, supposedly able to grow new tissue 'cell by cell', kill 'poison germs', and cure everything from piles to 'scalp disease'.[56] Other products on the market around that time included a 'Violet Ray' generator, for 'radiant health', pluggable into any light socket.[57] Some remedies were promoted—after the event—for supposed anti-flu properties.[58]

The Commission concluded that ignorance and the way that New Zealanders had simply continued everyday life despite the emergency had contributed to the problem:

ABOVE

ANZAC day processions in Wellington, 1920. Celebrations began as an essentially spontaneous event in 1916.

Photographer unidentified, Alexander Turnbull Library, G-116483-1/2)

...The infection was largely spread by the congregation of large crowds of people in the various centres in connection with the Armistice Celebrations, race meetings, the 'Carnival Week' in Christchurch...and the fact that no restriction was placed upon the movements of the people in travelling, even when they had individually been in contact with infected persons.[59]

The pandemic subdued the jubilation that came with the armistice in November 1918. In March 1919—as the former warring parties negotiated a settlement—the government decided to hold celebrations 'on the second Sunday, Monday and Tuesday after...the official announcement of preliminary peace having been signed.'[60]

OPPOSITE BELOW

'Inhalation chambers' were designed to kill the influenza virus in the throat. Although there was some evidence of the technique being effective, communal treatment probably also served to spread the virus.

Photographer unidentified, *The Press* (Christchurch) Collection, Alexander Turnbull Library G-8545-1/1

Dominions and jazz

Like most Western states, New Zealand left the war with an intrusive administration.[61] In many respects it was inevitable. Exigencies such as the British 'commandeer' prompted the government to establish a Board of Trade, authorised to control prices and prevent profiteering. Wartime censorship boosted pressure to legislate everything from films to drinking times and places—and had to be developed for state apparatus to administer them. Few wartime measures were dropped afterwards. In this, New Zealand reflected a world trend, and parties of

ABOVE

Influenza and disabled soldiers highlighted the need for hospitals and care in New Zealand. This is a maternity hospital around 1920.

Photographer unidentified, *The Press* (Christchurch) Collection, Alexander Turnbull Library, PAColl-3031, F-55156-1/2

both left and right embraced big government as a means of guiding, improving and asserting national power—filtered in New Zealand's case by the idea of being Britain's 'chief junior'. It has been argued that both trends helped define New Zealand as an entity.[62]

To some extent the expansion of the state, by definition, meant intervention—but in practice it simply reframed existing ideals, a movement along the small to large government continuum. Wartime promises to look after returned soldiers did not reflect an ideological sea-change at a time when governments were growing in any event, and in 1921, MP Sir Francis Bell declared that government should not start 'poking its nose in…to provide employment.'[63] But amid criticism that he had broken the government 'pledge to the soldiers',[64] he did endorse larger public works schemes. This was more Vogelian than Fabian, highlighting the point that the left-right split was operating at the 'big' end of the government spectrum—it was not a question of 'big' versus 'small' government, but which flavour of 'big' was going to be pursued.

Ward left the coalition in 1919, hoping to lead the Liberals into victory by seizing ground held by a still-radicalised Labour party. But his proposed state-owned bank, nationalised coalfields and freezing works, all funded by new overseas loans, were rejected by the electorate. As a Catholic, he was not helped by the Protestant Political Association, which lobbied against him.[65] The result was a crashing defeat; even Ward lost his seat. Labour were also spurned—their 40-hour week and plans to nationalise banks, shipping, factories and farms were too radical for a conservative populace, and Massey's Reform Party came to power with 43 seats and 36 percent of the vote, much of it from the rural sector.

The inter-war years were the first great age of the medium farmers, the group born of the dairying and frozen-meat revolution of the 1880s and nurtured by the Liberal land reforms. War gave them income; their products were snatched up by the British market. Pastoral industries provided 91.2 percent of all exports in 1919,[66] and even after the 'commandeer' ended in 1920, these products held disproportionate sway.

The economic strength of the farming sector was further reinforced during the 1920s by a pastoral revolution on the back of Nauru superphosphate, initially spread by hand or with 'blower' trucks. Mechanisation helped—internal combustion engines registered on farms rose from 13,981 to 18,321 during the decade. The dairying sector took up new machinery with alacrity. In 1920, there were 26,678 cream separators and 8806 milking plants. By 1928 there were 45,246 and 18,049 respectively. Most were electrically driven, reflected by an increase from 640 electric motors on farms in 1921 to 10,806 in 1928.[67]

Rising productivity embedded the new farming class in New Zealand's economy, and new technology—notably the telephone—had a social spinoff. Rural party lines were adopted early and spread rapidly, reinforcing bonds between sometimes far-flung but nonetheless sociable rural communities. This new breed of farmers were inelegant in their dress: gumboots, gaberdine trousers or shorts, black singlets and battered fedora were standard on farms, often topped in winter by the tartan bush shirt invented by New Plymouth tailor William Brougham in 1913—the classic 'Swanndri'. When these farmers dressed up for town—often to visit the saleyards—they inevitably arrived in tweed jackets, still wearing the fedora. None of it could be called sartorial, but the look was practical, effective—and defined the feel of New Zealand's rural life for half a century.

Few of the new class of classic Kiwi farmers were large landholders; just under 41 percent worked properties of between 100 and 640 acres by 1930.[68]

LEFT

Pomp of government: the Legislative Council chamber, William Massey on the left.

Photographer unidentified, Alexander Turnbull Library, F-31486-1/2

ABOVE

William Ferguson Massey (1856–1925), 'Farmer Bill', lifelong champion of the New Zealand farmer, was son of an Irish tenant-farmer and followed his family to New Zealand in 1870, aged 14. By the 1880s he was a self-employed farmer, but he had political ambition and became president of the Mangere Farmers Club in 1890, then provincial leader of the Auckland Agricultural Association. He entered Parliament in 1894 on the National Association platform, and presided over the decline of the Liberals and the rise of the small-holder in New Zealand.

Herman John Schmidt, Schmidt Collection, Alexander Turnbull Library, PAColl-3059, G-1533-1/1

They focussed on dairy, lamb, beef and wool, but did not quite overwhelm the big sheep runs—a few of which still operated in back-country Hawke's Bay and Canterbury. In these places old money still held sway.

This was the New Zealand of Fred Dagg and Wal Footrot, a ruralised, practical land of laconic, hard-working medium-holders whose world lasted, by and large, for 60 years or so. A good number of New Zealanders wanted in during the rugged years after the First World War and newspapers of the period were flooded with advertisements asking for rural land. 'Wellington city property,' one request read, 'Exchange for sound Dairy or mixed farm.' Hicks and Bull of Whanganui wanted 'land to sell' to clients in the Manawatu district.[69] However, the door was not opened to many. In 1919, there were 116,059 New Zealanders in pastoral occupations, including dairying. By 1929 there were 124,451.[70] Nonetheless, they gained power; pastoral products never fell below 91 percent of New Zealand's total exports in the 1920s, peaking in 1924, 1925 and 1929 at 94.2 percent.[71]

Under these circumstances it was perhaps understandable that returned soldiers were thanked with land. Some 6363 servicemen had been helped into urban properties by the end of the 1919–1920 financial year, aided by advances of up to £1,000 each—though as an official report remarked, 'already the soldiers are selling the houses at a profit to civilians or men not entitled to benefits under the Discharged Soldiers Settlement Act...'[72] Most sought further profit from the rural boom, and the prospect of quick wealth on the back of rising property prices lured others into orchards, market gardens, small sheep runs and dairy farms. By the end of the 1919–1920 financial year, more than 365,000 acres had been set aside for returned soldiers, some from existing runs, others from new land carved out of previously unsettled back-country. This was done in part by state loan; government forked out over £8.6 million to 12,415 soldiers by the end of March 1920.[73] Many were eager to accept, mortgaging themselves to the hilt in the hope that land values would continue to spiral upwards.

The growing relationship between hands-on government, economy and the farming sector also emerged in the public works of the period. The hot technologies of the twentieth century were electricity and cars. New Zealanders picked them up with alacrity, but as always the new carried a cost. Settler-age governments had wrestled with railway infrastructure. Building that network had been an expensive exercise, complicated by New Zealand's geographic reality and what by overseas standards was a sparse population. Relatively long distances had to be spanned to bring the far-flung colonial centres together with the iron horse, and that same sparsity of people also meant that both capital funding and likely revenues from the resulting lines were never going to be sparkling.

Now, in the unfolding third decade of the twentieth century the Massey administration faced the same issue again, this time twofold. The issue was

ABOVE

Auckland's War Memorial Museum was built in the late 1920s to a design by Grierson, Aimer and Draffin. A fair proportion of New Zealand's memorials were public buildings, often museums or libraries—an indication not simply of a pragmatic streak but, more poignantly, of the depth to which the wars shaped New Zealand's everyday life.

Photographer unidentified, Alexander Turnbull Library, PAColl-6997, C-14396-1/2

LEFT ABOVE

Snowy Battery, south of Waiuta, the quintessential West Coast mining town. When all the mines were worked out the town literally vanished—most of the buildings were physically removed.

Photographer unidentified, Derek French Collection, Alexander Turnbull Library, PAColl-4796, F-31558-1/2

broadly the same for both power and roading; old colonial-style administrative and funding structures had been built around localities. Early road-sealing and even power projects were often also locally initiated and funded by individual boroughs. But as demand kept spiralling these more local projects were becoming increasingly difficult to sustain in an age when cars could drive dozens and hundreds of miles and where the need for electricity was climbing sharply.

Roads had been a bugbear for years, and rural mechanisation added to the 30,000-odd cars already on New Zealand's roads by the late-war period, wearing

ABOVE

The rise of the 'classic' New Zealand farmer gave rural service towns a new flush of prosperity. This is Norsewood, probably during the 1920s.

Photographer unidentified, Alexander Turnbull Library, New Zealand Free Lance Collection, F-27116-1/2

RIGHT

Motor-buses were increasingly common on New Zealand's roads in the 1920s. This US-built REO Speed Wagon was owned by the Bell Bus Company of Wellington.

Photographer unidentified, F. R. Just Collection, Alexander Turnbull Library, F-71431-1/2

down roads built to handle horse traffic. Only about 40 percent of the national network was even metalled, and wartime production helped focus the crisis. Lobbying fermented during 1918 around the 'Good Roads Association'.[74] Part of the problem was that cars and trucks moved further than horses, straining a system based around separate local Road Boards funded by local users. Several Taranaki counties tried to toll 'foreign' vehicles,[75] setting a precedent that others looked likely to follow by the early 1920s. Voices of complaint from the Good

CHAPTER SEVEN
GOD'S OWN COUNTRY

LEFT

A Nelson charabanc, mid-1920s.

Frederick Nelson Jones, F. N. Jones Collection, Alexander Turnbull Library, PAColl-3051, G-9321-1/1

BELOW LEFT

The H. C. Baulf *Auckland Star* service car, between Frankton and Te Aroha around 1924.

Photographer unidentified, Alexander Turnbull Library, F-125498-1/2

BELOW RIGHT

A service car owned by Napier's Aard Motor Services gets a pull on the Wairoa road, mid-1920s. Founder G. Woodcock coined the name to get his company listed first in the phone book.

Photographer unidentified, Alexander Turnbull Library, F-89570-1/2

BOTTOM

Sealing was expensive and labour intensive; here, road-builders rake asphalt.

Photographer unidentified, Tyndall Collection, Alexander Turnbull Library, PAColl-0866, F-104338-1/2

275

NEW ZEALAND
AN ILLUSTRATED HISTORY

Roads Association were joined by others from the Automobile Association and Farmers' Union, and J. G. Coates proposed a 'Main Highways Bill' in 1921. County interests managed to delay it twelve months, but it was passed at the end of 1922 and came into being in April 1924, establishing a Main Highways Board and designating some 6000—later 10,000—miles of road under state control. Rebuilding and sealing these was a gargantuan task, and by 1929 some £59.5 million had been sunk into New Zealand's roads, most of it in the previous decade, outstripping rail for the first time. A further £49 million—around $4,462 million in early twenty-first-century money—had been spent on vehicles.[76]

The other big state money-soaker of the day was power generation, mostly through hydroelectric schemes. Demand for power was driven in part by demand from the rapidly electrifying dairy sector, but also by a proliferation of electric appliances. Government acquired national water rights in 1903, and the first state power station at Lake Coleridge was in operation by 1915, supplying up to 4500 kilowatts to Christchurch. Plans to reticulate the North Island were proposed in 1918 by Chief Electrical Engineer Evan Parry. He envisaged stations generating 150 watts per capita at Mangahao, north of Wellington; Waikaremoana, near Wairoa; and Arapuni on the Waikato.[77] Despite opposition from Hawke's Bay, priority went to the Mangahao scheme, which was finished in 1924. The Arapuni station was last, mainly because it required a high dam which seemed likely to bloat the price to £3 million—around $312 million in early twenty-first century money[78]— and demand had to top 27 megawatts to make the station economic. Teething problems with the dam delayed completion of the first stage until 1932.[79]

Massey's New Zealanders still defined themselves as double patriots. However, by the 1920s the inevitable generational shifts, intensified and accelerated by war experience, had changed this entwined complex of ideas into a new pattern that ranked local sentiment as highly as Imperial. As before the war, however, pro-British sentiment was not reciprocated. Although seeking new trade ties with her

OPPOSITE TOP

Putting the first coat of seal on the Paekakariki–Paraparaumu road, around 1930.

Photographer unidentified, Alexander Turnbull Library, F-61963-1/2

OPPOSITE BOTTOM

North Island power: Tuai hydroelectric station powerhouse under construction near Lake Waikaremoana, 1929.

A. Hardcastle, Alexander Turnbull Library, C-14298-1/2

BELOW

The powerhouse on Lake Coleridge opened with three of six planned 1500 kW turbo-generators in November 1914. The fourth was finished in 1917. Two 3000 kW units followed. Then two 7500 kW generators were added, requiring a second intake. Four 1500 hp U-boat diesels made up the shortfall in Christchurch, meanwhile.

Photographer unidentified, Alexander Turnbull Library, Making New Zealand Collection, F-564-1/4-MNZ

RIGHT

Engineers inspect the Arapuni dam after it had been drained, November 1930. An initial fill in 1929 produced cracks in the landscape around the head of the lake, traced to the weight of water, and the lake was drained while engineers dealt with the problem with advice from Sweden. The headrace was sealed and the station opened in 1932. Predictions that 27 mW capacity would be overkill were soon dashed, but the station had been designed with expansion in mind, and work began on the programme in 1934. When completed in 1946 the enlarged station had a capacity of 162 mW, then the largest in New Zealand.

E. C. Lackland, Alexander Turnbull Library, *Evening Post* Collection, C-27085-1/2

former colonies, the mother country had been pushing her children out of the Imperial nest for some time. New Zealand, like the other Dominions, separately signed the Treaty of Versailles, was a separate signatory of the naval arms limitation treaty signed in Washington in 1922, and was a founding member of the League of Nations.

The fact that New Zealand was entitled to a separate voice here was significant, but Massey went along with it under protest. His vision of Dominion partnership differed from Britain's plan to turn its Empire into a Commonwealth of independent nations. Partly for this reason Massey did not push New Zealand's independent role in the League of Nations.[80] Patriotism to Massey—and indeed to many New Zealanders—still meant loyalty to Imperial Britain. Schools still lined their children up, pseudo-military style, to salute the Union Jack or sing *God Save The Queen*. 'Our country' was New Zealand, but 'our nation' remained Imperial Britain. The political and economic realities of a post-First World War Empire, it seemed, counted for less in a Dominion that still counted itself as Britain's most loyal child.

This attitude stood alongside a heightened sense of local nationalism, a feeling that was yet another consequence of a more intrusive government, which by definition treated New Zealand as a nation. To a greater extent, though, it reflected front-line experience. During the war, New Zealand soldiers were treated as distinct by soldiers of other nations, including the British. Shared battlefield camaraderie reinforced the trend. More than half New Zealand's young men of the wartime generation had fought on the Western Front—and it was this battlefield, not Gallipoli, that became the birthplace of a New Zealand sense of nationalism. By the 1920s the idea of New Zealand as a nation stood in uneasy tension with the concept of New Zealand as 'junior partner' within the Empire. The oppositions survived for decades, and even in the late 1940s, when the British Empire was a faded glory, Peter Fraser was still trying to rationalise the concept in the Commonwealth context as 'independence with something added'.[81]

Defence policy reflected this curiously bipolar mind-set. Britain began pressuring the dominions to build their own navies after the 1923 Imperial Conference, and New Zealand received its first oil-fired cruiser in 1924. However, plans to acquire a second fell foul of Massey's intention to part-fund the Singapore naval base instead. His offer of £100,000 per annum for two years went down well with Australia and India, but Canada saw little sense in the strategy, and Britain's minority Labour government also disliked the idea. Singapore went on hold and Massey came under pressure to use the £100,000 for a second cruiser in the local naval division.[82] The New Zealand Parliament approved it in October but, almost simultaneously, the British government was defeated in a general election and the incoming Conservatives restarted Singapore.

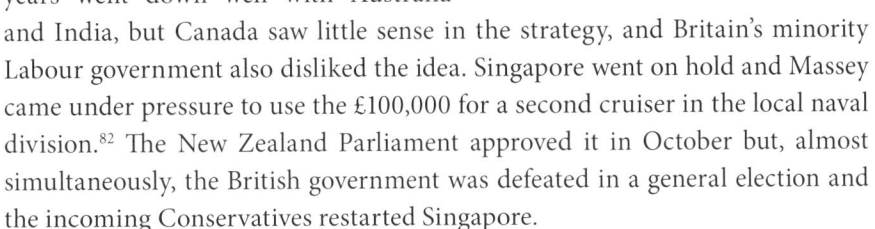

Massey wavered towards the cruiser, but wondered about taking out a loan for a £250,000 one-off grant for the base. The debate was inherited by his successor, J. G. Coates.[83] There were more calls for a third cruiser in early 1926,[84] but Coates was also pressed by the British to contribute £225,000 per annum to Singapore. The motive was financial, and while Coates refused to take over two sloops in New Zealand waters, he told the House in late 1926 that he would be guided by the Admiralty during the coming Imperial Conference. Here he 'sought the advice of Admiral Hotham',[85] attended meetings with other imperial leaders at Downing Street, and went on to the Admiralty, the War Office and the Air Ministry.[86] As a result Coates decided to cancel a third cruiser but replace the existing ships.

ABOVE

Passers-by stand for the camera in an Auckland street around 1924.

Photographer unidentified, Alexander Turnbull Library, PAColl-7433-47

LEFT

New Zealanders took to cars in the 1920s like ducks to water. Initial uptake was white collar and in the wealthier farming sector.

S. C. Smith, Alexander Turnbull Library, PAColl-3082, G-48844-1/2

RIGHT

J. G. Coates (1878–1943) at the Mahina-a-rangi meeting house, Ngaruawahia.

Photographer unidentified, Alexander Turnbull Library, F-59948-1/2

OPPOSITE TOP

New Zealand burst into the 'golden age' of aviation with several spectacular cross-country flights by rival air transport companies. This is the DH-9 of the Canterbury (NZ) Aviation Company in 1921 after an early flight to Nelson.

Frederick Nelson Jones, F. N. Jones Collection, Alexander Turnbull Library, PAColl-3051, G-28554-1/2

OPPOSITE BOTTOM

The public went wild when Charles Kingsford Smith flew his Fokker trimotor across the Tasman in September 1928, and 'Smithy' became an instant public hero on both sides of the Tasman. He is seen here at Wigram soon after his triumphant first landing. An effort by John Moncrieff and George Hood to fly a Ryan monoplane across earlier that year ended in what the *Auckland Star* called a 'futile tragedy'.

Photographer unidentified, Alexander Turnbull Library, PAColl-4273-3, F-30845-1/2

Meanwhile, he committed £1,000,000 to Singapore, by instalment—around $90.25 million in early twenty-first century money.[87]

On wider matters Coates, colourfully dubbed the 'Jazz Premier' by Labour member and war veteran John A. Lee,[88] proved very different from the autocratic Massey. New Zealand's main problem was an indifferent economy. The United States partied that decade, buoyed by the second industrial revolution and the European debt mountain, but Britain was in dire straits. A generation had died in the war, the Victorian inheritance had been spent, and the 1920s were spiritually and economically gloomy. New Zealand's own fortunes nose-dived when the 'commandeer' was cancelled. Some £44,344,503 worth of beef, mutton, lamb and other meat had been despatched under terms of the guaranteed purchase by the end of the 1919–20 fiscal year[89]—$3,815,076,855 in in early twenty-first century money—along with 2,898,294 crates of cheese worth £19,106,866,[90] 1,874,912 boxes of butter valued at £8,143,100,[91] £175,970 worth of the mineral scheelite, and wool worth £2,031,092.[92]

This cash cow came to an abrupt halt in 1920–21, contributing to a dive in New Zealand property prices that left many owners unable to repay mortgages. Exports picked up as the decade wore on, in part an outcome of a British drive to trade with its dominions rather than other nations. Dairy produce was in demand, but prices were never high, and apart from a slight surge in 1926–28 the decade consisted of an erratic lurch from one downturn to the next. Some economists have argued that New Zealand's whole inter-war period was depressed,[93] and there seems a good deal of truth in that. Massey's government responded conservatively, and there was a call for flat-rate income tax in 1924, accompanied by an abolition of land taxes. Coates, though sharing Forbes' attitudes to social policy, saw succour in a vigorous public works programme. He became Minister of Railways in 1924 and restarted a raft of pre-war proposals, including reconstructing the Auckland approaches, building a deviation out of Wellington and putting a new station in near Palmerston North. In an atmosphere

CHAPTER SEVEN
GOD'S OWN COUNTRY

MR HAWKER ARRIVES FROM BLENHEIM
WITH 2 PASSENGERS - MESSRS. PERANO
AND McARTNEY. NELSON 13.11.21. F.H.JONES.

RIGHT

Railway was one of the central pillars of New Zealand's public works programmes of the 1920s, and a focus for J. G. Coates, first as Minister of Railways and then Prime Minister. This is the Petone erecting shop in 1929.

Albert Percy Godber, A. P. Godber Collection, Alexander Turnbull Library, PAColl-3039, G-11880-1/2

RIGHT BELOW

Milson diversion under construction, Palmerston North, 1927.

Photographer unidentified, Alexander Turnbull Library, C-27172-1/2

where cars had made inroads into short-haul travel and were digging into longer routes, he called for new operating efficiencies and higher speeds.

To some extent this neo-Vogelism paid off. New Zealand already had an excellent light industrial base, pivoting around railways, and particularly wagon and locomotive construction. A good deal of the money spent on the railways was spent inside New Zealand, supporting that local industry and providing employment. Coates' initiatives also revived a railway system that seemed to be flagging in the face of motor transport. Goods being sent by rail rose by about 1.8 million tons per annum over the decade. Passenger numbers doubled.[94]

This policy—and other programmes that Coates inherited—outlasted his administration. Public works spending hovered around 21–22 percent of state spending during the war, dipped slightly in 1919, then began a steady climb to a high of 31.4 percent in 1931,[95] before plunging drastically. This was also the key focus of public spending at the time; direct social spending remained minimal, apart from education which absorbed around 10 percent of the state budget. Health budgets stood at around 3 percent of state spending in the first decades of the century, then plunged to under 2 percent through the 1920s.[96] Social welfare payments included war, old age and widows pensions, along with epidemic funds and a variety of annuities, and the net total in 1922, the peak year, amounted to 9.8 percent of all state expenditure.[97]

In the end, however, neither these public works with their infusion of vigour into the domestic economy, nor a bungled effort to hijack prices on the London dairy market, managed to pull the New Zealand economy out of the doldrums. The real problem was wider than New Zealand. The United States boomed during the 1920s, buoyed partly by the effects of the second industrial revolution with its mass production of relatively cheap consumer products. But nobody else flourished. Europe and Britain had been racked by war. Britain was in significant trouble, and that was where most of New Zealand's agrarian-focussed exports were going.

Seventy-two year old Sir Joseph Ward re-emerged as leader of a United Party in 1928, promising to cure all with new borrowing. Figures such as £70 million were bandied about after an address Ward gave in the Auckland Town Hall. In fact the plan was to borrow £7 million a year for a decade. Ward's error has been put down to failing eyesight and difficulty reading speech notes.[98] His party was elected as a minority government in November, but the decrepit ex-Liberal was not up to the job. His absences from the House became longer, his

ABOVE

An ageing J. G. Ward returned to politics in 1928. He stands here with his son Vincent Aubrey Ward.

Photographer unidentified, Alexander Turnbull Library, F-123686-1/2

BELOW

Francis Chichester's De Havilland DH-60G Gypsy Moth is unloaded at Wellington.

Photographer unidentified, Alexander Turnbull Library, PAColl-0614, G-32441-1/4

remarks vaguer, and his land-tax a political disaster. He made his last appearance in September 1929 with the claim that every New Zealander who wanted work would soon have it. This apparently reflected his misunderstanding of the £7 million loan, and Forbes had to issue a formal denial.[99] Ward was persuaded to resign in May 1930, handing the reins to Forbes, and the old Liberal warhorse died eight weeks later.

Puritans and parties

Life in New Zealand between wars was an exercise in extremes. An attitude that the war was over and it was time to party stood at odds with the flip-side reaction to the struggle, social purity—an exaltation of the puritanical attitudes that had been rising for the past generation. The more zealous advocates of social purity feared society was about to collapse in the face of unrestrained irreligious activity, seeing sexual misbehaviour and drunkenness around every corner. Protestant churches railed against contraception, joined by Baptists and Methodists as the decade went on. Family life was exalted by a cult of domesticity. Much of this extended previous idealism—the family had been evangelised in British cities and towns from the mid-nineteenth century,[100] However, all emerged in full flower after the war, a lurch to the safe and well-understood by a generation traumatised by events they had been unable to control or avoid.

A fair number of New Zealand's traditional institutions bent to the pressure.

BELOW

Crowds highlight the huge popularity of racing during the inter-war period.

John Reginald Wall, J. R. Wall Collection, Alexander Turnbull Library, PAColl-3065, G-17834-1/1

Racing was a particular target. Totalisator machines had been criticised since the 1880s, generating petitions to Parliament in 1903 and 1907—the last running neck-and-neck at 36,311 for and 36,471 against.[101] Ward's Gaming and Lotteries Act of 1908 compromised; off-course bookmaking was legalised and the totalisator entrenched, giving the government a percentage of the turnover. However, the system was a disaster and the moral evangelists prevailed in 1911 when bookmaking was made illegal. This did not reduce betting, and estimates suggest that illegal bookmaking up to 1946 topped £24 million. The ultimate answer was a government-run Totalisator Agency Board (TAB), established in 1949.[102]

The evangelists found another expression in Plunket, founded by asylum administrator Dr Truby King in 1907. His hygiene advice helped reduce the infant mortality rate, but his philosophy was unadulterated social purity, blended with period ideas of racial destiny and patriotic fervour. His prescription for new mothers involved large doses of discipline, obedience and enforced regular bowel movements.

Conformity, order and regimentation was certainly the name of the game during the inter-war decades. New Zealand's social norm was built around a narrow spectrum of acceptable thoughts and actions. Those who did not match up were defined as 'abnormal', in need of 'correction'—a mind-set that led, among other things, to some left-handers being forced to write with their right hand at school. This reduction of humanity to machine extended to thought, following the lead of thinkers such as Karl Jung who portrayed the psyche as a mechanistic

BELOW

Night races.

Photographer unidentified, Alexander Turnbull Library, C-27176-1/2

RIGHT

Quarter-acre paradise, early 1920s, complete with Dodge and Hupmobile. House, garden, berm and car defined the classic Kiwi suburban home for the rest of the century — only the details changed.

Henry Norford Whitehead, H. N. Whitehead Collection, Alexander Turnbull Library, PAColl-3068, G-4610-1/1

ABOVE

Clean, controllable heat made all the difference in the inter-war kitchen. This is a Wanganui Gas Company display in 1923.

Frank J. Denton, Tesla Collection, Alexander Turnbull Library, PAColl-3046, F-21467-1/1

system; and the mind-set devolved into eugenics, another world phenomenon which New Zealanders expressed in the absurd claim that the Dominion was 98.5 percent British—a remark that ignored Maori, Chinese, Irish and Scandinavians among others.

This new society also found new places to live. 'The homes of the town-workers,' John Mulgan wrote of these years, 'ate wide into the country, red-roofed, with their small gardens, concrete paths, and modern sanitation…'[103] Facilitated by car and mass transport, the new suburbs spread from inner-city Auckland, Wellington, Christchurch and Dunedin in particular. Some, like Johnsonville, were old villages; others were laid out from scratch. They brought a new look to the New Zealand urban landscape. Villas were passé; architects and draftsmen sought alternative inspiration in the Americas. California bungalows went up alongside English-cottage-style homes in the burgeoning suburbs,[104] interleaved with occasional Spanish Mission. Later they were joined by daring flat-roofed, speed-lined modernist styles, pastel-stuccoed expressions of the modernist age. In a few suburbs these styles predominated. All were set amid wide streets with roadside trees—often one to each berm—with space for parks, small shopping centres and schools.

Social utopia did not seem far away as garden beautification societies competed to make the neatest and most attractive properties. 'Scientific' home management was the order of the day.[105] Rooms gained new names; the verandah became the porch, parlour the living room, and many homes featured a 'sleeping porch'—designed to maximise fresh air by putting the slumbering home owner outside. As in the settler era, cleanliness had a moral dimension, helped in a physical sense by new technical advances that brought easy-clean materials to home interiors, notably chrome, ceramic and tiles in the bathrooms.[106]

These developments, sieved through the filter of apparent scientific certainties, stood against the other forces of the 1920s and 1930s. A new youth lifestyle emerged. This was the other reaction to wartime trauma; the lucky

LEFT

A well-packed Clyno and sidecar around 1920.

Photographer unidentified, *The Press* (Christchurch) Collection, Alexander Turnbull Library, PAColl-3031, G-8536-1/1

ones had come out alive and intended to live life to the full. Others had been children during the war and had no intention of suffering like their fathers or elder brothers. Their shared values were spread by radio, popular magazines and cinema, giving New Zealanders fresh impressions of life outside New Zealand and the British Empire. It was a world of temptation. Early Hollywood output

BELOW

Early bungalows brought twentieth-century styles to New Zealand.

Steffano Francis Webb, Steffano Webb Collection, Alexander Turnbull Library, PAColl-3061, F-3904-1/1

NEW ZEALAND
AN ILLUSTRATED HISTORY

was riddled with nudity, from 'what the butler saw' kinescopes to dancing girls in D. W. Griffiths' *Intolerance* of 1916. Films also peddled implicit sex, epitomised for many by screen vamp Theda Bara (*Arab Death*), whose performances pushed the boundaries of the period's moral sensibilities.

Lawn tennis, 'dates', outdoor picnics, parties and the Charleston combined with the latest New York or Parisian fashions in a new culture of youth and freedom. The main sources of inspiration were not surprising given the similarities between the New Zealand and American frontiers since the colonial period. Californian architecture had been in vogue across New Zealand since before the First World War. Parks and gardens were 'Americanised' with date palms. Shops and businesses reflected cross-Pacific inspiration in their window displays and range and style of products.

A good deal of this was made possible by the second industrial revolution—mass-production and the assembly line, kicked into high gear by the needs of the First World War. Cars poured into New Zealand, finding a ready market among white-collar workers, professionals, and the rising farming class.

New Zealand effectively motorised during the period.[107] Numbers of motor vehicles on the road rose from around 100,000 at the end of the First World War to nearly 300,000 by the end of the 1930s, and they were joined by trucks, tractors and buses. Horses and carts vanished virtually overnight—by the late 1920s only the domestic milk cart was still horse-drawn, and that for practical reasons. Horses survived, too, in the back-country. But in the towns and growing urban areas the whole focus was on the new. For the average family, transport in the late 1920s meant either taking the bus or train, or getting their own car. Around one in eight families had one by the 1930s, and garages vied for sales. 'The invincible Talbot,' intoned one Christchurch advertisement in 1928, offering a tourer for £575 and a saloon for £685.[108] These were significant sums—$41,332 and $49,239 respectively in early 21st-century money, but New Zealanders were prepared to pay them.[109] Many preferred American cars, such

OPPOSITE TOP

This large Auckland home was built to the latest inter-war styles.

Photographer unidentified, *Auckland Star* Collection, Alexander Turnbull Library, PAColl-3752, G-3158-1/1

OPPOSITE BOTTOM

Wellington expanded during the inter-war years as public transport and motor cars made suburban life practical. This is Wilton in 1932, looking towards the Karori cemetery. Otari Native Plant Museum stands on the left, established in 1927 by Leonard Cockayne and Director of Parks and Reserves J. G. MacKenzie.

Photographer unidentified, *Evening Post* Collection, Alexander Turnbull Library PAColl-0614, G-88436-1/2

LEFT

Avro Avian over Dannevirke, revealing a classic New Zealand street layout: neat grid with functional zones and, further away, quarter-acre sections

Newham, Alexander Turnbull Library, F-50990-1/2

TOP

Swimmers at Lyall Bay, 1920s.

Photographer unidentified, Alexander Turnbull Library C-120414-1/2

ABOVE

What the best-dressed tennis players wore in the 1920s

G. O. Burt, Alexander Turnbull Library, PAColl-4118, F-15412-1/1

as the Dodge 'Victory Six', a snap at £465 ($33,425), which was sold on the basis of safety features such as hydraulic four-wheel brakes,[110] or a 'turret-top' all-steel body.[111] In 1928, some £2.9 million ($208.46 million) worth of cars were imported from the United States and Canada, against just £800,000 ($57.5 million) worth from Britain.[112]

In this first age of mass-produced and disposable consumer goods; even poorer families could afford to buy products that had been luxury items 20 years earlier, including electric kettles, toasters, ranges and hotplates, water heaters, refrigerators, washing machines with electric wringers—even glow-in-the-dark 'radium' switches for those wanting to turn on the light without groping.[113] 'Pinnacles of perfection,' one advertisement for Moffat's 'Gold Medal Electric Ranges' declared.[114] Electricity also brought voices and music from afar. 'Stellar Altair' five-valve radios promised 'wide reception with true microphone reproduction' through an 8-inch speaker, with 'spin type tuning' for 'easier, quicker tuning.'[115] Other goods were gimmicky, such as the Roycroft 'Billiards & Dining Table Combined' that could be picked up for £45 'complete with cues, balls and marking board'—or easy terms of £2 10 shillings down and 7/6 weekly.[116] Many of these products came from the United States; imports from America hovered between £5 and £8 million—$359.41 and $575.06 million today—for much of the 1920s, and in 1926 was nearly half that imported from Britain.[117]

None of this went down well with the social purists. Dancing was too sexual, movies too corrupting, popular magazines and books too explicit. As late as 1937 *Truth* declared that 3 million books annually were pouring into the country and 'contaminating the mental outlook' of youth with 'sewer literature.'[118] This spoke more of social fears than realities. The attitude had its origins in jingo society, refocussed by war and technology. Regulations were already in force to restrict literature by 1913, and in 1917 attention swung to movies. The problem here was, it seemed, not so much their content as the apparently salacious manner in which they were being promoted and sold. The Minister of Internal Affairs warned local bodies about 'the exhibition on hoardings and in the vestibules

TOP

Worser Bay beach one hot summer's day in the early 1930s.

S. C. Smith, Alexander Turnbull Library, PAColl-3082, G-46931-1/2

LEFT

Outdoor pursuits gained popularity during the inter-war period. This is the Heretaunga Tramping Club in the late 1930s.

Photographer unidentified, Alexander Turnbull Library, PAColl-6181-03, F-84896-1/2

RIGHT

Hodson's Pioneer Motor Service, Ridgway Street, Whanganui.

Frank J. Denton, Alexander Turnbull Library, PAColl-3046, F-21107-1/1

OPPOSITE TOP

Cars at a sports meeting, 1920s.

Photographer unidentified, Alexander Turnbull Library, PAColl-0866, F-104319-1/2

OPPOSITE BOTTOM

Cars extended the tradition of the Sunday drive for many families.

H. N. Whitehead, Alexander Turnbull Library, PAColl-3068, G-4667-1/1

BELOW

Cars at a race meet near Stratford in 1927.

John Reginald Wall, J. R. Wall Collection, Alexander Turnbull Library, PAColl-3065, G-17853-1/2

of theatres and other places of objectionable posters'. If municipal authorities were not prepared to 'exercise their powers', he intoned, then the Government 'may consider it necessary to find some other means of coping with what is an undoubted evil, and which is calculated to undermine the morals of the juvenile population of the Dominion.'[119] That was telling them, and the battle for morality continued after the war, reinforced in May 1921 by an Order in Council banning any document inciting violence or sedition.[120]

CHAPTER SEVEN
GOD'S OWN COUNTRY

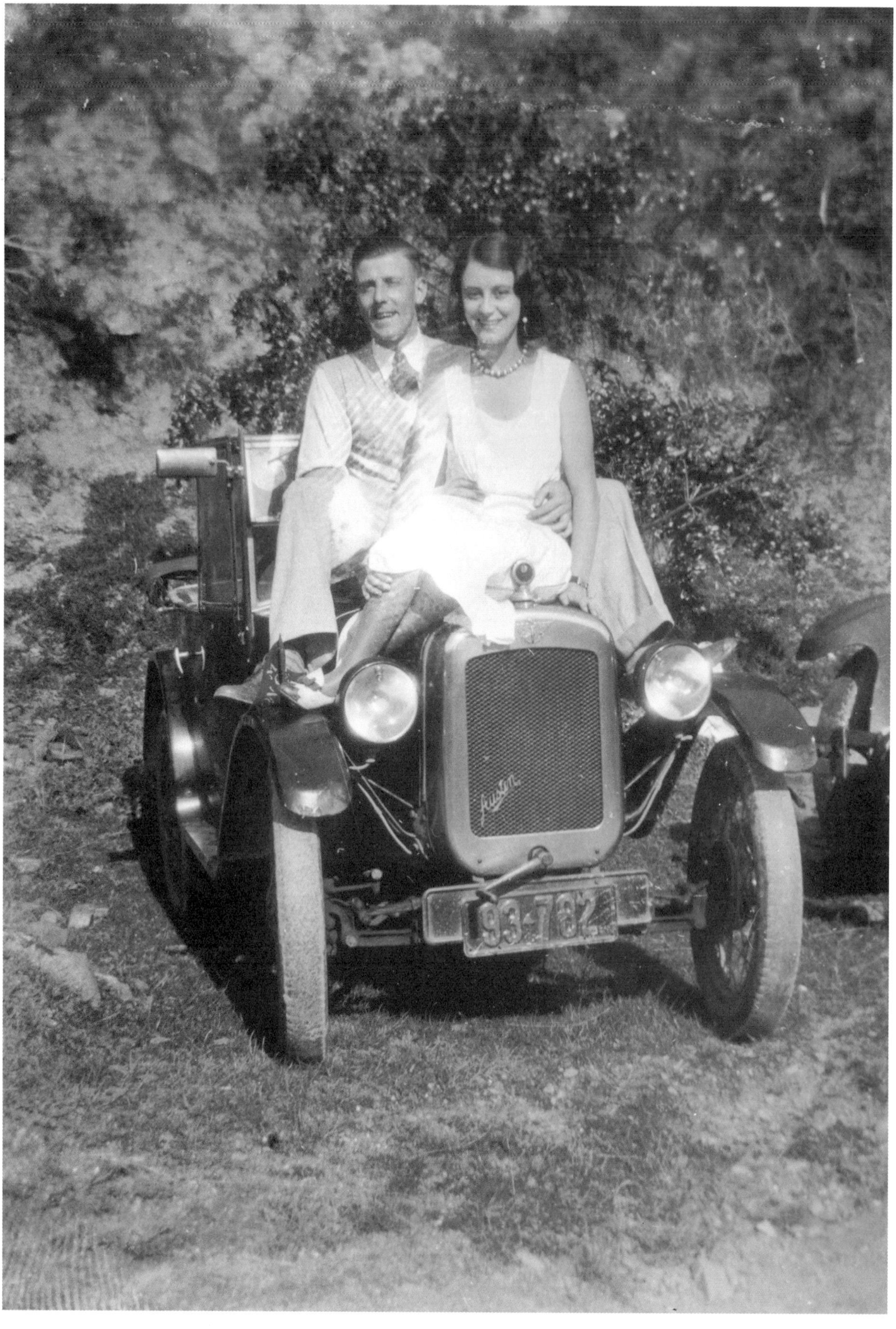
Austin
93-782

It was a largely male society. A blokeish world with its emphasis on alcohol, rowdiness and a professed indifference to the visceral had existed before the war as a part of labouring culture and the overall frontier environment. But the shared experiences on Gallipoli and the Western Front pushed the phenomenon in new directions and gave it new strengths, welding it to the family ethos and the rising world of dairy and sheep farmers. In many respects this became the definition of New Zealand culture as a whole for the next 60 years.

These traditions worked together to create an image of resourceful, independent, egalitarian, straight-talking, rugby-playing, hard-living outdoorsmen. This ideal drew inspiration from the 'working-class' ethos of the settler period. New emphasis on rugby and outdoor sporting pursuits was one of several factors driving the popularity of weekend hunting and tramping. What had been a way of life for hill-country shepherds emerged as a popular recreational activity, one also shared by women—but inevitably focussed on the image of the 'good keen man'. From this also emerged the twentieth-century notion of the gumbooted, laid-back 'Kiwi farmer' and his laconic 'she'll be right' attitude. Fred Dagg, Wal Footrot, and the imagery echoed in advertisements even into the twenty-first century stem from a frontier ethos brought together and refined by the traumatic lens of Gallipoli and Flanders.

New Zealand's bloke culture had its own customs, mostly to do with alcohol. The most prominent was 'shouting'—buying drinks for others in the group in even numbers. Beer was sold in jugs over the bar and 'chugged' in seven-ounce glasses. It was also watered down, a temperance-driven strategy that fostered consumption in quantity. Bloke culture had its own jargon—often derived from drinking, but also reflecting other facets of hands-on pastoral life. It was a white sub-culture, and it was wholly male. Even husbands tacitly behaved as single men when with their fellows, and wives were expected to be submissive stay-at-homes.

This ethos was reflected in sport; the inter-war years were in many ways a golden age of rugby. There were All Black tours of Australia in 1920 and 1922; and in 1924 a new team—including legendary fullback George Nepia—took on Britain, France and British Columbia. They played 32 games and won all of them, giving the team the epithet 'Invincibles'. Another tour of Australia followed in 1926, South Africa in 1928, Australia again in 1929, 1932, 1934 and 1938, and the British Isles and Canada in 1935.[121] War stopped the formal tours, but did not dim the enthusiasm, and 'friendlies' were occasionally organised at army level, as in North Africa where a team drawn from 2 NZ Division played another drawn from the South African force—an event requiring its own air

ABOVE

New Zealanders were not slow when it came to buying cars, and thanks in part to wartime exigencies when importers had to turn to North American suppliers, American models initially stood alongside English products. Every Kiwi family wanted one; the problem for most was affording them.

Samuel Heath Head, S. Head Collection, Alexander Turnbull Library, PAColl-3049, G-12090-1/1

OPPOSITE

Chummy motoring: a young couple with their Austin 7 around 1929.

Photographer unidentified, Bill Main (But Is It Art?) Collection, Alexander Turnbull Library, P(AColl-2489, C-15900-1/2

ABOVE

Legendary All Black from a legendary team: George Nepia (1905–1966), fullback with the 1924 'Invincibles', seen here in 1928.

S. P. Andrew, Alexander Turnbull Library, F-18732-1/1

RIGHT

The Invincibles return, 1925. There could be no doubt whatsoever about their popularity, or the status of rugby as a sport in New Zealand.

Photographer unidentified, Alexander Turnbull Library C-21948-1/2

cover. International matches by the All Blacks were backed by grassroots popularity, fostered by strong interprovincial rivalry based around the Ranfurly Shield. This had been established in 1902 as a gift from the Governor-General of the day, and came into its own in the 1920s. At this social level, rugby was part of the social flattening of the inter-war period, simultaneously a leveller that brought together people from all walks of life and a mechanism for exalting the heroes of the field as a national elite. It was also a permissible elite; herein lay one of the deeper issues of twentieth-century New Zealand. Local achievement was possible, local over-achievement even admired, but only through the filter of bloke culture and the sport that most New Zealand men had taken to heart. And even then, the real accolades only came when these local heroes were pitted against the best that the rest of the world could offer.

For New Zealanders who had a passion in other areas the local prognosis was often bleak; the cultural cringe and its flip-sides found new expression as the century aged. In the new environment, New Zealanders could still be the best of the best—indeed, were expected to be capable of it and admired only if they were. But the local door to that status was still firmly locked. Achievement could come only by being recognised overseas, by beating the best that the world could offer. One result was a disproportionate number of New Zealanders in high places outside the country, particularly in the arts and sciences. A list of names and barebones biographical information published in the 1966 *Encyclopedia of New Zealand* occupied more than 30 pages of close-printed text, listed by country.[122] By then there were prominent New Zealanders from Argentina to Zambia, where Leonard

Bean became one of nine Permanent Secretaries in 1960.[123] Most expatriates flourished in Britain, where there were high-achieving Kiwis everywhere from the armed services to the arts, photography, ballet, government offices, medicine, the sciences, academia and literature.

The reasons for going were not solely cringe-related. New Zealand simply did not offer opportunities for the ambitious. The key question is why there was such a disproportionate number of authors, poets and scientists among the migrants. Britain's community of talented expatriate Kiwi writers was well

TOP LEFT

Katherine Mansfield and John Middleton Murry at Menton, France, 1921.

Photographer unidentified, Alexander Turnbull Library, F-2593-1/2

ABOVE

New Zealand writers in Pat Lawlor's study, 1935. Back, L to R: Eric Bradwell, J. Wilson Hogg, O. N. Gillespie, Stuart Perry, Victor Lloyd, Alan Mulgan, Leo Fanning. Seated, L to R: C. A. L. Treadwell, Pat Lawlor, G. G. Stewart, Redmond Phillips.

S. P. Andrew, Alexander Turnbull Library 18216-1/1

LEFT

Ernest Rutherford and Hans Geiger (left) at Manchester University, 1912.

Photographer unidentified, Alexander Turnbull Library, F-65890-1/2

ABOVE

Deerstalkers in the 1930s.

Photographer unidentified, Alexander Turnbull Library F-1768-1/2-MNZ

known—their numbers during the century included Katherine Mansfield, Dan Davin, Geoffrey Cox, Alan Mulgan, Hector Bolitho and Dorothy Eden. Scientists included Ernest, Lord Rutherford, and the anthropologist Raymond Firth. Medical men were also prominent, notably Sir Robert Macintosh, George Maloney, James Murdoch and Arthur Mowlem.

Others followed their lead. But back home it was a different story. While the settler elite had pretensions to art and mind, the 'bloke' culture that had grown to dominate by the early twentieth century was superficially anti-intellectual. Work gangs had little time for the finer arts; and as twentieth-century conformity emerged, the rewards of being exceptional diminished. Settler literature had been neither snobbish nor wholly fictional; authors typically wrote lurid accounts of their experiences. Populist literature included pot-boiler fiction, serials, detective stories and romances, but there was almost nothing considered great literature by the high brow in-crowd. For a young Kathleen Beauchamp it was only in the opiate-riddled, sexually relaxed and generally dissipated Bloomsbury set in London that she could find like-minded literati to

ABOVE

Deer hunter at White Rock, South Wairarapa, in 1921.

Leslie Hinge, Leslie Hinge Collection, Alexander Turnbull Library, PAColl-3050, G-16902-1/4

BELOW

Record head shot in the Whitcombe watershed, Westland, around 1938.

G. G. Atkinson, Alexander Turnbull Library, F-1352-1/4-MNZ

whom she could relate. She left her name behind in New Zealand.[124]

Rutherford's situation was different. When the 'father of modern physics' graduated, he tried initially to find work as a teacher, then moved to Trinity College, Cambridge, in 1895. His professional career led him from McGill University—where he did the work that won him a Nobel Prize in 1907—to Manchester University, and in 1919 he became Professor of Experimental Physics at Cambridge, a post he held until his death in 1937. Rutherford helped define the theoretical basis of twentieth-century atomic theory, and at popular level remained best known for splitting the atom. The irony of it was that, although he showed it could be done, he did not himself see any particular use for what, to him, was essentially a party trick. His career encapsulated the paradox of the expatriate game; in practice, Rutherford became an Englishman. He visited New Zealand just four times during the twentieth century, yet—like Mansfield—remains a celebrated national hero in New Zealand.

The brain drain was not all one-way. Anti-Semitism in Germany and Austria prompted a wave of emigration by those who could afford it during the 1930s, among them many of Europe's top scientists and intellectuals. Some came to New Zealand, including Karl Popper (1902–1994), one of the great philosophers of the twentieth century, popularly known for his legendary 1946 'poker' debate with Ludwig Wittgenstein at the Cambridge University Moral Sciences Club. He taught at Canterbury University from 1937 to 1946 and produced one of his best-known works—*The Open Society and Its Enemies*—in New Zealand. As

ABOVE

Radio transmitters going up on Mount Victoria in 1927. Most homes had a valve receiver in that golden age of wireless; and many boys dreamed of building crystal sets.

Photographer unidentified, Alexander Turnbull Library, PAColl-0614, G-997-1/2-EP

an Austrian he did not subscribe to New Zealand's cultural cringe, though it subscribed to him. Local recognition of his genius had to wait until he moved to England in the wake of the Second World War.

Sugarbags and conservatives

There was food in New Zealand at this time, but the trains did not always load it. Rain fell that winter on empty docks. Did we hear, perhaps for the first time, the voice of a people that has recognised an injustice, that has perceived the possibility of disorganisation in its midst? Economists and old men told us that all this had happened before and would pass away, but this comfort was of philosophic form and our natures were sensuous and unsuited to philosophy.

– John Mulgan, *Report on Experience*.[125]

Mythology always attributes the Great Depression that swept the western world in the early 1930s to a 1929 Wall Street stock market crash, but the crisis actually reflected much deeper causes that reflected the costs of the First World War and which included the way the world was extracting itself from the 'gold standard'.[126] It was a time of unprecedented downturn; not any depression but *the* depression—a downturn so severe it gained its own name, the Great Depression. It brought tremendous hardship to the whole of the West, searing itself into the psyche of the century. The hurt, hunger and dreary hopelessness of it certainly defined mid-century New Zealand. Those who lived through it—among them a young boy named Robert David Muldoon—were determined that the pain should never be repeated. Many of the decisions and policies that followed in the 1940s and beyond were specifically moulded by that intent. The 'reform period' of the 1980s was a direct reaction to these developments, a generational rejection of the response to the Depression. As such, it must be considered part of that wider cycle—integral with the great sweep of New Zealand's twentieth century.

In a strict economic sense, New Zealand's Depression was relatively brief. The downturn hit New Zealand hardest between 1931–33, and estimates suggest that in 1933 perhaps 30 percent of the workforce were unemployed.[127] However, the economy recovered dramatically after 1934, and a study in 1935 reported 'satisfactory evidence of recovery'.[128] In an economic sense it was far less severe here than elsewhere; there was no default on sovereign debt, no banking crisis, and even the drop in gross domestic product was not so great. Estimates suggest that the per capita drop in GDP from 1929 until 1932 was 17.8 percent, which was less than in Australia, Germany, Canada and the US.[129]

New Zealand was drawn in largely through a sharp drop in export prices to Britain, the main market.[130] This was coupled with cross-contamination from an Australian balance-of-payments crisis; New Zealand's sterling reserves were mingled with Australia's in the same banks in London. New Zealand banks had trouble trading on London money markets to help compensate for the loss of export earnings. A depreciation of around 10 percent in the New Zealand pound against the British provoked alarm. All of this was very evident in New Zealand; as Tutira station owner Herbert Guthrie-Smith remarked, the 'harassed government' had lost its sources of income.[131]

However, Forbes sailed for the Imperial Conference in August 1930 with no cure to hand other than the 'sanity and sobriety' prescribed by visiting banker Sir Otto Neimeyer, meaning fiscal restraint.[132] This provided a background to cancelling several railway projects, throwing 1700 men out of work. In his absence, government passed an Unemployment Act, but Forbes returned in January 1931 to declare that the dole would be paid only to those who worked for it—which in the absence of a vigorous export sector meant make-work. Forbes also insisted that the state books had to be balanced, announcing reductions in relief wages and the salaries of all public servants.[133] The people, he declared, must return to the land, a remark that, as one historian has noted, made no sense when produce prices had plunged and the farming sector was in crisis.[134] Wages fell 10 percent in nominal terms in May 1931 on the back of arbitration. Guthrie-Smith's own net income from Tutira Station plunged from an unprecedented high of £5,722 in 1929

BELOW
New Zealand Prime Minister George Forbes (left) and British Prime Minister Ramsay MacDonald.
Photographer unidentified, Alexander Turnbull Library F-41881-1/2

NEW ZEALAND
AN ILLUSTRATED HISTORY

LEFT

Hastings was almost as heavily hammered as Napier. However, although both the borough powerhouse and most of the water pipes were damaged, there was enough water for fire-fighters to extinguish blazes before they spread.

S. C. Smith, Alexander Turnbull Library, PAColl-3082, G-47684-1/2

OPPOSITE TOP

The iconic image of the Hawke's Bay earthquake of 1931. Napier's Hastings Street could have been mistaken for a war zone in this classic image taken on the morning of 3 February 1931. A fireman walks away as a blaze rips through the ruined town centre. Although often captioned 'ten minutes after the quake', fire records show it was actually taken about 45 minutes later. Lack of water pressure—spurred by damage to the pipes, combined with power failure—hampered fire-fighting efforts.

Arthur Bendigo Hurst, P. T. W. Ashcroft Collection, Alexander Turnbull Library F-139885-1/2

OPPOSITE BOTTOM

Napier hospital—the only full-scale hospital in Hawke's Bay—was wrecked by the quake. Staff hastened to get patients and equipment out, setting up tents in the nearby Botanical Gardens.

Photographer unidentified, Williams Collection, Alexander Turnbull Library, F-29566-1/2

to a £4,276 loss in 1931. He was not alone, and remarked that by 1933, 'New Zealand sheep-farmers everywhere were temporarily bankrupt'.[135]

In some ways Forbes' policies—which reflected general world efforts to recover—were understandable. There was a warm memory of the halcyon days of 1913, and hope that these policies of restraint might revive those times. Actually there was no chance of that happening; the third decade of the twentieth century with its mass production, war reparations, large corporations, closed social mores and new technology was a very different environment. These difficulties were eventually realised, but meantime, as John Mulgan later put it, economists 'gained the status of witch doctors.'[136]

The crisis was compounded by a summer drought in early 1931—and then, just when it seemed New Zealand's fortunes were diving to rock bottom, Hawke's Bay was laid to ruin by a massive earthquake. It was New Zealand's most lethal natural disaster to that time. Victims ranged from six-week-old David Tripney to 92-year-old Gilbert Brown.[137] At one early stage authorities feared that up to 300 had died.[138] There were problems pinning the number. Some people were never found. Others took advantage of the confusion to change towns, change names and escape debts. One was found in Auckland. After an outstanding effort to locate and identify bodies, the official toll was 258—though this became 256 in the official report.[139] Over 400 were hospitalised with serious injuries. At least 2500 were cut, bruised, scratched and shocked, a toll never fully evaluated because few bothered to report trivial injuries. Damage stretched from Gisborne to Wanganui. Napier and Hastings were devastated.

For some the scenes of death and ruin were all too familiar. Former soldiers drew on reserves of emotional strength forged a dozen-odd years earlier in the trenches, making a difference in the minutes and hours after the shocks. The Western Front also laid important groundwork for post-quake organisation—in Hastings one wartime unit was even resurrected, and people fell back on the bonds built during the conflict. They were joined by civilians whose own responses

RIGHT AND BELOW RIGHT

Emergency depots in Hastings. The immediate priority in devastated Hawke's Bay was food, water and shelter. Many survivors were evacuated in the days that followed. Others took on the task of rebuilding.

Sydney Charles Smith, S. C. Smith Collection, Alexander Turnbull Library, PAColl-3082, G-47882-1/2 and Sydney Charles Smith, S. C. Smith Collection, Alexander Turnbull Library PAColl-3082, G-48308-1/2

were shaped by the organisation around them. 'Too much cannot be said of the splendid spirit of the Napier people,' a reporter wrote. 'There is something in big catastrophes that brings out the best in everyone, as did the Great War, and the way in which people are forgetting themselves to others strikes the stranger forcibly. Property is nothing. Fatigue and personal feelings do not count.'[140] Another contemporary account wrote of the way 'neighbour helped neighbour,' and 'for the time being, at least, there is a greater human understanding of each other than ever there was before. May it continue!'[141] Many laboured on despite personal loss, among them Constable Tripney who knew his wife and infant son had been killed, but 'continued to work…with rescue and search parties.'[142] At least one miscreant, under arrest in the police cells, did what he could to help and then turned himself in again.

ABOVE

Napier town centre reborn, seen here in 1934. Initial plans for block-spanning Spanish Mission-buildings and unified reconstruction had to be shelved in the face of Depression penury. The new Napier emerged as a cluster of small modernist buildings.

Photographer unidentified, National Publicity Studios, Alexander Turnbull Library, 4897, F-3628-1/2/Archives New Zealand/Te Whare Tohu Tuhituhinga O Aotearoa Wellington Office, AAQT 6403, 4897

Not everyone stood up to the strain. Some collapsed into what E. F. Scott called 'an attack of excitement hysteria.'[143] Others were effectively shell-shocked. One woman escaped from a collapsing store in Hastings only to see two friends crushed by the falling building. For some hours she and several others wandered 'aimlessly about the streets, which were piled up with wreckage. We were all dazed, and could only sit there and half realise what had happened. The most terrible feeling was that of helplessness.' She was found by a friend who 'took her to a place of refuge.'[144] Still others put on a brave face; W. Olphert thought the 'people of Napier were wonderfully cheerful',[145] but Agnes Bennett thought those she found on the Marine Parade the day after the quake were wrapped in 'an expression of dumb misery…even the children seemed toneless and wearied…'[146] In others the quake brought out the worst. 'A ghoul was seen stealing a wristwatch off a dead man lying on the pavement,' a horrified Dorothy Campbell wrote to her aunt, 'while articles of clothing were removed from living, wounded people. Houses were robbed while the owners were doing rescue work, goods & money were stolen from shops.'[147]

The war too dominated thoughts during the days and weeks afterwards. 'Scenes reminiscent of the war time in France,' read one caption in the 1931 book *Before and After*.[148] Others compared the destruction of the Napier Nurse's Home to the effects of shellfire.[149] The favourite comparison was Ypres, probably because it was well known. Dorothy Campbell heard former soldiers declare that damage

RIGHT

Crowds await election results on the corner of Mercer and Willis Streets, Wellington, in late 1931. Labour increased its support by 45,000 votes that year, and Forbes' United Party seemed set to lose. But a coalition deal with J. G. Coates' Reform Party kept them in power. The cost was a heavier defeat in 1935.

William Raine, Alexander Turnbull Library, F-66497-1/2

had been greater than several months' shelling.[150] Others found the exodus that followed reminiscent of war-torn France. 'The traffic on the road to Palmerston North was tremendous,' one reporter wrote. 'Cars, lorries, everything on wheels seemed to be there. They were full of furniture, bedding…prams, and all sorts of household utensils. It was a flight.'[151] Mary Hunter was driven south by a Feilding dairy factory manager at night, in a convoy of 'thousands of cars almost touching each other', though she saw 'almost as many going to Napier.' The lights of the vehicles 'looked like a fiery serpent when we got to the bends in the road.'[152] Hunter's estimate was no exaggeration. The 70,000-odd residents of Hawke's Bay owned just over 10,500 vehicles in 1931,[153] but literally tens of thousands of other vehicles drove in during the two days after the disaster to bring aid or evacuate refugees. Some 27,000 cars passed through Waipukurau in thirteen and a half hours on 5 February alone.[154]

Forbes did not change his attitudes in the face of the disaster. A rehabilitation loan offered by the Bank of England at peppercorn rates was turned down, and so was an offer by the Mayor of San Francisco to raise a Mansion House Fund. Contemporary estimates put earthquake losses at £3,685,450,[155] while a 1997 study suggested £3,402,500.[156] Both were far in excess of the £1.5 million granted by government under the Hawkes Bay Earthquake Act, of which £1,250,000 was earmarked for businesses and the rest to local bodies. This 'feeble start' represented all that the Forbes administration was prepared to provide,[157] and a study has shown that it did not stave off the Depression. Construction work in Hawke's Bay rose from the usual average of around 6 percent of the national total in 1930 to 13 percent in mid-1934, then fell to the usual 6 percent in 1935, with a net effect equal to about 2 percent of pre-quake GDP.[158] Specific job-creation figures are not available,[159] but figures such as 600 have been reported by non-economist historians,[160] while a more convincing 1997 study by a qualified economist identified 300 new jobs in 1932–1933.[161] Put another way, the earthquake was associated with a brief spike in employment, but there was no sustained reduction in unemployment afterwards.[162]

LEFT

Willis Street, Wellington, around 1930. Cars and electric trams jam the road, underlining the alacrity with which New Zealand picked up twentieth-century transport.

S. C. Smith, Alexander Turnbull Library, PAColl-3082, G-1792-10XB-

What it added up to was yet more misery. New Zealand slid through the year. National unemployment soared from 8000 to 27,000 during February 1931, in part a combination of the quake and changes in seasonal work. But it compounded the sense of calamity, and the Labour Party took up the cause, calling for industrial action if wage cuts were enforced. Three thousand workers marched on Parliament in March to support the call.[163] Late that year, Forbes—worried about the depths of the Depression—suggested the crisis had reached such dimensions as to demand wartime unity, proposing an all-Parliament government. Labour refused, but Coates—though he disliked Forbes—agreed, and a United-Reform coalition was announced in September. Labour increased its support in the election that year by 45,000 votes, but still held just 24 seats against the 51 that went to the United-Reform juggernaut.

Coates became Minister of Unemployment, then Minister of Finance after 1933—positions that, with a little post-fact help from Sidney Holland,[164] led to him becoming one of New Zealand's most hated politicians for 60 years. To some extent, such criticism is unfair. Coates had been an advocate of efforts to build private-sector prosperity through government construction and management of infrastructure, and he continued to hold these views into the 1930s—even setting up a think-tank in 1933 that included such left-leaning economists as W. B. Sutch and R. M. R. Campbell. He was the practical architect of the economic recovery from the Depression. The problem was that he did not engineer the moral recovery, which was as essential.

New Zealand's books were in trouble by 1932. National export receipts plunged from their 1929 high of £54.9 million to £34.9 million in the 1931–32 financial year.[165] The Coates-Forbes administration slashed state wages by 20 percent between 1931 and 1932. Pensions were cut 30 percent. Public works expenditure was cut by three-quarters, and hospitals were plunged into a funding crisis, forced to reuse disposable equipment and cut back on patient food.[166] The National Expenditure Adjustment Act of 1932 slashed bank deposit rates.

NEW ZEALAND
AN ILLUSTRATED HISTORY

Compulsory arbitration was cancelled, giving employers power to reduce wages and conditions. This burst of rectitude was meant to facilitate growth, but in fact only succeeded in taking money out of a depressed economy, intensifying the Depression.[167] As Guthrie-Smith remarked, 'every legislative enactment seemed to hinder not help.'[168] People could not buy what they needed to live, sometimes including food. Prices fell on the back of falling demand—precipitously. Deflation—a phenomenon more damaging to an economy than inflation—reached 12 percent in 1932, a disastrous level.[169]

The social cost was staggering. Children, often barefoot, were sent to school with Chelsea sugar-sacks as their only protection from winter rain. Once inside, many clustered around the classroom stove, their only source of warmth that day. Some had to work, outside school hours, on milk or paper runs—often still in bare feet. Every penny brought into the household counted, and even so, meals were often reduced to bread and butter, sometimes with jam if the family was lucky. Malnourished children grew into unhealthy adults, fuelling the rejection of so many New Zealanders as medically unfit for military service a few years later. Life became one of making do or doing without. Buckets, pots, pans and spades were repaired. Worn wallpaper, furniture and paint were lived with. Luckier families fell back on their 'quarter acre', using domestic chickens and vegetable gardens to supplement diets that might otherwise have fallen below subsistence. The garden as defence against starvation was well recognised;

ABOVE

Mount Victoria Tunnel, Wellington, under construction around 1930.

Photographer unidentified, Alexander Turnbull Library, PAColl-5448, G-25094-1/1

OPPOSITE TOP

Government slashed works budgets during the Depression and projects such as this Wellington reclamation slowed to a crawl.

Photographer unidentified, Alexander Turnbull Library, F-91142-1/2

OPPOSITE BOTTOM

Looking seawards over New Plymouth during the early 1930s.

John Wall, Alexander Turnbull Library, PAColl-3065, 13054-1/1

A World Land Speed Record attempt gave New Zealand brief distraction from the rigours of depression in February 1932. An Australian syndicate backed by Sydney businessman Fred Stewart used Ninety Mile Beach to race the Napier-engined *Fred H. Stewart Enterprise*. Designed by Don Harkness, the car was driven by Norman 'Wizard' Smith. They based themselves at Hukatere with the intent of cracking 300 miles an hour over the flying mile, but cooling problems forced Smith to add a locally fabricated radiator. Then they discovered the tyres were falling prey to toheroa shells. Smith failed to break the LSR, held by Henry Segrave at just over 231 mph. But he did break the world ten-mile record at 164.084 mph.

Photographer unidentified, New Zealand Free Lance Collection, Alexander Turnbull Library, F-154212-1/2

suburban garden clubs encouraged householders to cultivate their quarter acre, and there was even a competition in 1933 to find the best garden kept by an unemployed householder.[170]

The rural outlook was worse than the urban because the drop in producer prices meant that the full weight of the downturn fell on the countryside. Droughts in February 1932 prompted South Canterbury farmers to ask government for free rail transport as an offset, threatening to otherwise 'cut the throats' of their sheep and 'fill up the gullies with the carcases.'[171] The Farmer's Exchange Committee declared the same month that farms could become profitable if costs were slashed 30 to 40 percent—and as that was impossible, the only answer was dropping the exchange rate.[172] Marginal farms fell into ruin, including many of the remaining soldiers' settlements. Owners simply abandoned them to the banks, leaving behind their spirits with the magpies and the macrocarpas, unable to make ends meet in a world of depressed produce prices. Some of the unemployed became swaggers, roaming the roads in the way of their grandfathers 50 years earlier, hoping they might find work on farms here and there.

The imagery was enduring; and the idea that people chose unemployment out of laziness was hard to break. While relief schemes under the Unemployment Act of 1930 were not as soul-destroying as the prospect of a daily queue at the local post office for work, they were punitive enough. In part this was a consequence of government penury; they could not afford to be too generous because the money was simply not there. But in part it was deliberate; if government unemployment relief was simply a hand-out, it might become a lifestyle option for the lazy. Many unemployed came under Scheme 5, designed to subsidise local bodies who would, in turn, give the men work. Rates were miserly—14 shillings a day sustenance and 17 shillings relief for single men, graduated upwards for married men with children.[173] In theory this was meant to be enough to live off, but not so attractive as to deter the unemployed from finding proper paid work. In practice

LEFT

Smith's wife wishes him good luck before a record attempt on 3 February 1932.

Photographer unidentified, Alexander Turnbull Library, F-117660-1/2

the scheme simply prompted a new wave of impoverishment as businesses and local authorities sacked their employees and rehired them under the relief scheme.[174] Huge numbers of New Zealanders ended up in that position, and payments under the scheme totalled £4.2 million in the 1933–34 financial year.[175]

The effects on morale were devastating. Families were ripped apart as the breadwinners travelled to up-country work camps, there to face leaky tents, thin blankets and poor sanitation. Some of the tasks were useless make-work. Unemployed men, some of whom had been soldiers in the First World War and put their lives on the line for their country, were now made to drag ploughs.[176] Others laboured in drains, often waist-deep in water, never able to dry their clothes in the winter. Men chipped away at excavations that could have been done by heavy machinery. The work was mindless, sometimes pointless and always soul-destroying; yet it was often a case of doing it or starving. There was never enough money, and many families relied on charity to make good the difference. The Auckland City Mission dosshouse, during a seven-month period in 1932, apparently provided 37,000 beds and 102,080 meals to hungry New Zealanders.[177]

Unfortunately the plight of those with paid work was often also miserable. Some historians have argued that falls in wages were offset by falls in the official consumers' price index (CPI),[178] but that argument is misleading; the all-groups CPI represents an average-of-averages and does not capture all costs for different income groups.[179] A better indicator at the lower end of income is food, which for poorer families was often a significant part of the household budget. Here the picture was very different. Food prices initially fell faster than the CPI, but from 1932 were rising faster—in other words, the relative price of food rose through the Depression, and available data shows that quantities purchased fell.[180] The people were going hungry. And they also had to pay more tax; the Government introduced direct unemployment taxes, followed by a sales tax that yielded £1.8 million in 1933.[181] Average taxation per head in 1932 was £11/9/4; but by 1935 it

RIGHT

Wellington railway station under construction in 1934.

Photographer unidentified, Evening Post Collection, Alexander Turnbull Library, F-90785-1/2

was up to £15/18/4, most of the increase a result of the unemployment levies.[182] Those in debt were in particular trouble, because real interest rates did not fall as fast or quickly as the CPI. The relative cost of supporting debt, in short, rose.[183] All this was coupled with a near-total lack of job security, a direct outcome of Depression retractions at both state and private level. Nobody knew when their job might disappear, or if they would find themselves facing a take-it-or-leave-it ultimatum over pay cuts.

National morale was not helped by the fact that New Zealand's rich appeared to be staying that way. Old money had not disappeared, new money had emerged with new industries, and some of those who had it were unafraid to flaunt it. 'Here in Remuera,' John Mulgan wrote a little later, '...lived the aristocracy. Their daughters were lovely and satirical, drinking surreptitious gin in the half-empty cabarets.'[184] Landscape designers such as Alfred Buxton were in demand during the 1920s and 1930s, setting up impressive gardens around back-country estates, often blending 'arts and crafts' stylings with more traditional New Zealand forms. Some large suburban homes, too, were given massive and impressive surrounds.[185]

Many held government responsible for the 'ill-starred necessities' of Depression.[186] As one historian remarked in 1965, up to that time 'so much legislation that hurt so many people had never before been crammed into so brief a period.'[187] Hungry crowds stoned the Dunedin relief depot in April 1932 after the mayoress insisted on distributing food only after investigating each case. A few days later there was a mob attempt to break into the hospital, deflected by baton-wielding police. Riots followed in Auckland after a meeting to protest wage cuts, only stopped after ratings from HMNZS *Philomel* and firemen took to the fray. Queen Street was spattered with glass, and many shops were looted. John A. Lee—who was there—thought most of the rioters were 'so hungry, with families as hungry' that they had no choice but to make a 'desperate bid for food.'[188] There were more riots the following month in Wellington, where protestors were forbidden to congregate in Basin Reserve and stampeded into town, followed by a crowd, shattering windows as they made their way along Lambton Quay. In Christchurch, a tramway strike was brought to an end with batons.[189] Government responded with a punitive Public Safety and Conservation Act—but, as one historian has pointed out, the tensions ebbed, as if New Zealanders had gone to the brink but then pulled back.[190]

By September some 73,650 New Zealanders were unemployed, of whom 67,110 were on relief schemes.[191] More followed into 1933, reaching a high of 79,435, a figure not exceeded until the early 1990s.[192] Coates was widely—though wrongly—believed to have proclaimed that the needy could 'eat grass',[193] and in these desperate times some sought radical alternatives. The Soviet Union had sailed on apparently unaffected, and in Hastings there was even a 'communist' revolt among relief workers. In fact the apparent success of the Soviets was illusory; the collectivisation of farming resulted in mass famines in 1932–33.[194] However, the fact that some New Zealanders seriously considered such alternatives indicates the degree to which government response to the Depression had undermined society. In 1932 New Zealand was one of the half-dozen longest standing free democracies in the world. New Zealanders had fought and died to preserve it in the First World War, yet by 1932 dissent simmered from Kaitaia to Bluff. The following year the proto-fascist New Zealand Legion emerged as a pressure group.

BELOW

Depression-era hut in the Waimarino plains.

Samuel Heath Head, S. Head Collection, Alexander Turnbull Library, F-41332-1/2

ABOVE

Reverend Colin Graham Scrimgeour (1903–1987), Methodist minister and champion of the depression-era underdog. Known as 'Uncle Scrim', his radio programmes revealed him to be a staunch opponent of the puritanical Coates–Forbes government. He is seen here in 1938 broadcasting for 2YA.

Dorothy [?], Kenneally Collection, Alexander Turnbull Library, F-135748-1/2

The marriage rate fell with the economy; in 1929 it stood at 7.8 per 1000, but by 1932 it was down to 6.81.[195] People simply could not afford to get married and have children. Curiously, crime dropped during these years. Some 37,214 offences were reported in 1930 in a national population of 1,506,800; but by 1935 the figure was down to 33,168 offences.[196] This was the reverse of what might be expected during times of hardship, as both the nineteenth-century British pattern and the New Zealand experience of the 1984–99 period makes clear.[197] However, we do not have to look far to find the explanation; as the Hawke's Bay quake revealed, society of the 1930s had been shaped by the trauma of Flanders into something with real community spirit and genuine altruism.

Coates toyed with plans to settle the unemployed on small farms in 1933 but, as Lee put it, New Zealand's youth wanted more than to be just 'clothed and fed'.[198] New Zealand was facing a moral crisis of unprecedented dimension; but the opportunity for the electorate to speak was postponed with the general election, put off from 1934 to 1935. By this time the economy was already picking up—the Depression as a purely economic phenomenon was actually over by mid-1933. The reasons why have been debated. One of the triggers, arguably, was the decision to devalue the New Zealand pound by 25 percent against the pound sterling in January 1933, a controversial move that provoked Finance Minister Downie Stewart to resign and Coates to take up the position.[199] Although James Belich has argued that Coates' only successful policy was establishing the Reserve Bank,[200] the more compelling interpretation is that he was instrumental in engineering and guiding the recovery that took place in 1934. He set up a Dairy Board, retracted some of the more draconian policies, initiated public works schemes, and pushed for a central bank. Dairy prices remained depressed, but wool and meat prices doubled in 1934, and trade per capita began climbing back to 1929 levels.[201]

His problem was that recovery took time to develop, and the moral damage had been done. Better export prices and a rising tide of prosperity were little comfort for a people who had lost trust and confidence in the government, who felt punished for a misfortune that was not of their own making and which they had been powerless to control. Their unease was expressed in the desire for new political structures. There was talk of implementing proportional representation as an alternative to the 'first past the post' system, but it was 'urged upon the Government in vain.'[202]

During 1935 Coates made plans for further social spending, including introducing milk in schools. The New Zealand economy was on the way up, but too late to overcome the dismay of a cynical electorate. Government directives to quash dissent resulted in Post Office staff zealously jamming the Reverend C. G. Scrimgeour's popular 1ZB radio programme moments before he was due to explain why everyone should vote Labour.[203] The incident did Forbes no favours.

By this time Labour had emerged as a credible opposition. Radical leader Harry Holland died in late 1933 and was succeeded by Michael Joseph Savage, an Australian by birth who led the conservative faction of the party and whose warm persona contrasted with that of his predecessor.[204] Policies formulated by

BELOW

G. G. Martin's butchery, Cuba Street, Wellington, early 1930s.

Gordon Burt, Gordon Burt Collection, Alexander Turnbull Library, PAColl-4118, G-15384-1/2

Walter Nash and Peter Fraser, presented by the kindly Savage, offered a 'Way out of Chaos to a Land fit for Heroes'. Labour's new platform was built around conventional capitalism with a friendlier face, facilitated by state direction of the economy. Their manifesto of 1935, penned by Walter Nash, promised prosperity and work for all; and in the election that November, Labour won 53 seats to the government's 19, throwing the Coates-Forbes coalition into complete disarray.

There was a little cash left in the Consolidated Fund. Savage gave it to the unemployed as a Christmas bonus. To the hungry victims of the Great Depression it was like a gift from heaven.

CHAPTER EIGHT
The quest for security

The moral impact of the first Labour administration on Depression-racked New Zealand is difficult to overstate. C. G. Scrimgeour—'Uncle Scrim'—compared it to the sun shining 'for the first time in years'.[1] Although he had a particular axe to grind with the social policies of the Depression-era Forbes government, New Zealand of 1935 was spiritually depressed. The fact that the economy was recovering by then, on the back of policies developed by Gordon Coates, meant little to people who had lost faith and trust in the government, people yet to be touched by the warm glow of rising prosperity. When the election of 1935 came along, they looked to Labour for rescue. And Labour delivered. Savage gave New Zealanders what they wanted in the manner—as one historian put it—of a kind uncle.[2] What the people wanted was also clear: secure employment, security of accommodation through owning their quarter-acre section, and enough surplus cash to make life comfortable. It was something that New Zealanders had been trying to achieve since colonial times.

None of this was achieved overnight—indeed, New Zealand did not really approach the ideals and goals of Savage's administration until after it was gone from office 14 years later. But the journey itself was as important, and in the late 1930s it was enough for most New Zealanders to know that they were on the way. Positive attitudes counted, and although both times and fortunes were still deeply troubled in 1939, in other ways the country had been transformed into an optimistic, go-ahead nation, in stark contrast to the mood of gloom just five or six years earlier. The underlying joy was encapsulated in the Centennial celebrations of 1940, a dramatic combination of fairground attraction and industrial displays in Rongotai, near Wellington, which wartime exigencies

Michael Joseph Savage (1872–1940), seen here during the 1938 election campaign, remains one of New Zealand's historically best known—and best-loved—Prime Ministers. Born near Benalla, Victoria, he was working on the Victorian gold mines around 1900 when he met Paddy Webb, establishing the Political Labour League. Webb left for New Zealand, and Savage followed in 1907, joining the New Zealand Labour Party when it formed in 1916. He presented a warm family persona, and New Zealand mourned when he died in 1940.

Photographer unidentified, C. A. Jeffery Collection, Alexander Turnbull Library F-517934-1/2)

ABOVE

John Alexander Lee (1891–1982), novelist, soldier and *enfant terrible* of the Labour Party.

Photographer unidentified, Alexander Turnbull Library, F-49375-1/2

and strains did little to subdue. People had hope for the first time in years, and Savage was upheld as a national saviour; his portrait hung alongside that of Christ in many working-class homes. The effects were decisive; those who drew succour from these policies did not forget. Two generations of devoted Labour supporters followed, notably in major urban areas, standing against the more conservative rural districts, and broadly establishing the general pattern of New Zealand politics until the 1980s.

Radical conservatism and 'applied Christianity'

Despite the fears of the conservative farming lobby, the arrival of Labour's former pre-war radicals into power did not send New Zealand lurching wildly to the far left. Picking up where the Liberals left off, as Savage put it, was conservative by definition.[3] The key shift that Labour brought in was a change in the unwritten social contract between taxpayers and government. Savage and fellow Cabinet members Walter Nash, Peter Fraser and Robert Semple sought a new balance between nineteenth-century capitalism and the realities of the second industrial revolution, leavened with doses of Fabianism, to create the 'land fit for heroes'[4]

CHAPTER EIGHT
THE QUEST FOR SECURITY

that New Zealanders had been promised after the First World War. Capitalism would be harnessed, not destroyed.[5]

Labour was helped by the fact that economic recovery was well under way; farm output had fallen to a low of £49.2 million in the 1931–32 financial year, improved in 1933–34, and by 1935–36, when Labour started, was almost back to 1929 levels. Factory output followed a similar pattern.[6] Total trade per head, which had plunged to just over £39 in 1932, climbed away sharply after 1933 and returned to its 1929 levels late in 1936.[7] Various public works schemes were already under way when Labour came to power, including Wellington Railway Station.[8] Labour took the credit for this 'temple of transport' when it was completed in mid-1937.[9]

The architect of these policies was Coates, and it underscores one of the great myths of the Great Depression. Labour did not recover the economy in 1935; that had already been done by Coates who with hindsight was, as one historian has noted, closer to Labour than he was to Forbes.[10] While Labour took an active approach to the wellbeing of the people that had been rejected by the Coates–Forbes coalition,[11] some of the economic policies they wanted to bring in did not require radical changes from what was already under way and had been initiated by Coates. Repackaging and humanising was enough, as when the Unemployment Act 1930 was replaced by virtually the same thing in 1936—now called the Employment Promotion Act.[12] Work camps were still needed in 1936, but by

ABOVE

Wellington Railway Station in 1939. This 'temple of transport' was the largest single building in New Zealand when it was completed.

Photographer unidentified, Alexander Turnbull Library, F-21569-1/2

OPPOSITE BOTTOM

Robert Semple (1873–1955) was an early radical West Coast agitator, and the power behind the Miners Union formed in 1907. As Minister of Works in 1935 he set about replacing labour-intensive wheelbarrow gangs with bulldozers.

Photographer unidentified, *Evening Post* Collection, Alexander Turnbull Library, F-105128-1/2

ABOVE

Walter Nash (1882–1968), speaks to reporters on election night 1935. The former Kidderminster sweet shop owner was one of the key movers behind Labour's economic policies. Secretary of the Labour Party from 1922 to 1932, he held a variety of ministerial posts and was Deputy Prime Minister 1940–49, Prime Minister in the second Labour government in 1957–60, and retired from politics in 1963.

Photographer unidentified, *Evening Post* Collection, Alexander Turnbull Library, PAColl-0614, G-48791-1/4

mid-year most had been given recreation facilities, including some cinemas, accommodation was radically improved, and a new piece-work system effectively doubled the relief rate.[13] At a stroke, and at relatively low cost, the camps became places where New Zealanders could live with dignity and receive reasonable returns for their efforts.

Other economic policies certainly were more radical, based on centralising authority and insulating New Zealand's tiny and vulnerable economy from the vagaries of overseas markets.[14] But they did not recover the economy. Instead, they were designed to keep the recovery going and prevent a second depression. Walter Nash worked 18-hour days to develop the initial plan with input from Coates' former advisor William Sutch.[15] In many ways this was a radical policy shift—and yet, once again, the goals were relatively conservative, and the strategy was broadly maintained for the next four decades by centre-right and centre-left. Savage launched the plan as soon as Parliament met in March 1936. The Railways Board, Transport Co-ordination Board, Unemployment Board, Broadcasting Board, Dairy Export Control Board and Mortgage Corporation were abolished and their functions transferred to ministerial portfolios.[16] The Reserve Bank, founded as a semi-private organisation by the Coates–Forbes administration in 1934 on Neimeyer's recommendation, was nationalised and its lending limits eliminated.[17] Nash, meanwhile, organised his Primary Products Marketing Bill, designed to let the state buy dairy products at the average price

RIGHT

Children line up for porridge at the Sunlight League's Christchurch health camp, January 1936.

Photographer unidentified, Alexander Turnbull Library, C-16182-1/2

of the past decade. Semple worked up a three-year public works plan on a £17 million budget—$1481 million in early twenty-first-century money—covering roads, bridges, railway construction and new airfields. This was orthodox, though with a focus on mechanisation to save labour and avert humiliating make-work schemes. Semple symbolised the change by using one of the bulldozers to push a pile of wheelbarrows down a bank.[18]

Nash's first budget of August 1936 was surprisingly orthodox. The only radical idea was a proposal to borrow £5 million from the Reserve Bank to fund new state housing schemes. Yet this was pragmatic in many ways; new homes had become urgent. Nearly a third of all mortgages were foreclosed during the Depression and there had been little new construction. Many families were feeling the squeeze, and at a time when the nuclear family remained a mainstay of society, Labour intended to do something about it. Other works included improvements to the railway system, restarting the long-stalled East Coast Line and implementing ultra-modern electrified commuter rail in Wellington.[19]

Labour-market reforms followed. The cancellation of compulsory arbitration in 1932 had triggered an avalanche of unilateral reductions in wages and conditions, and unrest followed. Some 108,605 working days had been lost that year, more than double the loss for the year before.[20] New Minister of Labour H. T. Armstrong introduced a bill in April 1936 to restore arbitration, guarantee minimum wages and create a 40-hour working week.[21] Compulsory unionism for those covered by Arbitration Court awards followed, a more radical move that put a good deal of power into the hands of the 'Black Prince'—Fintan Patrick

ABOVE

English Electric EMU (electric multiple unit) at Kandallah, 1938. Labour restarted the long-delayed Tawa rail deviation out of Wellington, which reduced the Johnsonville stretch to a branch; but instead of ripping it up, the government decided to introduce an ultra-modern commuter service, serving the suburb. Services began in 1938. Virtually identical EMUs ordered in 1942 and 1946 defined the look of Wellington commuter rail for the rest of the century, and some were still rattling along Wellington commuter lines as late as 2012.

Albert Percy Godber, A. P. Godber Collection, Alexander Turnbull Library, PAColl-3039, G-1483-1/4-APG

ABOVE

Swimming, 1930s.

Photographer unidentified, Alexander Turnbull Library, F-67401-1/2

RIGHT

Forwards of the combined Thames, Waikato and King Country teams meet the Springboks in 1937. The South Africans won this particular game 6:3.

Weekly News, Making New Zealand Collection, Alexander Turnbull Library, F-2320-1/2

Walsh (1894–1963), who by 1937 was president of the Seaman's Union, secretary of the Wellington Clerical Workers Union, and president of the Wellington Trades Council, among other posts.[22]

These shifts won praise in the United States, which was looking for 'experiments that have been successful' which 'might be adapted to American requirements.'[23] Britain was less impressed, but the fact remains that Labour's policies worked in New Zealand. Morale recovered, and economic growth began to absorb the pool of unemployed. There were around 20,000 men on work schemes when Labour came to power; by 1938 this had dropped to 2735. Total unemployed fell from 56,502 in January 1936 to 29,899 in March 1938, although the figure fluctuated as seasonal work came and went, and the pool still had to be fully absorbed when the Second World War broke out.[24]

Labour's welfare reforms—which Savage classified as 'applied Christianity'[25]— took longer to organise. Early steps included improving existing benefits and

CHAPTER EIGHT
THE QUEST FOR SECURITY

ABOVE

Marching, as a competitive sport for women, was a New Zealand phenomenon. This is the Woolworths marching team in 1935.

Photographer unidentified, New Zealand Free Lance Collection, Alexander Turnbull Library, C-16178-1/2

LEFT

A skier on the Rangiwahia Ski Club grounds in the Ruahines, 1930s.

Bruce Valentine Davis, Making New Zealand Collection, Alexander Turnbull Library, F-2007-1/4-MNZ.

implementing a programme of state housing for the poor. Families who had been jammed cheek-by-jowl with extended family could have their own 'quarter acre'. Government took reform further during 1937–38, with a scheme to reorganise benefits into an encompassing system, including health care and low-cost state houses. While this, seen in hindsight, was essentially the start of a slippery slope to the welfare-bloat of the later twentieth century, the context of the late 1930s was very different. New Zealand of the 1930s did not have a comprehensive welfare system. The experience even of the 1880s remained within living memory, and that was without the immediate context of the Great Depression. To Savage and others in his Cabinet, human suffering of this kind could not be allowed to happen again; Labour envisaged the system providing a comprehensive safety-net for those unable to support themselves; a proper, thoughtful and caring backstop. Nor was this too great a risk in the late 1930s. Despite the nay-sayers

323

ABOVE

Michael Joseph Savage opens the Social Security and Health Department building on Aotea Quay, Wellington, 27 March 1939. During parliamentary debate over his 1938 welfare legislation, Savage referred to the new approach to public welfare as 'applied Christianity'.

Photographer unidentified, *Evening Post* Collection, Alexander Turnbull Library, G-49203-1/2

of the day, the fact was that prosperity was rising, and people were being thrown out of the system rather than into it. Welfare spending between 1937–38 and 1938–39 followed a slowly ascending curve, but this was mainly driven by old-age pensions, including the restoration of pre-Depression pension levels.[26]

However, the conservative rural sector remained a powerful voice against the new face of government. A National Party emerged from the ruins of United Reform in 1936. For a while there seemed little real threat from them, but that changed in the face of the 1938 elections. Voices against Labour's stance were growing. However, Savage felt he still had a task to complete, introducing new social welfare legislation as Labour's first term drew to a close. And then, in August, he collapsed in Auckland. The medical prognosis was grave; he had cancer. An immediate operation would likely cure it. But Savage decided he could not leave the field for the two months it would take to recuperate. He was the public face of Labour, an election loomed, and he had his legislation to push through. In the event, Labour won the 1938 elections with an increased majority—some 55 percent of the vote—and forged on.[27]

Savage underwent the delayed surgery, but it was too late. His genuine desire to change the everyday attitude of government towards its people—to make things better—and his need to make sure that the momentum was not derailed by the loss of an election, paid off. But it came at the cost of his life. He carried on through 1939, but faded through the year, and died in March 1940.

The Social Security Act for which Savage, in effect, sacrificed his life—the legislation that he called 'applied Christianity'—created a new department and consolidated all public benefits under one roof. Available benefits up to 1938 included limited superannuation, unemployment benefits under various schemes, another for miners disabled by their work, for the blind, among others. The new legislation replaced all of these. It included universal superannuation for those over 65, without a means test; a special benefit for those over 60, subject to a means test; a widows' benefit, an orphans' benefit; a family benefit for children under 16; a miners' benefit for those who had become ill from that work; an invalids' benefit; and an unemployment benefit. This last was not a lifestyle choice; the legislation made clear that it was for those who were ready and able for work, who had been looking, but who could not immediately find it. That underscored the context of the new legislation in the aftermath of the Great

Depression and of New Zealand's earlier times of hardship. But the legislation did not stop there. For those who could not get any of these benefits immediately, but were in need, there was an emergency benefit.

When put into due historical context and the mind-set of those enacting it, the main pillars of the first Labour administration's term —welfare and regulation— were clearly responses, filtered by their brand of conservative radicalism and Savage's notions of a government's responsibility towards constituents, to New Zealand's experience in general and the Great Depression in particular. However, at the time these steps were controversial, and no more so than in Britain where the New Zealand Government was obliged to get loans to help fund the costs incurred by their programmes.

Education also came in for attention during Labour's second term, starting with the primary schools. The entry age was dropped to five—a reversal of Depression measures when it was raised to cut costs—and government-funded milk was made available to all primary schools. Coates had been thinking of doing the same thing, but as with a number of Coates' initiatives, including the Wellington Railway Station, it was Labour that brought it in, and who got the credit. The practice continued until 1967, but the eventual notoriety of tepid 'school milk' did not offset the value of this service in its earliest years. In 1930s New Zealand, children were hungry. Some schools also received apples. Education itself was a priority, and Dr C. E. Beeby was appointed Director-General of Education to reform the national school system on a secular basis.

ABOVE

Children pose for the photographer in a new upstairs classroom at Newtown school in June 1939, the day it was opened by Minister of Education Peter Fraser. Wider corridors opened the classrooms to 'sun and air', both considered essential for children. The classroom was a product of Labour education reforms, implemented in the late 1930s and organised by Dr C. E. Beeby.

Photographer unidentified, Alexander Turnbull Library, PAColl-0614, F-96818-1/2

NEW ZEALAND
AN ILLUSTRATED HISTORY

CHAPTER EIGHT
THE QUEST FOR SECURITY

LEFT

Grocery shopping, late 1930s.

Photographer unidentified, National Publicity Studios Collection, Alexander Turnbull Library, 7357, F-116978-1/2, Archives New Zealand/Te Whare Tohu Tuhituhinga O Aotearoa Wellington Office, AAQT 6403, 7357

OPPOSITE TOP

This Lockheed Electra 10, one of half a dozen ultra-modern monoplanes brought into main-trunk services in 1937, captured the excitement of the age as New Zealand emerged from a depression that had collapsed morale.

Photographer unidentified, Evening Post Collection, Alexander Turnbull Library, PAColl-0614, G-32345-1/4

OPPOSITE BOTTOM

American and British interests pioneered flying-boat routes into New Zealand during 1937–1938. Plans were also pushed ahead to set up a trans-Tasman service under the aegis of Tasman Empire Airways Ltd (TEAL). Here, Captain J. Burgess brings *Aotearoa* into Wellington in January 1940, with officials bound for the centennial celebrations. By 1941, *Aotearoa* and her sister-boat were the only long-range aircraft in New Zealand, perforce swapping some passenger duties for urgent war work.

Photographer unidentified, Making New Zealand Collection, Alexander Turnbull Library, F-2052-1/4-MNZ

Plugging in to modernism

The 1930s were the world's great age of modernism—a range of styles that shed the last vestiges of nineteenth-century art nouveau, which exploited the possibilities of steel, chrome and glass, and which not only defined the main look of the mid-twentieth century but also encapsulated the essence of its technological jump from the wood-and-horse world of earlier days. Streamlined shapes entered everyday life, generally inspired by the practical shapes demanded of the higher-performance aircraft appearing in the skies. Bulbous cars shook off the last vestiges of their ancestry as coaches. Consumer products—static, immobile clocks and radios among them—took on streamlined characteristics, too, not because they had to deflect a slipstream, but because it looked good. The word for it in a later age might have been coolness.

The spread of all these things in New Zealand was helped by the recovery of the late 1930s. 'Step up to the V8 class', buyers were urged in one advertisement for 'Built-in-New Zealand' Ford saloons.[28] Other cars were sold on the basis of new technical features ranging from pre-selector automatic gearboxes to suspension systems.

Local manufacture was a particular selling point at a time when government was urging 'buy New Zealand'. The country had yet to adopt television—picked up in Britain and Germany at the end of the 1930s—but radios with 'streamlined' design features began appearing on mantelpieces. Some were even sold as 'TV-ready', meaning they could be used as an external speaker when television finally arrived.

The coal stoves and candles of earlier years had been almost completely supplanted by gas and electrical appliances by 1939. The Hawke's Bay Electric Power Board promised cooking for 'as little as 8/- a month' with its electric ovens. 'Stop wasting money on antiquated cooking methods... You'll know what it means to cook more enticing meals in a better, cleaner, cheaper and easier way

RIGHT

Department store, late 1930s.

Gordon Burt, Gordon Burt Collection, Alexander Turnbull Library, PAColl-4118, F-15466-1/1

RIGHT BELOW

The 1920s and 1930s were the 'golden age' of wireless in New Zealand. These modernist 1938 examples were made by His Master's Voice (HMV), a British electronics company that also made gramphones, records and refrigerators.

Photographer unidentified, EMI Collection, Alexander Turnbull Library F122054-1/2

OPPOSITE

Gas oven and hot water made this kitchen one of the more up-to-date of its day. Many New Zealanders were able to afford such facilities by the late 1930s; all that is missing from the line-up is a refrigerator. 'Odourless' models using freon rather than ammonia were on sale, but manufacturers were still selling the concept. 'Leftovers normally thrown away during hot spells can be kept and made up into delicious salads and cold dishes,' one advertisement declared. 'You'll never worry again when friends drop in unexpectedly,' trumpeted another. Most fridges could be bought for around £40, but whether householders had that to spare in the wake of the Depression was another matter — it amounted to over $3,500 in early twenty-first century money.

Gordon Burt, Gordon Burt Collection, Alexander Turnbull Library, F-15754-1/2

than you have ever done before.'[29] Other technology had to be sold as a concept. 'Come on the telephone,' one advertisement declared. 'The telephone, for social and domestic purposes. A swift and reliable messenger. Always a comfort and convenience.'[30] Refrigerators were another new appliance waiting for use. Automatic washing machines remained in the future, but manufacturers lost no time finding ways of easing the load on wash day. In 1935 consumers were urged to say 'goodbye to washing-day drudgery' with the aid of the 'oxygen charged suds' offered by one soap manufacturer. The 'gentle, cleansing oxygen bubbles' were guaranteed to 'do the work for you.'[31]

All of these appliances were snapped up by modern-minded New Zealanders. Despite a self-image of being somehow provincial, backward or otherwise socially behind the times, the fact was that New Zealanders were quick to pick

CHAPTER EIGHT
THE QUEST FOR SECURITY

RIGHT

The DIC window, Whanganui.

Frank J. Denton, Alexander Turnbull Library, PAColl-3046, F-22324-1/1

BELOW

The MLC building on Wellington's Lambton Quay around 1940.

Gordon Burt, Making New Zealand Collection, Alexander Turnbull Library, 2633-MNZ

up on the latest technological trends. They had motorised faster than most other countries outside North America, including Britain; and now they were picking up all the electrical inventions of the second industrial revolution as quickly as possible. The price of long-standing gear such as electric lights and telephones fell; other tech-miracles were flooding the market. By the late 1930s available household gadgets in New Zealand ranged from fluorocarbon-cooled refrigerators to electrical and gas ovens, washing machines, vacuum cleaners, radios, gramophones. electric clocks, electric jugs, toasters and even electric organs.

Even more was on the horizon; by 1938 television was available elsewhere in the world, and daring punters in the United States could even buy a polyphonic synthesiser, the Novachord, which inventor Laurens Hammond intended for the consumer market even though its electronic sounds were alien to the 1930s ear.

The only limit to the whole tech-adventure from New Zealand's perspective was the ability to pay for it; and therein lay the reason why mid-twentieth-century New Zealand sometimes perceived itself as hidebound. Depression penury gave way in the late 1930s to post-Depression government controls on foreign exchange. What people wanted, and what they could actually get in New Zealand shops or otherwise by import, sometimes became two different things. Still, the wider world was available in other ways. The movies, for example. Kiwis needed no persuasion to go to the 'flicks' during the 1930s; and here, too, New Zealand kept fairly well up with overseas trends. Cinema gained sound at the beginning of the decade, then burst into glorious colour. *The Wizard of Oz* and *Gone with the Wind* made a splash like few others.

Food gained new sophistication that decade as well, following overseas trends and again giving the lie to the popular notion that the country was backwards. The second industrial revolution brought more than cheap cars; it also created industries to mass-produce, process and package food, notably beakfast cereals. By the late 1930s cheese was being sold in handy pre-packed slices: 'Pixie segments...so tasty...so handy!'[32] Although the age of ubiquitous convenience food was still half a century away, it was a clear sign of the direction things were moving. Foods also broadened; customers at any grocery were advised to try 'Dr William's Health Loaf' and Vienna bread, or 'Morah Cooking Margarine' produced by Abels Ltd of Auckland. The Dominion Compressed Yeast Company of Christchurch and Auckland offered consumers the 'Malt that Makes the Difference'—DYC Mellowed Malt Vinegar, 'bottled in the scrupulously hygienic modern plant of the Dominion Yeast Company'. This 'product of sun-ripened grain' was available in screw-top bottles from most grocers. A pound of Roma 'Dust Freed' Tea was another addition to any shopping basket.[33]

Ngata and Ratana

The twentieth century brought opportunity and challenge for Maori. Opportunity in the sense that although Maori as a percentage of the total New Zealand population did not change, absolute numbers rose from 42,113 in 1896 to 52,723 in 1911 and 83,326 by 1936,[34] not including Maori of part-European descent who were living as Europeans.[35] The new century was a challenge in the sense that Pakeha society was monocultural and exclusive, though its racism was not that of other countries. Maori had been thought of as 'better natives' by the British, an attitude reflected in settler society, and there were even turn-of-the-century efforts to suggest they were Aryan.[36]

A 'gruelling game' between Maori and Springboks at Napier's McLean Park in September 1921 brought it all into focus.[37] One Springbok was disgusted at 'thousands of Europeans cheering on [a] band of coloured men to defeat members of their own race'.[38] This assertion—published in the local newspaper—met a vigorous rejoinder from one correspondent, who pointed out that the Springboks had been royally entertained by Maori and 'if they so despised the Natives why did they accept their hospitality as they did?'[39] An editorial declared that New Zealand could 'take pride in the fact that this noble people, so far from being exterminated by war or disease, are a virile and increasing community.' In period style, the paper then warned that in future a Maori would 'find it more and more difficult to maintain his racial purity'—leading to a future subsumed by 'the newcomers'.[40]

Such sentiment summed up the attitudes of the day. In fact, Maori and Pakeha societies were still effectively segregated—most Maori lived rurally. Yet Maori had no option but to find ways of engaging Pakeha culture if they were to improve their position. Early twentieth-century strategies for doing so continued the approaches begun in the nineteenth. Rangatira such as Te Heuheu

NEW ZEALAND
AN ILLUSTRATED HISTORY

332

Tukino picked up the sceptre during the 1890s, and for a while—as one historian notes—a sense of 'Maoriness' seemed about to overtake tribal feeling.[41] However, Kotahitanga was effectively defused by the Maori Councils Act of 1900, and in other respects overtaken by the Young Maori Party, an ostensibly political movement which originated among some Te Aute old boys. These people, all highly educated and 'Europeanised' Maori, sought to push the cause from within the framework of jingo society. Theirs was not strictly a political party—indeed, it had been originally known as the 'Association for the Amelioration of the Conditions of the Maori Race'.[42]

Prime movers included Te Rangi Hiroa (Peter Buck), Apirana Ngata and Maui Pomare. It was another bold effort, but did not last at political level. Pomare joined Reform in 1912, and Ngata became a Liberal. However, the strategy of engaging jingo society itself was more successful; young Maori supporters worked to promote Maori through the public service

The strategy of high-level engagement was also taken up by Eastern Maori MP and former kupapa James Carroll, as Native Minister during the first decade of the century. He slowed the process of land sales, but his efforts stood in opposition to other movements, and accusations that he continued to act as a kupapa during his Parliamentary term never completely evaporated. For all that, Carroll was less controversial than Pomare, who became a pariah for what arguably amounted to an imposition of settler values,[43] including an effort to get rid of practices such as hui and tangihanga. But this is not to under-rate his other achievements, such as taking charge of Maori recruitment for the government during the First World War, forming a committee, and going out to collect volunteers. Some Maori

ABOVE

Food preparation at Ohinemutu.

Photographer unidentified, Alexander Turnbull Library, F-56337-1/2

OPPOSITE, TOP

Ohinemutu around 1874.

Photographer unidentified, Alexander Turnbull Library, F-37827-1/2

OPPOSITE, BOTTOM

Ohinemutu, early one morning in March 1907.

Photographer unidentified, Hislop Album, Alexander Turnbull Library, C-2498-1/2

ABOVE

Wairoa-born James Carroll (1853–1926) fought with government forces against Te Kooti in 1871 and was twice Acting Prime Minister. A leading member of the Liberal Party, Carroll was Minister of Native Affairs under John Ballance.

Photographer unidentified, General Assembly Library Collection, Alexander Turnbull Library, F-136-35mm-D

ABOVE RIGHT

Tama te Kapua meeting house, Ohinemutu.

Alexander Turnbull Library 47253-1/2

served in the front line at Gallipoli. There were hopes that a good performance on the Western Front might enhance Maori status back home afterwards. In the event these hopes were dashed; the Maori Pioneer Battalion was a construction unit. But this was not through want of trying.

Apirana Ngata (1874–1950) of Ngati Porou became perhaps the most successful of the Te Aute graduates. After leaving the school he attended Canterbury University College, where he graduated BA (Hons) in political science in 1893. Later he studied for an MA and was given an honorary doctorate in 1948. He became involved in politics through the Te Aute Old Boys Association, which became the Young Maori Party. Ngata himself remained Liberal until 1928. He prodded Coates, Native Minister in 1921, into establishing the Maori Purposes Fund Board, designed to promote Maori cultural activities. From this flowed the Maori Arts and Crafts Act of 1926, and a Board of Ethnological Research to refocus academic attention on Maori language and culture. To some extent this was predicated on the notion that Maori culture had to be recorded for posterity before it disappeared, and by the thinking of that time, that was not an entirely unfounded assumption. While it had become clear by the 1920s that Maori themselves were not doomed to extinction in the sense imagined by the nineteenth-century settlers, there was certainly good reason to think that the old ways might well be lost or swamped. Ngata was not alone in such thinking, or in the Maori response. Te Puea followed suit at Turangawaewae, reviving carving, and organising touring concert parties.

To this was added a government-backed Te Arawa effort to promote Rotorua as a tourist mecca. The town had been founded by government in the early 1880s to take advantage of local thermal attractions, a strategy which Te Arawa eagerly engaged at every level. Although this raised tensions with other tribes—who felt Te Arawa were getting unfair advantage—it did help raise the profile of wider Maori cultural issues. The Rotorua Carving School, established with Ngata's help in the late 1920s, was intended to educate a new generation

CHAPTER EIGHT
THE QUEST FOR SECURITY

LEFT

Children from Tokomaru Bay School visit Wellington Zoo in 1943.

John Dobree Pascoe, John Pascoe Collection, Alexander Turnbull Library, PAColl-0783, F-846-1/4

BELOW

The infant room at Auckland's Horo Horo School.

Photographer unidentified, Alexander Turnbull Library, A2468, F-33925-1/2

335

ABOVE

Te Puea Herangi (1883–1950).

William Archer Price, William A. Price Collection, Alexander Turnbull Library, PAColl-3057, G-1920-1/2

in traditional methods, and some graduates moved on to Turangawaewae to start their own carving school. One result was new emphasis on the physical aspects of Maori culture, notably traditional carving, art, poi dances and songs. By the 1930s, Maori motifs had entered mainstream art and design, as in rebuilt Napier where some buildings featured Maori motifs, adapted to modernist styles.[44] However, other aspects of traditional culture, including hui and tangi, were not pushed so hard, arguably because it was more difficult to assert these in the wider post-war environment of moral evangelism and renewed attention to Christian doctrine. To some extent there was also indifference. Ngata was able to get Te Reo (the language) adopted as a university subject in 1923, but few students took it up.

Ngata went on to back an effort by Te Arawa to claim the lake beds in the Rotorua region.[45] He also became Minister of Maori Affairs during the Depression and pushed for funds to build meeting houses, money to improve Maori welfare, money for cultural events and promotions. He often got it, despite general government penury and an attitude of individual self-help as first port of call. Ngata also slowed, but did not stop, ongoing land sales. However, a 1933 investigation uncovered evidence of false accounts and misappropriation in the Native Department. While Ngata was not involved, he felt obligated to resign his portfolio. But he continued to push Maori matters privately, and was a prime mover behind the Maori Battalion a few years later.

These efforts to promote Maori from within the framework of Pakeha society were paralleled by Maori efforts to promote traditional culture. King Mahuta tried working with government along these lines on the advice of Henare Kaihau, during the first decade of the century. Perhaps the key leader of the period was Te Puea Herangi (1883–1950), of Tainui, who rose to particular attention through her opposition to conscription among her people. Afterwards she moved to Ngaruawahia where she established Turangawaewae marae, which by the end of the decade had become a focus for nationwide Maori sentiment. She developed a close association with Coates, whose own plans for assisting Maori through agriculture coincided with hers. She maintained a relentless effort to support, develop and promote Maori until her death in 1950.

Religion provided the mechanism for the most successful Maori association with Pakeha society. Te Kooti's spiritual successor, Rua Kenana, led a new millenarian movement at Maungapohatu in the depths of the Urewera during the first years of the twentieth century. He was tolerated but not welcomed by government, dogged by ongoing accusations of sly-grogging. Government finally sent armed police to arrest him on that pretext in April 1916, in what amounted to a pseudo-military operation. One reason for the disproportionate government reaction was rumour that Rua had German connections—enough, at a time of frothing anti-German sentiment, to prompt decisive steps. Another was what Rua symbolised—independence.

A new and enduring religious movement emerged after the First World War, founded by Tahupotiki Wiremu Ratana. The Rangitikei ploughman received divine revelations in 1918, and as the Mangai (mouthpiece), attracted a substantial following in the early 1920s, focussing a sense of Maori unity. Specifically why this happened has been debated; Ratana was not rangatira but, like Te Kooti, drew power from his adaptation of Christian teaching, including faith healing,[46] and it has been argued that his teachings struck a chord at a time when Maori had been doubly dislocated by both war and the influenza epidemic.[47] Former servicemen, in particular, expected better than they had received. Followers were often affiliated with other denominations, but the duality was not considered a problem and Ratana swiftly became a focus for a Maori renaissance. The movement was politicised; Ratana took up the Treaty of Waitangi as his sword and went to see King George V as early as 1924 to protest Maori treatment. Later he launched a petition calling for ratification of the treaty, accumulating over 30,000 signatures, which he presented to Parliament in 1932.[48]

Ratana turned to politics. His son almost dislodged Maui Pomare from his seat in the 1922 election, and from this flowed a strategy to put Ratana members into all Maori seats. Ratana fielded four candidates in 1928, and Eruera Tirakatene became an Independent Ratana member for Southern Maori after a by-election in 1932. Ratana had been attempting to woo various political leaders in the hope of finding allies in the House, and approached Holland with the offer to deliver 38,000 Ratana supporters to the Labour camp if Labour, in turn, took up Maori causes, including ratifying the Treaty of Waitangi and addressing a range of land grievances. Holland agreed. When Labour became government, Ratana visited Savage to remind him of the agreement. As a result, the two Ratana members, joined by a third in 1938, voted with Labour. By this time up to half of all Maori were associated with the movement.

ABOVE

Apirana Turupa Ngata (1874–1950), Ngati Porou leader and Te Aute graduate who, as member for Eastern Maori from 1905 until 1934, championed the Maori cause.

William Henshaw Clarke, General Assembly Library Collection, Alexander Turnbull Library, PAColl-0838, F-94-35mm-D

Labour made good on the promises, allowing Maori to draw equal benefit from the new welfare state established during the late 1930s. Health and education were extended to Maori, helping establish the basis for a post-war Maori population boom. There was also new focus on the Treaty of Waitangi, and the remains of the original document were put on display at Waitangi for the 1940 centenary. In the 1943 election all four Maori seats went to Ratana-Labour members, an arrangement that held good until Labour shifted ground in the 1980s.

Commonwealth conundrums

New Zealand's curious double patriotism flourished through the 1920s and 1930s, pushed by an ongoing—and reciprocated—trade focus on the mother country. The influx of American goods and movies during the 1920s coloured but did not dislodge these links; while 'buy New Zealand' refocussed attention on the New Zealand part of the equation, it is debatable whether this reflected nationalism at the expense of Imperial ties. The relationship Labour developed with the League of Nations gives a clue; Savage pursued closer ties, and New Zealand was elected to the League Council in 1936.[49] Some historians have argued that this reflected a partially independent foreign policy,[50] a point given weight by Savage's criticism of British 'appeasement', including New Zealand's refusal to recognise Italian-conquered Abyssinia.[51] New Zealand stood alone in the Commonwealth on this issue, but the real target was fascism, which the Savage administration—like Winston Churchill—regarded as a threat. The British government seemed disinclined to act, so New Zealand did, and to this extent the policy was in line with pre-war Liberal policies. It reflected New Zealand's ideas about what was best for Empire—whether Britain and the rest agreed or not—and by the 1930s one of the mechanisms for pursuing international policies was the League of Nations.

This point is underscored by the fact that when war broke out in September 1939, Savage instantly threw New Zealand's lot in with that of Britain. It was the British, not New Zealand, who shifted relative to fascism. Nor did dissent from the Imperial line reduce ties; British links through the inter-war period were reinforced as Britain turned to the Dominions for trading partners. Of the £58.4 million in goods exported by New Zealand in 1938, £48.9 million went to Britain, and the majority of imports—nearly three-quarters—came from Britain.[52] The whole has to be seen in the context of the British-driven conversion of Empire to Commonwealth in the 1930s. Here, New Zealand was dragging the chain, displaying tensions between national identity and Imperial loyalty that no other dominion experienced to that extent.

All this was a legacy of jingoism, sustained past its use-by date in part by the dairy, meat and wool trade, in part by the 'cultural cringe', in part by habit. People still spoke openly of 'home', meaning Britain, even if they had not been born there. The Union Jack was saluted at schools, the national anthem was *God Save The Queen*—*God Defend New Zealand* was the 'national hymn'—and overseas travel invariably meant a pilgrimage to the United Kingdom. This dichotomy was not a problem at everyday level. The practical difficulty—as always—came when

ABOVE

Bristol Fighter F2B of the New Zealand Permanent Air Force in 1928.

Photographer unidentified, *Evening Post* Collection, Alexander Turnbull Library, PAColl-0614, G-8669-1/4-EP

government faced the problem of reconciling Pacific defence with the European situation. New Zealand penury was matched by British weakness. Technology and lateral thinking offered prospects; and in January 1936 Labour's *enfant terrible*, John A. Lee, called for a modernised local air force. He followed that in March with the argument that naval policy was subservient to British whim. The country was isolated by ocean, he argued, and even disruption of trade would not 'afflict us with hunger.'[53] This was untrue; New Zealand had effectively mechanised its farms on the basis of imported fuel. But it sounded compelling.

These ideas were discussed by Cabinet in May, where there was talk of concentrating all spending on air forces. The debate encapsulated New Zealand's mind-set. Lee had been looking at the problem in a nationalistic sense; cabinet saw it as a way of addressing Commonwealth issues. As Savage told the House while discussing a separate air service in 1936, 'The general European situation is not one to make us feel that we can afford to be indifferent to defence matters.'[54] Air also had modernist connotations at a time when Labour were eager to bring new technology into the country. At practical level it was a means of reducing defence expenditure, driven by a need to economise in order to fund the social programme.

Tensions between national and Imperial priorities simmered through 1936. Lee swung to the former. So did the services, though perhaps for different reasons. British estimates of the likely scale of attack on New Zealand had not changed in 30 years, but New Zealand's Director of Air Services, Wing Commander T. M.

Wilkes, believed 'the previously accepted scale...can no longer be regarded as a maximum.' Warning that Singapore reinforcements might have to come via the Cape of Good Hope if the Mediterranean situation deteriorated, he argued that a 'fairly strong naval force' might overwhelm local defence, destroy local shipping, bombard the main centres, and occupy Auckland. It might take six months to repel them. A secret appendix—'The case for a Japanese invasion of New Zealand'—argued that Japan could 'launch a limited overseas attack without warning' and the strength of Singapore might force Japanese planners to seek targets further south.[55]

These oppositions forced a compromise. The whole Cabinet favoured an air force, but the Cabinet Defence Committee thought naval expenditure was the way to go. When the British government offered to send an officer to report on the New Zealand air defence situation in August,[56] Cabinet clutched the straw. However, Wing Commander Ralph Cochrane wrote his report during the journey to New Zealand, indicating he had no intention of taking local need into account. 'The rapid strengthening of the defences of Singapore and the decision of the United Kingdom government to press forward with its programme of rearmament,' he wrote 'promises an increasing measure of security.'[57] An air force would operate in conjunction with 'the general naval dispositions' and 'local forces and defences'.[58]

Cabinet acceptance did not resolve tensions within New Zealand, nor allay perception of a Japanese threat, particularly as Britain could not maintain its 'main fleet to Singapore' strategy.[59] This became explicit in 1938, and Cochrane proposed air reconnaissance from Fiji. That contributed to a New Zealand government decision in May 1938 to request a Pacific Defence Conference. It was held in Wellington 11 months later, attended by British, New Zealand and Australian delegates, each with their own agenda.[60] What emerged was a plan for a New Zealand and Australian patrol line from Port Moresby to Tongatabu, using aircraft based at Port Moresby and Suva. Cabinet accepted most of the recommendations in May, but nothing had been implemented by September when German dictator Adolf Hitler invaded Poland and—for the second time in a generation—Europe was plunged into war..

Savage promptly extended the 'fullest assurance of all possible support' to the mother country.[61] To the people he was more direct. 'Where Britain goes,' he declared, 'we go.'[62] The phrase echoed through the years, superficially a poignant summary of New Zealand's sentiment towards the mother country. 'Why are you New Zealanders fighting?' Field Marshal Erwin Rommel demanded of Brigadier George Clifton in mid-1942, 'This is a European war, not yours! Are you here for the sport?'[63] Clifton struggled to explain, 'never having previously tried to put into words the...self-evident fact that if Britain fought then we fought too.'[64]

That summed up the whole issue; and as always, it was far more complex than a simple sense of being British. At popular level it was emotional, a concrete expression of the double patriotism that all New Zealanders lived and breathed—and it was unique, a truly New Zealand sentiment that few outside could visualise or understand. These sentiments were also felt in New Zealand government circles. However, for government there was also a deep streak of pragmatism, even a cynical acceptance of the realities. Labour had resolutely stood against fascism, even when that took New Zealand down a different road from mother country and Commonwealth. These overlaid a third factor—the economic relationship. In 1939 New Zealand relied absolutely on the mother country for prosperity. If Britain fell, New Zealand's future would have been bleak. On a more subtle plane, the country had also just faced a difficult battle to renew state loans—Bernard Ashwin classified British proposals as 'severe' and effectively 'putting in a receiver'.[65] The new loans were due in 1940 and it seems likely that Savage had a little quid pro quo at the back of his mind when he jumped behind the Chamberlain government.

Beneath all of this, though, lay a fundamental and—for Labour at least—over-arching motive. The early twentieth century had seen the end of the old order and the rise of the new—a world in which democracy ran a poor third to the rising forces of totalitarianism, both in its fascist and communist flavours. Hitler, in particular, threatened the survival of Western democracies. Labour had already been opposing fascism wherever it occurred during the late 1930s. Now Hitler was on the warpath. He had to be stopped—whatever the cost. There was no choice. And in that southern spring of 1939, joining Britain for what seemed to be a limited European conflict did not seem a large step.

For a few months, that was where things stood. The war, it seemed, was 'phoney', played out in the air and mainly across the waters of the Atlantic. But then, in 1940, Hitler finally put Western Europe to the torch; by June, Britain was on her knees, and New Zealand was drawn into the maelstrom.

ABOVE

HMS *Achilles*, victor at the Battle of the River Plate in December 1939 and—with her sister ship *Leander*—one of the mainstays of the New Zealand naval effort during the Second World War. After a refit during 1943–1944 she joined the Far Eastern Fleet and took part in the naval campaign against the Japanese mainland in early 1945.

Photographer unidentified, Alexander Turnbull Library F-49007-1/2

Total war

'...to-night we are facing dangers such as we have never known in these islands... at this critical hour we must face the future with good heart and deep determination to do all and give all in the struggle for our country...'
– Peter Fraser, 8 March 1942[66]

The Second World War engulfed every New Zealander able to work or fight[67]— and the effort continued, through domestic rationing and participation in occupation forces —notably in Japan—well after the fighting ended. It was a total war in every respect, an extraordinary effort that allowed a country of just over 1.7 million to make a disproportionate contribution.

Pre-war dissonance between local and British defence priorities intensified as the conflict deepened, though what followed was not a simple shift by New Zealand from British to Pacific priorities. The local defence scheme laid out

RIGHT
The funeral procession of Michael Joseph Savage moves towards the railway station, Wellington, 31 March 1940. The funeral train made 20 stops on the journey north to Auckland, where he was buried. He died after a long battle with cancer, and the public outpouring of grief was without parallel in New Zealand's history.
William Hall Raine, W. H. Raine Collection, Alexander Turnbull Library, G-21743-1/1

during the 1939 Pacific Defence Conference relied on air power, but the teeth were drawn by the decision on the outbreak of war to hand the RNZAF's 30 Wellington bombers to the RAF.[68] This was a reasonable gesture in 1939, but it became a problem in 1940 when German raiders appeared in New Zealand waters. Sea forces alone could not find them, and the only long-range aircraft in New Zealand were two passenger flying boats and a handful of airliners.[69] Fraser's efforts to get patrol bombers were rebuffed, and as he told new British Prime Minister Sir Winston Churchill in June 1940:

ABOVE
Peter Fraser (1884–1950), Minister of Education in the late 1930s and Prime Minister 1940–1949. He was an effective war leader who did not hesitate to champion New Zealand's cause with Britain.
Photographer unidentified, Alexander Turnbull Library, A20185, F-5064-1/2

> ...we wonder if it is fully realised in the United Kingdom how helpless this Dominion is against attacks from seaward. As you know, the whole of our defence measures were built on the assurance that in time of potential trouble in these waters adequate naval forces would be available. They are not... We believe we are the only Dominion in this situation, and we are reminded every day that we would not have been in this situation had we not, voluntarily and unasked, decided to release the Wellingtons...[70]

When Churchill demurred, Fraser—who had a Japanese threat at the back of his mind—proposed sending a New Zealand minister to America 'in the hope of strengthening the security of the Pacific'. This was not to push an independent line but a way of 'reinforcing the representations already made to President Roosevelt...'[71] Churchill disagreed; he was already treading a delicate line between the hawkish Roosevelt and isolationist Congress, fearing a New Zealand move might be misinterpreted as an attempt to influence domestic US politics. The crisis was brought to a head when Britain bowed to Japanese pressure to close the Burma Road, through which Chiang Kai-shek's armies were supplied.[72] Fraser responded in no uncertain terms; appeasement was 'no more likely to be successful in the Far East than it was in Europe.'[73]

The War Cabinet considered the Pacific situation so threatening that by August 1940 there was talk of holding the Third Echelon back.[74] Churchill wanted part of this force in Britain, and finally told Fraser that if, 'contrary to prudence and self-interest' the Japanese attacked Australia or New Zealand, 'I have the explicit authority of Cabinet to assure you that we should then cut our losses in the Mediterranean and proceed to your aid, sacrificing every interest except only the defence of...this Island on which all depends.'[75] Churchill made the same assurance to Roosevelt, though he was concerned by the 'disastrous military possibilities'.[76] It was the concession Fraser had been looking for; he dropped his plan to send a delegation to Washington and suggested they might set up a diplomatic post. Churchill agreed. These moves have invariably been interpreted as an assertion of nationhood,[77] but it seems clear that Fraser's plans were

ABOVE

Ration queues, Second World War.

Photographer unidentified, New Zealand Free Lance Collection, Alexander Turnbull Library, PAColl-0785, G-41096-1/2

BELOW

Island Bay Emergency Precautions Service exercise, May 1941.

Photographer unidentified, *Evening Post* Collection, Alexander Turnbull Library, G-123828-1/2

geared within the framework of Commonwealth and the dissonance between local and Imperial threat perception. Even his threat to send an independent minister, which New Zealand was legally entitled to do, was couched within those parameters.

Tensions with Japan rose, driven by British and United States support for China. The fall of France left its Indo-Chinese colonies unprotected, and by early 1941 a crisis was brewing. Early in the year, the New Zealand government invited General Sir Guy Williams to help develop anti-invasion precautions. His recommendations included harbour-defence booms and minefields, and after a vigorous dispute, 200 mines were finally laid off Auckland in March.[78] Other minefields followed. In August the War Cabinet decided to train the Home Defence Forces 'to the standard of overseas troops'. Nash gave Churchill a shopping list that included 38,000 rifles and bayonets, 582 anti-tank guns, 2500 Bren guns, and 170 M3 light tanks.[79] Coates discussed war material with US representatives without success.

The Pacific crisis erupted in December. Popular fears of a Japanese invasion were exaggerated, but there were already shortages of fuel and industrial goods as a result of the European war, and German raiding vessels had shown that even inter-island connections could be threatened. War with Japan prompted more extreme measures. Because local coal production only just met needs,[80] rail travel was limited to 100-mile (160-km) journeys with no guarantee that return trips would be possible. Some people panicked, 'besieging petrol service stations' in an 'attempt to exchange whatever December and January coupons they held for precious benzine.'[81] Government withdrew some coupons,[82] then banned petrol sales altogether on 15 December to prevent stocks running dry.[83] The sense of crisis was fuelled by reverses in North Africa, where 2 NZ Division pulled the 8th Army's irons out of the fire outside Tobruk, but suffered heavy losses in the process. Long casualty lists appeared in New Zealand papers alongside news of Japanese successes in the Pacific.[84]

Japan conducted a small but sustained submarine campaign into the South Pacific through the first year of the Pacific war.[85] Their ocean-going submarine I-20 was off Fiji in January 1942, while I-29 entered Cook Strait in February, looking for troop transports, and Pilot Fujita Nobuo reconnoitred Port Nicholson with a floatplane. The submarine I-25 arrived in the South Pacific during March, encountering the armed merchant ship *Tongariro*. I-21 made a similar sortie in May, when Lieutenant Isumo Ito took a floatplane over Auckland 'and observed some small boats which he thought were fishing craft

LEFT

Although Fraser and leading members of his War Cabinet had been conscientious objectors in the First World War, they did not hesitate to have objectors imprisoned in the second. Harold Hansen, Bernard Giles, Tom Smith, Colin Clark and Jack Hammerton stand behind the wire at the Hautu Detention Camp, 1943.

Photographer unidentified, A. C. Barrington Collection, Alexander Turnbull Library, PAColl-3955, F-37726-1/2

lying in the harbour.'[86] A submarine attack on Sydney prompted precautions against similar raids in New Zealand.[87]

Invasion was another matter. The British Chiefs of Staff thought Japan might deploy a brigade group—a few thousand men—but New Zealand's Chief of General Staff, Lieutenant-General Sir Edward Puttick, thought a range of scenarios more likely,[88] and Fraser warned Churchill that British assessments were an 'attempt to think in terms of the past'. He added: 'if this line of thought is persisted in we must brace ourselves to meet the fate of Malaya and with infinitely less reason or excuse.'[89] In January 1942 government ordered full mobilisation. By this time 27,000 men were in training, many for a new armoured brigade

LEFT

Sign of the times: blackout warnings on the Hutt Road, 1943. This stretch was visible from the sea, through the harbour heads. Roadside hoarding is advertising Brasso, a polishing agent.

Photographer unidentified, *Evening Post* Collection, Alexander Turnbull Library, G-123929-1/2

ABOVE

A US Navy dance at the Majestic Cabaret, Wellington. American GIs and sailors made a splash with New Zealand women, raising tensions with New Zealand men for whom the epithet 'over-paid, over-sexed and over here' seemed all too true. Racial issues prompted tensions, as did lavish American military supplies in a nation starved of imports.

Photographer unidentified, E. M. Alderdice Collection, Alexander Turnbull Library, PAColl-0089-26, C-16005-1/2

which government decided to retain in New Zealand. A total of around 50,000 men were under arms, and some 18 battalions, nine rifle regiments and four field regiments were in formation. A further 17,500—including married men with children—were called up in March. Newspapers warned men to 'place their private and business affairs in order immediately'.[90]

The total number in the forces—including 61,368 overseas, but not the Home Guard—amounted to '...7.6 percent of the total population and 38 percent of the men within the age groups from which they were drawn.'[91] They were backed by several batteries of six-inch guns, 36 25-pounders and 50 18-pounders.[92] There was consequently no government clamour for the return of forces serving in the Middle East[93] but, as Fraser remarked, 'the success of anti-invasion operations depends to the greatest extent on air superiority, without which our land forces and coast defences will be at the worst possible disadvantage.'[94] The problem was that New Zealand had no modern fighters and, in early 1942, over 100 De Havilland DH 82 Tiger Moth trainers were nominated for combat duties.[95] These were moves of desperation. Fraser put the issue to Churchill:

> ...no reasonable security against carrier-borne air attack can be provided unless the limited air striking forces available are provided with fighter protection. In addition... [we]...consider that some fighter protection in the form of interceptor aircraft is essential for the protection of at least the two main ports of Auckland and Wellington...[96]

Britain could provide just 18 fighters.[97] An alarmed Fraser protested,[98] but Britain could only promise to 'do our best to help in consultation with the Americans.'[99] In the end the United States accepted the 'heavy responsibility...for

CHAPTER EIGHT
THE QUEST FOR SECURITY

the defence of Australia, New Zealand, and sea approaches,'[100] but only because US military chiefs decided they needed 'New Zealand and the Fiji islands', which '...together with Australia, must be held and used as bases for an offensive against Japan.'[101]

America came to town—and it was a culture shock. Although Hollywood had given New Zealand audiences a window on America, the Marines and GIs who arrived in Auckland and Wellington during mid-1942 were foreigners. And they brought everything they needed with them, including logistics support in what to ration-weary and import-starved New Zealand was astonishing quantity. Jeeps poured off the wharves at Aotea Quay along with Chevrolet 'deuce-and-a-half' trucks and other vehicles. The petrol to run them came ashore too, tinted red to stop it being on-sold or pilfered by New Zealanders. But a lot of it apparently ended up in New Zealand tanks anyway.

The biggest impact, however, was social. Quiet-spoken young Americans flooded into the milk-bars, into the streets, particularly in Wellington which was the main port of call. Most had not been outside the United States before, and for many the army was also their first time away from home, legacy of their youth and the fact that the US economy was still soaking up the unemployment legacies of the Great Depression. They had been ordered to be well-behaved, and most of them were, often by nature in any event. But common language disguised significant cultural divides. And they were well-paid by New Zealand standards, arriving in a country whose own young men were, as often as not, serving overseas. To young New Zealand women, these Marines, GIs and naval personnel were exotic, polite, attractive. Romances flourished, often fostered by dances

LEFT
Lack of air power dogged New Zealand during the early years of the war. Here, New Zealand's WAAF wireless operators are ready for a training flight. The De Havilland is one of several airliners impressed for war service.
William George Weigel, Weigel Collection, Alexander Turnbull Library, PAColl-5469-007, C-23048-1/2

ABOVE

Gun drill on a Fairmile launch. The Royal New Zealand Navy ran an anti-submarine campaign in local waters using boats built locally to British designs.

John Dobree Pascoe, John Pascoe Collection, Alexander Turnbull Library, PAColl-0783, F-490-1/4

RIGHT

Women outside Westfield Freezing Works, Otahuhu, September 1943 after a visit by Eleanor Roosevelt.

John Dobree Pascoe, John Pascoe Collection, Alexander Turnbull Library, PAColl-0783, F-573-1/4

held at the service clubs or on some of the bases, such as the sprawling United States Marines camp at Motukaraka Point at the head of the Pauatahanui Inlet. What followed was perhaps inevitable. Disputes over women and United States attitudes to race often flared into violence, notably triggering the 'battle for Manners Street', which has been dismissed by one historian as a myth,[102] but which actually occurred, and generally for the reasons attributed at the time.[103]

New Zealand's wider problem was meeting its self-imposed contribution to the war effort. The main problem was finding enough people both to sustain the promised agrarian and light industrial contributon to the war effort, and to meet ongoing commitments to air, land and sea combat forces, New Zealand's own and also, particularly, the Royal Air Force. This last reflected long-standing pre-war commitments to the British service, and the Air Force headed the priority list issued by the War Cabinet in 1942, followed by the Navy, local industry, and finally the Army. Women began working in jobs previously held by men, notably including farming. The United States had 'Rosie the Riveter'; New Zealand's equivalent were the 'land girls'. However, even with the introduction of draconian

ABOVE

Women watch celebrations marking the VC posthumously awarded to Moana Nui-a-Kiwa Ngarimu of 28 (Maori) Battalion for his actions in Tebaga Gap, southern Tunisia.

John Dobree Pascoe, John Pascoe Collection, Alexander Turnbull Library, PAColl-0783, F-696-1/4

LEFT

An Infantry Mk III Valentine tank being transferred to the floating crane *Hikitea* from the merchant ship *Akaroa* in 1943. Although obsolescent by European standards, the Valentine was adequate against Japan's tanks, and some were deployed to the Solomons.

John Dobree Pascoe, John Pascoe Collection, Alexander Turnbull Library, DA-01791, F-70-1/4

ABOVE AND LEFT

Children at Otaki health camp, 1945.

John Dobree Pascoe, John Pascoe Collection, Alexander Turnbull Library, PAColl-0783, F-1213-1/4; and John Dobree Pascoe, John Pascoe Collection, Alexander Turnbull Library, PAColl-0783, F-1201-1/4

'manpower' controls, designed to properly manage all the available national resource, New Zealand was soon stretched. Raising a second division for Pacific service during 1942 meant a manpower crisis was inevitable, and it was finally triggered by the 1943 mutton season. The prognosis for the 1944–45 season was worse and it was clear one of the army divisions would have to be disbanded. This was not an easy decision; New Zealand's contribution in all aspects of the war was being pushed to the very edges of the possible by deliberate government decision, particularly in the Pacific theatre where Fraser and his administration wanted to 'ensure that when the future of the Pacific is being considered after the war we … are in the most favourable possible political position'.[104]

The reasoning was overt; they had been, in effect, let down by British weakness during the crisis years of the war and the War Cabinet were determined that this

RIGHT

Dunedin women's lifesaving team in 1944.

Photographer unidentified, Alexander Turnbull Library, C-27162-1/2

would not happen again. Contributing to the direct war effort offered prospects of a quid pro quo in later negotiations. By 1943, however, this no longer seemed possible, and Fraser sought opinion from the Allies. New Zealand was groping for direction:

> How can New Zealand best serve? (a) By maintaining and expanding its air forces? (b) By maintaining its present naval strength? (c) …its Division in Europe? (d) …its forces in the Pacific zone? (e) By maintaining and if possible expanding its production of food supplies, particularly butter, cheese and meat?[105]

The question is whether all this was an assertion of New Zealand within the framework of Commonwealth, or whether it had changed to what F. L. W. Wood called a 'small power rampant',[106] an assertion on the world stage. Wood's observation runs at odds with the point that New Zealand, in Churchill's words,

ABOVE

Grasmere station, 1944. Wool and meat were mainstays of New Zealand's war production, pumped out to Britain at the expense of local need well after fighting ended.

John Dobree Pascoe, John Pascoe Collection, Alexander Turnbull Library, PAColl-0783, F-898-1/4

ABOVE

Peter Fraser attends a United Nations Conference on International Organisation session, San Francisco, 21 June 1945.

Photographer unidentified, Alexander Turnbull Library, 42356-FO, F-160156-1/2

was 'with' Britain 'from the moment when … war was loosed upon the world'.[107] The paradox has attracted extensive analysis,[108] but is explicable in context of Fraser's concept of New Zealand within the Commonwealth as 'independence with something added.'[109]

That approach was reflected in the way New Zealand handled its expeditionary force. The government was determined to have its main field division, making clear that its command was answerable solely to the New Zealand government. There would be no more Gallipolis or Passchendaeles. However, this was not understood by Middle East Command, who viewed it as a division within the British forces in theatre. The problem was compounded by the fact that the expeditionary force commander—Major-General Bernard Freyberg—had been brought up in New Zealand but was a serving British officer, and treated as such by his superiors. Freyberg, however, considered that he was reporting first to the New Zealand Government. There was a sharp intra-service spat within Middle East Command during 1940 as a result.[110]

The Crete debacle of late May 1941 brought all the issues to the fore, along with British use of the New Zealand force without proper air support. The island was lost because the defenders lacked air power and heavy weapons—something well in evidence before the battle began.[111] New Zealand did remarkably well despite the odds.[112] However. the battle went into legend, keying directly into New Zealand's self-image of being able to punch above its weight but never quite managing to achieve the results. The battle had gone against the British because of New Zealand failures at Maleme airfield and in organising counter-attacks afterwards. New Zealand's military historians since have inevitably pivoted their arguments around the issue of blame. This has been at the expense of a more useful understanding of what was actually going on in 1941, though it is perhaps explicable; the debate not only keyed into New Zealand's self-image of near-run defeats, but was laid out in the days after the battle, when the New Zealand brigadiers who had been in charge of the defences began scurrying to deflect any blame from themselves.

The limited extent to which these politics influenced Fraser at the time is made clear by the fact that Freyberg kept his job. Questions were raised, but the reality came out soon enough. The men had been committed to battle without heavy equipment or aircraft. Freyberg had never thought the island could be held in the face of these disadvantages, and had told General Archibald Wavell as much beforehand; the battle had panned out just as he had thought it would. An alarmed New Zealand government demanded 'a full appreciation of the question of air support.'[113] And while neither Prime Minister Peter Fraser nor the War Cabinet recommended withdrawing the division from North Africa,[114] Fraser was dismayed enough to head on to London where he pressed for better care of the New Zealand forces, and for other support.

Churchill was eager to oil the waters, particularly as Australia was threatening to withdraw from North Africa. It is an indication of the New Zealand mood—as a loyal part of the Commonwealth—that for all the disputes, Fraser never used 2 NZ Division or New Zealand's other forces in Europe as a bargaining counter. There were points during the North African campaign when the force could have been withdrawn—for example, after the victory at El Alamein in October–November 1942. However, government also demurred from withdrawing after Axis forces had been driven out of North Africa in May 1943. Instead, after much debate, the division went to Italy.[115]

Here too there were break points—such as the fall of Rome in mid-1944, where there was discussion of a withdrawal; but the New Zealanders went on to the end.[116] The contribution to the RAF, Royal Navy, Royal Marines and merchant marine was also kept up. In other words, although Fraser's government pursued a more energetic international policy during the last two years of the war, it was not at the expense of the pro-British war effort. The failure of collective Commonwealth security in the early war years did not destroy long-term faith in the institution. New Zealand continued to step forth, as Churchill put it, to the 'rescue and liberation' of the old world,[117] pushed—in Fraser's words—'to the fullest extent of our capacity'.[118]

New Zealand's apparent international 'rampancy' of 1943–44, which culminated in the Canberra Pact, still has to be explained; but in many respects this was the Pacific-versus-Europe tension writ large. That had dogged New Zealand's defence policy-making for decades, and came to a head during the desperate years of 1942–43 when the failure of pre-war collective security hit home. To this was added an apparent failure of the usual quid pro quo associated with war contributions. Despite providing disproportionate forces, producing virtually all the food for the Pacific war effort, and providing base facilities for US troops, New Zealand was excluded from the 1943 Cairo Agreement on post-war Pacific affairs. So was Australia, and there was a direct link between the Pacific carve-up in the Cairo Declaration and the Australian-initiated Canberra Pact—with its assertion of Australasian interests.[119]

Yet it is difficult to place the responses that followed in anything other than the context of Commonwealth. As in Seddon's day, Fraser's government was flexing its international muscles but in broader mind-set remained very much within the British framework, and if the Canberra Pact can be called rampancy it was short-lived. New Zealand sprang back into Commonwealth structures after the war. To Fraser, the Commonwealth was an 'association of independent democratic nations',[120] and within that New Zealand had—as he put it—'independence with something added'.[121]

Marching into history

They were mature men, these New Zealanders of the desert, quiet and shrewd and sceptical. They had none of the tired patience of the Englishman, nor that automatic discipline that never questions orders to see if they make sense. Moving in a body, detached from their homeland, they remained quiet and aloof and self-contained. They had confidence in themselves, such as New Zealanders rarely have, knowing themselves as good as the best the world could bring against them…Everything that was good from that small, remote country had gone into them—sunshine and strength, good sense, patience, the versatility of practical men. And they marched into history.

– John Mulgan, *Report on Experience*, 1945[122]

Between 1939 and 1945 New Zealanders fought in virtually every theatre of war from the Arctic to the Pacific Islands. They fought in the skies, on the oceans, in the deserts and in fields and towns. And they fought on to the very end; New Zealand forces fired the last shots of the Italian campaign in early May 1945; a few months later HMNZS *Gambia* fired the last shots of the war at the Japanese mainland. Soon after, she came under the very last attack of the war, targeted by a kamikaze that dived on her minutes after the Japanese surrender.[123]

Achieving this world-spanning effort within New Zealand's limited resources was not easy. Pilot training programmes and the RNZAF got first call on available manpower.[124] Equipped with US aircraft, the RNZAF deployed a number of fighter and bomber squadrons into the Pacific, and although New Zealand forces were excluded by the US from front-line work in 1944, the RNZAF continued to support Australian mopping-up operations in the Solomons until the end of the war.[125]

At sea, the New Zealand Naval Division—Royal New Zealand Navy after late 1941—operated from the South Atlantic to the Mediterranean, Pacific and Indian Oceans, making a direct contribution to the war effort and offering indirect protection for New Zealand's world-spanning trade links. The service also ran a sustained campaign into the Pacific islands from 1942 until the end of the war and maintained coastal defences around New Zealand throughout, including minesweeping and anti-submarine work. New Zealand's naval forces also fought with the British Pacific Fleet off Japan in 1945.

'All the sorrow in the world,' the original caption reads, 'finds expression in the mother's last embrace.' Men of 28 (Maori) Battalion leaving for war.

John Dobree Pascoe, John Pascoe Collection, Alexander Turnbull Library, PAColl-0783, F-831-1/4

The largest direct contribution, as in the First World War, was on land, principally in the Mediterranean. The Second New Zealand Expeditionary Force—meaning its component division—fought alongside British and Commonwealth forces in mainland Greece, Crete, Egypt, Syria, Libya, Tunisia and Italy. Unit battle honours read like a tour itinerary, a testament to the duration and intensity of the campaigns into which the Second New Zealand Expeditionary Force and its component division was deployed between 1940 and 1945. Maadi, Cairo, Maleme, Canea, Benghazi, Tobruk, Minqar Qaim, El Alamein, Tripoli, Medennine, Tebaga, Mareth, Takrouna, the Sangro, Cassino, Florence, Rimini, the Senio, the Gaiana, Venice and Trieste all held places in the hearts and minds of the New Zealanders who fought there. And, as John Mulgan put it, they 'carried New Zealand with them' as they went.[126]

Other participation was by proxy through British services. Kiwis were prominent in the RAF from the outset as a result of pre-war service schemes.

New Zealanders fought in the skies during the Battle of Britain—many led by Air Vice Marshal Keith Park, who had been with the RAF since 1919, and when Britain's darkest hour came was in command of No. 11 Fighter Group, covering south-east England. Seven New Zealand bomber squadrons were also formed within the RAF, at the insistence of the New Zealand government, but the squadrons were never fully 'Kiwified' by comparison with similar units developed for the Canadians and Australians. Later commanders included Air Vice Marshal Arthur 'Mary' Coningham, who served prominently in North Africa. New Zealanders also served with the Royal Navy, Royal Marines and the British Merchant Marine. More than 150 went down with HMS *Neptune* off Tripoli one stormy night in late 1941. Others worked in defence establishments, as engineers or technicians, and others made scientific contributions, including—directly—to the atomic bomb.[127]

This effort drew in a high proportion of New Zealand's young men and women. Around 105,000 New Zealanders served on land with the Second New Zealand Expeditionary Force between 1940 and 1945, one in 17 of New Zealand's total population, and a high proportion of military-age men. Casualties amounted to 6829 killed, 16,543 wounded and 8395 taken prisoner. Over 6000 other New Zealanders served with the RNZN, others with the RN and Royal Marines. Others served with the RNZAF, and more than 500 were with the RAF when war broke out, largely a result of the 1937 short-service scheme. More followed, and by December 1943, 2537 Kiwi airmen had become casualties, plus 59 who died in Canada during training. A significant proportion were with the bomber squadrons—put into brutal figures, the 1680 New Zealanders killed while serving with Bomber Command during the Second World War made up 47 percent of the fatalities suffered by New Zealand airmen with the RAF and RNZAF worldwide, and 52 percent of Kiwi air casualties in the whole of the European, Middle Eastern and South-East Asian theatres.[128]

All these people went knowing what had happened to their fathers in the First World War, but there was no shortage of volunteers. They were motivated by a range of attitudes, including lingering jingoism, pro-Imperial feeling, and family sentiment. 'I will never regret that I am able to do what I can,' one RNZAF volunteer wrote, 'to prevent, even in the smallest and most indirect way, the war ever coming to New Zealand.'[129] In 1939 there was also the fact that—as one soldier remarked—nobody 'knew, or could possibly realise, the magnitude of the coming struggle.'[130] Between October 1939 and May 1940, the war was fought low-key at sea and in the skies—the 'phoney war' that might yet have been resolvable by diplomacy.[131] Early battles such as the battle of the River Plate, where a squadron that included the New Zealand light cruiser *Achilles* came up against the *Graf Spee*, were greeted with fervour in New Zealand.[132] However, even after the war turned into a long struggle, New Zealanders continued to join up.

Like their fathers, most servicemen played tourist. Henry Miller—sailing to join the RAF in 1940—was entranced by his first sight of foreign shores, discovering Bermuda was an island paradise filled with Americans. 'The Americans think a terrible lot of us and are always wishing they could do anything for us,' he wrote. When he got to England he had time to see London, a 'dirty place and very smelly,' though he thought it would be 'wonderful during peacetime when there would be no blackout.'¹³³ Soldiers in Egypt were within easy striking distance of exotic destinations such as Karnak, Luxor, the Valley of the Kings and the pyramids. Palestine was crammed with places known to many through Sunday school or church. Later, tour parties were organised to Rome—and the 'eternal city' was a popular destination for New Zealand forces from its fall in May 1944 until the end of the war.

New Zealand's forces earned a significant reputation in the field, though the realities were later questioned. By the 1980s, many truths had been buried beneath myth, nostalgia and time. A second generation of war historians looked to cut through those layers; but efforts to demythologise over-compensated.¹³⁴ To some extent this reflected 1980s thinking, which portrayed New Zealand as a small, hidebound former colony that needed to play catch-up. Perceptions of the war, in short, suffered from the 'cultural cringe'.

Such argument diminished the genuine and significant effort New Zealand

ABOVE

Training at Baggush, mid-1941. Divisional commander Bernard Freyberg insisted that exercises should be as realistic as possible, to the point of detonating mines to simulate shellfire. The result, as General Archibald Wavell put it, was 'one of the best trained, disciplined and fittest divisions I have ever seen'.

Photographer unidentified, War History Collection, Alexander Turnbull Library, DA-02096, F-2096-1/4-DA

made during the war. It was not a huge contribution by the scale of that war—but New Zealanders fought in a wide range of theatres of war, and did so usually with distinction. Kiwi aviators put up a noteworthy performance in the RAF and Fleet Air Arm. Apart from Park's command of the key air battles, there were personal heroics such as A. C. Deere's exploits before and during the Battle of Britain and James Ward's climb on to the burning wing of his Wellington to extinguish the fire.[135] As a report noted in 1943, 'New Zealanders have earned the reputation of taking part in every operation worthwhile on every fighting front where the RAF operates.'[136] The performance at sea, particularly with the Fleet Air Arm, was no less spectacular. New Zealanders joined a risky and difficult attack on the *Tirpitz* in late 1944, and later played a significant part against Japanese air forces in the Pacific. The RNZAF gained a solid reputation among New Zealand, Australian and American forces in the same theatre.[137]

Perhaps the greatest debate has swirled around the performance of the Second New Zealand Division, the principal combat force deployed to the European theatre. This too was swept up in the 1980s revision of New Zealand's view of itself; but the realities seem clear. Middle East Commander in Chief, General Archibald Wavell, told Fraser in mid-1941 that 2 NZ Division was 'one of the best trained, disciplined and fittest divisions I have ever seen.'[138] Their performance won respect from their enemies. Rommel regarded the New Zealanders as 'among

ABOVE

Bringing the wounded down from Takrouna, May 1943. 28 (Maori) Battalion distinguished itself on this Tunisian peak as the North African campaign drew to a close.

Dr C. N. D. D'Arcy, War History Collection, Alexander Turnbull Library, DA14028, F-14028-1/41/4

RIGHT

Period sketch map of North Africa.

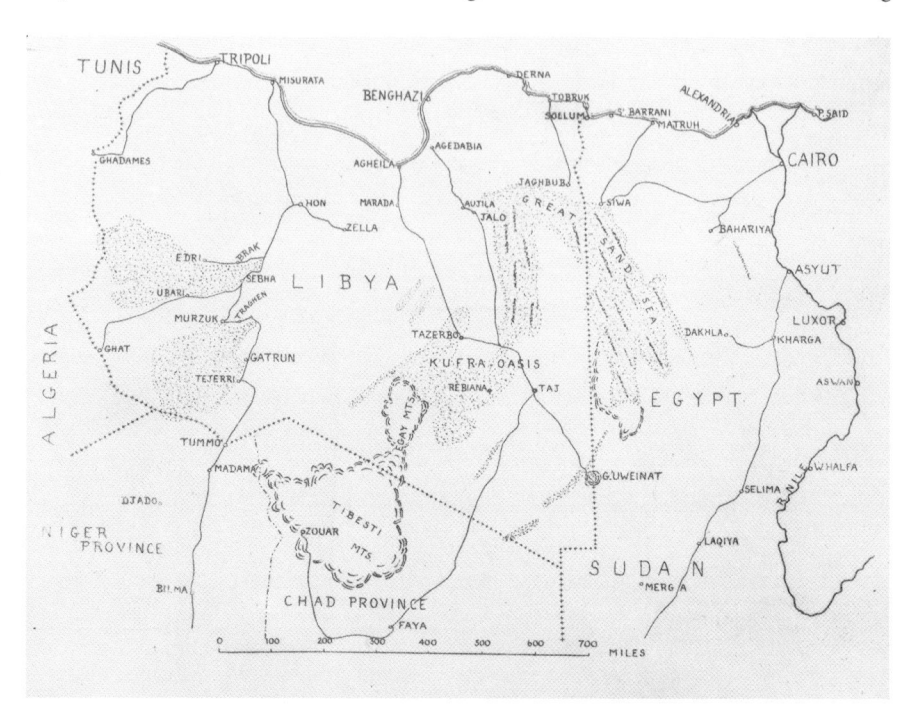

Photographer unidentified, War History Collection, Alexander Turnbull Library, DA-02096, F-2096-1/4-DA

the elite of the British Army,'[139] and by 1944 the Germans were issuing official warnings about the force and its 'dangerous' commander, Lieutenant-General Sir Bernard Freyberg.[140]

Friendly opinion was glowing. 'New Zealand Division,' US Middle East Intelligence reported in June 1942, 'is by far the best fighting unit in the Middle East.'[141] Lieutenant-General Bernard Montgomery offered fulsome praise. 'The Battle of Egypt,' he wrote in December 1942, 'was won by the good fighting qualities of the soldiers of Empire. Of all these soldiers, none were finer than the fighting men of New Zealand…The Division was splendidly led and fought magnificently…' In a reference to the role divisional commander Lieutenant-General Sir Bernard Freyberg had played in the battle at El Alamein, he added 'Possibly I myself am the only one who really knows the extent to which the action of the New Zealand Division contributed towards the victory.'[142] Lieutenant-General Richard McCreery, last commander of the 8th Army, was of the opinion that 2 NZ Division's 'splendid fighting qualities' had 'achieved successes that have often been decisive to the operations of the Army as a whole.'[143]

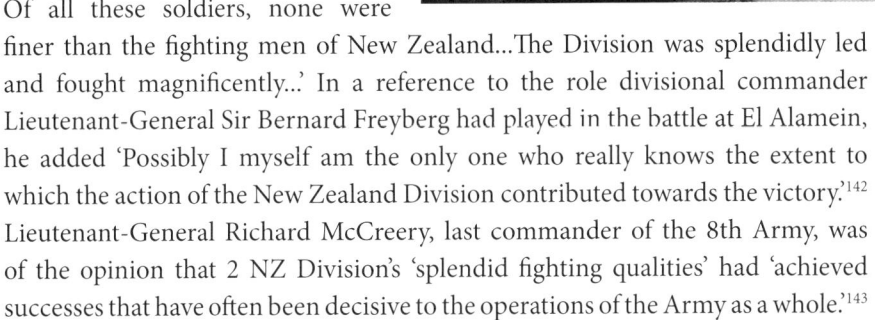

Such widely sourced sentiments cannot be wholly dismissed as wartime overstatement. The fact that the division was explicitly given the difficult jobs makes clear the reputation was genuine.

The real question is how that came about. One of the persistent—and false—myths of the day was that New Zealanders were somehow natural-born soldiers. In fact they were not. Although New Zealand styled itself the 'Prussia of the Pacific' in the early years of the twentieth century, building a self-professed tradition of combat excellence from the foundations of the Boer War, the idea that New Zealand had become a nation of expert militarists is pure mythology. Mistakes were made, particularly in the first years of the war, and some New Zealand commanders were well aware of their early inexperience.[144]

Like any soldiers, New Zealanders had to be trained to become good. It was not natural. Four factors seem to have contributed to the performance of the Division. First was enthusiasm and potential—a mix largely founded in the legacy of a rugged, physical, do-anything frontier ethos and its successor, the 'Kiwi bloke' do-it-yourself all-rounder. This was filtered and expressed through the egalitarian ethos, a thinking that allowed the men to focus less on protocols than on getting the job done. The result was a skill- and mind-set well suited for the battlefield. Freyberg recognised the point, remarking in March 1941 that:

> I am back with the NZers [sic] after twenty-six years absence. I find in them qualities of heart and mind that in my youth were not apparent to my unskilled eye. I believe

ABOVE

New Zealand forces landing on Nissan Island, part of the Green Islands Group, in early 1944.

Photographer unidentified, Alexander Turnbull Library, PAColl-4164, F-44747-1/2

ABOVE

New Zealand soldiers at Cassino, March 1944. This picture was probably taken before the main battle for the town, but reveals something of the conditions.

George Kaye, War History Collection, Alexander Turnbull Library F-5499-1/2

that there is a higher standard of talent and character in the ranks of the men of the New Zealand division than any troops I have seen.[145]

This was not something to be wasted, but it might have been if the division had been led by an average British officer, or one who did not have a charter laying out his powers and lines of responsibility. The differences between the colonial ethos and that of the British Army were clear.[146]

In the event the division was led by an extraordinary officer. Freyberg, a career British soldier who been brought up in New Zealand, later received his own share of the 1980s effort to invalidate past achievements;[147] but the realities again seem clear.[148] Freyberg was the second factor behind the New Zealand divisional performance in the war, a 'very great leader of men'[149] who imposed exacting standards and inspired his soldiers to great things. 'A difficult old cuss at times,' one officer opined. 'But we'd do anything for him.'[150] New Zealand battlefield superiority, which in the First World War had been an aspiration born of hope and jingoistic idealism, became reality under Freyberg.[151]

Composition, size and equipment contributed to the mix. The New Zealand division was the only fully motorised infantry force in North Africa, and by the second battle of El Alamein had become one of a handful of light divisions—two-thirds infantry, one-third armour, with artillery and armoured 'cavalry' in support. It was larger than an equivalent British unit. The final factor was that the division also had the knack, as Freyberg put it, of 'sitting over the vital point at the vital time'.[152] He made this observation of the desert war, but it also seems true of the Italian campaign, though this was not wholly chance.[153] For much of the 1941–43 period, 2 NZ Division made up a significant proportion of the 8th

Army—usually one of six divisions, and at one stage in June 1942, one of only two that remained intact. As its reputation grew, British commanders deliberately used the Kiwi force for the hard tasks.

The results were decisive. New Zealand soldiers, under their extraordinary fighting commander, turned the battle for Tobruk into victory in December 1941, hampered the German advance into Egypt six months later, led the main advance at El Alamein that defeated Rommel's *Panzerarmee Afrika* in the field of battle; and were in the vanguard of the break-through battle at Tebaga Gap that opened the way to final victory in Africa in May 1943. They repeated the performance in Italy between 1943 and 1945. During that 20-month campaign, New Zealanders made significant inroads into the toughest fortifications ever developed during the war, contributed to the drive north of Rome, and were instrumental in the destruction of the German armies in Lombardy in April 1945. Finally they led the dash to Trieste and the first confrontation of the Cold War.[154] It was an enviable record.

As in the First World War, the struggle focussed, honed and recast New Zealand's long-standing social ideals, including egalitarianism, job security and home ownership. For those overseas—a socially significant proportion of New Zealand's youth—there was exposure to other cultures, along with the experience of the war itself. Battlefield comradeship became a binding force in post-war New Zealand, adding to and shaping existing ties and cultural norms. The servicemen also had ideas about the kind of society they wanted to live in. 'We spent a lot of time,' John Mulgan wrote in 1945, 'talking about the world after the war. Some of this discussion was organised by the Army on highly creditable lines, but as usually happens, the basic conclusions were arrived at more crudely and

ABOVE

War's end. G. Hammond (Hawke's Bay), C. H. Thompson (Christchurch), W. G. Warner (Wanganui) and B. S. N. Berry (Dannevirke) in Trieste, May 1945. The dash by 2 NZ Division to Trieste during the last hours of the war in Italy, there to face Yugoslav communist forces, remains one of its more spectacular achievements. The New Zealand force had come a long, long way since 1939.

Photographer unidentified, war history collection, Alexander Turnbull Library, DA9389, F-9389-35mm-DA

personally.'[155] Soldiers from all nationalities shared the experience. Most wanted simply to 'feel well and happy in themselves,' and as Mulgan put it:

> Most of the men that I knew asked for very little beyond this. Every sensible man wants a home and the woman that he wants to live with and room for his children to move in. And besides that he wants some work to do. It doesn't matter at all what the work is, whether it is making roads or making books, although it is better if it is work that he can do satisfactorily or with belief...[156]

The role of 2 New Zealand Division in defining New Zealand's future hopes was significant, largely because this force drew in such a disproportionate percentage of the total who served into a single, integrated and proud unit. It was deployed into the field for six years, developing a social environment of its own—described by one officer as 'home'.[157] In part this environment derived from divisional leadership. Freyberg had the knack of focussing the strengths of his men and, in consequence, their values. It seems clear that 2 NZ Division encapsulated the usual comradeship of the field in ways that could not be matched even in the Pacific's 3 NZ Division or in the New Zealand squadrons of the RAF, which between them made up New Zealand's other big contributions to the war. This fed back into post-war society on two levels: in a general sense through the experiences shared by tens of thousands of New Zealanders in the division, and specifically because many of those in the divisional officer corps were professionals in civilian life, and returned to their normal work after the war, where they became significant movers and shakers in fields from education to the judiciary. Some entered Parliament—notably Robert Muldoon, a corporal with 9 Brigade in 1944–45.[158]

This thinking added a dimension to the general shifts in thought, behaviour and attitude that war brought to every New Zealander. They had come out of the Great Depression, been briefly offered hope by the Labour government, and then been plunged into total mobilisation, the threat of starvation or invasion, renewed shortages, blackouts, and devastating family loss. The crisis extended the exigencies of that depression. At the same time the war opened the eyes of service personnel and civilians to the wider world, epitomised for many New Zealanders by the arrival of American troops in 1942. All this helped define new expectations. The joyous crowds that surged into the streets to celebrate victory over Europe in May 1945 and—six months later—the surrender of Japan, were also marking the end of an era and expressing their hopes for a new and brighter future.

CHAPTER NINE
Slices of heaven

The safe, secure, conservative world that New Zealanders had sought for so long finally came to reality in the wake of the Second World War—a reality that British journalist Austin Mitchell whimsically classified as the 'half-gallon, quarter-acre, pavlova paradise'.[1] This paradise, as Gordon McLauchlan later observed, was also 'passionless'.[2] Yet that should not be taken as too deep a criticism. Much of New Zealand's mid-century blandness was intentional, and there were good reasons why that was so. New Zealanders had struggled, suffered and died to achieve a prosperous, stable, family-oriented society since the settler period. This long-sought nirvana had been achieved only after two devastating wars and the worst depression Western economies had seen to that time—a turbulent age of loss, sacrifice and high drama. By the late 1940s most New Zealanders wanted a peaceful life. The 'passionless' people of the 1950s and beyond were deliberately so.

This society was not perfect. Like the settler and jingo-era societies from which it developed, New Zealand's pavlova world pivoted around in-built contradictions, dissonances encapsulated in the ongoing tensions between moral evangelism and drinking. Both urban and rural society remained quintessentially white, blokeish and conservative. Maori, though moving to the towns and cities in ever-greater numbers, were firmly second-class in this triumphal Pakeha world; the social issues that flowed from the urban drift of Maori whose lives had, for much of the early twentieth century, been ruralised and marginalised, were not effectively addressed. Other perceived problems within the pavlova world itself ranged from drunken brawling to teenage rebellion, this last gaining disproportionate attention.

Yet from the wider historical perspective these issues did not diminish the triumph of the age. For 30-odd years from the early 1950s, more New Zealanders enjoyed a better life than they could have had in previous years, and their world—

ABOVE

Climbers watch the Ruapehu crater lake during the 1945 eruption.

Bruce Valentine Davis, B. Davis Collection, Alexander Turnbull Library, F-698- 35mm-B

which we might with due respect call the 'pavlova-era' New Zealand—survived for the active adult lives of those who built it. This remarkable longevity was achieved in part because this society was artificially preserved past its 'use-by' date, in part because its success diminished the motive to change.

A nation for heroes

The object of all economic activity is the satisfaction of human needs. But it is sometimes forgotten that human beings have needs and desires apart from those which can be satisfied by purely economic means. It is proposed now to open up this aspect, and to indicate forms of national development which, while not economic, must be given due place...
– Organisation for National Development, 'Interim Report on Post-war Reconstruction and National Development', July 1944[3]

New Zealand's pavlova era was founded in long-standing hopes and dreams, brought to reality by policies that evolved through the war, founded in a drive to get New Zealand back on its feet. The country was still in trouble in 1939, highlighted by the foreign loan crisis that year, and 1940 looked likely to bring fresh financial difficulties. Fraser's War Cabinet consciously took the opportunity to cure the problem, facilitated by the internal belt-tightening that went with the war, which the electorate stoically accepted in a way not possible during

BELOW

Devon Street, New Plymouth, 1948.

Photographer unidentified, Alexander Turnbull Library, 7210, F-27094-1/2

ABOVE

Loading timber for Australian housing at Tauranga, early 1950s.

Photographer unidentified, New Zealand Free Lance Collection, Alexander Turnbull Library, C-23029-1/2

peacetime. British purchase of available produce, plus war production, created income that Fraser's War Cabinet used to repay foreign debt. This had peaked in 1931 and been slowly pegged back, but still stood at 51.8 percent of total state debt in 1939. By 1945 that had plunged to just 20.4 percent, and successive governments continued the policy, bottoming the external debt in 1953, when it was at a historic low in percentage and absolute terms.[4]

Government turned its attention to the wider future as the war drew to a close.[5] The Organisation for National Development laid out a comprehensive vision for the post-war period in 1944.[6] The mistakes of 1919–21 would not be repeated. What followed was driven by the wartime sectoral compact between state and unions—to some extent a reflection of the personal friendship between Fraser and Walsh—and by Treasury's wartime secretary, Bernard Ashwin. 'The Labour movement,' Walsh wrote in a 1944 paper, 'is interested in improving its conditions and in raising the real standard of living'—to the benefit of 'the whole country.'[7]

It worked. New Zealand was ideally placed to grow in the new post-war world, nor was it alone in the desire to avoid the pitfalls of 1919. Agreements reached at a series of international meetings at Bretton Woods—attended by Walter Nash—laid the foundation for post-war co-operation. The pace was accelerated by the wool boom of the early 1950s, fuelled by the Korean War. Greasy wool prices rose from 37.98 pence per pound in 1949–50 to 87.47 pence per pound the following year.[8] Export returns soared; in 1945 they had been £62 million, by

ABOVE

Karapiro dam under construction, 1946.

Photographer unidentified, Alexander Turnbull Library 29435-1/2

1950 they were £183 million and the wool boom pushed them to £248 million in 1951. Returns continued to climb, reaching £277 million in 1957,[9] albeit eroded somewhat by inflation.[10]

New Zealand was able to meet post-war demand with the help of the second agrarian revolution. Giant discing and aerial topdressing brought marginal land into production in the early 1950s and sent lowland prosperity soaring. Tiger Moths buzzed back-country hills, replaced in the 1960s by De Havilland Beavers and other agricultural aircraft, even DC-3 airliners.[11] By 1954, there were around 90,000 farms in the country, of which 64 percent were less than 200 acres. Little remained of the old oligarch pattern of land holding—there were just six properties of more than 50,000 acres.[12] But some old pastoral patterns remained; sheep were concentrated on the east coasts of both islands, the Manawatu and Waikato; cows and cattle in Taranaki, the Waikato and Auckland.[13]

The economic power of the farmers belied their numbers. By the mid-1950s, around a quarter of the workforce were in manufacturing, and nearly 56 percent of all New Zealanders were in the so-called 'tertiary industries', building construction, power supply, transport, finance, domestic service, administration and the professions.[14] Most of this was supported by prosperity deriving from the 18 percent who worked on the farms. High prices for lamb, mutton, butter, wool and beef made the 1950s the most prosperous years New Zealand had enjoyed. Downturns, as in 1957–58, were the exception, and New Zealand soared on world prosperity rankings—though, in perspective, this was partly a function of the fact that other nations were down in the wake of the most destructive war in recent history. Even so, New Zealand's average growth between 1955 and 1973 amounted to around 4 percent per annum,[15] far in excess of what was achieved during the 1973–1999 period.

All this provided a foundation for the 'nation of heroes' promised a generation earlier. Government backed it with a comprehensive welfare state—though this was not the profligacy it might seem. In 1950 there were 38 registered unemployed in New Zealand, and the figure stayed below a hundred until 1956. All of them, the joke went, were known by name to the Prime Minister. To some extent this understates the level, because seasonal work accounted for several thousand who worked only periodically but did not register. Even so, the figure was significantly less than the 342,000 unemployed in Britain—2 percent of the workforce—in 1949.[16] New Zealand's prosperity was rising, and government could afford to be inclusive and generous. There were big rises in health spending, which had been hovering at 4–6 percent of state expenditure since the early 1930s. It climbed to 11.6 percent in 1958, and by the early 1960s was around 15 percent.[17] Public works expenditure also climbed, topping more than 20 percent of state spending in 1949, rising to nearly a third in 1956. It did not drop much below 20 percent until the early 1970s.[18]

Specific direction was guided by the consensus vision laid out during the last year of the Second World War by the Treasury, unions, the Economic Stabilisation Commission and the Organisation for National Development,

ABOVE

An RNZAF Grumman Avenger trials aerial topdressing at Ohakea, late 1940s. This technique prompted a new agrarian revolution. By the early 1950s, hundreds of former wartime pilots were working as topdressers, initially in Tiger Moths, later in purpose-built aircraft. Pastoral productivity jumped dramatically.

Photographer unidentified, Evatt Collection, Alexander Turnbull Library, PAColl-5546, F-106439-1/2

KOROPIO
ZK-AOP

NEW ZEALAND NATIONAL AIRWAYS CORPORATION
PARERA
ZK-AZA

among others. The latter's 1944 report included a call for 'long-range plans' to build roads, hydroelectric stations, bridges, railways, airfields, housing, factories, water systems, drainage, hospitals, and schools.[19] This was broadly implemented, leading to a 30-year arc of infrastructure projects ranging from large-scale highway sealing and urban motorway systems to flood-control schemes—notably in the Manawatu and Wairarapa—and world-scale hydroelectric development.[20] Some of these schemes broke new ground, notably the High Voltage Direct Current link from Benmore to Haywards, designed to bring power from a new rolled-earth dam at Benmore to the North Island. Nobody had built a DC transmission system of the scale envisaged by State Hydroelectric Department Chief Engineer M. V. Latta, but it was done with Swedish help. By the late 1990s the cable was carrying up to a third of the North Island's power.[21] These projects were themselves dwarfed by the Upper Waitaki power development of the 1970s, one of the largest hydro schemes in the world, including 58 km of canals, designed to boost the Waitaki river hydro output to 7640 gWH per annum.[22]

South Island 'hydro-towns' such as Roxburgh and Twizel were matched in the North Island by 'timber-towns' that included Kawerau and Tokoroa, built to house workers harvesting the maturing radiata forests of the central North Island—some of which were legacies of Great Depression-era make-work schemes. These were home to hundreds of 20-something New Zealanders, many of them with young families. Some flourished; Turangi, built as a tourist town, developed a life of its own fairly quickly. Others did not. Otematata, established to house the Benmore workforce, had a population of 3993 by 1966—but at the expense of Roxburgh Hydro, which provided many of the houses.

All was not rosy in this emerging utopia. An electorate that had supported Labour through the late 1930s and the war emergency of 1942–43 was less happy to find wartime hardships continuing. Labour's first hurdle was the Cold War. New Zealanders had been in on it from the outset—facing down Tito's troops in Trieste at the end of April 1945. The last New Zealand soldier killed during the European war fell to a Yugoslav bullet.[23] Fraser proved an enthusiastic 'cold warrior', perhaps over-enthusiastic; his reintroduction of conscription in 1949 was unprecedented, but less unpopular than the continuation of wartime rationing so that produce could be sent to a hungry Britain. Perhaps more crucial from the electorate viewpoint was the fact that in other respects Labour seemed merely to be offering more of the same. At the very moment when the long-promised future was upon New Zealand, it seemed Labour had no new ideas with which to guide the country into it.

This apparent intellectual exhaustion needs explanation, and it is hard to go beyond the point made by Bill Parry in 1947. Labour had won. They had achieved all their aims; everything they had fought for was in place. The political war was over.[24]

Yet many post-war problems remained to be tackled. The main popular gripe by this time was the delay in finding homes for returned servicemen and their families. This assumed near-crisis proportions in the late war period, a legacy of Depression-era housing shortages when extended families crammed into single homes out of necessity. Housing was 'already far short of requirements' as early as 1944, and planners expected that skilled builders would be 'required in record

OPPOSITE ABOVE

This Lockheed Lodestar operating in passenger service with the National Airways Corporation (NAC) had a curious life. It was originally built as a C-60A-5-LO in 1943, transferred to the RAAF later that year, and then in January 1947 sold to the New Zealand National Airways Corporation for £1900, about $150,000 in early twenty-first century money. In NAC service the aircraft became ZK-AOP *Koropiro*. It was sold to buyers in the US in 1952 and left New Zealand, but was still flying in US skies as late as 1977, when it was apparently impounded for drug running.

Gordon Onslow Hilbury Burt, G. O. Burt Collection, Alexander Turnbull Library, G-36727-1/2

OPPOSITE BELOW

A NAC DC-3 at Paraparaumu in 1953. Air travel came into its own after the Second World War, still an expensive luxury but increasingly affordable. Passenger numbers soared during the 1950s. Around 150,000 New Zealanders flew in 1948, more than double that by 1953, and in 1964 passenger numbers rose to one in three New Zealanders. Post-war services were initially operated by the RNZAF, then taken over by the new National Airways Corporation. DC-3s were the backbone of the fleet until the mid-1960s.

Photographer unidentified, Alexander Turnbull Library, F-58295-1/2

OPPOSITE ABOVE

Post-war rail; an oil-fired Ka-class locomotive hauls the Daylight Limited across the Hapuawhenua viaduct, main trunkline.

Photographer unidentified, Alexander Turnbull Library F-20339-1/2

OPPOSITE BELOW

Tasman Pulp and Paper mill under construction near Kawerau, September 1955.

E. Woolett, Alexander Turnbull Library, A41 844, F-34603-1/2, Archives New Zealand/Te Whare Tohu Tuhituhinga O Aotearoa Wellington Office, AAQT 6426/11

numbers', calling for training schemes. Demand for everything from furniture to 'floor coverings, stoves, utensils, linen, gardening implements, and all the other supplies which go with the establishment of homes', was expected to be 'acute'.[25]

Large-scale housing projects began in 1944, and 70–80 percent of all construction in the country during 1945 was of new homes. But it was still not enough.[26] Extended families lived cheek-by-jowl, even using tents as extra bedrooms, and after wartime sacrifices the people expected better. Fraser's government staggered through the 1946 election, framing their responses within the ideals they had fought to achieve, but the writing was on the wall. 'It's YOUR money they're spending on SUPER-DUPER CARS FOR MINISTERS,' National party posters declared in the build-up to the 1949 elections, capitalising on car-hunger among voters.[27] What finally did the damage was the housing crisis. 'We will house ALL the people QUICKLY!' another 1949 National slogan screamed.[28] The party came into power in that year's election with a twelve-seat majority.[29]

Prime Minister Sidney Holland distanced his party from the Forbes-Coates coalition, but while electioneering focussed on state retraction, the new government did not actually make fundamental changes. Withdrawing state control from urban land prices, cancelling rationing and opening up state housing to private purchase were mere tid-bits. The big pillars of Labour's 1930s initiatives, including state control of produce marketing, were virtually untouched—and emphasis on home ownership, this time via state loans, extended what Labour had begun with its state housing schemes. The difference was that where Labour provided the houses on a mildly more socialist basis, National did so within a mildly more private framework—but the net result was that government money underwrote the quarter-acre paradise by one mechanism or another. National also extended the welfare state, as did Labour when it came back in the 1957 election. This pattern of short-term moderately centre-left interspersed with longer-term centre-right governments dominated politics for a generation, and by later standards there was often little to choose between the two parties. Although

RIGHT

Sorting peas at Wattie's, 1948. The Hastings-based company produced military rations during the war. Neither were suited to the post-war civilian market, but owner James Wattie swiftly sought new lines. Much of the produce came from company-owned farms on the nearby Heretaunga plains.

Photographer unidentified, New Zealand Free Lance Collection, Alexander Turnbull Library, PAColl-5469-023, F-160227-1/2

CHAPTER NINE
SLICES OF HEAVEN

RIGHT

Opposition leader Walter Nash (left) with Prime Minister Sid Holland at the ceremony to open the new Rimutaka tunnel in November 1955.

Graeme Ayson, New Zealand Free Lance Collection, Alexander Turnbull Library F-65448-1/2

BELOW

Forestry housing under construction at Kaingaroa, central plateau.

Edward Percival Christensen, National Publicity Studios Collection, Alexander Turnbull Library A2397, F-34608-1/2, Archives New Zealand/Te Whare Tohu Tuhituhinga O Aotearoa Wellington Office, AAQT 6401, A2397

superficially offering flavours of 'private' or 'public', none particularly questioned the prevailing twentieth-century notion of big and intrusive government.

New Zealand's welfare system was upheld as a model alongside some of the Scandinavian systems, but this was the great age of John Keynes. Planning was in vogue around the Western world as the victorious powers sought to avoid the pitfalls of unregulated economies, looking instead to build a practical environment within which to promote their market system.[30] It was an age of pragmatism, not of policies adopted because ideology demanded them. The so-called 'black budget' of Labour Finance minister Arnold Nordmeyer in 1958, for instance, doubled duties on tobacco, alcohol and cars—and could easily have been a United-Reform measure.[31]

The response of the New Zealand electorate was certainly clear. Politics were split almost exactly between National and Labour—the parties each typically attracted between 41 and 47 percent of the vote until the early 1980s, with around 10 percent going to Social Credit after 1954. Labour leaned left, National leaned right; but by comparison with the politics of other days, they were remarkably similar. When the pattern did change, it was at the expense of both parties—the razor-tight election of 1981 slashed support for Labour and National, and both were separated by just 0.2 percent of the vote.[32] Such fortunes betrayed a society that sought stability. Who delivered it was less critical.

That did not stop the issues of the day being as hotly argued as those of any era. Many of the problems that successive governments had to tackle during the

BELOW

Returned servicemen joined others in the building industry during the last years of the war. This is part of Naenae under construction in September 1944.

John Dobree Pascoe, John Pascoe Collection, Alexander Turnbull Library, PAColl-0783, F-1171-1/4

NEW ZEALAND
AN ILLUSTRATED HISTORY

CHAPTER NINE
SLICES OF HEAVEN

LEFT AND BELOW

Ian Holmes and his family in 1944, outside one of more than 5500 state houses built by the Labour government in the Hutt Valley.

John Dobree Pascoe, John Pascoe Collection, Alexander Turnbull Library, F-1168-1/4 (left) AND F-1176-1/4 (below).

OPPOSITE TOP

Suburban dreams, under construction late 1944. Eighth-acre sections, curved streets, concrete footpaths and berms defined New Zealand's post-war urban landscape.

(Photographer unidentified, *Evening Post* Collection, Alexander Turnbull Library, PAColl-0614, F-35249-1/2

OPPOSITE BOTTOM

Suburban rail under construction, Hutt Valley, 1944.

Photographer unidentified, *Evening Post* Collection, Alexander Turnbull Library, PAColl-0614, C-27127-1/2

post-war decades stemmed from an unprecedented baby boom. This was another phenomenon that New Zealand shared with the world, and had its origins during the war; the non-Maori birth rate hovered around 16–17 per thousand in the 1930s, began climbing during the conflict, reached 25–26 per thousand in 1946 and stayed around the 24–25 per thousand mark until the mid-1960s. The phenomenon was partly a reflection of rising prosperity and the greater sense of security now felt by New Zealanders. It was also facilitated by a fall in marriage age. Post-war couples typically married in their early twenties, and were also urged to marry for romantic reasons. This differed from the 1920s when marriage was expected as a duty. It was a sign of yet another shift in generational attitudes; times were changing, and the old ideals of social purity were giving way to less strict ideals, though many were often still tightly conservative. There was a swing away from an emphasis on family as a cog in the machine, to family as a social experience.

The Pakeha birth-boom was matched by an even larger jump in the birth rate among Maori, where the figure climbed from 23.22 births per 1000 in 1927 to 46.64 ten years later. Such a jump among a people who even in the 1940s were still a largely marginalised rural group, living

375

ABOVE

State housing in upper Champion Street, Porirua, early 1960s.

Photographer unidentified, New Zealand Free Lance Collection, Alexander Turnbull Library, F-51884-1/2

BELOW

Naenae around 1960.

Photographer unidentified, silver gelatin print, New Zealand Free Lance Collection, Alexander Turnbull Library, PAColl-6303-08, C-9624-1/2

effectively separate lives from the white-dominated urban areas and wealthier farming communities, demands explanation. To a large degree it seems to have been a reflection of the Labour-led push to improve Maori health, and the birth rate did not drop below 40 births per 1000 until 1964.[33]

The 'baby boom' put rolling pressure on services and facilities, starting with schools and going on to universities, jobs and, eventually, pensions, over the lifespan of those born during the 15 to 20 years after the end of the Second World War. The rising birth rate also extended the immediate post-war housing crisis, complicating efforts by successive governments to cure it.[34] In 1954 just on a third of all new privately owned houses were built with state support, some 5402 in total, and though National focussed on supporting private owners, state

CHAPTER NINE
SLICES OF HEAVEN

ABOVE

Suburban shopping centres sprang up in the new suburbs of the 1950s. These are the Hutt Valley Consumers Co-operative Society stores at Naenae, built with voluntary labour. The pre-war car is noteworthy; older vehicles predominated on New Zealand roads for much of the twentieth century.

Photographer unidentified, Alexander Turnbull Library, 7680, F-116976-1/2, Archives New Zealand/Te Whare Tohu Tuhituhinga O Aotearoa Wellington Office, AAQT 6403, 7680

rental housing was still some 17.8 percent of all new construction. But it was not all plain sailing. The legacy of wartime restrictions and friction between Housing Minister W. S. Goosman and the building industry, added controversies.[35] Plans floated in 1953 called for 206,000 houses to be built nationally within the next decade, and differential interest rates were set for state loans to induce would-be owners to build rather than buy. The policy eventually spanned the political spectrum.

Most of the new houses went up in 'dormitory' suburbs, conceived around the combination of car and quarter- or eighth-acre sections. The first and largest were in South Auckland and greater Wellington. Nicknames such as 'nappy valley' (Wainuiomata) and 'stork's gully' (Stokes Valley) left no doubt as to their role. By 1954, some 41.7 percent of all New Zealanders were living in the four main centres, out of a total town-dwelling percentage of just over 70 percent.[36] These suburbs also introduced new lifestyles. Shopping centres had been features of a few late pre-war suburbs, and came into their own in the post-war period—as did the supermarket. The antecedent was the 'Four Square' grocery, the ubiquitous chain-store almost synonymous with the 1950s. Supermarkets with their vast range of products and total self-service ethos were a different phenomenon and something quite new for adults who had been children or teenagers during the Great Depression. It was a sign, in some ways, of how far prosperity had come in the years since; of the success of the conscious drive to create a better New Zealand. The first supermarkets in New Zealand opened in the mid-1950s, and

377

BELOW

Wave of the future: Wardell's self-service 'super market' in May 1956. Self-service was a novelty for a generation brought up with the helpful owner of the local 'corner store' or able to buy food from door-to-door vendors. To those whose childhood had been characterised by the Great Depression, both the range and quantity of stock were simply astonishing. And these shops only got bigger and more impersonal as the century went on.

E. Woollett, Alexander Turnbull Library, A45368, F-34159-1/2, Archives New Zealand/Te Whare Tohu Tuhituhinga O Aotearoa Wellington Office

by the end of the decade these self-service stores on steroids were widespread, dislodging older grocery outlets.

The mid-century suburban experience was not all positive. Multi-unit state housing zones became ghettos for lower socio-economic groups. These included youthful blue-collar workers and their families, and a rapidly urbanising and detribalising Maori, whose economic position did not improve much with the shift to town.[37] Social problems were evident as early as the 1960s, made worse as the pavlova society stagnated the following decade.[38]

Efforts to cure these problems underpinned the development of second-stage suburbs such as Hastings' Flaxmere. This was planned during the early 1960s as an 'elite subdivision',[39] a modern suburb of modern homes with ranchslider doors and other innovations that would shuck off the stigma of welfare-dependent state housing ghettoes. The idea failed, spectacularly and perhaps embarrassingly for the Hastings Borough Council and the suburban planners.

Other new suburbs in centres such as Hamilton, Napier and Whanganui swiftly gained their own reputations as troubled communities, welfare-dependent, prone to crime, their streets and properties littered, some homes reversing pride in the quarter acre by planting an inverted car on an uncut front lawn. Reputation was often worse than the reality; but concerted efforts by local authorities, residents' associations and community groups to address the difficulties were often ineffective. So were schemes to eliminate the problem by 'pepper-potting'—putting state houses amongst privately owned dwellings in newer suburbs. That simply reduced the whole area to the lowest denominator, and New Zealand families with reasonable means had little real desire to go and live in such places.

Pavlova world

> If the old world ends now with this war...I have had visions and dreamed dreams of another New Zealand that might grow into this future on the foundations of the old. The country would have more people to share in it... Few would be rich, none would be poor. They would fill the land and make it a nation.
> – John Mulgan, *Report On Experience*, 1945[40]

New Zealand's society of the 1950s and 1960s brought together many of the ideals, hopes and dreams that had been sought by the settlers, and at its ideal best was a secure world, framed around a comprehensive welfare state, full employment, private home ownership, and suspicion of any new trend that might upset the apple-cart. And although there were dark sides, that ideal was approached more closely than we might imagine. The quarter-acre paradise was pushed by policy, demanded by the people, built by deliberate intent. Increasingly urbanised New Zealanders spread into the burgeoning suburbs. Yet this did not diminish the populist image of a nation built around blokeish farmers. Indeed, the conservative, true-blue, prosperous farming sector was the key pillar that made everything possible.

Most mid-century New Zealanders felt they had earned it. Two generations of misery had, at last, given way to prosperity and comfort. Most of the adults of the 1950s and 1960s remembered family loss in the wake of the First World War, going to bed hungry or darting to school with bare feet in winter rain during the Great Depression, then the hardships of the Second World War. When good fortune finally came, largely as a result of their own efforts, mid-century New Zealanders embraced it with all their hearts.

In many ways it was a conservative and conformist world, harking back to the flatter ethos of the 1920s, and though Truby King's ideals were tempered for young mothers by the less puritanical thoughts of Benjamin Spock, society in general was still restrained. It was also an age of regularity. The weekday usually ended on a Friday, for men at least, with a drink at the pub, less hasty after six o'clock closing was abandoned by referendum in 1967—after which Kiwi blokes were allowed to continue the swill until the unheard of hour of 10.00 p.m. Women stayed at home, often all week, and even on Saturday as 'rugby widows' forbidden to

BELOW

Pavlova ideals were less strict in some senses than the social purity of the 1920s, but drew in many ways from those earlier values. The argument for 'six o'clock closing' still boiled down to family values versus alcohol, epitomised by this 1948 poster.

Artist unknown, Alexander Turnbull Library Eph-A-ALCOHOL-Hours-1948-01

ABOVE

Beachgoers at Days' Bay, Eastbourne, 1950.

S. C. Smith Collection, Alexander Turnbull Library, PAColl-3082, G-47360-1/2

OPPOSITE TOP

Auckland families relax at Mission Bay, early 1950s.

Photographer unidentified, New Zealand Free Lance Collection, Alexander Turnbull Library C-27126-1/2

OPPOSITE BOTTOM

Mission Bay from Bastion Point, October 1952.

Edward Percival Christensen, Alexander Turnbull Library, A-28502, F-18973-1/2, Archives New Zealand/Te Whare Tohu Tuhituhinga O Aotearoa Wellington Office, AAQT 6401, A29867

enter the sacred halls of men's society. It was a significant slide to the conservative; women had made a brief appearance in male worlds during the war when over 30,000 of them did everything from driving tractors to ticket-collecting. But when the men returned, women were pushed aside. Women in the 1950s were expected to be submissive homemakers, responsible for the front garden with its flowers and shrubs and, later, able to drive the second car. A few found jobs, often part-time, as the pavlova era unfolded; but for many the 1950s and 1960s were years of dull, often lonely domesticity.

The world of pavlova-age men also had its problems. Large-scale punch-ups in city backstreets were not unknown, though seldom reported. Some people felt stultified by the regulations that limited access to overseas goods, or by the ethos of conformity. Most men resented the drinking laws.

Perhaps the biggest problem was government fear of communism. Peter Fraser embraced the Cold War, and even the Holland administration feared 'reds' might lurk in New Zealand bedrooms through the 1950s. This had its effect on foreign policy, but there was also an internal consequence, and New Zealand's miniscule communist party—with its even tinier band of genuine communists—received undue attention. So did government officials with apparent left-leaning tendencies, including William Sutch, part-architect of New Zealand's mid-1930s socioeconomic changes. This tarring came back to haunt him a quarter-century later. However, none of this attracted much public attention, and there was little of the witch-hunting hysteria that accompanied US anti-communist rhetoric. Nor was there any real substance behind most

CHAPTER NINE
SLICES OF HEAVEN

381

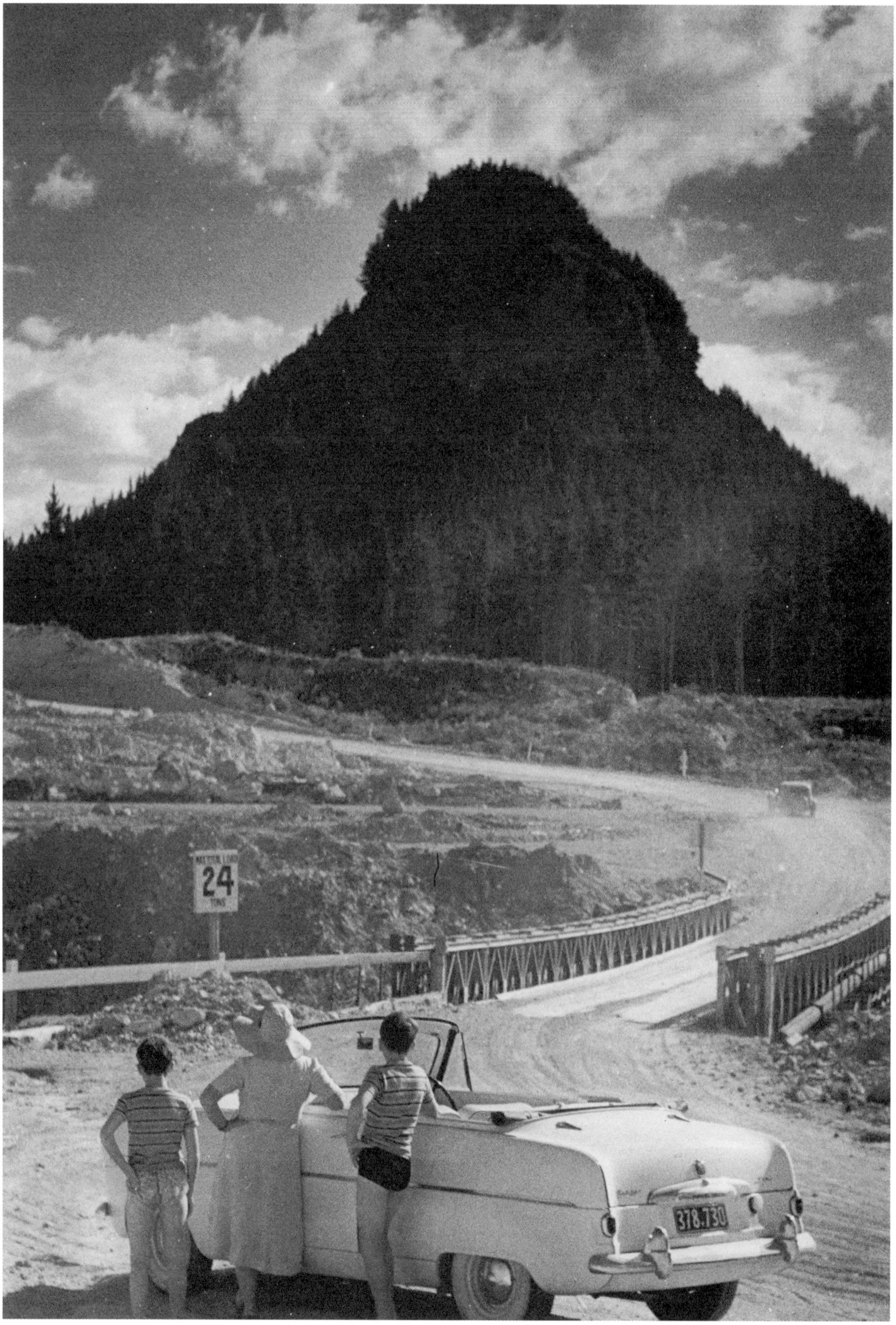
24
378.730

of the allegations, as officials such as Alister McIntosh realised.[41] The historical reality, missed at the time, was that communism had originally emerged in response to a set of European socio-economic circumstances that did not exist in New Zealand. It had been spread by conquest through Eastern Europe and parts of Asia during the 1940s, circumstances that again were not shared by any South Pacific nation. In any case, by the 1950s New Zealanders were enjoying one of the highest standards of living in the world. They had achieved nirvana; for all but a few radicals, there was no need for a revolution.

At a time of rising prosperity, even ordinary working-class families had the time and money to go to the beach, have picnics, and travel the country. Yet that did not mean ostentation. New Zealand holidays were an extension of home; a switch from suburban house to the beach-side bach, or perhaps a motel—where the rituals of home cooking, cleaning and regular meals were repeated. Some took their homes with them, packing clothes and children into the car and towing a caravan to one of the camping grounds that became a common destination for holidaymakers of the day

New Zealanders of this era often played harder than they worked. Prosperity and full employment, coupled with the occasionally abrasive but generally successful populist compact between government and union after 1951, produced a working environment where watersiders ran systems of 'spelling'—taking unauthorised breaks—and where government servants operated on 'glide

ABOVE

Mourere motor camp in 1953. Cars, caravans and camping grounds allowed pavlova-era New Zealanders to take their lifestyle with them.

W. Walker, Alexander Turnbull Library, A 29864, F-27534-1/2, Archives New Zealand/Te Whare Tohu Tuhituhinga O Aotearoa Wellington Office, AAQT 6401, A29864

OPPOSITE

The pine-clothed slopes of Powhaturoa rise before this family and their Mk I Zephyr near Atiamuri, August 1955. This car, with its American-style influence, was the latest in chic at the time.

Photographer unidentified, *Evening Post* Collection, Alexander Turnbull Library, PAColl-0614, F-164517-1/2

NEW ZEALAND
AN ILLUSTRATED HISTORY

LEFT

Skating on Lake Ida, mid-1950.

K. V. Bigwood, Alexander Turnbull Library F-34514-1/2, Archives New Zealand/ Te Whare Tohu Tuhituhinga O Aotearoa Wellington Office

BELOW

Yachting in Keneperu sound, March 1952. One of the ambitions of many mid-century Kiwi families, and achieved by a surprising number, was owning a boat.

K. V. Bigwood, Alexander Turnbull Library, A26 867, F- 27295-1/2, Archives New Zealand/Te Whare Tohu Tuhituhinga O Aotearoa Wellington Office, AAQT 6401, A26867

OPPOSITE TOP

Salmon fishers at the mouth of the Rangitata river in 1958.

Photographer unidentified, New Zealand Free Lance Collection, Alexander Turnbull Library, C-27124-1/2

OPPOSITE BOTTOM

Riverslea school float at the Blossom Festival, Hastings, 1958. Greater Hastings Incorporated came up with the idea of a spring promotion in the late 1940s and the first Blossom Festival was held in 1950. At its peak these festivals attracted up to 50,000 visitors. The key to success was correlation with contemporary ideals and values—a link that contributed to its decline. The last old-style festival was held in 1973, but they were revived in the late 1990s.

New Zealand Free Lance Collection, Alexander Turnbull Library C-27125-1/2

time'—which sometimes meant 'gliding' at both ends of the day. Yet when Kiwi men got home of an evening they worked with demoniac intensity on do-it-yourself home projects, fearlessly making furniture, repainting or adding extra rooms to the family home.

Weekends did not slow the pace. Saturday mornings echoed to the roar of the rotocut as men harvested the quarter-acre lawn, often going on to dig the vegetable patch or work on the car. They were frequently joined by their wives, who tilled the flower beds—inevitably, at the front. Saturday afternoon was

ABOVE AND BELOW

Interior of Napier record shop and electrical retailer 'Melody House', opened in 1958 using display and marketing methods, including 'bins' of records in alphabetical order and window display techniques brought across from London. These were novelties in pavlova-era New Zealand but were effective, and quickly picked up by record retailers across the country.

John Wright/Author collection

reserved for organised sport: rugby in winter, cricket in the summer, beer afterwards in the sports club. Sundays were less devoted to church than in the 1920s, more to family. The day often included a 'Sunday drive' or picnic, leavened with cone ice-cream from a corner dairy—often 'hokey pokey', New Zealand's own flavour.

This focus underscored what was important to mid-century New Zealanders; a predictable, controllable and secure family life of the kind that had been wanted but denied for so many decades. However, it came with a cost; a limit on other lifestyles, and Kiwis, paradoxically, objected to those restrictions.

The way these limits were perceived was often subtle. Overseas imports were limited by draconian foreign exchange regulations, and during the 1950s much of what consumers could buy was made or assembled in New Zealand, ranging from cars to gramophone records, some electronic apparatus, shoes and other products of light industry, all of them a consequence of pre-war focus on making and buying everything in New Zealand.

Some of this was done under licence. Records were made for New Zealand consumption from imported master discs in factories in places such as the Hutt Valley. But with these and other goods and entertainments there was always a feeling that local availability lagged, that it was behind the times. Domestic music was available, but again, it was always perceived as not quite the same as what might be available overseas, The cringe, it seemed, was operating at full volume; but in other ways the perception of backwardness had some basis in fact. Part of it was communication. Foreign trends simply did not filter quickly into New Zealand, and when opportunity came to bring in an international practice, such as ways of displaying retail goods and promoting them, innovations were picked up with alacrity.

However, other international developments were less eagerly adopted, particularly when it came to eating out. Pavlova-era New Zealand did not have a cafe culture as such. In the 1950s and 1960s, eating out for most New Zealanders often meant picnics on the beach or riverbank, washed down with lukewarm tea from the thermos. Sometimes there was more; an American import—the barbecue took quintessential Kiwi form as a 'sausage sizzle', often modified to sausages scorched, Boy Scout or

LEFT

Ford Mk I Zephyr being steam-cleaned at the Ford Motor Company plant in Lower Hutt, August 1951. Local car assembly from knocked-down kits imported mostly from Britain fostered local light industry, but import restrictions kept numbers well below demand and engendered frustration in Kiwi consumers, fuelling a sense of provincialism.

Edward Percival Christensen, Alexander Turnbull Library, A 25216, F-30407-1/2, Archives New Zealand/Te Whare Tohu Tuhituhinga O Aotearoa Wellington Office, AAQT 6401, A25216)

Girl Guide style, over open campfires on sticks. 'Bought food' was less common. Dairies stocked hot pies, and there were daytime sandwich bars serving eccles and butterfly cakes, neenish tarts, club sandwiches, milkshakes, tea and filter coffee. Milk bars were popular evening venues for teenage youth. But for adults or families, dinner-time options beyond the ritual Friday packet of 'greasies' from the local fish and chip shop were spartan. Most hotels operated a dining room, but broadly there were two choices—silver service or the pie cart. Part of the reason was licensing laws, which prevented many restaurants serving liquor. Occasionally teapots did not contain what they appeared to, but tastes also played a part.

This, too, fuelled a sense of being behind the times, of New Zealand as a backwater. What was less obvious was the fact that while Kiwis looked enviously at French cafe street culture and American diners, practical Kiwi tastes of the day simply did not stretch very far. Even cordon bleu was daring in pavlova-era New Zealand, and many mid-century Kiwis were reluctant to explore culinary options much beyond traditional meat-and-three-veg roasts, steak, chips, and the pie-cart repertoire of beans, eggs, and sausages on toast.

The real issue was alcohol. By the 1950s; state restrictions on availability, bar opening times, and licensing rules around restaurants and liquor were irritating for everyday Kiwi consumers and one of the major contributors to the popular perception of mid-century New Zealand as a cultural backwater. There was no question that New Zealand was not up with the play by comparison with more relaxed European nations which enjoyed more liberal laws, not least of which was the ability of bars to stay open beyond 6.00 pm.

BELOW

A Columbus valve radio with built-in monophonic record player and storage cupboards.

Gordon Burt, Gordon Burt Collection, Alexander Turnbull Library, PAColl-4118, F-15789-1/1

NEW ZEALAND
AN ILLUSTRATED HISTORY

RIGHT

Hotel bar, 1950s style.

Gordon Burt, Gordon Burt Collection, Alexander Turnbull Library, PAColl-4118, G-15560-1/2

BELOW

The Auckland Community Arts Ensemble touring 'La Serva Padrona' in 1953.

Steele Photography, D. Munro Collection, Alexander Turnbull Library, PAColl-0230

The legacies of social purity died hard. Successive governments resisted popular pressure to change licensing laws during the 1950s. It was not until 1960 that the Holyoake government began seriously considering reform. The Licensing Amendment Bill of 1961 increased the number of licences that could be issued. Other amendments during the decade opened up opportunities for 'family restaurants', large-scale eating houses often attached to public bars, typically offering steak, salad and chips, with pavlova and ice-cream desserts to follow.

Local perceptions of mid-century New Zealand as a cultural desert were compounded by the popular idea that 'culture' referred exclusively to the higher arts, something New Zealand also perceived itself lacking as the war ended. Although art was gaining ground—notably in the work of Peter McIntyre and Frances Hodgkins, among others—late-1940s Kiwis hoping to make good in opera, on stage or as writers still had to do so overseas—typically in Britain. Yet where it counted, at the populist level, New Zealand enjoyed a vigorous culture. Sport was a mainstay of male social activity, and cinema flourished. Matinees and evening features were the reality of New Zealand's cultural life, a mass opiate which made the transition in the 1950s to colour and, in some cinemas, 3D. These were the true expressions of New Zealand's 1950s art and culture.

The 'higher' arts were not altogether forgotten. 'In making her way toward national maturity,' a 1944 report on New Zealand's post-war direction declared:

…it is essential that New Zealand's own voice and character should not be drowned in the flood of machine-made music, exotic literature, and imported films…New Zealand's own voice, her national consciousness, and the sense of nearness of her

LEFT

The New Zealand National Orchestra rehearsing in July 1951 before a concert with Yehudi Menuhin.

W. Walker, Alexander Turnbull Library, A 24 029, F-34512-1/2

people to the higher forms of culture, can best be developed through a policy of positively searching out and promoting the development of such talent as may appear anywhere among her people...[42]

This meant overcoming the cringe; but there were signs that this was happening. Amateur operatic and dramatic societies went from strength to strength. The Auckland Community Arts Service brought opera to the city in the early 1950s, and in 1954 the New Zealand Opera Company was established, largely at the behest of Donald Munro. Ballet emerged from the Auckland Light Opera Club with support from the Auckland Community Arts Service in 1953. By the early 1960s, New Zealand Ballet was performing to packed houses, and in 1970 it sent dancers to the widely promoted 'Expo 70' in Japan.

Literature engaged pavlova society at its dominant edge—blokes and beer. Local production was nurtured by Christchurch-based Caxton Press, a pre-war company founded by Denis Glover and John Drew, pioneering the 'slim volume' format by which local poets could get their work into print. Another vehicle for verse was *Landfall*, founded by Charles Brasch. All met with surprising success. A. R. D. Fairburn's *Collected Poems* shifted around 6000 copies, high by world standards, and Alistair Campbell's 1950 *Mine Eyes Dazzle* went into a second edition. Popular literature did even better. War literature was significant, including novels such as Errol Braithwaite's *Fear in the Night* (1959). Jim Henderson's memoir *Gunner Inglorious* apparently sold around 90,000 copies in hard and soft-cover form. However, the path to populist fiction was bush-bashed by Barry Crump, a deer-hunter turned raconteur whose *Good Keen Man* of 1960 was published by A. H. & A. W. Reed, evidently shifting more than 80,000 copies in its first decade in print.[43]

This book and its sequels made Crump a New Zealand icon for a generation. Books with titles like *Bastards I Have Met* were certainly more likely to sell in

ABOVE

Frank Sargeson (1903–1982) at home, around 1947.

John Reece Cole Collection, Alexander Turnbull Library, PAColl-4063, F-3138-1/2

quantity to a culture that exalted blokeish masculinity than slim volumes like Anton Vogt's *Love Poems*. However, the relative success of 'high brow' works makes it clear that the literati also struck a chord, and Crump's appeal to Kiwi blokeishness highlighted the way ahead for the whole community. Poets and writers successfully engaged pavlova society at this level, some mixing pubs with poetry and popularising the medium to an unprecedented degree during the 1960s and 1970s. Pavlova-era New Zealand was not merely literate, but eagerly so. 'Bloke books' were only part of a brisk market that was well-filled by writers ranging from good keen Kiwis to thoughtful academics. Some writers shone as truly extraordinary—notably Janet Frame, whose 1957 book *Owls Do Cry* established her as one of New Zealand's leading novelists.

When it came to numbers, however, literature ran second place to practical living. New Zealand's most popular tome of all time was the *Edmonds Cookery Book*. Originally a promotion for a Christchurch-based baking-powder manufacturer, the recipe book became a pillar of New Zealand domestic culture. The *De Luxe* version went through 38 editions between 1955 and 1995, totalling some 2,556,000 copies.[44]

All of this was played out to a backdrop of rising lifestyle and increasing affluence. As in the 1920s there was a rapid uptake of new technology. The 1950s and 1960s brought a wave of increasingly sophisticated gadgets to the domestic scene, including electric eggbeaters, transistor radios, hairdryers, and stereo record players. They were not cheap. A Leonard refrigerator in 1957, offering 8½ cubic feet of storage space, retailed for £123/10/-, around $4400 in early twenty-first century money.[45]

Cars were in high demand. Although New Zealand motorised rapidly in the 1920s, vehicles remained unaffordable for most blue-collar workers. That changed after the war when rising relative wages made cars more affordable,

ABOVE

Broadway, Matamata, in March 1954; pre-war cars still feature, highlighting the car-hunger that created a culture of 20-year-old cars and high-value second-hand vehicles.

Edward Percival Christensen, National Publicity Studios, Alexander Turnbull Library A 34 703, F-32717-1/2, Archives New Zealand/Te Whare Tohu Tuhituhinga O Aotearoa Wellington Office, AAQT 6401, A34703

though they were still not cheap. By the late 1950s registrations were running at around 50,000 per annum, double that of late 1930s figures. The majority were British: Vauxhalls, Austins, Hillmans, Humbers and the classic Morris Minor. The latter were assembled in Auckland from knocked-down kits and came in several flavours including wood-panel vans, two-door and four-door saloons, and with a steady increase in engine size from the 850cc side-valve motor of the earliest models of 'Minor', to the 981cc unit that gained the 'Thousand' moniker, and further increases in the 1960s. A lot of New Zealanders, it seemed, had the money around to buy a 'Morrie Thou'; they became ubiquitous on New Zealand roads, often as a second car for families; and then as the 'first car' of teenagers in the 1970s. Their engine bay, originally intended for an air-cooled power plant, could accommodate much bigger motors, the construction was amenable enough to be 'hotted up' in other ways with suspension, carburettors and other add-ons. Some enthusiastic young Kiwis blokes did just that as time went on. They were still common enough in the 1980s.

British cars of various shapes and sizes were joined by Holdens, a General Motors product from Australia that became New Zealand's motoring gold standard. These big, robust vehicles were ideal for New Zealand conditions, epitomised by the HQ Holden and its successors of the early 1970s.

However, although more cars than ever were being built and sold, foreign exchange restrictions left demand soaring well above supply. Prices

RIGHT
More cars demanded more roads, and in the main centres the spread of new 'car' suburbs overloaded existing systems. In Wellington the problem was compounded by the fact that the Hutt road, seen here, already occupied most of the available space around the edge of the harbour. This picture was snapped over Ngauranga at the height of the morning rush hour in December 1962. In the event, road improvements were matched by rising traffic volumes.

Photographer unidentified, *Evening Post* Collection, Alexander Turnbull Library, PAColl-0614, F-55130-1/2

ABOVE

Racing on the Levin circuit around 1956.

Photographer unidentified, B. Davis Collection, Alexander Turnbull Library, F-811-35mm-E

were theoretically fixed, waiting lists long. At times, second-hand vehicles appreciated. A few families took advantage of the 'no-remittance' licensing regime by which those with money overseas could use it to bring goods in. New Zealanders purchased 1998 cars that way during 1955. By 1960 the figure was up to 4482 and five years later it topped 14,116.[46] Shortages fuelled a brisk second-hand market, and in the early 1950s even pre-war cars were selling for up to half their original value.[47] Newer cars were even more valuable. A 1954 two-door Morris Minor was advertised in 1957 for £525—some $19,600 in early twenty-first century money.[48] There was cash to be made for those quick enough off the mark. 'As new,' another advertisement that year declared about a 1956 Humber. '£850 for quick sale.'[49] New cars were frequently advertised as a safe investment. 'Available only on overseas funds,' one dealer declared as late as 1972, 'These models protect your resale value!'[50] The market was liberalised that year, but a car-culture based around 15- or 20-year old vehicles—unique by world standards—held sway until the mid-1980s.

Television arrived late. Part of the delay was financial, part of it cultural. Successive governments felt New Zealand did not need it, and during the 1950s television was—wrongly—thought to be the death-knell of cinema and—rightly—considered likely to change lifestyles. There was also a practical problem; the system was going to soak up precious foreign exchange, and for all these reasons, television arrived well after it had in Britain and the United States. The first broadcasts were in 1960, three evenings a week; first in Wellington, then Auckland—broadcast separately—then Christchurch. Dunedin followed in 1962. The provinces took a little longer, but by the end of the decade virtually the whole country had television, supported by a network of private translators that helped extend coverage. Even by international standards of the day these broadcasts were often basic, but Kiwis took to the new technology like ducks to water. Television sets had to be licensed after 1961, in part as a way of funding the broadcasts, and by the following year there were 65,000 of them, a figure that more than doubled in 1963 and topped more than half a million by 1968. It seemed that every family had to have one, although early sets were expensive and some consumers turned to hiring as a cheaper option.

Initial programming—featuring the *Flintstones* as prime-time Saturday viewing—was followed by more sophisticated offerings. Selwyn Toogood's popular quiz *It's In the Bag*, which ran to more than 500 radio shows in the ten years from 1954, made the transition to television in the late 1960s. Other local shows included *Country Calendar* and Peter Read's *The Night Sky*, broadly modelled on Patrick Moore's English equivalent, which began broadcasting in 1963. Chef Graham Kerr introduced New Zealanders to different styles of cooking. Music shows such as *Happen Inn* and *C'Mon* catered for a new generation of 1960s youth, though how well they addressed the needs of that generation remains debatable. But it was 1970 before a national network emerged, and despite various proposals, colour did not arrive until 1973—later in the regions—although in some ways that was no bad thing because it allowed New Zealand to adopt the technically superior PAL system.

Equality and conformity

The unfolding pavlova society refocussed attention on New Zealand's other settler-age ideal—equality. By assertion and popular mythology, the people of 1950s Godzone were not merely social but also economic equals, all apparently enjoying much the same middle-class standards of living, opportunities and incomes. This pleasant fantasy was fuelled by the rise and spread of new suburbs, all buoyed by the new prosperity of the age. To some extent it was even true; a mid-1970s study of socio-economic groups in Auckland suburbs revealed that 31.3 percent could be classified as middle class and 54.5 percent as lower middle or working class.[51]

However, the same study also identified a rich elite of 5.7 percent and an impoverished underclass of 8.5 percent,[52] and in practice the gulf between very rich and very poor was larger than ever throughout the period. It was also racially based. Many Maori, both rural and new urban, remained poor, a situation that persisted to the end of the century. They were joined by Pacific Islanders during the 1970s. Unemployment in these groups was endemic, and while the welfare state of the day meant they did not suffer Depression-style hardship, their lives invariably bumped along the poverty line.

This contrasted with extraordinary wealth at the top of the pavlova world. The gap between rich New Zealanders and the average Kiwi family in the 1950s and 1960s was vastly greater than that between the average family and the poor. A few farmers became very wealthy indeed on the back of the wool boom and second-stage pastoral revolution. Elsewhere, old money still held sway, and there was also a class of new industrial and commercial rich who emerged in spite of—and in some instances, because of—hardships and war. A 1936 list of New Zealand's ten richest people includes three brewers, three car dealers and one dairy magnate. Four of the ten were beneficiaries of old money, filtered through death duties—indicating that rich families, once they had made their pile, usually found ways of keeping it.[53] They were joined in the pavlova era by people who flourished on the back of the twentieth-century revolution. Car makers—notably the Todd family—topped the rich list in 1966, followed by cinema magnate Sir Robert Kerridge (1901–1979), a crop of brewers, a timber miller, and a significant number of businessmen who had founded their wealth in the construction and food processing, packaging and transport industries. There was one investor—Ronald Brierley.[54]

The difference between Kiwi wealthy and the rich elsewhere was that the rich farmers and wise 'old money' families usually did not display their fortunes in spectacular ways. There were individual exceptions,[55] but in general, pavlova-era displays of wealth were restrained, even disguised. The rich might buy a new car—but it would be a top-of-the-range Holden rather than a Rolls Royce. Others bought several cars of the same make, colour and model. In short, although all New Zealanders were not financially equal, most behaved as if they were. In behaviour and attitude, New Zealand was a nation of peers. As late as the 1960s, Prime Minister Keith Holyoake had his home address and phone number listed in the Wellington phone directory; ordinary New Zealanders could—and did—ring him up.[56] Norman Kirk was another who felt he should be personally accessible to the electorate. In the 1950s, Sidney Holland occasionally fell in

BELOW
Prime Minister Walter Nash, seen here in Sydney in March 1958, felt obligated to tell reporters why he wore two wristwatches when travelling—one was set to New Zealand time, the other locally.
Photographer unidentified, *Evening Post* Collection, Alexander Turnbull Library, PAColl-0614, F-76226-1/2

ABOVE

K. Kotua shearing on a farm near Nelson, mid-1950s.

Photographer unidentified, New Zealand Free Lance Collection, Alexander Turnbull Library: PAColl-6303-03

with other commuters while walking to Parliament from his Prime Ministerial residence in Thorndon.

Like its inter-war predecessor, pavlova society frowned on dissent. Schoolchildren were dressed in strictly policed uniforms and made to march to 'Colonel Bogey' as late as the 1970s, the boys exhorted to ready themselves for army life. This was 1939 thinking, increasingly out of date as Vietnam came to its unpopular conclusion, though explicable because schools of the day had to appeal to parents whose own formative years had been during the Second World War and its aftermath. This was accompanied by a surprising degree of institutionalised violence. Section 59 of the Crimes Act 1961 allowed teachers to use 'reasonable force' against children entrusted to their care, but it was questionable whether such practices as routinely hitting classes of eight-year-olds about the legs with 'the strap' or intimidating them with a three-foot blackboard ruler fell into that category.[57] A 1972 study of a Christchurch high school revealed that canings were meted out for behaviour typical of children—a pattern that had not changed in 80 years. But no canings were recorded for vandalism, assault and drug-abuse, and it has been argued, compellingly, that the purpose was classroom control—not actual discipline.[58]

Pavlova conservatism also had its effect on youth culture. Parents in the 1940s had frowned on their daughters jitterbugging with GIs, but the music of

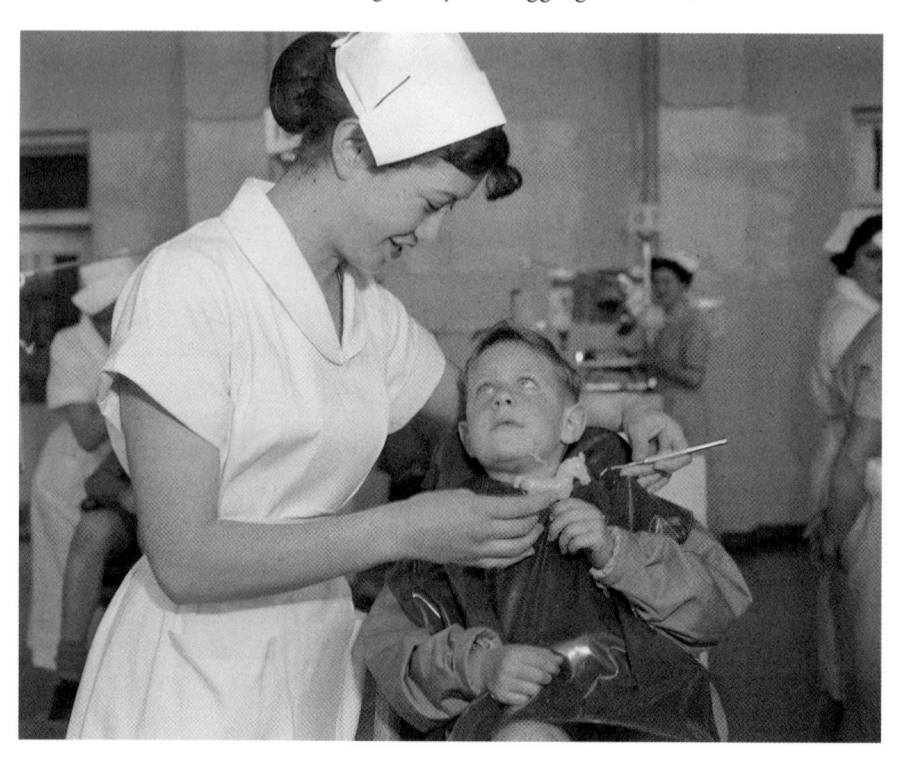

RIGHT

State support reached virtually every New Zealander during the 1950s, not least through school dental clinics. Visits to the 'murder house' were feared by generations of schoolchildren, even threatened as punishment by some teachers.

Edward Percival Christensen, Alexander Turnbull Library, A 36 966, F-33382-1/2, Archives New Zealand/Te Whare Tohu Tuhituhinga O Aotearoa Wellington Office, AAQT 6401, A36966

the 1950s posed a moral threat of another order of magnitude. By the early 1950s New Zealand had its own population of teenagers who frequented milk bars and conducted themselves badly, Brando-style. Getting the real Chuck Berry songs in New Zealand was hard, but local bands filled the gap and by the late 1950s New Zealand even had its own rock 'n' roll hero, Johnny Devlin—better than Elvis, because he was accessible. It did not take long for women at his concerts to start taking his clothes.

Teenagers gained notoriety as a sub-culture in 1953 when nearly 60 adolescents were arrested at Lower Hutt's Elbe Milk Bar for various sex offences. None of the girls became pregnant, but that merely compounded the scandal because they had clearly obtained contraception. It was a national scandal, and amid ministerial-level talk of 'terrible laxity', the Holland administration asked a committee led by Oswald Mazengarb to investigate the whole affair. The report that emerged—sent by a zealous and morally worried government to every householder in 1954—blamed 'oversexed' adolescent girls and lack of domestic guidance, citing mothers' absence at work.[59] This was a curious explanation at a time when most New Zealand wives were actually at home, but it underscored the way that the whole issue had floated on overwrought reactions.

None of these developments particularly dented the pavlova world that New Zealanders had built for themselves in the wake of the Second World War. Home life remained pivotal to New Zealand's sense of self. Rising urban populations prompted a new wave of suburban expansion from the late 1950s, gaining pace into the 1960s and this time featuring new architectural styles. Modernism was out, a dated relic of the inter-war years by late 1950s standards. New building materials and new attitudes to style produced a whole new look; it was the age of ranchsliders, wide glassed doors initially made in wood, later aluminium. It was, advertisers insisted, the 'sliding age'. Floor-to-ceiling windows, slanted to

ABOVE

Kenepuru under construction in April 1963.

Photographer unidentified, Evening Post Collection, Alexander Turnbull Library, PAColl-0614, C-27161-1/2

ABOVE
New architectural styles produced a new 'look' by the 1960s. Concrete paths, 'Morrie Thou' in the carport—another period innovation—and close-cut lawns typify suburban New Zealand.

Duncan Winder, Duncan Winder Collection, Alexander Turnbull Library
F-2508-1/2-DW

RIGHT
Lylian Shuker in her Titahi Bay home kitchen, well lit with tall windows that stood in contrast to earlier modernist designs.

Duncan Winder, Duncan Winder Collection, Alexander Turnbull Library
F-1045-1/2-DW

CHAPTER NINE
SLICES OF HEAVEN

fit the roofline, added light and a sense of the new. The change was matched with new building materials, especially 'fibrolite', sheets of cement and asbestos that became the vogue exterior cladding of the day, replacing weatherboard. Garages and concreted driveways nodded to the prosperity of the times; by the late 1950s every New Zealander could afford a car, and some had two. Life inside these new-style suburban homes, however, continued much as it always had; like their modernist predecessors, these three-bedroom houses were surrounded by the inevitable close-trimmed lawns, front and back, with vegetable garden and flower beds in all the proper places.

But the clouds of change seemed to be roiling around this tight pavlova world. If the youth culture of the 1950s and its supposed delinquents had been a threat to pavlova society, that of the early-to-mid 1960s was seen as a positive menace. Here, perhaps, was the real difference between inter-war culture and that of the 1950s. The bodgies of the 1950s with their motorcycles and distinctive clothing gave way to a youth movement inspired by overseas trends. The way was led by the Beatles, and New Zealand's own 'mop tops' soon emerged—a charge led by Ray Columbus and the Invaders. All were viewed with suitable shock by the older generation. The Rolling Stones toured in 1965, their bad-boy stage image somehow epitomising the whole threat to the old. The Stones and similar bands that came later in the decade made the Beatles look innocuous. Sympathy for

ABOVE

A Napier house, mid-1960s. Ranchslider doors, fibrolite cladding and floor-to-ceiling windows broke with tradition. By the 1970s, wood framing had given way to aluminium. Neatly trimmed lawns and gardens remained features of the New Zealand suburban landscape.

Duncan Winder, Duncan Winder Collection, Alexander Turnbull Library, F-875-1/2-DW

ABOVE

Sir Edmund Hillary (1919–2008). His 1953 conquest of Everest and epic 1958 crossing of Antarctica made him one of New Zealand's best-known and most popular figures.

Photographer unidentified, John Pascoe Collection, Alexander Turnbull Library, F-F-20196-1/2

rock was, it seemed to many older New Zealanders, indeed sympathy for the devil.

Society overseas, it seemed, was changing, and the essential liberalisation of what became known as the 'generation gap' had its effects in New Zealand, not least via publications such as the *Little Red Schoolbook*, a controversial and subversive effort to educate teenagers about sex. These shifts stood directly against the social purity of New Zealand's older generation, challenging some of the key tenets of the pavlova world, and they could not entirely be shut out. Some railed against what they considered threats to standards, but although campaigners such as Patricia Bartlett struck chords in some sectors, the effort to preserve an idealised social purity swiftly discredited itself. By the 1960s the world had moved on, and even regulated, exchange-controlled New Zealand could not shut itself away.

Yet rock music, television and the youth culture of the early-to-mid-1960s did not fundamentally destroy New Zealand's post-war society. Not then. Despite the fears of the time, the basic ideals of mid-century New Zealand were resilient, accommodating the teens of the 1950s as they became adults in the 1960s, accomodating the young adults of the early 1960s as they grew up later in the decade and began starting families and buying homes. Aspects of life changed, new ideas flowed, some things could be done or talked about without society frowning. Pavlova society shifted ground within its framework, but although—with some benefit of hindsight—the writing was on the wall, this world did not collapse. Part of it was the momentum of government regulation; but part of it was also a genuine streak of conservatism. And to this extent, New Zealand did lag somewhat behind the rest of the world.

Colony to nation?

The 'generation gap' and the social shifts of the 1960s were not the only things challenging New Zealand's mid-century pavlova paradise. There was also the issue of national self-image, and the love-affair with Britain that had dominated the national mind-set since Seddon's day was looking increasingly out of place in a world where Britain was actively shedding her Empire and looking to closer ties with Europe.

However, traditional double patriotism remained a force to be reckoned with through the 1950s, though this did not prevent changes in foreign policy. That demands explanation. Some historians have argued that international relations during the pavlova era were a separate issue from continued economic and emotional adherence to Britain,[60] and in part this is true. New Zealand had always had regional defence issues, even at the height of its jingo mentality in the years before the First World War, and British withdrawal from its world defence obligations could not be ignored. This contrasted with attitudes to the British economic withdrawal, where successive New Zealand governments, manufacturers and producers studiously pretended that the British drive to join the Common Market from the late 1950s did not matter. Only a few voices rang out in warning—notably that of W. B. Sutch, who saw undiversified adherence to British markets as colonial and dangerous.[61] Time proved him right; but in the mid-1960s he was a lone voice in the wilderness.[62]

The desire to hold on was predictable. Pavlova-era nationalism was founded in large part on the ideals of the 1920s. Schoolchildren still saluted the Union Jack, *God Save The Queen* was sung before the national hymn, *God Defend New Zealand*. The 'overseas experience' meant Britain, and those who went elsewhere were thought not to have properly travelled. When the new Queen toured New Zealand during 1953 she was feted wherever she went.

The question, then, is not whether New Zealand made the transition from colony to nation during these years—for in the social sense it did not—but why it seems to have done so in terms of its international relationships.

In fact there was no choice. New Zealand adhered to the Commonwealth structure immediately after the war, but such views were increasingly out of step with a world polarised between two superpowers, neither of them Britain. The nations of Oceania occupied a key geographical position relative to the Pacific—not the other zone of contention in Europe.[63] Against this backdrop, local issues that had always stood at tension with European priorities gained new importance. Old habits died hard; New Zealand policy makers recognised the change as it began, but initially saw the Commonwealth as a credible third player, despite once again being in a minority. Peter Fraser alone argued for a Commonwealth in 1949, within which he viewed New Zealand as an independent nation.[64] Sentiment was matched with action; frigates and aircraft were sent to back British forces in the Mediterranean from 1950–51, by way of helping deflect a possible Soviet threat to British interests in the region.[65] The big event of the early 1950s was the Korean War, which New Zealand joined at sea and on land, again within the British framework. Cabinet decided to move after consulting Field Marshal William Slim. A 2000-strong Army contingent joined a British Commonwealth contribution, and New Zealand naval forces operated under British command in Korean waters.[66]

However, Korea was also a harbinger of change. United States efforts to 'contain' communism led them to conclude a favourable peace treaty with the Japanese. That set alarm bells ringing in Australia and New Zealand, where memory of 1942 was too close. The prospect of alliance with the US against a re-armed Japan was raised by the Australians when Secretary of State John Foster Dulles visited Canberra in February 1951, and after a painful gestation the ANZUS pact came into force in April the following year. It promised consultation in the event of war in the Pacific, but as one historian has observed it was more to bolt the door against Japan than a swing away from Britain.[67] Indeed, the ANZUS arrangements acknowledged that New Zealand and Australia had military

Above
'Kiwi Keith'—Keith Jacka Holyoake (1904–1983)—entered Parliament in 1932 as Reform member for Motueka, lost the seat in the 1935 election, but returned as National member for Pahiatua in 1943, his home district. He was made deputy leader of the party in 1947 and briefly became Prime Minister in 1957 when Holland retired. He became Prime Minister once again in 1960 and led New Zealand through that turbulent decade. His conviction that the office made him a servant to the people led him to list his home address and phone number in the Wellington directory. He retired from politics in 1972 and became Governor-General.

Photographer unidentified, Alexander Turnbull Library, C-10579-1/2

obligations outside the Pacific area and, as late as 1955, Holland was describing the United Kingdom as having 'a great deal to offer as an ally.'[68] Pacific policies were also framed within the British ambit. New Zealand supported the Colombo Plan as a means of defeating Asian communism through economic means and gave arms to support the French in Indo-China during 1952.

South-East Asia continued to drive shifts in New Zealand perception, helping guide the policy of forward defence, which itself demanded alliance ties with nations that shared New Zealand's strategic views—essentially, Australia and the United States. After the siege of Dien Bien Phu in early 1954, New Zealand Minister of External Affairs, T. C. Webb, agreed with US and British proposals for new collective security arrangements in South-East Asia. If the strategically important and resource-rich nations in South-East Asia fell to communism, he argued, 'Australia and New Zealand would be gravely threatened.'[69] As a result, New Zealand joined the South-East Asia Collective Defence Treaty and Pacific Charter, which created the South-East Asian Treaty Organisation. A state of emergency was declared in Malaysia in 1948 in response to activity by 'communist terrorists'. To Holland, it had become 'increasingly clear' that the 'security of South-East Asia, and…Malaya, are of special significance to New Zealand.'[70] Cabinet discussed withdrawing 14 Squadron from Cyprus early in 1955. However, the New Zealand contribution to the struggle was still framed in traditional Commonwealth-centric terms; during a meeting in London, Holland couched the move in terms of relieving the British defence burden in Malaya.

They left one jump ahead of the Suez Crisis of 1956. This underscored Britain's long decline as a first-rate power, and in its wake Britain began actively moving

ABOVE

The Hawke's Bay Farmers Co-Operative store in Dannevirke. Department stores came into their own during the 1960s.

Duncan Winder, Duncan Winder Collection, Alexander Turnbull Library, F-900-1/2-DW

CHAPTER NINE
SLICES OF HEAVEN

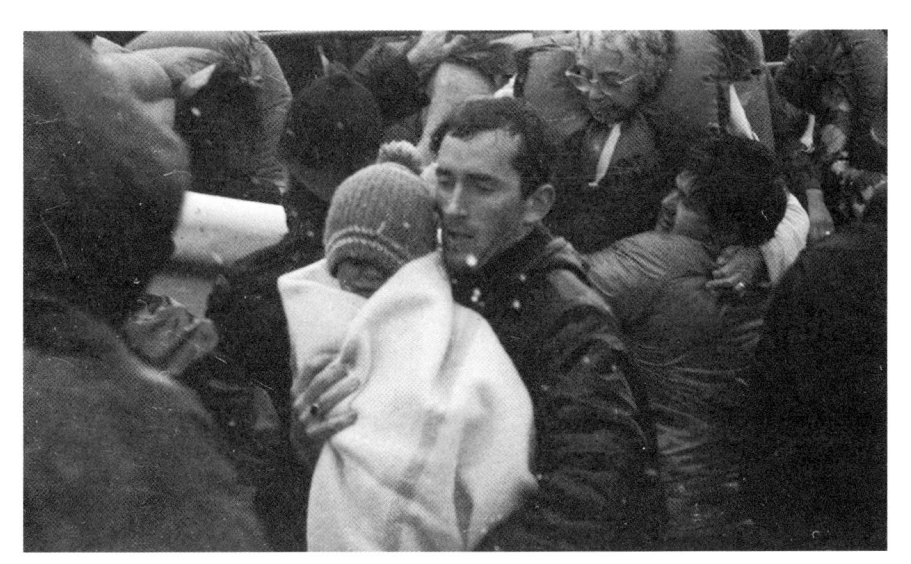

LEFT

The roll-on, roll-off inter-island ferry *Wahine* goes down off Seatoun after striking Barrett's Reef in a storm, 10 April 1968. It seemed unthinkable that a ship could go down like this in the harbour entrance of New Zealand's capital; but it did, and the images of the disaster became iconic.

Photographer unidentified, *Evening Post* Collection, Alexander Turnbull Library, PAColl-0614, F-1149-35mm-28

CENTRE

Survivors coming ashore at Seatoun wharf. Half the lifeboats were unusable as a result of the list, and rescue vessels—including the rail ferry *Aramoana*, tugs, a naval launch and the university research launch—were hampered by 70-knot winds. The *Aramoana* launched lifeboats, some of which were swamped, and the sloop *Tahi Miranda* was wrecked during the rescue effort.

Photographer unidentified, Alexander Turnbull Library, PAColl-0614, F-148061-1/2

BOTTOM

Safe at last. More than 500 were rescued from the *Wahine*, and none went down with the ship. Nevertheless, 51 lives were lost during the disaster. Some drowned when the S1 lifeboat was swamped, others died after being cast ashore south of Eastbourne in freezing conditions.

Photographer unidentified, *Evening Post* Collection, Alexander Turnbull Library, PAColl-0614, F-1161-35mm-20

ABOVE

Willis Street, Wellington, 1969.

Photographer unidentified, *Evening Post* Collection, Alexander Turnbull Library, PAColl-0614, F-16394-1/4

away from world obligations and collective Commonwealth security. The change continued into the 1960s, accelerated by a British White Paper of 1966 which foreshadowed reduction in British defence interests in the Far East. The same year, New Zealand and Australia joined the Asian and Pacific Council (ASPAC), a loose association that included Japan, Malaysia, Thailand and South Vietnam. New Zealand gained observer status with the Association of Southeast Asian Nations (ASEAN), formed in 1967.

None of this was achieved without a good deal of argument. Some voices pushed the line that New Zealand should sink or swim on its own.[71] In the broader sense, however, these policies were a reaction both to rising regional defence imperatives and to British withdrawal, both of which were beyond New Zealand's control and could not be ignored. The Cold War was impossible to avoid, so dominating that by the 1970s, international analysts framed all their thoughts around it,[72] and even major third-player developments were portrayed as shifts in the super-power balance rather than anything new.[73] New Zealand was integrally aligned with the West from the outset, and the geographical position in Oceania, coupled with the progressive British admission of second-line status, essentially dictated an orientation with American—and Australian—interests.

The practical transition was complete when the government decided to deploy 550 troops and RNZAF units into Vietnam, attached to Australian units. This was wholly independent of any British ties, and in July 1965 the service airlifted No. 161 Artillery Battery to Bien Hoa. Although it was later announced on television, the moment of departure was kept secret to avoid protests by the Progressive Youth Movement—even the aircrew believed they were only going to

Singapore until shortly before the first flight. RNZAF Bristol Freighters operated on a weekly basis into South Vietnam between 1968 and 1971.

New Zealand kept British ties via the Five Power Defence Arrangement (FPDA), and other arrangements, including officer exchange. However, by the mid-1970s, the hoped-for special Commonwealth arrangement was gone. Even hardware was not always procured from Britain, and the decision by the Muldoon administration to send a frigate into the Middle East to help the British naval recovery of the Falkland Islands in 1982 was a last salute to tradition. Politically, New Zealand's international disengagement from Empire was complete by the early 1980s. Despite the fond ties of memory, Britain had become, in practice, but one ally among several. The question was whether people, society and economy could follow.

Snakes in paradise

...economics is not money, or wealth, or resources, but people; their hopes, their fears, their reactions to stimuli or adversity...
– Robert Muldoon[74]

Although the British withdrawal from its Pacific and Far Eastern interests—coupled with efforts to join the European Economic Community (EEC) from the late 1950s—prompted a response at foreign policy level, New Zealand remained heavily committed to the British meat and dairy market. Some 65.5 percent of all exports went to Britain in 1952, down from the levels of the previous 50 years, but still under the ambit of wartime bulk purchase arrangements. These were renewed in 1944 and 1948 for butter and meat, but all ended in 1954, at which point New Zealand returned to the open market.[75] This forced a return to exchange controls after a brief taste of freedom. Large-scale British exports continued, but at volatile prices—contributing to another exchange crisis in 1957–58, and although the percentage of New Zealand's exports sold to Britain fell to 50.8 percent of New Zealand's total exports by 1965, New Zealand was still one of the two least diversified exporters in the OECD, beaten only by Iceland.[76]

New Zealand's response to the threat of Britain joining the EEC was to pursue the British harder, seeking access to the European market, a reaction partly driven by the fact that it was too late to change tack. A 1961 list of 'desired goods' New Zealand wanted to sell into that market included butter, cheese, milk products, beef, sheep meat and fruit. By 1967 this had been cut back to butter, cheese and sheep meat, and the actual access arrangements of 1972 allowed just butter and cheese.[77] Britain made a case to the EEC, to no avail.[78] It was obvious early on that the writing was on the wall for New Zealand's one-stop export shop, and W. B. Sutch warned of the consequences.[79] Few listened; at the time, Sutch was a voice in the wilderness, and no new policies followed a wake-up call in 1967, a foreign-exchange crisis that resulted in a near-20 percent devaluation of the dollar.[80]

The main problem was that pavlova society had been too successful; it had brought to reality the world New Zealanders had sought since before the First World War, and there seemed little reason to question either the thinking or

ABOVE

Norman Kirk (1923–1974) presides over a press conference in his office after returning from an Asian tour, 1974. Camera crew are noteworthy; the age of TV politicians had arrived.

Photographer unidentified, *Evening Post* Collection, Alexander Turnbull Library, PAColl-0614, F-21519-1/4

mechanisms behind it. This included the image of Britain as 'home', and the point that by the 1960s British markets had taken everything New Zealand could supply for two generations. The issue was not that New Zealand policy-makers and businessmen failed to consider the consequences of the failure of the British market, but that they reacted to it by trying to find ways of preserving the old, familiar and comfortable. In a psychological sense it reflected a fundamental insecurity, the colonial cringe writ anew. Such thinking was also expressed in the ostrich-like reluctance to diversify—in effect, a subconscious denial of change. Ultimately, faced with a threat to the umbilical cord, New Zealand also sought solace in the bosom of Mother England.

Yet not everybody had this view. It has been argued that Labour leader Norman Kirk—reflecting a significant portion of his own party and similar views in the electorate—took a nationalist perspective. As Opposition leader in early 1972 he criticised Common Market access provisions, declaring that New Zealand was living in a 'fool's paradise' and calling for diversification.[81] Once in power he began implementing the vision, evidenced by his foreign policies which oriented New Zealand as a small nation on the world stage.[82] His aims included nationalising the oil companies and breaking with Britain,[83] and the brief economic buoyancy of the early 1970s helped convince the Kirk administration that their policies might lead New Zealand into a new future, adapting the pavlova society to suit and sailing high in world rankings. Terms of trade rose, and the dollar was revalued 10 percent in late 1973.

However, Kirk reckoned without the decision by the Organisation of Petroleum Exporting Countries (OPEC) to raise the price of oil that year—itself a long downstream consequence of British withdrawal from the Middle East. The shift hammered Western economies and burst New Zealand's brief prosperity bubble. Inflation had re-emerged in the late 1960s and was fuelled by the oil shock. Government efforts to control it began as early as October 1973 with measures to spread price stabilisation measures across all sectors.[84] By 1974, New Zealand faced problems, but how Kirk might have tackled them longer term is a moot point. The popular Prime Minister, dubbed 'Big Norm' by his supporters, and subject of wide adulation—even a pop song—died in office in August 1974.

A shocked nation went into mourning, and Kirk into legend. The tantalising question always remained—where would New Zealand have gone had he remained in power? The immediate problem for Kirk's successor, former Finance Minister Wallace (Bill) Rowling, was the economic tightening of 1974–75, but he never had the opportunity to find longer-term answers. Labour was swept from power in the 1975 election, largely because National Party leader Robert Muldoon promised a universal superannuation benefit at age 60, set at 80 percent of the median wage, no strings attached.[85] Voters looking down the barrel of retirement were reputedly queuing up to vote for him.

As Prime Minister, Muldoon—Finance Minister in the previous National government—again took up the reins of the economy, combining two offices of considerable power. He had rescued New Zealand from the shocks of 1966–67, and apparently hoped to do so again in 1975. Nor was this out of line with the electorate. His own background as a child of the Great Depression, Second World War serviceman and rising National Party star during the 1950s and 1960s, struck a chord with others of the same generation. He dominated New Zealand politics from 1975 until a snap election in 1984, and along the way became one of New Zealand's most powerful historic figures, a Prime Minister whose impact put him easily in the league of Seddon, Massey and Savage.[86]

How Muldoon kept the trust of the electorate while implementing policies that were increasingly out of step with world trends and with the wants of a growing proportion of his electorate remains a key historical question. To some extent he failed; Labour gained more votes in the 1978 and 1981 elections. But despite increasing isolation from the right wing of his own party,[87] and the attempted 'Colonels Coup' of 1980, Muldoon kept an iron grip on the caucus, and his grassroots supporters—'Rob's Mob'—stuck with him through thick and thin. Muldoon's longevity was also a function of the executive powers of government, which he aggrandised to himself, combined with a personal style that inevitably polarised opposition against him. He was extraordinarily astute, quick in debate, and backed his points with in-depth and accurate data. That allowed him to

ABOVE

Wallace Rowling (1922–1995), Prime Minister after Norman Kirk's death, announcing new wage restraints late in 1974. Minister of Finance Bob Tizard sits behind him.

Photographer unidentified, *Evening Post* Collection, Alexander Turnbull Library, PAColl-0614, F-22016-1/4

ABOVE

Robert Muldoon (1921–1992) on the campaign trail, April 1975. Muldoon served with the Second New Zealand Division in Italy while completing his accountancy qualifications. He entered Parliament in 1960 as National MP for Tamaki, a seat he held until 1991. By 1967 he was finance minister, rescuing New Zealand from a crisis that year. He became Prime Minister in the landslide National victory of 1975, well aware of the problems New Zealand faced; but his combative and abrasive political style polarised popular opinion, disguising his genuine concerns for ordinary New Zealanders.

Photographer unidentified, *Evening Post* Collection, Alexander Turnbull Library PAColl-0614, F-22486-1/4

dominate the caucus and browbeat leading public servants. His disputes with those who objected to his ideas were legendary, and he extended this approach to his enemies—notably journalists, cartoonists and academics. One analyst considered him a 'political thug',[88] yet while there were clear elements of Seddon-like thuggishness about his approach, Muldoon also remained brutally honest. He invariably did what he said he would. Few were prepared to stand up to him and, as his biographer notes, some colleagues did not frankly criticise Muldoon until he was gone from power. A few waited until he was dead.[89]

This combative public persona contrasted with that of the private Muldoon, who genuinely and deeply cared for the society in which he lived. He was also loyal to his supporters, notably the slice of middle New Zealand who had backed him into power in 1975, and this proved his undoing. He preserved their society for them as best he could, against all odds and well past the point where a man of lesser conviction and ability might have given up. His biographer has argued, convincingly, that although the voices for liberalisation were growing by the late 1970s, the human cost of disentangling New Zealand from 50 years of intervention was not acceptable to Muldoon. Depression-era experience had left him acutely aware of the pain governments could bring, and he was determined to minimise the hurt at all costs.[90]

That cost was significant, in part because Muldoon inherited an invidious situation. By 1975 New Zealand had survived Britain's entry to the EEC and exporters were diversifying, but it was a late effort, undermined by the oil shock. Inflation was rising. New Zealand's had been below the OECD average between 1954–55 and 1968–69,[91] but in 1975 the all-groups consumers price index (CPI) stood at over 14 percent. By 1976 it was nearly 17 percent.[92] This

LEFT

Fire sale at McKenzie's Wellington branch, 1975.

Photographer unidentified, Evening Post Collection, Alexander Turnbull Library, PAColl-0614, F-22834-1/2

spurred lobby groups such as CARP—the 'campaign against rising prices'—and bargaining to keep wages up gave new weight to the unions. Other difficulties were of Muldoon's own making. The pension scheme had to be paid for, and suggestions that it might be scarcely more expensive than Labour's compulsory actuarial system were soon scotched. Muldoon nevertheless honoured the promise, and pension payments that stood at $140 million in 1975 soared to $926 million three years later. By 1984—when Muldoon went out of office—they stood at some $2.5 billion.[93] This was partly inflation, partly rising numbers of elderly as the wartime generation retired, but all had to be paid for out of the consolidated fund.

Muldoon's policies for handling these issues were more sophisticated than

ABOVE

All Blacks in action against Scotland at Eden Park, 14 June 1975. They won the game 24- nil.

Photographer unidentified, *Evening Post* Collection, Alexander Turnbull Library, PAColl-0614, F-22740-1/4

some of his successors were prepared to admit. To survive, aspects of New Zealand's systems had to be carefully modernised, and while he extended the interventionist state with one hand, he also pushed change with the other, including some of the reforms for which later governments took the credit. Muldoon's first act in 1976 was to implement Treasury recommendations to liberalise aspects of the financial sector. Then he was told it was cheaper to import pillow-cases, towels and sheets than to import cloth for local industry to make them, implemented reforms designed to allow imports, and 'gradually worked through the whole range of industries'.[94] Railway reform—completed in 1993 when the taxpayer-owned asset was sold—began in 1979 as a Muldoon-era initiative.[95] The local body restructuring of the late 1980s was actually part of a 15-year process initiated by the Kirk administration, though Muldoon put his stamp on it, as did his successors.[96]

These liberalisations were matched by new forms of intervention, most of them designed to support the agrarian output on which the economy still pivoted. In the hope of boosting both the farming sector and export earnings, Muldoon initiated a Livestock Incentive Scheme, low-interest rural loans and a Supplementary Minimum Payments system, this last effectively a way of compensating farmers for low prices. He apparently intended this to be a short-term measure to keep the farmers on their feet while they developed new markets, though the system did not quite pan out that way. Other interventions, again geared towards preserving the old-style pavlova world, included state supplements to freezing workers wages in 1978. Muldoon also expanded the welfare system; new sickness and domestic purposes benefits, the latter introduced in 1975, joined the queue for state cash. Although superficially contradictory, this policy mix was consistent—it was a pragmatic attempt to manage change. As his biographer argues, Muldoon found the alternatives—including tight monetary and fiscal policies—unacceptable because of the likely social and political cost.[97]

ABOVE

High inflation during the 1970s raised pressure on wages. Here, unions take part in a march to restore free wage bargaining.

Photographer unidentified, *Evening Post* Collection, Alexander Turnbull Library, PAColl-0614, F-26-35mm-C

Voices of change

The economic upheavals of the early 1970s joined a wide range of social pressures nudging New Zealand away from its mid-century pavlova paradise. The 'generation gap' added impetus from the late 1960s. As we have seen, pavlova society was able to absorb many of the social changes of the 1950s and early 1960s; but the values that emerged locally in the youth generation towards the end of that decade were another matter. These reflected overseas trends, but lagged somewhat behind them, though not by much. And the values, expectations and hopes of this new generation differed very sharply from that of their parents and grandparents.

In this, New Zealand shared a world trend. A discontinuity of this kind had not existed previously between generations—not to this extent. Yet in hindsight it was explicable, a product, largely, of the wider historical cycles of the twentieth century and particularly the way that two generations from 1914 had been shaped by the experiences of total war and depression. From this flowed a characteristic society—socially tighter, seeking security. New Zealand's experience of it was intensified, in part, by the 'cringe' and by the notion that the country was somehow backward.

NEW ZEALAND
AN ILLUSTRATED HISTORY

Much of the impetus for change in the 1960s came from the fact that the generation coming to adulthood then had not known war, depression and hardship as their parents and grandparents had. They were products of the safe, comfortable, conservative and at times outright boring society of the 1950s, and New Zealand's youth were far from alone; the 'generation gap' of the baby boomers was a world phenomenon. By the 1960s young 20-somethings throughout the West were tired of living in a world that still defined itself by war in various ways, both in popular memory and through the immediate oppositions of the Cold War, which flared hot every so often on the fringes of the opposing power blocs. It was to all this complex array of pressures and experiences that the growing baby-boomer generation reacted. And it happened relatively suddenly, a latent trend that, in the event, was focussed in part by the rise of rock music, focussed in part by the response to the Vietnam War. Hippies 'happened' across the world from Monterey to Chelsea in 1967's 'summer of love'.

New Zealand lagged a little—in part because of the strength of New Zealand's post-war culture—but still had its own disaffected youth who saw inspiration in these overseas trends. People eager to drop out and find alternative ways of living were evident across New Zealand by the end of the 1960s and into the early 1970s.

The New Zealand variety drew inspiration from overseas, but in specific form can be traced largely to Jerry Rubin's 'yippie' movement, to the Haight-Ashbury district of San Francisco, and to the expressions of this thinking in rock festivals such as Woodstock. As overseas, anti-war sentiment gave power to the movement. Indeed, much of the counter-culture philosophy was founded in shallow, emotive and often sanctimonious anti-war assertions which demonised the superficial trappings of war without apparently understanding their context. In many ways this was ironic because aspects of expected counter-culture behaviour mirrored features of contemporary US army field life, including illicit drug-taking. New Zealand's incarnation of the movement also stirred in elements of British counter-culture, with its folkish and idealised view of pre-industrial life in a rose-tinted 'Merrie England'. These views were often mixed with selected and misunderstood elements of Indian tantric philosophy, taken out of original strict caste context and reinterpreted to suit the 'free love' ideas of a generation that, once again, believed it was the first to discover the opposite sex.

For a while, the counter-culture flourished, surging across the staid world of late pavlova-era New Zealand in a swirl of tie-tied, rainbow-coloured clothes and bright paint. They lived in communes, in down-at-heel houses, or in the back of house-trucks cobbled up from recycled timber and various doors and window-frames from house demolition sites.

To the 20-somethings of the counter-culture, 'dropping out' may have seemed like the wave of the future. But it was not, and for good reason; the ethos was shallow, a jackdaw pillaging of world trends that reversed a few ideas and mixed them with decontextualised concepts from other cultures. All leaned heavily on conventional society for prosperity. New Zealand's hippies could live what some imagined to be a pre-industrial or 'self-sufficient' lifestyle in Coromandel, Northland or Karamea because they could get modern antibiotics, obtain an unemployment or sickness benefit, or in some cases rely on wealthy parents

OPPOSITE TOP

Holden Monaro at speed, circa 1975.

Photographer unidentified, *Evening Post* Collection, Alexander Turnbull Library, PAColl-0614, F-22558-1/2

OPPOSITE BOTTOM

Rugby lost none of its popularity during the pavlova era; these boys are playing probably in the Wellington region during the 1977 season.

Photographer unidentified, *Evening Post* Collection, Alexander Turnbull Library PAColl-0614, F-28181-1/4

ABOVE

Air travel became ubiquitous during the 1970s. NAC operated Fokker Friendships and the larger Boeing 737-200 on internal routes.

Photographer unidentified, *Evening Post* Collection, Alexander Turnbull Library, PAColl-0614, F-23133-1/4

to prop up their bank accounts. Their self-sufficiency depended on high-yield varieties of traditional foods. 'Organic' gardening was made practical in some areas because pesticide-using neighbours held insects and crop disease at bay. Hippies could 'space out' to Bob Dylan, Jethro Tull, Pink Floyd, Joni Mitchell, the Moody Blues, Jimi Hendrix, Steeleye Span, England, Fairport Convention and Yes because they bought records and owned radios, stereo amplifiers, cassette decks and turntables. The music was produced with modern recording technology, and the defining sounds were created by the Moog synthesiser, fuzz-tone electric guitars and the Mellotron—all exploiting developments of the 1950s.[98]

Most hippies eventually re-entered mainstream society; but while the pure counter-culture was short-lived as a mass movement, its thinking quietly flowed into wider society, colouring the 1970s in new ways. Conservatives were horrified at the licentiousness, at the drug-taking, at the hair; and yet sexual liberation filtered into the mainstream at worldwide level, fuelling a wider swing away from the tighter society of the early twentieth century. Nudity re-emerged on stage, introduced to New Zealanders in 1972's *Hair*. New hippified clothing and longer hairstyles gained mainstream status as commercial enterprise latched on to the youth dollar. Short-back-and-sides were out for 1970s New Zealand men, replaced by longer styles even among white-collar professionals. Women's hair styling became even more adventurous.

This thinking joined an emerging matrix of post-colonial values, which gained ground worldwide during the post-war years in part as a reaction to the institutionalised atrocities of Nazi Germany, and in general as a product of de-colonialism. Opposition to nuclear weapons and emphasis on conservation were added in the 1960s, all outcomes of practical concern and of disillusion with

ABOVE

Back on the campaign trail: Robert Muldoon promotes National in 1978.

Matthew McKee, *Evening Post* Collection, Alexander Turnbull Library, PAColl-0614, F-530-35mm

an ever-more militarised and industrialised twentieth century. This thinking was not restricted to the youth generation. And again, it is not difficult to see how it arose. The bigger-is-better mind-set had won the Second World War for the Allies and soared on through the 1950s, peaking with the triumphal ascent of Wernher von Braun's super-V2, the Saturn 5, which took Americans to the moon. But there were limits. First-world pollution and third-world hunger were significant problems by the 1960s, and New Zealand's youth shared the rising tide of opposition to mid-century thinking. A controversial 1969 proposal to raise the level of Lake Manapouri to give extra capacity to a massive underground power station being built on its shores focussed attention. The Save Manapouri campaign quickly became a national effort, drawing in a wide cross-section of New Zealanders. It became an election issue in 1972, and the incoming Labour administration of Norman Kirk honoured promises not to raise the lake.

To this array of values was added an emotive rejection of war, fuelled by the fighting in Vietnam. That politically-inspired struggle was very different from the Second World War, partly because there was no popular emotional involvement with the cause. And it was in every living room every night. New Zealanders first learnt of their involvement—initially, an artillery battalion—when Prime Minister Keith Holyoake announced it on television. The same medium also brought images so graphic by the standards of the day that the wisdom of showing them in New Zealand was debated at official level. Even the government, in fact, had doubts about getting involved. And yet the campaign against the struggle by the new youth generation evolved into an emotive push not against war, but against what a generation who had never fought naively imagined war to be. It was as much a rejection of mid-century values as a

RIGHT

Windsurfers scud across Wellington's Oriental Bay in 1978.

Photographer unidentified, *Evening Post* Collection, Alexander Turnbull Library, PAColl-0614, F-32144-1/4

statement for peace; and the difference between their one-dimensional imagery and the deeper reality of the war that their parents had actually experienced, helped create and reinforce the so-called 'generation gap'.

That gap intensified in New Zealand because pavlova society preserved older thinking paying only lip-service to change—the reversion of women to the home is a case in point. A rare exception was populist opposition to nuclear weapons. New Zealand servicemen had observed British bomb tests in the 1950s,[99] but public opposition grew during the 1960s, reaching the point where the Kirk government despatched frigates to support a protest flotilla sailing to Mururoa Atoll in 1973, where the French had started atmospheric testing.

Successive governments of the 1960s and 1970s, though working towards change, evidenced by new legislation for equal pay, reform of marriage laws and the formation of the Waitangi Tribunal, were not moving quickly enough for the Vietnam generation. Perhaps for this reason, post-colonial thinking became de-colonialism in some circles, reversing the targets of old thinking without much changing the framework within which the concepts were expressed. In a social sense there were similarities between the post-colonialists of the late twentieth century and the moral evangelists of a century earlier. Both were a reaction to prevailing society, characterised by polarisation of opinion and alliances between otherwise disparate lobby groups. This was certainly a feature of New Zealand campus environments by the early 1980s, where some students displayed an unprecedented level of intolerant and humourless anger at the world.

Maori urbanisation and revival

New Zealand's Pakeha society was ferociously monocultural for much of the twentieth century and effectively separatist, Maori, for the most part, lived in their own areas in ruralised communities. Pakeha dwelt in the cities. The twain did meet, but not to any huge extent, and much of the myth that New Zealand had the best race relations in the world derived from this practical separation. The relationship never had to be really tested. The issue reflected both attitude and demography. Maori comprised just 5 percent of the population in 1936, some 87 percent lived in the country,[100] and as a people they were effectively segregated.[101] As we have seen, efforts by the Young Maori Party, Apirana Ngata and other leaders to bring change had some effect, but the main arbiter of Maori reassertion in the late twentieth century was a significant population recovery, backed by a shift in general attitude that was ultimately triggered by the Second World War.

Maori had been hammered by contact—which introduced weapons and diseases—and by the pressure of the colony. Although numbers began growing in the 1890s, the rate of increase remained slow until the mid-1930s. Then the Maori population exploded, rising from 82,000 in 1936 to 201,159 30 years later. This represented an increase from 5 to nearly 8 percent of the population of New Zealand,[102] and was due to two factors. The birth rate rose in the 1930s to around 45 per thousand, and stayed there until the mid-1960s—indeed, it did not drop below 30 per thousand until 1973. This increase was combined with a sharp fall in the death rate, which had stood at around 15–20 per thousand during the late 1930s and fell sharply in the late 1940s—an improvement that can be credited to a Labour government drive to improve sanitation. The death rate dropped below 10 per thousand in the 1950s and continued to drop until the late 1960s, when it hovered around 4–5 per thousand. This was two thirds the non-Maori death rate, though to some extent the comparison was deceptive because Maori were younger on average when they died.[103]

To this was added the social effect of the Second World War. Maori were closely involved with 2 NZ Division; 28 (Maori) Battalion was used as an elite unit,[104] and pulled the divisional irons out of the fire on several occasions.[105] There was even talk of raising a second Maori unit for Pacific service.[106] Afterwards, many veterans felt that they had suffered for the country—and expected more than they were getting. Although even settler society had considered Maori a superior 'native', they were still discriminated against, often in subtle ways. Some bars would not serve Maori, credit arrangements differed, and there were fewer job opportunities. However, the real arbiter of change was less the field performance of the battalion than the work of the Maori War Effort Organisation. War work pushed Maori into the towns, bringing the two peoples into effective contact for the first time in 80 years.

By 1945, around a quarter of Maori lived in towns, and that number exploded over the next two decades. The largest shift came between 1951 and 1966, when the rural Maori population dropped from 70 to 38 percent of the total. Rural numbers continued to trend down, falling to 19.8 percent by 1986.[107] This has been put down to snowballing—a few moved, and were then joined by relatives and friends, drawn by the opportunities of the urban environment.[108]

Urban drift was an effective arbiter of de-tribalisation. While some ties back to whanau and hapu were maintained—such as in a return for tangihanga—the shift generally broke old links. New forms of leadership had to be found, new social ties and connections forged, new ways of applying customary practices in an urban setting developed. These took time, and in the interim there was a sense

ABOVE

State houses under construction for Maori tenants at Waiwhetu, Lower Hutt, late 1947. These were an initiative of Ihaaia Puketapu and an early expression of Maori urban drift.

Photographer unidentified, *Evening Post* Collection, Alexander Turnbull Library F-160390-1/2

of separation. Even use of Te Reo fell away—a legacy in part of a mid-century notion that Maori people could integrate better if they spoke English—and a new generation emerged in the towns and cities who, in many cases, did not speak it. One result was the rise of gangs.

This was not the only issue. Many Maori found work in fields ranging from freezing works to construction, but these were not always well paid and usually the first to go in a downturn. Others found work as labourers, or with state organisations; Maori were over-represented in state employment such as the Railways or the Ministry of Works, under-represented in white-collar private enterprise, and skilled professions.[109] Just 6.56 percent of Maori, in 1956, worked in professional or managerial circles, as opposed to more than a quarter of non-Maori. The practical result was that Maori entered the urban world at its lower end and usually stayed there.[110] Maori were more liable than European to live in

RIGHT

Primary school pupils learning cardio-pulmonary resucitation, 1974.

Photographer unidentified, *Evening Post* Collection, Alexander Turnbull Library, PAColl-0614, F-21968-1/4

second-class housing, and the result was ghettoisation. However, proposals to 'pepper-pot' Maori housing among European were disliked by both peoples.[111]

The wider problems Maori faced were only sporadically addressed by government. The Maori Social and Economic Advancement Act of 1945 helped. Some officers of 28 (Maori) Battalion became public servants in the newly organised Department of Maori Affairs after the war, but the state moved with glacial pace and it was the early 1960s before steps were taken to address the issues that went with Maori urbanisation. Despite hints at an integrated future in the Hunn Report, and the Maori Welfare Act that followed in 1962, it was clear that government was only paying lip-service to Maori needs. By this time more than 100,000 Maori were living in Auckland alone. Nearly half were under 30, nearly half in unskilled employment. Maori also formed a disproportionate part of the jail population.[112]

This was new. In part it was due to dislocation, expressed through new rules of behaviour and new attitudes, all symptomatic both of the failure of pavlova society to properly engage with Maori at all levels—and of Maori to engage with the pavlova world. In the longer term it was an outcome of the marginalisation and segregation that had begun a century earlier. The issue was highlighted and to some extent perpetuated by a failure of the education system. Specialist Maori schools focussed on agriculture, which was not relevant to the urban environment. General schools were not geared for a de-tribalised urban population, and the syllabus was seldom relevant. In 1963, for instance, 93.3 percent of Maori boys left school without any qualifications, by comparison with 67.4 percent of European. Just 2.6 percent of Maori school leavers went on to full-time higher education, compared with 14 percent of Europeans.[113] Unqualified Maori had little option but to find unskilled work—perpetuating the cycle.

There were protests. The Kirk administration made 6 February a public holiday and renamed it Waitangi Day as a move towards biculturalism, and while the policy was arguably cut short by Kirk's demise in 1974, in a general sense it reflected both emerging post-colonial attitudes and a growing need to address Maori issues. Arguably government could have done this earlier; but in practice—given mid-century attitudes—action was not feasible until an improving position made it possible for Maori to capture government attention. It has also been argued that agitation was facilitated by urbanisation during the 1950s and 1960s.[114]

Land protest grew in the wake of the 1967 Maori Affairs Amendment Act and new rating legislation, which seemed likely to strip Maori of much remaining land because it had been abandoned to urban drift. Hapu could not afford to pay accumulating rates.[115] Protests culminated in a spectacular land march down the length of the North Island in 1975. This was not led by radical youth, but by a respected kuia, Whina Cooper (1895–1994), and attracted enormous attention. Cooper, born Josephine Te Wake, was one of a new generation of Maori leaders, a long-standing campaigner for Maori interests.[116] She led 50 followers from Te Hapua in March 1975, and thousands flocked to join the march as they reached Auckland. Core supporters went on to Wellington amid a blaze of publicity. Soon afterwards, Ngati Whatua began a 17-month occupation of Auckland's Bastion Point, and there was other action to recover land lost at Raglan during the Second World War. In 1979, Matiu Rata resigned his Northern Maori seat to found the Mana Motuhake Party, designed to promote Maori rights.[117]

Protests gained pace during the early 1980s. There was a second Bastion Point occupation and eviction in 1982. Meanwhile, groups such as the 'Waitangi Action Committee' drew new attention to the Treaty of Waitangi. Decried as a 'fraud',[118] the Treaty was on the back-burner at the time. The Waitangi Tribunal was formed in 1975, but could only handle contemporary grievance. Attention swung to protests at the Waitangi Marae on Waitangi Day, reaching the point where it became difficult for ceremonies to continue. The court cases that followed were used as a forum. Government listened, giving the Waitangi Tribunal power to hear retrospective claims in 1985, identifying where the treaty had been breached and making recommendations.[119] The following year a court ruling required government to take account of Maori claims in the state asset sale programme.

This was an effective shift, of which perhaps the most important aspect was the ability to claim retrospectively. That opened the flood-gates to a range of historical grievances, and far more claims than could be heard in a reasonable time poured in. However, the system also required the Tribunal to identify breaches of Treaty 'principles', which had not been envisaged by officials in 1840 and had to be created in the 1980s. Some commentators argued that the Waitangi Tribunal did so by means of 'instrumental presentism'—evaluating past events in terms of late twentieth-century values, rather than the factors that applied at the time.[120]

To some extent this reflected the judicial aspects of the settlement process, a function of the timelessness attributed to law.[121] And in some ways the approach was also reasonable; the settlement process was designed to reflect a late twentieth-century situation and priorities. However, the historical work done for the settlement process was also used in some cases as a contribution to general historiography; and this was not satisfactory. As more than one commentator observed, there were differences between the purpose-driven work done for the 'industry', in effect arguing prosecution cases, and the enquiry-driven approach required of abstract historical analysis.[122]

CHAPTER TEN
Extreme decades

New Zealand's twentieth century ended in a flurry of extremes as a new generation brought a ninety-year cycle of social, political and economic thinking to an apparent end. This phase of Pakeha New Zealand's long evolution away from its colonial origins opened in 1981 with unprecedented public demonstrations against a Springbok rugby tour. It continued with an unprecedented demonisation of most of the political, social and economic pillars that had defined New Zealand's century, a shift that, in many respects, can be considered New Zealand's own revolutionary period.

This change had been a long time coming; the practical end of New Zealand's ability to pursue its unrequited love affair with Britain had actually occurred decades before. The problem was admitting to it; as late as the 1970s the generation in power—the wartime generation—were reluctant to see the world they had fought for pass away. The result, ironically, mirrored the experience of a century earlier; an extreme rush to a protected, safe world of the immediate past. A rush which was then reversed into an equally impractical extreme the other way. It was very Kiwi.

Despite conceits at the time that the so-called 'new right' reforms had set New Zealand on a new course, these changes in fact reflected and rode on shifts that were already well under way by the 1980s. They were generational, and they reflected a new maturity in New Zealand's general outlook. By 1999, when a newly elected Labour government declared the neo-liberal socioeconomic experiment over, much had changed about New Zealand society and culture—and from the historical perspective of generational trend and social mechanism, much of the New Zealand world of the early twenty-first century happened in spite of, not because of, the reforms which, from this perspective, were merely symptomatic.

The new pattern was clear by the time the first decade of the twenty-first century came to an end. The classic age of the Kiwi farmer was essentially

ABOVE
Parliament buildings and grounds.
Matthew Wright/Author collection

finished. Echoes of the old ways still resounded, swathed now in a warm glow of nostalgia; but the close-knit, socially flattened, blokeish, conservative society of farms and urban quarter-acres that emerged from the crucible of the First World War had essentially run its course. In its place was a more metropolitan, more confident society—yet like all societies, still ultimately framed and guided by its own history, and still struggling with many legacies of the past, not least of them colonial-era race relations.

Thinking big

New Zealand faced serious challenges in 1980. Oil prices were up in the wake of the Iranian revolution. Inflation was high, debt spiralling and growth not what it had been. The Muldoon administration proposed to cure all these with a strategy dubbed 'Think Big'. In essence, it was twentieth-century Vogelism, projects built with borrowed money that—so the promise went—would provide 400,000 jobs, flood capital into the economy, and build a basis for the future. While there were obvious political motives for a plan announced amidst the lead-up to the 1981 election, the main rationale was energy self-sufficiency. And this was reasonable at the time; the spot price of imported crude skyrocketed from $12.88 a barrel in March 1979 to $41.50 in December 1981, with dire effect on New Zealand's balance of payments.[1] In any case, New Zealand had been committed by the Kirk administration to compulsory purchase when the Maui gas field began producing in 1979, and the gas had to be paid for whether used or not. So there was sense in finding ways of using it. The huge upper Waitaki hydro scheme was also about to come on line, transforming New Zealand's power calculations.

The three-leg strategy that emerged was designed to improve New Zealand's energy position via a synthetic fuel plant, which would turn Maui gas into methanol and then petrol; take advantage of an electricity surplus to add a steel plant and expand the Tiwai Point aluminium refinery; and boost the economy through projects that included rebuilding and electrifying the main trunk line. From an engineering standpoint 'think big' was innovative. The synthetic fuel plant was the first in the world to use the zeolite-catalyst method on a large scale,[2] and early estimates suggested New Zealand could be made 50 percent self-sufficient in petrol as a result.[3]

In the event, New Zealand's version of China's 'great leap forward' tripped at the first hurdle. The early 1980s brought an oil glut, the 400,000 jobs never eventuated, and government was pilloried for what at the time seemed to be an expensive error. The 'new right' who swept to power in 1984 shut down, sold and otherwise got rid of it as quickly as possible. Criticism of the projects was at times intense, at times polemic, caught up with the general demonisation of Muldoonism. Certainly it looked as if Muldoon and his advisors had missed a beat; oil prices came down, ruining the economics of the calculation. But in other ways, 'think big' was timeless. The energy calculations on which it was founded stemmed in part from the 1970s experience of constrained supply on the back of the collision between Middle Eastern and Cold War politics, and what the rising prices did to New Zealand's balance of payments.

CHAPTER TEN
EXTREME DECADES

What became obvious later was that 'think big' was a long-term investment. Even in the 1970s there was a clear understanding that oil would eventually run out and alternatives would be needed. The issue was price—the cost of exploiting difficult-to-reach reserves coupled with the inability of the industry to meet rising demand. And in due course it happened; the cheap energy of the late twentieth century gave way to spiralling energy prices in the early twenty-first. At that point the 'think big' energy schemes, for all the dubious promises, domestic politics and doubtful economics that had shrouded their launch, began looking like they would have been useful. Muldoon, it seemed, had been right after all, though not entirely for the reasons he envisaged at the time.

The other big issue of 1981 was a long-planned rugby tour by the Springboks. It was political at every level. South Africa's white minority government had been an international pariah for years for its apartheid policies, and official Commonwealth condemnation extended into the sporting arena, enshrined in the Gleneagles agreement of 1977. The problem for New Zealand rugby players and supporters was that the Springboks offered the only credible challenge on the field. Rivalry had been hot for years. A 1949 tour of South Africa by the All Blacks went 4–0 in favour of the Springboks. The All Blacks achieved a 3:1 series victory in 1956, and the tussle continued with successive tours into the 1960s. However, all this went ahead against the background of South Africa's unpalatable racial policies, and eventually the political issues became overwhelming. The All Black tour of South Africa in 1967 went ahead amid controversy. The Kirk administration cancelled a proposed return visit by the Springboks to New Zealand in 1973; and the All Black tour of South Africa in 1976 prompted the Gleneagles Agreement.

ABOVE

Protestors march against the Springbok tour, central Wellington, early July 1981.

Photographer unidentified, *Evening Post* Collection, Alexander Turnbull Library, PAColl-0614, F-1602-35mm-25

These wounds were reopened when the New Zealand Rugby Football Union Council decided to organise a Springbok tour for 1981. It stood against the clear opinions of many New Zealanders and, according to his biographer, Muldoon could 'see nothing but trouble' coming from it.[4] However, he refused to cancel the tour and instead made a television call on the NZRFU to think about it.[5] Politics by media was new for New Zealand, but with just five months before an election in which the stakes seemed evenly balanced, Muldoon was probably trying not to alienate part of the electorate. The result was that the tour went ahead amid public protest, rhetoric and invective on a scale New Zealand had not seen since the Red Feds of 1913.

The tour swiftly became about more than just rugby. It split the country down the middle. University students contributed some of the loudest voices; the issues keyed closely into a youthful sense of indignation at the injustices of a wider world, and at perceived attitudes by government towards student communities which, at times, provoked calls to 'fight back'. In Wellington, particularly, student anger over the tour swirled through campuses, and there was intense pressure to conform. Those who did not join the protests risked ostracism. Yet, for all the anger with which students joined the cause, the real power of the protests came from ordinary New Zealanders who took to the streets in numbers for the first time in decades, and they were mothers, fathers, brothers, sisters, grandparents, even children in some marches.

Protestors managed to stop a test match in Hamilton, where police protected them from the irate crowd, and violence escalated as the tour went on, reducing 'the tour' to a law-and-order issue as far as government was concerned. By August, even a small-scale and peaceful protest in a rain-soaked Napier was met

BELOW

Anti-Springbok tour protestors and police in Sydney Street East, later Kate Sheppard Place, near Parliament, mid-1981.

Photographer unidentified, *Evening Post* Collection, Alexander Turnbull Library, PAColl-0614, F-1391-35mm-20

by police in riot gear, wielding long batons—dubbed 'Minto bars'—backed by dump-bins. The battle ended a few weeks later at Eden Park, where the All Blacks won the tour two tests to one, while police battled protestors outside and a light aircraft dropped flour bombs onto the pitch. And then it was over, leaving behind the political and emotional detritus of a bitter winter.[6]

All this masked the real historical point about the tour, which was that a wide cross-section of ordinary New Zealanders had taken to the streets in unprecedented numbers. The emotion of it seemed disproportionate to the issues. On the face of it—and genuinely—the protests reflected a direct objection to apartheid. White South Africa's racial policies of the day were repugnant by any standards, out of step with human values, certainly divergent from those of the late twentieth century. It had made them international pariahs, and New Zealand risked being tarred with the same brush for indulging the sporting contact. Many ordinary Kiwis wanted to show the world that everyday folk did not share that view—and were taking a stand.

It worked; the anti-tour protests drew international attention. For the first time, a whole people had stood up to object. This was a far more significant signal than anti-apartheid proclamations by government officials around the world, and the minority white government in South Africa had to pay attention.

But there was a deeper level to the phenomenon, well beyond the immediate issues of race and rugby—one that explains a good deal about the unprecedented intensity of the whole affair. It was not just a protest against apartheid. The emotional response whipped up by the anti-tour movement, coupled with the fact that action escalated to large-scale street battles in which ordinary New Zealanders were opposing rugby games and literally hitting symbols of the

ABOVE

Elements of the anti-tour movement escalated tensions to the point where both police and protestors armed and armoured themselves. The resulting street violence was of a scale unseen in New Zealand since the industrial disruptions of 1913.

Photographer unidentified, *Evening Post* Collection, Alexander Turnbull Library, PAColl-0614, F-1392-35mm-11A

establishment—the police—made clear that the protests were also a metaphor for deeper matters internal to New Zealand.

It was no coincidence that this unprecedented level of public anger emerged at a time of growing frustration at mid-century protectionist policies, which were increasingly viewed not as sensible insulation from a wild and hostile world, but as outdated barriers to progress. From this perspective the real battle-lines in that dark winter of 1981 were drawn between old and new, between the overstretched norms of mid-century pavlova society and the changing world outside New Zealand's cossetted shores, framed by the emerging ideals of post-colonialism.

At this deeper level, change could not be regulated out of existence, and the popular response to the 1981 Springbok tour was less safety valve than gauge. Muldoon was re-elected by a whisker in that year.[7] He credited 'Think Big',[8] but the writing was on the wall, and his administration limped into a third term with the tides of change swirling around it.

Beating the cringe with culture

Agitation during that bleak winter of 1981 underscored New Zealand's frustration with its mid-century society and the apparent relentlessness of the regulatory world. But a deeper social change away from that mind-set was already under way, pivoting around a growing popular sense that local achievements in New Zealand were just as valid as the achievements of expats in London. And it came from a perhaps unexpected direction. The early 1980s brought a significant renaissance of local arts, particularly music, which transcended the 'cringe' and reflected a growing sense of national identity and, more to the point, national self-worth.

In some respects this extended trends that had been brewing away through the whole pavlova period. Literature led the way, and a 'New Zealand' voice emerged after the Second World War through the engagement between literature and popular culture. Other arts took longer. Movies languished; Rudall Heyward's populist *wanderjahr* from Northland to Bluff in the 1920s, making local movies for local people—epitomised by shorts such as *Natalie of Napier*—was a false dawn. Just five movies were made locally in three decades from 1940. Part of the reason was financial, part the notion that anything New Zealand produced would be inferior.

That changed in the mid-1970s. The renaissance was led by *Sleeping Dogs* (1977), an adaptation of C. K. Stead's novel *Smith's Dream*. The break with the 'cringe' finally came with Geoff Murphy's *Goodbye Pork Pie* (1981), a quintessential road movie set in classic New Zealand, easily comparable with anything else in that genre on a world stage. It became an iconic expression of Kiwiness, the imagery of rebel-in-a-yellow-Mini still instantly recognisable 20 years later when a music video paid homage to it. A full-length cartoon, *Footrot Flats—A Dog's Tale* (1985), celebrated mid-century rural New Zealand, arguably gaining popularity because that culture was dying as the film came out. The 'splatter' comedy *Bad Taste* (1988) started the career of Wellington film-maker Sir Peter Jackson. By the 1990s New Zealand was producing movies the equal of any overseas, and

LEFT
Public events and displays, including this theatre-front diorama, marked the release of the first part of Peter Jackson's three-part adaptation of J. R. R. Tolkien's novel *The Hobbit*, in November 2012. The scale of these events, capturing attention across New Zealand, underscored the way local film-making had been transformed into an international industry, much of it thanks to Jackson's work.

Matthew Wright/Author Collection

the local voice was clear in *Topless Women Talk About Their Lives* (1997) and *Savage Honeymoon* (2000), the latter poking gentle fun at Auckland's 'Westie' subculture. Maori priorities were explored by *Whale Rider* (2003), an adaptation of the Witi Ihimaera novel which met unprecedented international success; later, by the comedy *Boy* (2009).

A reputation for top-rate production values, spectacular scenery and a favourable exchange rate prompted interest from United States television producers in the mid-1990s. Several 'sword-and-sorcery' fantasy movies and TV serials were filmed in Auckland. Meanwhile Jackson's ranking as one of the world's greatest film-makers was cemented through 2001 to 2003 with his epic three-part adaptation of J. R. R. Tolkien's classic novel *The Lord of the Rings*, followed a decade later by his three-part adaptation of *The Hobbit*. By the first decade of the twenty-first century, thanks largely to Jackson, New Zealand was attracting major international productions such as James Cameron's *Avatar* (2009) and Steven Spielberg's *Tintin* (2011). Although international, these films and others like them carried a huge Kiwi infusion via local production in Jackson's Miramar-based studio complex and Sir Richard Taylor's Weta Workshop. The standards were not merely world class; they were world-leading.

Music, like film, had lagged when it came to a local voice. Douglas Lilburn penned orchestral pieces with local flavour from the 1940s, but there were practical and financial barriers to performance in mid-century New Zealand and audiences were limited. Local jazz and swing bands were more popular. The baby boomers picked up rock music, but it took a while for local bands to play their own compositions, longer still for a 'New Zealand' sound to emerge. Ray Columbus and the Invaders paved the way; Fourmyula's 'Nature' of 1969 defined one local sound, Bruno Lawrence's Electric Revelation and Travelling Apparition (Blerta) another, captured in their 1972 single 'Dance All Around The World'. This hit No. 13 on local charts. But there was still a feeling that serious musicians only existed overseas, and New Zealand bands had to 'make it' in Sydney or Melbourne or London first. Dragon, Split Enz and Th' Dudes, among others, made the trans-Tasman journey in the late 1970s.

ABOVE

A dose of culture. Robert Muldoon shows his earplugs to Steve Gilpin, Don Martin and Kevin Stanton of Mi-Sex, June 1980. The band invited the Prime Minister to attend a concert in response to Muldoon's comments that rock music was not cultural. 'About as much culture as the rugby league test on Sunday,' he quipped afterwards. He knew very well what he meant. In retirement, Muldoon went on to star as the Narrator in a local version of Richard O'Brien's *The Rocky Horror Show*.

Photographer unidentified, *Dominion Post* Collection, Alexander Turnbull Library, PAColl-7327, EP/1980/1962/28

Part of the issue was practical; there were few places starting bands could play to small audiences in New Zealand. However, new drinking laws turned pubs into concert venues, eventually transforming the scene. Split Enz pioneered the push back into New Zealand at the end of the 1970s, and local music entered a renaissance, effectively validated from the top in 1980 when Prime Minister Robert Muldoon suggested rock music was not 'cultural'. The Knobz responded with the satirical 'Culture'—and Muldoon saw the joke, accepting an invitation to attend a concert by rockers Mi-Sex.

New Zealand music went from strength to strength over the next few years; The Swingers' fun 'Counting the Beat' was New Zealand's third-best selling single of 1981.[9] Other songs keyed into the mood of a restless people. 'There is No Depression in New Zealand,' Blam Blam Blam's take on the national plight, soared high in the charts the same year on the back of anti-Springbok tour protests.

In a clear sign of an emerging independence and maturity of self as a nation, New Zealand had found its own distinct 'sound' by this time. Songs such as Split Enz's 'Six Months in a Leaky Boat', or DD Smash's 'Devil You Know' were thoroughly Kiwi. In 1984, Dalvanius Prime's Patea Maori Club released 'Poi E', which became the best selling song in New Zealand that year, beating Stevie Wonder, Bob Marley and Bruce Springsteen, among others.[10] Dave Dobbyn, meanwhile, wrote songs that captured quintessential New Zealand-ness with his bands Th' Dudes and DD Smash, then went on to write the soundtrack for the *Footrot Flats* movie. This included 'Slice of Heaven', which Dobbyn performed with the band Herbs, in many ways an anthem to the spirit of New Zealand.

By the mid-1980s New Zealand was also producing regional styles, including the 'Dunedin sound' of The Chills and Netherworld Dancing Toys. The ultimate

ABOVE

Lampshades, glass barrels and acetylene containers provide instruments for this 'Scratch' orchestra from Auckland performing at the Wellington Teachers' College, 1974.

Photographer unidentified, Alexander Turnbull Library, PAColl-0614, F-21698-1/4

power-band was The Gordons, who anticipated thrash-metal by nearly two decades and carried a raw energy that left overseas punk in the shade.

All these bands expressed, nurtured and reflected an emerging general feeling during the early 1980s that local achievement did not have to be validated by success overseas. The shift of mood pre-dated the 'reform' period, underscoring the fact that the real changes in attitude of the day were generational—and that the 'reforms' did not create a new sense of mature nationhood. That shift was already bubbling along beneath the surface, well before government began dismantling the world of pavlova-era regulation. And the popular way to this new understanding was, in part, led by music.

Disengaging paradise

Faced with falling standards of living, rising unemployment and a burgeoning welfare bill, Muldoon turned to ever-tighter controls during the early 1980s in an effort to preserve the pavlova world he and his supporters had been brought up with. Much of this was personally directed and, as Muldoon's biographer remarks, by 1982 there was a 'widely held view' that Cabinet had 'become largely unaccountable to the caucus'—which could not 'check the Prime Minister and Finance Minister.'[11] In mid-1982, Muldoon implemented a wage-and-price freeze.[12] It was stop-gap, and Muldoon knew it. New Zealand's overseas debt rose from $1436 million in 1976 to $7764 million in 1983.[13] This represented a near-threefold increase once corrected for inflation,[14] highlighting the fact that

ABOVE

Robert Muldoon with his wife Thea during a press conference in the 'Beehive' theatrette, 15 June 1984, the morning after he had precipitately called a snap election.

Photographer unidentified, Alexander Turnbull Library, PAColl-7327, EP/1984/2786

OPPOSITE TOP

By the 1980s New Zealand had a long tradition of protesting matters nuclear, including at official level; the government had sent a frigate to Mururoa atoll in 1973 in opposition to French nuclear testing there. Here the yacht *Phoenix* readies to oppose the visit to Wellington of the US nuclear-powered missile cruiser USS *Truxtun*, August 1976.

Photographer unidentified, *Evening Post* Collection, Alexander Turnbull Library, PAColl-0614, F-69-35mm-B

OPPOSITE BOTTOM

Anti-nuclear protest march through Wellington, Hiroshima Day, 6 August 1987.

Photographer unidentified, *Dominion Post* Collection, Alexander Turnbull Library, EP/1987/3990/22

New Zealand was living beyond its means.[15] New arrangements with Australia—Closer Economic Relations—underscored trans-Tasman trade, which had been improving for a while. But it was not enough, and in 1983 Muldoon accepted recommendations from The Treasury to end Supplementary Minimum Payments to farmers. It was clear from Muldoon's calls for a new Bretton Woods agreement that he hoped rescue might come by external readjustment.

By now Muldoon faced dissent within the ranks, although calls for free-market reforms by new MPs elected in 1981[16] were not regarded as serious by many at the time.[17] The end came suddenly. The 1981 election left Muldoon with a working majority of one,[18] and in mid-June 1984, Marilyn Waring and Mike Minogue crossed the floor to support a private 'Nuclear-Free New Zealand' bill. A meeting with Waring on the evening of 14 June left Muldoon and senior members of caucus convinced that their only option was an early election, and an apparently alcohol-fuelled Prime Minister made the announcement to stunned journalists late in the evening.[19]

The notion that Muldoon precipitately called the 'snap' election after one too many drinks at Bellamy's became one of the supposed truths of this dramatic moment. In fact Muldoon discussed the options extensively during the evening with available members of caucus, including the President of the National Party who flew down from Auckland for the purpose;[20] and Muldoon's biographer has argued that diabetes medication, frustration and exhaustion contributed to Muldoon's demeanour when he faced the cameras.[21] Nor was a snap election such a huge gamble; at the time odds were on that he would get away with it. Labour won the election largely because the conservative vote was split by the recently formed New Zealand Party.[22]

However, although New Zealand was in a mood for change, much of what followed came as a surprise, in part because the 'reforms' that followed stood against the values Labour had historically stood for, in part because the snap election prevented the party issuing a full manifesto, and in part because other events competed for attention in 1985. The drama included the sinking of the Greenpeace protest vessel *Rainbow Warrior* in Auckland harbour by French government agents. One man died. Public imagination was captured for much of the year by the 'nuclear ships' row that erupted when New Zealand forbad nuclear power and weapons in its waters. This mirrored a populist worldwide swing against all things nuclear. However, New Zealand was well ahead of the pack at popular and policy levels—no other government in the main alliances had moved to a full ban. In this respect New Zealand was indeed 'leading the bloody world', and it came at a price. In the mid-1980s the Cold War was entering its last dangerous spasm. The US suspended the ANZUS alliance.

In March, Prime Minister David Lange—against advice, and in an unprecedented step for a national leader—took on US 'televangelist' Jerry Falwell

CHAPTER TEN
EXTREME DECADES

431

at the Oxford Union Debate in Britain, arguing that nuclear weapons were morally indefensible. The encounter was televised nationally in New Zealand. Amidst the emotion, Lange's classic riposte 'I can smell the uranium on your breath' won the moment and went down in legend.

Lange's triumph at Oxford marked the moment when New Zealand stood, effectively for the first time, as an independent nation on the world stage, with its own voice—a voice, furthermore, that stood against the wishes of close allies. But even as these dramatic events seized national attention, Finance Minister Roger Douglas was announcing a very different course from the policies that Michael Joseph Savage called 'applied Christianity', which had characterised New Zealand's governmental approach in various flavours for nigh on half a century. The new agenda was laid out in a briefing paper prepared by The Treasury in August 1984,[23] matching ideas that a small 'think tank' of intellectuals, businessmen and politicians had been tossing into the ring for some years.[24]

It reflected prevailing international trends. The 1980s were an age of renewed liberal conservatism across the Western world, epitomised by policies introduced just a few years earlier by US President Ronald Reagan and British Prime Minister Margaret Thatcher. Inspiration came from liberal evangelists such as Frederich Hayek and Milton Friedman, who opposed the philosophies of mid-century economists such as John Maynard Keynes; and they gained ground worldwide partly in reaction to the mid-twentieth century experience, partly spurred by the oil shocks, partly in reaction to the extreme bloating of welfare states around the world, and partly from ongoing ideological tensions between communism and capitalism. The Cold War was entering another dangerous spasm; capitalism was flexing its muscles.

The New Zealand approach was nicknamed 'Rogernomics', a play on the 'Reaganomics' of the contemporary United States, and a choice that highlighted one of New Zealand's differences. By contrast with America, the New Zealand version got the first name of its chief architect. Douglas was hardly original in his thinking; but he imposed the new faith with more speed and zeal than anybody else, attempting to reconstruct New Zealand's economy, government and, by extension, society around theoretical concepts of free-market enterprise and a minimalist state.

The change was as dramatic as it was swift, putting its own stamp on the reviews of local bodies and railways that had been initiated by Muldoon, and kicking others into action with what, at times, seemed frenetic haste. Tasks previously conducted by government were devolved to communities—the numbers of boards, councils and authorities were whittled back by about 80 percent.[25] State departments such as New Zealand Railways, the

BELOW

Deregulation during the late 1980s extended to the drinking laws, spurring a new wave of late-night cafes and small bars. New Zealand entered the sophisticated world of cafe culture with a rush, although the fad for over-priced, under-sized food was more device for displaying status and wealth than a practical answer to hunger. This is a bar in central Wellington, 1987.

Matthew Wright/Author Collection

Forest Service, the Post Office and State Coal Service were restructured into 'corporate' entities, shedding staff and premises along the way.[26] This had significant effect on rural communities, particularly as the Post Office began closing branches previously kept open in back-country districts for social reasons.

Economic protections were slashed. The dramatic disengagement from 'fortress New Zealand' provoked massive upheaval in the pastoral sector. Some of what followed was overdue adjustment for the loss of the British markets, and SMP's were already being withdrawn by the Muldoon administration—but now their loss came on top of the general retraction of other rural services.[27] The combination created rural impoverishment unseen for 60 years.[28] By 1986, some farmers were talking about abandoning the back country.[29] Provincial centres suffered. Shops and businesses closed. A new generation of youth walked the streets with little hope of finding the work that had once been readily available.

Much of this downside was masked in the major cities. The precipitate removal of the regulatory regime—in particular, the elimination of exchange controls—unleashed pent-up demand for everything from cars to cell phones. Money saved under old rules flooded into the pockets of consumers, and for a while, city-dwelling New Zealanders partied. For many twenty-something urbanites the mid-to-late 1980s were indulgent years of youthful hedonism, an entitled lifestyle awash with fat expense accounts, champagne, caviar, over-priced and under-sized *nouvelle cuisine*, 'brick' cellphones and luxury cars. It was the age of power: power lunches, power dressing, even power naps, a world of big hair, big shoulder pads and bold clothing styles, an age when to be seen to spend became a mark of power and hence of social status—a conspicuous assertion of self in every respect. The transformation was aided and abetted by liberalised drinking

ABOVE

The 'Six-Hour' superbike race at Manfeild, near Palmerston North, 1987. The mid-1980s were New Zealand's golden age of sports bikes, and interest in them was high among 20-something young men whose wallets did not stretch to high-performance cars. That changed with deregulation.

Matthew Wright/Author Collection

LEFT

State houses being re-piled and refurbished in Naenae, November 1985.

Ian Chappell Mackley, *Dominion Post* Collection, AlexanderTurnbull Library, EP/1985/4943/6

ABOVE

Glitz in a Wellington central city mall, 1987. The 1980s brought a new world to New Zealand of hard-edged, angular styling in glass and chrome, matched by boxy vehicle styles that at times looked like a collision of wedges and which, somehow, summed up the mind-set of the age.
Matthew Wright/Author Collection

laws, which contributed to a new 'cafe culture' that transformed eating out.

New Zealand had come a long way from the laconic and undemonstrative mind-set of the mid-twentieth century. Part of the new ethos was generational, and like many trends mirrored what was happening overseas. Those who had never known hardship rejected what they supposed was the boring world of their parents and grandparents. The New Zealand edition, however, was framed and flavoured by local thinking and experience. And therein lay the problem. As one commentator remarked, New Zealanders had been penned up for three generations behind protectionist walls. The 'cringe' fuelled a belief that the country was provincialised, trapped in a time-warp, missing out on what everybody imagined was happening overseas. Now the restrictions were gone, and nobody knew quite how to behave. The result was a naive, adolescent excess.[30]

It was not surprising. Ninety years earlier, New Zealanders had been naive, wide-eyed jingoes, pro-Imperial zealots and an Imperial laughing stock on the back of boy-scout enthusiasms. In the late 1980s, after three generations of state controls, New Zealanders were over-eager boy scouts once again.

The financial sector became a significant field of play. The late 1980s brought an age of financial novelty and of financial innocence to New Zealand. Money became a commodity to be transacted, and New Zealanders engaged world money markets with vigour. They also plunged into the share market with a joyful enthusiasm and a sense that, after being held back by stuffy protectionism for years, they had finally been given the keys to wealth. Or at least the toy cupboard. Everyone had a stock broker, it seemed, and there was status to be gained from ringing that broker on a brick-sized cell phone during a champagne-drenched 'power' lunch. Corporate raiders emerged, companies whose function was to buy and sell the stocks of other companies—including, at times, those of other raiders. Stocks soared. There was even a brisk market in 'futures'—gambling on later prices which, in the heat of the moment, seemed likely only to go up.

It did not take long for the edifice to come unstuck. The New Zealand stock market crashed three months after the 'Rogernomes' were re-elected in August 1987. It was a worldwide phenomenon, but the New Zealand market was heavily hit. It stood at a total value of $45 billion before the crash, lost $9.9 billion in one day, and was down to $24.2 billion by the end of the year.[31] There was a scrabble to find blame. Government initiated a Ministerial Commission of Enquiry in 1988.[32] The real problem, one observer suggested, was that New Zealanders were market cowboys.[33] Others thought ethical standards had slipped.[34] Wealth certainly did; by late 1991 the local share market was valued at just $14.5 billion.[35]

CHAPTER TEN
EXTREME DECADES

LEFT

Stock-market crash in progress, 23 October 1987. At the height of the collapse, New Zealand stocks and shares lost just under 20 percent of their value in a single day.

Ross Giblin, *Dominion Post* Collection, Alexander Turnbull Library, EP/1987/5980

BELOW

The asset sales programme swiftly drew opposition from ordinary Kiwis reluctant to see the family silver sold off. Here, Tainui women sing hymns against the sale of Coalcorp, outside the Court of Appeal, 28 August 1989.

Ross Giblin, *Dominion Post* Collection, Alexander Turnbull Library, EP-Ethnology-Maori Land from1976-03

The average Kiwi's flirtation with stocks and shares was over, and it hit most in the pocket. Many lost retirement savings, some their homes. Businesses fell on hard times, an unprecedented number of bankruptcies followed

The reform juggernaut rumbled on.[36] The new target was key public infrastructure such as the postal system, telecommunications system, railways and national airline. The sale programme laid out by Douglas in 1988 was advertised as bringing in $14 billion.[37] But even after the national telecommunications network was sold as a monopoly for $4.25 billion, the net return on public assets that had taken taxpayers a century or more to build up was just $8.3 billion.[38] The immediate wake of the stock-market crash was not, it seemed, the moment to pass taxpayer-owned property over to foreign private enterprise—and the effort did not go down well with an electorate that viewed the whole process as giving away the family silver.

Growing popular unease with the reform programme was reflected by ructions within the Labour Party. Lange suggested pausing the programme for what he called a 'cup

435

ABOVE

Finance Minister Ruth Richardson jogs to work along Wellington's Aotea Quay with a member of the Diplomatic Protection Squad, 1991.

Photographer unidentified, *Dominion Post* Collection, PAColl-7327, EP/1991/1054/17

of tea', and then sacked Douglas as finance minister in December 1988, a day when central Wellington was blacked out by a power cut caused by an exploding transformer. But the pro-change lobby could not be so easily quelled, and when the Cabinet voted for Douglas' return in August the following year, Lange resigned. The administration went into the 1990 general election with its third Prime Minister in eighteen months. A last-minute 'growth agreement' with the unions was launched by a Labour leadership mugging for the cameras,[39] but was ineffective as a vote-buyer. Labour slumped to just 29 seats.

The incoming National government faced several serious problems. The Bank of New Zealand had to be shored up.[40] Then the credit rating agency Standard and Poor's signalled a possible reduction in New Zealand's rating.[41] Despite painful reforms that had alienated the electorate, government debt had risen from $21,879 million in 1984 to $44,347 million in 1990. One component was a rise in health costs, spurred by the advent of high-tech medicine. Another was rising pension costs—a direct legacy of Muldoon's 1975 scheme. However, a significant part of the increase was a rising welfare bill, caused by unemployment flowing from restructuring, particularly of the public sector. By 1991, labour-force unemployment rates had reached levels similar to those of the Great Depression, more than double those of the mid-1980s.[42] Unemployment benefit payments that stood at $195.2 million in 1984 had risen by 1991 to $1.4 billion.[43] There was no sign of the promised prosperity. By 1991 many world economies were booming, but New Zealand's shrank by 0.8 percent.[44]

National extended the reforms to the social and labour sectors. The Employment Contracts Act broke the compact that had existed between unions and employers since the early 1950s. Finance Minister Ruth Richardson's

'Mother of all Budgets' slashed welfare support and introduced direct charges on taxpayer-funded health services and essential medicines. That shaved 0.9 percent off the external debt.[45] Unemployment peaked nationally in 1992 at 11.2 percent, some 172,600 individuals,[46] a high that exceeded the Great Depression of the 1930s.

Times became grim. Even those with work found themselves staring down the barrel of unemployment as government and industries restructured. The buzzword of the day was 'service', sometimes taken by those with money and power to mean 'servility'. Employees whose job security had vanished were fed corporate platitudes about formation-honking geese, patronised with empty promises of 'empowerment' that did little to disguise the fact that, as always in times of downturn, power over their future was the one commodity that most ordinary New Zealanders did not seem to have.

A stroll down Wellington's Lambton Quay—the 'golden mile' of New Zealand retail—revealed empty retail spaces, temporary shops and yellowing sale signs.[47] Crime soared, in contrast to the experience of the Great Depression. Then, some 37,214 offences were reported in 1930 on a national population of 1,506,800. This dropped to 33,168 offences in 1935. By contrast, rates climbed from 349,193 reported crimes in 1980 to 1,049,915 in 1994, on a national population of just over 3,325,900.[48] This was 15 times the per-capita Great Depression figures and could not solely be explained by the inclusion of traffic offences in the statistics.[49]

Government popularity plunged to record lows. Richardson—whose policies were dubbed 'Ruthenasia'—received police protection,[50] previously unheard of in a country where Prime Ministers once had their home addresses and numbers in the phone book. Polls showed that trust in politicians had slumped to just four percent by 1992, dramatically down from the 32 percent of 1975.[51]

Despite a public groundswell against the reforms, government continued to sell taxpayer-owned assets as monopolies. The railway system was sold, just before the 1993 election, to a consortium of US interests and merchant bankers Fay Richwhite. The price of $328 million was little more than had been spent rebuilding the main trunk line a few years earlier.[52] This rapid-fire shedding of public property completed the electorate disillusion with the reform process. Change had been pushed, originally, as essential medicine—short-term pain for long-term gain. But by the early 1990s the reforms had been pushed further, harder and faster than anywhere else in the world, and there was no sign either of an end to the pain, or of the gains that had been promised.

The electorate had certainly had enough; National kept power with a one-seat majority in the 1993 election,

ABOVE
Finance Minister Ruth Richardson, Council of Trade Unions president Ken Douglas, and media in Parliament buildings.
John Nicholson, *Dominion Post* Collection, Alexander Turnbull Library EP/1990/4080/30

BELOW
Brush Electric EF-class locomotive hauling the Overlander on the Raurimu Spiral, 2005. The 1993 sale of the national railway system as a monopoly to private hands returned little more than had been spent on refurbishing the main trunk line less than a decade earlier
Matthew Wright/Author Collection

ABOVE

Nelson, winter 2009. The city had come a long way since its founding in 1842.

Matthew Wright/Author Collection

BELOW

Trucks in the Farmers Transport yard, Hastings, 2006.

Matthew Wright/Author Collection

partly because Labour had not been quite forgiven. Voter frustrations at lack of apparent options were instead expressed in the vote for a new electoral system. The idea of changing New Zealand's 'first past the post' (FPP) system to proportional representation had been bandied about since the mid-1980s. Provision was made for a referendum in the Electoral Act 1993, and it went to the polls that year. The result favoured mixed-member proportional representation, which under the circumstance was a vote against the reforms.

A relatively new party, New Zealand First, held the balance of power after the first MMP election in 1996—choosing, after some weeks, to support a National coalition. The reforms continued, extending to the break-up of the national power generation and distribution system. This had been built as a balanced network, and its conversion into competing generation and lines companies—set up to fight each other for market share, on an artificial spot price—defeated the intention of the original design, which was built around the principle of balancing different generation methods and distributing that power where it was needed.

Labour, with the help of a resurgent Alliance Party—in many ways the spiritual descendant of the values espoused by Michael Joseph Savage—won the 1999 election by a decisive majority. Incoming Prime Minister Helen Clark, the first elected woman Prime Minister in New Zealand's history, declared that New Zealanders were 'weary of radical restructuring'.[53] The experiment was over. And the policies that followed underlined the point.⁵⁴ Government departments began moving away from what one commentator called 'narrow and prescriptive analysis', to a more 'reflective' and 'open-minded' perspective that 'acknowledges the wider significance of social factors.'⁵⁵

Labour stayed in power for three terms, repeating the pattern that had followed the Great Depression of the 1930s, when the conservative right discredited itself so badly they stayed out of power for half a generation. Some national infrastructure was re-acquired; government took a stake in Air New Zealand and in 2007 repurchased the railway system. Labour won its third term in office in 2005, but it did not get a fourth. A National government was elected in 2008 on the promise that they would not run an asset sales programme in their first term. They kept it; the programme was not implemented until a few days after they had been re-elected for a second term in 2011.

Not all the challenges faced by the government and people of New Zealand in the first years of the twenty-first century were locally driven. The new millennium opened with some of the most disruptive international developments seen in years, starting with international terror attacks on New York. New Zealand was drawn into the war on terrorism that followed, contributing forces to international efforts in Afghanistan. They were principally used in humanitarian and peace-keeping roles. However, combat forces from the Special Air Service (SAS) were deployed to the war zone. And in July 2007, Corporal Willy Apiata was awarded the New Zealand VC for outstanding bravery in the field three years earlier. He was the first recipient of this medal under a New Zealand honours system, and the first New Zealand combatant to receive the VC since the Second World War.

Other events flowed across and around New Zealand, including the so-called 'General Financial Crisis' that began in 2007. All these offered challenges, joined by local events that in November 2010 included the worst mine accident since 1914. Twenty-nine of the 31 men working in the Pike River coal mine were killed by explosions and fire.

This was a disaster by any measure, and it came amidst another calamity unfolding with remorseless pace on the other side of the South Island; a succession of quakes that essentially shook Christchurch, Lyttleton and the surrounding area to pieces. The cycle began in the pre-dawn hours of 4 September 2010 when a quake of magnitude 7.1 struck around 30 km from central Christchurch. It was felt as far away as New Plymouth, woke sleepers in Wellington, and did massive damage around Christchurch. Buildings were cracked and broken, chimneys fell through houses, masonry houses were ruined, and liquefaction sent mud pouring through suburban streets and homes. But by astonishing good fortune the quake struck while most people were asleep in their beds. Some were hurt, two seriously; and there was one death from a heart attack perhaps brought on by the quake. But nobody was killed directly. It was a remarkable escape from what

ABOVE

Jet boat pulling a power-spin near the Huka Falls, January 2005. Water-jet propulsion for high-speed, high-manoeuvrability boats suitable for shallow river work was a New Zealand invention, and jet boating was one of a raft of adventure tourism activities that began drawing international crowds to New Zealand in the early twenty-first century, and tourism in general became a significant part of the New Zealand economy.

Matthew Wright/Author Collection

ABOVE

Public performance at the Christchurch arts festival, 2009. Within a year the city had been devastated by a succession of earthquakes.

Matthew Wright/Author Collection

could have been a significant tragedy had it occurred in office hours.

Despite a barrage of aftershocks, some of them remarkably strong, Christchurch—New Zealand's third largest city—began to recover. Residents began the long job of excavating the liquid mud that had boiled up from former swampland. Buildings were demolished, others re-occupied. The central city came back to life. But then, at 12.51 p.m. on 22 February 2011, another heavy shake rocked the city. At an absolute magnitude of 6.3, this did not seem too great by quake standards, but the energy was focussed on the Christchurch area and the 'felt effects' were intense. It devastated the city. Buildings weakened by the earlier shakes cracked and some fell. Debris showered on central city streets, catching people rushing outside to escape. The cathedral—the icon of the city, symbol of its historical *raison d'etre*—cracked and broke. More liquid mud erupted into suburban areas, inundating houses.

The official death toll reached 185, of whom 115 were lost in the collapsed CTV building. Some survived the fall of this six-storey structure, but could not be rescued before they died, and in a sign of the poignancy that twenty-first century technology can lend to such moments, some were able to talk to loved ones while their cellphone batteries lasted.

The response by survivors highlighted much about the New Zealand spirit. Over 70

years earlier, the people of Hawke's Bay had faced a similar crisis. Then, the legacy of the First World War had stood them in good stead. Most of the men in 1931 Hawke's Bay had been on the Western Front and had faced crisis before; they knew what to do. The society of the early twenty-first century was different. Here were a people who had not experienced war, who had no experience of being hit by sudden danger. But they were not found wanting. Rescuers hurried at once to help the injured. They worked without stint, without pause, to save lives, displays of selflessness and courage that underscored many of the the qualities of humanity in general, and of New Zealand's expression of them in particular.

ABOVE
There were no casualties in the first Christchurch quake of 10 September 2010, but damage was widespread and many buildings destroyed, including the historic Deans homestead.
Photo: Martin Hunter

LEFT
The quake of 22 February 2011 left parts of Christchurch in ruins, including the city's iconic cathedral. By the time this picture was taken, two years on, debate still raged over whether to demolish the remains.
Photo: Matthew Wright

FAR LEFT
Shops at Merivale devastated by the earthquake of 2011.
Photo: EdStock

Time and tide

By the second decade of the twenty-first century there was no question that New Zealand was on a new course, informed and shaped by the experiences of the nineteenth and twentieth centuries, but different from them in many ways. The New Zealand of the new millennium was a more confident country, less prone to the 'cultural cringe', more accepting of its position as a small but capable and independent player on the world stage. This shift of mood was in part generational, but some of the specifics were also a legacy of the way that New Zealand had disengaged from the shapes and patterns of life in the twentieth century.

Some at the time, and even historians, have called the shifts of the late twentieth century a revolution. The more compelling argument, however, is that it was an evolution—a generational growth of New Zealand's psyche away from its colonial origins, away from the social frameworks of the twentieth century. This evolution was partially facilitated and given superficial character by the 'reform' period, but ultimately was a change of much deeper scope and power. Indeed, both Muldoonism and the reforms were in many ways symptomatic of the wider move away from earlier ideals. New Zealand reacted by lurching to a tighter hold on pavlova lifestyle as it faded, a lurch made possible in part by personality politics—Muldoonism. Then, New Zealand lurched to its opposing pole—Rogernomics. Neither stood particularly easily with the broader shapes and patterns of society, evidenced by the way the extremes of both were eventually rejected by the electorate, clear decisions which underscore the fact that the reforms, in particular, were not 'revolutionary' in themselves.

Still, from a historical perspective, the reform period from the mid-1980s to the end of the twentieth century demands an explanation. Muldoonism was more readily explicable; it was more of the same, of the familiar, however out of date that had become, however much it was pushed by Muldoon's particular brand of abrasive personality politics. But the reform era was a flirtation with purist socioeconomic ideology that apparently stood against the wider historical trends and values that characterised New Zealand.

What happened? Contemporary analysts—some with axes to grind—saw the reforms in polemic terms, classifying the changes as everything from essential medicine to a 'con' driven by theoretical ideology.[56] There was, it seemed, no middle ground or more abstract view. Part of the difficulty was emotional entanglement. The 1984–99 era had been fraught by any standards; both at the time and later, the reforms were presented by their advocates as all-or-nothing, prosecuted on the syllogism that the reforms were the only fix, and any who

ABOVE

Te Papa Tongarewa, New Zealand's national museum, opened in 1997 and was a remarkable feat of engineering, with a 150-year life, quake-proofed via lead-rubber bearings. It was built to the latest thinking about museums and featured the Treaty of Waitangi at the thick end of a large wedge-shaped chamber separating the Maori and Pakeha galleries.
Matthew Wright/Author Collection

OPPOSITE BOTTOM

Waitangi Park, Wellington waterfront, 2012
Matthew Wright/Author Collection

objected were advocating 'Muldoonism'. There was even an acronym, TINA, 'there is no alternative'. Actually there were alternatives, including the path taken by Australia, or strategies suggested by some businessmen.[57]

This is not to deny the issues that had to be faced; the hard fact was that by the late 1970s New Zealand had manifestly failed to adapt to a changing world. Britain was gone—and the writing for that shift had been on the wall long before the Suez Crisis. Meanwhile, 40 years had bloated the 'cradle to grave' welfare state into a corpulent beast well removed from its origins. The bloat was compounded by the sinking economy of the day, which threw people into the system, contrasting with the situation on its introduction in 1938, when prosperity was rising and people were being thrown out of the system. Indeed, the state system of 1980 was far more comprehensive than that of 1938, in many ways, because it included indirect support in the form of deliberately over-staffed departments—notably railways—subsidies, grants, rebates, and a universal no-fault accident compensation system. After two generations, some New Zealanders viewed welfare as a lifestyle, and many availed themselves of state padding

ABOVE
Diversification transformed pastoral provinces. Hawke's Bay, and particularly the horticultural regions around Havelock North and Hastings, became a significant wine-making region. This is the Craggy Range winery in 2009.
Matthew Wright/Author Collection

ABOVE

Over 100,000 Wellingtonians, most of the population of the downtown city, turned out to honour the Unknown Warrior, New Zealand's tribute to our dead of the First World War. He was buried, with all the pomp and circumstance the country could muster, beneath the National War Memorial in Buckle Street, on 11 November 2004. The scale of the crowd, roughly matching the number sent to fight in that war, was indicative of the new sense of national history.

Matthew Wright/Author Collection

in other ways. To this was added the walls of 'Fortress New Zealand', which by the early 1980s included subsidy schemes for farmers, work schemes to entice employers to hire youth, and make-work subsidies for local councils. This was insupportable and, although Muldoon recognised the point, his efforts to manage the process without pain were too slow to be workable, too heavily tinged with personality politics to be really palatable.

All these problems were genuine and serious for New Zealand. State sector restructuring after 1985 gave an overdue correction to some of the direct issues that had emerged from 40 years of the welfare state, protectionism and, in many respects, complacency. There was an absolute improvement in the level of government service. Many liberalisations were necessary to set New Zealand up to compete well on the world stage; other relaxations allowed New Zealanders to enjoy lifestyles previously envied as available only to those overseas. The reforms accelerated existing trends towards diversification and away from reliance on a single market. This was, in many respects, overdue medicine.

The fact that New Zealand needed modernising gave power to the initial changes, and partly explains how the package was sold to an electorate brought up on Savage's 'applied Christianity'. That question certainly puzzled commentators at the time. Some historians have considered it a 'coup',[58] purist policies forced on an unwilling electorate by a small group of politicians with the aid of the three-year Parliamentary mandate.[59] There is some validity in such a view, but the more compelling reason is that the early phases of the reforms in the mid-1980s were welcomed. New Zealanders were in a mood for change, wanting freer access to imported goods, easier overseas travel, a less regulated lifestyle, and opportunity to keep up with what were perceived to be overseas trends. At its best, neo-libertarian New Zealand was an exciting, urbanised nirvana of cafés, late-night clubs and shopping malls—novelties to the generation that first experienced them.

Curiously, a good deal of the popularity of this lifestyle stemmed from the fact that, while it seemed to transcend the limits regulation had imposed on earlier generations, it also celebrated the essence of New Zealanders' general ambition all along: having a nice life, with security, and ideally without working too hard for it. The pavlova world had offered one way of doing that, one that spoke to the needs and values of that age. The reform period offered another, this time keying into the new ideals of the baby boomers, and apparently without the downside of the protectionist limits experienced during the pavlova era.

CHAPTER TEN
EXTREME DECADES

ABOVE AND LEFT

Art deco wekend, Napier 2012. Napier's 1930s post-quake heritage gained a new lease of life in the 1990s on the back of a revival of interest in art deco. Napier had one of the world's best collections of small modernist buildings. Some had already succumbed to the wrecking ball; but the theme was picked up as a city promotion and celebrated. Events included a light-hearted annual 'art deco' weekend which by the early twenty-first century was beineing tens of thousands of people to the city every February. This is the 2012 weekend.

Matthew Wright/Author Collection

The problem was that this joyful lifestyle was only part of the deal, and the reforms did not take long to go well beyond what most everyday New Zealanders felt acceptable. It was not just the unpopular state asset sales programmes. Virtually every facet of government activity was reviewed, then reduced or eliminated in what by the early 1990s was beginning to look less like practical medicine and more like an ideological crusade. Public services gained a commercial price. Markets were imposed across every aspect of government business and

ABOVE

New Zealand's spectacular scenery gained new dimension in the face of a twenty-first-century tourist boom, in part fuelled by the identification of New Zealand with J. R. R. Tolkien's Middle Earth, on the back of Peter Jackson's *The Lord Of The Rings* movies. These are the Southern Alps, winter 2009.

Matthew Wright/Author Collection

behaviour, locally and centrally, and apparently whether this idea fitted or not.[60]

This was something new. Bruce Jesson looked on it as the colonisation of New Zealand by a 'culture of finance'.[61] Other commentators argued that much of it was applied as an exercise in theoretical purism, without much reference to the complexities of a real society.[62] Indeed, while the doctrines of leading Chicago School economist Frederich von Hayek influenced some New Zealand policy papers of the day,[63] some reformers—as more than one observer noted—had apparently not read his teachings.[64] That rendered the more extreme reforms matters of faith—products of conviction. Books by New Zealand's main movers-and-shakers of the period, another commentator argued, displayed 'intellectual shallowness', masked by 'cocksure arrogance'.[65]

The final arbiter remained the practical results. In some ways the reformers opened doors for a generation of New Zealanders who already had different aspirations from their parents and grandparents, who were already developing a sense of local validation. But the whole reform package was sold on the claim that the pain of adjustment was going to be short. Longer term gain would follow. In fact, New Zealand's average annual economic growth rate between 1984 and 1999 was just 0.5 percent. This was no better than typical 1970s figures, worse than 1950s levels, and well below that of unreformed countries such as Australia.[66] Taking housing out of the equation, the net wealth of the average New Zealand household fell by half between 1978 and 2003. The cause was debt rising faster than assets, an issue masked by a rise in housing values.[67] By these figures, then, the reforms had made no difference; they had not even stemmed the falling tide of prosperity.

The reformers countered the failure to produce promised results with the claim that change had not been pursued hard or fast enough. Actually, by the mid-1990s, New Zealand had pushed further down the pure theoretical neo-liberal line than most other western countries, noticeably further than Australia. And there was a huge social cost. Among other groups, a whole generation in their fifties were sacrificed to the reforms, particularly government employees who had dedicated their lives to their work and were then dismissed, left feeling worthless. Indeed, for a while in the early 1990s, anybody over 40 was thought unemployable. It was a sign of just how disconnected the ideology of the day had become, and the rationales were as shallow as they were facile: 'the *market* has *spoken*'; 'you can't stop progress'; change was 'inevitable'. Sometimes it was portrayed as a personal failure; those dispossessed by forces beyond their control were 'Neanderthals', lumbering and obsolescent 'dinosaurs' who had failed to adapt, by nature doomed by the forces of the future. Apparently.

In the end, while a few individuals caught the wave of the deregulating economy, many did not; and the fact that the pie did not grow much makes clear that the new rich became so by further impoverishing the poor. The mechanisms were not direct, but the results were clear. In 1997—more than ten years after the reforms began, and after the bulk were over, a third of Maori women reported that their families could eat properly only occasionally. By 2000–01, 22.6 percent of the population were surviving on less than three-fifths of the average income. This included 29.1 percent of all children, 32 percent of all Maori families, 40 percent of all Pacific Island families and 66.3 percent of all solo-parent families.[68]

These were very different figures from those of the classic pavlova era, and many problems of poverty had also re-emerged by the turn of the century,

BELOW
Some things changed little in the twenty-first century. Customising cars had been a popular hobby in New Zealand since the 1960s. This is a 1949 Mercury.
Matthew Wright/Author Collection

ABOVE

The 'Treaty House', flagstaff and grounds at Waitangi, restored, preserved and given historical meaning with interpretation boards. In some ways the scene on this January day in 2011 was not much different from what William Hobson and his officials would have seen in 1840. The marquee erected for the official signing ceremony stood on the grass in the left foreground of this picture.

Matthew Wright/Author Collection

including 'third world' diseases such as tuberculosis. An OECD report also showed that New Zealand had one of the world's highest rates of youth suicide, teen pregnancies and drug use.[69] Part of this was due to generational change that would likely have occurred in any event. However, the reforms played their part in driving this social outcome. And as the twentieth century drew to a close, many Kiwis were sick of it. New Zealanders, one commentator explained in 2003, had been 'flagellating ourselves at the altar of economic orthodoxy'—a push for 'purity' for which, in practice, country and people had paid heavily.[70] Perhaps the most telling opinion was external. New Zealand's 'radical free-market reformers,' one Australian magazine declared, had been 'peddling damaged goods.'[71]

In many ways, however, New Zealand's late twentieth-century lurches between extremes of protectionism and free market were historically fitting. In 1840, Wakefield had founded a New Zealand colony in an attempt to engineer a society around economic idealism. It was perhaps appropriate that the colonial era should stutter to a ragged close, 150-odd years later, with yet another flawed effort to impose simplistic theory across the complexities of the human condition.

For this was the problem with the reform period; it was framed by what had gone before and in many ways defined what was to be demonised by its immediate past. From this perspective, the reforms were not forward-looking, still less revolutionary; they were a product of their time, defined by their past and just as hidebound by the 'cringe' with its over-compensation for perceived inferiority as anything that had gone before. From the historical perspective, the experience had been another object lesson in the same old try-hard ethos that had dogged New Zealand since the 1880s. The late twentieth century was the world's great age of neo-liberal evangelism and, as always, Kiwis had taken the ideas to an extreme. And New Zealand's experience as a 'free-market laboratory'[72] had a clear downside. Socioeconomic purism had not made New Zealanders generally wealthy, but it did create a new class of poor.

The new mind-set of a more confident, more independent New Zealand had been bubbling away for a while, generationally, beneath all these upheavals, and finally became a force to be reckoned with during the first decade of the twenty-first century. The same sense that New Zealand had its own place in the world. after all. also brought a long look backwards by grass-roots New Zealanders. It was no coincidence that general interest in New Zealand's own history enjoyed a renaissance during the early twenty-first century. For the first time, Kiwis realised, we actually had a history; we were not just a barnacle on the British story. Michael King's *The Penguin History of New Zealand* was released in 2003 and became one of New Zealand's best-selling books of all time, with over 250,000 copies sold as the second decade of the twenty-first century opened.

This new interest in history was symptomatic of the way New Zealanders were handling the discovery of a more confident sense of self-identity. It took early form in a revival of Anzac Day attendance, including ever-larger pilgrimages by New Zealanders to the beaches of Gallipoli on the day itself. The motives went further than simply discovering what their grandparents did in 'the war'. It was also an exaltation of New Zealand's identity as a place different from mother England, a place with its own history and culture.

These shifts helped focus an emerging sense of national maturity, something that had been growing before the 'reform' period—a developing notion that New Zealanders could achieve great things by world standards without having to be boy-scout try-hards. The fact was that Kiwis had been quietly achieving things, in an unassuming way, behind the scenes, for decades. During the twentieth century, Kiwis around the world had been responsible for splitting the atom, pioneering key techniques of plastic surgery and climbing Mount Everest. They included scientists such as William Pickering, who ran the Jet Propulsion Laboratory for years, or Max Planck Institute head Sir Ian Axford—who came from Napier—who were at the very top of their profession, worldwide. Their experiences showed that New Zealanders were as capable as anybody else, and by the twenty-first century there was a sense that Kiwis did not have to achieve recognition overseas before they could be accepted at home.

This sense of self-validation had emerged before the 'reform' period, driven

ABOVE

In the early twenty-first century, New Zealand effectively discovered its vibrant, exciting and integral history. Much of this past could be found and experienced without looking too hard. This is the graveyard at Russell. A headstone here marks those killed during the battle here in 1845. Bullet holes from the battle can still be found in the church walls. This is real history that can be seen and touched.

Matthew Wright/Author Collection

as we have seen in part by the local music scene. It gained further momentum in the twenty-first century from the information revolution, born on the back of the World Wide Web, and which New Zealanders embraced. The social consequences had not been fully predicted, except by British science fiction writer and social futurist Arthur C. Clarke, who as early as 1964 laid out the specific consequences of worldwide information exchange being made cheap, easy and ubiquitous.[73] He got it right. The internet and its main application, the World Wide Web, meant social contact without knowing location; a commonality of shared information; and a breaking down of boundaries, all underscoring New Zealand's shift of mind-set away from that of provincial backwater.

New Zealand's course seemed well set as the twenty-first century entered its second decade. Like all trends, the new was complex and multi-faceted, founded in the past, but laying new ideals over old. It brought the first real steps away from a society moulded by failed colonial dreams, by world-engulfing war and by its own flawed sense of identity. Kiwis of the early twenty-first century were more confident, more self-assured, and more focussed on self-determination, defined in part by a pluralist emphasis on rights.

These changes also underscored another point; the Pakeha of the early twenty-first century were not transplanted British folk, but had an identity of their own. New Zealand was their country too. Their fathers and grandfathers had fought and died for it. This society and people stood alongside a resurgent Maori culture, alongside other cultures gaining ground as New Zealand became overtly multi-racial, multicultural and multi-faceted in ways that could not have been contemplated even 30 years earlier. The issues were complex. And yet, despite an unprecedented combination of new rich, new poor, new language and new attitudes, New Zealand ideals were still shaped by some of the concepts on which colonial society had been founded nearly two centuries earlier—house-ownership, the quarter-acre section, lip-service egalitarianism and employment security. As always, the legacy of New Zealand's past continued to shape the unknown future.

Notes

Introduction
1. Accepted date is 1280 AD +/- 30 years, see Chapter 1.
2. http://en.wikipedia.org/wiki/History_of_gunpowder, accessed 6 March 2012.
3. Keith Sinclair, *A History of New Zealand*, Penguin, Auckland 1959, revised Pelican edition 1988; W. H. Oliver, *The Story of New Zealand*, Faber and Faber, London 1960.
4. Michael King, *The Penguin History of New Zealand*, Penguin, Auckland 2003.
5. Keith Sinclair, *A History of New Zealand*, Penguin, Auckland 1959, revised Pelican edition 1988.
6. See, e.g., Paul Moon, *New Zealand in the Twentieth Century*, HarperCollins, Auckland 2011.

Chapter One
1. R. P. Suggate (ed), *The Geology of New Zealand*, Vol. II, Government Print, Wellington, 1978, p. 741; Stevens and McCulloch p. 90.
2. C. M. Lees, V. E. Neall, A. S. Palmer, 'Forest persistence at coastal Waikato, 24,000 b.p. to present', *Journal of the Royal Society of New Zealand*, No. 28, No. 1, March 1998, pp. 55–81.
3. See R. P. Suggate (ed), *The Geology of New Zealand*, Vol. II, Government Print, Wellington, 1978, pp. 736–741; Malcolm McKinnon (ed), *New Zealand Historical Atlas*, Bateman, Auckland 2000, Plate 7, and Brian Enting and Les Molloy, *The Ancient Islands,* Port Nicholson Press, Wellington 1982, esp. Ch 1. For the cultural implications of the end of glaciation see also Jared Diamond, *Guns, Germs and Steel*, Vintage, London 1998.
4. W. H. Oliver, *The Story of New Zealand*, Faber and Faber, London 1960, p. 27.
5. See, e.g., Gary J. Cook and Thomas J. Brown, *The Secret Land: People Before*, StonePrint Press, Christchurch 1999; John Tasker, *Secret Landscape*, Kanuka Press, Hastings 2000; John Tasker, *Myth and Mystery*, Tandem Press, Auckland 1997.
6. William Colenso, 'On the Māori Races of New Zealand', *Transactions and Proceedings of the New Zealand Institute 1868*, Vol. 1, Wellington 1869, p. 56.
7. For rebuttal, see, e.g., Pugsley, Christopher, 'Maori did not invent trench warfare', *New Zealand Defence Quarterly*, No. 22, Spring 1998.
8. Described in M. P. K. Sorrenson, *Maori Origins and Migrations*, Auckland University Press, Auckland 1979, p. 41 and 44.
9. K. R. Howe, *The Quest for Origins*, Penguin, Auckland 2003, p. 171.
10. Michael King, *The Penguin History of New Zealand*, Penguin, Auckland 2003, pp. 39–40, 46.
11. W. T. L. Travers, 'Notes of the traditions and manners and customs of the Mori-oris', *Transactions of the New Zealand Institute*, Vol. 9, Wellington 1875, p. 15.
12. Worthy and Holdaway, pp. 24–25; Anderson, *Prodigious Birds*, p. 178.
13. K. R. Howe, 'Western ideas about islanders origins' in K. R. Howe (ed), *Vaka Moana: voyages of the ancestors, the discovery and settlement of the Pacific*, David Bateman, Auckland 2006, p. 284
14. Noted in King, *The Penguin History of New Zealand*, p. 49.
15. See J. D. H. Buchanan (ed D. R. Simmons), *The Maori History and Place Names of Hawke's Bay*, A. H. & A. W. Reed Ltd, Wellington, 1973, p. 5.
16. Ibid, p. 51.
17. David Simmonds, *The Great New Zealand Myth*, A. H. & A. W. Reed, Wellington 1976; Howe, pp. 161–164.
18. See, e.g., Martin Doutré, *Ancient Celtic New Zealand*, Dé Danaan Publishers, Auckland 1999; Ross Wiseman, *New Zealand's Hidden Past*, Discovery Press, Auckland 2003.
19. Howe, pp. 153–154.
20. Richard Walter, 'New Zealand Archaeology and its Polynesian Connections' in Furey and Holdaway, p. 134
21. Geoffrey Irwin, *The Prehistoric Exploration and Colonisation of the Pacific*, Cambridge University Press, Cambridge 1992, p. 108.
22. Ibid, pp. 16–18.
23. McKinnon (ed), Plate 10; also J. H. Parry (ed), *The European Reconnaissance*, selected documents, Harper Torchbooks, New York 1968, Maps.
24. Patrick J. Grant, 'Climate, Geomorphology and Vegetation', p. 166.
25. King, *The Penguin History of New Zealand*, p. 51.
26. Prickett, *Maori Origins*, p. 25. See also H. B. Elliott, B. Striewski, J. R. Flenley, J. H. Kirkman and D. G. Sutton, 'A 4300 year palynological and sedimentological record of environmental change and human impact from Wharau road

27. H. S. McGlone, A. Anderson, R. N. Holdaway, 'An ecological approach', in Douglas G. Sutton (ed) *The Origins of the First New Zealanders*, Auckland University Press, Auckland 1994., p. 148.
28. McGlone, M. S., Anderson, A., Holdaway, R. N., 'An ecological approach', p. 147.
29. Noted in King, *The Penguin History of New Zealand*, p. 49.
30. Davidson, p. 129.
31. McGlone, M. S., Anderson, A., Holdaway, R. N., 'An ecological approach', p. 149.
32. Michael King, *Nga Iwi O Te Motu*, revised edition, Reed, Auckland, 2001, p. 15.
33. Geoffrey Irwin, 'Voyaging and Settlement' in K. R. Howe (ed), *Vaka Moana: Voyages of the ancestors, the discovery and settlement of the Pacific*, David Bateman, Auckland 2006, pp. 90–91.
34. Patrick J. Grant, 'Climate, Geomorphology and Vegetation', in Douglas G. Sutton (ed) *The Origins of the First New Zealanders*, Auckland University Press, Auckland 1994, p. 166.
35. Higham and Jones, p. 229.
36. Atholl Anderson, *Prodigious Birds—Moas and moa hunting in prehistoric New Zealand*, Cambridge University Press, Melbourne, 1989, p. 176; Margaret Orbell, *Hawaiki—a new approach to Maori tradition*, p. 59
37. J. D. H. Buchanan (ed J. D. Simmons), *The Maori History and Place Names of Hawke's Bay*, A. H. & A. W. Reed, Wellington, 1973, p. 43.
38. See Philip Houghton 'A Vigorous People' in John Wilson (ed), *From the Beginning, the Archaeology of the Maori*, Penguin, Auckland 1987, pp. 36–42.
39. Anderson, p. 179, Davidson p. 57.
40. Davidson, pp. 166–167.
41. Anderson, p. 181.
42. Beverley McCulloch and Michael Trotter, *Digging Up the Past*, p. 50
43. Patrick J. Grant, 'Climate, Geomorphology and Vegetation', p. 166. This is not Grant's argument.
44. Beverley McCulloch, illus. Geoffey Cox, *Moas—Lost Giants of New Zealand*, HarperCollins, Auckland 1992, pp. 41–43.
45. Anderson, p. 98.
46. McCulloch, *Moas—Lost giants of New Zealand*, pp. 54–55.
47. Anderson, pp. 178–187
48. Beverley McCulloch and Michael Trotter, *Digging Up the Past, New Zealand's archaeological history*, revised ed. Penguin, Middlesex, 1997 p. 51
49. King, *The Penguin History of New Zealand*, p. 66, suggests 150.
50. Anderson, pp. 171–176.
51. Ibid, p. 157.
52. Garry Law, 'Coromandel Peninsula and Great Barrier Island' in Nigel Prickett (ed) *The First Thousand Years*, Dunmore Press, Palmerston North 1982, p. 56
53. See David Lewis and Werner Forman, *The Maori: Heirs of Tane*, Orbis, London 1982, p. 24
54. Anderson, p. 178. As Anderson notes, suggestions that moa survived into the European period can be discounted.
55. — 'Social Progress at the Antipodes', transcript, Misc MSS, NAMU, also Atholl Anderson 'Food from Forest and Coast' in John Wilson, pp. 73–84.
56. Anderson, p. 176.
57. Davidson, pp. 134–135.
58. Holdaway, Jones and Beavan Athfield, p. 654.
59. See Atholl Anderson 'Canterbury and Marlborough' in Nigel Prickett *The First Thousand Years*, Dunmore Press, Palmerston North 1982, p. 89.
60. See, e.g. N. L. Elder *Vegetation of the Ruahine Range: An Introduction*, Royal Society of New Zealand, Wellington 1965.
61. Argued by Grant, *Hawke's Bay Forests of Yesterday*.
62. See, e.g. Ash Cunningham, 'The Indigenous Forests of East Coast—Poverty Bay, Hawke's Bay' and N. L. Elder, 'Maori Cultivation and the Retreat of Forest', talk given 9 October 1956
63. Grant, *Forests*, pp. 219–224 provides a summary.
64. See also NZHA Plate 12.
65. Stevens, McGlone and McCulloch, p. 118–119.
66. Davidson, p. 41.
67. King, *The Penguin History of New Zealand*, p. 71.
68. James R. Goff and Bruce G. McFadgen, 'Nationwide tsunami during prehistoric Maori occupation, New Zealand', ITS 2001 Proceedings, Session 3, No. 3-1, pp. 469–476.
69. Atholl Anderson 'North and Central Otago' in Nigel Prickett (ed), *The First Thousand Years*, p. 124, notes the distinction between lowland 'archaic' sites and 'classic' habitations on defensible headlands.
70. Argued by Fagan, pp. xiv–xv.
71. King, *The Penguin History of New Zealand*, p. 41.
72. Philip Houghton, *The First New Zealanders*, Hodder & Stoughton, Auckland, 1980, p. 77.
73. Douglas G. Sutton (ed), *The Archaeology of the Kainga*, Auckland University Press, Auckland, 1990, second edition 1994, p. ix.
74. H. S. McGlone, Anderson, A., Holdaway, R. N., 'An ecological approach', in Douglas G. Sutton (ed) *The Origins of the First New Zealanders*, Auckland University Press, Auckland 1994, p. 156.
75. Kevin Jones, 'Skill with Stone and Wood' in John Wilson pp 57–72
76. H. S. McGlone, A. Anderson, R. N. Holdaway, 'An ecological approach', p. 152, 160.
77. Davidson, pp. 184, 188.
78. Colenso, 'On the Māori Races of New Zealand', p. 9.
79. Davidson, p. 147.
80. Sutton (ed), p. 33, 47.
81. Davidson, p. 128.
82. Davidson, pp. 134–35.
83. Colenso, 'On the Māori Races of New Zealand', p. 9.
84. Colenso, 'On the Māori Races of New Zealand', p. 9.
85. Houghton, p. 126–127.
86. Philip Houghton, *The First New Zealanders*, Hodder & Stoughton, Auckland, 1980, p. 115.
87. Ibid, p. 117.
88. Philip Houghton, *The First New Zealanders*, Hodder & Stoughton, Auckland, 1980, p. 96.
89. F. E. Maning, *Old New Zealand: a tale of the good old times by a Pakeha Māori*, Golden Press, Auckland and Christchurch, 1975, p. 102.
90. See, e.g. Ballara, *Taua*, pp. 71–73.
91. Davidson, p. 181.
92. J. D. H. Buchanan, *The Maori history and place names of Hawke's Bay*, A. H. & A. W. Reed, Wellington 1975, p. 17.
93. McNab, I, King Papers, 'New Zealand Natives', pp. 266–67.
94. Ballara, *Taua*, pp. 127–128
95. Ballara, *Taua*, pp. 128–129.

96 http://www.nzherald.co.nz/Māori/news/article.cfm?c_id=252&objectid=10529179, accessed 6 June 2010.
97 Savage, *Some Account of New Zealand*, p. 34.
98 See, e.g. Eric Schwimmer, 'The Maori Hapu: A generative model', in *Journal of Polynesian Studies*, Vol. 99, No.3, September 1990.
99 McGlone, Anderson and Holdaway, p. 156, following Parsonson.
100 Evison, *The Ngāi Tahu Deeds*, p. 18.
101 Ibid, p. 57.
102 Evison, *The Ngāi Tahu Deeds*, p. 19.
103 Robert MacNab, *Historical Records of New Zealand*, Vol. II, Government Printer, Wellington, 1914, 'Tasman's Journal', p. 18.
104 See, e.g. H. R. Trevor-Roper, 'The General Crisis of the Seventeenth Century', *Past and Present* No. 16, 1959; Andrew Sharp, 'More blood out of Stone; what was the crisis of the aristocracy?', *Historical News*, March 1969 pp. 6–8; Michael Cullen, 'Lawrence Stone, the Manors and other ruins', *Historical News*, March 1969, pp. 8–10; Robert Ashton, 'Aristocracy in Transition', *Economic History Review*, Vol. 22, 1969; Hexter, Robert, 'The English Aristocracy, its Crises, and the English Revolution, 1558–1660', *Journal of British Studies*, Vol. VIII, 1968.
105 See, e.g. Fagan, pp. 101–112.
106 Theodore K. Rabb, *The Struggle for Stability in Early Modern Europe*, Oxford University Press, New York 1975, pp. 116–145
107 Grahame Anderson, pp. 31–32; see also 'Mar di India', print of c 1630 map in author collection.
108 Edwards (ed), pp. xlviii–xlix; map between pp lxii and lxiii.
109 Anderson, Grahame, *The Merchant of the Zeehaen – Isaac Gilsemans and the Voyages of Abel Tasman*, Te Papa Press, Wellington 2001, p. 32.
110 Philip Edwards (ed), *The Journals of Captain Cook: Prepared from original manuscripts by J. C. Beaglehole for the Hakluyt Society, 1955–1967*, Penguin, London 1999, p. lvii.
111 McNab, Vol. II, 'Resolution of the Dutch East India Company', p. 3
112 McNab, Vol. II, 'Tasman's Instructions' *see below*, p. 11.
113 Salmond, p. 73.
114 Ibid, p. 20.
115 Ibid, p. 21.
116 Salmond, p. 78.
117 King, *The Penguin History of New Zealand*, p. 96.
118 McNab, 'Tasman's Journal', p. 21.
119 Ibid, p. 21.
120 McNab, 'Tasman's Journal', pp. 21–22.
121 McNab, 'Tasman's Journal', p. 22. This translation differs from that used by Grahame Anderson, see e.g. Anderson p. 92.
122 McNab, 'Tasman's Journal', pp. 22–23.
123 Ibid, p. 23.
124 Ibid p. 23.
125 Graeme Anderson, p. 100.
126 McNab, 'Tasman's Journal', p. 26.
127 Ibid, p. 29.
128 'Gereduceerde Kaart vant Zuid-Land', print in author collection.
129 Beaglehole (ed), p. c.
130 McNab, Vol. II, footnote p. 84.
131 Beaglehole (ed), Friday May 27th to Friday July 29th, p. 1. Cook's original spelling and capitalisations have been preserved.
132 McNab, Vol. II, The Lords of the Admiralty to Lieutenant Cook, 30 July 1768, pp. 54–55.
133 Beaglehole, 'Additional Instructions for Lt James Cook', p. cclxxxii.
134 Cited in Salmond, *Two Worlds*, p. 124.
135 Cited in Beaglehole (ed), p. 169.
136 Bruce Biggs, 'Does Maori have a closest relative?', in Douglas G. Sutton (ed), *The Origins of the First New Zealanders*, Auckland University Press, Auckland 1994, pp. 96–97.
137 Beaglehole (ed), Monday 9th October 1769, p. 169.
138 Cited in Beaglehole (ed), p. 169, n. 2.
139 Salmond, *Two Worlds*, pp. 126–127; Beaglehole (ed), p 170.

Chapter Two
1 McNab, Vol. I, John Thomson to Henry Dundas, 22 November 1792, pp. 584–85.
2 Anne Salmond, *Between Worlds*, Viking, Auckland 1997, p. 205.
3 McNab Vol. II, 'The Plan', p. 47.
4 McNab, Vol. I, Lord Sydney to the Lords Commissioners of the Treasury, 18 August 1786, pp. 50–51.
5 McNab, Vol. I, 'Governor Phillip to Under-Secretary Nepean', March 1 1787, p. 71.
6 Salmond, *Between Worlds*, pp. 207–08.
7 Ibid, p. 250.
8 McNab, I., J. M. Haite and W. Fenwick, Chatham Rope Yard, 10 June 1818.
9 Matthew Wright, *Convicts – New Zealand's Hidden Criminal Past*, Penguin, Auckland 2012, p. 42.
10 McNab, I., Governor King to Earl Camden, 30 April 1805, p. 254.
11 Alan Moorhead *The Fatal Impact*, Hamish Hamilton, London 1966, pp. 3–8. While the term was coined by Moorhead, the idea was widespread well before then.
12 McNab, I., Governor King to Earl Camden, 30 April 1805, p. 254.
13 Colenso, 'On the Māori races', p. 49.
14 Jameson, p. 184.
15 William Yate, *An Account of New Zealand*, Seeley and Burnside, London, 1835, pp. 105–106.
16 Augustus Earle, *A narrative of a nine months' residence in New Zealand in 1827; together with a journal of a residence in Tristan D'Acunha*, Longman, Rees, Orme, Brown, Green & Longman, London 1832, p. 259.
17 William Barrett Marshall, *A personal narrative of two visits to New Zealand in HM Ship Alligator, AD 1834*, James Nisbet, London 1836, p. 187.
18 William Williams, *Christianity Among The New Zealanders*, Seeley, Jackson and Halliday, London 1867, p. 19.
19 McNab, Vol. 1, King Papers, 'New Zealand Natives', p. 264.
20 John Marmon, 'The Life and Adventures of John Marmon, the Hokianga Pakeha Pakeha Maori: or, seventy-five years in New Zealand', *Auckland Star*, 7 January 1882.
21 Peter Adams, *A Fatal Necessity*, Auckland University Press, Auckland 1977, pp. 39–40
22 F. E. Maning, *Old New Zealand*, Golden Press reprint, Auckland 1987, p 213.
23 Judith Binney, 'The Expansion of the Missions', *New Zealand's Heritage*, Vol. I, Part 11, p. 282.
24 A. N. Brown, Diary, cited in Bronwyn Elsmore *Like Them that Dream*, Reed, Auckland 2000, p. 19.
25 Cited in Dom Felice Vaggioli, *History of New Zealand and its inhabitants*, trans. John Crockett, Otago University Press, Dunedin

26. McNab, Vol. I, 'Government and General Orders', 9 November 1814, p. 428.
27. McNab, Vol. I, 'Extract from the Report of the Committee delivered to the Annual Meeting held May 4, 1819, at Freemason's Hall, Great Queen Street: Australasia Mission' p. 434
28. McNab, Vol. I, 'Extract from the Report of the Committee delivered to the Annual Meeting held May 4, 1819, at Freemason's Hall, Great Queen Street: Australasia Mission' p. 434
29. King, *The Penguin History of New Zealand*, p. 141.
30. Adams, p. 43.
31. Maning, pp. 106–107.
32. McNab, Vol. I, Governor King to Earl Camden, 30 April 1805, p. 254.
33. McNab, Vol. I, 'Commissioner Bigge's Enquiry', p. 540.
34. McNab, Vol. I, 'Commissioner Bigge's Enquiry', p. 539.
35. Cited in Judith Binney, 'The Expansion of the Missions', *New Zealand's Heritage*, Vol. I, Part 11, p. 282.
36. McNab, Vol. I, 'Commissioner Bigge's Enquiry', p. 540. See also NZHA, Plate 28.
37. McNab, Vol. I, 'Commissioner Bigge's Enquiry', p. 561.
38. McNab, I, p. 712, Ralph Darling to Sir George Murray, 22 September 1830.
39. Ibid.
40. Matthew Wright, *Town and Country — The History of Hastings and District*, Hastings District Council, Hastings 2001, p. 20.
41. Graeme Hunt, 'Ignorance lets Tuia spread her poisoned gospel', *National Business Review*, 8 September 2000.
42. Dom Felice Vaggioli, *History of New Zealand and its Inhabitants*, trans. John Crockett, Otago University Press, Dunedin 2000, p. 51.
43. Ibid, p. 51.
44. See, e.g. general argument in Ballara, *Taua*.
45. Trevor Bentley, 'Tribal Guns, Tribal Gunners: a study of acculturation by Māori of European military technology during the New Zealand intertribal musket wars', MPhil thesis, University of Waikato 1977, glossary p. 206.
46. Matthew Wright, *Guns and Utu*, Penguin, Auckland 2011, pp. 52–56.
47. Ibid.
48. Crosby, p. 357.
49. Noted in Binney, 'The Expansion of the Missions', p. 283.
50. Ballara, *Taua*, p. 455.
51. See, e.g. Matthew Wright, *Town and Country*, pp. 32–44.
52. See, Wright, *Guns and Utu*, pp. 190–196.
53. Patricia Burns, *Fatal Success—A History of the New Zealand Company*, Heinemann-Reed, Auckland 1989, p. 136.
54. WTu MS 1232, Donald McLean Journal, 18 April 1851
55. Ballara, *Taua*, pp. 454–457
56. Adams, pp. 21, 25.
57. McNab, Vol. I, Darling to Murray, 22 September 1830, enclosure, p. 713.
58. Ibid, p. 29.
59. McNab, Vol. I, 'Letter from Baron de Thierry to the Editor of the Sydney Gazette', 17 December 1837, p. 726.
60. Thomson, p. 259.
61. Ibid, p. 191.
62. McNab, II, 'Commissioner Bigge's Report', pp. 587–596
63. Adams, pp. 66–67.
64. Ibid, p. 274.
65. Adams, p. 70.
66. Cited in Matthew Wright, *Hawke's Bay — The History of a Province*, Dunmore Press, Palmerston North 1994, p. 24.
67. Binney, 'The Expansion of the Missions', *New Zealand's Heritage*, Vol. I, Part 11, p. 285.
68. Elsmore, p. 75.
69. Burns, p. 27.
70. Cited in Claudia Orange, *The Treaty of Waitangi*, Bridget Williams Books, Wellington 1987, p. 20.
71. Cited in A. H. McLintock, *Crown Colony Government in New Zealand*, Government Print, Wellington 1958, p. 23, n.3.
72. Orange, p. 21.
73. Adams, p. 76.
74. But see Orange, p. 21; also Appendix 2, p. 258.
75. McNab, I, 'Baron de Thierry', pp. 724–728.
76. Adams, p. 79.
77. Cited in McClintock *Crown Colony Government in New Zealand*, p. 25.
78. Cited in ibid, p. 26.
79. Orange, p. 25.
80. Jack Lee, *The Old Land Claims in New Zealand* NHPS, Kerikeri 1993, pp. 33–34.
81. Orange, pp. 24–25.
82. McNab, Vol. I, J. Stephen esq to John Backhouse, 12 December 1838, p. 742.
83. Patricia Burns, *Fatal Success—A History of the New Zealand Company*, Heinemann-Reed, Auckland 1989, p. 133
84. McLintock, *Crown Colony Government in New Zealand*, p. 48.
85. See Orange, pp. 28–29.
86. McNab, Vol. I, Marquess Normanby to Mr Attorney-General, 30 May 1839, p. 740.
87. McLintock, *Crown Colony Government in New Zealand*, p. 48.
88. McNab, Vol. I, G. J. Pennington, Pro-Secretary, to James Stephen, esq., 22 June 1839, pp. 745–46.
89. Argued by McLintock, *Crown Colony Government in New Zealand*, p. 48.
90. McNab, Vol. I, Normanby to Hobson, 15 August 1839, pp. 731, 734.
91. McNab, Vol. I, Marquess Normanby to Captain Hobson, 15 August 1839, p. 731.
92. Ibid, p. 734.
93. Ibid.
94. Ibid, p. 735.
95. McNab, Vol. I, Captain Hobson to the Under Secretary of State, Colonial Department, August 1839, p. 750.
96. McNab, Vol. I.
97. E. Jerningham Wakefield, *Adventure in New Zealand*, ed. Joan Stevens, Golden Press, Auckland, 1975, p. 35.
98. Cited in J. G. Wilson (ed), *History of Hawke's Bay*, A. H. & A. W. Reed, Wellington, 1939 p. 144.
99. McLintock, p. 50
100. Ibid, p. 58, n. 6.
101. WTu MS-Papers-1983, Busby, James, 'Three documents by or relating to James Busby, 1840'.
102. R. M. Ross, 'Te Tiriti Waitangi'. in Judith Binney (ed), *The Shaping of History*, Bridget Williams Books, Wellington 2001, p. 100; see also Orange, p. 40.
103. Michael King, *Nga Iwi Te Motu*, p. 33–34; see also Michael King, *The Penguin History of New Zealand*, p. 160.
104. King, *The Penguin History of New Zealand*, p. 160.
105. Ross, p. 100.
106. Wu-MS-Papers f-76-048 Colenso, William, 1811–1899: letter from

James Busby to William Colenso and other papers, letter by Waka Nene and others (fragment).
107 Vaggioli, p. 96
108 For discussion see Oliver, 'The future behind us', pp. 26-27.
109 Belich, *Making Peoples*, p. 194.
110 Cited in Alan Ward, *A Show of Justice*, ANU Press 1974., p. 88.
111 William Colenso, 'The Authentic and Genuine History of the Signing of the Treaty of Waitangi', Government Print 1890; 'Wednesday, February 5th.'
112 Ibid.
113 Ibid.
114 Ibid.
115 Orange, p. 56
116 William Colenso, 'The Authentic and Genuine History of the Signing of the Treaty of Waitangi', Government Print 1890; 'Wednesday, February 5th.'
117 Ibid.
118 WTu MS Papers 1983 Busby, James Papers 'Three documents by or relating to James Busby, 1840'
119 Orange, p. 53, see also MS Papers 1983 Busby, James Papers 'Three documents by or relating to James Busby, 1840'
120 King, *The Penguin History of New Zealand*, p. 163.
121 WTu MS Papers 1983, Busby, James Papers 'Three documents by or relating to James Busby, 1840'
122 Vaggioli, p. 115.
123 WTu MS-Papers-1611, Colenso, William Papers, 'Memoranda of the Arrival of Lieut. Governor Hobson in New Zealand'. This is the 'first draft' of Colenso's later 'Authentic and Genuine' history and its emendations suggests it was written at or soon after the meeting. Compare 'Authentic', Thursday February 6th.
124 William Colenso, *The Authentic and Genuine History of the Signing of the Treaty of Waitangi*, Government Print 1890; 'Thursday, February 6th.'
125 Claudia Orange, *The Treaty of Waitangi*, Wellington, Bridget Williams Books, Wellington 1987, p 71.
126 Wilson, p. 140.
127 The Waitangi Tribunal were askd by Ahuriri claimants in 1994 to rule that Ngati Kahungunu had signed the Treaty of Waitangi, but were unable to do so because most Ngati Kahungunu had not been signatories. Wai 55 p. 32.
128 William Colenso, 'The Authentic and Genuine History of the Signing of the Treaty of Waitangi', Government Print 1890; 'Wednesday, February 5th.'
129 Argued by Paul Moon, *Hone Heke*, David Ling, Auckland 2001, p. 18.
130 Maning, p. 247.
131 William Colenso, *The Authentic and Genuine History of the Signing of the Treaty of Waitangi*, Government Print 1890; 'Wednesday, February 5th.'
132 Cited in Vaggioli, p. 96.
133 Maning, p. 247.
134 Orange, p. 66.
135 Ibid, p. 67.
136 Maning, p. 243.
137 Ibid, p. 243.
138 Cited in Matthew Wright, *Town and Country*, p. 23.

Chapter Three
1 Philip Temple, *A Sort of Conscience—The Wakefields*, Auckland University Press, Auckland 2002, p. 4
2 Temple, pp. 537–539.
3 Matthew Wright, *Old South*, Penguin, Auckland 2009, pp. 122–123.
4 Noted in Temple, p. 39.
5 *The New Zealand Gazette and Wellington Spectator*, 13 June 1840.
6 Ibid.
7 Ibid.
8 Evison, *Ngai Tahu Deeds*, p. 38.
9 Ward, p. 105.
10 *The New Zealand Gazette and Wellington Spectator*, 13 June 1840.
11 Ibid.
12 Burns, p. 30.
13 Ibid, p. 41.
14 Ibid, pp. 19–21.
15 Cited in ibid, p. 44.
16 John Ward, *Information Relative to New Zealand*.
17 Temple, pp. 226–227.
18 *The New Zealand Gazette*, 21 August 1839. Ward, p. 147, cites £400,000.
19 Listed in *The New Zealand Gazette and Wellington Spectator*, 14 August 1841, p. 4.
20 Burns, p. 107.
21 Ward, p. 149.
22 *The Times*, 27 July 1840, reproduced in Burns p. 146.
23 *New Zealand Gazette*, 21 August 1839.
24 Quoted in Burns, p. 110.
25 Ward, p. 136.
26 Temple, pp. 231–232.
27 Ibid, pp. 242–246
28 Michael King, *Moriori—A People Rediscovered*, Penguin, Auckland, revised edition 2001.
29 Temple, p. 248.
30 Cited in Ward, pp. 118–19.
31 Ibid, p. 120.
32 Clarke, p. 49.
33 E. Jerningham Wakefield, *Adventure in New Zealand*, ed. Joan Stevens, Golden Press, Auckland, 1975, p. 34, footnote.
34 Burns, p. 115.
35 Ward, p. 122.
36 E. Jerningham Wakefield, *Adventure in New Zealand*, p. 35.
37 Temple, p. 252.
38 Wright, *Guns and Utu*, p.175.
39 Temple, p. 253.
40 Reeves, *The Long White Cloud*, p. 142.
41 Wtu MSO-Papers-3730, Wakefield, William 1801–1848, Deeds of Sale of Maori Land, fourth sheet; Matthew Wright, *Two Peoples, One Land*, Reed, Auckland 2006, p. 180.
42 Clarke, *Notes on Early Life in New Zealand*, p. 49.
43 Edward Hopper, cited in Burns, p. 132.
44 E. Jerningham Wakefield, *Adventure in New Zealand*, p. 26.
45 Cited in Caughey, p. 140.
46 Caughey, pp 140–43.
47 *The New Zealand Gazette*, 21 August 1839.
48 Ibid.
49 *New Zealand Gazette*, 13 June 1840.
50 Ibid.
51 Ibid.
52 Matthew Wright, *Old South*, Penguin, Auckland 2009, pp. 72–76.
53 Ibid, Wakefield to Wakefield, 8 January 1842.
54 Ibid, Wakefield to Wakefield 8 April 1842.
55 Nelson Provincial Museum, Qms LET, Petition to Captain Wakefield from the Working Men of Nelson, 14 January 1843.
56 Burns, pp. 237–238.
57 Caughey, pp. 33, 48, 50.
58 NZHA, Plate 31.
59 Burns, pp. 137–143
60 Ibid, p. 155.
61 Cited in the Ngai Tahu Report 1991 p. 257; see also Adams, p. 180.
62 Cited in Adams, p. 184.
63 W. P. Morrell, *The Provincial System in New Zealand, 1852–76*, Whitcombe & Tombs, Wellington 1964, pp. 32–33.
64 T. L. Buck, *New Zealand's First War, the rebellion of Hone*

65. Maning, p. 249.
66. Ibid.
67. Argued by Belich, *The New Zealand Wars*, pp. 31–33
68. Maning, p. 250.
69. Buick, p. 49.
70. Vaggioli, p. 116.
71. Maning, pp. 252–53.
72. Ibid.
73. Buick, p. 74.
74. Vaggioli, p. 122.
75. Buick, p. 79, footnote.
76. Belich, *Wars*, p. 79 cites 140; Buick, p. 117, cites 300.
77. Cited in Buick, p. 147.
78. Maning, p. 339.
79. Vaggioli, p. 129.
80. Maning, p. 343.
81. Chris Pugsley, 'Walking Heke's War', *Defence Quarterly*, No. 4, Autumn 1994, p. 32.
82. Maning, p. 348.
83. Buick, pp. 272.
84. See, e.g. Belich, *Wars*, p. 70; King, *The Penguin History of New Zealand*, p. 185.
85. Cited in Vaggioli, p. 124.
86. Ballara, *Taua*, p. 67.
87. Henry Yule, *Fortification for Officers of the Army and Students of Military History*, William Blackwood, Edinburgh 1851, pp. 80–4.
88. Royal Military College, A Course of Lectures on Fortification, Military Tactics and Perspective; with the attack and defence of fortresses, Royal Military College, Third Edition, London, 1852, p. 45.
89. Yule, p. 4.
90. Tim Ryan and Brian Parham, *The Colonial New Zealand Wars*, p. 87.
91. T. Lindsay Buick, *New Zealand's First War*, Government Printer, Wellington 1926, p. 155.
92. James Cowan, *The Maoris in the Great War: a history of the New Zealand Native Contingent and Pioneer Battalion*, Gallipoli 1915, France and Flanders 1916–1918, Whitcombe & Tombs Ltd, Auckland, 1926, p. 3, http://www.nzetc.org/tm/scholarly/tei-CowMaor-t1-body-d2.html, accessed 8 November 2009; see also David G., Chandler, *Atlas of Military Strategy: the art, theory and practice of war 1618–1878*, Arms and Armour Press, London, 1980, pp. 40–41, 50–51, 140–41.
93. James Cowan, *The New Zealand Wars*, Vol. 1, http://www.nzetc.org/tm/scholarly/tei-Cow01NewZ-c7.html accessed 4 February 2012.
94. James Belich, *The New Zealand Wars*, Penguin, Auckland 1986, p. 52.
95. Ross Calman, *The New Zealand Wars*, Reed, Auckland 2004, p. 29, compare with Belich, pp., 296–298.
96. King Papers, 'New Zealand Natives', in McNab, Vol. I, p. 264.
97. QMS-0160, Berard, Auguste, Report of Captain Berard, 4 July 1844–31 January 1846.
98. Wright, *Guns and Utu*, pp. 100–103.
99. Ibid, pp. 151–153.
100. John Marmon, 'The Life and Adventures of John Marmon', *Auckland Star*, 7 January 1882.
101. Compare Belich, *The New Zealand Wars* pp. 49–52; with Peter Harrington, *English Civil War Fortifications*, Osprey, Oxford 2003, pp. 21–23. Earthern ramparts in the English version took the place of Kawiti's wooden inner fence.
102. Maning, p. 338.
103. *New Zealand Spectator and Cook Strait Guardian*, 18 January 1845.
104. See, e.g. Tom Gibson, *The Maori Wars*, A. H. & A. W. Reed, Wellington 1974.
105. Quoted in McKillop, p. 242.
106. *New Zealand Spectator and Cooks' Strait Guardian*, 19 August 1846.
107. Sinclair, *Maori Times*, p. 184.
108. WTu MS-Papers 1234, Donald McLean, Diary 11 November 1851. My italics.
109. Great Britain Parliamentary Papers Vol. 5, 1846–47, Earl Grey to Governor Grey, 23/12/1846, pp 67–69.
110. AJHR 1890 G1, Sir William Martin, Pamphlet of 1848, p 3.
111. Great Britain Parliamentary Papers, Vol. 6, 1847–1850, Governor Grey to Earl Grey, 15/5/1848, p 24.
112. Ibid.
113. WTu MS-Papers 1286, McLean Diary 8 April 1851 .
114. See, e.g. AJHR 1886 G-1 'Reports from Officers in Native Districts'.
115. See, e.g. AJHR 1858 E-1 'Report of Ahuriri Native Industrial School 1856'.
116. AJHR 1862 E-4 'Report of Inspectors on Native Schools', 'Report on the Te Aute Native Industrial School in the Province of Hawke's Bay', 25 June 1862.
117. Op cit, 'Report from W. R. Baker, esq, on the Waerengaahika (Turanga) School, 6th May 1862.
118. Ann Parsonson, 'The Pursuit of Mana' in W. H. Oliver *The Oxford History of New Zealand*, OUP, Auckland 1981. p. 153.
119. Sutch p. 39.
120. AJHR 1862 C-1 No. 74, Cooper to McLean 20th June 1861.
121. AJHR 1861 E-9 'Minutes of Proceedings of the Kohimarama Conference' p 25
122. A. McKirdy, 'Maori-Pakeha Pakeha Land Transactions in Hawke's Bay 1848–1864,' MA Thesis, VUW 1994, pp 82–83
123. Cited in R. M. Ross 'Te Tiriti o Waitangi', in Judith Binney (ed), *The Shaping of History*, Bridget Williams Books, Wellington 2001, p. 101
124. Hawke's Bay Museum, Resident Magistrate's Letterbook, Domett to Harawera 1 October 1855
125. WTu MS 1234, McLean journal, 30 March 1851.
126. See, e.g. M. P. K. Sorrenson, 'Maori and Pakeha Pakeha' in W. H. Oliver (ed) *The Oxford History of New Zealand*, Oxford, Auckland 1981
127. R. D. Hill 'Pastoralism in the Wairarapa, 1844–53', in R. F. Watters (ed), *Land and Society in New Zealand*, A. H. & A. W. Reed, Wellington 1965, reprint 1967, p. 29; also A. G. Bagnall *Wairarapa: An Historical Excursion*, Masterton 1976, pp 23–24.
128. Bagnall p. 48
129. Hill, pp. 33–34.
130. Bagnall p 84.
131. *Government Gazette of the Province of New Munster*, 9 October 1847.
132. See, e.g. M. P. K. Sorrenson, 'Maori and Pakeha' in W. H. Oliver (ed), *The Oxford History of New Zealand*, Oxford, Auckland 1981, p. 175.
133. Archives New Zealand NM 10/9 Series 10/9, 'Colonial Secretary's Inwards Correspondence, 28 Apr 1848–4 Sep 1848', Domett to Native Secretary 26 September 1848; Domett to Kemp, 12 October 1848.
134. Archives New Zealand NM 10/9 Series 10/9, 'Colonial Secretary's Inwards Correspondence, 28 Apr 1848–4 Sep 1848' Domett to Kemp, 12 October 1848.
135. Archives New Zealand, NM 8/35,

1849/39, 'Colonial Secretary's Inwards Correspondence, 1849', Colenso to Domett, 23 December 1848
136 Archives New Zealand NM 10/9 Series 10/9, 'Colonial Secretary's Inwards Correspondence, 28 Apr 1848–4 Sep 1848', Domett to Colenso, 17 January 1849
137 Colenso Journal entry October 4th 1847, quoted in Wilson p. 247.
138 Archives New Zealand G7/6/61, Te Pohipi, Na Hou and Hoani Waikau to Governor Grey, 12 April 1849, translation and transcript 9.
139 Hawke's Bay Museum, McLean inwards letterbook Vol. 24, Eyre to McLean, 24 September 1849.
140 Hawke's Bay Museum, McLean Inwards Letterbook, transcript, Vol. 24, Fox to Domett, 3 July 1850.
141 Op cit, McLean to Domett [n.d]
142 Archives New Zealand, Series 2/4 'Inwards Despatches from Governor-In-Chief, 24 Jan–23 Dec 1850', Grey to Eyre, 14 September 1850.
143 Archives New Zealand, Series 10/10, 1850/746 'Colonial Secretary's Outwards Correspondence, 1850', S. E. Grimstone to McLean 7 October 1850.
144 Op cit, 14 November 1850.
145 Hawke's Bay Museum McLean Inwards Letterbook Vol. 28, Journal 14 October 1850. This line was omitted from the version published by the Waitangi Tribunal.
146 AJHR 1862 C-1, Enclosure No.1 in No. 6, Te Hapuku to Grey, 3 May 1851.
147 AJHR 1862 C-1,
148 This differs from the assertion in a 1994 background report commissioned by the Waitangi Tribunal. Angela Ballara and Gary Scott, 'Crown Purchases of Land in Early Provincial Hawke's Bay', Waitangi Tribunal Wai 201, January 1994, p. 81.
149 McKirdy, p. 90.
150 Ibid, pp. 4, 90-91.
151 Ray Fargher, *The Best Man Who Ever Served The Crown? A Life of Donald McLean*, Victoria UniversityPress, Wellington 2006, pp. 103–105.
152 Keith Sinclair, *A History of New Zealand*, Penguin, Auckland 1959, revised edition 1988, pp. 119–122.
153 AJHR 1858 C-1 Native Land Purchases; Summary of Purchases Effected from 1st March 1856 to 30th June 1856 and 1st July 1856 to 31st March 1858.
154 Noted in Parsonson, p. 153.
155 Ibid.
156 Matthew Wright, *Town and Country: the history of Hastings and district*, Hastings District Council, Hastings 2000, pp. 40–41.
157 David Thorns and Charles Sedgwick, *Understanding Aotearoa/New Zealand: Historical Statistics*, Dunmore Press, Palmerston North 1997, p. 32.

Chapter Four
1 John Ralston Saul, *Voltaire's Bastards*, Penguin, Canada 1992, pp. 38–76; Eric Hobsbawm, *The Age of Revolution*, Abacus, London 1977.
2 Matthew Wright, *New Zealand's Engineering Heritage*, Reed NZ, Auckland 1999, pp. 2–4.
3 W. Cooke Taylor, 'Notes of a Tour in the Manufacturing Districts of Lancashire', 1842, in B. I. Coleman (ed) *The Idea of the City in Nineteenth Century Britain*, Routledge and Kegan Paul, London 1973, p. 81.
4 Edwin Chadwick, 'Report on the Sanitary Conditions of the Labouring Population of Great Britain', in B. I. Coleman (ed) *The Idea of the City in Nineteenth Century Britain*, pp. 77–81.
5 Tony Simpson, *A Distant Feast*, Godwit, Auckland 1999, p. 39, 49.
6 Eric Hobsbawm, *On History*, Abacus, London 1998, p. 155.
7 McNab, Vol. I, n.d. pp. 41–42; McLintock, *Crown Colony Government in New Zealand*, p. 8
8 'The Goose and the Commons', quoted from http://www.wealthandwant.com/docs/Goose_commons.htm, accessed 15 June 2011.
9 Fagan, pp. 174–180.
10 R. Vaughan, 'The Age of Great Cities', 1843, in B. I. Coleman (ed) *The Idea of the City in Nineteenth Century Britain*, p. 89
11 Smith referred to 'an' not 'the'. Quoted in Bruce Jesson, *Only Their Purpose is Mad*, Dunmore Press, Palmerston North 1999, pp. 26–29.
12 Keith Rankin, 'Approach is orthodox but so is burning witches', *New Zealand Herald*, 2 March 2000.
13 Hobsbawm *On History*, p. 179.
14 Cited in Tony Simpson, *The Immigrants*, Godwit, Auckland 1997, p. 40.
15 David Thomson, *England in the Nineteenth Century*, Penguin, London 1950, p. 77
16 Fagan, p. 179.
17 Argued by Thomson, pp. 80-81.
18 Ian Tattersall, *The Fossil Trail*, Oxford University Press, Oxford 1995, pp. 18–19; also Steven Jay Gould, *Ever Since Darwin*, Penguin, London 1991, pp. 21–45.
19 Cited in David Taylor, *Poverty*, Heinemann Educational, Oxford 1990.
20 Eric Hobsbawm, *On History*, p.130.
21 G. R. Hawke, *Railways and Economic Growth in England And Wales 1840–1870*, Clarendon Press, Oxford 1970, pp. 363–366.
22 See Mark Blaug, *Great Economists Before Keynes*, Wheatsheaf Books, Brighton, 1986.
23 Simpson, *The Immigrants*, pp. 41–43.
24 Miles Fairburn, *The Ideal Society and Its Enemies*, Auckland University Press, Auckland 1989, pp. 26-27.
25 Rodger D. Win, *Who Ploughed So Well*, private publication, Nelson 1996.
26 Thorns and Sedgwick, p. 33.
27 Ibid, p. 37.
28 AJHR 1863, D-6, 'The Otago Gold Fields' p. 10.
29 Rollo Arnold, *The Farthest Promised Land*, Victoria University Press and Price Milburn, Wellington 1981, pp. 18–19.
30 NZEH, Plate 49.
31 Ibid.
32 F. W. Campbell, 'Early Days in New Zealand', Noble-Campbell Papers.
33 WTU MS-Papers-3779–1/2, Hay Family: Papers, Letters from William and Mary Hay, William Hay to his mother, August 13, 1865.
34 F. W. Campbell, 'Early Days in New Zealand', Noble-Campbell Papers.
35 Matthew Wright, *Havelock North — The History of a Village*, HDC, Hastings 2001, p. 44.
36 Simpson, *A Distant Feast*, p. 66.
37 WTu MS-Papers-4328, Hamilton, Francis William, 1840–1901: Outward letters, letter to Mr J. Morton, 7 January 1862.
38 Havelock North Public Library,

39. Charlotte Godley, *Letters from Early New Zealand*, Whitcombe and Tombs, Auckland 1951 p. 8.
40. Havelock North Public Library, A/397/1879, William Rainbow, diary, 6 January 1880.
41. Ibid, 11 January 1880.
42. Godley, p. 1.
43. Havelock North Public Library, A/397/1879, William Rainbow, diary, 8 January 1880.
44. Ibid, 12 January 1880.
45. Ibid, 6 February 1880.
46. Godley, p. 7.
47. WTu MS-0667, Davie, Cyrus Papers, 'Journal of a voyage on board the Sir George Seymour and Randolph of 850 tons from Plymouth to Port Victoria, New Zealand.'
48. Godley, p. 8.
49. Cited in Simpson, *A Distant Feast*, p. 65.
50. Havelock North Public Library, A/397/1879, William Rainbow, diary, 31 December 1879.
51. Godley, p. 3.
52. Ibid, p. 3.
53. Ibid, p. 13.
54. Godley, p. 61. Godley was referring to a railway magnate.
55. *Hawke's Bay Herald* 10 and 12 March 1868.
56. Charlotte Macdonald, *A Woman of Good Character*, Allen and Unwin/Historical Branch, Wellington 1990, table p. 49.
57. Calculated from M. F. Lloyd Prichard, *An Economic History of New Zealand to 1939*, Collins, Auckland 1970, p. 60
58. Lloyd-Prichard, p. 63.
59. Thorns and Sedgwick, pp. 61–62. See also Lloyd-Prichard, p. 100.
60. Hocken MS-0079, Courage, Sarah Amelia, 'Lights and Shadows of Colonial Life'.
61. Cited in Alison Drummond and L. R. Drummond, *At Home in New Zealand*, p. 32.
62. Frances Porter, *Born to New Zealand, a biography of Jane Maria Atkinson*, Bridget Williams Books, Wellington 1995, p.
63. WTu MS-Papers-3205, Rose, Conway Lucas, fl. 1851–1853, letters to his sister Issie about life in the Canterbury settlement, letter 25 March 1852.
64. Macdonald, p. 124
65. Cited in Drummond, p. 158.
66. Claire Toynbee, 'Class and Social Structure in Nineteenth Century New Zealand' and Tom Brooking, 'Commentaries', in D. A. Hamer (ed) *New Zealand Social History, Papers from the Turnbull Conference on New Zealand Social History, 1978*, University of Auckland, Auckland 1978.
67. Erik Olssen, *Building the New World, work, politics and society in Caversham, 1880s-1920s*, AUP, Auckland 1995, pp. 8–11.
68. Claire Toynbee, 'Class and social structure in nineteenth century New Zealand' in D.A. Hamer (ed), *New Zealand Social History, Papers from the Turnbull Conference on New Zealand Social History, 1978*, University of Auckland, Auckland 1978.
69. Matthew Wright, *Town and Country* p. 241, also D. P. Balfour, 'His Life, By Himself'.
70. Matthew Wright, *Hawke's Bay—The History of a Province* esp. Chs 4–5.
71. Stevan Eldred-Grigg, *A Southern Gentry*, p. 105.
72. Noted in John. E. Martin, *The Forgotten Worker*, Allen and Unwin, Wellington 1990, p. 10.
73. Cited in King, *The Penguin History of New Zealand*, p. 225.
74. Hill, p. 34.
75. Ibid, p. 41.
76. Ibid, p. 43.
77. WTu MS-Papers-3520, Smith, Hector William Pope, 1837–1878, Extracts from journal
78. For details see Matthew Wright, *Old South*, pp. 151–157.
79. McLintock, Vol. 3, p. 113.
80. Cited in Cherry A. Hankin, *Life in a Young Colony*, Whitcoulls, Christchurch, 1981, p. 78.
81. Ibid, p. 81.
82. Lloyd-Prichard, p. 84
83. Thorns and Sedgwick, p. 61.
84. Cited in Martin, p. 12.
85. Ibid, p. 101.
86. *Hawke's Bay Herald*, 11 April 1876.
87. Martin, p. 13.
88. McLintock, Vol. 2, p. 716.
89. Belich, *Making Peoples*, p. 397.
90. Cited in Drummond, p. 150.
91. Alison Drummond and L. R. Drummond, *At Home in New Zealand — an illustrated history of everyday things before 1865*, Blackwood and Janet Paul, Auckland 1967, p. 127
92. Notably Sir Keith Holyoake, see Ken Comber 'Personal reflections on my father in law', in Margaret Clark (ed) *Sir Keith Holyoake, Towards a Political Biography*, Dunmore Press, Palmerston North, 1997, esp. pp. 21, 23.
93. *Otago Witness*, 17 October 1874.
94. Eldred-Grigg, *A Southern Gentry*, A. H. & A. W. Reed, Wellington 1980, pp. 119–120; see also David Thomson, *A World Without Welfare, New Zealand's Colonial Experiment*, Auckland University Press/Bridget Williams Books, Wellington 1998, p. 69.
95. *Hawke's Bay Herald*, 30 December 1892.
96. Ibid.
97. Hawke's Bay Museum, D. P. Balfour, *His Life, By Himself*, typescript.
98. Eldred-Grigg, *A Southern Gentry*, pp. 87–88.
99. *Hawke's Bay Herald*, 27 October 1876.
100. Matthew Wright, *Town and Country*, HDC, Hastings 2001, pp. 178–179.
101. Eldred-Grigg, *A Southern Gentry*, p. 85
102. For a description of the British ethos see Leonore Davidoff and Catherine Hall, 'The architecture of public and private life, English middle class society in a provincial town, 1780 to 1850', in Derek Fraser and A. Sutcliffe (eds), *The Pursuit of Urban History*, Edward Arnold, London 1983.
103. Eldred-Grigg, *A Southern Gentry*, p. 98.
104. Campbell, p. 15.
105. Eldred-Grigg, *A Southern Gentry*, p. 99.
106. A. H. McLintock, *An Encyclopaedia of New Zealand*, Vol. 1, p. 322.
107. McLintock (ed), Vol. 1., p. 688.
108. Cited in Hankin, pp. 132–133.
109. *Hawke's Bay Herald*, 19 December 1892.
110. Eldred-Grigg, *A Southern Gentry*, p. 104.
111. Matthew Wright, *Hawke's Bay, The History of a Province*, p. 42
112. Matthew Wright, *Town and Country*, p. 92.
113. WTu MS Papers 1635-05 Monro, David (Sir), Papers. Statements of assets and monies owing.
114. David Thomson, *A World Without Welfare, New Zealand's Colonial Experiment*, Auckland University Press/Bridget Williams Books, Wellington 1998, p. 69.
115. *Hawke's Bay Herald*, 27 October 1876.
116. Guthrie-Smith, p. 139
117. Guy H. Scholefield (ed), *The*

Richmond-Atkinson Papers, II p. 341
118 Ibid, p.141
119 P. R. Stephens, 'The Age of the Great Sheep Runs' in Watters (ed), p. 58.
120 *Hawke's Bay Herald*, 17 September 1880.
121 Stephens, p. 56
122 WTu MS-Papers-4328, Hamilton, Francis William, 1840–1901: Outward letters, letter to Mr J. Morton, 13 November 1861. £65 in 1861 money translates to about $13,000 in early 21st-century dollars.
123 Guthrie-Smith, p. 157
124 Ibid.
125 WTu MS-Papers-4328, Hamilton, Francis William, 1840–1901: Outward letters, letter to his sister 30 January 1862.
126 *Daily Telegraph* 15 March 1877
127 Matthew Wright, *Town and Country*, p. 59, 98.
128 McLintock, Vol. 2, p. 27.
129 Cited in Martin, p.12.
130 Matthew Wright, *Town and Country*, p. 235
131 Cited in Hankin, p. 228.
132 Martin, p. 21.
133 Lloyd-Prichard, p. 63
134 WTu MS-Papers-3895-06 Haslam family: family papers, Typed transcripts of the letters from Sarah Ann Self (Haslam), letter 26 January 1863.
135 Op cit, 4 February 1864.
136 Lloyd-Prichard, p. 60.
137 Martin, p. 15.
138 Matthew Wright, *Havelock North—The History of a Village*, p. 45.
139 Martin, p. 144.
140 John E. Martin, *The Forgotten Worker*, p. 99 provides a useful diagram.
141 Cited in Hankey, p. 113.
142 Eldred-Grigg, *A Southern Gentry*, p. 101.
143 Cited in Oliver (ed), *The Oxford History of New Zealand*, p. 136.
144 Thorns and Sedgwick, p. 54.
145 Martin, p., 21.
146 David Hamer, 'Towns in Nineteenth Century New Zealand' in D. A. Hamer (ed), *New Zealand Social History, Papers from the Turnbull Conference on New Zealand Social History, 1978*, University of Auckland, Auckland 1978, pp. 16–17.
147 *Hawke's Bay Herald* 31/05/1889
148 Giselle Byrnes, *Boundary Markers*, Bridget Williams Books, Wellington 2001, p. 50.
149 Cited in ibid, p. 55.
150 See Asa Briggs, *Victorian Cities*, Pelican, London 1968, p. 135, for a discussion of middle-class association between dirt, poor and nature.
151 Harding, p. 9.
152 Cited in Briggs, p. 26.
153 Byrnes, pp. 55–56.
154 Archives New Zealand, LS Misc 2044 Samuel Cobham Wellington street plan.
155 Byrnes, p. 82.
156 Matthew Wright, *Havelock North—The History of a Village*, HDC, Hastings 1996, p. 22.
157 Simpson, *A Distant Feast*, pp. 70–71.
158 See Matthew Wright, *Havelock North—The History of a Village*.
159 Eric Hobsbawm, *On History*, Abacus, London 1998, pp. 97–98. See also, Peter Laslett, *Family Life and Illicit Love in Earlier Generations*, Cambridge University Press, Cambridge 1977, pp. 102–155.
160 See Fairburn, pp. 213–214, 225.
161 Ibid, pp. 10–11, pp. 191–233.
162 Fairburn, 'Local Community or Atomized Society', p. 243.
163 Caroline Daley, 'Taradale Meets the Ideal Society and its Enemies', in Binney (ed), pp. 267–282, p. 282.
164 Calculated from Thorns & Sedgwick, p. 40.
165 Stevan Eldred-Grigg, *Pleasures of the Flesh*, A. H. & A. W. Reed, Wellington 1984, p 24
166 Population Census 1891, Part V, Conjugal Condition of the People.
167 Population Census 1881, Part III, Conjugal Condition of the People.
168 Stevan Eldred-Grigg, *Pleasures of the Flesh*, p. 12
169 Macdonald, Table 1.1, p. 21.
170 Ibid.
171 Eldred-Grigg, *Pleasures of the Flesh*, p 24
172 Macdonald, Table 2.8, p. 68.
173 Cited in Hankin, p. 225.
174 Cited in Macdonald, p. 140.
175 *New Zealand Times*, 5 July 1877; also cited in Fairburn *The Ideal Society and Its Enemies*, p. 217.
176 Duncan Mackay, 'The Orderly Frontier', in Binney (ed), pp. 257–265.
177 Hawke's Bay Museum, Extracts from the Diary of C. C. Weston, 10-30 April 1888.
178 David Balfour, *His Life, by Himself*, typescript.
179 Ibid.

Chapter Five
1 Hawke's Bay Museum, McLean Papers, typescript Vol. 15, A. Alexander to McLean, 7 January 1858.
2 Op cit, Vol. 12, Domett to McLean, 12 July 1854.
3 Op cit, T. H. Fitzgerald to McLean, 14 December 1858.
4 Sinclair, p. 109.
5 Matthew Wright, *New Zealand's Engineering Heritage*, Reed, Auckland 1999, pp. 12–14.
6 Matthew Wright, *Hawke's Bay— The History of a Province*, pp. 72–73.
7 Sorrenson, 'Maori and Pakeha', in W. H. Oliver (ed) *The Oxford History of New Zealand*, Oxford University Press, Oxford 1981, reprinted 1991, p. 180.
8 AJHR C-1, 1862, The District Commissioner to the Chief Commissioner, 29 November 1856.
9 Sorrenson, 'Maori and Pakeha ', p. 180.
10 Parsonson, p. 156.
11 AJHR 1862 C-1 No. 43, Cooper to McLean, 29 July 1858
12 Vaggioli, p. 169.
13 AJHR 1862 C-1 Nol. 67, Cooper to McLean, 12 March 1860.
14 AJHR 1860 E-2, Extract from Sub-Protector Clarke's Report to the Chief Protector, 29 June 1844, p. 11.
15 Op cit, 'Report from District Commissioner Cooper, 8 August 1854'.
16 Op cit, 'Report from Native Secretary, 27 January 1855'
17 Op cit, 'Proclamation by the Governor, 12 February 1858'.
18 Sinclair, p. 124.
19 Ibid, p. 125.
20 Belich, *Wars*, esp. p. 298.
21 Compare Belich with, e.g. Pugsley, 'Walking Heke's War', p. 33; see also Matthew Wright *Two Peoples, One Land*, Reed, Auckland 2006, general thesis of book.
22 Tim Ryan and Bill Parham, *The Colonial New Zealand Wars*, Grantham House, Wellington 1986, pp. 39–48; Belich, *Wars*, pp. 109–112.
23 Wright, *Two Peoples, One Land*, p. 111.
24 Ibid, pp. 128–129.
25 Prickett, *Landscapes*, pp. 81–84.
26 Wright, Two Peoples, One Land, pp. 140–141.

27. Byron Farwell, *Queen Victoria's Little Wars*, Allen Lane, London 1973, p. 163.
28. Ibid, p. 170–171.
29. AJHR 1864 E-3 'Further Papers Relative to the Native Insurrection', Enclosure in No. 24, 'Account of Wiremu Nero's Visit to Maungatautari'.
30. See, e.g. Farwell pp. 160–161,
31. AJHR 1874 E-2, 'Further Papers relative to peace and confiscation of native lands', Te Waharoa Tamihana to Pompallier, Enclosure in No.1 and Memorandum by the Governor. Two different translations of the letter were published.
32. *New Zealand Herald*, 6 April 1864.
33. AJHR 1864 E-3 'Further Papers Relative to the Native Insurrection', Lieutenant-General Cameron to His Excellency Sir George Grey, 5 May 1864.
34. *New Zealand Herald*, 2 May 1864.
35. Matthew Wright, *Two Peoples, One Land*, Reed, Auckland 2006, p. 145.
36. Belich, *Wars*, pp. 185–186.
37. Belich, *Wars*, p. 297.
38. See, e.g. Wright, *Shattered Glory*, pp. 210–212.
39. Wright, *Two Peoples, One Land*, p. 147.
40. Cited in Lloyd-Prichard, p. 109.
41. Lloyd-Prichard p. 87.
42. Ibid, p. 119.
43. Matthew Wright, *Town and Country*, p. 178.
44. Thomson, *A World Without Welfare*, p. 69.
45. P. R. Stephens, 'The Age of the Great Sheep Runs' in Watters (ed), *Land and Society in New Zealand*, A. H. & A. W. Reed, Wellington 1965, reprint 1967, p. 60.
46. Cited in Lloyd-Prichard, p. 77.
47. Ibid, p. 108.
48. Ibid, p. 101.
49. Ibid, p. 102.
50. Ibid, p. 108.
51. Ibid, p. 113.
52. James Belich, *Paradise Reforged*, Allen Lane, Auckland 2001, pp. 54–55.
53. AJHR 1863, D-6, 'The Otago Gold Fields', p. 8.
54. Cited in Lloyd-Prichard, p. 116.
55. Ibid, p. 115.
56. James Forrest, 'Otago During the Goldrushes', in Watters (ed), p. 83.
57. AJHR 1863, D-6, 'The Otago Gold Fields', Vincent Pyke, esq. to the Superintendent of Otago, p. 2.
58. Ibid.
59. Ibid.
60. Ibid, citing Read to Richardson, 4 June 1861.
61. Ibid.
62. AJHR 1863, D-6, 'The Otago Gold Fields', p. 10. See also Forrest, Table 1, p. 86.
63. Op cit, Vincent Pyke to he Superintendent of Otago, p. 3.
64. Op cit, pp. 10–11. See also in Forrest, Table 1, p. 86.
65. Ibid, p. 84.
66. Sinclair, p. 107.
67. Cited in Lloyd-Prichard, p. 84.
68. Forrest, p. 98.
69. AJHR 1863, D-6, 'The Otago Gold Fields', p. 13.
70. Ibid, p. 8.
71. AJHR 1866, D-11, 'Return showing the amount of gold exported from the various ports in the colony for the year commencing on 1st April 1865, and ending the 31st March 1866.
72. See W. B. Sutch *Colony or Nation?* pp. 3–34; W. J. Gardner, 'A Colonial Economy' from W. H. Oliver & B. R. Williams (eds) *The Oxford History of New Zealand* pp. 57–86; and Brian Easton 'Three New Zealand DepressionDepressions' from W. E. Willmot (ed) *New Zealand and the World*, University of Canterbury, Christchurch 1980.
73. *Hawke's Bay Herald*, 24 March 1868.
74. WTu Micro-MS-0425, Maunder, George, Letters written from Hawke's Bay to his sister Jane, and to his mother.
75. Elsmore, esp. pp. 87–90.
76. See, e.g. Paul Clark, *Hauhau, The Pai Marire Search for Maori Identity*, Auckland University Press, Auckland 1975.
77. AJHR 1864 E-6 'Papers Relative to the Pai Marire Religion, etc', Lieutenant-Colonel Logan to the Assistant Military Secretary, 2 July 1864, and enclosures.
78. AJHR 1865 E-5 'Papers Relative to the murder of the Rev. Carl Sylvius Volkner by the Hau Hau Fanatics', Extract of a letter from Miss Wallace, 21 February 1865.
79. Prickett, *Landscapes*, p. 114.
80. Matthew Wright, *Town and Country*, pp. 71–72.
81. Belich, *Wars*, p. 210; Richard Boast, 'Esk Forest Claim: Report on the Mohaka-Waikare confiscation', p. 43.
82. Matthew Wright, *Town and Country*, pp. 71–72.
83. AJHR 1867 A-1a, sub-enclosure 1 to Enclosure in No. 30, McLean to Stafford, 9 October 1866.
84. Ibid.
85. Belich, *Wars*, pp. 254–255; compare Wright, *Two Peoples, One Land*, pp. 194–195.
86. Wright, *Two Peoples, One Land*, pp. 216–217.
87. Maurice Gee's novel *Season of the Jew* gives an excellent, if fictionalised, account of Te Kooti.
88. For more details see Wright *History of a Province,* Ch 6.
89. Balfour, *His Life, By Himself*, typescript, p. 84.
90. Reported in the *Hawke's Bay Herald*, 16 September 1868.
91. *Hawke's Bay Herald*, December 1868.
92. Ibid, p. 84.
93. WTu MS-Papers-MS-Papers-0069-049, Copy of journal of the capture of the Ngatapa by A. Kempthorne. See also Matthew Wright 'Pressure on Whitmore for victory in the east', *Daily Telegraph*, 3 September 1998.
94. For further details see Whitmore, pp. 79–88, Belich, pp. 258–67.
95. Balfour, *His Life, By Himself*, typescript.
96. Judith Binney *Redemption Songs*, Bridget Williams Books, Wellington 1995, p. 160
97. Whitmore p. 187.
98. Quoted in the W. H. Oliver and Claudia Orange (eds), *The Dictionary of New Zealand Biography*, Vol. I, BWB, Wellington 1997, p. 325.
99. *Hawke's Bay Herald*, 12 October 1869.
100. Whitmore p. 189.
101. Ibid, p. 191.
102. Sinclair, p. 153.
103. Ibid, p. 153, citing R. M. Burdon.
104. AJHR 1867 F4 'Railway Gauge Committee'.
105. AJHR 1885 D6 'The North Island Trunk Railway' p. 3; Matthew Wright *New Zealand's Engineering Heritage*, p. 38.
106. *Supplement to the New Zealand Gazette* No. 48, 'The Railways Act 1870', 13 September 1870.
107. AJHR 1874 E-8 Appendices to the Public Works Statement 1874, Appendix A.
108. AJHR 1879 E-1 Appendix M 'Annual Report on Working Railways by the Commissioner of Railways for the Middle Island'.
109. AJHR 1879 E-1 Appendix L, 'Annual Report on Working Railways by the Commissioner of

Railways, North Island'.
110 Calculated from AJHR 1879 E-1 Appendix L, 'Annual Report on Working Railways by the Commissioner of Railways, North Island', Tables 1 and 2.
111 Thorns and Sedgwick, p. 33.
112 Ibid, p. 37.
113 Arnold, *The Farthest Promised Land*, p. 18.
114 Ibid, p. 103.
115 M. Wynn Papers, 'Pratly, Pratley and Prattley Reunion, Timaru, 15 May 1993', see also Arnold *The Farthest Promised Land*, p. 128. Privately held Pratley family records indicate these events took place in 1873, not 1874 as implied by Arnold.
116 M. Wynn Papers, 'Pratly, Pratley and Prattley Reunion, Timaru, 15 May 1993', see also Arnold *The Farthest Promised Land*, p. 128.
117 Arnold, p. 162.
118 Ibid, p. 220–223.
119 AJHR 1874 D-2, 'Immigration to New Zealand', Hon. J. Vogel to the Agent General, 22 October 1873.
120 Op cit, Commissioner's Report on ship *Salisbury*, 26 January 1874.
121 Op cit, Commissioner's Report on ship *St. Leonards*, 28 September 1873.
122 Op cit, Commissioner's Report on ship *Brerar*, 4 September 1873.
123 Op cit, Commissioner's Report on ship *Helen Denny*, 27 November 1873.
124 Op cit, Memorandum by Mr Diver for Mr Haughton, enclosure in Hon. J. Vogel to Agent-General, 6 February 1874.
125 Op cit, Commissioner's Report on ship *Columbus*, 18 September 1873.
126 Op cit, His Honor J. D. Ormond to the Hon J. Vogel, 9 December 1873.
127 Op cit, Commissioner's Report on ship *Star of India*, enclosure in Hon. J. Vogel to Agent-General, 6 February 1874.
128 Op cit, Hon. J. Vogel to Agent-General, 6 February 1874.
129 Op cit, Report by Immigration Commissioners on Ship *Woodlark*, 6 April 1874.
130 Op cit, Hon J. Vogel to His Honor the Superintendent, Otago, 12 March 1874, and enclosures.
131 Matthew Wright, *Hawke's Bay—The History of a Province*, p. 106.
132 G. C. Petersen, *Pioneering the North Island Bush*, in Watters, p. 66.
133 Scholefield, 1904, cited in Petersen, p. 73.
134 Ibid, p. 73.
135 J. G. Wilson, *The History of Umutaoroa 1896–1956*, Dannevirke Publishing Company Ltd, Dannevirke, 1956.
136 Petersen, p. 77.
137 AJHR 1884, D-1, 'Return of immigration from 1st July 1883 to 30th June 1884, Nationalities of Immigrants'.

Chapter Six
1 Sinclair, *A History of New Zealand*, p. 172.
2 See, e.g. *New Zealand's Heritage*, Vol. 5., Part 56, introduction. Keith Sinclair, *A History of New Zealand*, p. 172.
3 Lloyd-Prichard, p. 156.
4 Ibid, Table 11 (Appendix), p. 408.
5 Thorns and Sedgwick, p. 64.
6 Ibid, p. 64.
7 Ibid, p. 113.
8 Ibid, p. 108.
9 *New Zealand Herald*, 3 January 1884.
10 Matthew Wright, *Town and Country*, pp. 178–180.
11 Thomson, p. 22.
12 See, e.g. R. J. Morris 'Voluntary Societies and British Urban Elites, 1780–1850', *Historical Journal*, Vol. 26 No.1, March 1983.
13 Thomson, pp. 21–28.
14 Thomson, p. 85.
15 Matthew Wright, *Hawke's Bay—The History of a Province*, p. 120.
16 Thomson, p. 94.
17 Ibid, pp. 29-31.
18 Judith Bassett, 'The Exodus', *New Zealand's Heritage*, Paul Hamlyn, Auckland 1971, Part 54, pp. 1506.
19 Cited in Martin, p. 44.
20 Hawke's Bay Museum, Extracts from the Diary of E. C. Weston, 10-30 April 1888.
21 AJHR 1885 D-6, 'The North Island Trunk Railway', p. 3.
22 *Hawke's Bay Herald*, 15 and 16 June 1882.
23 AJHR 1883 D-1 p 38. Te Kooti had taken refuge in the King Country in the early 1870s.
24 AJHR 1885, D-6, 'The North Island Trunk Railway', p. 2.
25 Ibid.
26 G. S. Cooper to Donald McLean, 12 March 1860, AJHR 1862 C-1.
27 King, *The Penguin History of New Zealand*, pp. 251–256.
28 NZPD 1885.
29 AJHR 1871 A-2a, 'Memorandum on the Operation of the Native Lands Court by Sir William Martin'.
30 AJHR 1873 G-7, 'Report of the Hawke's Bay Native Lands Alienation Commission', p.18.
31 *Hawke's Bay Herald*, 15 January 1877.
32 Matthew Wright, *Town and Country*, pp. 50–53
33 AJHR 1867 A-15, 'Report by Mr G. S. Cooper on the subject of native lands in the province of Hawke's Bay', G. S. Cooper to J. C. Richmond, 14 August 1867.
34 Matthew Wright, 'Hawke's Bay was home of land rings', *Daily Telegraph*, 18 June 1994
35 AJHR 1873 G-7, 'Report of the Hawke's Bay Native Lands Alienation Commission', p. 18.
36 Ibid.
37 Ibid, p. 19
38 AJHR 1874, G-2, Resident Magistrate Richard Woon to Native Under-Secretary, 16 June 1874.
39 Matthew Wright, *Town and Country*, pp. 84-86, 91-95.
40 AJHR 1878 G-1, 'Reports from Officers in Native Districts', RM Richard Woon to Native Under-Secretary, 28 May 1878.
41 AJHR 1879, G-1, 'Reports from Officers in Native Districts', RM Richard Woon to Native Under-Secretary, 24 May 1879.
42 For example, see the expenses account of Te Meihana Takihi in AJHR 1873 G-7 Appendix 3 p. 162
43 Phil Briggs, *Looking at the numbers, a view of New Zealand's economic history*, New Zealand Institute of Economic Research, Wellington 2003, p. 43
44 See, e.g. Keith Sinclair, 'The Liberals Come to Power' in *New Zealand's Heritage*, Vol. 5, Part 56; Sinclair, *A History of New Zealand*, pp. 172–188.
45 Len Richardson 'Parties and political change' in W. H. Oliver (ed) *The Oxford History of New Zealand*, Oxford University Press, Auckland, 1981, reprinted 1991, p. 205
46 *New Zealand Herald*, 6 October 1890.
47 Ibid.
48 *New Zealand Herald*, 4 September 1893.
49 Lloyd-Prichard, pp. 175–177.
50 King, *The Penguin History of New Zealand*, p. 265.
51 See Patricia Grimshaw, *Women's Suffrage in New Zealand*,

52. *New Zealand Herald*, 6 October 1890.
53. Micro-MS-0425, George Maunder, Letters written from Hawke's Bay to his sister Jane, and to his mother.
54. *Grey River Argus*, 12 March 1885.
55. *Otago Witness*, 31 December 1896.
56. Ibid, 14 May 1886.
57. Ibid.
58. Noted in Grimshaw, p. 37
59. Quoted in ibid, p. 42.
60. Ibid, pp. 41–44.
61. Quoted in Grimshaw, p. 46.
62. *New Zealand Herald*, 4 September 1893.
63. *New Zealand Herald*, 11 September 1893.
64. *New Zealand Herald*, 20 September 1893.
65. *New Zealand Herald*, 11 September 1893.
66. *New Zealand Herald*, 20 September 1893.
67. Matthew Wright, *Town and Country*, pp. 255-256.
68. Reproduced in *New Zealand's Heritage*, Vol. 58, pp. 1608–1609.
69. See Chapter 8.
70. Sinclair, *A History of New Zealand*, p. 171.
71. *Hawke's Bay Herald*, 4 July 1891.
72. Richardson, 'Parties and Political Change', p. 201
73. Eldred-Grigg, *A Southern Gentry*, pp. 132-33.
74. Len Richardson and W. David McIntyre (eds) *Provincial Perspectives*, University of Canterbury, Christchurch 1980, p. 200.
75. Richardson 'Parties and Political Change', pp. 200-201.
76. £60,000 was equivalent to around $11 million in early 21st century money.
77. Lloyd-Prichard, p. 138.
78. Ibid, p. 194.
79. Ibid
80. Ibid
81. Tom Brooking '"Bursting up" the Greatest Estate of All' in Binney (ed),*The Shaping of History*, Bridget Williams Books, Wellington 2001, p. 167.
82. Ibid, p. 213.
83. Guthrie-Smith, p. 401.
84. Author collection, Lands & Survey Auction Map 12/10/05.
85. Lloyd-Prichard, p. 146.
86. Ibid.
87. Joan Burnett 'The Impact of Dairying on the Landscape of Lowland Taranaki', in R. F. Watters (ed), *Land and Society in New Zealand*, A. H. & A. W. Reed, Wellington 1965, reprint 1967, pp. 101–119, esp. p. 104.
88. Michael King *Nga Iwi o Te Motu*, p. 61.
89. Eldred-Grigg, *A Southern Gentry*, p. 115.
90. Douglas MacLean changed the spelling of his surname; his father was Donald McLean.
91. Eldred-Grigg, *A Southern Gentry*, p. 115.
92. *Hawke's Bay Herald*, 4 April 1894.
93. Eldred-Grigg, p. 161.
94. Ibid, p. 171.
95. Matthew Wright, *New Zealand's Engineering Heritage*, Reed, Auckland 1999, pp. 57–59; *Hawke's Bay Herald*, 29 December 1892.
96. Matthew Wright, *Town and Country*, p. 307.
97. Cited in ibid, p. 308.
98. Eldred-Grigg, *A Southern Gentry*, p. 162.
99. *Hawke's Bay Herald*, 19 December 1892.
100. *Hawke's Bay Herald*, 17 March 1897.
101. Eldred-Grigg, *A Southern Gentry*, p. 151.
102. Ibid, p. 167.
103. WTu MS Cha 1911, letter from John Chambers to directors of the *Hawke's Bay Tribune* 23/1/1911.
104. Ibid
105. Ibid
106. Ibid
107. Matthew Wright, *Town and Country*, p. 285.
108. *New Zealand Herald*, 22 September 1890.
109. Olssen, p. 257.
110. *New Zealand Herald*, 4 November 1890.
111. Not to be confused with his son John Chambers (1854–1946).
112. Quoted in S. Grant *In Other Days—A History of the Chambers Family of Te Mata, Havelock North*, CHB Printers, Waipukurau 1980, p. 54.
113. *Hawke's Bay Herald* 7 September 1885
114. Lloyd-Prichard, pp. 162-63.
115. *Hawke's Bay Herald,* 2 September 1882 and 20 October 1882.
116. W. Nelson 'The Tomoana Freezing Works' in *Hastings, The Hub of Hawke's Bay, New Zealand.*
117. Ibid.
118. Matthew Wright *New Zealand's Engineering Heritage*, Reed, Auckland 1999, p. 73.
119. Ibid, p. 132.
120. Burnett 'The Impact of Dairying on the Landscape of Lowland Taranaki', pp. 101–119, esp. p. 104.
121. Cited in Lloyd-Prichard, p. 113.
122. *New Zealand Herald*, 4 November 1890.
123. See figures in Lloyd-Prichard, p. 204.
124. See figures in ibid, p. 209. The term 'trend' excludes atypical data spikes.
125. See figures in ibid, p. 204.
126. See figures in ibid, p. 291.
127. See figures in ibid, p. 293.
128. Matthew Wright 'Australia, New Zealand and Imperial Naval Defence', MA Thesis, Massey University 1986.
129. See, e.g. F. L. W. Wood *New Zealand In<cap?> the World*, Department of Internal Affairs, Wellington 1940, p. 91.
130. Brian Easton, 'Beyond the Cringe', *New Zealand Listener*, 20 October 2001.
131. Belich, *Paradise Reforged*, p. 30.
132. Matthew Wright, 'Australia, New Zealand and Imperial Naval Defence', MA Thesis, Massey University 1986; Matthew Wright, 'Sir Joseph Ward and New Zealand Naval Defence, 1907–13', *Political Science*, Vol. 41, No. 1, July 1989. See also Matthew Wright, *Blue Water Kiwis*, Reed, Auckland 2001, esp. Ch 1.
133. See, e.g. James Morris *Pax Britannica*, Faber and Faber, London 1968, p. 404.
134. Cited in ibid, p. 118.
135. Ibid, p. 404.
136. Farwell, pp. 339-353.
137. Laurie Barber, *A Short History of New Zealand*, Century Hutchinson, Auckland 1981, p. 79.
138. Barber, p. 81.
139. Morris, p. 115.
140. Glynn Barratt, *Russophobia in New Zealand*, Dunmore Press, Palmerston North 1981, p 78.
141. Wright, *Blue Water Kiwis*, Reed, Auckland 2001, pp. 11–12.
142. *New Zealand Herald* 17 March 1885
143. AJHR 1885 A-6, 'Naval Defence of the Colony'
144. *New Zealand Statutes 1887*, 51 Vict, pp 129–31.
145. New Zealand Parliamentary Debates (NZPD) 1909 Vol. 148 p. 809.
146. Wood, *New Zealand in the World*,

147 Ibid, p. 91.
148 Matthew Wright, *Blue Water Kiwis*, Reed, Auckland 2001, p. 19.
149 F. L. W. Wood, 'Why did New Zealand not join the Australian Commonwealth in 1900–1901', *New Zealand Journal of History* Vol. 2, No. 2, October 1968, pp. 115–129.
150 Argued by Wood 'Why did New Zealand not join the Australian Commonwealth in 1900–1901', p. 127.
151 R. M. Burdon *The New Dominion*, A. H. & A. W. Reed, Auckland, 1965, p. 3.
152 A. R. Barclay 'The Premier and his troubles', Pamphlet, S. Lister, Printer, Dunedin 1909, p. 11.
153 Neville Meaney *The Search for Security in the Pacific* I, Sydney University Press, Sydney 1976, p. 177.
154 F. L. W. Wood *New Zealand In the World*, Department of Internal Affairs, Wellington, 1940, pp. 82-85.
155 R. A. Loughmann, *Life of Sir Joseph Ward*, New Century Press, Wellington 1929, pp 50, 145-46.
156 CD 3523 'Minutes of the Proceedings of the Colonial Conference, 1907', pp 134-36, 153-55.
157 Ibid, p 134.
158 CD 4325 'Correspondence Relating to the Naval Defence of Australia and New Zealand' p 40.
159 Archives New Zealand G2/17 'Confidential Inwards despatches from the Secretary of State, 29 Jun 1909-22 Feb 1910', 'Dominions No. 5' p 176
160 Archives New Zealand G2/16 'Confidential Outwards despatches from the Secretary of State, 29 Jun 1909-22 Feb 1910', Despatch No. 696/09 pp 4-7.
161 Archives New Zealand G2/17 'Confidential Inwards despatches from the Secretary of State, 29 Jun 1909-22 Feb 1910', 'Dominions No. 7', pp. 70, 175-78.
162 Peter Padfield *The Great Naval Race* Hart-Davis, London 1974, pp 194-232: W. S. Churchill *The World Crisis*, 1911–1918, p. 31.
163 New Zealand Parliamentary Debates, Vol. 146, 1909 p 154–169, *AJHR*, 1909 A-5 'Imperial Naval Conference—proceedings of informal meeting of members of the House of Representatives on the Question of the representation of New Zealand at the.' p 20, Archives New Zealand Series 1, 22/6/9 'Naval Defence', from the file 'Naval Defence — Policy and Agreement, NZ Prior 1914, 1905–1914', statement by Massey.
164 Archives New Zealand G2/16 'Confidential Outwards despatches from the Secretary of State, 29 Jun 1909-22 Feb 1910' 'Governor-General's Secret Quarterly Report', May 1909, p 6.
165 *Evening Post* 18-22 March 1909.
166 Argued in Matthew Wright, *Blue Water Kiwis*, pp. 26-28.
167 *Evening Post*, 22nd-27th March 1909; CD 4948 p 3
168 Archives New Zealand G2/16 'Confidential Outwards despatches from the Secretary of State, 29 Jun 1909-22 Feb 1910' Despatch No. 696/09 'Dominions No. 16' pp 7-8.
169 Archives New Zealand G2/16 'Confidential Outwards despatches from the Secretary of State, 29 Jun 1909-22 Feb 1910' 'Dominions No. 17' p 30.
170 CD 4949 'Conference' p 26.
171 Matthew Wright, *Blue Water Kiwis*, pp. 28-30.
172 Ibid, pp. 34-37.
173 Sergei Eisenstein, *Battleship Potemkin* (1925). Eric Hobsbawm, *Age of Extremes: The Short Twentieth Century 1941–1991*, Abacus, London 1994, pp. 54-60; David Thomson *Europe Since Napoleon*, Pelican, London, 1966, pp. 370-375, 391–408.
174 Barber, p. 89.
175 Oliver, *The Story of New Zealand*, p. 161.
176 Barber, p. 78.
177 Guthrie-Smith, p. 411.

Chapter Seven
1 Eric Hobsbawm, *Age of Extremes—The Short Twentieth Century 1914–1991*, Abacus, London 1994, reprinted 1998, pp 2–11.
2 Ibid, pp. 8–10.
3 Eric Hobsbawm, *Age of Extremes: the short twentieth century 1914–1991*, Abacus, London 1995, pp. 5–11.
4 Winston S. Churchill, *The World Crisis 1911–1918*, Four Square, London 1960, p. 7.
5 A. J. P. Taylor, *How Wars Begin*, pp. Book Club Associates, London 1979, pp. 99–122; Winston S. Churchill, *The World Crisis 1911–1918*, Four Square, London 1960, pp. 113–145
6 See, e.g. Leon Wolff, *In Flanders Fields*, Longmans, Green & Co., London 1959, p. 24.
7 Lloyd-Prichard, p. 266. Various figures have been given, see, e.g. AJHR 1921–22, H-19 'Defence Forces of New Zealand', report of General Officer Commanding, for period from 1st July 1920 to 30th June 1921', p. 2
8 Lloyd-Prichard, p. 266.
9 AJHR 1921–22, H-19, p. 2
10 Lloyd-Prichard, p. 266.
11 WTu MS Papers 2392, 'A Soldier's Book of Life' by Aubrey Tronson.
12 Matthew Wright, *Blue Water Kiwis*, Reed, Auckland 2001, p. 41.
13 R. L. Weitzel, 'Pacifists and anti-militarists in New Zealand, 1909–1914', *New Zealand Journal of History*, Vol.7, No. 2, October 1973, p. 129.
14 Matthew Wright, *Blue Water Kiwis*, pp. 42
15 WTu MS Papers 2477-2, Diary of Louisa Higginson, typescript
16 Churchill, *The World Crisis*, pp. 399-407, esp. pp. 400-01.
17 WTu MS-Papers-2350, Bollinger, George Wallace 1890–1917, Diary and letters.
18 MS-Papers-2393, Tronson, Aubrey de Coudrey 1892–1957, A soldier's book of life.
19 Nicholas Boyack, *Behind the Lines*, Allen & Unwin, Wellington 1989, pp 19-22
20 WTu MS-Papers-2477-2, Higginson, Louisa 1885–1978, Diaries/transcribed by Mrs R. L. Wilson.
21 Churchill, *The World Crisis*, p. 403-04.
22 Ibid, especially pp. 268-314.
23 WTu MS-Papers-2477-2, Higginson, Louisa 1885–1978, Diaries/transcribed by Mrs R. L. Wilson.
24 *New Zealand Herald*, 26 April 1916.
25 Allen, J., Box 9, Correspondence with Colonels Birdwood and Russell, 1914–1920, Allen to Birdwood, 3 September 1918.
26 King, *Nga Iwi o Te Motu*, p. 89.
27 Matthew Wright, *Shattered Glory*, Penguin, Auckland 2010, pp. 180–181.
28 Ibid, pp. 273–277.
29 Matthew Wright, 'Now we lie in Flanders fields', *New Zealand Listener*, 13–19 October 2007.
30 WTu MS-Papers-7198, Stayte, Jesse William (1875–1918), 'Rough notes from my diary', 16

October 1917.
31. Matthew Wright, *Italian Odyssey*, Reed, Auckland 2003, pp. 107–109, and supporting documentation.
32. Lloyd Clark, *World War I: An Illustrated History*, Helicon, Oxford 2001, pp. 199-200.
33. For a personal account of their genesis see Churchill, *The World Crisis*, pp. 350-353
34. WTu MS-Papers-2295, Hassell, N. E., 'Memories of 1914'
35. WTu MS-Papers-1703, Speedy, Fanny Hakna, fl. 1915–1919, diaries, diary 11 November 1918.
36. See, e.g. King, *Nga Iwi o Te Motu*, p. 71; Belich, *Paradise Reforged*, p. 196.
37. Lloyd-Prichard, p. 251
38. Matthew Wright, *Town and Country*, p. 340.
39. King, *The Penguin History of New Zealand*, p. 315-316.
40. AJHR 1920 H-37, 'No License<Licence?> Districts'
41. AJHR 1920 H-37b, 'No License<Licence?> Districts'.
42. AJHR 1920 H-37a, 'No License<Licence?> Districts', Table V.
43. Poster reproduced in R. M. Burdon, *The New Dominion*, A. H. & A. W. Reed, Wellington 1965, facing p. 119.
44. Burdon, p. 21.
45. *The Press*, 3 September 1928.
46. Ibid.
47. AJHR 1919 H-31, Appendix A, 'Influenza Pandemic report on the epidemic in New Zealand by Dr H. H. Mackgill, District Health Officer, Auckland.'
48. Ibid.
49. Ibid.
50. AJHR 1919 H-31, Appendix A, 'Influenza Pandemic report on the epidemic in New Zealand by Dr H. H. Mackgill, District Health Officer, Auckland.'
51. AJHR 1919 H-31a, 'Report of the Influenza Epidemic Commission'
52. AJHR 1919 H-31, Appendix A, 'Influenza Pandemic report on the epidemic in New Zealand by Dr H. H. Mackgill, District Health Officer, Auckland.'
53. AJHR 1919 H-31a, 'Report of the Influenza Epidemic Commission'
54. AJHR 1919 H-31, Appendix A, 'Influenza Pandemic report on the epidemic in New Zealand by Dr H. H. Mackgill, District Health Officer, Auckland.'
55. Reproduced in AJHR 1919 H-31a, 'Report of the Influenza Epidemic Commission'; see also Hastings District Council archive HN 103 New Zealand Public Health Department Bulletin No. 2a 'Protect Yourself Against Influenza', 5 June 1919.
56. *The Press*, 13 September 1928.
57. *Daily Telegraph*, 10 September 1921.
58. *Daily Telegraph*, 10 September 1921.
59. AJHR 1919 H-31a, 'Report of the Influenza Epidemic Commission'.
60. Cited in Matthew Wright, *Town and Country*, p.350
61. Sinclair, *New Zealand*, p. 241.
62. Brian Easton, *The Nationbuilders*, Auckland University Press, Auckland 2001, pp. 8-9.
63. *Daily Telegraph*, 10 September 1921.
64. Ibid.
65. Michael King, *The Penguin History of New Zealand*, p. 315-316.
66. Lloyd-Prichard p. 291.
67. Ibid, p. 280.
68. Ibid, p. 336.
69. Dominion, 3 January 1919.
70. Calculated from Lloyd-Prichard, p. 279.
71. Ibid, p. 291.
72. AJHR 1920, C-9, 'Discharged Soldiers Settlement', p. 3.
73. Ibid, p. 6.
74. Burdon, pp. 104–105.
75. Ibid, p. 105.
76. Duncan Waterson 'Transport in New Zealand 1900–1930', in Watters, pp. 120–138, p. 121. Conversion using Statistics New Zealand figures, Reserve Bank of New Zealand CPI calculator, to 2011Q4 figures.
77. Burdon, p. 114. Matthew Wright, *New Zealand's Engineering Heritage*, Reed, Auckland 1999, pp. 74-75.
78. Conversion using Statistics New Zealand figures, Reserve Bank of New Zealand CPI calculator, 1932Q1 to 2011Q1.
79. Matthew Wright, *New Zealand's Engineering Heritage*, Reed, Auckland 1999, pp. 75-76.
80. Sinclair, *A History of New Zealand*, p. 246.
81. Cited in W. D. McIntyre 'Peter Fraser's Commonwealth: New Zealand and the Origins of the New Commonwealth in the 1940s', in *New Zealand in World Affairs*, Vol. 1, Price Milburn for the New Zealand Institute of International Affairs, Wellington 1977, p. 39.
82. *Evening Post*, 29 April 1924.
83. Archives New Zealand Series 1, 6/1/4, 'Addition of Third Cruiser' from the file 'H. M. Ships attached to N.Z. Division, addition of third cruiser, 1935-42' *Evening Post* clipping 24 September 1925.
84. Op cit, *New Zealand Times* clipping 17 July 1926.
85. AJHR 1927 A-7 'Singapore and Naval Defence' p. 2.
86. AJHR 1927 A-6 'Imperial Conference 1926: Summary of Proceedings' p. 21
87. AJHR 1927 A-7 'Singapore and Naval Defence' p. 2. Conversion using Statistics New Zealand figures, Reserve Bank of New Zealand CPI calculator, 1926Q4 to 2011Q4 figures.
88. Michael Bassett, *Coates of Kaipara*, AUP, Auckland 1995, pp. 94-95.
89. AJHR 1920 H-38 'Department of Imperial Government Supplies', p. 1. Conversion using Statistics New Zealand figures, RBNZ Calculator, 1920Q1 to 2011Q4.
90. Ibid, p. 3.
91. Ibid, p. 4.
92. Ibid, p. 7.
93. Brian Easton *In Stormy Seas*, University of Otago Press, Dunedin, 1997, p. 68.
94. Matthew Wright, *New Zealand's Engineering Heritage*, pp. 85-89.
95. Thorns and Sedgwick, p. 108.
96. Ibid, p. 113.
97. Calculated from *ibid*, p. 103.
98. Burdon, pp. 120–121.
99. Ibid, p. 124.
100. Leonore Davidoff and Catherine Hall, 'The architecture of public and private life, English middle class society in a provincial town, 1780 to 1850', in Derek Fraser and A. Sutcliffe (eds), *The Pursuit of Urban History*, Edward Arnold, London 1983, p. 325.
101. McLintock, *The Encyclopedia of New Zealand*, Vol. 3, p. 19.
102. Ibid, pp. 19-20.
103. Mulgan, pp. 11–12.
104. Jeremy Salmond, *Old New Zealand Houses 1800–1940*, Reed, Auckland 1986, reprint 1991, pp 189-211, 212-215.
105. Matthew Bradbury (ed), *A History of the Garden in New Zealand*, Viking, Auckland 1995, pp. 135-36.
106. Jeremy Salmond, pp. 200, 211.
107. Matthew Wright, *Cars Around New Zealand*, Whitcoulls, Auckland 2005, pp. 31–32.
108. *The Press*, 12 September 1928.

109 Conversion using Statistics New Zealand figures, Reserve Bank of New Zealand CPI calculator, to 2003Q1 figures.
110 *The Press*, 12 September 1928.
111 *Dominion*, 16 November 1935.
112 Lloyd Prichard, p. 298.
113 Jeremy Salmond, pp. 206-207.
114 *The Press*, 12 September 1928.
115 Quoted in Matthew Wright, *Town and Country*, p. 509.
116 *The Press*, 12 September 1928.
117 Lloyd Prichard, p. 299.
118 Cited in David McGill *Guardians at the Gate*, Silver Owl Press, Wellington 1991, pp. 122–123.
119 Hastings District Council Archive, HN 102, Minister of Internal Affairs Circular Letter, 04/05/1917
120 Ibid, p. 123.
121 McLintock, *An Encyclopedia of New Zealand*, Vol. 3., p. 144.
122 McLintock, *Encyclopedia of New Zealand*, Vol. I., pp. 573-604.
123 Ibid, Vol. I, p. 575, 604.
124 Antony Alpers, *The Life of Katherine Mansfield*, Oxford University Press, Oxford, reprint 1983; esp. pp. 87–106, 148-49.
125 Mulgan, p. 12.
126 Wright, 'Mordacious Years', pp. 44-45.
127 Keith Rankin, 'New Zealand's Gross National Product', *Review of Income and Wealth*, Vol. 38, No. 1, March 1992, p. 61.
128 R. Boulter and T. G. A. Muntz, 'Report on economic and commercial conditions in New Zealand', HM Stationery Office, London 1936, p. 6.
129 Ola Honningdal Grytten, 'Why was the Great DepressionDepression not so great in the Nordic countries? Economic policy and unemployment', Department of Economics, Norwegian School of Economics and Business Administration, n.d., p.6.
130 L. A. Paish, 'Economic Conditions in the Dominion of New Zealand to March 1931', HM Stationery Office, London 1931, p. 9.
131 Guthrie-Smith, p. 414.
132 Burdon, p. 129.
133 Ibid, p. 127, 132.
134 Tony Simpson, *The Road to Erewhon*, Beaux Arts, Auckland 1976, p. 86.
135 Guthrie-Smith, p. 414.
136 Mulgan, p. 10.
137 *Hawke's Bay—Before and After*, Daily Telegraph, Napier 1931, reprint 1981, p. 66.
138 "The Full Story of the Great Earthquake Disaster", *The Weekender*, Third Overseas Edition.
139 J. G. Wilson *History of Hawke's Bay* p. 451 cited 246 casualties, possibly a typographical error for 256. A. H. McLintock (ed) *An Encyclopedia of New Zealand*, Government Print,Wellington 1966, Vol. 1 p. 475 cited 256 casualties, 161 in Napier, 93 in Hastings and 2 in Wairoa. This is the official tally. Geoff Conly *The Shock of '31*, A. H. & A. W. Reed, Wellington 1980, pp. 232-235 listed 258 names comprising 140 in Napier and 22 unidentified, 87 in Hastings and 6 unidentified, and 3 in Wairoa.
140 *Hawke's Bay—Before and After*, p. 69.
141 Ibid, p. 74.
142 *New Zealand Herald*, 5 February 1931
143 Scott, p. 5.
144 *Hawke's Bay—Before and After*, p. 78.
145 Quoted in Matthew Wright, *Quake—Hawke's Bay 1931*, Reed, Auckland 2001, p. 102.
146 Ibid, p. 82.
147 Ibid, p. 93
148 *Hawke's Bay—Before and After*, p. 100.
149 *New Zealand Herald*, 6 February 1931
150 WTu MS-Papers-5814, Campbell, Dorothy Beatrice, 1903–1975, Letter
151 *Hawke's Bay—Before and After*, p. 77.
152 Quoted in Matthew Wright, *Quake—Hawke's Bay 1931*, Reed, Auckland 2001, p. 98.
153 Chapple<?> p. 12. About 100 vehicles were destroyed in the earthquake.
154 *Hawke's Bay—Before and After*, p. 118.
155 Chapple, p. 50.
156 Ibid, p. 26.
157 Comment by H. M. Campbell, M.P. for Hawke's Bay, quoted in Conly *Shock of '31* , p 182.
158 Chapple, pp. 37–38, citing *New Zealand Yearbooks*.
159 Boyd and Chapple provided estimates only.
160 Boyd, p. 270.
161 Chapple, p. 44.
162 Figures from Chapple, p. 44. My interpretation differs from Chapple.
163 Burdon, p. 133.
164 Noted by Simpson, *The Road to Erewhon*, p. 89.
165 Lloyd Prichard, p. 354.
166 Tony Simpson, *The Sugarbag Years*, p. 13.
167 Barber, p. 131.
168 Guthrie-Smith, p. 414.
169 Wright, 'Mordacious Years', p. 48.
170 Bradbury (ed), p. 145–146.
171 *New Zealand Herald*, 2 February 1932.
172 *New Zealand Herald*, 2 February 1932.
173 Lloyd Prichard, p. 380.
174 Simpson, *The Sugarbag Years*, pp. 14–15.
175 Lloyd Prichard,<?>
176 C. G. Scrimgeour, John A. Lee and Tony Simpson, *The Scrim-Lee Papers*, A. H. & A. W. Reed, Welliington 1976, p. 26.
177 Cited in Burdon, p. 140.
178 Summarised in Belich, *Paradise Reforged*, p. 255.
179 See, e.g. Matthew Wright and Graham Howard, 'The Reserve Bank Inflation Calculator'<see earlier>, Reserve Bank of New Zealand *Bulletin*, Vol. 66, No.4, pp. 66-67.
180 Matthew Wright, 'Mordacious years': socio-economic aspects and outcomes
of New Zealand's experience in the Great Depression', Reserve Bank of New Zealand *Bulletin*, Vol. 72, No. 3, p. 49.
Matthew Wright
181 Lloyd Prichard, p. 385.
182 Ibid, p. 384.
183 Wright, 'Mordacious Years', p. 49.
184 Mulgan, pp. 11–12.
185 Bradbury (ed) pp. 150–151, 156.
186 Mulgan, p. 12.
187 Burdon, p. 145.
188 Scrimgeour, Lee and Simpson, p. 32.
189 Simpson, *The Road To Erewhon*, p. 85.
190 Michael King, *The Penguin History of New Zealand*, p. 348.
191 Burdon, p. 142.
192 Thorns and Sedgwick, p. 74; Lloyd Prichard p. 379.
193 Simpson *The Sugarbag Years* is illustrative, also Laurie Barber *New Zealand: A Short History*, pp. 124-32.
194 Hobsbawm, *Age of Extremes*, p. 247 noted this was still the case in the 1980s.
195 Lloyd Prichard, p. 383.
196 Thorns and Sedgwick, pp. 131–132.

197 Ibid, pp. 131–132.
198 Cited in Burdon, p. 147.
199 David Greasley and Les Oxley (2002), 'Regime shift and fast recovery on the periphery: New Zealand in the 1930s', *Economic History Review*, LV(4), p. 698.
200 Belich, *Reforging Paradise*, p. 257.
201 Wright, 'Mordacious Years', p. 54.
202 *Dominion*, Editorial, 'A Labour Government', 27 November 1935.
203 Scrimgeour, Lee and Simpson, pp. 48-49.
204 For description see Sinclair, p. 266.

Chapter Eight
1 Scrimgeour, Lee and Simpson, p. 55.
2 Ibid, p. 59.
3 Argued by Simpson, *The Road to Erewhon*, p. 99; also Sinclair, p. 289.
4 Labour election manifesto reproduced in Simpson, *The Road to Erewhon*, p. 93.
5 Easton, *The Nationbuilders*, p. 93, citing Bruce Jesson *Fragments of Labour*, p. 17.
6 Lloyd Prichard, p. 333.
7 Ibid, p. 349.
8 Matthew Wright, *New Zealand's Engineering Heritage*, pp. 86-87.
9 Ibid, p. 85.
10 Oliver, *The Story of New Zealand*, p. 189.
11 Sinclair, p. 289.
12 Lloyd Prichard, p. 378.
13 Burdon, p. 225.
14 Easton *The Nationbuilders*, p. 93.
15 Ibid, p. 126.
16 Burdon, p. 215.
17 Ibid, p. 218.
18 Oliver, *The Story of New Zealand*, p. 190.
19 Matthew Wright, *Rails Across<cap?> New Zealand*, p. 69, 78-79.
20 Thorns and Sedgwick, p. 70.
21 Burdon, pp. 223-224.
22 Easton, *The Nationbuilders*, pp. 91-97.
23 *New Zealand Herald*, 9 March 1937.
24 Lloyd Prichard, p. 379.
25 King, *The Penguin History of New Zealand*, p. 354.
26 Figures in Thorns and Sedgwick, p. 115.
27 Cited in Belich, *Paradise Reforged*, p. 261.
28 *New Zealand Herald*, 2 March 1937.
29 Matthew Wright, *Town and Country*, p. 507.
30 *New Zealand Herald*, 2 March 1937.
31 *The Dominion*, 8 November 1935.
32 *New Zealand Herald*, 2 March 1937.
33 Matthew Wright, *Town and Country*, p. 509.
34 Thorns and Sedgwick, pp. 32-33.
35 *Daily Telegraph*, 7 September 1921.
36 Belich, *Reforging Paradise*, p. 207.
37 *Daily Telegraph*, 8 September 1921.
38 *Daily Telegraph*, 9 September 1921.
39 *Daily Telegraph*, 10 September 1921.
40 *Daily Telegraph*, 7 September 1921.
41 King, *The Penguin History of New Zealand*, p. 328.
42 Ibid, p. 329.
43 Walker, pp. 180–181.
44 Matthew Wright, *Quake—Hawke's Bay 1931*, p. 124.
45 Ranginui Walker, *Struggle Without End*, Penguin, Auckland 1990, p. 191.
46 e.g. *Daily Telegraph*, 27 July 1921.
47 Argued by Michael King, *Nga Iwi o Te Motu*, p. 77.
48 Walker, pp. 195–196.
49 Sinclair, p. 277.
50 Belich, *Paradise Reforged*, pp. 265-266.
51 Sinclair, p. 277.
52 Lloyd Prichard, p. 354, 358.
53 Cited in Matthew Wright *Pacific War*, Reed, Auckland 2003, p. 36.
54 New Zealand Parliamentary Debates, Vol. 246 p. 539.
55 Matthew Wright, *Kiwi Air Power*, Reed, Auckland 1998, p. 24.
56 Archives New Zealand G5/111, Series 5/111 'Inwards telegrams and acknowledgements of telegrams received, 1 Aug 1936 (1282)-19 Nov 1937 (1827), SSDA to Governor General, 5 August 1937.<end quote?>
57 Archives New Zealand 'R. A. Cochrane: Report on the Air Aspect of the Defence Problems of New Zealand, including the suggested duties, strength and organisation of the New Zealand Air Force' from the file 'Pubs and Docs: RNZAF His. 1 w/c Cochrane 1937'
58 Ibid.
59 Matthew Wright, *Pacific War*, pp. 14–16.
60 Archives New Zealand 'R. A. Cochrane: Report on the Air Aspect of the Defence Problems of New Zealand, including the suggested duties, strength and organisation of the New Zealand Air Force' from the file 'Pubs and Docs: RNZAF His. 1 w/c Cochrane 1937'
61 Kippenberger, H. (ed), *Documents Relating to New Zealand's Participation in the Second World War*, War History Branch, Department of Internal Affairs, Wellington 1949, Vol. 1., No. 9, Governor <hyphen?>General of New Zealand to the Secretary of State for Dominion Affairs, 4 September 1939 (1.55 a.m.), pp 6–7. Hereafter referred to as *Documents*.
62 Cited in Matthew Wright, *Desert Duel*, Reed, Auckland 2002, p. 11.
63 George Clifton, *The Happy Hunted*, Cassell & Co., London, 1952, p. 225.
64 Ibid.
65 Cited in Brian Easton, *The Nationbuilders*, p. 48.
66 Ibid, p. 22.
67 Matthew Wright, *Pacific War*, Reed, Auckland 2003, p.156.
68 Matthew Wright, *Kiwi Air Power*, Reed, Auckland 1998, pp. 31, 46.
69 See Matthew Wright *Blue Water Kiwis*, Reed, Auckland 2001, pp. 91-98.
70 *Documents*, III, No. 191 Governor-General of New Zealand to the SSDA, 4 December 1940.
71 F. L. W. Wood, *Political and External Affairs*, War Histories Branch, Wellington 1958, p. 198.
72 *Documents*, III, SSDA to the High Commissioner for the United Kingdom (Wellington), 14 July 1940, p. 1
73 Op cit, Governor-General of New Zealand to the SSDA, 30 July 1940, p. 14.
74 Op cit, Governor-General of New Zealand to the SSDA, 5 August 1940, pp. 207-08.
75 Op cit, SSDA to the High Commissioner for the United Kingdom (Wellington), 11 August 1940, pp. 18–19.
76 W. S. Churchill *The Second World War*, Vol. III, Clarendon Press, London 1950, pp 157–58.
77 See, e.g. Michael Ashby, 'Fraser's Foreign Policy', in Margaret Clark (ed) *Peter Fraser, Master Politician*, Dunmore Press, Palmerston North, 1998, p. 169.
78 S. D. Waters, *The Royal New Zealand Navy*, War Histories Branch, Wellington 1956, pp. 223-

79 *Documents*, III, No. 193, Acting Prime Minister of New Zealand to the SSDA, 4 September 1941.
80 Matthew Wright, *Rails Across New Zealand*, Whitcoulls, Auckland 2003, p. 79.
81 *New Zealand Herald*, 9 December 1941.
82 Ibid.
83 *New Zealand Herald*, 15 December 1941.
84 Matthew Wright, *Desert Duel*, Reed, Auckland 2002, pp. 67-68.
85 Waters, p. 212.
86 *Southern Cross*, 26 July 1949.
87 *Evening Post*, 27 July 1942.
88 *Documents*, III, No. 209, Prime Minister to the New Zealand Minister, Washington, 13 March 1942, p. 236.
89 Op cit, Prime Minister of New Zealand to the Prime Minister of the United Kingdom, 28 February 1942.
90 *New Zealand Herald*, 9 March 1942.
91 *Documents*, III, Fraser to Nash, 13 March 1942, Section IV, p. 241
92 Op cit, Chief of the General Staff to General Freyberg, GOC 2nd NZEF (Egypt), 2 January 1942, pp.217-218.
93 *Auckland Star*, 11 March 1942.
94 Ibid.
95 *Documents*, III, Prime Minister of New Zealand to the SSDA, 19 February 1942, p. 228.
96 Op cit, Prime Minister of New Zealand to the SSDA, 30 January 1942, p. 218.
97 Op cit, SSDA to the Prime Minister of New Zealand, 3 February 1942, p. 219-220.
98 Op cit, Prime Minister of New Zealand to the SSDA, 4 February 1942, pp. 220-21.
99 Op cit, SSDA to the Prime Minister of New Zealand, 3 February 1942, p. 222-23.
100 *Documents*, III, SSDA to the Prime Minister of New Zealand, 23 March 1942, enclosures, p.180.
101 Op cit, New Zealand Minister, Washington, to the Prime Minister, 24 March 1942, p. 249.
102 Belich, *Reforging Paradise*, p. 290.
103 M. Wynn, pers. comm.
104 Cited in Oliver A. Gillespie, *The Pacific*, War History Branch, Department of Internal Affairs, p. 107.
105 *Documents*, II, letter from the Hon. W. Nash, New Zealand Minister at Washington, to President Roosevelt, 24 January 1944, p. 333.
106 F. L. W. Wood, *Political and External Affairs*, Historical Publications Branch, Wellington, 1958, title of Chapter 26.
107 *Documents*, III, Prime Minister of the United Kingdom to the Prime Minister of New Zealand, 15 August 1945, p. 508.
108 W. D. McIntyre 'Peter Fraser's Commonwealth: New Zealand and the Origins of the New Commonwealth in the 1940s', in *New Zealand in World Affairs*, Vol. 1, Price Milburn for the New Zealand Institute of International Affairs, Wellington 1977, pp. 9-36; Wood, pp. 370-384; Michael Ashby 'Fraser's Foreign Policy' in Margaret Clark (ed) *Peter Fraser: Master Politician*, The Dunmore Press, Palmerston North, 1998.
109 Cited in McIntyre, p. 39.
110 Matthew Wright, *Desert Duel*, Reed, Auckland 2002, pp. 18–19.
111 Matthew Wright, *Battle for Crete*, Reed, Auckland 1999, reprint 2003, pp. 112–114.
112 See ibid, esp. Chs 2-4.
113 *Documents*, I No. 444, Nash to Fraser 5 June 1941
114 Loc cit, No. 447, Fraser to Nash 7 June 1941
115 Matthew Wright, *Italian Odyssey*, Reed, Auckland 2003, pp. 16-24.
116 Ibid, pp. 116–118, 157–158.
117 David Cannadine (ed) *The Speeches of Winston S. Churchill*, Penguin, London 1989, p. 165
118 Cited in Gillespie, p. 103.
119 M. P. Lissington, *New Zealand and the United States*, Government Print, Wellington 1972, p. 84.
120 Cited in McIntyre, p. 40.
121 Cited in ibid, p. 39.
122 Mulgan, p. 15.
123 Matthew Wright, *Pacific War*, Reed, Auckland 2003, p. 155, 160.
124 Matthew Wright, *Pacific War*, Reed, Auckland 2003, p. 57.
125 Matthew Wright, *Kiwi Air Power*, Reed, Auckland 1998, pp. 111–114.
126 Mulgan, p. 14.
127 Matthew Wright, *Pacific War*, Reed, Auckland 2003, p. 159.
128 Archives New Zealand AIR 118/8 'Information Concerning New Zealand's Air Effort during the Second World War, Section A: Statistics relating to New Zealand's Air Effort' from the file 'NZ Air Effort during the Second World War'
129 Cited in Matthew Wright, *Kiwi Air Power*, Reed, Auckland 1998, p. 63.
130 Uren, p. 9.
131 Andrew Roberts 'Prime Minister Halifax' in Robert Cowley (ed) *What If? 2*, Berkley, New York 2001, pp. 281–290; Heinz Magnenheimer, *Hitler's War*, Cassell, London 1997, argues pp. 277-283 that Germany only moved away from political solutions after 1941–42.
132 Matthew Wright, *Blue Water Kiwis*, Reed, Auckland 2001, pp. 88, 90.
133 WTu MS-Papers-2446, Miller, Henry G., d 1940, Outward letters
134 See, e.g. John McLeod, *Myth and Reality, The New Zealand Soldier in World War II*, Heinemann Reed, Auckland 1986, esp. pp. 6–7, 190–191.
135 Matthew Wright, *Kiwi Air Power*, Reed, Auckland 1998, pp. 47–48.
136 MS-Papers-2183-09, Royal New Zealand Air Force—Review for the Hon Minister of Defence, secret 1943 report.
137 Matthew Wright, *Kiwi Air Power*, p. 108
138 Cited in Paul Freyberg *Bernard Freyberg VC—Soldier of Two Nations*, Hodder & Stoughton, London p. 328.
139 Basil Liddell-Hart (ed) *The Rommel Papers*, Collins, London 1953, trans. Paul Findlay. (German original written by Erwin Rommel and edited by Fritz Bayerlein, Lucie-Maria Rommel and Manfred Rommel) p. 240
140 Cited in Sir John White 'Hard Lessons Learned from another war', *Dominion*, 20 April 2000.
141 Archives New Zealand, WAII, 11/7, 'R. Walker's Notes, Minqar Qaim, Ruweisat etc; correspondence on the Minqar Qaim period: extracts from cables USAFIME to General Marshall', from the file 'R. Walker's Notes; Battle for Egypt, Syria, Minqar Qaim'; Maxwell to Marshall (II), 27 June 1942.
142 Sir John White Papers, 'The New Zealand Division in Egypt and Libya, Operations Lightfoot and Supercharge', Foreword.
143 Sir John White Papers, 'Message from the Army Commander to All Ranks 2nd New Zealand Expeditionary Force, 21 July 1943.
144 See, e.g. *Desert Duel*, pp. 94-99.
145 Matthew Wright, *Italian Odyssey*

146 Matthew Wright, *Desert Duel*, p. 18.
147 See summary in, e.g. Matthew Wright, *The Battle for Crete: New Zealand's Near-Run Affair*, Reed, Auckland 1999, reprinted 200, pp. 110–111.
148 See, e.g. Matthew Wright, *Desert Duel*, pp. 169–170; Paul Freyberg, *Bernard Freyberg VC, Soldier of Two Nations*, Hodder & Stoughton, London 1991; Laurie Barber and John Tonkin-Covell, *Freyberg: Churchill's Salamander*, Century Hutchinson, Auckland 1989.
149 Matthew Wright, *Freyberg's War*, Penguin, Auckland 2005, p. 115.
150 Cited in Fred Madjalany, *Cassino, Portrait of a Battle*, Longmans, Green & Co., London 1957, p. 102
151 Argued by Matthew Wright, *Desert Duel*, pp. 168–170; Matthew Wright, *Italian Odyssey*, pp. 169–170.
152 Cited in ibid, p. 170.
153 Matthew Wright, *Italian Odyssey*, p. 151.
154 Ibid, p. 170.
155 John Mulgan, *Report on Experience*, p. 138.
156 Ibid, p. 139.
157 Matthew Wright, *Italian Odyssey*, p. 27.
158 Barry Gustafson, *His Way, a Biography of Robert Muldoon*, Auckland University Press 2000, paperback edition 2001, pp. 37–38.

Chapter Nine
1 Austin Mitchell, *The Quarter-Acre, Half-Gallon, Pavlova Paradise*, Whitcombe and Tombs, Christchurch 1972.
2 Gordon McLauchlan, *The Passionless People*, Cassell, Auckland 1976.
3 Organisation for National Development, 'Interim Report on Post-war Reconstruction and National Development', July 1944, p. 34.
4 Thorns and Sedgwick, p. 104.
5 Archives New Zealand, Series 11, 11/6 'Papers on Economic Stabilisation: memorandum of future stabilisation policy' from the file 'Correspondence of Maj. Gen. H. Kippenberger, 1947–55'
6 Organisation for National Development, 'Interim Report on Post-war Reconstruction and National Development', July 1944.
7 Archives New Zealand, Series 11, 11/6 'Papers on Economic Stabilisation: memorandum of future stabilisation policy' from the file 'Correspondence of Maj. Gen. H. Kippenberger, 1947–55', F. P. Walsh 'Economic Stabilisation in the Post-War years.'
8 W. B. Sutch, *The Quest for Security in New Zealand 1940 to 1966*, Oxford University Press, London 1966, p. 409
9 Sutch, p. 411
10 Thorns and Sedgwick, p. 64.
11 Matthew Wright, *Wings Over New Zealand*, p. 94.
12 Kenneth B. Cumberland and J. W. Fox, *New Zealand: A Regional View*, Whitcombe and Tombs, Auckland 1958, second printing 1959, p. 23
13 Ibid, pp. 24-25.
14 Ibid, p. 29.
15 Sinclair, *New Zealand*, p. 288.
16 Sutch, p. 440.
17 Thorns and Sedgwick, pp. 113–114.
18 Ibid, p. 108.
19 Organisation for National Development, 'Interim Report on Post-War Reconstruction and National Development', p. 30
20 Matthew Wright, *New Zealand's Engineering Heritage*, pp. 104–138.
21 Ibid, pp. 121–122.
22 Ibid, pp. 136–138.
23 Matthew Wright, *Italian Odyssey*, p. 163.
24 King, *The Penguin History of New Zealand*, p. 420.
25 Organisation for National Development, 'Interim Report on Post-war Reconstruction and National Development', July 1944, p. 4.
26 See, e.g. Hastings District Council Archive, HBC 46/64 Transit Camp Temporary Housing Windsor Park 1946, Rainbow to Jones 04/09/1945.
27 Reproduced in *New Zealand's Heritage* p. 3528
28 Gale Ferguson, *Building the New Zealand Dream*, Dunmore Press, Palmerston North 1994, p. 178.
29 Sinclair, p. 287.
30 Martin Walker *The Cold War*, Viking, London 1993, pp 230-251.
31 Ibid, p. 293.
32 Thorns and Sedgwick, p. 175.
33 Ibid, p. 41.
34 Ferguson, pp. 177-79.
35 Ibid, p. 181.
36 Cumberland and Fox, p. 32
37 See, e.g. Michael King *Nga Iwi o Te Motu*, p. 102
38 Noted in Ferguson, p. 204.
39 Cited in Matthew Wright *Town and Country*, p. 648.
40 Mulgan, p. 15.
41 King, *The Penguin History of New Zealand*, p. 426.
42 Organisation for National Development, 'Interim Report on Post-war Reconstruction and National Development', July 1944, p. 39.
43 Sales figures from *New Zealand's Heritage*, pp. 2701–2705.
44 *Edmonds Cookery Book*, Bluebird Foods, Auckland, 38th Edition 1995.
45 *Evening Post*, 11 February 1957
46 Sutch, p. 419.
47 Graham Howard and Matthew Wright 'The Reserve Bank Inflation Calculator', *Reserve Bank Bulletin*, Vol. 66, No. 4, December 2003.
48 *Evening Post*, 5 February 1957. Conversion by Reserve Bank Inflation Calculator, Statistics New Zealand figures.
49 *Evening Post*, 3 February 1957.
50 *Evening Post*, 21 February 1972.
51 Peter Davis, 'Stratification and Class' in Paul Soonley, David Pearson and Ian Shirley (eds), *New Zealand Sociological Perspectives*, Dunmore Press, Palmerston North 1972, p. 127.
52 Ibid.
53 Graeme Hunt, *The Rich List*, Reed, Auckland 1999, p. 173.
54 Ibid, p. 194.
55 Noted in Hunt, *The Rich List*, p. 197.
56 Ken Comber, 'Personal reflections on my father-in-law', from Margaret Clark (ed), *Sir Keith Holyoake, Towards a Political Biography*, Dunmore Press, Palmerston North, 1997, p. 22.
57 Author observation. See also James Marshall and Dominique Marshall, *Discipline and Punishment in New Zealand Education*, Dunmore Press, Palmerston North 1997, p. 106.
58 Marshall and Marshall, p. 108.
59 King, *The Penguin History of New Zealand*, p. 431
60 Sinclair, *A History of New Zealand*, esp. pp. 310-311; Oliver, *The Story of New Zealand*, p. 227.
61 See, e.g. W. B. Sutch *Colony or Nation?*, Sydney University Press 1966, second edition 1968.

62. Brian Easton, *The Nationbuilders*, p. 169
63. See, e.g. Colin S. Gray, *The Geopolitics of the Nuclear Era*, Crane, Russak & Co., Inc., 1977, esp. pp 14-32.
64. W. D. McIntyre 'Peter Fraser's Commonwealth' in Alistair McIntosh (ed), *New Zealand in World Affairs*, Price, Milburn, and Company, Wellington 1977, p. 81.
65. Matthew Wright, *Kiwi Air Power*, p. 120.
66. Matthew Wright, *Blue Water Kiwis*, pp. 156–158.
67. Sinclair, *A History of New Zealand*, p. 304.
68. —<?> *NZ Foreign Policy Statements and Documents 1943-57*, Foreign Affairs, Government Print, Wellington 1972, Doc 106, p 391.
69. Ibid, Doc 86, pp 336-37.
70. Ibid, Doc 102, p 382.
71. Easton, *The Nationbuilders*, p. 184.
72. See, e.g. Robert J. Lieber, *Theory and World Politics*, Winthrop Publishers 1972, esp. pp. 38-67, 120–145.
73. Geoffrey Kemp, 'The New Strategic Map', from Uri Ra'anan, *Arms Transfers to the Third World*, Westview Press, 1978, pp. 3–18.
74. R. D. Muldoon, *The Rise and Fall of a Young Turk*, A. H. & A. W. Reed, Wellington 1981, p. 195.
75. Bruce Brown, 'Foreign Policy is Trade: Trade is Foreign Policy' in Ann Trotter (ed) *Fifty Years of New Zealand Foreign Policy Making*, University of Otago Press, Dunedin 1993, pp. 59-60
76. Brian Easton, *In Stormy Seas*, University of Otago Press, Dunedin, 1997, Table 9.2, p. 142.
77. Brown, p. 65, note 24.
78. Ibid, p. 68.
79. See, e.g. W. B. Sutch *Colony or Nation?*, esp. pp. 181–182.
80. Easton, *In Stormy Seas*, p. 102
81. *The Post*, 21 February 1972.
82. See, e.g. Easton, *The Nationbuilders*, pp. 184–186.
83. Bruce Jesson, *Only Their Purpose Is Mad*, Dunmore Press, Palmerston North, 1999, p. 74.
84. Geoff Conly *Wattie's—The First Fifty Years*, p. 145.
85. Barry Gustafson, *His Way: A biography of Robert Muldoon*, Auckland University Press, Auckland 2000, p. 238
86. Easton, *The Nationbuilders*, pp. 250-252; see also Gustafson, p. 469.
87. Noted in Gustafson, p. 267.
88. Easton, *The Nationbuilders*, p. 250.
89. Gustafson, p. 470.
90. Ibid, p. 6–7. See also Easton, *The Nationbuilders*, p. 249.
91. Easton, *In Stormy Seas*, p. 102.
92. Thorns and Sedgwick, p. 64.
93. Ibid, p. 119.
94. R. D. Muldoon, *The New Zealand Economy, a personal view*, Endeavour Press, Auckland, 1985, p. 105.
95. Matthew Wright, *Rails Across New Zealand*, Whitcoulls, Auckland 2003, pp. 122–123.
96. Matthew Wright, *Town and Country*, p. 663.
97. Gustafson, p. 274.
98. Paul Stumpf *The Music's All That Matters*, Quartet, London 1997, pp 197-99.
99. Matthew Wright, *Blue Water Kiwis*, p. 172.
100. Thorns and Sedgwick, p. 54.
101. Noted by, e.g. Michael King *Nga Iwi O Te Motu*, p. 96.
102. Sutch, *Colony or Nation?*, p. 157.
103. Thorns and Sedgwick, pp. 40-41.
104. Matthew Wright, *Italian Odyssey*, pp. 73-77.
105. e.g. at Minqar Qaim, see Matthew Wright, *Desert Duel*, p. 83.
106. Matthew Wright, *Pacific War*, Reed, Auckland 2003, pp. 65-66.
107. Thorns and Sedgwick, p. 54.
108. King, *Nga Iwi o Te Motu*, pp. 103–104.
109. Sutch, *Colony or Nation?*, p. 157.
110. King, *The Penguin History of New Zealand*, p. 473.
111. Ibid, pp. 470-472.
112. Simpson, *The Road to Erewhon*, pp. 141–42.
113. Calculated from Table XLI in W. B. Sutch *Colony or Nation?*, p. 159.
114. Argued by Michael King, *Being Pakeha Pakeha Now*, Penguin, Auckland 1999, p. 116.
115. Walker, p. 212.
116. King, *The Penguin History of New Zealand*, p. 476.
117. Walker, p. 222.
118. Ibid, p. 221.
119. Orange, p. 250.
120. W. H. Oliver 'The Future Behind Us', in Andrew Sharp and P. G. McHugh (eds), *Histories, Power and Loss*, BWB, Wellington 2001, pp. 10, 12, 27, 29; Paul Moon, *The Path to the Treaty of Waitangi*, David Ling Publishing, Auckland 2002; Andrew Sharp 'Recent Juridical and Constitutional Histories of Maori', in Sharp and McHugh p. 31.
121. Argued in Sharp, p. 32.
122. Michael King, *Being Pakeha Now*, pp. 206-207; Paul Moon, *The Path to the Treaty of Waitangi*, David Ling Publishing, Auckland 2002, p. 11; Andrew Sharp 'Recent Juridical and Constitutional Histories of Maori', in Sharp and McHugh. esp. pp. 30-36.

Chapter Ten
1. Gusfafson, p. 278.
2. For background, see, e.g. Mike Paterson *The Point At Issue*, HarperCollins, Auckland 1991, pp. 110–116.
3. Matthew Wright, *New Zealand's Engineering Heritage*, pp. 138–140, 148–149.
4. Gustafson, p. 311.
5. Watched by the author. Also cited in Gustafson p. 312.
6. For another view see King, p. 485.
7. Gustafson, p. 319.
8. Muldoon, *The New Zealand Economy*, p. 118.
9. Stephen Stratford, *The Dirty Decade—New Zealand in the 80's*, Tandem Press, Auckland, 2002, p. 16.
10. Stratford, p. 37.
11. Gustafson, p. 335.
12. Ruth Richardson, *Making a Difference*, Shoal Bay Press, Christchurch 1995, pp. 31–32.
13. Thorns and Sedgwick, p. 104.
14. The 1983 figure was $3168.7 million in 1976 dollars. Statistics New Zealand figures; RBNZ Inflation Calculator.
15. Donald Brash 'Economy' in George Bryant (ed) *New Zealand 2001*, Cassell, Auckland 1981, pp. 33-34. This was written in March 1980.
16. Richardson, pp. 24-27
17. Jesson, p. 12.
18. Muldoon, *The New Zealand Economy*, p. 119.
19. Jesson p. 31.
20. Muldoon, *The New Zealand Economy*, p. 125.
21. Gustafson, pp. 372-373.
22. Sinclair, *A History of New Zealand*, p. 320.
23. The Treasury, *Economic Management*, The Treasury, 14 July 1984.
24. Brash, 'New Zealand's Remarkable Reforms', p. 20; Sinclair, *A History of New Zealand*, p. 322.
25. Michael King, The Penguin History of New Zealand, p. 488.
26. Marcia Russell, *Revolution*,

Hodder Moa Beckett, Auckland 1996, p. 119.
27 For commentary see also Jesson, pp. 34-36.
28 Russell, p. 127.
29 Interviewed by the author.
30 Stratford, p. 7.
31 Jesson, p. 104
32 Graeme Hunt, p. 63
33 Stratford, p. 77.
34 Jesson, p. 126.
35 Belich, *Reforging Paradise*, pp. 406-407.
36 Roger Douglas, *Unfinished Business*, Random House, Auckland 1993, reprint 1994, p. 222
37 Russell, p. 212.
38 Ibid, p. 212.
39 Author present at the press conference.
40 Richardson, pp. 74-76.
41 Ibid, pp. 94-95.
42 Briggs, p. 89.
43 Thorns and Sedgwick, p. 119. Briggs, Figure 54, p. 111 is illustrative.
44 Thorns and Sedgwick, p 74.
45 Thorns and Sedgwick, p. 104.
46 Thorns and Sedgwick, p 74.
47 Author observation.
48 Thorns and Sedgwick pp. 131–132. Traffic offences contributed to the 1994 rate. Eric Hobsbawm, *Age of Extremes—The Short Twentieth Century, 1914–1991*, Abacus 1994, especially pp. 49-51, pp. 336-343, p. 565, argued that the twentieth century brought general degradation of standards worldwide.
49 Thorns and Sedgwick, p. 132.
50 Richardson, p. 99.
51 King, *The Penguin History of New Zealand*, p. 490.
52 Matthew Wright, *New Zealand's Engineering Heritage*, p. 149.
53 See, e.g. *Wanganui Chronicle*, 22 December 1999; Tracey Lowndes, 'Economy a case of "minor adjustment"', *Otago Daily Times*, 4 January 2000; *Hawke's Bay Today*, 21 December 1999.
54 Ray Lilley 'Labour-Alliance prepares for great tax leap backward', *National Business Review*, 10 December 1999; see also *Hawke's Bay Today*, 21 December 1999; 'Government delivers on Super promise', *New Zealand Herald*, 28 January 2000.
55 Jeff Gamlin, 'Treasury's white paper implies country is at a crossroads', *National Business Review*, 28 January 2000. See also Ruth Laugesen 'Clark finds new energy', *Sunday Star-Times*, 23 January 2000.
56 Gordon McLauchlan, *The Big Con*, Government Print, Wellington 1992.
57 Jesson, pp. 77-78.
58 Belich, *Reforging Paradise*. p. 411.
59 Jesson, p. 13.
60 Jesson, p. 145.
61 Jesson, p. 144.
62 McLauchlan, *The Big Con*, p. 124.
63 See, e.g. The Treasury 'Government Management', The Treasury, Wellington 1987 (2 Vols), especially Annex 1.
64 Brash, p. 18; Jesson, p. 22
65 Jesson, p. 22.
66 'Kiwis turn their backs on failed reforms—academic', *Evening Post*, 05/12/1999.
67 See, e.g. 'By The Numbers', *New Zealand Herald*, 19 July 2003.
68 Simon Collins 'Good, but could be better', *New Zealand Herald*, 18 February 2003.
69 Ibid.
70 Peter Lyons 'Purity could be costly', Southland Times, 1 December 2003.
71 John Quiggin, 'Change long overdue in New Zealand', Australian Financial Review, 2 December 1999.
72 Graeme Peters, 'Time to ask if reform pain brought gain', *Evening Post*, 3 July 1999.
73 http://www.openculture.com/2011/09/arthur_c_clarke_looks_into_the_future_1964.html, accessed 3 March 2012.

Glossary

Aotearoa	North Island or Great Barrier Island; later applied to New Zealand generally
baby boomer	generation born between the Second World War and mid-1960s
brown bess	nickname for the Pattern musket, an eighteenth-century British weapon built to a particular standard
CMS	Church Missionary Society, the Church of England organisation responsible for setting up missions in British territories and protectorates, among other places.
generation x	children of the baby boomers
hapu	a key Maori social grouping usually comprised of several whanau
heke	migration
iwi	grouping of hapu
kaumatua	elder, possibly under 40 in pre-European times
nappy valley	specific nickname for Wainuiomata; generic term for any post-war 'baby boomer' suburb
pukaea	wooden trumpet
regiment	the main organisational unit of the nineteenth-century British army, with a social dimension
taua	war party
toa	warrior
utu	reciprocal debt
VOC	Vereenigde Oostinsche Compagnie—Dutch East India Company
whanau	extended family in Maori society

Bibliography

Alexander Turnbull Library (WTu)

Micro-MS-0425, George Maunder, Letters written from Hawke's Bay to his sister Jane, and to his mother.
MS Cha 1911, letter from John Chambers to directors of the Hawke's Bay Tribune.
MS Papers 1635-05 Monro, David (Sir), Papers. Statements of assets and monies owing.
MS-1194-1214, McLean, Donald (Sir) 1820–1877, Diaries.
MS-1215-1282, McLean, Donald (Sir) 1820–1877, Diaries and notebooks.
MS-1284-1287, McLean, Donald (Sir) 1820–1877, Journal (typescript of selected diaries and notebooks)
MS-Group-0556, Cordery, Eric Leofwin, Papers.
MS-Papers f-76-048 - Colenso, William, 1811–1899: letter from James Busby to William Colenso and other papers, letter by Waka Nene and others (fragment).
MS-Papers-0032 McLean, Donald (Sir), 1820–1877, Papers.
MS-Papers-0069-049, Copy of journal of the capture of the *Ngatapa* by A. Kempthorne.
MS-Papers-0667, Davie, Cyrus Papers, 'Journal of a voyage on board the *Sir George Seymour* and *Randolph* of 850 tons from Plymouth to Port Victoria, New Zealand.'
MS-Papers-1346, Bennett, Agnes Elizabeth Lloyd, 1872-1960, Papers.
MS-Papers-1611, Colenso, William Papers, Memoranda of the Arrival of Lieut. Governor Hobson in New Zealand.
MS-Papers-1983, Busby, James, 'Three documents by or relating to James Busby, 1840.
MS-Papers-2183-09, Royal New Zealand Air Force—Review for the Hon Minister of Defence.
MS-Papers-2350, Bollinger, George Wallace 1890–1917, Diary and letters.
MS-Papers-2393, Tronson, Aubrey de Coudrey 1892–1957, *A soldier's book of life*.
MS-Papers-2418, Folder 4, W. J. Ashcroft, writing of the quake in 'The Apiarist' in 'The New Zealand Smallholder', 16 March 1931.
MS-Papers-2481, Bourke, Henry O'Donel, Diary 1917–1918.
MS-Papers-2446, Miller, Henry G, d 1940, Outward letters.
MS-Papers-2477, Higginson, Louisa 1885–1978, Diaries/transcribed by Mrs R L Wilson.
MS-Papers-3520, Smith, Hector William Pope, 1837–1878, Extracts from journal.
MS-Papers-3779-1/2, Hay Family: Papers, Letters from William and Mary Hay.
MS-Papers-3895-06 Haslam family: family papers, Typed transcripts of the letters from Sarah Ann Self (Haslam).
MS-Papers-3975, Chapman, Leslie Walter, 1913–1985, Papers.
MS-Papers-4328, Hamilton, Francis William, 1840–1901: Outward letters.
MS-Papers-5814, Campbell, Dorothy Beatrice, 1903–1975, Letter.
MSO-Papers-3730, Wakefield, William 1801–1848, Deeds of Sale of Maori Land, fourth sheet.
QMS-0160, Berard, Auguste, Report of Captain Berard, 4 July 1844–31 January 1846.
WTu MS-Papers-2295, Hassell, N. E., 'Memories of 1914'.
WTu MS-Papers-1703, Speedy, Fanny Hakna, fl. 1915-1919, diaries, diary 11 November 1918.
WTu MS-Papers-2477-2, Higginson, Louisa 1885–1978, Diaries/transcribed by Mrs R L Wilson.

Archives New Zealand/Te Whare Tohu Tuhituhinga O Aotearoa

Wellington Office
Air Department (AIR)
Series 1, 102/4/1 'R. A. Cochrane: Report on the Air Aspect of the Defence Problems of New Zealand, including

the suggested duties, strength and organisation of the New Zealand Air Force' from the file 'Pubs and Docs: RNZAF His. 1 w/c Cochrane 1937'.
Series 118/8 'Information Concerning New Zealand's Air Effort during the Second World War, Section A: Statistics relating to New Zealand's Air Effort' from the file 'NZ Air Effort during the Second World War'.

Allen Papers
Box 9

Navy Department (N)
Series 1, 6/1/4, 'Addition of Third Cruiser' from the file 'H. M. Ships attached to N.Z. Division, addition of third cruiser, 1935–42'.
Series 1, 22/6/9 'Naval Defence', from the file 'Naval Defence—Policy and Agreement, NZ Prior 1914, 1905–1914'.

War Archives, World War Two (WAII)
Series 11, 11/7, 'R. Walker's Notes, Minqar Qaim, Ruweisat etc; correspondence on the Minqar Qaim period: extracts from cables USAFIME to General Marshall', from the file 'R. Walker's Notes; Battle for Egypt, Syria, Minqar Qaim'.
Series 11, 11/6 'Papers on Economic Stabilisation: memorandum of future stabilisation policy' from the file 'Correspondence of Maj. Gen. H. Kippenberger, 1947–55'.

New Munster Province (NM)
Series 2/4 'Inwards Despatches from Governor-In-Chief, 24 Jan–23 Dec 1850'.
Series 8/35, 1849/39, 'Colonial Secretary's Inwards Correspondence, 1849'.
Series 10/10, 1850/746 'Colonial Secretary's Outwards Correspondence, 1850'.
Series 10/9, 'Colonial Secretary's Inwards Correspondence, 28 Apr 1848–4 Sep 1848'.

Governor (G)
Series 2/17 'Confidential Inwards despatches from the Secretary of State, 29 Jun 1909–22 Feb 1910'.
Series 5/111 'Inwards telegrams and acknowledgements of telegrams received, 1 Aug 1936 (1282)–19 Nov 1937 (1827).
Series 7/6,61 'Inwards despatches from Lieutenant-Governor Eyre, New Munster, 2 June–11 July 1849.
Communicate New Zealand, Series 6401 and 6403.

Nelson Provincial Museum
Qms LET, Petition to Captain Wakefield from the Working men of Nelson, 14 January 1843.

Hawke's Bay Museum
Resident Magistrate's Letterbook.
Donald McLean Inwards Letterbook.
Donald McLean Papers, typescript volumes.
Extracts from the Diary of E. C. Weston, 10–30 April 1888.

Havelock North Public Library
A/397/1879, William Rainbow diary, typescript.

Hastings District Council archive
HN 102.
HBC 46/64 Transit Camp Temporary Housing Windsor Park 1946.
HNL 98/1100 'The Hawke's Bay Master Builders Assn. In Conjunction with the Hastings City Council presents Flaxmere Parade of Homes'.
HCC577 Finance, 'A Financial Report, Flaxmere 1963–1987'.

Great Britain Parliamentary Papers (GBPP)
Vol 5, 1846–47.

Appendices to the Journal of the House of Representatives (AJHR)
1858, C-1, Native Land Purchases.
1858, E-1, Report of Ahuriri Native Industrial School 1856.
1861, E-9, Minutes of Proceedings of the Kohimarama Conference.
1862, C-1, Correspondence.
1862, E-4, Report of Inspectors on Native Schools, 'Report on the Te Aute Native Industrial School in the Province of Hawke's Bay.
1862, E-4, Report from W. R. Baker, esq, on the Waerengaahika (Turanga) School, 6th May 1862.
1863, D-6, 'The Otago Gold Fields'.
1866, D-11, 'Return showing the amount of gold exported from the various ports in the colony for the year commencing on 1st April 1865, and ending the 31st March 1866.
1860, E-2, Extract from Sub-Protector Clarke's Report to the Chief Protector, 29 June 1844.
1864, E-3, 'Further Papers Relative to the Native Insurrection'.
1874, E-2, 'Further Papers relative to peace and confiscation of native lands'.
1864, E-6, 'Papers Relative to the Pai Marire Religion, etc'.
1865, E-5, 'Papers Relative to the murder of the Rev. Carl Sylvius Volkner by the Hau Hau Fanatics'.
1867, A-1a.
1867, A-15, 'Report by Mr G. S. Cooper on the subject of native lands in the province of Hawke's Bay'.
1867, F4, 'Railway Gauge Committee'.
1871, A-2a, 'Memorandum on the Operation of the Native

Lands Court by Sir William Martin'.
1873, G-7, 'Report of the Hawke's Bay Native Lands Alienation Commission'.
1874, D-2, 'Immigration to New Zealand'.
1874, E-8, Appendices to the Public Works Statement 1874.
1874, G-2.
1878, G-1, 'Reports from officers in Native Districts'.
1879, E-1, Appendix M 'Annual Report on Working Railways by the Commissioner of Railways for the Middle Island'.
1879, E-1, Appendix L, 'Annual Report on Working Railways by the Commissioner of Railways, North Island'.
1879, G-1, 'Reports from Officers in Native Districts'.
1884, D-1, 'Return of immigration from 1st July 1883 to 30th June 1884, Nationalities of Immigrants'.
1885, A-6, 'Naval Defence of the Colony.'
1885, D6, 'The North Island Trunk Railway'.
1886, G-1, 'Reports from Officers in Native Districts'.
1890, G-1, 'Opinions of various authorities on native tenure'.
1890, G-1, 'Sir William Martin, Pamphlet of 1848'.
1909, A-5, 'Imperial Naval Conference—proceedings of informal meeting of members of the House of Representatives on the Question of the representation of New Zealand at the.'
1921–22, H-19, 'Defence forces of New Zealand, report of General Officer Commanding for period from 1st July 1920, to 30th June 1921.
1920, H-37a, 'No Licence Districts'.
1920, H-37b, 'No Licence Districts'.
1919, H-31, Appendix A, 'Influenza Pandemic report on the epidemic in New Zealand by Dr H. H. Mackgill, District Health Officer, Auckland.'
1919, H-31a, 'Report of the Influenza Epidemic Commission'.
1920, H-19a, 'War Expenses Account'.
1920, H-38, 'Department of Imperial Government Supplies'.
1921–22, H-19, '23rd Annual Report of the Pensions Department.'
1920, C-9, 'Discharged Soldiers Settlement'.
1927, A-7, 'Singapore and Naval Defence'.
1927, A-6, 'Imperial Conference 1926: Summary of Proceedings'.

Other government publications
Command Papers
Government Gazette of the Province of New Munster
New Zealand Parliamentary Debates
New Zealand Statutes
Population Census
Supplement to the New Zealand Gazette
The New Zealand Gazette

Online sources
http://en.wikipedia.org/wiki/History_of_gunpowder
http://www.nzetc.org

Newspapers
Evening Post
Hawke's Bay Herald
National Business Review
New Zealand Herald
New Zealand Times
Southern Cross
The Daily Telegraph
The Dominion
The Dominion-Post
The New Zealand Gazette and Port Nicholson Advertiser
The Press
The Weekender

Private papers and collections
Noble-Campbell Papers
Sir John White Papers
M. Wynn Papers

Author Collection
Cunningham, Ashley, 'The Indigenous Forests of East Coast, Poverty Bay, Hawke's Bay' and Elder, N. L., 'Maori Cultivation and the Retreat of Forest', talk given 9 October 1956.
'Mar di India', print of c 1630 map.
Lands and Survey Auction Map, 12 October 1905.
Letter and newspaper files.

Published books, papers and reports
– *Economic Management*, The Treasury, Wellington, 14 July 1984.
– *Government Management, Briefing to the Incoming Government*, Vols I and II, The Treasury, Wellington, 1987.
– *Hastings, The Hub of Hawke's Bay, New Zealand.*, Hastings Borough Council, n.d.
– *Hawke's Bay—Before and After, Daily Telegraph*, Napier 1931, reprint 1981.
– *New Zealand Foreign Policy Statements and Documents 1943–57*, Foreign Affairs, Government Print, Wellington 1972.
– *Edmonds Cookery Book*, Bluebird Foods, Auckland, 38th Edition 1995.
Adams, Peter, *A Fatal Necessity*, Auckland University Press, Auckland 1977.
Aitken, Jefley J., *Rocked and Ruptured, Geological Faults*

in New Zealand, Reed Publishing (NZ) Ltd, Auckland 1999.

Anderson, Atholl, *Prodigious Birds—Moas and moa hunting in prehistoric New Zealand*, Cambridge University Press, Melbourne, 1989.

Anderson, Atholl, 'Canterbury and Marlborough' in Nigel Prickett (ed), *The First Thousand Years*, Dunmore Press, Palmerston North, 1982.

Anderson, Atholl, 'North and Central Otago' in Nigel Prickett (ed), *The First Thousand Years*, Dunmore Press, Palmerston North 1982.

Anderson, Grahame, *The Merchant of the Zeehaen—Isaac Gilsemans and the Voyages of Abel Tasman*, Te Papa Press, Wellington, 2001.

Arnold, Rollo, *The Farthest Promised Land*, Victoria University Press and Price Milburn, Wellington 1981.

Ashby, Michael, 'Fraser's Foreign Policy', in Margaret Clark (ed), *Peter Fraser, Master Politician*, Dunmore Press, Palmerston North, 1998.

Ashton, Robert, 'Aristocracy in Transition', *Economic History Review*, Vol. 22, 1969.

Bagnall, A. G., *Wairarapa: An Historical Excursion*, Masterton, 1976.

Ballara, Angela and Gary Scott, 'Crown Purchases of Land in Early Provincial Hawke's Bay', Waitangi Tribunal Wai 201, Wellington, 1994.

Ballara, Angela, *Taua*, Penguin, Auckland 2003.

Barber, Laurie and John Tonkin-Covell, *Freyberg: Churchill's Salamander*, Century Hutchinson, Auckland 1989.

Barber, Laurie, *A Short History of New Zealand*, Century Hutchinson, Auckland, 1981.

Barclay, A. R., 'The Premier and his troubles', Pamphlet, S. Lister, Printer, Dunedin, 1909.

Barratt, Glynn, *Russophobia in New Zealand*, Dunmore Press, Palmerston North, 1981.

Bassett, Judith, 'The Exodus', *New Zealand's Heritage*, Paul Hamlyn, Auckland, 1971, Part 54.

Bassett, Michael, *Coates of Kaipara*, AUP, Auckland, 1995.

Beckham, A. J. (ed), *The Discovery of the Maori*, Pemaka Press, Whitcombe & Tombs, Wellington, 1969.

Belich, James, *Making Peoples*, Penguin, Auckland 1996.

Belich, James, *Paradise Reforged*, Allen Lane, Auckland, 2001.

Belich, James, *The New Zealand Wars*, Penguin, Auckland, 1985.

Bentley, Trevor, 'Tribal Guns, Tribal Gunners: a study of acculturation by Māori of European military technology during the New Zealand inter-tribal musket wars', MPhil thesis, University of Waikato, 1977.

Binney, Judith, 'The Expansion of the Missions', *New Zealand's Heritage*, Vol. I, Part 11.

Binney, Judith, 'The Expansion of a Competitive Society', in David Hamer 'Towns in Nineteenth Century New Zealand' in D. A. Hamer (ed) *New Zealand Social History, Papers from the Turnbull Conference on New Zealand Social History, 1978*, University of Auckland, Auckland, 1978.

Binney, Judith, *Redemption Songs*, Bridget Williams Books, Wellington, 1995.

Blaug, Mark, *Great Economists Before Keynes*, Wheatsheaf Books, Brighton, 1986.

Boast, Richard, 'Esk Forest Claim: Report on the Mohaka-Waikare confiscation', Waitangi Tribunal, Wellington.

Boyack, Nicholas, *Behind the Lines*, Allen & Unwin, Wellington, 1989.

Boyd, Mary, *City Of the Plains*, Hastings City Council, Hastings, 1984.

Bradbury, Matthew (ed), *A History of the Garden in New Zealand*, Viking, Auckland, 1995.

Brash, Donald, 'Economy' in George Bryant (ed) *New Zealand 2001*, Cassell New Zealand, Auckland, 1981.

Brash, Donald., *New Zealand's Remarkable Reforms*, Institute of Economic Affairs, London, 1996.

Briggs, Asa, *Victorian Cities*, Pelican, London, 1968.

Briggs, Phil, *Looking at the numbers, a view of New Zealand's economic history*, New Zealand Institute of Economic Research, Wellington, 2003.

Brooking, Tom, '"Bursting up" the Greatest Estate of All' in Judith Binney (ed), *The Shaping of History*, Bridget Williams Books, Wellington, 2001.

Brooking, Tom, 'Commentaries', in D. A. Hamer (ed), *New Zealand Social History, Papers from the Turnbull Conference on New Zealand Social History, 1978*, University of Auckland, Auckland, 1978.

Brown, Bruce, 'Foreign Policy is Trade: Trade is Foreign Policy' in Ann Troter (ed) *Fifty Years of New Zealand Foreign Policy Making*, University of Otago Press, Dunedin, 1993.

Buchanan, J. D. (ed, J. D. Simmons), *The Maori History and Place Names of Hawke's Bay*, A. H. & A. W. Reed, Wellington, 1973.

Buck, T. L., *New Zealand's First War, the rebellion of Hone Heke*, Capper Press, reprint, Christchurch, 1976.

Buick, T. Lindsay *New Zealand's First War*, Government Printer, Wellington, 1926.

Burdon, R. M., *The New Dominion*, A. H. & A. W. Reed, Auckland, 1965.

Burnett, Joan, 'The Impact of Dairying on the Landscape of Lowland Taranaki', in R. F. Watters (ed) *Land and Society in New Zealand*, A. H. & A. W. Reed, Wellington, 1965, reprint 1967.

Burns, Patricia, *Fatal Success—A History of the New Zealand Company*, Heinemann-Reed, Auckland, 1989.

Byrnes, Giselle, *Boundary Markers*, Bridget Williams Books, Wellington, 2001.

Calman, Ross, *The New Zealand Wars*, Reed, Auckland, 2004.

Cannadine, David (ed), *The Speeches of Winston S. Churchill*, Penguin, London, 1989.

Caughey, Angela, *The Interpreter—The Biography of Richard 'Dicky' Barrett*, David Bateman, Auckland, 1998.

Chadwick, Edwin, 'Report on the Sanitary Conditions of the Labouring Population of Great Britain', in B. I. Coleman (ed) *The Idea of the City in Nineteenth Century Britain*, Routledge and Kegan Paul, London, 1973.

Chandler, David G., *Atlas of Military Strategy: the art, theory and practice of war 1618–1878*, Arms and Armour Press, London, 1980.

Chapple, Simon, *The economic effects of the 1931 Hawke's Bay Earthquake*, New Zealand Institute of Economic Research (Inc), Working Paper 97/7, Wellington, August 1997.

Chrisp, Stephen, 'The Maori occupation of Wairarapa: orthodox and nonorthodox versions', Journal of the Polynesian Society, Vol. 102, No. 1, March 1993.

Churchill, W. S., *The Second World War* (6 Vols), Clarendon Press, London, 1948–1954.

Churchill, W. S., *The World Crisis, 1911–1918*, Four Square, London, 1960.

Clark, Lloyd, *World War I: An Illustrated History*, Helicon, Oxford, 2001.

Clark, Paul, *Hauhau, The Pai Marire Search for Maori Identity*, Auckland University Press, Auckland, 1975.

Clifton, George, *The Happy Hunted*, Cassell & Co., London, 1952.

Colenso, William, 'On the Māori Races of New Zealand', Transactions and Proceedings of the New Zealand Institute 1868, Vol. 1, Wellington, 1869.

Colenso, William, 'The Authentic and Genuine History of the Signing of the Treaty of Waitangi', Government Print, 1890.

Comber, Ken, 'Personal reflections on my father-in-law', from Margaret Clark (ed) *Sir Keith Holyoake, Towards a Political Biography*, Dunmore Press, Palmerston North, 1997.

Conly, Geoff, *Wattie's—The First Fifty Years*, J. Wattie Canneries Ltd, Hastings, 1984.

Cook, Gary J. and Thomas J. Brown, *The Secret Land: People Before*, StonePrint Press, Christchurch, 1999.

Cooke Taylor, W., 'Notes of a Tour in the Manufacturing Districts of Lancashire', 1842, in B. I. Coleman (ed) *The Idea of the City in Nineteenth Century Britain*, Routledge and Kegan Paul, London, 1973.

Cowan, James, *The Maoris in the Great War: a history of the New Zealand Native Contingent and Pioneer Battalion, Gallipoli 1915, France and Flanders 1916–1918*, Whitcombe & Tombs Ltd, Auckland, 1926.

Cowan, James, *The New Zealand Wars*, Volume 1: 1845-64, Government Printer, Wellington, 1922.

Cowan, James, *The New Zealand Wars*, Volume 2: The Hauhau Wars, Government Print, Wellington, 1923.

Crawford, John and Ellen Ellis, *To Fight for the Empire: An Illustrated History of New Zealand and the South African War, 1899–1902*, Reed NZ Ltd, Auckland, 1999.

Crosby, R. O., *The Musket Wars*, Reed, Auckland 2000.

Cullen, Michael, 'Lawrence Stone, the Manors and other ruins', *Historical News*, March 1969.

Cumberland, Kenneth B., and J. W. Fox, *New Zealand: A Regional View*, Whitcombe & Tombs, Auckland 1958, second printing 1959.

Czerkas, Sylvia A., and Stephen A. Czerkas, *Dinosaurs: A Global View*, Dragons World, London, 1990.

Daley, Caroline, 'Taradale Meets the Ideal Society and its Enemies', in Judith Binney (ed) *The Shaping of History*, Bridget Williams Books, Wellington, 2001.

Davidoff, Leonore and Catherine Hall, 'The architecture of public and private life, English middle class society in a provincial town, 1780 to 1850', in Derek Fraser and A. Sutcliffe (eds) *The Pursuit of Urban History*, Edward Arnold, London, 1983.

Davidson, Janet, 'Auckland' in Nigel Prickett (ed) *The First Thousand Years*, Dunmore Press, Palmerston North, 1982.

Davidson, Janet, *The Prehistory of New Zealand*, Longman Paul, Auckland, 1984.

Davis, Peter, 'Stratification and Class' in Paul Spoonley, David Pearson and Ian Shirley (eds), *New Zealand Sociological Perspectives*, Dunmore Press, Palmerston North, 1982.

Diamond, Jared, *Guns, Germs and Steel*, Vintage, London, 1998.

Douglas, Roger, *Unfinished Business*, Random House, Auckland, 1993, reprint 1994.

Dowrick, David, 'Damage and Intensities in the Magnitude 7.8 1931 Hawke's Bay, New Zealand earthquake', *Bulletin of the New Zealand National Society for Earthquake Engineering*, Vol 31, No. 3, September 1998.

Drummond, Alison and L. R. Drummond, *At Home in New Zealand—an illustrated history of everyday things before 1865*, Blackwood and Janet Paul, Auckland, 1967.

Earle, Augustus, *A narrative of a nine months' residence in New Zealand in 1827; together with a journal of a residence in Tristan D'Acunha*, Longman, Rees, Orme, Brown, Green & Longman, London, 1832.

Easton, Brian, 'Beyond the Cringe', *New Zealand Listener*, 20 October 2001.

Easton, Brian, 'Three New Zealand Depressions' from W. E. Willmot (ed), *New Zealand and the World*, University of Canterbury, Christchurch, 1980.

Easton, Brian, *In Stormy Seas*, University of Otago Press, Dunedin, 1997.

Easton, Brian, *The Nationbuilders*, Auckland University Press, Auckland, 2001.

Edwards, Philip (ed), *The Journals of Captain Cook: Prepared from original manuscripts by J. C. Beaglehole for the Haklyut Society, 1955–1967*, Penguin, London, 1999.

Elder, N. L., *Vegetation of the Ruahine Range: An Introduction*, Royal Society of New Zealand, Wellington, 1965.

Eldred-Grigg, Stevan, *A Southern Gentry*, A. H. & A. W. Reed, Wellington, 1980.

Eldred-Grigg, Stevan, *Pleasures of the Flesh*, A. H. & A. W. Reed, Wellington, 1984.

Elliott, H. B., B. Striewski, J. R. Flenley, J. H. Kirkman, and D. G. Sutton, 'A 4300 year palynological and sedimentological record of environmental change and human impact from Wharau road swamp, Northland, New Zealand', *Journal of the Royal Society of New Zealand*, No. 27, No. 4, December 1997.

Elsmore, Bronwyn, *Like Them that Dream*, Reed, Auckland, 2000.

Enting, Brian and Les Molloy, *The Ancient Islands*, Port Nicholson Press, Wellington, 1982.

Evans, Geoff, *The Discovery of Aotearoa*, Reed, Auckland, 1998.

Fagan, Brian, *The Little Ice Age—How the Climate Made History*, Basic Books, New York, 2000.

Fairburn, Miles, 'Local Community or Atomized Society', in Judith Binney (ed) *The Shaping of History*, Bridget Williams Books, Wellington, 2001.

Fairburn, Miles, *The Ideal Society and its Enemies*, Auckland University Press, Auckland, 1989.

Farwell, Byron, *Queen Victoria's Little Wars*, Allen Lane, London, 1973.

Ferguson, Gael, *Building the New Zealand Dream*, Dunmore Press, Palmerston North, 1994.

Finney, Ben, 'Experimental Voyaging and Maori Settlement' in Douglas G. Sutton (ed) *The Origins of the First New Zealanders*, Auckland University Press, Auckland, 1994.

Forrest, James, 'Otago During the Goldrushes', in R. F. Watters (ed) *Land and Society in New Zealand*, A. H. & A. W. Reed, Wellington 1965, reprint 1967.

Fox, Aileen, 'Hawke's Bay', in *The First Thousand Years*, Dunmore Press, Palmerston North, 1982.

Freyberg, Paul, *Bernard Freyberg VC—Soldier of Two Nations*, Hodder & Stoughton, London, 1991.

Gamlin, Jeff, 'Treasury's white paper implies country is at a crossroads', *National Business Review*, 28 January 2000.

Gardner, W. J., 'A Colonial Economy' from W. H. Oliver & B. R. Williams (eds) *The Oxford History of New Zealand*, Oxford University Press, Auckland, 1981.

Conly, Geoff, *The Shock of '31*, A H & A W Reed, Wellington, 1980.

Gibson, Tom, *The Maori Wars*, A. H. & A. W. Reed, Wellington, 1974

Gillespie, Oliver A., *The Pacific*, War History Branch, Department of Internal Affairs, Wellington, 1952.

Goff, James R. and Bruce G. McFadgen, 'Nationwide tsunami during prehistoric Maori occupation, New Zealand', ITS 2001 Proceedings, Session 3, No. 3-1

Gould, Steven Jay, *Ever Since Darwin*, Penguin, London, 1991.

Grant, Patrick J., 'Climate, Geomorphology and Vegetation' in Douglas G. Sutton (ed), *The Origins of the First New Zealanders*, Auckland University Press, Auckland, 1994.

Grant, Patrick J., *Hawke's Bay Forests of Yesterday*, CHB Print, Waipukurau, 1996.

Grant, S., *In Other Days—A History of the Chambers Family of Te Mata, Havelock North*, CHB Printers, Waipukurau, 1980.

Gray, Colin S., *The Geopolitics of the Nuclear Era*, Crane, Russak & Co., Inc., 1977.

Greasley, David and Les Oxley (2002), 'Regime shift and fast recovery on the periphery: New Zealand in the 1930s', *Economic History Review*, LV(4).

Grimshaw, Patricia, *Women's Suffrage in New Zealand*, Auckland University Press, Auckland, second edition 1987.

Grytten, Ola Honningdal, 'Why was the Great Depression not so great in the Nordic countries? Economic policy and unemployment', Department of Economics, Norwegian School of Economics and Business Administration, n.d.

Gustafson, Barry, *His Way, A Biography of Robert Muldoon*, Auckland University Press, Auckland, 2000, paperback edition 2001.

Guthrie-Smith, H., *Tutira*, 3rd ed, William Blackwood & Sons, London, 1951.

Hamer, David, 'Towns in Nineteenth Century New Zealand' in D. A. Hamer (ed) *New Zealand Social History, Papers from the Turnbull Conference on New Zealand Social History, 1978*, University of Auckland, Auckland, 1978.

Hankin, Cherry A., *Life in a Young Colony*, Whitcoulls, Christchurch, 1981.

Harrington, Peter, *English Civil War Fortifications*, Osprey, Oxford, 2003.

Harris, Paul and Linda Twiname, *First Knights*, Howling at

the Moon Press, Auckland, 1998.

Hawke. G. R., *Railways and Economic Growth in England and Wales 1840–1870*, Clarendon Press, Oxford, 1970.

Hesselberg, Erik, *Kon Tiki and I*, Allen & Unwin, London, 1949.

Hexter, Robert, 'The English Aristocracy, its Crises, and the English Revolution, 1558–1660', *Journal of British Studies*, Vol. VIII, 1968.

Hill, R. D., 'Pastoralism in the Wairarapa, 1844–53', in R. F. Watters (ed) *Land and Society in New Zealand*, A. H. & A. W. Reed, Wellington 1965, reprint 1967.

Hobsbawm, Eric, *On History*, Abacus, London, 1998.

Hobsbawm, Eric, *Age of Extremes; The Short Twentieth Century 1941–1991*, Abacus, London, 1994.

Hobsbawm, Eric, *The Age of Revolution*, Abacus, London, 1977.

Hogg, Ian V., *The Machine Gun*, Phoebus, London, 1976.

Holdaway, R. N. and T. H. Worthy, 'A reappraisal of the later Quaternary fossil vertebrates of Pyramid Valley swamp, North Canterbury, New Zealand', *New Zealand Journal of Zoology*, Vol. 24, 1997.

Holdaway, Richard N., Roberts, Richard G., Beavan-Athfield, Nancy R., Olley, John M., and Trevor H. Worthy, 'Optical dating of quartz sediments and accelerator mass spectrometry 14C dating of bone gelatin and moa eggshell: a comparison of age estimates for non-archaeological deposits in New Zealand', *Journal of the Royal Society of New Zealand*, Vol. 32, No. 3, September 2002.

Holdaway, Richard N., 'A spatio-temporal model for the invasion of the New Zealand archipelago by the Pacific rat Rattus Exulans', *Journal of the Royal Society of New Zealand*, No. 29, No. 2, June 1999.

Houghton, Philip, 'A Vigorous People', in John Wilson (ed), *From the Beginning, the Archaeology of the Maori*, Penguin, Auckland, 1987.

Houghton, Philip, *The First New Zealanders*, Hodder & Stoughton, Auckland, 1980.

Howe, K. R., 'Western ideas about islanders origins' in K. R. Howe (ed), *Vaka Moana: voyages of the ancestors, the discovery and settlement of the Pacific*, David Bateman, Auckland, 2006.

Howe, K. R., *The Quest for Origins*, Penguin, Auckland, 2003.

Hunt, Graeme, *The Rich List*, Reed, Auckland, 1999.

Irwin, Geoffrey, 'Voyaging and Settlement' in K. R. Howe (ed) *Vaka Moana: Voyages of the ancestors, the discovery and settlement of the Pacific*, David Bateman, Auckland, 2006.

Irwin, Geoffrey, *The Prehistoric Exploration and Colonisation of the Pacific*, Cambridge University Press, Cambridge, 1992.

Jesson, Bruce, *Only Their Purpose Is Mad*, Dunmore Press, Palmerston North, 1999.

Jones, Kevin, 'Skill with Stone and Wood' in John Wilson (ed) *From the Beginning, the Archaeology of the Maori*, Penguin, Auckland, 1987.

Kemp, Geoffrey, 'The New Strategic Map', from Uri Ra'anan, *Arms Transfers to the Third World*, Westview Press, 1978.

King, Michael, *Moriori—A People Rediscovered*, Penguin, Auckland, revised edition 2001.

King, Michael, *Being Pakeha Now*, Penguin, Auckland, 1999.

King, Michael, *Nga Iwi O Te Motu*, revised edition, Reed, Auckland, 2001.

King, Michael, *The Penguin History of New Zealand*, Penguin, Auckland, 2003.

Kippenberger, H. K. (ed), *Documents Relating to New Zealand's Participation in the Second World War,* War History Branch, Department of Internal Affairs, 3 Vols, Wellington 1949, 1951 and 1963

Laugesen, Ruth, 'Clark finds new energy', *Sunday Star-Times,* 23 January 2000.

Law, R. Garry, 'Multiple settlement in Eastern Polynesia', in Douglas G. Sutton (ed) *The Origins of the First New Zealanders*, Auckland University Press, Auckland, 1994.

Lee, Jack, *The Old Land Claims In New Zealand* NHPS, Kerikeri, 1993.

Lees, C. M., V. E. Nealland A. S. Palmer, 'Forest persistence at coastal Waikato, 24,000 b.p. to present', *Journal of the Royal Society of New Zealand*, Vol. 28, No. 1, March 1998.

Lewis, David and Werner Forman, *The Maori: Heirs of Tane*, Orbis, London, 1982.

Liddell-Hart, Basil (ed), *The Rommel Papers*, Collins, London 1953, trans. Paul Findlay. (German original written by Erwin Rommel and edited by Fritz Bayerlein, Lucie-Maria Rommel and Manfred Rommel).

Lilley, Ray, 'Labour-Alliance prepares for great tax leap backward', *National Business Review*, 10 December 1999.

Lissington, M. P., *New Zealand and the United States*, Government Print, Wellington, 1972.

Lloyd-Prichard, M. F., *An Economic History of New Zealand to 1939*, Collins, Auckland, 1970.

Loughmann, R. A., *Life of Sir Joseph Ward*, New Century Press, Wellington, 1929.

Lowndes, Tracey, 'Economy a case of "minor adjustment"', *Otago Daily Times,* 4 January 2000.

Macdonald, Charlotte, *A Woman of Good Character*, Allen & Unwin/Historical Branch, Wellington, 1990.

Mackay, Duncan, 'The Orderly Frontier', in Judith Binney (ed) *The Shaping of History,* Bridget Williams Books,

Wellington, 2001.

MacLaren, A. A., 'Class Formation and Class Fractions, the Aberdeen bourgeoise 1830–1850', in G. Gordon and B. Dicks (eds) *Scottish Urban History*, Aberdeen University Press, Aberdeen, 1983.

MacNab, Robert, *Historical Records of New Zealand*, Vols I and II, Government Printer, Wellington, 1908 and 1914.

Madjalany, Fred, *Cassino, Portrait of a Battle*, Longmans, Green & Co., London, 1957.

Magnenheimer, Heinz, *Hitler's War*, Cassell, London, 1997.

Maning, F. E., *Old New Zealand*, Golden Press reprint, Auckland, 1987.

Marmon, John, 'The Life and Adventures of John Marmon, the Hokianga Pakeha Maori: or, seventy-five years in New Zealand', *Auckland Star*, 7 January 1882.

Marshall, William Barrett, *A personal narrative of two visits to New Zealand in HM Ship* Alligator, *AD 1834*, James Nisbet, London, 1836.

Martin, John E., *The Forgotten Worker*, Allen & Unwin, Wellington, 1990.

McCulloch, Beverley, illus. Geoffrey Cox, *Moas—Lost Giants of New Zealand*, HarperCollins, Auckland, 1992.

McGill, David, *Guardians at the Gate*, Silver Owl Press, Wellington, 1991.

McGlone, H. S., A. F. Mark and D. Bell, 'Late Pleistocene and Holocene vegetation history, Central Otago, South Island, New Zealand', *Journal of the Royal Society of New Zealand*, Vol. 25, No. 1, March 1995.

McGlone, H. S., A. Anderson and R. N. Holdaway, 'An ecological approach', in Douglas G. Sutton (ed) *The Origins of the First New Zealanders*, Auckland University Press, Auckland, 1994.

McIntyre, W. D., 'Peter Fraser's Commonwealth' in Alistair McIntosh (ed) *New Zealand in World Affairs*, Price, Milburn and Co., Wellington, 1977.

McKinnon, Malcolm (ed), *The New Zealand Historical Atlas*, Bateman, Auckland, 2000.

McKirdy, A., 'Maori-Pakeha Land Transactions in Hawke's Bay 1848–1864,' MA Thesis, Victoria University of Wellington, 1994.

McLauchlan, Gordon, *The Big Con*, Government Print, Wellington, 1992.

McLauchlan, Gordon, *The Passionless People*, Cassell, Auckland, 1976.

McLeod, John, *Myth and Reality, The New Zealand Soldier in World War II*, Heinemann Reed, Auckland, 1986.

McLintock, A. H., *Crown Colony Government in New Zealand*, Government Print, Wellington, 1958.

McLintock, A. H. (ed), *A Descriptive Atlas of New Zealand*, Government Printer, Wellington, 1959, second edition 1960.

Meaney, Neville, *The Search for Security in the Pacific* I, Sydney University Press, Sydney, 1976.

Metge, Joan and P. Kinloch, *Talking Past Each Other: Problems in Cross-Cultural Communication*, Victoria University Press, Wellington, 1984.

Mitchell, Austin, *The Quarter-Acre, Half-Gallon, Pavlova Paradise*, Whitcombe & Tombs, Christchurch, 1972.

Moon, Paul, *New Zealand in the Twentieth Century*, HarperCollins, Auckland, 2011.

Moon, Paul, *Hone Heke*, David Ling Publishing, Auckland, 2001.

Moon, Paul, *The Path to the Treaty of Waitangi*, David Ling Publishing, Auckland, 2002.

Moorhead, Alan, *The Fatal Impact*, Hamish Hamilton, London, 1966.

Morris, James, *Pax Britannica*, Faber & Faber, London, 1968.

Morris, R. J., 'The Middle Class and British Towns and Cities of the Industrial Revolution, 1780–1870', in Derek Fraser and A. Sutcliffe (eds) *The Pursuit of Urban History*, Edward Arnold, London, 1983.

Morris, R. J., 'Voluntary Societies and British Urban Elites, 1780-1850', *Historical Journal*, Vol. 26 No.1, March 1983.

Muldoon, R. D., *The Rise and Fall of a Young Turk*, A. H. & A. W. Reed, Wellington, 1972.

Muldoon, R. D., *The New Zealand Economy, a personal view*, Endeavour Press, Auckland, 1985.

O'Malley, Vincent, *The Ahuriri Purchase*, Crown Forestry Rental Trust, Wellington, 1995.

Oliver, W. H., *The Story of New Zealand*, Faber & Faber, London, 1960.

Oliver, W. H., 'The Future Behind Us', in Andrew Sharp and P. G. McHugh (eds) *Histories, Power and Loss*, Bridget Williams Books, Wellington, 2001.

Olssen, Erik, *Building the New World, work, politics and society in Caversham, 1880s–1920s*, Auckland University Press, Auckland 1995.

Orange, Claudia, *The Treaty of Waitangi*, Bridget Williams Books, Wellington, 1987.

Orbell, Margaret, *Hawaiki—a new approach to Maori tradition*, University of Canterbury, Christchurch, 1985.

Organisation for National Development, 'Interim Report on Post-war Reconstruction and National Development', July 1944.

Padfield, Peter, *The Great Naval Race*, Hart-Davis, London, 1974.

Paish, L.A., 'Economic Conditions in the Dominion of New Zealand to March 1931', HM Stationery Office, London, 1931.

Parsonson, Ann, 'The Pursuit of Mana' in W. H. Oliver *The Oxford History of New Zealand*, Oxford University Press, Auckland, 1981.

Patterson, Mike, *The Point at Issue*, HarperCollins, Auckland, 1991.

Petersen, G. C., 'Pioneering the North Island Bush', in R. F. Watters (ed) *Land and Society in New Zealand*, A. H. & A. W. Reed, Wellington, 1965, reprint 1967.

Porter, Frances, *Born to New Zealand, a biography of Jane Maria Atkinson*, Bridget Williams Books, Wellington, 1995.

Prickett, Nigel, *Landcapes of Conflict—A Field Guide to the New Zealand Wars*, Random House, Auckland, 2001.

Prickett, Nigel, *Maori Origins—from Asia to Aotearoa*, David Bateman, Auckland, 2001.

Pugsley, Chris, 'Walking Heke's War', *Defence Quarterly*, No. 4, Autumn 1994.

Quiggan, John, 'Change long overdue in New Zealand', *Australian Financial Review*, 2 December 1999.

R. Boulter and T. G. A. Muntz, 'Report on economic and commercial conditions in New Zealand', HM Stationery Office, London, 1936.

Rabb, Theodore K., *The Struggle for Stability in Early Modern Europe*, Oxford University Press, New York, 1975.

Rankin, Keith, 'New Zealand's Gross National Product', *Review of Income and Wealth*, Vol. 38, No. 1, March 1992.

Richards, Rhys, 'Rongotute, Stivers and "Other Visitors" to New Zealand', *Journal of the Polynesian Society*, Volume 102, No. 1, March 1993.

Richardson, Len, 'Parties and political change' in W. H. Oliver (ed) *The Oxford History of New Zealand*, Oxford University Press, Auckland, 1981, reprinted 1991.

Richardson, Len and W. David McIntyre (eds), *Provincial Perspectives*, University of Canterbury, Christchurch, 1980.

Richardson, Ruth, *Making a Difference*, Shoal Bay Press, Christchurch, 1995.

Roberts, Andrew, 'Prime Minister Halifax' in Robert Cowley (ed) *What If? 2*, Berkley, New York, 2001.

Ross, R. M., 'Te Tiriti o Waitangi', in Judith Binney (ed) *The Shaping of History*, Bridget Williams Books, Wellington, 2001.

Royal Military College, *A Course of Lectures on Fortification, Military Tactics and Perspective; with the attack and defence of fortresses*, Royal Military College, Third Edition, London, 1852.

Ryan, Tim and Bill Parham, *The Colonial New Zealand Wars*, Grantham House, Wellington, 1986.

Salmond, Ann, *Between Worlds*, Viking, Auckland, 1997.

Salmond, Ann, *Two Worlds*, Viking, Auckland, 1991.

Saul, John Ralston, *Voltaire's Bastards*, Penguin, Canada, 1992.

Schwimmer, Eric, 'The Maori Hapu: A generative model', in *Journal of Polynesian Studies*, Vol. 99, No.3, September 1990.

Scrimgeour, C. G., John A. Lee and Tony Simpson, *The Scrim-Lee Papers*, A. H. & A. W. Reed, Wellington, 1976.

Sharp, Andrew, 'More blood out of Stone; what was the crisis of the aristocracy?', *Historical News*, March 1969.

Sharp, Andrew, 'Recent Juridical and Constitutional Histories of Maori', in Andrew Sharp and Paul McHugh, *Histories Power and Loss*, Bridget Williams Books, Wellington, 2001.

Simpson, Tony, *The Sugarbag Years*, Hodder & Stoughton, Auckland, 1974, new edition 1984.

Simpson, Tony, *A Distant Feast*, Godwit, Auckland, 1999.

Simpson, Tony, *The Immigrants*, Godwit, Auckland, 1997.

Simpson, Tony, *The Road to Erewhon*, Beaux Arts, Auckland, 1976.

Simpson, Tony, *The Slump: The 1930s Depression, its origins and aftermath*, Penguin, Auckland, 1990.

Sinclair, Keith, 'The Liberals Come to Power', in *New Zealand's Heritage*, Paul Hamlyn, Auckland 1971, Part 56.

Sinclair, Keith, *A History of New Zealand*, Penguin, Auckland 1959, revised edition 1988.

Sorrenson, M. P. K., Maori Origins and Migrations, Auckland University Press, Auckland, 1979.

Sorrenson, M. P. K., 'Maori and Pakeha' in W. H. Oliver (ed) *The Oxford History of New Zealand*, Oxford University Press, Auckland, 1981, reprint 1991.

Stephens, P. R., 'The Age of the Great Sheep Runs' in R. F. Watters (ed) *Land and Society in New Zealand*, A. H. & A. W. Reed, Wellington 1965, reprint 1967.

Stevens, Graeme and Beverley McCulloch, *Prehistoric New Zealand*, Heinemann Reed, Auckland, 1988.

Stone, R. C. J., *From Tamaki-Makau-Rau to Auckland*, Auckland University Press, Auckland, 2001.

Stratford, Stephen, *The Dirty Decade—New Zealand in the 80's*, Tandem Press, Auckland, 2002.

Stumpf, Paul, *The Music's All That Matters*, Quartet, London, 1997.

Suggate, R. P. (ed), *The Geology of New Zealand*, Government Printer, Wellington, 1978.

Sutch, W. B., *Colony or Nation?*, Sydney University Press 1966, second edition 1968.

Sutch, W. B., *The Quest for Security in New Zealand 1940 to 1966*, Oxford University Press, London, 1966.

Sutton, Douglas G. (ed), *The Archaeology of the Kainga*, Auckland University Press, Auckland, 1990, second edition 1994.

Tasker, John, *Myth and Mystery*, Tandem Press, Auckland, 1997.

Tasker, John, *Secret Landscape*, Kanuka Press, Hastings,

2000.
Tattersall, Ian *The Fossil Trail*, Oxford University Press, Oxford, 1995.
Taylor, A. J. P., *How Wars Begin*, Book Club Associates, London, 1979.
Taylor, David, *Poverty*, Heinemann Educational, Oxford, 1990.
Temple, Philip, *A Sort of Conscience—The Wakefields*, Auckland University Press, Auckland, 2002.
Thomson, David, *A World Without Welfare, New Zealand's Colonial Experiment*, Auckland University Press/Bridget Williams Books, Wellington, 1998.
Thomson, David, *England in the Nineteenth Century*, Penguin, London, 1950.
Thorns, David and Charles Sedgwick, *Understanding Aotearoa/New Zealand: Historical Statistics*, Dunmore Press, Palmerston North, 1997.
Toynbee, Claire, 'Class and Social Structure in Nineteenth Century New Zealand' in D. A. Hamer (ed) *New Zealand Social History, Papers from the Turnbull Conference on New Zealand Social History, 1978*, University of Auckland, Auckland, 1978.
Travers, W. T. L., 'Notes of the traditions and manners and customs of the Mori-oris', *Transactions of the New Zealand Institute*, Vol. 9, Wellington, 1875.
Trevor-Roper, H. R., 'The General Crisis of the Seventeenth Century', *Past and Present* No. 16, 1959.
Trotter, Michael and Beverley McCulloch, *Digging up the Past—New Zealand's archaeological history*, revised ed. Penguin, London, 1997.
Tylecote, Andrew, *The long wave in the world economy, the present crisis in historical perspective*, Routledge, London 1991.
Vaggioli, Domenico Felice, *History of New Zealand and its inhabitants*, trans. John Crockett, Otago University Press, Dunedin, 2000.
Vandergoes, Marcus J., Sean J. Fitzsimons and Rewi M. Newnham, 'Late glacial to Holocene vegetation change in the eastern Takitimu mountains, western Southland, New Zealand', *Journal of the Royal Society of New Zealand*, Vol. 27, No. 1, March 1997.
Vaughan, R., 'The Age of Great Cities' in B. I. Coleman (ed) *The Idea of the City in Nineteenth Century Britain*, Routledge and Kegan Paul, London, 1973.
Waitangi Tribunal, *Muriwhenua Land Report*, Wellington, 1997.
Waitangi Tribunal, *Ngai Tahu Report 1991*, Wellington, 1991.
Morrell, W. P., *The Provincial System in New Zealand, 1852-76*, Whitcombe & Tombs, Wellington, 1964.
Wakefield, E. Jerningham, *Adventure in New Zealand*, ed. Joan Stevens, Golden Press, Auckland, 1975.

Walker, Martin, *The Cold War*, Viking, London, 1993.
Walker, Ranginui, *Struggle Without End*, Penguin, Auckland, 1990.
Ward, Alan, *A Show of Justice*, ANU Press, 1974.
Ward, David, 'The Victorian Slum: An enduring myth', *Annals of the Association of American Geographers*, Vol. 66, 1976.
Ward, John, *Information Relative to New Zealand Compiled for the Use of the Colonists*, John W. Parker, London 1840; Capper Press reprint, Christchurch, 1975.
Waters, S. D., *The Royal New Zealand Navy*, War Histories Branch, Wellington, 1956.
Waterson, Duncan, 'Transport in New Zealand 1900–1930', in R. F. Watters (ed) *Land and Society in New Zealand*, A. H. & A. W. Reed, Wellington, 1965, reprint 1967.
Weitzel, R. L., 'Pacifists and anti-militarists in New Zealand, 1909-1914', *New Zealand Journal of History*, Vol. 7, No. 2, October 1973.
Wells, Andrew, Glenn H. Stewart and Richard P. Duncan, 'Evidence of widespread, synchronous, disturbance-initiated forest establishment in Westland, New Zealand', *Journal of the Royal Society of New Zealand*, No. 28, No. 2, June 1998.
Whitmore, G. S., *The Last Maori War in New Zealand*, Sampson, Low, Marston & Co., London, 1902.
Williams, William, *Christianity Among the New Zealanders*, Seeley, Jackson and Halliday, London, 1867.
Wilson, J. G. (ed), *History of Hawke's Bay*, A. H. & A. W. Reed, Wellington, 1939.
Wilson, J. G., *The History of Umutaoroa 1896–1956*, Dannevirke Publishing Company Ltd, Dannevirke, 1956.
Win, Roger D., *Who Ploughed So Well*, private publication, Nelson, 1996.
Wolff, Leon, *In Flanders Fields*, Longmans, Green & Co., London, 1959.
Wood, F. L. W., 'Why did New Zealand not join the Australian Commonwealth in 1900–1901', *New Zealand Journal of History* Vol. 2, No. 2, October 1968.
Wood, F. L. W., *New Zealand in the World*, Department of Internal Affairs, Wellington, 1940.
Wood, F. L. W., *Political and External Affairs*, War Histories Branch, Wellington, 1958.
Wright, Matthew and Graham Howard, 'The Reserve Bank Inflation Calculator', Reserve Bank of New Zealand *Bulletin*, Vol. 66, No.4.
Wright, Matthew, *Havelock North—The History of a Village*, HDC, Hastings, 1996.
Wright, Matthew, *New Zealand's Engineering Heritage*, Reed NZ, Auckland, 1999.
Wright, Matthew, 'Australia, New Zealand and Imperial

Naval Defence', MA Thesis, Massey University 1986.

Wright, Matthew, 'Mordacious years': socio-economic aspects and outcomes of New Zealand's experience in the Great Depression, Reserve Bank of New Zealand *Bulletin*, Vol.72, No. 3. 2009.

Wright, Matthew, 'Sir Joseph Ward and New Zealand Naval Defence, 1907–13', *Political Science*, Vol. 41, No. 1, July 1989.

Wright, Matthew, *Battle for Crete*, Reed, Auckland, 1999, reprint 2003.

Wright, Matthew, *Blue Water Kiwis*, Reed, Auckland, 2001.

Wright, Matthew, *Cars Around New Zealand*, Whitcoulls, Auckland, 2005.

Wright, Matthew, *Desert Duel*, Reed, Auckland, 2002.

Wright, Matthew, *Hawke's Bay—The History of a Province*, Dunmore Press, Palmerston North 1994.

Wright, Matthew, *Italian Odyssey*, Reed, Auckland, 2003.

Wright, Matthew, *Kiwi Air Power*, Reed, Auckland, 1998.

Wright, Matthew, *New Zealand's Engineering Heritage*, Reed, Auckland, 1999.

Wright, Matthew, 'Now we lie in Flanders fields', *New Zealand Listener*, 13–19 October 2007.

Wright, Matthew, *Old South*, Penguin, Auckland, 2009.

Wright, Matthew, *Pacific War*, Reed, Auckland, 2003.

Wright, Matthew, *Rails across New Zealand*, Whitcoulls, Auckland, 2003.

Wright, Matthew, *Two Peoples, One Land*, Reed NZ Ltd, Auckland, 2006.

Wright, Matthew, *New Zealand's Military Heroism*, Reed, Auckland, 2007.

Wright, Matthew, *Shattered Glory*, Penguin, Auckland, 2010.

Wright, Matthew, *Wings over New Zealand*, Whitcoulls, Auckland, 2002.

Wright, Matthew, *Town and Country—The History of Hastings and District*, Hastings District Council, Hastings, 2001.

Wright, Matthew, *Guns and Utu*, Penguin, Auckland, 2011.

Wright, Matthew, *Convicts: New Zealand's Hidden Criminal Past*, Penguin, Auckland, 2012.

Yate, William, *An Account of New Zealand*, Seeley and Burnside, London, 1835.

Yule, Henry, *Fortification for Officers of the Army and Students of Military History*, William Blackwood, Edinburgh, 1851.

Index

agrarian revolution 271, 366
Alexander, Alexander, 148
Alexandra, 166
All Blacks, 203, 204, 224, 296, 410, 423, 425
Alligator, HMS, 49
anti-nuclear protests, 430–431
Anzac Cove, 257
ANZUS, 410, 430
Aotearoa, origins, 18
Arapuni, 277
Armstrong, H. T., 321
Arrow River, 164
Art deco — *see* modernism
Ashwin, Bernard, 341, 365
Astrolabe, 31
Atiamuri, 383
Atkinson, Henry, 189, 190, 201, 205, 208, 211, 215
Atkinson, Jane, 108–109
Auckland City Mission, 311
Auckland Community Arts Ensemble, 388
Auckland Savings Bank, 202
Auckland, 73–74, 76, 84, 95, 108, 127, 130–131, 135, 145, 147–148, 160–161, 174, 190, 208, 230–231, 233, 236, 242, 250, 273, 312, 346–347, 377, 380–381, 393, 419, 430
Australia, union with, 243–244
Australia and New Zealand Corps (ANZAC), 257, ANZAC Day, 269

baby boom 375–376, 413, 427, 445
Balfour, David P., 110, 121, 146, 165, 170, 172
Ballance, John, 200, 206, 209, 210, 248, 334
Barrett, Richard (Dicky), 45, 65, 87
Bartlett, Patricia, 400
Bastion Point, 419
Battle for Manners Street, 349

Bay of Islands, 34, 38, 40, 45, 48, 51, 75, 76, 95
Bay of Plenty, 14, 93, 168
Beauchamp, Kathleen, 217, 298, *see also* Mansfield, Katherine
Beeby, Dr. C. E., 325
Bell Block, 151
Bell, Sir Francis, 227, 270
Benmore, power station, 369
Bennett, Agnes, 305
Bidwill, C. R., 92
Bishop, William, 113
Bluff, 46, 218, 316
Board of Trade, 269
Boer War, 233, 234, 256, 359
Bollinger, George, 256
Bourke, Harry, 263
Bourke, Richard 49, 51
Brees, S. C., 30–31
Bretton Woods, 365, 430
Bridge, Major Cyprian, 19, 38, 40, 77, 79, 81
Broughton, Charles, 168
Brown, Ohiwi, 129
Buchanan, J. B. H., 16
Buck, Peter *see* Hiroa, Te Rangi
Buller, 165
Bunbury, Thomas, 58–60
Burns, Barnet, 49
Busby, James, 48–52, 54–56
Butler, Samuel, 115

Cameron, Duncan, 147, 154, 157, 159, 167, 170
Cameron, Sarah Ann, 124
Campbell, Alistair, 389
Campbell, Dorothy, 305
Canterbury Association, 91, 102, 141
Canterbury Aviation Company, 280
Canterbury, 109, 112, 113, 116, 117, 122, 124, 128, 147, 149, 159, 161, 163, 174, 252, 254, 272, 441

Carlyon, George, 115, 124
Carrington, Frederick, 139
Carroll, James, 212, 333–334
Carruthers, John, 195
cars, 272–275, 279, 286, 289–290, 292–295, 390–393
Cawthron, Thomas, 119
Caxton Press, 389
Centennial celebrations, 317
censorship, 269, 290
Chambers, John (jnr), 214, 215, 216
Chambers, John, 121, 218
Chichester, Francis, 283
Christchurch Club, 238
Christchurch, 61, 102, 117, 120, 127, 134–136, 139, 253, 266, 267, 277, 286, 313, 320, 393, 396, 439, 440, 441
Church Missionary Society, (CMS), 36–38
Churchill, Sir Winston, 256, 338, 343–345, 346, 351, 353
Clark, Helen, 438
Clifton, George, 340
Coates, J. G., 277, 279, 280, 282, 306, 307, 313–315, 317, 319, 320, 325, 334, 336, 344, 370
cold war, 251, 361, 369, 380, 404, 413, 422, 432
Colenso, William, 12–14, 19, 22, 35, 49, 55–56, 86, 91–92
Colonial Conference 1887, 237; 1897, 241; 1902, 241
Colonial Office, 49–54, 62, 64, 73–74, 85–86, 147, 201
Columbus, Ray, 399, 427
Common Market, 401, 406
Communist Party, 380
Coningham, Air Vice Marshal Arthur, 356
Cook strait, 11, 27
Cook, James, 22, 27, 28, 29, 30, 32

483

Cooper, Whina, 419
Cox, Geoffrey, 298
Cromwell, 137, 165
Crump, Barry, 389, 390
cultural cringe, 225, 236, 252, 258, 296, 300, 338, 357, 442, and try-hard ethos, 225–227, 449

d'Urville, Jules Sebastien Cesar Dumont, 21, 31, 32
Dagg, Fred, 272, 295
dairy farming, 132, 180–184, 189, 220–222, 271–272, 277, 280, 314–315, 320, 405
Dannevirke, 183, 289, 407
Davie, Cyrus, 105
Davin, Dan, 298
De Surville, Jean, 29
de Thierry, Baron Charles Phillipe Hippolyte, 50–51
Declaration of Independence, 51, 55, 58
deer hunting, 299, 389
defence, 236–246, 339–344; Singapore, 279–280, 340
Defence Act 1909, 256
depressions: Great Depression, 300–301, 305–314, 316–317, 319–321, 323–325, 328–330; Long, 167, 186
Despard, Colonel Henry, 79–80
Devlin, Johnny, 397
Dieffenbach, Ernest, 65
Discharged Soldiers Settlement Act, 272
Dobbyn, Dave, 428
Dobson, Arthur, 128
Dobson, Edward, 128
Domett, Alfred, 75, 90, 91, 92, 140, 148, 197
Dominion, ideas of, 239, 245
Donnelly, G. P., 214
New Zealand and double patriotism, 251, 338, 340, 400
Douglas, Ken, 437
Douglas, Roger, 432, 435–436
du Fresne, Marion, 31
Duff, Roger, 16
Dundas, Henry, 31
Dunedin Sound, 428
Dunedin, 117, 118, 133–135, 137, 163, 165, 166, 230, 235, 286, 312, 350, 393
Dunedin (ship), 218

economic: crises, 159–161, 280–283; recovery, 315, 365–367; restructuring, 436–438, 444–447
Eden, Dorothy, 298
Emergency Precautions Service, 344
Empire Defence Fund, 263
Endeavour, HMS, 27–29
Eyre, Edward, 74, 88, 92–94

Featherston, Dr Isaac, 110, 119
Federation of Labour, 249

First World War, 251–256, 258, 264, 444
Firth, Josiah, 128, 170
Firth, Raymond, 298
Fitzgerald, James, 119
FitzRoy, Robert, 73–74, 76–77, 79–80, 84
Five Power Defence Arrangement (FPDA), 405
Footrot, Wal, 272, 295
Forbes, George, 280, 284, 301, 303, 306–307, 314–317, 319–320
Four Square Groceries, 377
Fox, William, 109, 165, 170, 173, 197, 204
Foxton, 174, 181–182
Frame, Janet, 390
Fraser, Peter, 263, 278, 316, 318, 325, 342–343, 345–346, 350–354, 358, 364–365, 369–370, 380, 401
Freyberg, Lieutenant-General Sir Bernard, 352–353, 357, 359–360, 362

Gallipoli, 258–259, 295
Gate Pa, 147, 157–158
General Assembly, 74, 148
gentry life, 110–120
Gisborne, 170, 242, 303
Gleneagles Agreement, 423
Glenelg, Lord, 50, 52
Glenmark Station, 115, 120
Glover, Denis, 389
Godley, Charlotte, 91, 105, 107–108
Godley, John Robert, 91, 102
Godley, Major-General Sir Alexander, 256
gold mining, 161–167
gold rush, 102
Golden Bay, 25, 27, 29
Good Roads Association, 274
Goodbye Pork Pie, 426
Goosman, W. S., 377
Gore-Browne, Thomas, 95, 150, 197
government: big, 270; settler, 72–75
Great Depression *see* depression
Great White Fleet, 242
Greer, H. H., 157, 159
Grey, George, 74, 79–81, 84–95, 147, 154, 156–157, 175, 188–189, 200
Greymouth, 204, 229
Guthrie-Smith, Herbert, 121, 211, 250, 301, 309

Haast, Julius, 12
Hall, Sir John, 205
Hamilton, 78, 140, 378, 424
Hamilton, F. W., 104, 122, 124
Hapuawhenua viaduct, 370–371
Harding, John, 115
Hastings, 117, 136, 140, 303–305, 313, 370, 378; blossom festival, 385
Haumene, Te Ua, 167
Havelock North, 140, 142

Hawke's Bay, 42, 46, 53, 58, 90, 92–96, 112, 114, 116–118, 120, 124, 129, 144, 148–149, 160–161, 167–168, 170–174, 178–184, 189, 191, 194–195, 198, 210–215, 218, 272, 303–304, 306, 443
Heaphy, Charles, 61, 69, 80
Heemskirck, 25
Heke, Hone, 56, 59, 75
Henderson, Jim, 389
Herangi, Te Puea, 263, 334, 336
Hewitt, Ellen, 145
Heyward, Rudall, 426
Higginson, Louisa, 256, 257
High Voltage DC Cable, 369
Hika, Hongi, 37, 43–44, 77, 83
Hillary, Edmund, 400
hippies, 413–414
Hiroa, Te Rangi, 12, 13, 333
Hobhouse, Mary, 109, 112, 114
Hobson, William, 46, 51–59, 69, 72–75, 86
Hodgkins, Frances, 388
Holland, Harry, 315, 337
Holland, Sidney, 307, 370, 372, 380, 395, 397, 402
Holyoake, Sir Keith Jacka, 388, 395, 401, 415
housing, styles 286–287, 375; shortages 369–370
Hulme, Lieutenant-Colonel William, 77
Hunter, Mary, 306
Hursthouse, C. W., 195
Hutt Valley, 66, 71, 82–84; housing 374–375, 377

Ihimaera, Witi, 427
Imperial Conferences, 239, 245
influenza epidemic, 255, 266–270
information revolution, 450
Invercargill, 140, 186, 190
Invincibles, The, 295–296

Jackson, Sir Peter, 433
Jervois, Sir William, 116
jingoism, 234–239
Johnsonville, 289

Kaingaroa, 372
Kaitaia, 248
Kapiti island, 18
Karapiro dam, 366
Kaskowiski hoax, 236
Kawerau, 369–371
Kawhia, 44
Kawiti, Te Ruki, 75, 77, 79–81
Kemp, Henry, 87
Kenana, Rua, 336
Kerikeri, 38, 39, 46
Kerr, Graham, 394
Kerridge, Sir Robert, 395
King Country, 154, 156, 173–175, 185, 194–195, 263

King Movement *see* Kingitanga
King, Lieutenant-Governor Philip, 32, 34, 38
King, Michael, 449
King, Truby, 285, 379
Kingitanga, 150–151, 197
Kingsford Smith, Charles, 280
Kirk, Norman, 406–407, 410, 415–416, 419, 422–423
Kohimarama conference, 89
Korean war, 401
Kororareka (Russell), 35, 46–48, 76–77, 79
Kotahitanga movement, 333

Labour market reforms, 321
Labour party, 200, 270, 307, 370–373, 406–409, 417, 421, 430, 435; elected 1935, 318, 320; welfare as applied Christianity, 322, 324; and defence, 338–342, 369, 406–409, 417, 421, 430, 435; elected 1984, 436; elected 1999, 430, 438–439
Lake Coleridge, 277
Lake Manapouri, 415
Lake Waikaremoana, 277
Land Claims Court, 54
land purchases, 84–96
Larnach, W. J., 117
Latta, M. V., 369
Lawlor, Pat, 297
League of Nations, 278, 338
Lee, John A., 312, 314, 318, 339
Levin, 135, 393
Levin, William Hort, 116, 135, 188
Liberal Party, 199–201, 206–207, 209, 216, 248–249, 270, 272, 334; land reforms, 200, 207, 209–212, 215–216, 271
liberal thinking, 239
literature, 389; settler, 298
Lower Hutt, 387, 418
Luckie, D. M., 242
Lyttleton, 100-101, 103

Macintosh, Sir Robert, 298
MacLean, Douglas, 212
Mahia, 49, 53
Mair, William, 157
Manawatu, 11, 93, 94, 129, 135, 182, 184, 188, 191, 194, 272, 366, 369
Maney, Richard D., 128, 198
Maniapoto, Rewi, 155, 195
Maning, Frederick, 21, 35, 37, 40, 59
Mansfield, Katherine, 297–299
Mantell, Walter, 16, 87
Maori Arts and Crafts Act 1926, 334
Maori Battalion, 336, 349, 355, 358, 417, 419
Maori Pioneer Battalion, 259, 334
Maori War Effort Organisation, 417
Maori, origins 12–15, population growth 15, impact on New Zealand 15, 17, classic society 18–19, warfare 21–22, tools 20, European trade 34–35, European disease 36–37, missionaries 37–39, muskets 40–46, potato 40–41, and assimilation 88, response to settler expansion 196–198, demographic change 375, re-assertion, 422, urbanisation 417, population recovery 417, post-war economic position 418–419, cultural revival 419–420
Marlborough, 112, 116, 147, 161
marriage, 40, 109, 119, 129, 144–146, 314, 375
Marsden, Samuel, 37–39
Martin, Sir William, 86,198
Martinborough, 140
Massey, William Ferguson, 244, 248, 250, 264, 267, 270–272, 277–280
Massey's Cossacks, 250
Masterton, 138, 143
Matamata, 391
Mathew, Felton, 138
Mazengarb, Oswald, 397
McDonnell, Colonel Thomas, 173
McIntosh, Alister, 383
McIntyre, Peter, 388
McKenzie, John, 209–210
McKenzie, Thomas, 248, 250
McLean, Allan, 213
McLean, Sir Donald, 65, 86–87, 89–96, 108, 112–113, 117–118, 148–149, 152, 168–171, 173, 198, 207
meat industry, 120, 161, 218–221, 271, 280, 315, 351, 405
Mercer, Henry, 155
Meremere, 154–155
Methodist Missionary Society, 39
migration: 100–107, 131–132, 175, 177–185, 299; Maori, 12–14
missionaries, 36–39, 41, 44–45
Mixed-member proportional representation (MMP), 438
Moa, 12–13, extinction 15–17
Modernism, 327–331, 397
Mohaka massacre, 172
Monro, Sir David, 120
Moore, G. H., 115, 120
Moorehouse, William, 149
Morris 1000, 391, 393
Mount Algidus, 112
Mount Egmont (Taranaki), 220
Mount Ruapehu, 363
Muldoon, Sir Robert, 362, 405, 407–411, 415, 422–424, 426, 428–430, 432–433, 436, 442–444
Mulgan, Alan, 297–298
Mulgan, John, 286, 300, 303, 312, 354–355, 361–362, 379
Munro, Donald, 389
Murphy, Geoff, 426
Mururoa Atoll, 416, 430

musket pa, 46, 79, 83

Nanto-Bordelaise Company, 72, 74
Napier, 92, 108, 117–118, 129, 135, 140, 168, 170–171, 173, 179, 181, 190, 214, 218, 220, 242, 445; earthquake, 302–306
Nash, Walter, 318, 320–321, 344, 365, 372, 395
National Airways Corporation (NAC), 369
National Expenditure Adjustment Act, 307
National Party: founded 324; comparison with Labour, 370–373, 407, 421, 436
Nelson Football Club, 224
Nelson, 69–71, 74–75, 140, 147, 438
Nelson, William, 218, 220
Nene, Tamati Waka, 39, 54–56, 59, 75–79
Nepia, George, 295–296
New Munster, 74
New Plymouth, 61, 71–72, 84, 135, 139–140, 144, 151–152, 220–221, 309, 364
New Zealand and Australia Land Company, 113
New Zealand Ballet, 389
New Zealand Company, 52, 54, 61–64, 72–74, 83, 86, 88, 90–92, 101–102, 140, 151
New Zealand Farmers Union, 248
New Zealand First Party, 438
New Zealand Land Company, 63
New Zealand Legion, 313
New Zealand National Orchestra, 389
New Zealand Permanent Air Force, 339
New Zealand Railways, 432
New Zealand, HMS, 241
Ngapuhi, 34, 41, 50, 75, 80, 83
Ngai Tahu, 24, 48
Ngaruawahia, 154, 156–157, 280, 336
Ngata, Sir Apirana Turupa, 333–334, 336–337, 417
Ngati Hineuru, 168
Ngati Kahungunu, 13, 59, 86, 90, 92–94, 96, 112, 168, 171, 173, 197–198
Ngati Mutunga, 64, 67
Ngati Raukawa, 64, 81, 155
Ngati Toa, 42, 43, 65-66, 83, 84
Ngati Tumatakokiri, 25
Ngati Whatua, 46, 419
Niagara, SS, 267
Normanby, Lord, 52–54
Norsewood, 183, 274
North Island main trunk line 175, 185, 193–194, 196, 242, 422, 437
Northland, 11
Nugent, C. L., 151

OECD, 405, 408, 448
Ohinemutu, 332–334

oil, 406–408, 422–423
Old Age Pensions Act 1898, 249
Onehunga, 131, 205
Opotiki, 168
Organisation of Petroleum Exporting Nations (OPEC), 406
Ormond, John, 113–114, 117–118, 120, 170, 173, 181, 198, 216
Otago, 11, 14, 92, 112–113, 122, 147–149, 160–167, 174–175, 190, 218
Otemata, 369

Pacific Defence Conference, 340, 343
Pacific island territories, 237
Pai Marire, 167–169, 197
Pakiaka, 45
Palliser Bay, 18
Palmerston North, 140, 280, 282
Paraparaumu, 277, 369
Paremata, 33
Parihaka, 194
Park, Sir Keith, 356
Parkinson, Sidney, 22, 28
Parry, Evan, 277
Passchendaele, 259, 261
pastoralism, 110–124
'Pavlova' society, 363–364, 378
Petone, 209, 282
Petre (Wanganui), 72
Pickering, William, 449
Pipitea Pa, 66
Pito-One (Petone), 65
Plimmer, John, 188
Polack, Joel, 35, 49, 77
Pomare, Maui, 259, 333
Popper, Karl, 299
Port Nicholson, 65
Poverty Bay, 168, 170–171
Pratley, Philip, 178
Protestant Political Association, 264, 270

quarter-acre ideal, 136, 141, 286, 317, 363, 370, 379, 422
Queen Charlotte Sound, 16, 30
Queenstown, 166

Rainbow Warrior, 430
Rainbow, William, 104–106
Rangiriri, 154–155, 157
Rangitata River, 385
Rangitata (orogeny), 11
Rangitikei, 122
Rata, Matiu, 420
Ratana movement 337–338, and Labour 338
Ratana, Tahupotiki Wiremu, 337
Rattlesnake, HMS, 51
Read, Gabriel, 162, 164, 166
Red Feds, 246–249
Reeves, William Pember, 117, 200–203, 208–210, 217, 247
Reform Party, 248, 264, 270, 306

Reform Political League, 248
Repudiation movement, 197–198
Rhodes, Heaton, 213
Rhodes, W. B. (Barney), 53
Riccarton, 225
Richardson, Ruth, 436–437
Richmond, C. W., 121, 149, 198
Richmond, J. C., 170–171, 198
Rimutaka incline, 202
Ringatu, 170, 197
Rogernomics, 432, 442
Rolleston, William, 111–112, 217
Rotorua Carving School, 334
Rotorua, 230, 334
Rowling, Wallace, 407
Roxburgh, 369
Ruatara (Duaterra), 38–39
Russell (Kororareka), 449
Russell, Henry, 115, 120, 148, 198
Russell, Lord John, 73
Russell, Major-General Sir Andrew, 259
Russell, Purvis, 210
Russell, Sir William, 207, 248
Russell, Thomas, 111
Rutherford, Ernest, 297–299

Sargeson, Frank, 390
Savage, Michael Joseph, 209, 247, 252, 315–318, 320, 322–325, 337–342, 407, 432, 438, 444
Scandinavian settlers, 179, 181–184
school milk, 325
Scrimgeour, Reverend Colin, 314–315, 317
Second New Zealand Division, 350, 358, 408
Second World War, 322, 341, 342, and double patriotism 338, 340, economic realities 341, rationing 342, local defence 346, Japanese threat 343–345, war with Japan 347, 354, women workers, 349, defence of New Zealand 354, rampancy 353–354, land, air and naval campaigns 354–356, reputation 357–359, social legacy 361
Seddon, Richard ('King Dick'), 200, 202, 205–209, 227–228, 233, 237–238, 241, 248–249, 254
Self, Sarah, 131
Semple, Robert, 247, 318
settlements, early, 61–71
Shacklock, Henry, 128
sheep *see* pastoralism
Sheppard, Kate, 203, 205
Shortland, Willoughby, 58, 73–74
Shrimpton, Walter, 209
Sinclair, Keith, 7
six o'clock closing, 264–265, 379
Smith, Hector, 112, 119
Smith, Norman 'Wizard', 310
Smith, S. Percy, 12–14

Smith, William Mein, 65–66, 90, 140
social: complexity, 199–201; purity, 284–286, 290
Social Democrat Party, 250
Socialist Party, 247
Somes, Joseph, 63
South Auckland, 377
Southland, 148, 160
Spain, William, 151
Split Enz, 427
Spock, Benjamin, 379
Springboks, 331, versus Maoris 331, 1981 tour 421, 423–424, 426, and students 428
Stead, C. K., 426
Stewart Island, 30
Stewart, Adela, 119
Stokes, Robert, 91
Stout, Sir Robert, 175, 193
Stratford, 122
Supplementary Minimum Payments (SMP's), 410, 430, 433
Sutch, W. B., 307, 320, 380, 401, 405
Sutton, Frederick, 198

Tainui, 197, 336, 435
Taitapu (Golden Bay), 25
Tamatea, 15
Tamihana, Wiremu, 150, 157
Tanner, Thomas, 103, 117, 189, 198, 207
Taranaki, 7, 11, 14, 16, 21, 39, 40, 51–52, 63, 65, 89, 116, 151–154, 167, 170, 174, 184, 194–195, 212, 220, 274
Tarawera, eruption c1314, 14, eruption 1886 191–192
Tasman Empire Air Lines (TEAL), 327
Tasman, Abel, 24–29
Taupo, 11, 150, 194–195
Tauranga, 139, 157–158, 365
Tawhiao, 150, 154, 156, 173, 194–196, 263
Taylor, Mary, 129
Taylor, Richard, 127
Taylor, Sir Richard, 427
Taylor, T. E., 233
taxation, 167, 210–212, 215, 280, 284, 311
Te Arawa, 44, 157, 173, 334
Te Ati Awa, 63–65, 259
Te Aute College, 87–88, 334, 337
Te Awamutu, 154, 194–196
Te Hapuku, 46, 58, 60, 94–96
Te Heuheu, Horonuku, 150, 331
Te Kooti, 170–173, 195
Te Kuiti, 196
Te Moananui, Kurupo, 96
Te Pahi (Tippahee), 36, 82
Te Puni Kokopu, Honiana (Epuni), 64–65
Te Rangitake, 152–153
Te Rau, Kereropa, 168
Te Rauparaha, 37, 42–44, 48, 63, 65, 83–85

Te Wharepouri, 64–67
Te Wherowhero, 96, 150
television, 393
temperance, 185, 199, 203–204, 264–265, 267, 295
Thames, 165, 167
Think Big, 422–423, 426
Three Kings Islands, 27
Tiffen, Henry, 112, 120, 124, 140, 148
Timaru, 131, 254
Tirikatene, Eruera, 337
Titokowaru, 170, 173
Tolaga Bay, 31
Tollemache, Algernon, 107, 112, 119–120
Tollemache, Frances Louise, 160
Toogood, Selwyn, 394
totalisator machines, 285
trade: early, 31–32; frozen meat, 218–221
traders, early, 32–33
Tregear, Edward, 207
Trentham Camp, 263
Tronson, Aubrey, 256
Tuckett, Frederick, 140
Turanga (Gisborne), 58
Turanga-nui, 28 *see also* Poverty Bay
Turangawaewae, 334, 336
Turangi, 369
Twizel, 369

unemployment, 189, 201, 301, 306–307, 310–312, 319, 394, 429, 436–437
Union Steamship Company, 220
United Party, 283
urban development: settler period 133–141; ideal towns 138–139
Urewera, 171, 173, 336
Utting, Frederick, 139

Vaggioli, Domenico, 43, 55
Valpy, Arabella, 230
Vietnam war, 404–405, 413
VOC (Veernigde Oostinche Compagnie), 24–25
Vogel rail, 173–177
Vogel, Sir Julius, 173–175, 177–178, 181º184, 187, 190, 205, 229
Vogt, Anton, 390
Volkner, Carl Sylvius, 169
von Tempsky, Gustavus Ferdinand, 154

Wahine, 403
Waihi Miners Union, 249
Waihi, 246, 247, 250
Waikato, 58, 96, 150–151, 154–157, 173–174, 196, 366
Waimakariri River, 124
Waiouru, 118
Waipukurau, 94, 115
Wairarapa, 89–95, 112, 122, 182, 184, 194, 202, 299, 369
Wairau incident, 74
Wairoa, 168, 170–172, 187, 211, 275, 277
Waitangi Tribunal, 416, 420
Waitangi, Treaty of: origins 50–51; drafted 54–55; finalised 55; and sovereignty 54–55; debated 56; signed 56–59; and waste lands 54, 73, 86; war over 75–76; declared injudicious 86,152; and Ratana 337–338; principles defined 420
Waitara, 152–153, 195, 218
Waitemata, 46, 58–59, 73, 75, 96, 236
Waiuta, 273
Wakefield, Arthur, 65, 70
Wakefield, Edward Gibbon: 61–62; colonisation scheme 63–65, 67, 70–72, 75, 91–92, 96, 101–102, 107, 110–111
Wakefield, Edward Jerningham, 53, 63–65, 67, 69–70
Wakefield, William, 45, 63, 66–67, 69–70, 86
Walsh, Fintan Patrick, 322, 365
Wanganui, 665, 87, 168, 199, 208, 286, 303
Ward, John, 71
Ward, Sir Joseph, 200, 237, 246, 248, 267, 270, 283, 284–285
Waterhouse, Reverend J., 7
Wattie's, 370
Webb, Paddy, 317
Weld, Frederick, 92, 112, 160
Wellington and Manawatu Railway Company, 116, 188
Wellington Provincial Council, 62
Wellington Railway Station, 319, 325
Wellington, 45, 65, 66, 70, 73–75, 84, 87, 109, 110, 112, 127, 140–142, 147, 148, 160, 176, 193, 202, 226, 233, 242, 248, 250, 269, 277, 280, 289, 306–312, 315, 321, 324, 327, 330, 377, 392, 404, 423, 424, 430, 436–437, 442
Wentworth, W. C., 52
Weston, Ernest, 146, 191
whalers, 33–34
Whanganui River, 14, 23
Whitmore, George S., 119, 167, 170–173, 236
Williams, Henry, 44, 49, 54–56, 76
Williams, Samuel, 87–88, 96
Williams, William, 49, 58–59, 189, 195, 197
wine, 443
wireless, 300, 328
Women's Christian Temperance Union (WCTU), 205
Woodville, 184, 242
wool, 111–113, 120–122, 166–167, 212, 217–218, 221, 272, 280, 315, 351, 365–366, 394
working classes, 129–131, 141, 247, 295, 383, 394

Yate, William, 37
Yates, Elizabeth, 205
Young Maori Party, 334–334, 417
youth, 286–289

Zeehaen, 22

About the author

Matthew Wright is one of New Zealand's most published historians and writers. He has qualifications in music, history and anthropology, among other fields, holds post-graduate degrees in history, and is a Fellow of the Royal Historical Society at University College, London. He published his first short story in 1976 and since the early 1980s has worked extensively as a writer, professional historian, reviewer and journalist. His work includes more than 500 articles, academic papers, reviews and 50 books on topics ranging from travel guides to biography, engineering, military and social history.